Health Systems Governance i

There is a fundamental contradiction at the core of health policy in the European Union (EU) that makes it difficult to draw a line between EU and Member State responsibilities. This raises a number of difficult questions for policy makers and practitioners as they struggle to interpret both 'hard' and 'soft' laws at EU and Member State level and to reconcile tensions between economic and social imperatives in health care. The book addresses these complex questions by combining analysis of the underlying issues with carefully chosen case studies that illustrate how broader principles are played out in practice. Each chapter addresses a topical area in which there is considerable debate and potential uncertainty.

The book thus offers a comprehensive discussion of a number of current and emerging governance issues in EU health policy, including regulatory, legal, 'new governance' and policy-making dynamics, and the application of the legal framework in these areas.

Edited by
Elias Mossialos is Brian Abel-Smith Professor of Health Policy and Director of LSE Health at the London School of Economics and Political Science.

Govin Permanand is Programme Manager of the Health Evidence Network at the World Health Organization Regional Office for Europe, Copenhagen, and Research Fellow, LSE Health at the London School of Economics and Political Science.

Rita Baeten is Senior Policy Analyst at the OSE, European Social Observatory, Brussels.

Tamara Hervey is Professor of Law at the University of Sheffield.

Health Economics, Policy and Management

Series Editor: Professor Elias Mossialos, London School of Economics and Political Science

This series is for scholars in health policy, economics and management. It publishes texts that provide innovative discourses, comprehensive accounts and authoritative approaches to scholarhip. It also creates a forum for researchers to participate in interdisciplinary conversations on contemporary issues in healthcare. Concerns in health policy, economics and management will be featured in the context of international healthcare practices and on-going discussions on the latest developments in scholarly research and theoretical issues from a variety of perspectives.

Presenting clear, concise and balanced accounts of topics, particularly those that have developed in the field in the last decade, the series will appeal to healthcare scholars, policy makers, practitioners and students.

Performance Measurement for Health System Improvement: Experiences, Challenges and Prospects

Edited by Peter C. Smith, Elias Mossialos, Irene Papanicolas and Sheila Leatherman

Private Health Insurance and Medical Savings Accounts: History, Politics, Performance

Edited by Sarah Thomson, Elias Mossialos and Robert G. Evans

Health Systems Governance in Europe

The Role of European Union Law and Policy

Edited by

ELIAS MOSSIALOS
London School of Economics and Political Science

GOVIN PERMANAND
World Health Organization and London School of Economics and Political Science

RITA BAETEN
OSE, European Social Observatory

TAMARA HERVEY
University of Sheffield

CAMBRIDGE
UNIVERSITY PRESS

CAMBRIDGE UNIVERSITY PRESS
Cambridge, New York, Melbourne, Madrid, Cape Town, Singapore,
São Paulo, Delhi, Dubai, Tokyo

Cambridge University Press
The Edinburgh Building, Cambridge CB2 8RU, UK

Published in the United States of America by Cambridge University Press,
New York

www.cambridge.org
Information on this title: www.cambridge.org/9780521747561

First published 2010

Printed in the United Kingdom at the University Press, Cambridge

A catalogue record for this publication is available from the British Library

Library of Congress Cataloguing in Publication data
Health systems governance in Europe : the role of EU law and policy / [edited by] Elias
    Mossialos ... [et al.].
    p.   cm. – (Health economics, policy and management)
    ISBN 978-0-521-76138-3 (hardback)
    1. Medical policy–European Union countries.   2. Medical laws and legislation–European Union
    countries.   3. Medical care–Law and legislation–European Union countries.   4. Public health–
    European Union countries.   I. Mossialos, Elias.   II. Title.   III. Series.
    KJE6206.H43   2010
    344.24′0321–dc22
    2009042032

ISBN 978-0-521-76138-3 Hardback
ISBN 978-0-521-74756-1 Paperback

This project was commissioned and funded by the Belgian National Institute for Health and Disability
Insurance (NIHDI) and the Belgian Federal Public Service 'Public Health, Food Chain Safety and
Environment', and carried out by the Observatoire social européen, together with the European
Observatory on Health Systems and Policies.

Contents

Figure

Tables

Boxes

Contributors

RITA BAETEN OSE, European Social Observatory

STEFAAN CALLENS Callens Law Firm; KU Leuven, Centre for Biomedical Ethics and Law

WOUTER GEKIERE Université Libre de Bruxelles, Institut d'études européennes

ANNA GILMORE University of Bath, School for Health

IRENE A. GLINOS OSE, European Social Observatory, European Observatory on Health Systems and Policies; Maastricht University, Faculty of Health, Medicine and Life Sciences

SCOTT L. GREER University of Michigan, School of Public Health; London School of Economics and Political Science, LSE Health and Social Care

LEIGH HANCHER Allen & Overy LLP; University of Tilburg

VASSILIS HATZOPOULOS Democritus University of Thrace; College of Europe; University of Nottingham

TAMARA HERVEY University of Sheffield, School of Law

BEATRIX KARL Karl-Franzens-Universität Graz, Institut für Arbeitsrecht und Sozialrecht

JULIA LEAR International Labour Organization

JEAN MCHALE University of Birmingham, Birmingham Law School

MARTIN MCKEE London School of Hygiene and Tropical Medicine; European Observatory on Health Systems and Policies

SHERRY MERKUR London School of Economics and Political Science, LSE Health and Social Care; European Observatory on Health Systems and Policies

ELIAS MOSSIALOS London School of Economics and Political Science, LSE Health and Social Care; European Observatory on Health Systems and Policies

WILLY PALM European Observatory on Health Systems and Policies

MIEK PEETERS Zorgnet Vlaanderen

GOVIN PERMANAND World Health Organization, Regional Office for Europe; London School of Economics and Political Science, LSE Health and Social Care

TONY PROSSER University of Bristol, School of Law

SARAH THOMSON London School of Economics and Political Science, LSE Health and Social Care; European Observatory on Health Systems and Policies

BART VANHERCKE University of Amsterdam (ASSR); European Social Observatory (OSE); University of Leuven (CESO)

ELLEN VOS Maastricht University, Faculty of Law

Foreword

It is a great pleasure to introduce this volume edited by Elias Mossialos, Govin Permanand, Rita Baeten and Tamara Hervey. It is a volume which continues the success of two earlier books commissioned by the Belgian government and published by Peter Lang Publishing Group in 2002.[1] The topic of this contribution is a crucial one. Indeed, one can hardly imagine a subject closer to the lives of European Union (EU) citizens than an exploration of how EU law and policy has influenced, and will continue to influence, the health systems of the 27 Member States. This two-dimensional perspective means that this work will certainly be studied with great interest by all concerned with the functioning of the EU as well as by those wanting to discover more about national health systems.

In principle, in light of Article 152 of the EC Treaty, national authorities are solely responsible for health care. Yet, though the Member States are free to decide how to deliver and organize health services, they must do so in compliance with other aspects of the Treaty, in particular with the fundamental freedoms and elements of competition law. Put differently, national health systems are not enclaves of national sovereignty insulated from European market integration. While EU legislators may not regulate health care as a means of promoting social cohesion, they may, however, enact legislation relating to those aspects affecting the establishment and functioning of the internal market. Given that national health systems are deeply rooted in social solidarity and welfare, the "constitutional asymmetry" (to borrow the term used by Fritz Scharpf) laid down in the Treaty gives rise to important tensions.

---

[1] Mossialos, Elias and McKee, Martin (2002) *The influence of EU law on the social character of health care systems*. P.I.E. – Peter Lang, Brussels; and McKee, M and Mossialos, Elias and Baeten, R (2002) *The impact of EU law on health care systems*. Peter Lang Publishers, Brussels.

Outside the framework of the internal market, not only is EU legislative action to promote social protection founded on a weak Treaty basis, but it is also hard to achieve politically. Taking the view that the Europeanization of health care might be excessively market driven, the Member States fear that transferring too much power to the EU would amount to losing control over welfare entitlements. Besides, due to the large diversity among the different national (and regional) health systems, the significant economic differences among the Member States, and citizens' national allegiances, reaching an EU agreement more ambitious than adopting general guidelines seems a challenging endeavour. Accordingly, it is not surprising that a political deadlock has forced the European Court of Justice (ECJ) to step forward by incorporating social protection considerations when evaluating the validity of limitations on market integration. However, in spite of its best efforts to reconcile the fundamental freedoms and competition provisions with social solidarity, the ECJ may only provide partial answers on a case-by-case basis. Additionally, the ECJ must respect the constitutional settings put in place by the EC Treaty. As a consequence, its capacity to enhance social cohesion at the expense of market integration is somewhat limited.

These constitutional and political restrictions imposed on the *"méthode communautaire"* have given rise to alternative modes of governance at EU level, which are friendlier towards the aspirations of a Social Europe. For instance, the creation of EU agencies, such as the European Medicines Agency (EMEA) or the European Food Safety Authority (EFSA), and the adoption of soft law have contributed to bringing clarity into the realm of health care. Because they are less hierarchical, not legally binding, and less focused on attaining uniformity, these new modes of governance encourage the Member States to engage in a constructive dialogue. They are not, however, free from shortcomings. Doubts may arise regarding the normative effectiveness of sharing information, dissemination of best practices, and mutual learning by monitoring. Likewise, these alternatives may not suffice to reduce drastically the economic and political differences between the Member States. Most importantly, these new modes of governance appear to bypass traditional accountability checks which are responsible for ensuring democratic legitimacy.

As a result, when looking at the interaction between the EU and national health systems, the picture that then emerges is that of a complex patchwork composed of legislation, case-law, differing policy approaches and priorities, and new modes of governance. Additionally, this complexity is further intensified by the current trend towards liberalizing health care as a response to rising costs, greater expectations from civil society, and changes in the population pyramid. Indeed, in the domain of health care there is currently no clear-cut division between activities reserved to the public sphere and activities governed by the market: the vertical (EU versus Member States) and horizontal (regulation versus market) dimensions of national health systems thus become more intertwined.

In a multidisciplinary approach that reflects the operation and governance of national health systems in the EU, this book provides an up-to-date, thorough and innovative insight into how political actors, courts and stakeholders have coped with the challenges of the internal market and social solidarity trade-offs. Owing to the quality of the contributors, this volume offers a critical assessment throughout its 15 chapters which clearly illuminates the virtues and vices of the decisions taken by the EU from both policy and legal angles. Legal arguments are placed in a historical, factual and political context that enables the reader to better understand how law is influenced by politics and vice versa. Very much appreciated is the special attention paid to future developments and proposed strategies to improve the current situation.

On all accounts, legal and policy scholars and practitioners will benefit from this book.

Koen Lenaerts
Professor of European Law, Institute for European Law,
Katholieke Universiteit Leuven
Judge of the Court of Justice of the
European Communities

Acknowledgments

We would firstly like to thank Mr Jo De Cock, General Manager of the Belgian National Institute for Health and Disability Insurance (NIHDI), who invited us to write this book. We extend our gratitude also to Dirk Cuypers, President of the Management Board, and Leen Meulenbergs, Head of Service, International Relations Department, both from the Belgian Federal Public Service 'Public Health, Food Chain Safety and Environment'. Without the financial support of these partners, this book would not have been possible. We also owe them our thanks for commenting on several earlier drafts of this book and for facilitating the meetings between the authors.

Our special thanks go to Minister Laurette Onkelinx, Belgian Deputy Prime Minister and Minister for Social Affairs and Public Health, for her highly appreciated support in organizing the conference on 'Health Systems Governance in Europe: the Role of EU Law and Policy', held in Brussels on 11 December 2008, where the main findings of this book were first presented. The support of her collaborators Stefaan Thijs, Serge Wauthier and Marleen Steenbrugghe has also been invaluable in organizing this conference.

For the book itself, we particularly appreciate the detailed and very constructive comments of several external reviewers, and in particular those who participated in the workshop held on 27 September 2007 in Brussels. Here we would like to especially mention Mathias Wismar, Senior Health Policy Analyst at the European Observatory on Health Systems and Policies, Herwig Verschueren, Professor of International and European Social Law at the University of Antwerp and at the Free University of Brussels, Nick Fahy, Head of Unit of the Health Information Section at the Directorate-General for Health and Consumer Protection of the European Commission, Chris Segaert, Attaché at the International Relations Department of the Belgian National Institute for Health and Disability Insurance, Taco Brandsen, Associate Professor at the Radboud University of Nijmegen, Mark

Flear, Lecturer at Queen's University Belfast, and Philippe Pochet, former Director of the Observatoire social européen.

We are further grateful to Valérie Cotulleli and Françoise Verri from the Observatoire social européen for having ensured, together with several staff members from the Belgian National Institute for Health and Invalidity Insurance, the smooth organization of the workshop in Brussels. We also would like to acknowledge Candice Lambeth and Scarlett McArdle, both student research assistants at the University of Sheffield, and Valérie Cotulleli for having meticulously checked all the references and retrieved many often obscure references. Our thanks go also to Ian Loasby of the University of Sheffield for his IT assistance.

Additional thanks and much appreciation go to our copy-editors, Anna Maresso, from the European Observatory on Health Systems and Policies, and Matt Ward. We are grateful to Jonathan North, Publications Officer at the European Observatory on Health Systems and Policies, for ensuring page layout and typesetting of the text. Last but not least, our special thanks go to Irene A. Glinos from the OSE, European Observatory on Health Systems and Policies for her invaluable feedback on our work, and for her overall support in ensuring that drafts were circulated at the right moment and that deadlines were respected.

It remains the case that the views expressed in this book are those of the authors alone and should not be taken as representing those of any of the organizations with which they are affiliated.

Elias Mossialos, Govin Permanand,
Rita Baeten and Tamara Hervey.

Abbreviations

AIM	Association Internationale de la Mutualité
All ER	All England Reports
ASL	Local Health Authority (Italy)
AURE	Alliance of United Kingdom Health Regulators on Europe
BAT	British American Tobacco
BEPA	Bureau of European Policy Advisors
BSE	bovine spongiform encephalopathy
CAT	Competition Appeal Tribunal
CECCM	Confederation of European Community Cigarette Manufacturers
CFI	Court of First Instance
CFT	Commission for Fair Trading (Malta)
CHMP	Committee for Medicinal Products for Human Use
CME	continuing medical education
COMP	Committee for Orphan Medicinal Products
Comp AR	Competition Appeal Reports
CPD	continuing professional development
CPMP	Committee for Proprietary Medicinal Products
CSOPH	Committee of Senior Officials on Public Health
DCA	Dutch Competition Authority
DG	Directorate-General
DG Agriculture	Directorate-General for Agriculture and Rural Development
DG Competition	Directorate-General for Competition
DG Environment	Directorate-General for Environment, Nuclear Safety and Civil Protection
DG Industry	Directorate-General for Enterprise and Industry

DG Internal Policies	Directorate-General for Internal Policies of the Union
DG Justice	Directorate-General for Justice, Freedom and Security
DG MARKT	Directorate-General for the Internal Market and Services
DG Research	Directorate-General for Science, Research and Development
DG SANCO	Directorate-General for Health and Consumer Protection
DG Social Affairs	Directorate-General for Employment, Social Affairs and Equal Opportunities
DHA	Dutch Healthcare Authority
DR	European Commission of Human Rights Decisions and Reports
DRG	diagnosis-related group
EACCME	European Accreditation Council for Continuing Medical Education
EACP	Europe against Cancer Programme
EC	European Community
EC Treaty	Treaty establishing the European Community
ECC	European Commercial Cases
ECDC	European Centre for Disease Prevention and Control
ECHR	European Convention for the Protection of Human Rights and Fundamental Freedoms
ECJ	European Court of Justice
ECN	European Competition Network
ECOFIN	Economic and Financial Affairs Council
ECR	European Court Reports
ECtHR	European Court of Human Rights
EEA	European Economic Area
EEC	European Economic Community
EEC Treaty	Treaty establishing the European Economic Community
EFPIA	European Federation of the Pharmaceutical Industries and Associations
EFSA	European Food Safety Authority
EGA	European Generics Medicines Association

EHIC	European Health Insurance Card
EHR	electronic health records
EHRR	European Human Rights Reports
EISS	European Influenza Surveillance Scheme
EMEA	European Medicines Agency
EMU	Economic and Monetary Union
EPC	Economic Policy Committee
EPC/AWG	Economic Policy Committee/Ageing Working Group
EPHA	European Public Health Alliance
EPIET	European Programme for Intervention Epidemiology Training
EPP	evaluation of professional practices
EPSCO	Employment, Social Policy, Health and Consumer Affairs Council
EPSU	European Federation of Public Service Unions
ERDF	European Regional Development Fund
ESF	European Social Fund
ESIP	European Social Insurance Partners
ESM	European Social Model
EuroHIV	European Centre for the Epidemiological Monitoring of AIDS
EU-SILC	European Union Statistics on Income and Living Conditions
EWHC (Admin)	England & Wales High Court (Administrative Court)
EWHC (Ch)	England & Wales High Court (Chancery Division)
EWRS	Early Warning and Response System
Fam	Law Reports, Family Division
FCA	Finnish Competition Authority
FCTC	Framework Convention on Tobacco Control
FDA	Food and Drug Administration (USA)
FENIN	Federación Española de Empresas de Tecnología Sanitaria
FFSA	French Federation of Insurance Companies
FT	Foundation Trust (United Kingdom)
FVO	Food and Veterinary Office
GCA	German Competition Authority

GM	genetically modified
GMOs	genetically-modified organisms
GP	general practitioner
GSK	GlaxoSmithKline
HCC	Hungarian Competition Council
HFEA	Human Fertilisation and Embryology Authority
HIA	Health Insurance Authority (Ireland)
HLG	High Level Group on Health Services and Medical Care
HLPR	High Level Process of Reflection
HMPC	Committee on Herbal Medicinal Products
HOSPEEM	European Hospital and Healthcare Employers Association
IAA	Italian Antitrust Authority
IARC	International Agency for Research on Cancer
ICT	information and communication technology
IESC	Supreme Court of Ireland
IHR	International Health Regulations
IMS	Intercontinental Marketing Services
IVF	in vitro fertilization
JTI	Japan Tobacco International
MEP	Member of the European Parliament
MRP	mutual recognition procedure
NAP/Inclusion	National Action Plan on Social Inclusion
NBTC	National Blood Transfusion Centre
NCA	national competition authority
NCE	new chemical entity
NHA	National Health Accounts of the World Health Organization
NHS	National Health Service (United Kingdom)
NIHDI	National Institute for Health and Disability Insurance (Belgium)
NMG	new modes of governance
NTPF	National Treatment Purchase Fund (Ireland)
OECD	Organisation for Economic Co-operation and Development
OFT	Office of Fair Trading (United Kingdom)
OJ	Official Journal
OMC	open method of coordination

OTC	over the counter
PASA	Purchasing and Supply Agency (United Kingdom)
PCT	Primary Care Trust (United Kingdom)
PDCO	Paediatric Committee
PFI	Private Funding Initiative
PHEA	Executive Agency for the Public Health Programme
PMI	private medical insurance
PPP	public–private partnership
PPRS	price and profit regulation scheme
QB	Law Reports, Queen's Bench
R&D	research and development
RMS	reference Member State
SCA	Swedish Competition Authority
SCF	Scientific Committee for Food
SEA	Single European Act
SEM	single European market
SGEI	services of general economic interest
SGI	services of general interest
SHA	Strategic Health Authority (United Kingdom)
SHA-OECD	System of Health Accounts of the Organisation for Economic Co-operation and Development
SHARE	Supporting and Structuring HealthGrid Activities and Research in Europe
SHI	Social Health Insurance (Germany)
SPC	Social Protection Committee
SPaC	supplementary patent certificate
SSGI	social services of general interest
StCF	Standing Committee on Foodstuffs
TEU	Treaty on European Union
TFEU	Treaty on the Functioning of the European Union
WHO	World Health Organization
WLR	Weekly Law Reports

1 | Health systems governance in Europe: the role of European Union law and policy

ELIAS MOSSIALOS, GOVIN PERMANAND,
RITA BAETEN AND TAMARA HERVEY

1. The scope and aims of this book

This volume assesses the impact of European Union (EU) policy and law on Member States' health systems and their governance in a number of key areas. In so doing, it builds on two earlier books[1] that sought to assess the changing legal and policy dynamics for health care in the wake of the European Court of Justice's (ECJ) seminal rulings in the *Kohll* and *Decker* cases.[2] These books showed that, despite widely held views to the contrary, national health care systems in the EU were not as shielded from the influence of EU law as originally thought.[3] The explicit stipulations of Article 152 EC (as amended by the Amsterdam Treaty) that health is an area of specific Member State competence, and implicit understanding of the subsidiarity principle where policy is undertaken at the lowest level appropriate to its effective implementation, proved not to be the 'guarantees' of no EU interference in national health care services that they were often held to be. As the raft of legal cases and degree of academic attention that followed have shown, *Kohll* and *Decker* were certainly not the 'one-offs' many policy-makers hoped they would be.[4] In fact,

---

[1] M. McKee, E. Mossialos and R. Baeten (eds.), *The imapct of EU law on health care systems* (Brussels: PIE-Peter Lang, 2002); E. Mossialos and M. McKee (with W. Palm, B. Karl and F. Marhold), *EU law and the social character of health care* (Brussels: PIE-Peter Lang, 2002).

[2] Case C-120/95, *Decker* v. *Caisse de Maladie des Employes Prives* [1998] ECR 1831; Case C-158/96, *Kohll* v. *Union des Caisses de Maladie* [1998] ECR I-1931.

[3] T. Hervey and J. McHale, *Health law and the European Union* (Cambridge: Cambridge University Press, 2004); M. McKee, E. Mossialos and P. Belcher, 'The influence of European Union law on national health policy', *Journal of European Social Policy* 6 (1996), 263–86.

[4] K. Lenaerts and T. Heremans, 'Contours of a European social union in the case-law of the European Court of Justice', *European Constitutional*

they are widely held to have set precedent in terms of the application of market-related rules to health care, which in turn 'allowed the EU into' the health care arena. As the growing number of national level analyses of the impact of EU law on health care systems highlight,[5] it is clear then that careful scrutiny is needed in future in order to ensure the balance between creating and sustaining the internal market and the maintenance of a European social model in health care. So, ten years on from *Kohll* and *Decker*, how has the EU health care landscape changed, and what now are the pressing issues? These are two of the underlying questions with which this book is concerned.

In addressing such questions, and particularly in view of the need to balance the internal market with the European social model in health care, it is worth noting that there are three EU policy types, as discerned by Sbragia and Stolfi.[6] Market-building policies emphasize liberalization and are generally regulatory, reflecting the 'Community method'[7] and with a leading role for the European institutions. These are the typical internal market, trade, competition and commercial policy related rules, including those around economic and monetary union (EMU). Market-correcting policies aim to protect citizens and producers from market forces and tend to be redistributive rather than regulatory, thereby involving intergovernmental bargaining. The Common Agricultural Policy and EU Structural Funds are examples. There are also market-cushioning policies, which are again regulatory in nature, and, as they are intended to mitigate the harm that economic activities can bring to individuals, are shared EU–Member State competences. We see this in the case of environmental policy

Law Review 2 (2006), 101–15; E. Mossialos and W. Palm, 'The European Court of Justice and the free movement of patients in the European Union', *International Social Security Review* 56 (2003), 3–29.
[5] See, for example, D. Martinsen and K. Vrangbaek, 'The Europeanization of health care governance: implementing the market imperatives of Europe', *Public Administration* 86 (2007), 169–84.
[6] A. Sbragia and F. Stolfi, 'Key policies', in E. Bomberg, J. Peterson and A. Stubb (eds.), *The European Union: how does it work?* Second edition (Oxford: Oxford University Press, 2008).
[7] The 'Community method' refers to the institutional operating mode for the first pillar of the European Union and follows an integrationist logic with the following key features: the European Commission has the right of initiative; qualified majority voting is generally employed in the Council of Ministers; the European Parliament has a significant role reading and co-legislating with the Council; and where the European Court of Justice ensures the uniform interpretation and application of Community law.

and occupational health and safety. Economic integration, which began with market-building policies, has, given the pressure it exerts also in other areas, seen the development of market-correcting and, now, market-cushioning policies at EU level. This implies a recognition of the welfare and social policy impacts of policies taken from an otherwise economic perspective.

In view of the *Kohll* and *Decker* 'fallout', and given the considerable autonomy exercised by the Commission in this area, our focus in this book is on the first category of policy – market-building – and the effects this has on health policy. We seek to examine these effects, what they mean from the perspective of EU law and the ECJ's role, and their impact on Member State health care systems. In particular, competition law, which is a core EU policy area (where the Commission can be very active), falls under the market-building category and has a profound impact on EU health policy. Market-correcting and market-cushioning policies are not so relevant to health policy given that the EU has little direct competence here – with some ECJ rulings corresponding to the former, and some aspects of public health falling under the latter.

Involving a cadre of leading experts, this volume thus proposes an interdisciplinary treatment of the subject-matter, drawing primarily from the legal and policy spheres. Aimed at an informed audience, the contributors offer a critical examination in crucial and emerging areas of EU law and health care, as well as assessing potential policy implications given changing governance dynamics[8] at the EU level. Among the more specific questions and issues addressed are: what are key areas of concern in health care and law at the EU and Member State levels? How is the Court's role viewed and how has it developed? What do the increasing number of EU soft law instruments and measures

---

[8] By 'governance', we mean all 'steering' carried out by public bodies that seeks to constrain, encourage or otherwise influence acts of private and public parties. We also include structures that 'delegate' the steering capacity to non-public bodies (i.e. professional associations). By 'steering', we mean to include binding regulatory measures (laws) and other measures that are sometimes called 'new governance' measures – that is, 'a range of processes and practices that have a normative dimension but do not operate primarily or at all through the formal mechanism of traditional command-and-control-type legal institutions'. See G. de Búrca and J. Scott, 'Introduction: new governance, law and constitutionalism', in G. de Búrca and J. Scott (eds.), *New governance and constitutionalism in Europe and the US* (Oxford: Hart, 2006).

mean for health care? What challenges and opportunities exist? And
what might the future hold in terms of reconciling continued tensions
between economic and social imperatives in the health (care) domain?
The book thus provides not only a broad understanding of the issues,
but also analyses of their specific interpretation and application in
practice through the use of issue-specific chapters/case-studies. And
while it is clear that such a volume cannot be exhaustive in its coverage, and some issues or policy areas have not been included, each chapter addresses a topical area in which there is considerable debate and
potential uncertainty. The chapters thus offer a comprehensive discussion of a number of current and emerging governance issues, including
regulatory, legal, 'new governance' and policy-making dynamics, and
the application of the legal framework in these areas.

The remainder of this chapter is divided into two sections. The first
offers an initial snapshot of the current status of health (care) policy
in the EU before examining specific challenges facing policy-makers.
While the focus of the book is less about theory than about the legal
situation and its policy impact, some elements from the relevant theoretical literature are raised in order to help better set the scene. These
relate to the different (in part explanatory) perspectives on how policies
have developed (why and why not) and where the constraints lie. The
second section reflects the structure of the remainder of the volume,
providing an introduction to the content of each chapter, as well as an
in-depth discussion of the main findings and policy relevance in each
case. This opening chapter is therefore written both as an introduction
to the book, and as a key contribution to the volume in its own right.

2. EU health policy: contradictions and challenges

Health policy in the European Union (EU) has a fundamental
contradiction at its core. On the one hand, the EC Treaty, as the
definitive statement on the scope of EU law, states explicitly that
health care is the responsibility of the Member States.[9] On the
other hand, as Member State health systems involve interactions
with people (e.g. staff and patients), goods (e.g. pharmaceuticals
and devices) and services (e.g. provided by health care funders and
providers), all of which are granted freedom of movement across

---

[9] Article 152(5) EC.

borders by the same Treaty,[10] many national health activities are in fact subject to EU law and policy.[11] For instance, when national health systems seek to purchase medicines or medical equipment, or to recruit health professionals – what would appear to be clear local health care policy choices – we see that their scope to act is now determined largely by EU legislation.[12] Further, when the citizens of a Member State travel outside their national frontiers, they are now often entitled to receive health care should they need it, and have it reimbursed by their home (national) authority. We thus have a situation where national health care systems officially fall outside EU law, but elements relating to their financing, delivery and provision are directly affected by EU law.

In addition to this overarching contradiction, the EU has, since the 1992 Maastricht Treaty, been required to 'contribute to the attainment of a high level of health protection' for its citizens.[13] This is an understandable and important objective in its own right, and there is compelling evidence that access to timely and effective health care makes an important contribution to overall population health – so-called 'amenable mortality'.[14] But, notwithstanding the EU's commitment to various important public health programmes and initiatives, how are EU policy-makers to pursue this goal of a high level of health attainment when they lack Treaty-based competences to ensure that national health systems are providing effective care to their populations? How can they ensure that health systems promote a high level of health and, indeed, social cohesion, and that they comply with the single market's economic rules (particularly regarding the free movement principles) when health care is an explicit Member State competence?

In this regard, EU health (care) policy can be seen to be affected by what Scharpf terms the 'constitutional asymmetry' between EU policies to promote market efficiency and those to promote social

---

[10] Articles 18, 39, 43, 28 and 49 EC.
[11] McKee, Mossialos and Baeten (eds.), *The impact of EU law*, above n.1; Mossialos and McKee, *EU law and the social character of health care*, above n.1.
[12] Hervey and McHale, *Health law*, above n.3; McKee, Mossialos and Belcher, 'The influence of European Union law', above n.3.
[13] Article 3(1)(p) EC.
[14] E. Nolte and M. McKee, *Does health care save lives? Avoidable mortality revisited* (London: Nuffield Trust, 2004).

protection.[15] That is, the EU has a strong regulatory role in respect of the former, but weak redistributive powers as requisite for the latter. This can be ascribed to the Member States' interest in developing a common market while seeking to retain social policy at the national level. More widely, this conforms with Tsoukalis' view that while welfare and solidarity remain national level prerogatives, many issues affecting the daily life and collective prosperity of individuals are dependent on EU level actions, mainly in economic policy spheres.[16] This reflects what he identifies as the 'gap' between politics and economics in the EU system: 'the democratic process of popular participation and accountability has not caught up with this development [an expanding EU policy agenda driven primarily from an economic perspective]'.[17] Rather than a strong political base, therefore, the EU system relies on an increasingly complex institutional arrangement, a growing depoliticization of the issues, and rules set by legislators and experts. This gap is an important reflection on the EU as a whole – in part encompassing what others have identified as the 'democratic deficit' of the EU[18] – and appears of especial relevance to health and social policy where the economic impetus has set much of the path in the absence of a Treaty-based (political) mandate.

In the health (care) arena, we further see that the constitutional asymmetry is exacerbated by a dissonance between the Commission's policy-initiating role in respect of single market free movement concerns and the Member States' right to set their own social priorities. Wismar and colleagues have noted the 'subordinate role' of health within the broader European integration process,[19] and others have highlighted that health policy in the EU has, in large part, evolved within the

---

[15] F. Scharpf, 'The European social model: coping with the challenges of diversity', *Journal of Common Market Studies* 40 (2002), 645–70.

[16] L. Tsoukalis, *What kind of Europe?* (Oxford: Oxford University Press, 2005).

[17] *Ibid.*, 42.

[18] For a detailed discussion on the merits and failings of the democratic deficit argument in respect of the EU, see A. Follesdal and S. Hix, 'Why there is a democratic deficit in the EU: a response to Majone and Moravscik', European Governance Papers (EUROGOV) No. C-05–02 (2005), www.connex-network.org/eurogov/pdf/egp-connex-C-05–02.pdf.

[19] M. Wismar, R. Busse and P. Berman, 'The European Union and health services – the context', in R. Busse, M. Wismar and P. Berman (eds.), *The European Union and health services: the impact of the single European market on Member States* (Amsterdam: IOS Press, 2002).

context of the economic aims of the single market programme.[20] This has led to a situation in which the Member States have conceded the need for the EU to play a role in health (care), even if only a limited one, and in ill-defined circumstances. As Tsoukalis' view on the politics–economics 'gap' allows us to highlight, this is in part because the EU continues to lack a sufficient political base, not just in health policy but across the board. It has also seen an ad hoc development of measures and, crucially, an ongoing tension between economic and social priorities in the provision of health care. This is in stark contrast to environmental protection, as another area of EU policy, where the EU is given explicit competence under Title XIX of the EC Treaty.[21] This is not to equate health/social policy and environmental policy. But it is simply to highlight that a greater policy mandate for areas outside (though related to) the single market could be accorded to the EU via the Treaties if desired, and that the asymmetry need not be as clear or as limiting as it appears to be for health. This suggests a redefinition or, at least, a reorganization and re-prioritization of health at the EU level, and one that would change current policy-making dynamics.

A. Constraints and parameters: theoretical perspectives on EU health policy-making

Beyond the constitutional asymmetry, which represents an overarching constraint on the development of health (care) policies, there are other perspectives that are useful in explaining the conditions under which policies can be pursued and implemented. And while a theoretical treatment of the issues or the development of an encompassing conceptual framework[22] is not our aim, we can discern three main perspectives that can help us to better understand where policies can or cannot be agreed.

[20] See, for instance, W. W. Holland, E. Mossialos and G. Permanand, 'Public health priorities in Europe', in W. W. Holland and E. Mossialos (eds.), *Public health policies in the European Union* (Aldershot: Ashgate, 1999); B. Duncan, 'Health policy in the European Union: how it's made and how to influence it', *British Medical Journal* 324 (2002), 1027–30.

[21] Articles 174–6 EC.

[22] The evolution of the European Community into an organization with supranational qualities has been explored extensively in the academic literature on European integration. For an analysis of the theories and debates that emerged see, for example, B. Rosamond, *Theories of*

The first is a group of rationalist perspectives,[23] where, for instance, Wilson's 'politics of policy' typology[24] provides a useful illustrative backdrop.[25] Here, policy-making is divided into four categories according to the costs and benefits to the affected stakeholders: majoritarian politics (diffuse/diffuse); client politics (diffuse/concentrated); entrepreneurial politics (concentrated/diffuse); and interest group politics (concentrated/concentrated). In the case of EU health (care) policy, we can define the main stakeholders as the Commission (in some cases, specific Directorates-General), the Member States and, to a degree, the European Court of Justice and industry (in particular, the health-related industries). These actors all have vested interests – often in specific outcomes – and either directly contribute to, or else indirectly affect, policy development. If we are to consider key elements of the EU's current health policies and competences, we see that aspects of public health policy are majoritarian; much pharmaceutical policy is client-based; occupational health and safety or even food safety is entrepreneurial; while the Commission has very little say over those areas that are interest group-oriented and thus fall within the purview of the Member States. It may be the case that aspects of soft law, and the open method of coordination in particular (see below), can play a role in addressing issues within this latter category.

European integration (Basingstoke: Macmillan, 2000); M. Cini and A. Bourne, *European Union studies* (Basingstoke: Palgrave Macmillan, 2006); M. Eilstrup-Sangiovanni, *Debates on European integration* (Basingstoke: Palgrave Macmillan, 2006); I. Bache and S. George, *Politics in the European Union* (Oxford: Oxford University Press, 2006), Chapters 1–4. See also E. Mossialos and G. Permanand, 'Public health in the European Union: making it relevant', LSE Health Discussion Paper No. 17 (2000), for a discussion specific to EU health competencies in respect of theories of European integration.

23 T. Börzel and T. Risse, 'When Europe hits home. Europeanization and domestic change', *European Integration Online Papers* 4 (2000), http://eiop.or.at/eiop/texte/2000–015a.htm; Bache and George, *Politics in the European Union*, above n.22, Chapters 1–2.

24 J. Q. Wilson, *The politics of regulation* (New York: Basic Books, 1980).

25 This is an approach that has already been used to explain the development and orientation of EU public health policy. See Mossialos and Permanand, 'Public health in the European Union', above n.22; G. Permanand and E. Mossialos, 'Constitutional asymmetry and pharmaceutical policy-making in the European Union', *Journal of European Public Policy* 12 (2005), 687–709.

Given our interest in EU law specifically, as the Court's role in health policy is primarily oriented towards free movement, we see that client-based and entrepreneurial politics are the most feasible avenues of action for the Court (e.g., anti-discrimination or cross-border care). The Court steers clear of majoritarian and interest group politics, such as where financial benefits or other redistributive policies are involved, and where it is for the Member States to agree between themselves. Indeed, the Court may deliver judgements relating to the nature of the Member States' social security systems, but has not sought to rule against them in addressing issues such as reimbursement and pricing, except from an EU-wide free movement perspective.[26]

A second group of perspectives is oriented around constructivism,[27] one where the gradual development and building up of capacity and policies is possible. We see this best reflected in the so-called 'new modes of governance' approaches, where Member States seek mutual learning and progress on sensitive and potentially partisan issues via benchmarking and sharing of best practices. The open method of coordination (OMC) is a clear example, and is in stark contrast to the interest group dynamic under the politics of policy view, where the Member States may engage directly with one another, albeit behind the scenes rather than in a transparent manner, and often without much concrete evidence of change. Issues of entrepreneurial politics, with their concentrated costs but diffuse benefits, may also lend themselves to the OMC.

A third view is the broader one represented by the 'grand' international relations theories of European integration. Intergovernmentalism,[28] for instance, which asserts the pre-eminence of the governments of the Member States in the integration process (i.e.,

---

[26] Case C-238/82, *Duphar* v. *Netherlands* [1994] ECR 523. The *Duphar* case has been widely invoked to support the argument that Community law does not detract from the powers of the Member States to organize their social security systems. See D. Pieters and S. van den Bogaert, *The consequences of European competition law for national health policies* (Antwerp: Maklu Uitgevers, 1997).

[27] Börzel and Risse, 'When Europe hits home', above n.23; Bache and George, *Politics in the European Union*, above n.22, pp. 27–8, 43–7.

[28] A. Moravscik, 'Preferences and power in the European Community: a liberal intergovernmentalist approach', *Journal of Common Market Studies* 31 (1993), 473–524.

that national governments remain very much at the helm in deciding the course of Europeanization), distinguishes between issues deemed to be of high politics (defence, foreign policy) and those of low politics (economic interests, welfare policy). The latter are much easier to secure Member State agreement on than the former. And while the distinction would not appear to hold true for health policy as an ostensibly low politics issue over which agreement should be reachable, it is the case that Member States are more or less agreed on the social welfare underpinnings (low politics) but not so over the health care planning and financing elements (high politics). It is these latter elements that in large part represent the stumbling blocks given the loss of national control and consequent budgetary implications of EU competence here. In the case of neo-functionalism,[29] as the other grand international relations theory in respect of the European Union, we see that its central tenet of 'spillover' also carries some explanatory value. Spillover asserts that the pressure to integrate or harmonize in one sector can spill over or demand similar integration in another sector; this seems most relevant to the economic and free movement imperatives of the single market programme, which extended into social policy areas as well. For instance, we have seen how, in order to avoid a situation of social and ecological dumping,[30] and to establish a level playing field for business, the European Community sought to pre-emptively avoid a weakening of countries' health and safety legislation by explicitly strengthening such legislation for coal and steel workers under the original European Coal and Steel Community (ECSC) and European Economic Community (EEC) Treaties. This has since evolved to broader health protection for EU citizens more widely. These bird's eye view perspectives often miss the detail, particularly at the level of policy-making itself, but they do help us to understand the broader roles and interests of different stakeholders – be they those of the European institutions or of stakeholders within the Member States – and they help to establish an overall contextual backdrop to the more immediate political and legal discussions.

---

[29] E. Haas, *The uniting of Europe: political, social and economic forces* (Palo Alto: Stanford University Press, 1968).

[30] V. Eichener, 'Effective European problem-solving: lessons from the regulation of occupational safety and environmental protection', *Journal of European Public Policy* 4 (1997), 591–608.

In addition to the constraints represented by these perspectives, it would appear that the EU health (care) legal and policy framework is itself more broadly grounded around free movement rights and rules and principles pertaining to non-discrimination on grounds of nationality. For the most part, legislation and policies thus have to do with entitlements to free movement and 'negative integration'. This implies the removal of (national regulatory) obstacles to market access, as opposed to positive integration that involves the EU-level approximation of laws and standards, which then replace the different national frameworks. Whether relating to trade, imports, services, free movement or foreign providers, the majority of EU initiatives can be viewed from this free movement rights and non-discrimination perspective. It should not, therefore, be surprising that this is often the view taken by the Commission when seeking to enact policies.

Again, we are not proposing a definitive theoretical framework for understanding how EU health (care) policies have evolved or within what parameters they can or cannot develop; it is not clear that any single framework will be able to do this. But we do see each of the perspectives mentioned above, despite their individual limitations, as capable of helping us better understand the dynamics and constraints at play, which are in addition to the overriding constitutional asymmetry. That is, they help to establish the contextual backdrop to the interplay between interests and actors, and to shape the parameters within which the patchwork of health competences can be executed.

B. Taking EU Policy forward?

The development and application of a prospective and coherent EU legal framework to address the issues mentioned here, including a bridging of the asymmetry and economics–politics gap, if seen as desirable, would face a number of hurdles. In the first place, and reflecting the societal preferences of their citizens, Member States have chosen different ways to organize their health care systems. The overall design of any system is often based on specific national histories, such that commonly accepted norms are important.[31] So,

---

[31] J. Figueras, R. Saltman and C. Sakellarides (eds.), *Critical challenges for health care reform* (Buckingham: Open University Press, 1998); A. Oliver and E. Mossialos, 'Health system reform in Europe: looking back to see

while social insurance systems require an existing set of relationships between employers, trade unions and government, national health services imply a different relationship – one in which social partners play a less prominent role and governments become more important. Patterns of funding reflect views about the balance between individual and collective financing of health services, as well as the amount of redistribution that each society believes to be desirable. Methods of provision reflect views on the balance between professional and organizational autonomy and the role of the state in ensuring effective treatment and an equitable distribution of facilities. The ways in which these varying goals are achieved highlight differing interpretations about the legitimacy of regulation, incentives and other levers to bring about change. And, while the Member States' systems are often thought of as falling within broad categories, such as Bismarckian or Beveridge, it is important to note that each national health care system is in fact unique. An EU-level 'policy' or legal framework would need to take account of such differences, and not seek to minimize or de-emphasize them.

Despite the challenges posed by these differences, a further difficulty for policy-makers in fact stems from a similarity between the Member States' health systems. Among at least the longer standing EU Member States, there is a common model or approach to health care provision based on social solidarity and universal coverage. This approach has several important features that distinguish health care from a normally traded good or service, and this complicates the application of economic rules to the governance[32] of health care. In particular, the European social model is based on a complex system of cross-subsidies, from rich to poor, from well to ill, from young to old, from single people to families, and from workers to the non-active.[33] This model has continued to attract popular support, reflecting the historical

---

forward?', *Journal of Health Policy Politics and Law* 30 (2005), 7–28; E. Mossialos, A. Dixon, J. Figueras and J. Kutzin (eds.), Funding health care: options for Europe (Buckingham: Open University Press, 2002).

[32] See above n.8 for our understanding and use of the term governance throughout this volume.

[33] This is not to suggest a clear definition of the European social model – see below n.58 – but to acknowledge its importance as an underpinning set of values or approach among EU Member States.

necessities from which it emerged and the deeply rooted values of solidarity in Europe.[34] It also recognizes that a market for health care is inevitably imperfect; individuals may not always be in the best position to assess their health needs, whether because they are unaware of the nature of their health need or are simply unable to voice it effectively. In part as a consequence, Member States have explicitly stated in the Treaties that the organization and delivery of health services and medical care remains a matter of national competence.

Yet it is clear that health care cannot be ignored by European legislators and policy-makers. Health care is not something that stands alone, isolated from the wider economy. In fact, many individual elements of health care are, entirely reasonably, subject to market principles. For instance, with the exception of some vaccines and drugs with specialized applications related to national security, governments generally do not produce or distribute pharmaceuticals. Health facilities purchase equipment, whether clinical or otherwise, on the open market. Both medical equipment and technology are freely traded internationally. Many health professionals are self-employed, engaging in contracts with health authorities or funds. Patients may pay for treatment outside the statutory health care system, either in their own country or abroad. Pharmaceuticals or technology are traded across borders, and their production, distribution and purchase are all legitimately governed by the provisions of the single market. Health care workers also have free movement, and Member States cannot simply exclude providers from another Member State without objective justification. Indeed, given the failure of many Member States to produce or retain sufficient numbers of their own health care professionals, they are often desperately in need of those from elsewhere in Europe and

[34] See P. Taylor-Gooby, 'Open markets and welfare values', *European Societies* 6 (2004), 29–48; S. Stjernø, *Solidarity in Europe: the history of an idea* (Cambridge: Cambridge University Press, 2005). Indeed, health care is increasingly complex, creating major informational asymmetries that present scope for opportunistic exploitative behaviour by providers and thus reflect a need for effective systems of regulation and oversight. For these reasons, all industrialized countries have taken an active role in the organization of health care. Even the United States has established a substantial public sector, covering about 40% of the population, to address at least some of the more obvious symptoms of market failure.

abroad.[35] All of these matters are entirely legitimate subjects for the application of internal market and competition law; indeed, the 'fundamental freedoms' enshrined in the Treaties require that such transactions be transparent and non-discriminatory on grounds of nationality.

At the same time, it needs to be recognized that policies developed to sustain the principle of solidarity, with its complex system of cross-subsidies, are especially vulnerable to policies whose roots are in market principles. Unregulated competition in health care will, almost inevitably, reduce equity because of the incentive to select those whose health needs are least, making it difficult or expensive for those in greatest need to obtain cover. Risk adjustment systems can be established, but are far from perfect, especially in an intensely competitive environment.[36] Cost containment policies may be based on restricting supply, such as the number of health facilities.[37] Such policies may be undermined if patients can require their funders to pay for treatment elsewhere. Policies that address the issue of informational asymmetry may involve selective contracting with providers, but this requires the existence of agreed uniform standards. Concerns about information have also caused European governments to reject policies, such as direct-to-consumer advertising of pharmaceuticals, which may seem superficially to redress this asymmetry, on the basis of empirical evidence that it is often misleading and drives up health care costs while bringing few if any benefits to patients. This is, however, clearly an interference with the working of the market. In other words, even for those elements of health care that are covered by internal market provisions, both the Member States and the EU acknowledge that the effects of the market must be constrained.

As a result of such concerns, EU Member States have now explicitly stated that equitable effective health care systems are a means

[35] S. Bach, 'International mobility of health professionals: brain drain or brain exchange?', Research Paper No. 2006/82, UNU-World Institute for Development Economics Research (2006); and M. Vujicic and P. Zurn, 'The dynamics of the health labour market', *International Journal of Health Planning and Management* 21 (2006), 101–15.

[36] W. van de Ven *et al.*, 'Risk adjustment and risk selection in Europe: 6 years later', *Health Policy* 83 (2007), 162–79.

[37] E. Mossialos and J. Le Grand (eds.), *Health care and cost containment in the European Union* (Aldershot: Ashgate, 1999).

of promoting both economic growth and social cohesion in Europe. This is reflected, for instance, in the Council Conclusions on common values and principles in European Union health systems of 2006.[38] There is, therefore, a broad consensus on basic values that would underpin a so-called 'European health policy'. For instance – and perhaps most fundamentally – while greater efficiency is welcomed, there is little interest in radical reforms that risk changing (undermining) the welfare-state constellation.[39] European health care systems have survived largely intact in the face of undulating economic fortunes. And, where fundamental changes have been attempted, they have often failed or been rejected by a public that places a high value on the underlying concept of social solidarity. In considering a wider role for the EU, therefore, it is important to bear in mind the value placed by Europe's citizens on the social model that they have helped to create at home. This allows us to ask whether policies that emerge at the EU level, and the impact of EU law on national health care systems, are consistent with these values. For while Majone has argued that, 'rather than undermining the achievements of the welfare state, [the European Union] is in fact addressing many quality-of-life issues which traditional social polices have neglected – consumer protection and equal treatment for men and women, for example',[40] the issue is that, especially in relation to health, it is doing so often in the context of spillover rather than in a proactive fashion.

An important outcome of the lack of clarity and, in some cases, conflict between the objectives of national and EU policies is the emergence of a leading role for the European Court of Justice in the field of health (care) policy. In a series of seminal decisions, the Court

---

[38] Council Conclusions on common values and principles in European Union health systems, OJ 2006 No. C146/1. These Conclusions are also reflected in European Commission, 'Proposal for a Directive of the European Parliament and the Council on the application of patients rights in cross-border health care', COM (2008) 414 final, 2 July 2008. We see also a broader political commitment expressed by European member states in the 2008 World Health Organization's Tallinn Charter on Health Systems, Health and Wealth, Tallinn, 27 June 2008, www.euro.who.int/document/E91438.pdf.

[39] See T. Hervey, 'The European Union's governance of health care and the welfare modernization agenda', *Regulation and Governance* 2 (2008), 103–20.

[40] G. Majone, 'The European Community between social policy and social regulation', *Journal of Common Market Studies* 31 (1993), 153–70, at 168.

has set crucial precedents in areas such as patient mobility and the reimbursement of medical costs. Through its 'teleological' approach to the interpretation of very general Treaty and legislative texts, and given the institutional constraints upon the EU legislature already highlighted, the Court can in fact be seen to be setting policy directions, and doing so on the basis of 'atypical cases' within the single market and, to some extent, competition law rules.[41]

The thrust of the Court's role is to fill in gaps that have developed in the creation of the single market. The peculiar status of health policy – both an economic and social concern, and with (de facto) shared EU and national levels of competence – means in essence that an unelected and unrepresentative body is in large part constraining the context in which decisions may be taken on social policy matters in relation to Member States' health systems.[42] Moreover, such decisions and the policies they subsequently generate, involving the EU legislative and administrative institutions, are generally subject to scrutiny by people who often have little idea of what they will lead to. Most single market-related policies, even those relevant to health care, will be initiated by the European Commission's Directorate-General for Internal Market and Services, debated by the Member States' economic or competition ministers at their Council meeting, and in turn examined by the European Parliament's committees on the internal market or industry, before being forwarded for approval. Those with an interest or expertise in health care or public health usually have little say. This, in part, reflects the constitutional asymmetry between EU policies that promote the single market and those that promote social protection, but so too the lack of recognition within the Treaty framework that health is in fact an area of shared competence (contrast environmental policy). The result is a patchwork of health competences, legal provisions and measures, some with a market-oriented focus and others with more social solidarity underpinnings, and increasing areas of tension between the EU

---

[41] E. Mossialos and M. McKee, 'Is a European health care policy emerging?', *British Medical Journal* 323 (2001), 248; M. McKee and E. Mossialos, 'Health policy and European law: closing the gaps', *Public Health* 120 (2006) Supp: 16–21; and G. Permanand, 'Commentary on "health policy and European law: closing the gaps"', *Public Health* 120 (2006), Supp: 21–2.

[42] G. Permanand, 'Commentary on health policy and European law', *Public Health* 120 (2006), Supp: 21–2.

legislature (and the Court) and the Member States in the area of health (care) policy.

The patchwork and the resulting tension are further manifest in concerns over the potential erosion of the social values intrinsic to European health care systems, as raised earlier.[43] It is feared that, via the strict application of EU law – particularly as a means of redressing gaps in the single market rules – solidarity will become a secondary priority behind, for example, free movement or free competition. We see this particularly in the impact of competition law on the regulation of public and private actors involved in providing health care. Indeed, competition law has been shown to impact on public services in general[44] – the impact on health needs more exploration – and there are limits on the provision of state aid and indirect subsidies via both primary and secondary legislation.[45] And, while competition law may not apply in certain cases, such as those involving 'services of general economic interest', the question is whether this will in turn be thinned via further policies and case-law. Unsurprisingly, some commentators would argue the former, while others foresee the latter.

Overall, therefore, there is a gap in the EU approach to health (care) policy, especially in relation to the delivery and funding of health care services. The Treaties state that it is a matter for Member States, yet it is clear that many aspects are within the ambit of EU law. Member States decide the goals they wish to pursue, such as equity and more effective care, and must then find mechanisms by which to do this that are consistent with EU law. The inability of the legislative bodies of the EU to deal with the issues that arise, or to deal with them in a way that takes account of the specificities of health systems, means that it has often fallen to the Court to make law as it goes along. Moreover, much of the relevant EU law has emerged from rulings that have either arisen from considerations in other sectors, or by addressing only the issues in a single case, thereby leaving issues of

---

[43] T. Hervey, 'EU law and national health policies: problem or opportunity?', *Health Economics, Policy and Law* 2 (2007), 1–6.

[44] T. Prosser, *Competition law and public service in the European Union and the United States* (Oxford: Oxford University Press, 2005).

[45] V. Hatzopoulos, 'Health law and policy: the impact of the EU', in G. de Búrca (ed.), *EU law and the welfare state: in search of solidarity* (Oxford: Oxford University Press, 2005).

broader applicability unresolved. All of this suggests that there is a need for a clear future health care policy agenda in the EU.

This must be an agenda that can reconcile the often conflicting imperatives already highlighted, but that also respects the wide diversity that exists. Ideally, it would allow the Member States to cooperate where necessary and to learn from each other on the basis of best practices and evidence-informed approaches. Such an agenda should aim to ensure that the EU's citizens benefit from health care systems that concomitantly support solidarity and economic growth. In pursuing such an agenda, however, policy and law-makers will also need to be aware that a deregulation-oriented approach to the rules of the single market will, if not sensitively applied, undermine the social principles upon which European health care systems, and the European social model in general, are based.

In view of not just the policy issues and difficulties, but so too the environment, constraints and (theoretical) perspectives outlined above, it becomes necessary to take a closer look at the impact of EU law and the rulings of the European Court of Justice, and what the response and results have been. This is the primary purpose of this book. We do so because the Court is seen by many as a driving force behind the health care policy agenda in the context of the constitutional asymmetry, and is playing this role through the strict and potentially insensitive application of the single market rules. Does the Court sufficiently take into account the peculiarities of health care (that is, as more than a simple product or commodity subject to normal market rules)? Are the Member States' interests and their diversity respected and, indeed, reflected in decisions? How have EU policy-makers responded? And what measures are being pursued to 'soften' the Court's role, or at least lessen its impact on solidarity and social policy grounds? Indeed, Scharpf's broad constitutional asymmetery view is useful in understanding the tension between market-enhancing and market-correcting policies, but it perhaps underplays the influences, over time, of ideas that become embedded in (internal market) law and policy-making processes – this includes the jurisprudence of the Court – among which are the traditionally non-market based conceptions of public health care provision in European contexts.[46] This book considers such questions, and

---

[46] See Hervey, 'The European Union's governance', above n.39.

asks about the wider impact of EU law and governance on national health care systems.

3. EU Law and (the erosion/protection of) national social policies

As the process of Europeanization[47] continues, a gradual redrawing of national and European identities and a (partial) dismantling of Member State social policy would appear to be following.[48] Welfare systems seem to have become insufficient in the face of growing difficulties to the task of balancing national commitments to the welfare state and EU internal market objectives. Welfare and the internal market may therefore be juxtaposed as incompatible, but, at the same time, both ideals are central tenets of European identity and valued by EU citizens. Consequently, it is often argued that an EU-level equilibrium between market efficiency and social protection policies is necessary.[49] Although some theorists focus on the inherent limitations of EU governance and the need for decentralized decision-making, others emphasize EU capabilities to both influence Member State welfare priorities[50] and to protect them in global contexts. In this regard, a stronger role for the EU in welfare contexts is perhaps envisaged.

Three main roles are ascribed to the modern state: regulation, redistribution and stabilization – essentially, a need exists for market-building,

[47] For a useful overview of the uses of 'Europeanization' in research on the EU, see I. Bache and A. Jordan, 'Britain in Europe and Europe in Britain', in I. Bache and A. Jordan (eds.), *The Europeanization of British politics* (Basingstoke: Palgrave Macmillan, 2008), pp. 12–5; C. Radaelli, 'Europeanization: solution or problem?', in M. Cini and A. Bourne (eds.), *European Union studies* (Basingstoke: Palgrave Macmillan, 2006).

[48] For example, S. Leibfried and P. Pierson, *European social policy: between fragmentation and integration* (Washington: Brookings, 1995); M. Ferrera, *The boundaries of welfare: European integration and the new spatial politics of social protection* (Oxford: Oxford University Press, 2005); T. Hervey, *European social law and policy* (London: Longman, 1998).

[49] P. Taylor-Gooby, 'Introduction. Open markets versus welfare citizenship: conflicting approaches to policy convergence in Europe', *Social Policy and Administration* 37 (2003), 539–54.

[50] See, for instance, F. Scharpf, *Governing in Europe: effective and democratic?* (Oxford: Oxford University Press, 1999), on the one hand; and B. Eberlein and D. Kerwer, 'New governance in the European Union: a theoretical perspective', *Journal of Common Market Studies* 42 (2004), 121–42, on the other.

market-correcting and market-cushioning public policy – but the rise of the European Union as what Majone calls a 'regulatory state' (a state-like body with regulatory powers to create the internal market) was intentionally not accompanied by the development of a corresponding set of redistributive mechanisms or financing capacity.[51] Although the EEC had (and the EU still has) modest redistributive powers in the context of the Common Agricultural Policy (CAP), the Structural Funds (European Regional Development Fund, European Social Fund), and its poverty and social inclusion programmes, the amounts involved are insignificant in comparison with national welfare budgets. This imbalance between market-building and market-correcting/cushioning competences at the EU level suggests that the EU's contribution to social policies is likely to be to undermine their provisions over time. It also allows us to ask what options are available to the Member States given the otherwise primarily economic (market-building) nature of the EU's health competences.

Indeed, because of this imbalance, many national governments are hesitant to engage in dialogue about the Europeanization of welfare. They fear that closer integration will mean loss of national gate-keeping control over welfare entitlements. Nonetheless, discussions of inputs (who gives) and outputs (who gets) are an important component of a state's legitimacy vis-à-vis its citizens, and the EU – where it fulfils these state-like functions – is no exception.[52] The EU's founding Treaties, as interpreted by the Court, have established a rudimentary 'constitutional' definition of EU citizenship based on safeguarding fundamental civil, political and social rights, though enforcement and implementation are left to the national level. This suggests the existence of a baseline EU-level moral commitment to social solidarity,[53] and most Europeans profess a commitment to the ideals of equality, cooperation and helping those in need;[54] social solidarity appears a

[51] G. Majone, 'A European regulatory state', in J. Richardson (ed.), *European Union: power and policy-making* (London: Routledge, 1996); G. Majone, *Regulating Europe* (London: Routledge, 1996).

[52] F. Scharpf, 'Problem-Solving Effectiveness and Democratic Accountability in the EU', Max Planck Institute for the Study of Societies Working Paper No. 03/1 (2003).

[53] J. H. H. Weiler, 'A constitution for Europe? Some hard choices', *Journal of Common Market Studies* 40 (2002), 563–80.

[54] Ferrera, *The boundaries of welfare*, above n.48.

source of pride in the national identity of many Europeans.[55] And while the evolution of a dual European and national identity is underway, national allegiances still supersede EU loyalty for most citizens. Ferrera considers this tendency a reflection of people's conceptions of national boundaries. Yet European integration is challenging such spatial boundaries as borders are continuing to open as a result of the single market.[56] Where identity evolves to take into account these new spatial conceptions, an EU-level version of values, such as solidarity and equal access to welfare based on need, may become articulated, and eventually embedded in EU law and policy.

Some degree of solidarity has already been evidenced between subnational regions within the EU, due in part to EU supranational patronage, for instance, through the EU's Structural Funds.[57] These activities of the EU might diminish the role of national governments as gatekeepers of social policy, and may result in tensions between different geographical areas, if 'those who give' resent giving to 'those who get', as we do see in respect of the CAP. But an EU-level commitment to a shared social welfare policy may equally have positive effects, such as encouraging innovation and efficiency. In the context of global trade, EU-level solidarity may contribute to shoring up the 'European social model'[58] vis-à-vis alternative welfare models in the rest of the world (such as the approach to welfare and health care found in the United States), though this is not clear. The implication of this observation is that the EU's contribution to national social policies is likely to be to protect 'European' welfare values over time. Or else, as Majone has described it, the 'social Europe' of the future, based also on key jurisprudence from the Court,

---

[55] Weiler, 'A constitution for Europe?', above n.53.
[56] M. Ferrera, 'European integration and national social citizenship: changing boundaries, new structuring?', *Comparative Political Studies* 33 (2003), 611–52.
[57] Ferrera, *The boundaries of welfare*, above n.48.
[58] There is no formal legal definition of the 'European social model'. For a discussion of the meaning of the phrase, see T. Hervey, 'Social solidarity: a buttress against internal market law?', in J. Shaw (ed.), *Social law and policy in an evolving European Union* (Oxford: Hart, 2000), 31–47, in which is also cited Commissioner Flynn's speech to the Conference on 'Visions of European Governance', Harvard University, Cambridge, MA, 2 March 1999: '[t]he European Social Model ... has been conceived and is applied in many different ways. ... All the variants reflect and respect two common and balancing principles. One is competition ... the other is solidarity between citizens.'

'will be, not a supranational welfare state, but an increasingly rich space of social-regulatory policies and institutions'.[59]

We can discern two types of challenges to EU-level articulations of the values of social solidarity, or development of EU social policy. The first concerns the wide variety in approaches to welfare and the economic disparities between the Member States. Establishing a common EU-level social and health policy framework would be challenging in view of the great disparities that exist between Member States in ability to pay for health and social services and also in varying conceptions of social solidarity. Four broad regional models of welfare solidarity exist within the EU: Scandinavian, Anglo-Saxon (the United Kingdom and Ireland), Continental and Southern European.[60] Additionally, new Member States have attempted to reconcile communist legacies and, in some cases, post-communist worldviews, with free market principles. These groups of countries differ in their sources of funding, relative levels of taxation, social service spending, priorities and contribution rates.[61] Inevitably, solidarity evokes varying levels of commitments, inputs and outputs in different nations.[62] And, for the newer Member States, given their different traditions of welfare and state development, and recent changes in priorities, is their adherence to social protection and social solidarity still as strong (or likely to remain as strong)? Conversely, rich Member States may fear that EU social citizenship could also lead to increased supranational redistribution between Member States, while relatively poorer nations might worry that EU regulation would place unduly lofty demands given limited resources, funding and capacity. EU-level social policy (set at the more generous welfare levels that arguably only the richer Member States can afford) here becomes a form of protectionism for the wealthier EU Member States.[63] However, we might observe that similar challenges pose barriers to the creation of an EU-level environmental policy, and yet such a policy exists.

The second type of challenge to the feasibility of developing EU-level social policy concerns the as-yet (and perhaps always to be)

---

[59] Majone, 'The European Community', above n.40, 168.
[60] G. Esping-Anderson, *The three worlds of welfare capitalism* (London: Polity Press, 1989); Scharpf, 'The European social model', above n.15; J. Alber, 'The European social model and the United States', *European Union Politics* 7 (2006), 393–419.
[61] Scharpf, *Governing in Europe*, above n.50.
[62] Weiler, 'A constitution for Europe?', above n.53.
[63] Hervey, *Social Solidarity*, above n.58, p. 8.

brittle concept of supranational solidarity. Although EU citizenship and EU solidarity can be seen to have a discernible influence on the legal and political stage, at least at the level of political discourse, for most citizens national loyalty still takes precedence over EU loyalty. This may, in part, be due to the fact that EU citizenship seems defined primarily in terms of free movement rights and anti-discrimination rules, where some countries initially favoured including citizenship and human rights in the Treaties, while others were less supportive.

For instance, the 1992 Maastricht Treaty granted EU citizens political rights, the right of free movement, the right to diplomatic protection and the right to appeal to the European Parliament. Following this, while several Member States supported further strengthening of citizenship rights, under German and French impetus, the United Kingdom instead pushed for a 'partnership of nations'. Amsterdam represented something of a disappointment to those favouring stronger citizenship provisions. The result of this still inconclusive understanding of EU citizenship may be the diminished loyalties that are evidenced towards foreigners and immigrants from within the EU (i.e., neighbouring Member States).[64] Fears of 'EU benefit tourism' could spur increasingly protectionist national responses and a restriction of welfare entitlement eligibility.[65] Indeed, a balancing act must occur between voices against the entry of foreign migrants and the outsourcing of domestic firms with petitions to opt out of social insurance policies or to enter domestic markets.[66] The *Pierik* rulings[67] clarified that authorization for treatment abroad was always to be granted when the treatment in question could not be given at home, irrespective of the coverage rules of the insurance scheme and of financial considerations. In a reaction to these rulings, the Member States forced a restrictive amendment of the

---

[64] Ferrera, *The boundaries of welfare*, above n.48.
[65] M. Ferrera, 'Towards an 'open' social citizenship? The new boundaries of welfare in the European Union', in de Búrca, *EU law and the welfare state*, above n.45.
[66] See the cases of Case C-438/05, *The International Transport Workers' Federation and The Finnish Seamen's Union* [2007] ECR I-10779; Case C-341/05, *Laval* [2007] ECR I-11767; and Case C-346/06, *Rüffert* [2008] ECR I-1989.
[67] Case 117/77, *Bestuur van het Algemeen Ziekenfonds Drenthe-Platteland* v. *G. Pierik* [1978] ECR 825; and Case 182/78, *Bestuur van het Algemeen Ziekenfonds Drenthe-Platteland* v. *G. Pierik* [1979] ECR 1977.

relevant Regulation,[68] effectively blocking a Court-led stream of negative integration.[69] Additionally, political mobilization to sway rulings of the Court has also been evidenced – for example, the French Government's campaigns in the *Poucet and Pistre* case (see below).[70] Repeat litigation,[71] delay tactics and deliberate non-compliance have also been seen, such as the Spanish request for further clarifications around cross-border health service provision.[72]

However, even without a centralized and coherent EU social policy framework, and irrespective of whether one is now or will ever be feasible, the boundaries of welfare are already being blurred as a result of EU internal market and other policies. The evolution of EU citizenship without a complementary EU welfarist framework decreases the legitimacy of the EU as a regulatory state and is subtly changing national welfare policies without transparency or careful consideration at either the EU or national levels.[73] The European regulatory state brings theoretical and practical challenges that must first be addressed in relation to social protection and European conceptions of redistributive justice.

We can identify five main areas of Europeanization that have restricted national welfare systems: economic and monetary policy; internal market policies; EU employment law; EU law on the free movement of human beings (including movement of workers and citizens within the EU, and immigration and asylum); and health related regulation (including environmental law and public health).[74] The EU's economic and monetary union policy adjusts exchange rates based on average conditions in the Eurozone, thus divesting Member States of the ability to adjust exchange and interest rates in relation to internal

---

[68] Council Regulation 1408/71/EEC on the application of social security schemes to employed persons and their families moving within the Community, OJ 1971 Sp.Ed. Series I, p. 416.

[69] Ferrera, *The boundaries of welfare*, above n.48.

[70] Joined Cases C-159/91 and 160/91, *Poucet and Pistre* [1993] ECR I-637.

[71] Such as in the context of German legislation on 'minimal workers'.

[72] J. Sylvest and C. Adamsen, 'The impact of the European Court of Justice case law on national systems for cross-border health services provision', Briefing Note, DG Internal Policies of the Union, IP/A/ALL/FWC/2006–105/LOT 3/C1/SC1 (2007).

[73] Ferrera, *The boundaries of welfare*, above n.48.

[74] Scharpf, *Governing in Europe*, above n.50; G. de Búrca, 'Towards European welfare?', in de Búrca, *EU law and the welfare state*, above n.45.

economic conditions. This has the potential to further encumber and punish countries with slow growth, while serving to exacerbate highly inflationary economies that may be overheating.[75] The budgetary commitments required by economic and monetary union imply increased financial pressure on national welfare systems.[76]

Internal market policies have fostered increased EU liberalization, deregulation policies and competition laws.[77] Economic integration has been promoted through legal mechanisms like deregulation. The EU Treaties prohibit restrictions on the provision of cross-border services and the movement of goods.[78] These directly-effective Treaty provisions are enforceable by individual litigation ('negative integration'). Even if these goods or services are affiliated with domestic social programmes, like government-sponsored health care or subsidized pharmaceuticals, directly effective EU Treaty law on free movement or competition is still applicable in principle, if these activities are deemed to be 'economic' and not purely welfare-based services.[79] This application of market models in welfare contexts seems to contradict European welfarist principles such as equal access and solidarity. EU internal market and competition law restrict the use of numerous Keynesian policies, such as increased state level employment and other traditional tools designed to cushion and boost economies in recession. Thus, EU internal market and competition law reduces the number of strategies a domestic government can use to stimulate its economy. As a result, instead of increased spending on social programmes, policy-makers may resort to supply-side measures like welfare reductions or tax cuts.[80]

EU employment law has attempted to prevent discrimination and protect employment rights, and a large body of EU worker health and safety legislation has been adopted, including employment rights during restructuring, non-discrimination clauses and directives on working

[75] Scharpf, 'The European social model', above n.15.
[76] P. Pestieau, *The welfare state in the European Union: economic and social perspectives* (Oxford: Oxford University Press, 2006), pp. 116–24.
[77] B. Eberlein and E. Grande, 'Beyond delegation: trans-national regulatory regimes and the EU regulatory state', *Journal of European Public Policy* 12 (2005), 89–112.
[78] Article 49 EC; Article 28 EC.
[79] Scharpf, 'The European social model', above n.15.
[80] Hervey, 'The European Union's governance', above n.39.

time.[81] However, EU regulators may not have considered the long run implications of such decisions, particularly as they apply to welfare institutions, which are often among the largest employers within a Member State. The increased cost of compliance with EU employment law may also have the effect of squeezing public welfare budgets.

Measures of EU law based on the protection of the rights of mobile workers[82] or, more recently, the emergent 'citizenship of the EU',[83] have influenced the movement of people in the EU. Such principles of free movement law, as applied to human beings, also affect domestic welfare programmes. Countries with generous social systems may reduce benefits in response to increased immigration or tighten eligibility regulation.[84] The creation of a mobile 'European' labour force is changing boundaries and eroding social sovereignty within Member States. This has resulted in the evolution of (semi) sovereign welfare states[85] within an EU regulatory structure, and a new era of governance and complexity.[86]

Finally, the obligations to comply with EU-level health-related regulation (in fields such as environmental law, food law and communicable diseases law) may restrict the ability of individual Member States to tailor responses to these threats to public health to their national (or even local) specificities. The need to comply with EU-level information-gathering, monitoring and reporting requirements alone – while it may be entirely appropriate, given the need to have a European (or even global) response to many public health threats – does require Member States to deploy human and other resources in ways that would not be mandatory were they not Member States of the EU.

[81] See C. Barnard, *EU Employment Law* (Oxford: Oxford University Press, 2006).

[82] Article 39 EC; Council Regulation 1612/68/EEC on freedom of movement for workers within the Community, OJ 1968 No. L257/2.

[83] Article 17 EC; Directive 2004/38/EC of the European Parliament and the Council on the right of citizens of the union and their family members to move and reside freely within the territory of the Member States, amending Regulation 1612/68/EEC and repealing Directives 64/221/EEC, 68/360/EEC, 72/194/EEC, 73/148/EEC, 75/34/EEC,75/35/EEC, 90/364/EEC, 90/365/EEC and 93/96/EEC, OJ 2004 No. L229/35.

[84] S. O'Leary, 'Solidarity and citizenship rights in the Charter of Fundamental Rights of the European Union', in de Búrca, *EU law and the welfare state*, above n.45.

[85] Leibfried and Pierson, *European social policy*, above n.48.

[86] G. Majone, 'The regulatory state and its legitimacy problems', *West European Politics* 22 (1999), 1–24.

As already noted, the jurisprudence of the European Court of Justice plays a pivotal role in EU-level law and policy-making, including in those areas just mentioned. The Court enjoys the exclusive power to provide authoritative interpretations of EU law, which is supreme and applies in preference to contradictory national law.[87] For instance, the Court has safeguarded the rights of transnational EU workers to social assistance entitlements[88] and cross-border health care access,[89] corresponding unemployment benefits and child support for migrant workers have been established,[90] along with the rights of other groups such as students.[91] Consequently, Court decisions have eroded national competence in several key areas of social policy, such as control over beneficiary restrictions, consumer choice in benefits consumption, coverage of non-national workers and access to foreign providers. Nonetheless, certain social rights gaps have not been accounted for by Court rulings in these areas, such as unemployed spouse benefits, children's access to social insurance schemes and discrimination against non-traditional family structures like homosexual couples. Such omissions, more or less mandated by the structure of internal market law, and the Court's limited jurisdiction (in this context, to hear references from national courts on questions of the interpretation of EU law under Article 234 EC), indicate that the Court's rulings focus primarily on protecting active members of the labour force.[92] Most Court rulings have focused on the concerns of relatively well-off income groups.[93] Better educated people with greater financial resources may have an easier time navigating through any court system, and the European Court of Justice is no exception. As a result, without explicit EU social legislation guaranteeing the rights of marginalized groups, leaving matters to the Court may unintentionally disadvantage those people who need social protection the most. In addition, it remains the case that the 'ambiguous' understanding of what a social dimension to Europe would mean, as

---

[87] Article 220 EC; Article 234 EC; Case 26/62, *Van Gend en Loos* [1963] ECR 1.
[88] Case C-456/02, *Trojani* [2004] ECR I-7573
[89] Case 159/90, *Grogan* [1991] ECR I-4741; Case C-120/95, *Decker*, above n.2; Case C-158/96, *Kohll*, above n.2.
[90] Case C-85/96, *Martinez Sala* [1998] ECR I-2691.
[91] Case C-184/99, *Grzelczyk* [2001] ECR I-6193; L. Conant, 'Individuals, courts, and the development of European social rights', *Comparative Political Studies* 39 (2006), 76–100.
[92] Conant, 'Individuals, courts', above n.91.
[93] Ferrera, 'European integration', above n.56.

already highlighted by Majone in the wake of the Treaty of Rome, remains in place. For while it is clear that neither a single (common) market, nor rulings by the ECJ can facilitate a 'social Europe', the question remains as to what extent the Member States are willing to themselves engender such a concept.

4. The role of the European Court of Justice in health care

Moving from such wider social policy questions to the Court's role in respect of health care specifically, many regard the Court's rulings in the *Kohll* and *Decker* cases as something of a *Wendezeit* – a turning point in European health policy development. From the point of view of health care policy, the decisions were an unanticipated 'endogenous shock', surprising many people, and policy-makers in particular, and they certainly contributed to the establishment of a so-called 'critical juncture'[94] in European health policy (at least in terms of becoming high profile cases). But, from the point of view of existing EU internal market law, *Kohll* and *Decker* did not represent anything new. The application of internal market (in this case, freedom of movement) rules to health services had already been recognized.[95] Regulation 1408/71/EEC[96] on the application of social security schemes to employed persons and their families moving within the EU, already allowed for health care to be provided in another Member State in specific circumstances. As part of its justification in delivering its decisions in *Kohll* and *Decker*, the Court reaffirmed the Regulation.[97] Just as importantly, the Court had already applied principles of internal market law in health care contexts. The

---

[94] S. Greer, *Power struggle: the politics and policy consequences of patient mobility in Europe* (Ann Arbor: University of Michigan School of Public Health, 2008); S. Greer, 'Choosing paths in European Union health services policy: a political analysis of a critical juncture', *Journal of European Social Policy* 18 (2008), 219–31.

[95] Joined Cases 286/82 and 26/83, *Luisi and Carbone* v. *Ministero del Tesoro* [1984] ECR 377, para. 16.

[96] Regulation 1408/71/EEC of the Council of 14 June 1971 on the application of social security schemes to employed persons and their families moving within the Community, OJ 1971 No. L149.

[97] The Court also held that, while the national Luxembourg rules that were being used to implement Regulation 1408/71 were in violation of the free movement principles under Articles (ex) 28–30 of the Treaty, the Regulation itself was not in violation.

1981 *Duphar* ruling[98] on the basis of the reimbursement of medicines (resulting in the wide-spread use of negative and positive lists in Europe), affirmed the Member States' right to organize their social security systems as appropriate. In the 1984 *Luisi and Carbone* case,[99] the Court established that tourists, business travellers, students and patients could travel to another Member State as a 'recipient of services'; the economic elements of free movement were thus already recognized as incorporating health services, falling within (then) Article 60 EEC (now Article 49 EC). As such, the extent of the Court's reference to the free movement provisions in *Kohll* and *Decker* should really not have been unexpected. Moreover, and more generally, the Court was in fact doing exactly what it is mandated to do – that is, to interpret and apply the available hard law (that is, the EC Treaty) in order to fill gaps uncovered by legal challenges.

A characterization of the Court's role as filling gaps is perhaps a statement of the obvious. We have already noted the confused and piecemeal status of health care policy in the EU. As such, the logic of the system would seem to be about plugging holes, smoothing inconsistencies and moving where possible in order to overcome the challenges and tensions mentioned earlier. Perhaps the real question in respect of the Court's role, therefore, is how the Court fills those gaps. Indeed, its role in interpreting the application of EU law in specific circumstances towards filling these gaps raises concerns. This is the case because these Court decisions establish generalized interpretations of the Treaty rules, which become precedents that must be applied in all similar circumstances. Moreover, there is a wide-spread concern that, in doing so, the Court has expressed an apparent leaning towards the application of internal market principles, or the adoption of an economic perspective, at the expense of either a more Member State-oriented approach (a wider 'margin of discretion' for Member States) or a more balanced interpretation of the place of welfare within the internal market. This is, however, perhaps an oversimplification of the position. The Court does try to balance the place of welfare within the internal market, by recognizing that the internal market is not simply a deregulated economic space, but one where social (and other non-economic, such as environmental) dimensions are also embedded in market-correcting or market-cushioning measures. Moreover, it is

[98] Case C-238/82, *Duphar* v. *Netherlands* [1994] ECR 523.
[99] Joined Cases 286/82 and 26/83, *Luisi and Carbone*, above n.95, para 16.

not just the Court that is 'interfering' in national health care policy. The Commission, too, has sought to use internal market principles in this way. For instance, the 'Bolkestein' Directive (and certainly its early drafts), were an attempt to free up the cross-border provision of services (including health care services) via internal market mechanisms, in particular the ill-fated 'country of origin' principle.[100]

The Court has determined that some 'public' provisions of welfare services, such as health care, are not exempt from the Treaty's free movement and competition law. Member States remain competent to organize their health care systems as they see fit, but they must do so in ways consistent with EU law.[101] Cross-border medical treatment is permitted in most cases, and, in many cases, the public purse is obliged to compensate the patient for treatment received in another Member State. In such a manner, the precedent of increased patient choice and mobility in alignment with EU internal market objectives was established. However, the Court has also sought to maintain the principles of solidarity, such as in the *Poucet and Pistre* ruling,[102] in which it was held that exit from compulsory national insurance schemes was not allowed on the basis of competition law,[103] and in the *Albany* case, in which it ruled that the sectoral pension scheme under question carried out an essential social function within the Dutch system.[104] Additionally, we see in such cases that public insurance monopolies have also been exempted from competition rulings with certain stipulations. The Court has also shown sensitivity in its interpretation of the term 'undertaking' where the Member States' organization of their social systems around

---

[100] According to the 'country of origin' principle, a service provider providing services anywhere in the EU would be subject only to the regulatory controls of their 'home state' – that is, the Member State in which they were established. This principle did not survive in the 'Services' Directive 2006/123/EC of the European Parliament and of the Council of 12 December 2006 on services in the internal market, OJ 2006 No. L376/36, as finally adopted.

[101] We see the point made by Damjanovic and De Witte, that the Lisbon Treaty makes welfare *values* far more pertinent at the level of EU policy-making, but that this is not reflected in a commitment to the future evolution of EU welfare *integration*. D. Damjanovic and B. De Witte, 'Welfare integration through EU law: the overall picture in the light of the Lisbon Treaty', EUI Working Paper LAW 2008/34 (2008).

[102] Joined Cases C-159/91 and 160/91, *Poucet and Pistre*, above n.70.

[103] Hatzopoulos, 'Health law and policy', above n.45.

[104] Case C-67/96, *Albany International* v. *Stichting Bedrijfspensioenfonds Textielindustrie* [1999] ECR I-5751.

the principle of solidarity is concerned.[105] And there have, of course, been several instances where the Court has specifically and explicitly qualified its decisions on the basis of non-economic policy objectives.

For instance, in *Preussen-Elektra*, a landmark 2001 ruling,[106] the Court upheld a German requirement that electricity distributors purchase from renewable energy suppliers at fixed minimum prices (where suppliers then compensated them), stating that this was not incompatible with the free movement of goods under internal market rules. Recalling the point made at the outset of this chapter, because commitment to environmental protection is explicitly included in the EU competences (see Title XIX EC), the Court was able to consider two equally footed EU-level polices: commitment to the environment versus internal market pricing stipulations.[107] Such a framing suggests that the explicit inclusion of social objectives in the EC Treaty could similarly help balance national policies promoting social protection, and reflects the Court's ability to be sensitive to a balanced approach to the internal market, particularly where the EC Treaty encourages it to do so. The Court also took into account that a further 'aim' of the German measure was public health protection. It is, of course, to be acknowledged that, like health, environmental policy is itself also a unique case. Nonetheless, other examples where the Court's approach to internal market law (including competition law) and welfare is more balanced include the Irish *BUPA* decision, where the Court of First Instance defended the state compensation scheme,[108] holding that it did not amount to state aid but rather a service of general interest within the scope of Article 86(2) EC, and *Kohll* and *Decker* themselves, where ensuring the financial sustainability of the social protection system was regarded as an important consideration. The Court has also referred to the Charter of Fundamental Rights in some instances.[109] Such cases may not be the norm, but it does need to be asked to what extent can the Court be expected to raise equity

---

[105] H. Schweitzer, 'Competition law and public policy: reconsidering an uneasy relationship. The example of Art. 81', EUI Working Papers 2007/30 (2007).

[106] Case C-379/98, *Preussen-Elektra AG v. Schleswag AG* [2001] ECR I-4473.

[107] Scharpf, 'The European social model', above n.15.

[108] CFI Judgement in Case T-289/03, *BUPA and Others v. Commission*, [2008] ECR II-81.

[109] Case C-173/99, *The Queen v. Secretary of State for Trade and Industry, ex parte Broadcasting, Entertainment, Cinematographic and Theatre Union*

and solidarity approaches to health care when these are only vaguely mentioned in the EC Treaty? The point to be made, therefore, is that the Court acts within the parameters available, and that it is responsive to Treaty amendments in policy areas other than internal market and competition law, as well as the 'background' of legislation, soft law, governance and policy activity. The Court's primarily internal market and free movement-oriented roles do, however, reflect its inability and unwillingness to address issues of a majoritarian politics nature.

Further, as the Court's role is to interpret and apply the rules that the Treaty sets out, then the argument may be made that it is not the Court that is responsible for making the rules per se, but the Member States as the *Herren der Verträge*. For, while the Court's decisions may bring prominence to an issue and focus attention, and may even go further than anticipated, the Court is not setting the rules as much as it is working within them. So, if the governments of the Members States are 'unhappy' with the Court's interpretation and application of the Treaties, can it not legitimately be asked whether they themselves are not at least in part responsible? Indeed, can such 'problems' not be addressed via new legislation? As Alter points out:

[I]f Member States cannot sway the interpretation of the Court, they may still be able to change the European law itself. This would not necessarily be an affront to the Court, nor would it necessarily undermine the Court's legitimacy. The political system is supposed to work by having legislators draft and change laws, and courts apply laws.[110]

During the 1990s, for instance, we saw the Member States move to protect specific practices with regard to private health insurance. As the legal framework for medical insurance was becoming clearer and more specific, the Member States were able to agree on and secure partial legislative exemptions aiming to protect social objectives. In future, we may also see the Member States actively move to protect practices that would otherwise constitute a violation of competition law, such as by subsidizing pharmacists to move into more rural areas.

(BECTU) [2001] ECR I-04881; and Joined Cases C-122/99 and C-125/99, *PD and Sweden* v. *Council* [2001] ECR 1-4319.

[110] K. J. Alter, *Establishing the supremacy of European law: the making of an international rule of law in Europe* (Oxford: Oxford University Press, 2001).

However, while in theory it should be easier now to change regulations and directives than in the earlier days of the EEC, because of the possibilities offered by qualified majority voting in the Council,[111] in practice we see that few Court interpretations have provoked legislative action to reverse the thrust of the decision. Alter notes that this is because:

[M]ost decisions of the European Court of Justice … affect Member States differently, so there is no coalition of support to change disputed legislation … After enough time passes, and enough protests or attempts to challenge ECJ jurisprudence lead nowhere, political passivity sets in … Inertia undermines the political will to effect change, and passivity is taken as a sign of tacit support.[112]

Although not our focus here, it is perhaps worth noting that Dehousse goes further, emphasizing that 'the tendency towards juridification may help to weaken the legitimacy of the integration process as a whole'.[113] Supposedly neutral debates on the interpretation of EU law considerably weaken the political process, and this adds to the perception of a democratic deficit in the EU more generally (even if the deficit itself is not a view shared by all scholars of European integration).[114] This offers opportunities to opponents of integration to claim that citizen's democracy is replaced by a form of 'judicial democracy'. Dehousse also points out that, because 'ECJ rulings may easily be perceived as intrusions calling into question the choices and traditions of national communities', the same process nonetheless enables EU law to protect individual rights against the decisions of national

---

[111] G. Tsebelis and G. Geoffrey, 'The institutional foundations of intergovernmentalism and supranationalism in the European Union', *International Organization* 55 (2001), 357–90.

[112] Alter, *Establishing the Supremacy*, above n.110.

[113] R. Dehouse, 'Constitutional reform in the European Community: are there alternatives to the majoritarian avenue?', *West European Politics* 18 (1995), 118–36.

[114] See, for example, G. Majone, 'Europe's "democratic deficit": the question of standards', *European Law Journal* 4 (1998), 5–28; A. Moravcsik, 'In defense of the "democratic deficit": reassessing the legitimacy of the European Union', *Journal of Common Market Studies* 40 (2002), 603–34; C. Crombez, 'The democratic deficit in the European Union: much ado about nothing?', *European Union Politics* 4 (2003), 101–20; Follesdal and Hix, 'Why there is a democratic deficit', above n.18.

administrations.[115] The point to be stressed, therefore, is that, in view of the joint decision trap, where sub-optimal policy outcomes tend to result, it is extremely difficult in practice for the Member States to reverse any Court advances that are based on the Treaty.

Given the Court's role, the parameters of the constitutional asymmetry, and recognizing the difficulties in overcoming Member State differences, EU policy-makers sought to reach their policy goals through alternative approaches, such as the development of transnational regulatory agencies. Attempts have also been made to strengthen the normative aspirations of 'social Europe' through 'new governance methods', employing soft law such as the open method of coordination (OMC). Such soft laws may be a first step in reconciling the constitutional asymmetry of the EU 'regulatory state', but their long run effectiveness and legitimacy remain in question.

5. New forms of governance and the role of soft law

Given the fundamental contradictions EU health (care) policy is confronted with, linked to the reluctance of Member States to transfer power in this field to the EU, while, at the same time, EU internal market policies might have adverse effects on national social policies, other policy approaches have developed over time, including in the field of health care. A wide variety of phenomena are associated with the concepts of 'new modes of governance', and the ambiguity of the notion may have contributed to its abundant popularity. Most do, however, refer to the relationship between state intervention, on the one hand, and societal autonomy, on the other.[116] 'New governance' refers to policy-making that is less prescriptive, less committed to uniform approaches and less hierarchical in nature.[117] In this section, we will shed light on the role of new modes of governance in EU health care policies. We will first consider the use of supranational agencies

---

[115] R. Dehouse, 'Integration through law revisited: some thoughts on the juridification of the European political process', in F. Snyder (ed.), *The Europeanisation of law: the legal effects of European integration* (Oxford: Hart, 2000).

[116] O. Treib, H. Bähr and G. Falkner, 'Modes of governance: a note towards conceptual clarification', Eurogov Paper No. N-05-02 (2000), available at www.mzes.uni-mannheim.de/projekte/typo3/site/fileadmin/wp/abstract/N-05-02.htm.

[117] See Chapter 4 in this volume.

as part of the new governance architecture, and then discuss the soft law instruments as non-legally binding EU rules of conduct, with a focus on the open method of coordination.

Looking first at the EU's use of supranational agencies, many of the current twenty-nine agencies have an impact, even if not direct competences, in health (care) policy fields. The two most relevant are the European Medicines Agency (EMEA), established in 1993, and the European Food Safety Authority, established in 2002 (EFSA).[118] Supranational agencies were set up primarily in response to the need to serve the 1992 Single Market Programme, where it became increasingly clear that the Commission had neither the functional nor technical expertise, far less the resources, to address the number of tasks associated with governing the internal market. It is also the case that the Member States were not in favour of any strengthening or expansion of the Commission. With independent regulatory agencies becoming an increasingly popular choice for governments at home, it was an approach that could be 'sold' to them, particularly so as these agencies were, on the one hand, decentralized, outside of the Commission bureaucracy and acting independently and, on the other, bodies that would regulate primarily in terms of gathering and disseminating information, without therefore interfering directly in Member State affairs. The European agency model was thus one that was more intergovernmental/technocratic than supranational. Not only did the agencies' management boards comprise Member State representatives, but the agency structure involved national regulatory authorities with the EU agency at the centre.[119]

None of the EU agencies are independent regulators in the sense of national regulatory authorities. Nonetheless, they do fill one or more governance roles, such as development of EU standards in the internal market;[120] information collection;[121] and the implementation of

---

[118] The afore-mentioned public health agency, as an 'executive agency' of the EU, is established for a limited time in order to administer the implementation of a specific Community programme and is not therefore a regulatory authority in the manner of the other EU agencies. The Executive Agency for the Public Health Programme is thus mandated to run from 1 January 2005 until 31 December 2010.

[119] Dehousse, 'Constitutional reform', above n.113.

[120] For example, the European Medicines Agency.

[121] For example, the European Environment Agency.

specialized programmes.[122] Despite their lack of executive powers, the use of agencies has been seen as filling the 'regulatory gap' at the EU level in terms of requiring the Member States, via their national regulatory authorities, to work together, rather than acting individually. The EU's agency model enables collective decisions to be taken that might otherwise have been hampered by the Member States' opposition to any further centralization of authority in the Commission. This 'softer' approach can therefore be seen as part of the 'new modes of governance' view of contemporary EU policy-making, marking a shift away from the long-standing, essentially top-down, rule-based 'Community method'. In this regard, many of the agencies represent the formalization into a single structure of what had previously been a series of loosely connected committees. This single committee structure can then work independently of both the Commission and the Member States – though this is not to say that the main committees are not subject to pressures from both, nor that their decisions or recommendations have never reflected these pressures – a fact that, in turn, generates its own credibility.

Essentially, an EU agency needs to be legitimate at both the EU and national levels, along with being effective at carrying out its assigned tasks. Many EU agencies have questionable power and legitimacy, leading to variability between Member States and decentralization.[123] Both the EMEA and EFSA rely on independent committees comprised of national experts to undertake assessments and work closely with the Member State agencies. Taking the risk assessment function away from the individual national bodies and assigning it to the relevant EU-level scientific committee or panel thus represents an attempt to depoliticize health protection and foster credibility in scientific decision-making in the EU. Nevertheless, in terms of their legitimacy at the EU and national levels, while EMEA is, in the main, well regarded, EFSA, even accounting for its relative youth, is regarded as weaker. This reflects the fact that the Commission tends to 'interfere' to a higher degree in the latter agency's work, where the College of Commissioners reviews the agency's recommendations. It also reflects that the Commission's decisions

---

[122] For example, the Executive Agency for Health and Consumers.

[123] Despite it not being an EU agency, it is worth highlighting in this context that, although DG SANCO is especially well regarded among national stakeholders, its lack of a clear legal competence to propose measures concerning health care hampers its abilities to effect comprehensive EU regulation change. Hervey, 'The European Union's governance', above n.39.

are put to the Council of Ministers for a vote, which introduces national sensitivities and politics into the food (safety) and agriculture sectors, as well as a high degree of politicking. This contributes to the agency's opinions being regarded as less credible than those of the EMEA. Nevertheless, the use of independent expert committees through hub and spoke arrangements via the agencies can be seen as part of the new governance architecture in the EU, as well as reflecting the EU health care governance 'patchwork'.[124]

Staying with the new modes of governance discussion, but moving perhaps a step beyond the agencies' policy-affecting role, soft law encapsulates non-legally binding EU rules of conduct.[125] There are three main categories of soft law: (a) preparatory information, including action programmes and communications; (b) interpretive and decisional tools intended to provide guidance in the application of EU law; and (c) policy coordination and steering instruments.[126] Such distinctions are often blurred in reality, as often soft law can evolve over time, including into hard law. For example, what began as a briefing on cancer screening evolved into a national policy steering instrument.[127]

The case can be made, relying on a constructivist approach, rather than the rational actor explanations that underpin intergovernmental explanations of EU-led policy change, that soft law can set the stage for policy change, through, for example, policy learning and sharing of best practice, by increasing dialogue and raising awareness. But limitations to effective policy learning arise due to financing disparities, differing capacities and asymmetric power between those 'at the table' in the process of articulating soft law measures. Without adequate financing mechanisms to back EU-led soft law suggestions for change, national policy change is unlikely. Even with adequate funding, best practice exchange between countries is not a given – measures pursued by one country will not

---

[124] See Chapter 2 in this volume.

[125] L. Senden, *Soft law in the European Community* (Oxford: Hart, 2004); L. Barani, 'Hard and soft law in the European Union: the case of social policy and the open method of coordination', The Constitutionalism Web-Papers No. p0011 (2006).

[126] Greer, 'Choosing paths', above n.94.

[127] L. G. Trubek, M. Nance and T. Hervey, 'The construction of a healthier Europe: lessons and questions for EU governance from the fight against cancer', 26 *Wisconsin International Law Journal* (2008), 804–43.

automatically work in another due to varying underlying conditions, especially if the 'learner' does not have the ability to facilitate
change.[128] Also, a middle of the road approach attempting to balance multiple development models may not be as efficient as pursuing one clear and well-coordinated strategy.[129] Member States may
also have the tendency to push forward soft laws that align with
their own domestic agendas, rather than policies that might better benefit the EU as a whole. Additionally, powerful lobbies such
as the pharmaceutical sector appear to have had success at getting their concerns on the EU soft law agenda, as evidenced by the
Pharmaceutical Forum.

The alignment of the requisite legal elements and key stakeholder
buy-in were important factors in the success of such examples.[130]
Ensuring that soft law is being developed and distributed to decision-
makers at the national level is also critical. Speed of uptake at the
national level may also be affected by how controversial the subject
matter is: contrast, for instance, the European Platform for Action on
Diet and Physical Activity and the work of the High Level Group on
Health Care in the internal market. On the other hand, soft laws such
as those promulgated through EU-level cancer and AIDS public health
programmes, funded by EU sources, have provided extremely helpful
research, guidelines and tools since inception. There is also evidence
that such programmes provide positive incentives for national governments to improve the quality and support of corresponding domestic
initiatives.[131]

Although such EU public health programmes may be well received,
Member States are quite sensitive to EU interference in welfare
domains like health care. Overall, despite the lack of formalized EU
welfare policies, a patchwork of law, governance and policy, especially
in the areas of public health, employee protection and cross-border
health care provision, is evident. The combination of formalized EU
regulation, Court rulings and the introduction of soft laws, leads to

[128] B. Eberlein, 'Formal and informal governance in Single Market regulation',
in T. Christiansen and S. Piattoni (eds.), *Informal governance in the EU*
(Cheltenham: Edward Elgar, 2004); Alber, 'The European social model',
above n.60.
[129] Alber, 'The European social model', above n.60.
[130] Scharpf, 'The European social model', above n.15.
[131] Trubek, Nance and Hervey, 'The construction of a healthier Europe',
above n.127.

'hybrid' policy channels.[132] Such 'amalgam' policies can help effect change and may be more politically feasible than policies relying solely on traditional regulatory (or redistributive) methods.

The open method of coordination (OMC) is the best-known example of soft law. The OMC, seen as a new mode of governance, serves to promote comparative evaluations of EU Member States' performance based on the voluntary sharing of information, dissemination of best practices and 'learning by monitoring'.[133] Although lacking formal sanction capabilities, the OMC establishes a benchmarking framework that respects national diversity and employs 'peer pressure tactics' (e.g., 'naming and shaming') to promote learning and achieve progress. It involves the European Commission as something of a broker or facilitator between Member States, with the burden of work falling to transnational networks of policy experts. The introduction of the OMC has prompted much debate over the role of such soft laws in EU governance.

Proponents contend that a 'gradual hardening' of OMC goals can be evidenced by the growing incorporation of social protection considerations in judicial rulings and in increased national implementations of soft laws.[134] They also point out that so-called 'hard law' may not, in practice, necessarily result in change on the ground, and that 'bottom-up' decision-making that engages those who will be responsible for actually implementing the decisions on the ground may be much more effective in practice than hard (but not necessarily observed) law. It is certainly the case that, with the EU political system dependent on consensus and (qualified) majority opinion, a dynamic based on peer pressure and benchmarking may help to move policy forward in intractable areas or those that are otherwise normally off-limits.

Sceptics of the use of soft law in this context raise five broad objections. They point out that soft law lacks specificity, enforceability and the ability to establish a concrete plan of action, fearing that it cannot counterbalance the hard laws defined around the internal market.[135] As Tsoukalis summarizes: '[i]n a political system consisting

[132] D. Trubek, P. Cottrell and M. Nance, *'Soft Law,' 'Hard Law,' and European Integration: Toward a Theory of Hybridity* (Madison: European Union Center of Excellence, University of Wisconsin, 2005).
[133] Scharpf, 'The European social model', above n.15.
[134] Ferrera, *The boundaries of welfare*, above n.48.
[135] Trubek, Cottrell and Nance, *'Soft Law'*, above n.132.

of (semi-) sovereign states, which retain in most cases the monopoly of implementation of joint decisions, discretion and brainstorming are usually a poor substitute for rules'.[136] Second, given a scenario of 'competitive solidarity', such soft laws may not be able to assuage tension between competing regions.[137] Third, soft law also bypasses traditional accountability mechanisms, such as public forums, which decreases transparency and may lead to an 'expert-ocracy' of sorts, as the process is often detached from the constituency of the EU citizen, and from traditional representative democratic bodies, such as parliaments.[138] This again reflects (and reinforces) the politics–economics gap already mentioned. The Lisbon Strategy, for instance, set out to make the EU the 'most competitive and dynamic knowledge-based economy in the world' by 2010. Notwithstanding the financial crisis ongoing at the time of writing, there has been but limited progress towards achieving this goal. Fourth, the application of the OMC to health care, in particular, raises a number of questions, particularly in respect of benchmarking and the extent to which demonstrable outcomes or cumulative progress can be ascertained.[139] The difficulties surrounding the health care strand of the social protection OMC, and the fact that the development of even base-line indicators has been significantly slower than in other strands of this OMC, further confirm these concerns. Fifth, Scharpf contends that the OMC cannot achieve constitutional parity due to the vulnerable state of national social protection policies in relation to economic integration objectives.[140] Using the Scandinavian welfare model as a case-study, Scharpf concludes that even such best-practice welfare models could hypothetically be dismantled by a Court ruling based on internal market free movement or competition law. However, others believe that the internal market's legal structure takes both economic and social protection considerations into account, and Hervey

---

[136] Tsoukalis, *What kind of Europe?*, above n.16, p. 34. He does, however, acknowledge that soft law approaches, and the OMC in particular, 'may have wider application in some new policy areas where national governments want to preserve a wide margin of discretion'. While not a new policy area, this designation would seem to apply to health policy.

[137] Trubek, Cottrell and Nance, '*Soft Law*', above n.132.

[138] Ferrera, 'European integration', above n.56; M. Bovens, 'New forms of accountability and EU governance', *Comparative European Politics* 5 (2007), 104–20.

[139] McKee and Mossialos, 'European health care policy', above n.41.

[140] Scharpf, 'The European social model', above n.15.

therefore maintains that elements of social protection can be firmly embedded in EU regulation of the internal market[141] – although this is not to say that they have (yet) been so embedded, in all circumstances where this might be desirable.

The difficult questions of whether soft laws are legitimate and effective must also be asked. In relation to legitimacy, many uncertainties persist. From misgivings about the very concept of EU-level solidarity, to tensions around the viability of soft and hard laws coexisting, and questions about the democratic nature of this non-consensus driven process, the legitimacy of soft policy is not guaranteed.[142] The flexible nature of soft law also makes it almost impossible to gauge its effectiveness.[143] Additionally, clarification is necessary around whether soft law efficacy is measured by its influence on national level policy change, institutional restructuring and/or vague conceptions of mutual learning.[144] Nonetheless, soft laws can be considered a 'democratic experimentation' of sorts that, albeit far from perfect, may be a critical first step in establishing EU-level social policy.[145] Hard laws in the realm of social Europe may not be politically tenable at this point in time, and a process like the OMC could help stakeholders gradually realize the need for (and possibly effectiveness of) enhanced EU-level social policy, including in health care fields. So, while soft laws, including the OMC, have the potential to be an important first step and to help shape national policies, it does not appear that soft law alone can resolve the constitutional asymmetry. Further, as Jorens notes, 'we should take care. In case we really want to guarantee that social policy

---

[141] T. Hervey and L. Trubek, 'Freedom to provide health care services in the EU: an opportunity for "hybrid government" ', *The Columbia Journal of European Law* 13 (2007), 623–45.

[142] B. Eberlein and D. Kerwer, 'Theorising the new modes of European Union governance', *European Integration Online Papers* 6 (2003), available at http://eiop.or.at/eiop/texte/2002–005a.htm; J. Zeitlin, 'Social Europe and experimentalist governance: towards a new constitutional compromise?', in de Búrca, *EU law and the welfare state*, above n.45.

[143] See, on the methodological impossibility of discerning whether national policy changes are attributable to the OMC, S. Borrás and B. Greve, 'Concluding remarks: new method or just cheap talk?', *Journal of European Public Policy* 11 (2004), 329–36, at 331–3.

[144] Zeitlin, 'Social Europe and experimentalist governance', above n.142.

[145] C. Sabel and J. Zeitlin, 'Learning from difference: the new architecture of experimentalist governance in the EU', *European Law Journal* 14 (2008), 271–327; Eberlein and Kerwer, 'Theorising the new modes', above n.142.

is a productive factor on an equal basis with economic and employment policy, there is a need for a better regulatory framework.'[146] This is the case in order to ensure that social objectives are not (implicitly) governed by economic or fiscal factors, for the extent to which the OMC can either bring tangible developments in health care policy at the EU level, or even lead to hard law more generally, remains unclear.

6. Key areas of EU legal and policy developments in health: the structure of the book

This section serves to apply the various elements of the above discussion to specific areas – current and emerging – in EU law and health care. These areas reflect the individual chapters of the book, and each subsection in the following provides a brief synopsis of the relevant chapter, as well as a more detailed examination of the policy questions and implications at hand.

The volume is roughly divided into two parts. Chapters 2–6 consider, broadly speaking, governance and policy-making arrangements at the EU and Member State levels in view of the impact of EU law on health. Chapters 7–15 then address individual areas of contention or interest given the incursion of EU law – primarily relating to free movement, but also competition law – and its effect on policy-making and outcomes. All of the chapters address both the tension between economic and social priorities in health care given the impact of EU law, and the impact on national health systems (in terms of issues raised and effects brought to bear). The discussion begins with a more detailed and critical exploration of the legal, governance and policy-making patchwork touched upon above.

A. *The legal–policy patchwork*

Chapter 2 provides an in-depth examination of the different EU-level responses to the myriad issues facing the Member States as the effects of EU law (and of European integration more widely) on their health care systems are felt. Taking as their starting point the somewhat paradoxical situation that national policies are increasingly influenced

---

[146] Y. Jorens, 'The evolution of social policy in the European Union', *Polityka Spoleczna* (2005), 26–9.

by EU legislative instruments and policies at the same time that EU level welfare policy is purposefully weak, Tamara Hervey and Bart Vanhercke explain how a 'patchwork' of EU law and policy has developed in relation to health care. An increased appreciation of the effects of European integration on national health care objectives has evolved over time, and the chapter provides an overview of this phenomenon. It makes the case that an EU health care policy sphere is evolving that balances formal EU legislation and judicial rulings, EU soft modes of governance, and defensive national level responses.

Providing something of an historical perspective, the chapter begins with an overview of formal EU laws around public health policy. The direct and unintended consequences of other EU laws and court cases on national health care systems are then critically assessed and numerous examples are provided. Specifically, the role of internal market, competition, social and employment law are evaluated. The fourth section explores the processes through which various sets of actors attempt to shape the EU health care debate. Five sets of key player are identified, which are labelled as 'public health', 'social affairs', 'internal market', 'enterprise' and 'economic' actors, who have crowded the health care arena and established various uncoordinated responses with varying impacts at the domestic (and, indeed, EU) level.

Public health is a separate policy domain from health care, but there is, of course, a high degree of overlap. EU public health policy is based on Article 152 of the EC Treaty, equipping the EU with instruments to regulate at the supranational level. Specifically, EU public health programmes, such as those on cancer and HIV/AIDS, appear to have had a positive impact, especially in increasing awareness of high priority health issues throughout the EU. The programmes' budgets, though modest, have nonetheless provided guidelines and positive incentives for change at the national health care policy level, especially in research and development. As a result, the public health programmes, administered by the Directorate-General for Health and Consumer Protection (DG SANCO), provide a platform from which health care governance can springboard.

EU legislation relating to other policy areas and decisions of the Court provide further avenues and legal instruments that have had profound influences on national health care systems. Despite a small budget, the extensive regulatory powers of the EC Treaty in internal market law have had a significant influence. Specifically, the principle of free movement of goods, services and professionals has been applied to the health care arena. Despite exceptions such as the 'protection of the health and life of humans' under Article 30 EC, and additional recognition of 'objective public interests', the encroachment of internal market law on national health care policies has occurred. The Court has attempted to balance such public interest with market objectives, but its jurisprudence has more explicit market-promoting guidelines in comparison to more vague welfare-promoting objectives.

Some formal regulation has been adopted concerning the manufacture, marketing and sale of pharmaceuticals and biomedical devices, as well as consumer protection measures (e.g., tobacco laws). It appears that the success of EU regulatory measures is contingent on the formal legal power to adopt such EU-level standards and the corresponding political will. Promoting competition and protecting services of general interest are also primary objectives of EU internal market policy. Articles 81 and 82 EC may apply to governmental services like health care, which has had repercussions on national health care and places a burden of proof on domestic governments, such as in respect of services of general economic interest (and this, in turn, depends on how these services are considered), as discussed in Chapters 7–9. Additionally, EU social and employment law, intended primarily to protect EU workers and promote non-discrimination, have also had unintended consequences in the health care setting. For example, the Working Time Directive's application to medical professionals may hamper domestic delivery of care.

In such a manner, the freedom of domestic stakeholders to organize their national health care systems is restrained by the growing influence of EU law, but the EU has limited specific legal competence in the health care field. Defensive responses to protect solidarity-based national models of health care by a multitude of actors and institutions have been evidenced. Nonetheless, health care has slowly but unmistakably found its way onto the EU agenda. A key initial milestone was the adoption of soft law such as the 1989 Community Charter of Fundamental Social Rights for Workers; Commission white papers on social protection have also played an instrumental role. Other Commission communications have spurred debates on topics like reducing costs, ageing and pensions. High profile court cases have also kick-started political momentum around social protection, especially in health care. And the EU Treaties have afforded various Directorates-General greater legitimacy, such as the increased role implied for DG SANCO under the Amsterdam Treaty.

'Enterprise' players, such as the pharmaceutical industry, have also played a profound role in pushing forward agendas such as competitiveness, direct-to-consumer advertising and transparency in pricing and reimbursement. The launch of the G10 Medicines Group to foster competitiveness is an example of a new informal mechanism that largely enables the Directorate-General for Enterprise and Industry (DG Industry) to weaken the position of the institutions involved in the legislative process on pharmaceuticals. Increasing awareness of such 'back door' internal market-promoting approaches and their influence on national health care systems is occurring. Nonetheless, EU level intervention remains very politically sensitive. National health ministers and DG SANCO have struggled to implement soft law recommendations such as those of the High Level Process of Reflection on Patient Mobility, or to implement the 'Concerted Strategy on Health Care for the Elderly'. Member States often seek to delay the processes. The European Commission succeeds in pushing soft law like the OMC forward by employing simple strategies such as shifting the wording of Council mandates from referencing 'health care' to 'health and long-term care for the elderly'.

Health will continue to be a highly constrained area of EU competence. But awareness of the influence of EU regulation on health care continues to increase. The case is made that greater governance does not appear to significantly destabilize the independent agency of the Commission, and public consultation is seen as a tool to legitimize further initiatives like soft law and legally-binding directives. The increasing interlinkage between classical EU law and new governance processes is evidenced. Such cross-fertilization is fostering hybrid policy instruments; however, it does not appear that such patchworks will result in a single unified EU approach to health care.

B. *Agencies and health (care) policy-making*

In Chapter 3, Govin Permanand and Ellen Vos look at the reasons behind the increasing number and influence of EU-level agencies, before focusing on the two with the most direct relevance to national health systems: the European Medicines Agency (EMEA) and the European Food and Safety Authority (EFSA). They highlight a general trend amongst European policy-makers to turn to executive or regulatory agencies that are outside of the Commission structure as a means of addressing specific areas of EU policy. The agencies are also seen as a means of generating objective assessments and disseminating information and examples of best practice. More widely, the chapter also considers agencies from the perspective of their being a central element in the new experimentalist governance architecture of EU policy-making, and considers the pharmaceuticals and foodstuffs agencies as examples in practice.

The authors trace the evolution of EU competence in health and the Europeanization of pharmaceutical and food safety as precursors to the eventual emergence of EFSA and the EMEA. The discussion looks at EU-level initiatives, the impact of the single market, and health crises in the respective domains, highlighting how this dual health protection and internal market facilitation role is reflected in both agencies' mandates and their execution of regulatory functions. These mandates are then examined in detail, especially their risk analysis functions. This reflection on their operations is tied to the EU's principles of good governance. The chapter thus offers a comparative analysis of the two agencies, considering their real and potential impact on Member State health systems. Throughout, concerns are raised around the independence, accountability and strength of both agencies, especially as their spheres of influence increase. The chapter further raises the question as to whether the agency approach, which is seen as a constituent element of new modes of governance approaches (see Chapter 4 in this volume), is likely to be relevant to other health-related areas as well.

The wider development of Community health competences can, however, be seen as a backdrop to the emergence of the EMEA and EFSA in terms of how health has permeated the EU agenda in the first place. Here, the discussion looks at the 1992 Maastricht Treaty's allowance of public health protection, the 1997 Treaty of Amsterdam's emphasis on human health safety, and ECJ rulings on the free movement of health care services and professionals. In identifying milestones in the development of the two agencies, we see that specific legislation and monitoring guidelines addressing the pharmaceutical sector, at both the national and EU levels, were first adopted in the aftermath of the thalidomide case. 'Mutual recognition' procedures aimed at reducing trade barriers to increase the speed of entry of new medicines were introduced in 1975 and further augmented by the 1986 Single European Act's emphasis on the free movement of goods, services and capital. Meanwhile, specific food safety oversight began in 1974 with the creation of a risk assessment body and was first seriously questioned in the wake of the bovine spongiform encephalopathy (BSE) crisis with the reorganization of scientific committees under the Directorate-General for Consumer Policy and Health Protection of the Commission (now DG SANCO). A new Community approach thus began to evolve with the adoption of the 2002 General Food Law[147] to address safety concerns and the creation of the centralized EFSA. Tension between balancing the objectives of the EU internal market, such as free movement and competition, and health safety is thus evidenced in both policy domains, and both agencies' remits reflect this in their regulatory mandates. Nonetheless, a bias towards market policy is suggested, indicating a need to better serve public health interests more directly.

The mandates and functions of the EU regulatory agencies reflect considerable variability in degree of authority, ranging from collecting and disseminating information, acting in an advisory capacity to the Commission and/or Member States, and providing direct oversight and guidance. As regards the medicines and foodstuffs agencies specifically, the underlining aims are shown to include securing political commitment for long-term goals in health, addressing uncertainties and risk analysis, enhancing credibility through greater independence from policy-makers and increasing efficiency. In this regard, both agencies are shown to be similar in their focus on guaranteeing product accessibility and safety, along with meeting consumer expectations by effectively communicating potential risks. Yet, while the EMEA is shown to be a 'strong' agency by virtue of its proximity to the Commission (where the Commission accepts the EMEA's opinions in the form that they are delivered), EFSA is shown to be comparatively weak, as its recommendations do not carry similar weight. A further crucial difference between the agencies lies in the timing of regulatory interventions: pharmacovigilance tends to focus especially on ex ante

---

[147] Regulation 178/2002/EC of the European Parliament and of the Council of 28 January 2002 laying down the general principles and requirements of food law, establishing the European Food Safety Authority and laying down procedures in matters of food safety, OJ 2002 No. L31/1.

regulation, while foodstuff testing generally occurs ex post market distribution. Regarding the latter, an increasing trend towards pre-market control is, however, the case.

Despite the agencies' need to be seen as credible, independent and accountable, and to espouse good communication practices, the chapter shows that both reveal some shortcomings in these areas. Even if not in the opinion-generating procedures per se, it is suggested that the influence of the governments of the Member States, the Commission and industry on the agencies may be too high, though understandable given their role in also promoting the single market. So, while both agencies attempt to maintain their independence – efforts have been made to strengthen the declaration of interests of agency committee and panel members, and greater public involvement has been sought, for example, through the EMEA's introduction of consumer and doctor representatives on its management board – we see that neither agency is immune to politics. This is especially the case for EFSA, where the communication of risk assessment findings is extremely political and challenging. Additionally, there are potential conflicts of interest in relation to industry sponsorship. Here, it is interesting to note that the instructive capacities of EMEA in helping to guide applicants on what is needed for a successful marketing authorization go considerably beyond that undertaken at a national level or by the United States Food and Drug Administration. Increased transparency is pivotal in building consumer trust, but also a challenge in light of commercial secrecy. And the fact that neither agency is entirely free from EU and national level politics – that the science is not properly divested from the politics – is also identified as an area of potential concern, given that both purport to protect public health according to the highest independent scientific standards. Overall, therefore, better balance between the agencies' commitment to hard science, stakeholder priorities and public opinion must be achieved.

The chapter also treats the agencies as part of the broader new modes of governance approach. As such, there are lessons to be learned from their design, their involvement of interests and their functioning in practice. This is especially the case given their impact on national health care systems. Can such agencies help to forward the more deliberative and participatory policy-making approaches required to address sensitive issues in health and health care? The discussion does not offer an unequivocal answer – it is not clear that one exists. But the discussion does strike a cautionary note in nonetheless endorsing the view that the agencies have an important role to play and may serve as something of a model for better balancing between the free movement of goods and public health priorities.

C. *Health care and the EU: the hard politics of soft law*

The shift away from the 'classic Community method' of regulation to more incorporative and less prescriptive approaches has led to an increasing literature of so-called 'new modes of governance' in the EU. Soft law, in general, and the OMC – the most institutionalized form of soft law – in particular, have so far been used with some success in various areas of social policy. Are these modes of governance relevant to health policy (making) in terms of helping to breach the constitutional asymmetry between EU-level regulatory internal market law and lack of redistributive power in welfare contexts? For, while the OMC may be useful in helping to overcome national divergence via a shared bottom-up approach, it is nevertheless grounded in an EU legal framework, which seeks deregulation of national markets and the promotion of competition. The question of how to achieve overall convergence while promoting individual competitiveness, and how to then balance this with appropriate and shared social protection guidelines, are among the challenges facing policy-makers who seek to use the OMC approach in health (care) policy.

Taking as their starting-point the conceptual difficulties and rather ambiguous definitions that mark much of the new modes of governance and soft law literature, in Chapter 4 Scott Greer and Bart Vanhercke seek to offer some clarity by focusing on four questions. What is new governance? Why and how has new governance developed in health care? Finally, they ask what it may do now in view of the challenges and sticking-points already mentioned several times. They discuss the new governance concept within the context of soft law more generally, and offer a case-study of OMC, as applied to health care, in terms of its theoretical origins and application in practice.

The authors highlight that specifying what new governance is and what is not 'new governance' is not an easy task given the degree of networked policy-making that characterizes the EU polity. Nonetheless, the Commission's increased use of: (a) green and white papers, action

programmes and information communications; (b) more formal
communications, guidelines and frameworks for action; and (c) steering instruments such as the OMC or the High Level Group on Health
Services and Medical Care reflects this less hierarchical and more
deliberative approach.

The OMC, as officially laid out at the Lisbon Summit in 2000, is
envisaged as an incremental mode of securing Member State approval
towards achieving consensus in areas that have otherwise defied harmonization. Via a commitment to agreed goals, benchmarking of
progress towards these goals, reporting mechanisms and sharing of
best practices, Member States can help each other develop and pursue
measures towards promoting convergence among them.

The authors found that the new governance mechanisms emerged
as a result of competition between different sets of actors to frame EU
health policy as an economic (internal market), social or health policy
issue, and that this developed as a reaction to the development of EU
law and decisions by the Court, as well as the pressures of Economic
and Monetary Union (EMU). The direction of Court decisions both
created an EU competency and gave it a concrete form – the internal
market (patient mobility), state aids, competition and public procurement law. That form did not reflect the priorities, values or the expertise of health systems or welfare states. Consequently, health ministries
and health interest groups were at least grudgingly receptive to the
Commission when it proposed new governance mechanisms such as
the OMC and the High Level Group on Health Services and Medical
Care. The emergence of soft law with regard to health care is thus the
result of bargaining between different sets of strategic actors, each with
specific, sometimes conflicting, interests. The authors found some evidence that illustrates that soft law is considered by some and in some
cases to ensure compliance with Court rulings (where soft law is seen as
a tool to implement hard law), whereas, in other circumstances and by
other actors, soft law is sometimes used to avoid specific legislation on
health care (e.g., through engaging and occupying the Commission).

The chapter outlines the necessary conditions for successful new
governance. Drawing on the work of Sabel and Zeitlin,[148] they substantiate that the first condition is uncertainty – i.e., lack of agreed

[148] Sabel and Zeitlin, 'Learning from difference', above n.145.

solutions (or problems) – which is the case in health. The second is a lack of hierarchy, with no single actor having the capacity to impose its own preferred solution. These two criteria are fertile grounds for networks. The third criterion is an unattractive penalty default for failure – i.e., something worse that will happen if the experimental governance fails, a destabilization regime. The authors consider the progressive submission to internal market law as extended in an unpredictable, case-by-case manner to be the penalty for lack of action. The ultimate question is, however, whether any of the soft law instruments will prevent the penalty default. This is not clear. The authors do, however, suggest that the Court has shown itself to be sensitive to the political consequences of its decisions. Furthermore, it is not clear that new governance mechanisms would have to actually affect health systems or policies in order to 'head off' the Court. New governance might affect policy without staving off the expansion of internal market law, and it might equally deter the Court and the Directorate-General for the Internal Market and Services (DG MARKT) without affecting a single doctor or patient.

Looking at the likely future of new governance, the authors conclude that the benefits for the EU institutions and Member States are sufficient to keep new governance alive, even if they might not be sufficient to carry the day for the social or health framing of EU health policy. New governance tools might be abandoned if Member States do not get adequate use out of them or if one or more EU institutions dislike the consequences. However, the Commission is the most active EU institution, and its fragmentation and internal competition generally enhance its entrepreneurialism. Therefore, the authors conclude that it is likely to continue to offer new governance mechanisms. New governance might do better than survive if new governance seems likely to prevent the 'default penalty' of internal market law. Conversely, if the OMC turns out to be a way to discuss health policy while the Court is rewriting the fundamental rules of the game, Member States might lose interest. But even if they never replace the Community method, and fail as the countermove to Court jurisprudence, the different mechanisms fulfil multiple functions, such as strengthening networks, contributing to epistemic Europeanization and shaping political consensus.

D. Public health in the EU

In Chapter 5, Tamara Hervey, Martin McKee and Anna Gilmore highlight that, at the same time as the EC Treaty enshrines the exclusive right of the Member States to set their own national health care policies, so too do they establish a set of obligations for the EU vis-à-vis public health requirements. Although the inherent difficulty (if not contradiction) in this position has been raised in Chapter 1, this chapter explores the range of competences exercised at the EU level in public health protection of EU citizens. The chapter sets out the legal framework, discussing the Treaty and the regulations governing the EU's public health programmes. It examines the challenges faced by the EU in developing public health policy through two case studies: communicable diseases and tobacco.

Throughout the chapter, the authors highlight the tensions with which the EU is confronted while discharging its obligations to develop and implement public health policy. The first tension relates to its positioning between nation states and international organizations. The EU lacks the public health expertise, resources and experience of international bodies. It also lacks the capacity – in particular, the financial and human resources – of a state, which would enable it to deliver public health policies. The chapter illustrates that, as a result, in some respects, the EU acts, or attempts to act, as if it were an international public health organization. In other respects, the EU acts, or attempts to act, as if it were a state. What emerges is a series of partially-connected EU laws and policies that have various effects on public health. Secondly, the EU has obligations concerning the protection and promotion of public health, but the organization and delivery of health care services is the responsibility of the Member States. Yet, in practice, public health measures can reduce the burden of disease falling on health care systems, while health promotion is a core function of a health care system. In practical terms, this can make it difficult to ascertain what is or is not within the scope of EU law. The third tension is between the imperative to promote public health and those elements designed to create the internal market. And finally, within the European Commission, one Directorate-General (DG SANCO) has a specific responsibility for public health, but many policies that might be considered to be directly relevant to public health are located elsewhere, often reflecting other priorities and underpinned by different values. For instance, DG SANCO has the responsibility to ensure that the EU is 'mainstreaming' health protection, by 'ensuring a high level of human health protection' in all its policies and activities, implying a duty to conduct health impact assessments of EU policies. However, DG SANCO's capacity to do so is extremely limited. The authors substantiate that, until these tensions can be resolved, if this is possible, the EU institutions, with their limited resources, will find it very difficult to develop a comprehensive public health policy.

The chapter further analyses how the powers of the EU in the field of public health extended mainly as a reaction to failings to address serious crises such as the BSE crisis or health scandals such as the one on the distribution and transfusion of HIV-infected blood and blood products. While Article 152 EC explicitly prohibits the adoption of binding EU-level laws designed to protect and improve human health, it has allowed the EU to develop its own public health programmes. According to the authors, it is difficult to assess the overall impact of the public health programmes, as they lack specific goals against which success can be measured. Furthermore, the extent to which the results of projects are subsequently embedded into national practices or fed into EU law and policy-making is unclear.

In order to illuminate some of the other means by which the EU fulfils its obligation to 'improve public health', the chapter examines policies with regard to communicable disease. The progressive dismantling of borders within Europe, with the resultant increase in mobility of people and goods, has greatly increased the opportunity for the spread of infectious diseases. There are, however, various safeguards in the Treaties that have been developed in subsequent legislation. Court rulings and specific legislation have clarified this further, allowing obstacles to the free movement of products where there is genuine doubt about the risk to health, or to the free movement of persons, although the circumstances in which the latter may be done are extremely limited. Article 152 EC provides the legal basis for establishing proactive mechanisms to combat communicable diseases. The EU accordingly established in 2004 a European Centre for Disease Prevention and Control (ECDC) to provide structured, systematic responses to the threats from communicable diseases and other serious health threats in Europe.

The chapter illustrates the wide spectrum of different roles for EU law and policy that are at play, ranging from regulation through the provisions of internal market law, through to soft law and the use of information to exercise control and effect change. At the more 'regulatory' end of the spectrum, Article 152 EC expressly excludes the ability to take harmonizing measures for public health purposes. On the other hand, restrictions on the free movement of persons and goods, in pursuit of protection of public health, are permitted within internal market law. There is EU-level regulation of the contents of products, and the labelling of products, that involve or may involve a public health risk. The chapter shows, however, a lack of 'fit' between the EU legal bases and the public health aims. Measures adopted under Article 95 EC must be proportionate (i.e., they must not go further than necessary in achieving the aim of ensuring the smooth functioning of the internal market). The EU may not lawfully use internal market law simply to achieve public health goals. This has left them open to challenge by lobbies, as illustrated through the major Tobacco Control Directives since 1989, which have all been challenged by the tobacco industry and its allies.

At the other end of the spectrum, there are areas where it is believed, according to the authors, that greater interaction between members of the public health community, supported by the EU, has played a role in the diffusion of ideas leading to convergence of national policies without any direct involvement of the EU institutions. The EU has exercised influence through information collection, dissemination, development of best practice and networking. As illustrated by the EU's activities in communicable disease control, the authors suggest that the judicious use of relatively small available funds, in carefully selected policy areas, can lead, through their own successes and also external pressures, to large scale, more integrated sets of policy-making tools and institutions, supported by a long term financial framework.

The authors conclude that, faced with the responsibility of developing public health policy, in the context of insufficient resources and competences to develop the full range of policies and practices that make up national public health and insufficient expertise and experience to become an international public health actor, the EU has adopted a piecemeal approach, based on the 'art of the possible'.

E. *Fundamental rights and their applicability to health care*

In Chapter 6, Jean McHale considers how and, indeed, whether fundamental human rights principles may be utilized in developing

EU law and policy in health. She looks, first, at how principles of fundamental human rights have been developed at the European level, both in respect of the Council of Europe (i.e., the European Court of Human Rights, the European Social Charter and the European Convention on Biomedicine) and the European Union (i.e., the Charter of Fundamental Rights of the European Union). The discussion considers their impact – real and potential – on health and health care in the Member States and raises, with examples, the potential conflicts between such initiatives and national laws, particularly in ethical and religious issues. Second, the chapter outlines the recently endorsed EU Charter of Fundamental Rights and newly created Fundamental Rights Agency. It further considers what impact, if any, they will have in general and on health and health care specifically. The discussion here is oriented around the question of whether an 'EU approach to fundamental rights in health and health care law' will develop.

With health and health care not explicitly delineated in the various human rights declarations relevant to the EU Member States (though they are implied or mentioned in passing), their impact has, in the main, been limited to legal challenges in related areas. These include abortion and the right to life, suicide and euthanasia, assisted reproductive technologies, access to care, and limitations placed on, for example, persons with HIV/AIDS. Nonetheless, the Charter of Fundamental Human Rights (agreed in 2000 and adopted in amended form by the Member States in 2007 within the context of the Lisbon Treaty)[149] has the potential to make more of an impact. For instance, the Commission will be able to challenge Member States should it perceive them to be in breach of the Charter in areas within the scope of EU law, and it may result in more (EU and national) legislation being framed in the language of fundamental rights. However, the aspirational language used, along with the considerable scope afforded in interpreting elements of the seven titles and fifty-four articles of the Charter suggests a degree of uncertainty. Indeed, Article 35, which is entitled 'Health Care', is broad-ranging, if not simplistic, in citing access subject to national laws and the need for the EU to take health into account when developing policies.

---

[149] The Lisbon Treaty entered into force on 1 December 2009.

Increased rhetoric and better-informed debate – an area in which the new Fundamental Rights Agency's primarily information-gathering and dissemination role can play a part – may not necessarily amount to a tangible (long-term) impact. Indeed, the agency is not designed to monitor human rights in the Member States. It is not to be a human rights 'watchdog': it cannot cite Member States or address citizens' complaints, and will be more focused on coordination within and between Member States over human rights issues. Additionally, while there is no specific reference to health or health care in the agency's mandate, health care has, in 2008, been added as a 'thematic area of work'. This reflects that some areas of its work in respect of discrimination (whether based on sex, race or ethnic origin, religion or belief, disability, age or sexual orientation, etc.), the rights of the child, and the respect for private life and protection of personal data have carried some health impact. The agency's work around health rights – mainly concerning access by minority groups or others excluded – has been oriented around (non-) discrimination. Given its limited mandate, therefore, the agency's work here is primarily in disseminating what the Member States are or are not doing. For instance, it highlights good and bad implementation of the EU's anti-discrimination legislation or good practice in tackling racism and discrimination (including as relates to health care). And an overall conclusion of this work is that the agency urges Member States, as well as the EU more generally, to encourage cultural sensitivity in the health care workforce.

Despite the Charter and the Agency, therefore, it remains unclear whether a health care dimension to fundamental rights in the EU, or a fundamental rights dimension to EU health care policy, will develop. While both Charter and Agency will contribute to greater awareness, and may have the longer-term effect of moving human rights from a soft to hard law context, perhaps their primary contribution may be in terms of the use of new modes of governance in the context of health and health care law and policy-making – that is, they will engage the Member States and other actors in a deliberative process to deal with complex and controversial issues in a sensitive manner towards enabling agreement and progress. For instance, if the Agency can contribute to better embedding the Charter into decision-making contexts, we may see more explicit EU policy emerge in the future.

F. EU competition law and public services, including health care

Chapters 7–9 analyse the applicability of EU competition rules to national health systems, and whether the case-law and Commission policy statements provide sufficient guidance to resolve the dilemmas that such an application raises. As the authors remind us, the creation of the single internal market characterized by open competition has been and remains an important tenet of European Union policy. Public services in many Member States are characterized by the principles of solidarity and citizenship, which may make the application of internal market and competition principles inappropriate. In Chapter 7, Tony Prosser first considers to what extent health services are subject to the competition norms of the internal market. Following from this, Julia Lear, Elias Mossialos and Beatrix Karl in Chapter 8 then ask when competition law applies to health care organizations. In Chapter 9, Vassilis Hatzopoulos considers how the rules of public procurement and state aid affect the organization of Member State health care systems. Neither the European Court of Justice, the Court of First Instance nor the Commission have defined sufficiently unambiguous responses to these questions.

The most important Treaty provisions for this purpose are Articles 81, 82 and 86 EC governing competition, and Article 87 EC covering aids granted by states. Article 81 bans cartel agreements, activities and practices that aim to or somehow affect the prevention, restriction or distortion of competition within the common market. Article 82 prohibits abuse of a dominant position by one or more undertakings. The term 'undertaking' is not defined in the Treaty, but case-law indicates that it does not matter whether the entity is public or private; the defining factor is whether the entity is engaged in economic activity. These rules make it difficult for market participants to attempt to coordinate activities with other market players or to attempt to exploit their monopoly position. Article 86 addresses both the activities of Member States directly and organizations involved in services of general economic interest. In the case of public undertakings and bodies given exclusive or special rights, Member States must not make or maintain in force measures contrary to Treaty rules, notably in relation to competition. Article 86(2) allows for an exemption from competition rules for services of general economic interest where market failures cannot be effectively remedied with market-based solutions. Article 87 EC prohibits Member States from granting public resources in a form that distorts or threatens to distort competition by favouring certain undertakings. Public funds must either be distributed following a competitive tender based on objective and transparent criteria, or must be specifically evaluated under the Treaty rules on state aids.

Within this context, Chapter 7 focuses on the conflict between economic policy and public services within EU law. The health sector offers an interesting case-study of this dilemma, as some Member States have begun to mix markets and solidarity-based provision of care. The evolving test for services of general economic interest is another point where the Court must determine whether the health sector should be subject to the rules on competition. Chapter 8 takes the next step in the analysis and offers cases from the Court, national courts and the national competition authorities to illustrate the complexities of applying EU competition law to the health sector. Since Regulation 1/2003/EC[150] modernized and decentralized enforcement authority, the protection of EU competition law by national courts and national competition authorities has created the opportunity for greater scrutiny of health care markets. Chapter 9 then explains the links between public procurement and state aid rules and further dissects the implications for financing, planning and contracting for health services.

The competition provisions are based on the argument that competitive markets are the best means of achieving two objectives: maximizing economic efficiency and augmenting consumer choice. Since the health care sector is plagued by market failures, including information asymmetry, moral hazard and uncertainty, Member States have traditionally defined policies to fund and provide services in an attempt to minimize these problems. Competition law may apply where governments mix markets and solidarity-based provision of health services. The distinction between social and economic activities used in the determination of whether competition law applies may seem intuitive at first glance. However, as the complexity of case-law around the health sector demonstrates, it is often unclear to what extent EU competition law is engaged when national health

---

[150] Council and European Parliament Regulation 1/2003/EC on the implementation of the rules on competition laid down in Articles 81 and 82 of the Treaty, OJ 2003 No. L1/1.

systems have introduced elements of competition. Some public health providers compete with private organizations for privately paying patients, such as between health care trusts in the United Kingdom, or some public hospitals in Finland. In other systems, private providers fulfil public service obligations under the principle of solidarity, such as health insurers in the Netherlands and Ireland. In many cases, there is no clear distinction between a service based on social solidarity and one based on markets and competition. As many of the examples have not been tested within legal proceedings, the question as to whether competition law applies has not been answered.

Once the determination that competition law applies has been made, prohibited conduct includes anti-competitive agreements or associations between undertakings and abuse of dominant positions. Numerous examples exist of agreements between pharmaceutical companies unlawfully colluding to fix prices, or of professional associations illegally encouraging their members to engage in unlawful concerted actions or raising anti-competitive barriers to entry. Some agreements are excluded from the prohibition, such as those resulting from state delegation of sovereign powers or where the restriction is deemed proportionate to protect a legitimate national state interest. Where an undertaking is dominant in a given market, it is prohibited from abusing that dominance to distort competition, as in the case where pharmaceutical companies exploit their market influence by engaging in predatory pricing, as seen in the *Napp* case.[151]

Another complication in the application of EU competition law is Article 86(2), which allows for a partial exemption of competition rules in cases where a Member State has proactively delineated the activity as a service of general economic interest to obtain immunity from competition law principles, for instance with regard to state aid, as the Court of First Instance held in the *BUPA* case.[152] Similarly, the Commission's White Paper on services of general interest affirms the importance of universal services for social and territorial cohesion and the need to respect the diversity of different types of services as defined

---

[151] Case 1001/1/1/01, *Napp Pharmaceuticals* v. *Director General of Fair Trading* [2002] CompAR 13.
[152] Case T-289/03, *British United Provident Association Ltd (BUPA) and Others* v. *Commission* [2008] ECR II-81.

by Member States. It is currently the role of Member States, rather than the Commission and EU law, to promote public service values and good governance in services of general interest. The Commission will only interfere with the Member States' discretion in cases of manifest error. However, there is still a role for the Commission to play by providing legal guidance on cross-cutting issues, such as the state aid rules, further developing sector-specific policies and monitoring and evaluating services on a sector-by-sector basis.

Although the national competition authorities of some Member States have been investigating and prosecuting health sector cases throughout the 1990s (including Finland, Italy and Germany), national authorities became much more active after the entry into force of Regulation 1/2003/EEC in May 2004.[153] Due to the Regulation's delegation of enforcement to national authorities and the proximity and familiarity of domestic legislation, competition authorities have had the opportunity to pursue anti-competitive practices in the health market with greater frequency than the Commission. As a result of decentralization tendencies, the role of the Commission has evolved from primary enforcer to steward of competition enforcement. The Commission has, in turn, begun to focus on priority setting, enforcing state aid rules and ensuring consistency among the national authorities through the European Competition Network. The scope of authority and financial resources delegated to the authorities varies among Member States, which could lead to a number of problems that have yet to be publicly evaluated by the Commission. Several Member States have employed their competition authorities to comment on health reform legislation and to make recommendations regarding market failures, for instance, leading to rising costs of pharmaceuticals.

The extent to which public procurement and state aid rules affect the organization of national health systems depends on the regulatory techniques used by Member States. The rules on state aids in Article 87 EC prohibit the use of public funds either indirectly through advantages or directly through subsidies, unless the Commission approves the grant following a notification procedure. The rules on public procurement defined in Directives 2004/17/EC and 2004/18/EC[154] require that public contracts are awarded following stringent

---

[153] Regulation 1/2003/EC, above n.130.
[154] For procurement in the utilities sector, Directive 2004/17/EC of the European Parliament and of the Council of 31 March 2004 coordinating the

conditions of publicity, transparency, mutual recognition and non-discrimination. While the rules of public procurement apply to public contracting entities, state aid rules apply where state resources are transferred to undertakings. Therefore, the rules apply in principle alternatively, and not simultaneously.

The Court formalized this link between the two sets of rules in the *Altmark* case,[155] holding that financial support does not constitute a state aid when four conditions are met cumulatively. The *Altmark* test requires: (a) clearly defined public service obligations; (b) compensation defined in advance in a transparent and objective manner; (c) stipulation that remuneration does not exceed costs; and (d) compensation that must be determined on the basis of an analysis of the costs that a typical undertaking, which is well run, would have incurred if the efficient provider had been found through a competitive tendering procedure. These criteria were most recently used, in a modified form, in the Irish *BUPA* case.[156] The Commission's Communication on the *de minimis* rules[157] limited the application of public procurement rules to contracts falling below a minimum threshold. The Communication goes on to explain the four principles of public procurement: non-discrimination, transparency, proportionality and mutual recognition. The so-called 'Altmark Decision'[158] considers public service compensation to small size service providers and hospitals to be lawful state aids, which need not be notified to the Commission. This Decision and related Commission publications have clarified state aid rules to an extent, but have fallen short of clearly delineating when hospitals or other health system providers are exempted as services of general interest. In an

procurement procedures of entities operating in the water, energy, transport and postal services sectors, OJ 2004 No. L134/1; and the 'General' Procurement Directive, Directive 2004/18/EC of the European Parliament and of the Council of 31 March 2004 on the coordination of procedures for the award of public works contracts, public supply contracts and public service contracts, OJ 2004 No. L134/114.

[155] Case C-280/00, *Altmark Trans GmbH* [2003] ECR I-7747.
[156] Case T-289/03, *BUPA v. Commission*, above n.152.
[157] European Commission, 'Interpretative Communication on the Community law applicable to contract awards not or not fully subject to the provisions of the public procurement directives', OJ 2006 No. C179/2.
[158] Commission Decision 2005/842/EC on the application of Article 86(2) of the EC Treaty to state aid in the form of public service compensation granted to certain undertakings entrusted with the operation of services of general economic interest, OJ 2005 No. L312/67.

effort to promote fairness, the Court has defined and the Commission has clarified the rules, requiring burdensome analyses rather than identifying with precision which entities qualify as 'contracting authorities' and which circumstances meet the *Altmark* requirements.

These rules will impact upon health systems depending upon the choices Member States make regarding the funding of health care. How the state defines the split in financing infrastructure versus costs associated directly with patient care could have an effect on how contracts should be tendered. Lack of transparency in cost calculation by private providers frustrates systems of public tendering. The 'Altmark Decision' raises a number of questions concerning the funding of hospitals entrusted with public service obligations. What is the state's obligation to monitor hospitals to determine whether these organizations fulfil their missions allowing for some reasonable profit, and what recourse must the state take if a hospital fails? If the organization qualifies as a contracting entity, there are still some circumstances where competitive tenders are not required. An example is if no contractual relationship exists because the services are provided between two public entities. What the discussion in this chapter thus shows us is that the general Treaty rules on prohibiting discrimination and restriction of free movement will continue to apply, and thereby result in continued confusion, without positive integration and measures to promote harmonization in the area of health care provision.

G. *Private health insurance*

In Chapter 10, Sarah Thomson and Elias Mossialos examine the impact of specific internal market laws and policies on the regulation of private health insurance, for the move into private health insurance at the EU level is itself a product of spillover from internal market-oriented policies, reflecting market-enhancing (-building) intentions on the part of the Commission. In 1992, the EU adopted the Third Non-life Insurance Directive[159] to facilitate the free movement of insurance services. The Directive prohibits insurance monopolies and requires equal treatment of insurers, along with forbidding

---

[159] The third 'Non-life Insurance' Directive, Council Directive 92/49/EEC on the coordination of laws, regulations and administrative provisions relating to direct insurance other than life assurance, OJ 1992 No. L228/23.

national governments from demanding ex ante claims approval or systematic supervision of policy conditions and premiums. Article 54 of the Directive includes specific rules for health insurance that constitute a 'complete or partial alternative' to statutory national health insurance plans provided by social security systems. In such cases, the Directive grants an exception and permits governments to impose material (as opposed to merely financial) regulation in the interest of the general good. Examples of permissible measures include open enrolment, community rating, standardized benefits packages and risk equalization schemes. The chapter analyses areas of uncertainty in interpreting the Directive, focusing on the lack of clarity around when and how governments may invoke Article 54 to justify intervention in health insurance markets. It also questions the Directive's capacity to promote consumer and social protection in health insurance markets. Analysis is based on discussion of case-law referred to the European Court of Justice under Article 234 EC concerning private health insurance and infringement procedures initiated by the European Commission under Article 226 EC.

The chapter provides evidence suggesting that material regulation is acceptable so long as private health insurance substitutes for cover that would otherwise be provided through social security. In allowing intervention under such circumstances, the Directive appears to support access to private health insurance where it contributes to social protection. The chapter argues that supplemental private health insurance may also enhance social protection – for example, if it covers reimbursement of user charges or health services excluded from a narrowly-defined statutory benefits package. However, the Directive's framework deems material regulation of such complementary private health insurance to be inappropriate. The Directive may therefore constrain government attempts to ensure access to supplementary private health insurance. This could, in turn, undermine social protection, particularly if insurers have incentives to deter people in poor health from purchasing private cover. Dissonance between recent Court decisions concerning the Irish market[160] and current European Commission infringement proceedings against Slovenia imply continued uncertainty in interpreting Article 54.

Other outstanding issues that the authors highlight include the extent to which private health insurance can be seen as a service of general

[160] Case T-289/03, *BUPA* v. *Commission*, above n.152.

economic interest (SGEI) – exempt from competition rules under Article 86(2) EC – and the degree to which the SGEI argument can be used to justify differential treatment of insurers. It is argued that the Directive's emphasis on financial regulation may not sufficiently protect consumers in markets where health insurance products are highly differentiated, potentially leading to risk selection and/or consumer confusion. Information problems appear to be growing in health insurance markets in some countries, but the Commission has yet to establish mechanisms to monitor anti-competitive behaviour by insurers.

As the chapter points out, the Directive reflects the regulatory norms of its time. When it was first introduced, the European Commission may have been convinced that Article 54 would provide ample scope for governments to protect consumers in substitutive markets, while in markets regarded as supplementary, the benefits of deregulation (increased choice and competition resulting in lower prices) were perceived to outweigh concerns about consumer protection. These assumptions are more problematic now, partly because there is no evidence to suggest that the expected benefits of competition have materialized, and also due to increased blurring of the boundaries between normal economic activity and social security. The latter is no longer the preserve of statutory institutions or public finance, but a result of increased complexity around welfare systems that is likely to bring new challenges for policy-makers. Greater obscurities around the public–private interface in health insurance give rise to challenges that the Directive does not seem equipped to address at present. In light of these complexities, it is suggested that it is perhaps time for a new debate about how best to update the Directive.

H. Free movement of services

In Chapter 11 on the free movement of services, Wouter Gekiere, Rita Baeten and Willy Palm focus on the direct application of the Treaty provisions on the freedom to provide services and the freedom of establishment to health care. The discussion considers the impact and extent to which the application of these rules to health care goes far beyond the issue of patient mobility and the reimbursement of health care costs received in another Member State. It illustrates how regulation in the health care sector is increasingly scrutinized as a potential obstacle to free movement, and considers that almost any regulatory or institutional aspect of health care provision can potentially be challenged under the free movement rules. The authors explore the conditions under which the Court accepts health care regulator justifications related to safeguarding public interests and clarify that, even for such measures, actions must be proportional. It becomes clear from the analysis that health authorities face a relatively high burden of proof, and that providing sufficient evidence to justify public intervention under the free movement rules is challenging. Regulatory bodies must demonstrate that general measures are also justified in single cases for an individual provider, and they are required to demonstrate what would happen if the measure were dropped. The authors then analyse the legislative process in a search for policy answers to the legal uncertainty and to the threat of a slippery slope of deregulation arising from these developments. They explain the complexity of the policy process and analyse why policy initiatives thus far have not succeeded in delivering appropriate answers.

The threshold for the application of free movement of services regulations on health services is relatively low. Furthermore, recent Court case-law shows that free movement rules come into play even if the regulatory measure that is under scrutiny lacks a specific potential cross-border element.[161] Nonetheless, as the chapter shows, the application of free movement rules in the field of health care is not unconditional. The Court is aware that important market failures might occur and the sustainability of national systems could be threatened when health care is delivered in an unregulated setting. The protection of public health, as well as the sustainability of national health care and the related social protection systems, are recognized as public interest objectives, which can serve as legitimate justifications for obstacles to free movement.

The true challenge rests not as much in the identification of the public interest objectives, but rather in providing the proof that the measures do not exceed what is necessary and that the result cannot be achieved by a less restrictive alternative. Member States will have to provide sufficient evidence demonstrating that the non-application of a restrictive measure in a particular case would jeopardize the public interest objective. Providing evidence of what would hypothetically

---

[161] Case C-55/94, *Gebhard* [1995] ECR I-4165, Case C-8/96, *Mac Quen* [2001] ECR I-837; and Case C-294/00, *Deutsche Paracelsus Schulen* v. *Gräbner* [2002] ECR I-6515.

occur without the restriction is problematic. Furthermore, even if a rule is generally justifiable, this does not automatically validate its application to every specific situation. As a consequence, health authorities face a relatively high burden of proof. The internal market approach dealing with individual services, and the structure of individual litigation relying on directly effective Treaty rules (negative integration), make it very difficult to consider the health system in its totality and ensure coherence in the government's role as a public payer or purchaser. As a consequence, there is a risk that the free movement provisions might lead to creeping deregulation in this intricately regulated sector.

Actors have gained an awareness of what is at stake in a piecemeal fashion. It appears to be extremely difficult to find an adequate policy response to these developments. The complexity of the issues at stake, the absence of a clear legal framework in the Treaty to deal with these questions and an inherent inertia stalling efforts to fundamentally change the rules of the game all play an important role. Furthering this challenge, stakeholders have discordant concerns, objectives and interests.

Governments of Member States are concerned with losing their steering capacity. However, codification of cross-border health care regulation would engage them to determine what aspects of health system organization and financing should be declared compatible with free movement under what conditions and which to exclude. Although, in principle, the Member States may favour EU-level legislation, in practice national policy-makers become extremely reluctant once concrete proposals have to be discussed. They seem to be caught in the paradox that, in order to safeguard their national autonomy, they have to accept some EU-level interference in their national policies.

Beyond the issue of patient mobility, the European Commission seems neither able nor willing to provide guidance on the specific application of the free movement rules to health care services. It is internally divided between the differing objectives and responsibilities of the Directorates-General, and is limited by its constrained powers. The power relations within the Commission reflect the respective importance of the Treaty provisions on which the areas of expertise of each Directorate-General are based. The voice of DG MARKT thus outweighs the voices of DG SANCO or the Directorate-General for Employment, Social Affairs and Equal Opportunities in the policy debates.

Health care regulation will thus inevitably come under increasing scrutiny on the grounds of its compatibility with the rules on freedom of service provision. The long-term effects thereof are rather unpredictable. Developments are likely to create more diversity in health care provision and increasingly fragmented health care systems. More choice for patients and providers might challenge public support for equity and the solidarity principles underpinning national systems.

I. Free movement of patients

Modest in size but high on the political agenda, attention surrounding patient mobility within the EU has gathered momentum over the last ten years. Two procedures for patients seeking medical treatment outside the state of affiliation now exist in parallel – one designed by Member States, acting through the EU legislature, in the form of Regulation 1408/71/EEC,[162] and one emerging as the Court applies the principles of free movement to health care.[163] This creates a complex legal picture. Compared to the traditional social security coordination mechanism, Court jurisprudence has created an alternative Treaty-based procedure with a different legal basis, and different conditions in terms of access to and reimbursement of care. Member States have been slow and reluctant to adapt to the new situation, and the revision of the social security coordination framework did not succeed in incorporating both procedures or in simplifying the existing Regulation.

In Chapter 12, Willy Palm and Irene Glinos analyse these issues ten years after the *Kohll* and *Decker* rulings,[164] and in the aftermath of the Commission's proposed directive on cross-border health care.[165] The focus of numerous Court rulings in this area has been on permitting the cross-border movement of patients and the subsequent reimbursement of their costs by the home health care budgets, at the same

---

[162] Regulation 1408/71/EEC, above n.97.

[163] Case C-120/95, *Decker*, above n.2; Case C-158/96, *Kohll*, above n.2; Case C-157/99, *Geraets-Smits and Peerbooms* [2001] ECR 5473; Case C-385/99, *Müller-Fauré* [2003] ECR 4509; Case C-372/04, *Watts* [2006] ECR I-4325; Case C-444/05, *Stamatelaki* [2007] ECR I-3185.

[164] Case C-120/95, *Decker*, above n.2; Case C-158/96, *Kohll*, above n.2.

[165] European Commission, 'Proposal for a Directive of the European Parliament and of the Council on the application of patients' rights in cross-border health care', COM (2008) 414 final, 2 July 2008.

time as seeking to entrench the right of the Member States to organize
their social security systems as they see fit. This seems somewhat odd
when the Member States are reticent about 'health tourism', given the
health care budgetary strains it implies. Differing national interpretation and implementation of the Court's rulings are a further complication. Deregulation of access to health care and free movement of
patients may seem a good idea in principle, but it is not clear that it is
desirable, far less widely evidenced, in practice. Nevertheless, we now
see growing interest in a set of patients' rights that are valid across
the EU and that go beyond the more traditional issues of financing to
covering quality of care, liability and compensation, conflict of laws,
etc. The chapter addresses these issues, while also considering the
need to balance the interests of the individual with the broader equity
and access requirements for all EU citizens.

   In order to first set the scene, the chapter reviews the status and evolution of the social security coordination mechanism and the case-law
of the Court, illustrating how the Court in consecutive rulings has
reinterpreted and by-passed Regulation 1408/71/EEC. By defining
medical activities as falling within the scope of the freedom to provide
services, the Court has reduced Member States' scope for denying cover
of treatment in another Member State and has created an alternative
Treaty-based route to access health care services outside the state of
affiliation. At the same time, the European Commission has pursued its
own political agenda, first pushing for 'more market' in health care by
including health services in the Horizontal Services Directive,[166] then
proposing a Community framework on cross-border health care.[167]

   Under pressure to admit internal market rules into national
health care systems and as the potential effects of Court judgments
slowly dawn on them, Member States have had to adjust. At the
national level, governments have adopted new legislation in conformity with the jurisprudence. At the EU level, efforts to retake
control of the situation have, however, remained limited. Initiatives
have amounted to high-level debates and non-binding guidelines,
as Member States are unable to agree on what action to take in the

---

[166] European Commission, 'Proposal for a European Parliament and Council
     Directive on services in the internal market', COM (2004) 2 final, 5 March
     2004
[167] European Commission, 'Proposal', above n.165.

form of hard law. Moving from this broader discussion, the chapter illustrates what the changing legal and policy environments at the EU and national levels have meant for EU citizens deliberately seeking treatment in another Member State and for those in need of care while temporarily abroad. For both groups, the possibilities to access care outside the state of affiliation have significantly increased as a result of the Court rulings and of developments in the field adopted by health care actors. The scope of prior authorization has been challenged, as has Member States' control over cross-border movements and ensuing costs. Potential tensions between national health policies and the values underlying European health systems, on the one hand, and Member States' obligations under EU law and the free movement of services logic, on the other, have emerged. This might explain why patient mobility has attracted considerable political attention over the years. Despite its limited extent, it has left health systems more exposed to the pressures of the internal market.

The pursuit of more EU-level governance on patient mobility is motivated partly by legal uncertainty as to the application of internal market rules to health care, and partly by diversifying mobility patterns and behaviours. The debate on patient mobility has changed to include issues such as quality of care, liability, responsibility and safety of care received abroad. These need to be addressed together with attempts to clarify the legal context. Following the exclusion of health care from the Services Directive in 2006, the Commission has finally been able to put forward an adapted legislative proposal incorporating flanking measures. The wording remains somewhat vague and the approach minimal, considering the diversity among health systems. It remains to be seen whether the proposal will, in fact, add clarity to outstanding legal issues or even reassure Member States concerned with their control over patient flows and financial implications.

Other developments are likely to entail challenges of a different kind. Increasingly aware patients, commercial incentives for health care stakeholders, novel possibilities through e-health and differing national legislations on interventions with important bioethical dimensions are likely to raise new legal and ethical questions. An EU-level framework should ideally be able to respond and adjust to evolving trends, and it is not clear that these proposals adequately account for this.

The question of who is steering the policy of increased mobility has become inescapable. Governments initiated the debate, but the European Commission has gradually taken over the reins of the process, albeit with different aims and methods depending on which Directorate-General is involved. While stakeholders and the European Parliament have succeeded in removing health services from a horizontal directive on services, high level groups involving Member States have found it difficult to come up with a suitable framework instead. Patients, administrators and actors are left without clear guidance in an environment of procedural and legal complexity and uncertainty. As long as policy makers do not fill the gap, the Court is bound to do so by continuing to apply primary and secondary EU law to the field of health care.

J. The status of e-health in the EU

E-health – defined here as the application of information and communication technologies across a range of functions that affect the health care sector – has grown and proliferated in recent years. At the same time, the European Commission has become increasingly interested in consolidating the EU as an information society. In Chapter 13, Stefaan Callens examines the place and role of e-health in the EU. Treated as a now important component of the single market, e-health is supported by the Commission as enabling higher quality, effective health care that is safe, empowering and accessible for patients and cost–effective for governments. The Commission thus appears to be pursuing numerous initiatives around e-health that are generating a potential legal framework for indirectly governing health systems. In the chapter, Callens therefore analyses how EU rules related to e-health have an important effect on national health care players and systems.

Given the breadth of understanding that surrounds the e-health concept, the chapter first provides a broad view and establishes some initial parameters. The second part of the discussion outlines key areas of e-health and the corresponding legislation that exists within the EU. The evolution of directives with relevance to e-health is described, and the influence on national health care programmes is then assessed along with current EU policies related to e-health. Callens' focus is on five directives relating to: data protection; e-commerce; medical devices; distance contracting; and electronic signatures. The third part of the chapter then looks at other current EU deliberations and policies in e-health – specifically, new (legal) challenges regarding e-health applications, guidelines on the reimbursement of telemedicine and liability issues vis-à-vis telemedicine – and considers how (in practice and in theory) EU rules related to e-health are affecting national health systems and health care players.

The European Commission sees e-health as central to making the EU a leading information society. More specifically, e-health is seen as a mechanism or instrument to restructure and promote citizen-centred health care systems, as well as promoting greater cooperation between actors in the health arena. The Commission is embracing e-health as an approach that also respects diversity in language and culture among its Member States, while enabling higher quality, cost- and clinically-effective care that is participatory and empowering. In this regard, the Commission's view on e-health broadly comprises: (a) clinical information systems; (b) telemedicine and home care, including personalized health systems and remote patient monitoring, teleconsultation, telecare, telemedicine itself and teleradiology; (c) integrated national and regional health networks, distributed electronic health record systems and associated services (e.g., e-prescriptions and e-referrals); and (d) secondary use non-clinical systems (e.g., support systems such as billing). These developments are interesting given that the EU has no formal competences in health care, a fact that also explains the Commission's considerable interest in pushing the area forward as a means of developing competence. A case is thus made that a more detailed legal framework governing e-health is necessary, especially in light of its influence on health care systems. Specific consideration of all vested interests, such as data protection, public health, quality and continuity of care, cost, etc., is therefore required.

At the same time as the number of initiatives and interest grows, Callens shows that e-health raises tricky questions relating to (data) privacy and confidentiality, liability and, potentially, competition law within the context of European Union rules. The EU has had legislation on data protection in place since 1995 (Directive

95/46/EC).[168] While, on the one hand, the Directive emphasizes the fundamental rights and freedoms of the individual in respect of confidential personal information being protected and secure, on the other it aims to promote the free movement of secure personal data within the internal market in instances where required or desirable. Additionally, many health care players do not always appear to know how to comply with the Data Protection Directive and may need further guidance. Taking the case of health grids, the chapter shows how ethical challenges emerge in implementation due to data sharing responsibilities across multiple controllers. The development of rigorous guidelines is pivotal in this example. The storing of genetic data on computers also raises an interesting dilemma in terms of ensuring privacy in genetic screening, but supplemental guidelines remain vague and ineffectual.

In the area of liability, the EU has several pieces of legislation in place to protect consumers from poor quality products. As such, the General Liability for Defective Products Directive (85/374/EEC)[169] may apply to e-health in some instances, so too may the General Product Safety Directive (2001/95/EC).[170] But, as e-health is not a traditional consumable in that it has several faces – for example, as consumer product, software application, medical device or Internet service – no single legislative approach is exhaustive in respect of liability considerations. Similarly, for EU competition law, there are numerous rules on specific elements (undertakings, services of general interest, regulatory competition, etc.), all of which are relevant, in different ways, to e-health (and the provision of health care in general). As is shown in the chapter, this all contributes to a somewhat confusing picture. For instance, specific questions arise in respect of whether, in shopping around, purchasing and drawing up contracts with specific suppliers for e-health services, health care providers are to be classified as engaging in economic activities or whether they are instead acting

[168] The 'Data Protection' Directive, Council Directive 95/46/EC on the protection of individuals with regard to the processing of personal data and on the free movement of such data, OJ 1995 No. L281/31.

[169] Council Directive 85/374/EEC on the approximation of the laws, regulations and administrative provisions of the Member States concerning liability for defective products, OJ 1985 No. L210/29.

[170] Directive 2001/95/EC of the European Parliament and of the Council of 3 December 2001 on general product safety, OJ 2002 No. L11/4–17.

as public entities. All of these issues may have impacts on, and raise concerns for, patients, clinicians and the medical profession more generally, producers, suppliers, purchasers and national governments.

In order for e-health to deliver on the promises of its exponents, or help to address the Commission's concern to promote cost–effective, patient-centred systems, the EU will need to address these data protection, liability and competition concerns in a firm manner. For, as Callens argues, the existing legal framework is often vague and remains unfinished in many areas. Questions surrounding the reimbursement of e-health activities and applications, and the (no-fault) liability issue in particular, will need solving. It is not yet clear that the Commission has the tools, far less the consensus, at hand to do this.

K. *EU law and health professionals*

In Chapter 14, Miek Peeters, Martin McKee and Sherry Merkur examine health professionals' mobility in the EU. Advantages of the free movement of health workers include increased quality of specialized care, greater collaboration in highly complex procedures, improved access for patients living close to national boundaries and allowances for professionals to move across borders. Potential drawbacks include exacerbating the 'brain drain' of medical professionals from new Member States, challenges in rotational programmes in western European countries and compromised continuity of care, especially for chronic disease management. A case is made that uncertainties around health professional mobility must be adequately addressed in order to legitimize this practice to EU citizens, and the unintended consequences of EU law in the unique realm of health care must also be carefully considered.

This chapter begins by analysing the EU legal framework within which health professionals operate, focusing specifically on the arrangements for worker mobility between Member States. Critically assessing both old and new legislation, the benefits, challenges and shortcomings, particularly in relation to patient safety, are addressed and extensive examples are provided. The Working Time Directive[171] is also examined in great detail to highlight the immense impact of EU legislation not specifically directed at the health sector.

---

[171] European Parliament and Council Directive 2003/88/EC concerning certain aspects of the organisation of working time, OJ 2003 No. L299/9.

This chapter is contextualized to highlight the effects and unintended consequences of the EU's deficient legal basis for health care, as well as the piecemeal role the Court has been forced to play. A case is made that mutual recognition and coordination of professional requirements has enabled increased cross-border mobility, but that such free movement also evokes concerns over professional qualifications and patient safety. The legal framework must strike a balance between the benefits of professional mobility and the safeguarding of quality by working to resolve current shortcomings and legal uncertainties.

Examples reviewed in this chapter include the lack of coordination of disciplinary proceedings, continuing educational requirements and cross-border reimbursement, along with the need for a clear definition of 'services' and increased clarity around telemedicines. Ethical issues also surround this question, related to the different ethos in different Member States, such as abortion or euthanasia practices, and different language certifications for various types of medical professionals. The legitimacy and oversight of minimum training requirements is also a source of great contention. The misgivings of European citizens around health worker mobility can be assuaged by increasing the transparency and oversight of training quality, along with resolving the remaining legal issues highlighted above.

The application of non-discrimination on grounds of nationality in the health care setting is also a challenging feat given the vagueness of guidelines offered in the Doctors' Directive.[172] Greater transparency and administrative oversight is needed, especially in coordinating medical education requirements. Balancing access to medical education with allowances for national priority-setting objectives is also necessary, such as safeguarding that an adequate number of medical professionals from a Member State's home country are educated. A challenge lies in the varying national interpretations and viewpoints surrounding acceptable levels of state intervention and regulation of health professionals. The Working Time Directive[173] highlights that the European legislature does not always take account of the specific characteristics of and implications for the health care sector. Through specific case studies, it is suggested that the implementation of the Directive will

---

[172] European Parliament and Council Directive 2005/36/EC on the recognition of professional qualifications, OJ 2005 No. L255/22–142.

[173] Directive 2003/88/EC, above n.171.

pose a threat to the staffing of hospitals, especially more remote and smaller facilities. The *SIMAP* and *Jaeger* cases,[174] in particular, have placed restrictions on varying Member State definitions of 'working time', in 'on-call' and 'stand-by' hours especially. Although the standardized 48-hour week and other requirements are intended to be implemented in 2009, the Member States can request a (further) delay and also allow individual workers to opt out of such restrictions. Several Member States have implemented such opt-out clauses in health care, and the United Kingdom has enabled all workers to do so. In spite of the fact that the Council has finally, in June 2008, reached a political agreement on 'on-call' time, stipulating that inactive on-call time does not have to be regarded as working time unless national law or a collective agreement so provides,[175] the European Parliament and Council have failed to find a compromise in the conciliation process. This is the first time that no agreement could be found via conciliation since the Amsterdam Treaty, which significantly extended the scope of the codecision procedure. Although enacted with good intentions, to help safeguard EU worker safety, the special nature of the health care sector makes such restrictions extremely difficult. The challenge rests in finding a balance between the objectives of promoting efficiency, equity, quality and access both for patients and medical professionals.

L. *EU pharmaceutical policy and law*

In Chapter 15, Leigh Hancher analyses the specific case of pharmaceuticals in the EU – an area where the clash between the EU's health considerations and economic interests is especially acute, and that has a direct impact on health care policy in the Member States. Hancher takes as her starting point that the EU's involvement in pharmaceutical policy reflects two, not always concordant, faces. First is the health protection face, through the promotion of innovation and enabling the market access of only those medicines that are deemed safe and effective. The second face is in the provision of incentives and a regulatory environment that is conducive to

---

[174] Case C-303/98, *SIMAP* [2000] ECR I-7963; Case C-151/02, *Jaeger* [2003] ECR I-8389.
[175] www.consilium.europa.eu/ueDocs/cms_Data/docs/pressData/en/lsa/101031.pdf.

a competitive pharmaceutical industry in Europe. In using the EU's aims to balance these two faces as the thread that keeps the various elements of her detailed discussion together, Hancher outlines the development and exercise of EU competence in respect of what she terms the 'regulatory pathway' – that is, licensing according to strict criteria – and the 'market pathway' – that is, the conditions under which medicines are made available in the Member States. The considerable imbalance between the EU's influence over the former in comparison to the latter is developed in detail, and the impact of each on three types of competition within the sector – therapeutic, generic (inter-brand) and intra-brand – is examined in view of recent changes and developments.

Looking at recent developments in the 'regulatory pathway', the chapter highlights legislative changes made with regard to widening the coverage of and speeding the marketing authorization processes for patented medicines. Within the context of these 2005 changes, attention is also given to generic competition and the major changes introduced by the Commission. In addition to such ex ante regulation, the Commission has also sought stricter ex post controls on certain practices of the research-based industry. Here, the discussion focuses on the application of EU competition law in respect of the Commission's fine of AstraZeneca for abuse of a dominant position – where it had tried to delay the market entry of generic versions of its best-selling proton pump inhibitor Losec – and the recent sector-wide inquiry that was instigated by concerns over insufficient enforcement of generic competition.

The discussion then considers recent developments in the 'market pathway' on the post-authorization of prescription medicines – specifically, pricing and patient information, which are traditionally the preserve of the Member States. The still-controversial practice of parallel trade in medicines is examined in view of the Commission's position that it remains a lawful form of trade, and the manufacturers' attempts to develop strategies to diminish its impact. Specific court rulings are profiled here, as well as Member State decisions.

Given the issues identified, the chapter then considers the emergence of the Pharmaceutical Forum as a mechanism to address competing challenges, and to do so in a way that ensures wide-spread stakeholder support. The discussion considers the Forum's potential role in developing both faces of EU pharmaceutical policy in tandem rather than in competition. This development can be seen as an example of the more incremental and discursive approach assumed under the new modes of governance discussion (see Chapter 4 in this volume). The discussion also touches on clinical trials and pharmacovigilance in view of a two-part consultation process, which is expected to result in the development and adoption of proposals that will introduce changes to the EMEA's roles and that will have repercussions for national systems as well.

For, while generic manufacturers have been offered opportunities, such as now being able to conduct research and development prior to patent expiry (an EU equivalent of the United States 'Bolar provision')[176] and a more efficient registration system, the overall time that they are required to wait before registering their products has been increased. These types of trade-offs reflect quite clearly the Commission's attempts to balance public health interests (access to affordable medicines), with measures to promote innovation and ensure a productive pharmaceutical industry in the EU.

More importantly, however, the two pathways are no longer as distinct as previously. The growing intersection between them is raising a host of challenges for national and EU-level stakeholders; challenges which may impact and have repercussions upon national policy-making.

7. Conclusions

By way of conclusion, we seek to raise some questions on the internal market/social solidarity trade-offs touched upon throughout this discussion, and which lie at the heart of the chapters to follow. These chapters discuss many of the places in health care policy where a blurring of 'social security' (associated with non-market, non-competitive

---

[176] The United States provision is an exemption that enables generic manufacturers to conduct research before the relevant patent expires without infringing the patent, and consequently to place the product on the market immediately the relevant patent expires. It was introduced in §271(e)(1) of the Hatch-Waxman Act 1984, Drug Price Competition and Patent Term Restoration Act of 1984, Pub. L. No. 98–417, 98 Stat. 1585 (1984), codified at 15 USC §§ 68b-68c, 70b (1994); 21 USC §§ 301 note, 355, 360cc (1994); 28 USC § 2201 (1994); 35 USC §§ 156, 271, 282 (1994), which was the legislative overruling of the decision in *Roche Products* v. *Bolar Pharmaceuticals*, 733 F.2d 858 (Fed. Cir. 1984).

structures, constrained within geographical borders, collective responsibility and redistribution – a matter for Member States) and 'normal
economic activity' (associated with markets and competition, free
movement across borders, individual rights and regulation – a matter
for the EU's internal market) has occurred. Indeed, where such blurring occurs and health care – which has otherwise been founded upon
a stark distinction between these two opposing concepts – interfaces
with EU law and policy, there are important challenges. Part of the
challenge for the future, then, is to reconceptualize this relationship
(social security/welfare as *part of* the internal market) so as to develop
robust and helpful contributions from EU law and policy to health
systems governance in Europe.

Health care systems in the Member States are evolving in response
to rising costs, rising population expectations and ageing societies.
The choice of reform or policy options adopted in response to these
changes may fall under the scrutiny of the Commission, under soft
law mechanisms or the Court applying economic legislation. In any
case, Member States can no longer rely on the EU's inertia in the field
of health policy. Once a Member State shifts its health services from
a model based essentially on solidarity to one including market-based
principles, the uncertainty surrounding the scope of application of EU
law could result in unintended consequences. Such reforms may unintentionally broaden the market's influence on health services, despite
the dampening effect of the 'services of general economic interest'
clause in the EC Treaty.

The leveraging of best practices and other soft law techniques must
be carefully considered in the context of each situation. Specific allowances for the protection of comprehensive national welfare systems
and the simultaneous capacity building of new Member State welfare
systems need to be inbuilt into long-term EU strategies. To achieve
this, additional EU enforcement capabilities, along with appropriate
incentive structures, are necessary. Additionally, neither increased
regulation nor soft law will resolve underlying national disparities
in power, financing and capacity. The safeguarding of strong welfare systems in wealthier nations and simultaneous strengthening of
social structures in new Member States is a challenging goal neces-
sitating a new transformative approach. Social protection and equality can best be augmented by establishing a robust and transparent
supranational policy framework, and one that can counterbalance the

acquis of EU internal market regulation. EU free-market ideals like patient choice resonate in many Court rulings and other aspects of EU regulation. However, the counterbalancing mention of solidarity and other welfarist principles appear to be less pronounced in much EU regulation.[177]

Having opened this chapter by highlighting the contradiction inherent in EU health policy and the constraints imposed by Scharpf's 'constitutional asymmetry', it has now become clear that this is not the whole story. First, there is always an interplay between trade and health interests, and not just at the EU level but also within the Member States themselves. The chapters that follow provide evidence of this. Second, there is clearly some flexibility at hand for an emerging EU health policy to incorporate welfare principles such as solidarity and equality of access based on medical need – as indicated in the discussion regarding the patchwork – in terms of the Court's role, and in possibilities for soft law. Moreover, there is perhaps scope for market-cushioning policies, in which the Member States can, despite the considerable implementation problems, shape them in a manner appropriate to their needs. The 'asymmetry' does not have to mean that policies cannot be implemented in a proactive manner: this is not a black and white view.

Still, the EU's constrained competence in health care does result in a tendency towards more internal market or competition regulatory elements rather than a clear *health care* policy focus or approach. Again, the constrained competence to adopt formal legal measures implies the use of incentives and very small scale redistributive policies, and an increased potential role for soft law mechanisms. And the Court's unwillingness to move into areas of majoritarian or interest group politics further hampers developments here. Additionally, the strength of the internal market as a basis for action, and the internal institutional structure of the Commission, mean that the Commission will always find it easier to give priority and greater attention to trade and free movement. Yet even measures based on free movement within the internal market can promote a high level of health protection.[178] What is clear in respect of the current 'asymmetry', however,

---

[177] Eberlein and Grande, 'Beyond delegation', above n.77.
[178] See, for instance, the Toy Safety Directive, Parliament and Council Directive 2005/84/EC amending for the 22nd time Council Directive 76/769/EEC on

is that long-term planning and a coherent policy framework would mitigate some of the negative impacts of the patchwork approach that otherwise results. We might point to the successes of EU environmental protection policy, where there is explicit Treaty stipulation of Community competences. At the same time, it is not immediately clear how best to bridge or remedy the gap between politics and economics in the health arena; at least not without making changes at the level of the Treaty.

The new modes of governance, soft law and open method of coordination, in particular, have been forwarded as a means to address the gap (these modes of governance have also been used with some degree of success in combination with hard laws in EU environmental policy). While such approaches have the potential to bring dividends in respect of Member States' and other stakeholders' mutual learning and in being an inclusive and deliberative dynamic, this is first contingent on the OMC and other soft law approaches generating meaningful results. Compared to internal market law, the OMC is still in something of an embryonic stage, and its results are therefore somewhat uncertain. One visible output is perhaps the proposal for a directive on the application of patients' rights in cross-border health care.[179] But it is worth asking whether this really is (or ought to be) a priority for the EU rather than for the Member States, such as through using ordinary 'conflict of laws' rules, which is what currently applies to questions of liability, etc. It can certainly be argued that there are more compelling (public) health issues to be addressed at the EU level, especially those relating more to the determinants of health. This is not to say that health care activities emanating from an EU level, whether via the OMC or otherwise, are unhelpful. Establishing a legal, or even soft law, framework is not a bad thing per se, and it need not necessarily erode social solidarity (but this depends on the Member States).

That said, some activities of the EU legislature have proved less helpful in terms of promoting robust health care policies for the future. For example, the private health insurance provisions do not provide for standardization of products, nor for monitoring competition rules

the approximation of the laws, regulations and administrative provisions of the Member States relating to restrictions on the marketing and use of certain dangerous substances and preparations (phthalates in toys and childcare articles), OJ 2005 No. L344/40.

[179] European Commission, 'Proposal', above n.166.

in the market. And, while the Commission's lack of capacity here is a limiting factor, this lack of a quality element to EU level policies is a common theme. In the pharmaceutical sector, for instance, we see much attention paid to the important issue of facilitating the industry's registration of new products, but other important issues such as comparative clinical trials or the use of comparative efficacy data by the EMEA (raised but not followed through) are less rigorously pursued.

Two further topical examples relate to the work of the European Centre for Disease Control (ECDC) and the issues of revalidation/recertification of health professionals. The ECDC continues to develop slowly and, despite its mandate to cover chronic diseases, this has not sufficiently been addressed. The formal justification for the establishment of the ECDC was Article 152 EC, but to what extent is it really executing a public health mandate? And, while the EU has done a great deal to seek the standardization of professional qualifications and to promote patient choice (including to cross-border care), the quality of care has not been given comparative attention – there are no provisions in respect of continuing professional development or quality of assessment of health professionals in the EU. Internal market legislation and policies thus concern qualifications and minimum standards, but they rarely tackle quality or what the Member States are doing within their own borders.

In terms of the Commission's own priorities and scope for action, again consider the disproportionate emphasis put on cross-border movement for patients compared to other areas. There is little to suggest that the currently miniscule number of individuals affected by, or likely to make use of, easier cross-border access to health care will increase dramatically with the new legislation. Moreover, it bears asking who the likely beneficiaries of such a policy are going to be: those with the most pressing health and clinical needs, irrespective of socioeconomic status, or those who are better-informed and with more means to be able to make use of it? The same is the case with the mobility of health workers, where much emphasis continues to be placed upon enabling free movement, such as through promoting the recognition of qualifications. Notwithstanding (some) Member States' fears, and the Commission's interest here, there have been changes in the patterns of labour flows generally, but net mobility has remained steady and at a fairly muted level. According to Hantrais, for instance, EU policies on the recognition of qualifications or the coordination of social protection systems have had some impact on formal obstacles to mobility. But other difficulties associated with linguistic and cultural traditions have mitigated this.[180] Again, why is the emphasis not on quality of care to patients by ensuring healthcare professionals remain competent and up-to-date? Surely it is here, rather than in promoting mutual recognition of qualifications, that EU policy-makers can make a greater contribution to the high level of health protection for European citizens called for under Article 152. Overall, therefore, in contrast to the level of attention paid to such areas where the Commission's competences are not yet well-defined, it remains regrettable that the Commission is not more proactive in respect of public health where it has a relatively clear mandate to act under Article 152. Yet, even here, much policy is driven by externalities rather than through concerted action by the Commission itself (e.g., the 'knee-jerk' establishment of the ECDC or the development of tobacco control policies). Acknowledging the practicalities of coordinating across Directorates-General and securing support, quite simply, there appears little initiative and forward-thinking by the Commission, not even where room to act exists.

The development of hybrid approaches incorporating soft and hard laws, judicial rulings, EU agencies and national policies in a patch-work arrangement has been referred to several times through this discussion and is the explicit focus of the next chapter. Currently, such a mix of supranational and domestic policies may be the most politically feasible option. At the same time, however, such an ad hoc approach is unlikely to be effective without in-built incentiviz-ing structures. Additionally, the development of a clear framework and the formation of an explicit EU welfarist structure to assist in decision-making and EU regulation are other pivotal success fac-tors. An explicitly legally adopted baseline set of social objectives to be applied to health care law and policy emerging at the EU level would better equip the Court in decision-making, and represent a more balanced framework for policy-makers to employ. Our con-cern here, therefore, is with the lack of a strong legal basis in the Treaty for health and social protection policies (including health

---

[180] L. Hantrais, *Social Policy in the European Union* (Basingstoke: Palgrave Macmillan, 2007).

care), and to what extent the resulting patchwork of legal and policy instruments that characterizes the EU health care arena can be better managed.

Balance is thus the challenge for the future. For, while focusing on individual patients is crucial, it should not be at the expense of other important issues, such as population public health policies more generally. The development of an EU agenda thus depends in large part on what the Member States themselves are doing at home, not just what the Commission or the Court may be pursuing. Indeed, the Commission's push for a directive on the application of patients' rights in cross-border health care may reflect a case of doing what it can where it can, and as a means of increasing its own scope of authority, rather than pursuing a more normative and coherent framework for health care and social policy in the EU. For the Member States, this raises a question in respect of protecting the social basis of their health systems and, indeed, social cohesion more generally. For it has been suggested that economic integration in Europe may lead to a 'gradual and indirect process of social policy erosion'.[181] Without necessarily endorsing this view – indeed, as Majone already noted some fifteen years ago, 'if there is a crisis of the welfare state ... this is because of factors which have nothing to do with the process of integration: demographic trends, the mounting costs of health care, the world crisis in social security, taxpayers' revolts, excessive bureaucratization and so on'[182] – it is clear that the Member States will have to be careful here. The EU framework is certainly more about trade than reflecting or protecting a social dimension to health policy. But, as this book endeavours to show, the Member States are nonetheless still able to defend the social character of their health systems. Rules on public procurement or services of general economic interest have a special status in respect of national health care systems. And it will be up to the Member States themselves to ensure that moves towards, for example, greater privatization of health services do not undermine the social model and its goals of equity and social cohesion, which otherwise underpin European health care systems.

[181] S. Leibfried and P. Pierson, 'Prospects for social Europe', *Politics and Society* 20 (1992), 333–66.
[182] Majone, 'The European Community', above n.40, at 160.

2 | Health care and the EU: the law and policy patchwork

TAMARA HERVEY AND BART VANHERCKE

1. Introduction

Governments of European welfare states face an uncomfortable predicament. To transfer their welfare-state obligations to the EU level would jeopardize the political basis of their legitimacy. However, since at least the mid-1980s, the processes of European integration, to which those governments are irreversibly committed, have become increasingly pervasive.[1] As a result, European integration creates a problem-solving gap in that 'member governments have lost more control over national welfare policies, in the face of the pressures of integrated markets, than the EU has gained de facto in transferred authority',[2] substantial though the latter may be.

The research for this chapter benefited from funding by the 'Shifts in Governance' programme of the Dutch Science Foundation (NWO) and the 'Society and Future' programme, implemented and financed by the Belgian Science Policy Office. We are grateful to Elias Mossialos, Rita Baeten, Govin Permanand, Matthias Wismar, Willy Palm and Szilvia Kalman for their helpful comments on earlier drafts. The usual disclaimer applies.

[1] See F. Scharpf, 'A new social contract? Negative and positive integration in the political economy of European welfare states', European University Institute Working Paper RSC 96/44 (1996); R. Dehousse, 'Integration v regulation? On the dynamics of regulation in the European Community', *Journal of Common Market Studies* 30 (1992), 383–402; G. Majone, 'The European Community between social policy and social regulation', *Journal of Common Market Studies* 31 (1993), 153–70; F. Scharpf, 'The European social model: coping with the challenges of diversity', *Journal of Common Market Studies* 40 (2002), 645–70; C. Offe, 'The European model of "social" capitalism: can it survive European integration?', *Journal of Political Philosophy* 11 (2003), 437–69; M. Ferrera, *The boundaries of welfare: European integration and the new spatial politics of social protection* (Oxford: Oxford University Press, 2005); L. Moreno and B. Palier, 'The Europeanisation of welfare: paradigm shifts and social policy reforms', in P. Taylor-Gooby (ed.), *Ideas and welfare state reform in Western Europe* (Basingstoke: Palgrave Macmillan, 2005), pp. 145–71.

[2] S. Leibfried, 'Social policy. Left to judges and the markets?', in H. Wallace, W. Wallace and M. Pollack (eds.), *Policy-making in the European Union* (Oxford: Oxford University Press, 2005), p. 243.

At face value, health care seems to be a case in point to illustrate this predicament. Indeed, generally speaking, with some limited exceptions, the European Union has no legal competence to adopt EU law in the field of health care,[3] this being a matter of national competence according to the EU's founding or 'constitutional' document, the EC Treaty (to be replaced by the Treaty of Lisbon[4] once it has been ratified by all the Member States). Unsurprisingly, both Member States and EU institutions are heavily bound in their ability and willingness (on account of national interests, political sensitivities and the huge diversity of health care systems in an EU of 27) to issue legislation in this area. Those who are (politically) responsible for health care at the domestic level are faced with a second problem: since the very beginnings of what is now the European Union, other areas of EU law have had unintended effects in health care contexts. The second section of this chapter provides an overview of the main examples of this phenomenon. It involves several areas of EU law. Their effects on health care in the Member States form a kind of patchwork, unconnected by legal or policy coherence.

In spite of this predicament, the EU has developed, since the early 1990s, its own health care policies in response to these unintended consequences of the application of EU law in health care settings and their consequent effects on the national health care systems of the Member States. Because the EU has no formal legal powers to develop its own health care law, the EU's emergent health care policy is also something of a patchwork. EU health care law and policy is formed from a variety of provisions that constitutionally 'belong' to different policy domains, principally those of the internal market, social affairs, public health, enterprise and economic policy. The third part

---

[3] Article 152(5) EC. See, for instance, Case 238/82, *Duphar* [1984] ECR 523, para. 16; Joined Cases C-159/91 and 160/91, *Poucet and Pistre* [1993] ECR I-637, para. 6; Case C-70/95, *Sodemare* [1997] ECR I-3395, para. 27; Case C-120/95, *Decker* v. *Caisse de Maladie des Employes Prives* [1998] ECR 1831, para. 21; Case C-158/96, *Kohll* v. *Union des Caisses de Maladie* [1998] ECR I-1931, para. 17; Case C-157/99, *Geraets-Smits and Peerbooms* [2001] ECR I-5473, para. 44. See also Consolidated Version of the Treaty on the Functioning of the European Union, OJ 2008 No. C115/1, which, if the Treaty of Lisbon of 17 December 2007, OJ 2007 No. C306/1, is ratified, confirms in a new Title I, Article 6, that the EU has competence to carry out actions to support, coordinate or supplement national actions in the fields, *inter alia*, of 'protection and improvement of human health'.

[4] Treaty of Lisbon, above n.3.

of the chapter explores the processes through which the various sets of actors representing these five policy domains at the EU level have tried to shape the terms of the EU health care debate and expand their influence upon it.

Both the substance of – and the institutional arrangements for – EU health care law and policy-making are therefore highly displaced, in comparison with national health care law and policy-making, which has its own constitutional structures and established mechanisms. While national health care policy tends to be the domain of national (political or administrative) 'health' experts, in the EU context most legal measures and policies that have implications for health care are adopted within institutional structures and procedures that were developed for quite different policy domains. Furthermore, EU-level health care law and policy occupies a highly contested space in the EU's current constitutional settlement. Traditionally understood, EU law and policy-making is legitimated through a constitutional settlement within which powers are formally conferred by the Member States, in a negotiated political settlement represented in legal documents (the EC and EU Treaties) to an institutional triptych of the European Commission, European Parliament and Council of Ministers. In policy areas outside those where the EU has competence to legislate, the Member States enjoy autonomy of action. Recently, however, this binary distinction between EU and national competence has been challenged by the emergence of new governance practices in the EU.[5] By 'new governance', we mean 'a range of processes and practices that have a normative dimension but do not operate primarily or at all through the formal mechanism of traditional command-and-

---

[5] These include, but are not limited to, the 'open method of coordination' (OMC), which was defined by one of its founding fathers in the social field as 'a mutual feedback process of planning, examination, comparison and adjustment of the policies of Member States, all of this on the basis of common objectives'. See F. Vandenbroucke, 'New policy perspectives for European cooperation in social policy', Speech at the European Conference 'Social and Labour Market Policies: Investing in Quality', Brussels, 22 February 2001. The OMC toolbox typically comprises joint (EU) objectives (political priorities), indicators, guidelines and sometimes targets; national reports or action plans to assess performance against objectives and metrics; peer review of national plans through mutual criticism and exchange of good practices. See also Chapter 4 in this volume.

control-type legal institutions'.[6] These apply in areas from which EU competence is formally excluded. But they involve the EU institutions (and especially the European Commission) in the creation of distinctly normative elements, including non-binding measures such as mutually agreed objectives, indicators and benchmarks, or mandatory reporting mechanisms, which are often embedded in participatory, non-hierarchical and iterative procedures.

Health care law, policy and governance in the EU can thus be understood through a metaphor of a double patchwork. Various parts of long-standing EU law have effects in health care policy settings. The EU institutions, as well as the Member States, have themselves responded to this phenomenon, again using a variety of different policy domains and discourses as their platform. It is our contention that, so far, these patchworks have largely developed in parallel (with governance processes being developed rather defensively in an attempt to soften the consequences of law), but that law and soft modes of health governance are becoming increasingly interwoven, thereby opening the door for hybrid EU policy instruments.

2. The EU's public health policy

Before we turn to the examples of ways in which EU law has affected national health care policies through non-health-care policy domains, we must first explore the major exception to the general principle that the EU has no competence in health: the field of public health. Public health and health care are, of course, discrete policy domains. But public health measures have important implications for health care systems, not least because preventative public health measures may reduce burdens on health care systems. The EU institutions – in particular, the Directorate-General for Health and Consumer Protection (DG SANCO) of the Commission – have therefore sought to use public health as one possible platform for health care policy. As we will see in the third section, public health is one of the five main policy domains or discourses that comprise the patchwork of EU health care law, policy and governance.

---

[6] G. de Búrca and J. Scott, 'Introduction: new governance, law and constitutionalism', in G. de Búrca and J. Scott (eds.), *New governance and constitutionalism in Europe and the US* (Oxford, Portland: Hart, 2006), p. 3.

The EU's public health policy is based on Article 152 EC. This gives the EU a very limited legislative competence to adopt EU-level harmonizing legal instruments such as directives and regulations.[7] However, it does provide an enabling competence to adopt 'incentive measures' – that is to say, programmes that are funded by EU resources and managed by the Commission and its committees or agencies. These general EU public health programmes have been running since 2003, although they have their roots in earlier programmes such as 'Europe against Cancer'[8] and 'Europe against AIDS'.[9] Note that a scientific evaluation concluded in 2003 that the 'Europe against Cancer' Programme (which included the European Code against Cancer) 'appears to have been associated with the avoidance of 92 573 cancer deaths in the year 2000', or a reduction of 10% in the EU overall.[10] Another key tool in this area are the EU Guidelines on Breast and Cervical Cancer Screening,[11] which are extremely influential, as they are being used as a reference manual by cancer professionals and medical practitioners throughout the EU. Furthermore, advocacy groups (such as the German women's associations) use them as leverage to encourage national governments and authorities to improve quality standards.[12]

---

[7] For instance, this power has been used to adopt EU law on blood safety: Directive 2002/98/EC setting standards of quality and safety for the collection, testing, processing, storage and distribution of human blood and blood components and amending Directive 2001/83/EC, OJ 2002 No. L33/30.

[8] See Council and Representatives of the Governments of the Member States Resolution on a programme of action of the European Communities against cancer, OJ 1986 No. C184/19; Council and Representatives of the Governments of the Member States Decision 88/351/EC adopting a 1988 to 1989 plan of action for an information and public awareness campaign in the context of the 'Europe against cancer' programme, OJ 1988 No. L160/52.

[9] Council and Ministers for Health of the Member States Decision 91/317/EEC adopting a plan of action in the framework of the 1991 to 1993 'Europe against AIDS' programme, OJ 1991 No. L175/26.

[10] P. Boyle *et al.*, 'Measuring progress against cancer in Europe: has the 15% decline targeted for 2000 come about?', *Annals of Oncology* 14 (2003), 1312–25.

[11] The latest versions are N. Perry *et al.*, *European guidelines for quality assurance in breast cancer screening and diagnosis* (Brussels: European Commission, 2006); and N. Perry *et al.*, *Guidance for the introduction of HPV vaccines in EU countries* (Stockholm: European Centre for Disease Prevention and Control, 2008). Guidelines for colorectal cancer screening should be produced by 2009, see Europa, Press Release 06/161, 7 April 2006.

[12] Interview with DG SANCO, February 2008.

It will come as no surprise, then, that the 'Europe against Cancer' programme became a template for all future EU health programmes.

The first public health programme (2003–08)[13] addressed three general objectives: improving health information and knowledge; responding rapidly to health threats; and addressing health determinants. These objectives are pursued by specific 'actions'. The programme is managed by the Executive Agency for the Public Health Programme,[14] which launches calls for proposals, negotiates grant agreements, manages projects and organizes conferences and meetings. Details of the more than 300 projects funded are available on the web site of DG SANCO.[15] The detail reflects a reasonably wide range of topical public health concerns of the EU Member States. Note that the Commission's proposals 'to stimulate EU-level action on comparing and assessing health care systems' through the programme were removed during the first reading in the co-decision procedure in 2001, highlighting great reluctance by the Member States to accept interference in this domain, even if it 'merely' implied comparisons of performance.[16]

The second public health programme, which for the first time explicitly deals with health care, will run from 2008–13,[17] with a budget of a similar size. Its objectives are to improve citizens' health security; to promote health; and to generate and disseminate health information and knowledge. Promoting health includes a reduction in health inequalities, which was added by the European Parliament at the second reading of the proposal.[18]

---

[13] European Parliament and Council Decision 1786/2002/EC adopting a programme of Community action in the field of public health (2003–2008) – Commission Statements, OJ 2002 No. L271/1.

[14] Commission Decision 2004/858/EC setting up an executive agency, the 'Executive Agency for the Public Health Programme', for the management of Community action in the field of public health – pursuant to Council Regulation 58/2003/EC, OJ 2004 No. L369/73.

[15] http://ec.europa.eu/health/ph_projects/project_En.htm.

[16] R. Baeten, 'Health care on the European political agenda', in C. Degryse and P. Pochet (eds.), *Social developments in the European Union 2002* (Brussels: ETUI, 2003).

[17] European Parliament and Council Decision 1350/2007/EC establishing a second programme of Community action in the field of health (2008–13), OJ 2007 No. L301/3.

[18] European Commission, European Parliament Legislative Resolution of 10 July 2007, OJ 2005 No. C172.

Although the budget for the EU's public health programmes is modest (as is the EU's budget as a whole), the significance of the programmes lies in the extent to which the EU institutions have used financial incentives to promote particular behaviour. This is governance through 'carrots' rather than 'sticks', and the mechanisms by which EU governance interacts with national health care policy in this domain are quite different from the areas discussed below, where 'direct effect' and 'supremacy' of EU law (at least potentially, where litigation is successful) have immediate implications for national health care systems. It is virtually impossible to determine a clear 'cause and effect' relationship between the EU's public health policies and national health care policies. However, it must be at least conceivable that the availability of funding from the EU for certain activities may encourage certain behaviour. It is also conceivable that the sharing of information and best practices across European networks (which is one of the main types of project funded under the public health programmes) will, over time, feed into national policy-making processes. Cancer screening seems to be a case in point. Furthermore, EU-level financial support may lead to the adoption of principles or values that eventually feed through to EU-level legislation.

If this is the case for EU funding available through the public health programmes, it may also be the case where other EU budget lines are used in areas that could affect national health care policy or practice. For instance, the EU general funding programmes for research and development (the latest of which is known as the 7th Framework Programme or 'FP7')[19] include strands on health. Indeed, under FP7, the first of the ten themes for international research collaboration is 'health'. This includes research on how to optimize the delivery of health care to citizens of the EU and how to promote high quality and efficient health care systems.[20] These could potentially have implications for health care professional practice and for national regulatory structures for health care.

---

[19] European Parliament and Council Decision 1982/2006/EC concerning the Seventh Framework Programme of the European Community for research, technological development and demonstration activities (2007–2013), OJ 2006 No. L412/1.

[20] *Ibid.*, p. 12.

Likewise, the EU's Structural Funds,[21] such as the European Social Fund (ESF)[22] and the European Regional Development Fund (ERDF),[23] which aim to reduce disparities in economic development across the EU, are already being used in health care settings. For example, Greece and Portugal have operational programmes exclusively dedicated to health,[24] in spite of the fact that 'health' was not at all central in the 2000–6 programming period (and was mainly linked to health and safety at work and the training of health personnel). Following a consultation,[25] in the new programming period (2007–13), actions such as 'preventing health risks' and 'filling the gaps in health infrastructure and promoting efficient provision of services' can be funded, either through the ERDF or the ESF.[26] The funds can support cross-border cooperation in the field of health care[27] and 'developing collaboration, capacity and joint use of infrastructures, in particular in sectors such as health'.[28] Thus, 'future cohesion policy will provide a broader scope for support in the area of health', even if the Commission finds that 'it must be stressed that the running of the healthcare system is not eligible under the Structural Funds'.[29] Again, the availability of financial support from the EU for such activities may prompt developments in national policy or practice – for example, by supporting '[d]esign, monitoring and evaluation

---

[21] Council Regulation 1083/2006/EC laying down general provisions on the European Regional Development Fund, the European Social Fund and the Cohesion Fund and repealing Regulation 1260/1999/EC, OJ 2006 No. L210/25.

[22] European Parliament and Council Regulation 1081/2006/EC on the European Social Fund and repealing Regulation 1784/1999/EC, OJ 2006 No. L210/12.

[23] *Ibid.*

[24] European Commission, *European social fund and health in the 2007–2013 programming period* (Brussels: EMPL A1, 2006), p. 3.

[25] European Commission, 'Working document of Directorate-General Regional Policy summarising the results of the public consultation on the Community Strategic Guidelines for Cohesion 2007–2013', 7 October 2005, pp. 2, 7, http://ec.europa.eu/regional_policy/sources/docoffic/2007/osc/report.pdf.

[26] Council Decision 2006/702/EC on Community strategic guidelines on cohesion, OJ 2006 No. L291/11.

[27] *Ibid.*, p. 32, para. 2.4.

[28] Article 6(1)(e), European Parliament and Council Regulation 1080/2006 on the European Regional Development Fund and repealing Regulation 1783/1999/EC, OJ 2006 No. L210/1, p. 5.

[29] European Commission, *European social fund*, above n.24, p. 4.

of health policies … as part of comprehensive reforms in the health system' or '[p]romoting partnership between private bodies and the social sector'. Other examples include 'investment in health information tools' and '[c]ontinuous updating of the skills of training personnel and workers in the health sector'.[30] The operational programmes of some of the central and eastern European Member States (e.g., Poland and Hungary) indicate that health care is indeed a priority for the new programming period. Even though a causal relationship between these funding mechanisms and the outcomes can at most be made 'plausible' (and is virtually impossible to prove), the European Commission will publish, by the end of 2008, an assessment of the impact of the 2000–6 ESF planning period in the area of health.

In sum, through these financial mechanisms, the public health programmes give the EU Commission, especially DG SANCO, a platform from which to engage in the governance of health care, given the connections between public health governance and health care governance. In addition, the unintended effects of other areas of EU law give further platforms or opportunities to develop policy discourse and even legal instruments that have effects on national health care systems. We now turn to the principal examples of these.

3. Effects of EU law on national health care systems

What are the main ways in which disparate areas of EU law have had effects on national health care systems? The EU's budget is small and the EU's budgetary powers are distinctly weak.[31] Nevertheless, the EU has used its meagre resources to influence policy discourses and policy learning – for instance, through the public health programmes and their precursors (see section two above). That said, the EU's main influence, in the field of health care, among others, is said to be through regulation, rather than redistribution.[32] One important (although not the only) mechanism by which the EU achieves its goals of (economic) integration is through regulatory activities, in the adoption and implementation of EU law.

---

[30] *Ibid.*, pp. 6–9.
[31] See B. Laffan and J. Lindner, 'The budget', in Wallace, Wallace and Pollack (eds.), *Policy-making*, above n.2.
[32] See G. Majone, *Regulating Europe* (London: Routledge, 1996).

The regulatory powers of the EU are governed by the Treaties. The legislative and executive institutions of the EU have limited competence and in legal terms may act only where the Treaties give them power to act, according to the principle of 'conferred powers'.[33] Actions taken outside those powers are unlawful and may be annulled by the European Court of Justice ('the Court').[34] In most contexts, including health, competence is shared between the institutions of the EU and those of the Member States.[35]

EU law enjoys unique qualities compared to those of either the national legal systems of its Member States or of traditional international law. EU law enjoys 'supremacy' or 'primacy' over contradictory national law, requiring national courts to 'set aside' any such contradictory national law and apply EU law in its place.[36] Some measures of EU law (regulations and decisions) take effect in the legal systems of Member States without the need for intervening action on the part of national legislatures or executives.[37] Further, the Court has found that certain provisions of EU law, including many key Treaty provisions, such as those establishing the internal market and the rules of competition law, have 'direct effect' – that is, they are enforceable at the suit of individuals, before national courts of the Member States.[38]

---

[33] Article 5(1) EC: 'the Community shall act within the limits of the powers conferred upon it by this Treaty and the objectives assigned to it therein'. If the Lisbon Treaty is ratified by all the Member States, Article 2 thereof will incorporate a new Title I into what is now the EC Treaty, which elaborates on the EU's competences.

[34] Under the procedures set out in Article 230 EC or Article 234 EC.

[35] See, for example, P. Craig and G. de Búrca, *EU law* (Oxford: Oxford University Press, 2007), pp. 88–107; S. Weatherill, 'Competence creep and competence control', *Yearbook of European Law* 23 (2004), 1–55. See also the Lisbon Treaty, Article 2, which, if ratified, will incorporate a new Title I, Article 2C into what is now the EC Treaty, which enumerates areas of shared competence.

[36] Case 6/64, *Costa* v. *ENEL* [1964] ECR 585; Case C-213/89, *Factortame* [1990] ECR I-2433.

[37] Article 249 EC.

[38] Case 26/62, *Van Gend en Loos* [1963] ECR 1; Case 43/75, *Defrenne* v. *SABENA (No. 2)* [1976] ECR 455; Case 39/72, *Commission* v. *Italy* [1973] ECR 101; Case 9/70, *Grad* v. *Finanzamt Traunstein* [1970] ECR 825; Case 104/81, *Kupferberg* [1982] ECR 3641; Case 41/74, *Van Duyn* v. *Home Office* [1974] ECR 1337; Case 148/78, *Ratti* [1979] ECR 1629; Case 152/84, *Marshall* [1986] ECR 723.

It is these two qualities of EU law – its supremacy and direct effect – that have the most wide-ranging implications for national health care systems. Unless a specific exemption is available, where elements of national health care systems fall within the scope of EU law, that law applies in priority over national law and is enforceable by individuals before national courts. Provisions of EU law that may have been adopted without consideration of their application in health care contexts may subsequently turn out to have unforeseen – and perhaps undesirable – implications in those contexts. These implications come to light through the adversarial processes of litigation, where there is a high degree of unpredictability of outcomes. This unpredictability makes it difficult for national health care institutions to respond or plan accordingly, and raises concerns that interests and implications outside those that arise in the particular circumstances of the litigation will not be properly taken into account. Within national constitutional structures, such destabilizing activity by the courts can be smoothed by political processes. In the EU context, as we shall see, although this does take place, it may be more difficult, in part because of the position of health care within the EU's current constitutional settlement – the patchwork noted above. We now explore three areas of that patchwork, where EU law has affected national health care systems: internal market law, competition law and social law.

A. *Internal market law: free movement, but not total deregulation*

Already in the 1950s, the EEC Treaty (now the EC Treaty) envisaged the unfettered movement of factors of production within the territory of the EU (the 'internal market'), and put in place legal mechanisms to create that internal market. One such legal mechanism is deregulation. The EC Treaty prohibits all unjustified restrictions on the freedom to provide services,[39] freedom of establishment[40] and free movement of persons,[41] as well as prohibiting measures that have equivalent effect to quantitative restrictions on free movement of goods.[42] The relevant Treaty provisions are directly effective and thus bestow enforceable

---

[39] Article 49 EC.   [40] Article 43 EC.   [41] Article 39 EC; Article 18 EC.
[42] Article 28 EC.

rights upon individuals.[43] Individuals may therefore bring proceedings before their national courts, to challenge any unjustified restrictions in national laws on freedom of movement. Following the supremacy principle, national courts must apply the Treaty provisions in priority over national law.

In principle, the Treaty provisions on free movement apply to all goods and services that form part of the national economies of the Member States. The fact that provision of a good or service forms part of a national health care system is not sufficient in itself to remove it from the application of EU law.[44] Thus, the Court has applied the Treaty rules on free movement of services to the service of health care given in non-hospital[45] and hospital settings;[46] those on freedom of establishment to third sector providers of health and social care;[47] those on free movement of goods to pharmaceuticals and medical devices;[48] and those on free movement of persons to health care professionals.[49]

The principle that EU internal market law applies to all goods and services is reflected in the significant body of legislation concerning public procurement – the purchase of goods and services by governments and public utilities.[50] The legislation[51] imposes obligations of non-discrimination and transparency upon authorities

---

[43] Case 74/76, *Iannelli and Volpi* [1977] ECR 557; Case 83/78, *Pigs Marketing Board* v. *Redmond* [1978] ECR 2347; Case 33/74, *Van Binsbergen* [1974] ECR 1299; Case 41/74, *Van Duyn* [1974] ECR 1337; Case C-413/99, *Baumbast* [2002] ECR I-7091; Case C-200/02, *Zhu and Chen* [2004] ECR I-9925.

[44] See Case C-120/95, *Decker*, above n.3; Case C-158/96, *Kohll*, above n.3; Case C-368/98, *Vanbraekel* [2001] ECR I-5363; Case C-157/99, *Geraets-Smits and Peerbooms*, above n.3.

[45] Case C-158/96, *Kohll*, above n.3.

[46] Case C-368/98, *Vanbraekel*, above n.44.

[47] Case C-70/95, *Sodemare*, above n.3.

[48] For example, Case 15/74, *Centrafarm* v. *Sterling Drug* [1974] ECR 1147; Case C-322/01, *DocMorris* [2003] ECR I-14887.

[49] Case 96/85, *Commission* v. *France* [1986] ECR 1475.

[50] See also Chapter 4 in this volume.

[51] European Parliament and Council Directive 2004/18/EC on the coordination of procedures for the award of public works contracts, public supply contracts and public service contracts, OJ 2004 No. L134/114, as amended, most recently by European Parliament and Council Directive 2009/81/EC on the coordination of procedures for the award of certain works contracts, supply contracts and service contracts OJ 2009 L216/76.

that enter into public supply or services contracts, where the public contracts meet certain thresholds.[52] Thus, purchasers cannot insulate their national suppliers within national markets, but are obliged to open their contracts to suppliers from anywhere within the internal market.

Given the internal market's underpinning ethos of openness of markets across the EU and efficiency resulting from unfettered competition between suppliers of goods and services within that single market, the application of internal market law to health care settings might be seen as setting in train processes of deregulation and liberalization that are in contradiction to European understandings of health care provision. In European settings, health care is based on principles of equality of access and solidarity in funding arrangements, whether that is primarily through taxation or through regulated social insurance. Generally speaking, European health care is not based on market deregulation or liberalization. However, such a hasty conclusion about the effects of EU law should be tempered by a more considered approach to the operation of internal market law and its detailed provisions. The free movement provisions in the EC Treaty do not operate purely as deregulatory mechanisms, and do not give rights without exceptions. The Court and the Commission have developed this understanding of the internal market since at least the 1970s.[53] It dovetails with the Commission's 'social Europe' discourse, which emerged from the mid-1980s onwards.[54] Unfettered application of deregulatory internal market law might pose significant threats to health (and health care) within the EU, as well as other public interest objectives that are served by national regulatory structures that keep the internal market divided in practice. The structures and details of internal market law, as understood by the Court and Commission, recognize this fact. Broadly speaking, three

---

[52] The Treaty rules apply to public contracts falling below those thresholds.

[53] Case 120/78, *Cassis de Dijon* [1979] ECR 649; Communication from the Commission concerning the consequences of the judgement given by the Court of Justice on 20 February 1979 in Case 120/78, *Cassis de Dijon*, OJ 1980 No. C256/2.

[54] See T. Hervey, *European social law and policy* (London: Longman, 1998), pp. 20–4; R. Geyer, *Exploring european social policy* (Cambridge: Polity Press, 2000), pp. 40–8; J. Kenner, *EU employment law: from Rome to Amsterdam and beyond* (Oxford: Hart, 2003), pp. 73–8.

types of responses to such potential threats are found within internal market law.[55]

First, the Treaty itself contains some specific exceptions to the general free movement rules. Article 30 EC provides that the Treaty does not preclude restrictions on imports of goods justified on the grounds of the 'protection of the health and life of humans'. A similar Treaty exemption is available for restrictions on freedom to provide services, freedom of establishment and free movement of persons, on the basis of 'protection of public health',[56] although the scope of application of this provision has been interpreted restrictively by the Court.[57]

The second response is a Court-developed exception to the free movement rules. The Court has recognized that non-discriminatory restrictions on freedom to provide services, freedom of establishment and free movement of persons are justified in pursuance of an 'objective public interest'.[58] The Court has recognized various interests that are directly relevant in health care contexts – for instance, the application of professional rules, including those relating to the organization of professions, qualifications or professional ethics, for the public good,[59] the social protection provided by national social security systems,[60] the financial viability of such social security systems,[61] and consumer protection.[62]

---

[55] See, further, T. Hervey and J. McHale, *Health law and the European Union* (Cambridge: Cambridge University Press, 2004), pp. 46–7.

[56] Article 46(1) EC.

[57] See, for example, Case 36/75, *Rutili* [1975] ECR 1219.

[58] The origins of this approach in the area of services lie in Case 33/74, *Van Binsbergen* [1974] ECR 1299, in which the Court held: 'taking into account the particular nature of the services to be provided, specific requirements imposed on the person providing the service cannot be considered incompatible with the Treaty where they have as their purpose the application of ... rules justified by the general good ... which are binding upon any person established in the State in which the service is provided'. See also Case 71/76, *Thieffry* [1977] ECR 765, para. 15; Case C-384/93, *Alpine Investments* [1995] ECR I-1141.

[59] Case 33/74, *Van Binsbergen*, above n.58, para. 14; Case 292/86, *Gulling* [1988] ECR 11, para. 29; Case C-106/91, *Ramrath* [1992] ECR I-3351.

[60] Case C-272/94, *Guiot and Climatec* [1996] ECR I-1905.

[61] Case C-120/95, *Decker*, above n.3; Case C-158/96, *Kohll*, above n.3; Case C-157/99, *Geraets-Smits and Peerbooms*, above n.3; Case C-368/86, *Vanbraekel*, above n.44; Case C-8/02, *Leichtle* [2004] ECR I-2641; Case C-372/04, *Watts* [2006] ECR I-4325.

[62] Case 205/84, *Commission v. Germany* [1986] ECR 3755, para. 30; Case C-288/89, *Gouda* [1991] ECR I-4007, para. 27; Case C-76/90, *Säger*

The willingness of the Court to take into account objective public interests and to apply these effectively in order to exempt national laws, policies, practices and structures needs to be taken into account in an assessment of the destabilizing impact of internal market law on national health care systems. It is not the case that the Court simply pursues a deregulatory agenda, to the detriment of national structures designed to protect legitimate objective public interests, such as those of solidarity, equality of access and financial sustainability, which underpin the national health care systems of the Member States. A more nuanced critique takes account of the Court's development and application of objective public interest justifications. The Court is sensitive to the potentially devastating application of internal market law in social contexts, including health care. The 'objective public interest' justification in the Court's jurisprudence allows a balance between the deregulatory impetus of internal market law, and the need to protect public interests that are not well served by EU-level deregulation. Of course, there must *be* a legitimate public interest that can be objectively articulated by the relevant Member State. It must not be disproportionate to the distortion to the internal market involved. It may not be a 'purely economic' aim.[63] If these criteria cannot be met, then without the intervention of the legislature, the consequences of internal market law for national health care systems may be more significant than the handful of cases decided so far suggests. But the structure of the Court's jurisprudence leaves the door open to the justification of national policies and practices.

The third response of EU law to threats to public interests, such as maintaining health protection and national health care systems in the face of the deregulatory impact of internal market law, is to regulate at EU level, in EU legislation such as regulations or directives. Different standards imposed at the national level create barriers to the establishment of the internal market, because goods and services moving across borders have to meet a dual standard, both

---

[1991] ECR I-4221, para. 15; Case C-275/92, *Schindler* [1994] ECR I-1039, para. 58.

[63] For a less optimistic assessment of the objective public interest justification in this context, see G. Davies, 'The process and side-effects of the harmonisation of European welfare states', Jean Monnet Working Paper No. 02/06 (2006), pp. 27–36.

that of the 'home' and the 'host' state. Harmonized regulatory standards, promulgated at EU level and applicable in all Member States, may achieve the dual objective of protecting public interests – in particular, those of consumers of goods and services – and creating the internal market.[64]

The EC Treaty gives legal power to adopt such measures in Articles 94, 95 and 308 EC. So, for instance, these provisions form the basis of the EU's long-standing and now extensive regulatory measures applicable to the manufacture, marketing and sale of pharmaceuticals and medical devices, designed to protect consumers.[65] The technical requirements for testing new medicinal products are regularly updated, in the light of scientific developments, using powers of delegated legislation, through EU agencies and regulatory or technical committees.[66]

Another example of internal market law with effects on health care is the regulation of tobacco manufacturing, presentation and sale,[67] and the advertising of tobacco in the internal market. Here, the precise scope of the competence provided by Article 95 EC has been the subject of significant litigation. The EU legislative institutions were forced to revise the original Tobacco Advertising Directive,[68] in response to

[64] However, there is a fundamental asymmetry in EU law between deregulation (or 'negative integration') supported by enforceable EU Treaty law, and re-regulation (or 'positive integration'), which is reliant upon the legal competence of the EU institutions to act, and the political will to reach agreement among the governments of the Member States meeting in Council. See J. H. H. Weiler, 'The Community system: the dual character of supranationalism', *Yearbook of European Law* 1 (1982), 267–306; F. Scharpf, *Governing in Europe: effective and democratic?* (Oxford: Oxford University Press, 1999), pp. 51–83; S. Weatherill, *Law and integration in the European Union* (Oxford: Clarendon, 1995); F. Scharpf, 'A new social contract?', above n.1; R. Dehousse, 'Integration v regulation? On the dynamics of regulation in the European Community', *Journal of Common Market Studies* 30 (1992), 383–402.

[65] These have been adopted since the 1960s and are now found in the Commission's (multi-volume) publication, 'The Rules Governing Medicinal Products within the European Union', the 'Eudralex Collection', http://ec.europa.eu/enterprise/pharmaceuticals/eudralex/index.htm.

[66] For details, see also Chapter 3 in this volume.

[67] European Parliament and Council Directive 2001/37/EC on the approximation of the laws, regulations and administrative provisions of the Member States concerning the manufacture, presentation and sale of tobacco products, OJ 2001 No. L194/26.

[68] European Parliament and Council Directive 98/43/EC on the approximation of the laws, regulations and administrative provisions of the Member States

litigation brought by various tobacco companies and by Germany.[69] However, the Court has found the revised version, Directive 2003/33/ EC, which prohibits press and radio advertising of tobacco products within the EU, to be valid.[70] More recently, the Commission launched a consultation on freeing Europe from exposure to environmental tobacco smoke (or 'passive smoking'), which may well lead to binding legislation aimed at banning smoking in work-places, or even in all enclosed public places.[71] Note that European legislation on tobacco has been inspired by – and based on – evidence that was collected through non-binding EU instruments, such as 'Europe against Cancer' and the Public Health Programme discussed above. We will return to this kind of cross-fertilization between formal law and governance in section four below.

Specific Treaty provisions, such as Articles 47 and 55 EC on free movement of persons, freedom of establishment and free movement of services, also give the EU power to adopt internal market laws that can have implications for national health care systems. Although the finally adopted version of the Directive on Services in the Internal Market does not apply to health care services,[72] earlier versions of the text did so,[73] and, in principle, such a directive could apply to health care services, so long as health care services meet the definition of 'services' for the purposes of EU law.[74] Article 57(2) EC on the free movement of capital is the basis for the Non-life Insurance

relating to the advertising and sponsorship of tobacco products, OJ 1998 No. L213/9.

[69] Case C-376/98, *Germany* v. *European Parliament and Council (Tobacco Advertising)* [2000] ECR I-8419; Case C-491/01, *R* v. *Secretary of State for Health, ex parte British American Tobacco and Imperial Tobacco* [2002] ECR I-11453.

[70] Case C-380/03, *Germany* v. *European Parliament and Council (Tobacco Advertising No. 2)* [2006] ECR I-11573.

[71] European Commission, 'Towards a Europe free from tobacco smoke: policy options at EU level', Green Paper, COM (2007) 27 final, 30 January 2007, p. 19.

[72] Article 2(2)(f), European Parliament and Council Directive 2006/123/EC on services in the internal market, OJ 2006 No. L376/36.

[73] Opinion of the European Economic and Social Committee on the Proposal for a Directive of the European Parliament and of the Council on services in the internal market, OJ 2005 No. C221/113.

[74] A 'service' in the sense of Article 49 EC must be provided for 'remuneration' – that is, consideration for the service in question. See Case 263/86, *Humbel* [1988] ECR 5365. The Commission has now proposed a

Directives, which have had significant implications for health insurance structures in Member States such as Ireland.[75]

The approach of adopting EU level regulatory measures is successful where there is both formal legal power to adopt such EU level standards, through measures of EU law, and the political will to do so. However, where one or both of these factors is missing, EU-level harmonization through law is not feasible. The EU institutions have experimented with different governance approaches in such contexts (see section four).[76]

B. EU competition law and services of general interest

Alongside the provisions on free movement, the EC Treaty seeks to create a system ensuring that competition within the internal market is not distorted.[77] The legal foundations of EU competition law and policy are found in Articles 81–9 EC, and a significant body of EU legislation, administrative decisions of the Commission, and jurisprudence of the Court. EU law prohibits anti-competitive agreements between firms (Article 81 EC), abuse of a dominant position by monopolies or groups of firms (Article 82 EC), and state aids to industry that distort competition.[78] As with the free movement provisions, in principle, the mere fact that an agreement, or abuse of a dominant position, or provision of a state aid, involves part of a national health care system is not *in itself* sufficient to remove it from the application of EU competition law.[79]

Directive on the application of patients' rights in cross-border health care (not on 'healthcare services in the internal market'). European Commission, 'Proposal for a Directive of the European Parliament and of the Council on the application of patients' rights in cross-border healthcare', COM (2008) 414 final, 2 July 2008. See also Chapter 11 in this volume.

[75] See Chapter 10 in this volume. See S. Thomson and E. Mossialos, 'Editorial: EU law and regulation of private health insurance', *Health Economics Policy and Law* 2 (2007), 117–24.

[76] See, further, T. Hervey, 'The European Union and the governance of healthcare', in de Búrca and Scott (eds.), *New governance and constitutionalism*, above n.6, pp. 179–210; T. Hervey, 'New governance responses to healthcare migration in the EU: the EU guidelines on block purchasing', *Maastricht Journal of European and Comparative Law* 14 (2007), 303–33.

[77] Article 3(g) EC.   [78] Article 87 EC.

[79] See, for example, Case C-475/99, *Ambulanz Glockner* [2001] ECR I-8089; the UK Competition Appeal Tribunal decision in *Bettercare* [2002] Comp

Both Articles 81 and 82 EC apply only to 'undertakings'.[80] Where a government department itself provides a service, such as defence or judicial services, it acts purely in the public domain and cannot be said to be an 'undertaking'. However, since the 1980s, the Member States of the EU have shown an increasing interest in involvement of private actors in the provision of services that were previously provided directly by the state, including in the health care domain. Where public health care provision is provided in this way, EU competition law may apply.

Even if the Treaty rules do apply – again, as is the case with internal market law – the Treaty does not envisage that its competition law rules will apply without exceptions. Values embedded in the constitutional and legal structures of Member States, such as that of solidarity, imply that free competition within markets is not always the optimal mode of delivery of certain types of goods or services, including those provided within public health care settings. These values are reflected in the EU's constituent Treaties. From the 1950s, the EC Treaty provided a specific legal exemption from competition law for 'undertakings entrusted with the operation of services of general economic interest' (such as telecommunications or postal services), to the extent that the application of EU competition law would prevent such firms from carrying out the particular tasks with which they are entrusted (Article 86(2) EC). The concept of 'services of general economic interest' has, over time, been developed alongside a related concept, not currently mentioned in the EU's constituent Treaties,[81] that of 'services of general interest'.[82] National health care systems within the EU provide services of general interest. It follows that the exception to EU competition law in Article 86(2) EC may apply to national health care systems.

C. *EU social and employment law*

Another policy domain of EU law that has had unexpected effects when applied within health care settings is that of the EU's social

---

AR 226; but contrast Case T-319/99, *FENIN* [2003] ECR II-357; which was upheld in Case C-205/03 P, *FENIN* [2006] ECR I-6295.

[80] For discussion of the definition of 'undertaking', see Chapter 8 in this volume.

[81] The Treaty of Lisbon, if ratified, will attach a Protocol on 'Services of General Interest' to the Treaties.

[82] 'Services of general interest' was used for the first time by the Commission in European Commission, 'Communication on services of general interest in Europe', OJ 1996 No. C281/3. Davies suggests that 'the Commission, and

and employment law. Article 137 EC gives the EU power to adopt directives in various employment-related fields – in particular, health and safety at work and working conditions. These directives only occasionally make special provision for health care professionals, but, provided that health care professionals satisfy the status of 'employee' or 'worker', simply treat them as all other workers are treated.[83] So, for instance, EU secondary legislation on health and safety at work,[84] employment rights in the event of restructuring of employers' enterprises,[85] and non-discrimination on grounds of

lawyers, now act as if the phrase "services of general economic interest" meant the same as "economic services of general interest" ', which he sees as 'an act of deliberate misinterpretation as linguistically grotesque as it may be justifiable in terms of policy'. See Davies, 'Process and side-effects', above n.63.

[83] Other sectors, such as transport, regularly enjoy special exemptions from measures of EU employment law. For instance, European Parliament and Council Directive 2003/88/EC concerning certain aspects of the organisation of working time, OJ 2003 No. L299/9 (the 'Working Time Directive'), does not apply to mobile workers engaging in offshore work (Article 20), or to workers on seagoing fishing vessels (Article 21).

[84] See the Council Framework Directive 89/391/EEC on the introduction of measures to encourage improvements in the safety and health of workers at work, OJ 1989 No. L183/1; as amended by Regulation 1882/2003/EC of the European Parliament and of the Council of 29 September 2003 adapting to Council Decision 1999/468/EC (Celex No. 31999D0468) the provisions relating to committees which assist the Commission in the exercise of its implementing powers laid down in instruments subject to the procedure referred to in Article 251 of the EC Treaty, OJ 2003 No. L284/1; Directive 2007/30/EC of 20 June 2007 amending Council Directive 89/391/EEC, its individual Directives and Council Directives 83/477/EEC, 91/383/EEC, 92/29/EEC and 94/33/EC with a view to simplifying and rationalising the reports on practical implementation, OJ 2007 No. L165/21; and Regulation 1137/2008/EC of the European Parliament and of the Council of 22 October 2008 adapting a number of instruments subject to the procedure laid down in Article 251 of the Treaty to Council Decision 1999/468/EC, with regard to the regulatory procedure with scrutiny – adaptation to the regulatory procedure with scrutiny, OJ 2008 No. L311/1; and the discussion of the EU's legal framework on health and safety at work in C. Barnard, *EC employment law* (Oxford: Oxford University Press, 2006), Chapters 11 and 12.

[85] See, for example, Council Directive 77/187/EEC on the approximation of the laws of the Member States relating to the safeguarding of employees' rights in the event of transfers of undertakings, businesses or parts of businesses, OJ 1977 No. L61/26 (now repealed and replaced by Directive 2001/23/EC of 12 March 2001 on the approximation of the laws of the Member States relating to the safeguarding of employees' rights in the event of transfers of

sex,[86] racial or ethnic origin, religion or belief, age, disability or sexual orientation[87] applies to employment in the health care field, just as in other fields.

In some circumstances, the fact that the general EU employment law provisions have not been tailored to the health care profession may cause difficulties in a Member State. This is the case with the EU law on working time provisions. The original Working Time Directive was heavily criticized by health care professionals and providers of health care in Member States such as the United Kingdom, Ireland and the Netherlands as being insufficiently sensitive to the traditional practices of their national health systems, and in particular for causing capacity problems, as junior doctors may no longer work the long hours that have historically formed part of their training.[88] Such criticisms led to an ongoing legislative process of amendment of EU working time law.[89]

Working time is an example where activity by the courts – especially the European Court of Justice – that jeopardized elements of national health care systems could be resolved, or at least alleviated, by EU-level political processes. However, in practice, proposals to amend the Working Time Directive are often stalled in the Council.

The elements of EU internal market law, competition law and employment law discussed above all have implications for national health care systems. They also illustrate the multiplicity of institutional and legal settings in which EU law may be important for national health

---

undertakings, businesses or parts of undertakings or businesses, OJ 2001 No. L82/16); Barnard, *EC employment law*, above n.84, Chapters 13 and 14.

[86] See, for example, Council Directive 76/207/EEC on the implementation of the principle of equal treatment for men and women as regards access to employment, vocational training and promotion, and working conditions, OJ 1976 No. L39/40 (now repealed and replaced by Directive 2006/54/EC of 5 July 2006 on the implementation of the principle of equal opportunities and equal treatment of men and women in matters of employment and occupation (recast), OJ 2006 No. L204/23); and the discussion of the EU's legal framework on sex equality in employment in Barnard, *EC employment law*, above n.84, Chapters 6–10.

[87] See Council Directive 2000/43/EC implementing the principle of equal treatment between persons irrespective of racial or ethnic origin, OJ 2000 No. L180/22; Council Directive 2000/78/EC establishing a general framework for equal treatment in employment and occupation, OJ 2000 No. L303/16, on forbidden grounds of discrimination in the labour market.

[88] See Hervey and McHale, *Health law*, above n.55, pp. 196–7.

[89] For further details, see Chapter 14 in this volume.

care policy, and also the fact that the relevant EU laws and policies are proposed by Directorates-General (DGs) of the Commission, and negotiated and adopted through European Parliamentary committees and meetings of the Council of Ministers, whose members have no specific expertise in health care. Coupled with the EU's public health competence, the EU health care law and policy domain emerges as a patchwork of different measures.

4. The 'governance' of health care in the EU

Section three illustrated that those who are (politically) responsible for health care at the domestic level are faced with a 'double bind'[90] from the EU level. Their freedom to organize their national health care systems is restrained by the important and growing influence of EU law, but the EU has limited specific legal competences, with even less political will to use them in health care fields. Moreover, a patchwork of actors and institutions decides and implements relevant EU legislation. While, in those circumstances, it is difficult to prepare an orchestrated response at the EU level, at the same time 'doing nothing' is not an option, precisely because of the unexpected influences of EU law, especially internal market and competition law, in health care areas, in the context of European solidarity-based models of health care. In this section, we will describe how EU policymakers have responded to this 'double bind' by establishing various types of EU-level health care governance. These include the (mere) promotion of exchange of information and debate, perhaps feeding into proposals for legislation adopted through traditional hierarchical models ('pre-law'), but also processes of non-hierarchical policy coordination and opportunities for mutual learning within networks, through the use of information gathering, knowledge dissemination, standard setting, benchmarking and monitoring, each of which involves a normative dimension. Governance equally involves the introduction of governance mechanisms within legislative instruments. For example, new governance practices in the field of health care in the United States could lead to the rethinking of three specific legal concepts: that of participation (in relation to social inclusion);

---

[90] A. Hemerijck, *Revisiting productive welfare for continental Europe* (The Hague: Netherlands Scientific Council for Government Policy, 2007), p. 25.

recalibrated federalism; and the role of government.[91] Others have argued that the practice of new governance could reshape and give renewed meaning to the concept of solidarity, which is also central in the context of health care (litigation).[92] Taken together, this patchwork implies implementation of EU health care policy through a hybrid mechanism of law and governance that mutually influence one another.

A. The slow move of health care to the EU agenda

'Health care' as a *sui generis* topic slowly found its way onto the EU agenda between the beginning of the 1990s and the turn of the century. Arguably, the Community Charter of Fundamental Social Rights of Workers constituted the first milestone in raising health care to the European agenda, almost two decades ago.[93] In 1992, within a wider social protection agenda, the Council of the European Union unanimously recommended that Member States should maintain and develop a high-quality health care system, geared to the evolving needs of the population, and ensure for all legal residents access to necessary health care and measures to prevent illness.[94] In order to implement this recommendation, the Council asked the Commission to 'submit regular reports to the Council on progress achieved in relation to the objectives set out above and to determine and develop, in cooperation with the Member States, the use of appropriate criteria

[91] L. Trubek, 'New governance practices in US healthcare', in de Búrca and Scott (eds.), *New governance and constitutionalism*, above n.6. For examples of interactions between governance mechanisms and legislation in the domain of drug authorization and health and safety, see C. Sabel and J. Zeitlin, 'Learning from difference: the new architecture of experimentalist governance in the European Union', *European Law Journal* 14 (2008), 271–327.

[92] C. Barnard, 'Solidarity and new governance in social policy', in de Búrca and Scott (eds.), *New governance and constitutionalism*, above n.6.

[93] The Community Charter of the Fundamental Social Rights of Workers, Solemn Declaration of the Heads of State or Government of 11 Member States of the EU [the 12 Member States of the time, but not the UK], Strasbourg, 9 December 1989, includes the right of access to preventive healthcare and the right to benefit from medical treatment, to improvement of living and working conditions, health and safety at work, and rights for people with disabilities and elderly people.

[94] Council Recommendation 92/442/EEC on the convergence of social protection objectives and policies, OJ 1992 No. L245/49, p. 51.

for that purpose'.[95] If one replaces the word 'criteria' with 'indicators', the method proposed at the time 'resembles a premature version of the OMC'.[96]

This early Council recommendation was followed by two Commission papers[97] and the 1993 report on social protection in Europe,[98] which 'for the very first time gave a common image of what social protection was in Europe'.[99] In a 1995 Communication, the Commission proposed a wide range of social protection issues for discussion[100] and, more importantly, sent an early warning to the Member States, through the following assessment and (in retrospect, rhetorical) question:

There is a grey area as to the extent to which compulsory affiliation to schemes which are not statutory schemes is compatible with European law. Whilst the European Court of Justice will rule on such questions on a case by case or scheme by scheme basis, is there a need to explore what general principles should be applied with a view to achieving the Community objective of providing a high level of social protection and to avoid unbalancing schemes, and predetermining Member States' choices in this area?[101]

A second Communication, in 1997, on 'modernising and improving social protection' focuses, as regards health care, on reducing costs.[102]

---

[95] *Ibid.*, p. 52.
[96] C. de la Porte and P. Pochet, 'Supple co-ordination at EU level and key actor's involvement', in C. de la Porte and P. Pochet (eds.), *Building social Europe through the open method of co-ordination* (Brussels: PIE-Peter Lang, 2002), p. 41.
[97] European Commission, 'Options for the Union', Green Paper, European Social Policy, COM (93) 551 final, 17 November 1993; European Commission, 'European social policy. A way forward for the Union', White Paper, COM (94) 333 final, 27 July 1994.
[98] European Commission, 'Social protection in Europe', COM (93) 531 final, 26 April 1994.
[99] Interview with DG Social Affairs, October 2007.
[100] The 1995 Communication suggests, for example, that 'at European level, it would appear useful to analyse whether, as a first step, efficiency gains could be made by improving the complementarity in the supply of specialised health care across borders'. European Commission, 'The future of social protection, framework for a European debate', COM (95) 466 final, 31 October 1995, p. 8.
[101] *Ibid.*, p. 9.
[102] European Commission, 'Modernising and improving social protection in the European Union', COM (97) 102 final, 12 March 1997, pp. 13–4.

But other than keeping the political debate alive, it seems that while the two Council recommendations of the beginning of the 1990s prepared the ground for enhanced EU cooperation based on common objectives and multilateral surveillance, the European level returned, by the end of the decade, to a scenario in which the direct involvement of the EU with social protection was 'limited to, first, the coordination of social security systems, with the aim of assuring free movement, and, second, to the nurturing of debates through communications (the European level as a platform for the exchange of experience)'.[103]

A number of landmark cases[104] in the Court 'kick-started' the political momentum that brought social protection (including health care) more firmly back to the European political agenda. This momentum was obviously strengthened by the entering into the Amsterdam Treaty on 1 May 1999, which confirmed that social policy falls under the joint responsibility of the EU and the Member States. The new Treaty granted the EU explicit competences with regard to combating social exclusion and social security and social protection of workers.[105] The Amsterdam Treaty also constitutionalized the European Employment Strategy,[106] which 'all of a sudden gave the Directorate-General for Employment, Social Affairs and Equal Opportunities (DG Social Affairs) much more legitimacy towards other DGs, and we felt strong enough to try this for social protection as well'.[107] Importantly, 'the Commission at that point was still in the post-Delors sort of expansion of competences

---

[103] B. Vanhercke, 'The social stakes of economic and monetary union: an overview', in P. Pochet and B. Vanhercke (eds.), *Social challenges of economic and monetary union*, Work and Society Series No. 18 (Brussels: European Interuniversity Press, 1998), pp. 19–20.

[104] These include Case C-70/95, *Sodemare*, above n.3; Case C-158/96, *Kohll*, above n.3; Case C-120/95, *Decker*, above n.3; and Case C-67/96, *Albany International* v. *Stichting Bedrijfspensioenfonds Textielindustrie* [1999] ECR I-5751.

[105] The Treaty of Amsterdam incorporated into the EC Treaty the Maastricht 'Agreement on Social Policy' (see Chapter 1 of the new Title XI and new Articles 136–145). Under Article 137, the Council may adopt, by qualified majority in co-decision with the Parliament, measures designed to encourage the combating of social exclusion. Unanimity in the Council remains the norm with regard to social security and social protection of workers.

[106] The Treaty of Amsterdam included a new Title (VIII) on employment, thereby giving a specific legal base to the Employment Process.

[107] Interview with DG Social Affairs, October 2007.

perspective, and was still willing to try to push and drag the Member States'.[108]

The resigning Santer Commission, which was still in office until a new Commission was in place, seized the opportunity and published (in July 1999) a Communication in which it proposed a 'concerted strategy for modernising social protection'.[109] What the Commission proposed was to launch a European strategy for social protection systems, which aims at deepening the cooperation between the Member States and the EU, based on common objectives, mechanisms for exchanging experience and monitoring of ongoing political developments in order to identify best practices.[110] Work would be organized around four key objectives, which are key issues of concern to all Member States:

- to make work pay and to provide secure income;
- to make pensions safe and pension systems sustainable;
- to promote social inclusion; and
- to ensure high quality and sustainable health care.[111]

The European Commission proposed that Member States would designate high level senior officials to act as focal points in this process. The result of the work (starting from the four key objectives) would be published by the Commission every year in a 'report on social protection', which would be based on contributions by the Member States and would be submitted to the Council together with the joint employment report.[112] In sum, the European Commission did no less than what the European Parliament had called on the institution to do: 'to set in motion a process of voluntary alignment of objectives and policies in the area of social protection, modelled on the European employment strategy'.[113]

The reason that the Commission could follow this proactive course of action seems to be the fact that, by the time of the publication

[108] Interview with DG SANCO, October 2007.
[109] European Commission, 'A concerted strategy for modernising social protection', COM (99) 347 final, 14 July 1999.
[110] *Ibid.*, p. 12. [111] *Ibid.*, pp. 12–4. [112] *Ibid.*, p. 15.
[113] European Parliament Resolution on the Commission report to the European Parliament, the Economic and Social Committee and the Committee of the Regions on social protection in Europe 1997, A4–0099/99, 25 February 1999, OJ 1999 No. C175/435.

of this Communication in 1999, eleven out of fifteen Member State governments were headed by social democrats, who tend to be more supportive of European social policy initiatives.[114] Consider the contrast with the situation at the beginning of the 1990s (see above), when only two out of twelve Member States were governed by the left.[115] This large support explains: (a) why the resigning Commission (and notably DG Social Affairs) dared to seize the window of opportunity; and (b) why the 'Social Affairs' Council of the European Union, merely four months after the publication of the Commission Communication, decided to launch a 'concerted strategy' on social protection (to be called 'OMC' a few years later, see below). The ministers for social affairs identified 'high quality and sustainable health care' as the fourth key objective that should be pursued at the EU level.[116]

Soon after, a so-called 'High Level Committee on Health'[117] received a strong (parallel) mandate from the Nice European Council to '[e]xamine, on the basis of studies undertaken by the Commission, the evolution of the situation with regard to cross-border access to quality health care and health products'.[118] Thus, a second set of players willing to make an issue of health care at the EU level entered the stage (i.e., those responsible for 'health').

In mid-March 2001, a third set of actors increased its efforts to influence the European health debate[119] – the 'enterprise' players. Our example below focuses upon the pharmaceutical industry: representatives of other industries, including medical devices, or insurance

---

[114] A. Schäfer, 'Beyond the community method: why the open method of coordination was introduced to EU policy-making', *European Integration Online Papers* 8 (2004), 10.

[115] *Ibid.*, 6.

[116] Council Conclusions on the strengthening of cooperation for modernising and improving social protection, OJ 2000 No. C8/7, p. 7.

[117] The High Level Committee on Health is composed of senior civil servants from the health ministries of the Member States. It meets two to three times a year and operates with a number of working groups. See http://ec.europa.eu/health/ph_overview/co_operation/high_level/high_level_En.htm.

[118] European Social Agenda, approved by the Nice European Council, 'Presidency Conclusions', Annex 1, OJ 2001 No. C157/4, para. 17.

[119] The G10 on medicines was in fact a follow-up to the 'Bangemann Roundtables' (named after Industry Commissioner Martin Bangemann) on the completion of the internal market for pharmaceuticals, held between 1996 and 1998.

might also have similar effects on the debate.[120] Although industry actors may not be interested in the EU health care debate per se, they are concerned where particular sectors are affected – here, the medicines sector – in matters such as industrial competitiveness, direct-to-consumer advertising, transparency of pricing and reimbursement, and the process of authorization for new medicinal products. The 'High Level Group on Innovation and Provision of Medicines in the EU' ('G10' Medicines Group), was set up by Enterprise Commissioner Erkki Liikanen and Health Commissioner David Byrne to explore ways of improving competitiveness in Europe while encouraging high levels of health protection. The Group consisted of health and industry ministers from five Member States, representation from different sectors of industry, mutual health funds and a specialist in patient issues,[121] and reported to Commission President Romano Prodi after one year.[122] It divided its work into three agenda areas: provision of medicines to patients; single market, competition and regulation; and innovation. The rationale and remit of the Group came in part from DG SANCO's role as co-initiator.

All of these issues reflect longstanding priorities of the pharmaceutical industry, which were also at stake during the revision of the EU pharmaceutical legislation (the 'Pharma Review'), launched in 2001,[123] running in parallel to the G10 activities. The Pharma Review, in fact, incorporated crucial G10 recommendations, for example, concerning data protection of innovative medicine.[124] Thus, the pharmaceutical industry (and the Directorate-General for Enterprise and Industry (DG Industry), which held the secretariat) successfully used the

---

[120] See Chapter 10 in this volume.
[121] The input into this 'Group of 10' (which actually consisted of thirteen members) from a wide variety of actors was obtained through a public consultation. The consultation document from DG Industry was issued on 27 September 2007; answers were due within two months.
[122] The G10 Medicines met for the first time on 26 March 2001, followed by meetings in September 2001 and February 2002. See http://ec.europa.eu/enterprise/phabiocom/g10home.htm.
[123] The three legislative proposals concerning the review of the Community Pharmaceutical Legislation can be found in European Commission, 'Proposal for a Directive of the European Parliament and of the Council amending Directive 2001/82/EC on the Community code relating to veterinary medicinal products', COM (2001) 404 final, 26 November 2001.
[124] European Parliament and Council Regulation 726/2004/EC laying down Community procedures for the authorisation and supervision of medicinal

informal G10 debates to bypass the traditional institutions involved in the Pharma Review, be they political (the Council, the European Parliament) or technical (the European Medicines Agency, whose members are not permitted to have any direct financial or other interests in the pharmaceutical industry). Without a doubt, part of this 'success' can be attributed to the fact that the G10, in contrast to its predecessors (such as the Bangemann Rounds), involved 'stakeholders', thereby drastically increasing its legitimacy, and thus its ability to exert pressure on decision-makers. The G10 reached agreement on fourteen recommendations,[125] and expressed a wish to continue its exercise. As we will see below, this continuation happened through a 'Pharmaceutical Forum'.

At the same time, the health care debate, as part of the 'concerted strategy on social protection', moved forward, albeit prudently (still, no formal reference was made to an 'open method of coordination' (OMC)). The Gothenburg European Council in June 2001 stipulated that further reflections should deal with 'healthcare and care for the elderly', which is now considered, together with pensions, to be part of the 'meeting the challenge of an ageing population' agenda.[126] Furthermore, the Council mandate makes it clear that another set of players needs to be taken into account in the EU health debate, by stipulating that an initial study on this issue should be prepared by the Social Protection Committee (SPC), an advisory body to the Social Affairs Council, *and* the Economic Policy Committee (EPC), which is the main advisory body to the Economic and Financial Affairs Council (ECOFIN).

The 'economic' players thereby strengthened their say in the debate. In fact, in the context of the Broad Economic Policy Guidelines,[127] Member States had already been invited to 'review pension and

products for human and veterinary use and establishing a European Medicines Agency, OJ 2004 No. L136/1.

[125] High Level Group on Innovation and Provision of Medicines in the EU, 'Recommendations for action', Brussels, 7 May 2002, p. 8, http://ec.europa.eu/enterprise/phabiocom/docs/g10-medicines.pdf.

[126] Göteborg European Council, 'Presidency Conclusions', Doc. No. SN 200/1/01 REV 1, 15–16 June 2001, para. 43.

[127] The 'Broad Economic Policy Guidelines' were introduced by the Treaty of Maastricht (1992) and involve non-binding recommendations from the Council to Member States to monitor the consistency of national economic policies with those of the European Monetary Union.

health care spending in order to be able to cope with the financial burden on welfare spending of the ageing population'.[128] However, until 2001, ministers for finance, who are obviously not in charge of health care polices at the national level, had little legitimacy to discuss these issues. The Gothenburg European Council increased this legitimacy considerably by giving them a place in the health care part of the concerted strategy. Later, in 2001 (November), the ECOFIN Council discussed a report prepared by the EPC on the 'budgetary challenges posed by ageing populations',[129] in which it addressed the expected increase in public spending regarding health care and long-term care up to the year 2050. The ECOFIN Council feared that, regarding health care and long-term care, Member States could face 'increases in expenditure levels over the fifty years to come of around 2 to 4 percentage points of GDP', and underlined in this context that ensuring sustainable public finances 'is a crucial challenge that Member States must address as soon as possible'.[130] ECOFIN also invited the EPC to repeat these projections every three to five years, thereby confirming itself as a regular player on the health care scene.

A few weeks after the EPC report, DG Social Affairs published a short Communication on 'the future of health care and care for the elderly', in which it concluded that health care systems in the EU all face the challenge of attaining simultaneously the threefold objective of access to health care for everyone, a high level of quality in health care and the financial viability of health care.[131] The 'concerted strategy' thus starts to take shape through provisional common objectives, progress towards which should be reported by the Member States in 'preliminary reports' (rather than forward-looking 'action

---

[128] Draft Report from the Council (ECOFIN) on the broad guidelines of the economic policies of the Member States and the Community, appended to the Presidency Conclusions of the Cologne European Council, Doc. No. 8586/99, 3–4 June 1999.

[129] Economic Policy Committee (EPC), 'Budgetary challenges posed by ageing populations: the impact on public spending on pensions, health and long-term care for the elderly and possible indicators of the long-term sustainability of public finances', Doc. No. EPC/ECFIN/630-EN (2001), p. 113.

[130] ECOFIN Council Conclusions, 'Report on budgetary challenges posed by ageing populations', Doc. No. SN 4406/1/01 REV 1 (2001), p. 2.

[131] European Commission, 'The future of health care and care for the elderly: guaranteeing accessibility, quality and financial viability', COM (2001) 723 final, 5 December 2001, p. 14.

plans') and all this without a set of commonly agreed indicators. Note that the European Commission reveals itself as a master of timing: the Communication on health care and care for the elderly was published, by no means coincidentally, a week before the Laeken Summit (December 2001) and two days before an international conference organized by the Belgian Presidency in December 2001 on 'European Integration and National Health Care Systems'.[132]

The Commission's timing seems to have worked well: the Laeken European Council (December 2001) called on the Council to prepare an initial study on health care and care for the elderly (requested at Gothenburg, see above) 'in the light of the Commission Communication' and endorsed, at this early stage, the broadly-based approach taken by the Commission in its Communication on health care and care for the elderly (balancing access, quality and financial sustainability).[133] In other words, the Commission successfully set the terms of the emerging EU health care debate. So, in spite of the fact that there is no legislation involved, the Commission seems to be holding on to its 'right to initiative' rather effectively.

Only a few days after the Laeken European Council, the aforementioned report of the High Level Committee on Health was published by Health Commissioner Byrne.[134] This happened rapidly,[135] and even before it was formally adopted.[136] Through this accelerated procedure, the Health Commissioner managed to secure his place in the European debate on health care services, which he was reluctant

---

[132] 'European Integration and National Health Care Systems: A Challenge for Social Policy', International Conference organized by the Belgian Presidency of the EU, Ghent, 7–8 December 2001. Note that the Belgian President of the Council of the EU Frank Vandenbroucke sent the scientific report, which was prepared by Mossialos *et al.* to underpin this conference, to each of his colleagues in the Council, as a preparation for the informal debate that would take place in Malaga (see below).

[133] Laeken European Council, 'Presidency Conclusions', Doc. No. SN 300/1/01 REV 1, 14–15 December 2001.

[134] European Commission, 'The internal market and health services', Report of the High Level Committee on Health, Brussels, 17 December 2001, p. 30, http://ec.europa.eu/health/ph_overview/Documents/key06_En.pdf.

[135] The Health Council 'took note of the Commission's intention to rapidly submit a report on the impact of the Court's judgements'. European Council, 2384th Council Meeting on Health, Doc. No. 13826/01 (Press 415), Brussels, 15 November 2001.

[136] The report was agreed by the Working Group in September 2001 and discussed by the Committee in October 2001. Committee members were

to leave to the Social Affairs Commissioner,[137] who was in charge of taking the 'concerted strategy' forward.

It seems that the establishment, in early 2001, of the EU Health Policy Forum[138] should be seen in the same light: through this platform of almost fifty umbrella organizations in the health sector, DG SANCO can test new ideas and gather stakeholder support. The recommendations of this Forum[139] (over which DG SANCO presides and provides the secretariat) usually comment on proposals issued by the Directorate-General for the Internal Market and Services (DG MARKT) or the Directorate-General for Employment, Social Affairs and Equal Opportunities.[140] With a view to creating a constituency for itself, DG SANCO also requested the creation of a 'European Patients Forum', and sent its officials to the annual European Health Forum in Gastein, which is a significant venue for networking among EU and national administrators and experts within the broader health community.

The Laeken European Council also backed the continuation of the debate desired by the 'health' players (mainly ministers for health and DG SANCO) in that it requested that '[p]articular attention will have to be given to the impact of European integration on Member States' health care systems'.[141] On this basis, and strengthened by a first ministerial debate on the issue during the Belgian Presidency,[142]

---

then asked for their agreement on the draft report in a written procedure. Eventually, the Committee formally approved the document in the spring of 2002. European Commission, 'The internal market', above n.134, p. 2.

[137] Anna Diamantopoulou at the time.

[138] See Chapter 4 in this volume. For further information, see http://ec.europa.eu/health/ph_overview/health_forum/health_forum_En.htm.

[139] EU Health Policy Forum (EHPF), 'Recommendations on EU social policy', Brussels, December 2003, p. 10; EHPF, 'Recommendations on mobility of health professionals', Brussels, December 2003, p 8; EHPF, 'Recommendations on health services and the internal market', Brussels, May 2005, p. 17.

[140] S. Greer, 'Choosing paths in European Union health policy: a political analysis of a critical juncture', *Journal of European Social Policy* 18 (2008), 219–31.

[141] Laeken European Council, 'Presidency Conclusions', above n.133, para. 30.

[142] The Council 'expressed its wish to hold a detailed discussion on this subject and welcomed the Spanish delegation's invitation to discuss this topic at the informal meeting scheduled during its Presidency (Malaga, February 2002)'. Council, 2384th Council Meeting on Health, above n.135, p. 8.

as well as new Court judgments,[143] the Spanish Presidency of the EU held an informal ministerial debate in February 2002 in Malaga. The Presidency focused the debate almost completely on patient mobility, afraid as they were of the consequences of large groups of European pensioners residing in the Spanish coastal regions.[144] This was a narrower focus than the Laeken Conclusions suggested. Commissioner Byrne remained remarkably prudent during the debate, as a consequence of a head of cabinet meeting during which it was agreed that, as long as it was unclear which DG within the Commission was to be 'pilot' for the European health care debate, it would adopt a low profile attitude.[145]

The Health Council of 26 June 2002 then endorsed Council Conclusions on patient mobility and health care in the internal market. Recognizing the importance of strengthening cooperation, the Council invited the Commission to launch a 'High Level Process of Reflection' (HLPR) to propose further action so that the Council could 'return to this issue at the next meeting of the Health Council'.[146] The launch of this HLPR was considered a 'milestone', since it recognized 'the potential value of European cooperation in helping Member States to achieve their health objectives'.[147]

Amazing as it may seem, given the increasing awareness that Europe is entering national health care systems by the back door of the internal market (see above), national governments continued to be strongly averse to formalizing the debate about health care at the EU level. Thus, a proposal to investigate the possibility of

---

[143] Case C-368/98, *Vanbraekel*, above n.44; Case C-157/99, *Geraets Smits and Peerbooms*, above n.3.

[144] The 'questions for debate' were redrafted four times by the Presidency, but remained confusing and lacked focus. A Presidency paper to prepare the debate was withdrawn at the request of a majority of the delegations. See 'The Europe of Health', unpublished paper from the Spanish Presidency of the EU in preparation of the informal ministerial debate in Malaga, 24 January 2002.

[145] Interview with DG SANCO, October 2007.

[146] Council, 2440th Council Meeting on Health, Doc. No. 10090/02 (Press 182), Luxembourg, 26 June 2002, p. 11.

[147] M. Kyprianou, 'The new European healthcare agenda', Speech at the European Voice Conference 'Healthcare: Is Europe Getting Better?', Brussels, 20 January 2005, p. 2; European Commission, 'Follow-up to the High Level Reflection Process on Patient Mobility and Healthcare Developments in the European Union', COM (2004) 301 final, 20 April 2004, p. 18.

applying the OMC in this High Level Process was debated, but not accepted, by the Council in June 2002 (a decade, we should recall, after the first Council recommendation calling for coordination in this area). Similarly, the Health Council could not agree on the creation of a formal 'committee' to underpin the Health Council. By opting for a High Level 'Process' launched and presided over by the Commission, and in which members participated 'on a personal basis', the Member States kept all the options open. The same fear that the EU would interfere in national systems, even through a non-binding reflection process, explains why there was considerable resistance (which was eventually overcome) to creating a working group within the High Level Process of Reflection on 'reconciling national health policy with European obligations', which would raise issues such as improving legal certainty for health services within the framework of EU law, as well as the need for new institutions or structures. It seems that Member States did not at all perceive this process, formally non-binding, as non-constraining or unimportant.

These topics remained very sensitive for the Member States, despite DG MARKT's further increase of pressure on the Member States, in the summer of 2002, by launching a consultation process on the follow-up of the Court's jurisprudence relating to the reimbursement of medical expenses incurred in another Member State.[148]

Thus, while the ministers of health, and especially DG SANCO, struggled with the practical launch of the HLPR on patient mobility, Member States were dragging their feet, in a very similar way, in the 'concerted strategy' on health care and care for the elderly. The above-mentioned initial study (requested by the Gothenburg European Council), was drafted by the SPC and the EPC at the beginning of 2002.[149] The Social Affairs Council adopted it, but was extremely prudent concerning the next steps. Whereas it had launched the

---

[148] European Commission, 'Report on the application of internal market rules to health services – implementation by the Member States of the Court's jurisprudence', Commission Staff Working Paper, SEC (2003) 900, 28 July 2003.

[149] The report recalled that the debate on health care and care for the elderly is still 'at an early stage' and that it is 'even a more complex process', making it necessary 'to involve those responsible for health policy'. Economic Policy Committee, Social Protection Committee (Joint EPC/SPC), 'Draft

OMC in the fields of social inclusion (2000) and pensions (2001), with regard to health care it merely 'agreed on the need to initiate and to develop cooperation between the Member States over 2002 and 2003',[150] leaving many doubts over the continuation of the process in the longer term. Nevertheless, both the EU Council[151] and the European Council[152] did confirm the three long-term objectives set out in the afore-mentioned Commission Communication (accessibility, quality and financial sustainability of systems) as a basis for information gathering and exploring possibilities for mutual learning and cooperation. Two examples can further illustrate the steering role of the European Commission in the development of these non-binding governance mechanisms.

First, the European Commission managed to shift the wording of the Council mandate, once again. The Council abandoned the reference to 'health care and care for the elderly', and instead referred to 'health and long-term care for the elderly'.[153] By entirely linking the debate to the 'elderly', the Commission succeeded in 'selling' the health care OMC as part of the ageing agenda, which was far less contested.

Second, during the first days of 2003, the Commission introduced the vocabulary of the OMC in the slowly emerging concerted strategy on health care and care for the elderly. It was no coincidence that the Commission decided to label a report it issued on this issue[154] a 'proposal

---

for a Council Report in the field of health care and care for the elderly', SPC/2002/Jan./01 en final, p. 3.

[150] Council Meeting on Employment, Social Policy, Health and Consumer Affairs, Doc. No. 14892/02 (Press 376), Brussels, 2–3 December 2002, para. 12.

[151] *Ibid.*

[152] Barcelona European Council, 'Presidency Conclusions', Doc. No. SN 100/1/02 REV 1, 15–16 March 2002, para. 25.

[153] The difference is subtle, yet crucial: whereas the former label could be read as a mandate to work on 'health care' (in general), on the one hand, and 'care for the elderly' (aimed at a specific age group), on the other, the new formulation clearly suggested that work deals with 'health care and long-term care', *both* with regard to the elderly. Thus, EU cooperation in this new policy area had moved, at least at the level of discourse, from 'health care' (with attention to the challenge of ageing), via 'health care and long-term care', to 'health care of the elderly' and 'long-term care'.

[154] The report was in fact a draft analysis of the Member States' replies to the 2002 questionnaire on health and long-term care for the elderly.

for a joint report'.[155] The 'joint report' had been a cornerstone of the 'up and running' OMCs, such as the employment strategy, for some years, and had already been prepared for more recent OMCs, such as those on social inclusion and pensions. Thus, in terms of wording, the association with an actual OMC became very strong. It is worth noting that an agreement on this joint report (an instrument of 'soft' governance) could only be reached after hard negotiations, and ultimately political compromises, between Member States and the Commission on controversial points such as the relationship between the state and the market as health care provider, and the level of resources 'necessary' for health care funding.[156] This again illustrates how Member States resisted EU involvement in 'their' health care systems, but also that governance is taken seriously (as opposed to being regarded as irrelevant) by Member States.

What happened with the afore-mentioned 'reflection process' of the health players in the meantime? The 'High Level Process of Reflection on Patient Mobility and Healthcare Developments in the European Union' began work at the beginning of 2003. In view of the initial difficulties (see above), there was an unexpected amount of interest from Member States in participating (both in plenary meetings and working groups). All fifteen ministers invited took part from the outset.[157] This may, of course, reflect a fear that issues would be discussed beyond their control, rather than their willingness to take EU initiatives on this subject. The High Level Process of Reflection adopted recommendations for action at EU level by the end of 2003.[158] For the

---

[155] European Commission, 'Proposal for a Joint Report. Health care and care for the elderly: supporting national strategies for ensuring a high level of social protection', COM (2002) 774 final, 3 January 2003.

[156] These controversies can be seen in the considerable differences between the Commission's draft report, and the Joint Report that was ultimately adopted by the ECOFIN and Social Affairs Council. ECOFIN and Social Affairs Council, 'Joint Report by the Commission and the Council on supporting national strategies for the future of health care and care for the elderly', Doc. No. 7166/03 (SOC 116), 10 March 2003.

[157] Luxembourg participated only in an administrative sense.

[158] These recommendations were structured around five themes: European cooperation to enable better use of resources; information requirements for patients, professionals and policy-makers; access to and quality of care; reconciling national health policy with European obligations; health-related issues and the EU's Cohesion and Structural Funds. European Commission, 'High Level Process on Patient Mobility and Healthcare Developments in

first time, Member States acknowledged that 'changing the Treaty' and 'secondary legislation' are options to improve legal certainty. The recommendations of the HLPR also invited the Commission to examine how the existing Community financial instruments could be used to facilitate investment in health, health infrastructure and skills development.[159] Crucially, the Commission was asked to propose a permanent mechanism at EU level to support European cooperation in the field of health care (not limited to patient mobility).[160]

Arguably, the HLPR was inspired by the outcome of the above-mentioned consultation process launched by DG MARKT on the application of internal market rules to health services.[161] In short, the Commission concluded that the 'Internal Market in health services is not functioning satisfactorily and European citizens are encountering unjustified or disproportionate obstacles when they apply for reimbursement'.[162] The Commission reconfirmed its preference for a constructive dialogue with Member States on their responses to the Court's judgments.[163]

In 2003, the economic players continued their work on the factors driving public expenditures on health care and long-term care, through a report by the EPC working group on ageing populations, adopted by the ECOFIN Council. The report acknowledged that: 'in practice demographic change has not been a significant driver of increasing levels of health and long-term care expenditures in recent decades, but rather demand and supply factors have prevailed'.[164] Furthermore, the results of a first study examining the impact of non-demographic drivers in shaping future public expenditures on long-term care 'show for the four Member States covered by the projection

the European Union, outcome of the reflection process', HLPR/2003/16, 9 December 2003.
[159] *Ibid.*, p. 11.   [160] *Ibid.*
[161] See Chapter 11 in this volume.
[162] European Commission, 'Report on the application of internal market rules', above n.148, p. 18.
[163] Among others, in the High Level Process of Reflection on Patient Mobility and the SOLVIT network, which links the national administrations of every Member State. Its task is to find rapid solutions to problems arising from the application by the Member States of the rules governing the internal market. See http://ec.europa.eu/solvit/site/index_En.htm.
[164] The suggestion was therefore made that, in the next round of common projections, an attempt should be made to model these non-demographic factors in a more explicit manner for all Member States. Economic

exercise, spending on long-term care as a share of GDP is projected to more than double between 2000 and 2050'.[165]

In sum, it seems that at least five different sets of actors tried to shape the terms of the EU health care debate, and expand their influence on it, between 2000 and 2003. We have simplified them as the 'social affairs', 'internal market', 'public health', 'economic' and 'enterprise' players. Together, they created, in a remarkably short time span, a very crowded law and policy-making space. Various governance tools began to take shape, but they remained very fragile, involving provisional institutional architectures that left doubts about their longer-term continuation. National governments remained involved, but the different Commission DGs set the pace.

B. After the Services Directive: operationalization of the EU health care governance toolbox

There is abundant evidence that it was the proposal for a services directive of January 2004[166] that boosted the operationalization of governance in the form of policy coordination on health care. There are at least two reasons for this, one substantive, the other procedural. Most obviously, in substantive terms, in its original version the 'Bolkestein Directive' was entirely applicable to health care services. Procedurally, many 'health players' were concerned that:

In spite of the fact that DG MARKT participated in the high level process on patient mobility, it did not at any point reveal its intention to launch the Directive [while this proposal] tackles crucial issues that were discussed during the high level process, such as the reimbursement of costs for care received in another Member State.[167]

Policy Committee (EPC), 'The impact of ageing populations on public finances: overview of analysis carried out at EU Level and proposals for a future work programme', Doc. No. EPC/ECFIN/435/03, 22 October 2003, p. 26.
[165] *Ibid.*, p. 27.
[166] European Commission, 'Proposal for a Directive of the European Parliament and of the Council on services in the internal market', COM (2004) 2 final, 5 March 2004.
[167] R. Baeten, 'Health care: after the Court, the policy-makers get down to work', in C. Degryse and P. Pochet (eds.), *Social developments in the European Union 2004* (Brussels: ETUI, 2005).

The release of the Directive within a few weeks after the final outcome
of the High Level Process explains why health players felt that the
Bolkestein Directive was deliberately kept in the drawers of DG
MARKT until the end of that Process. As a consequence of these substantive as well as procedural factors, the proposal 'provoked unpre-
cedented reactions from the public authorities responsible for health
policy and from the organizations concerned',[168] in that it 'opened
everyone's eyes'.[169] The European advisor to the Belgian Minister for
Health put it this way: 'if the Bolkestein Directive had not existed, we
would have had to invent it. It was the wake-up call we all desperately
needed.'[170]

DG SANCO seized the momentum created by the Bolkestein proposal: the speed with which it decided to create a 'High Level Group
on Health Services and Medical Care' to take forward the recommendations of the High Level Process of Reflection on Patient Mobility
'mirrors the competition between the "health" and "social" players
at EU level to take the lead in the process of European cooperation on
health care'.[171] On 1 July 2004, merely one month after the Group was
politically endorsed by the Health Council, the Commission launched
the Group through its first plenary meeting. It brings together civil
servants from all the Member States[172] and the Commission (which
presides over the plenary meetings and holds the secretariat), working in seven priority areas, with the help of working groups.[173] It also
contributes to other work relevant to health services, including, on
paper, the OMC on health care. In practice, however:

[W]e should have been involved, and to be fair to our colleagues in DG
Employment, we have been asked to contribute at every opportunity, but
it is physically not possible with the staff we have to do also the analytical
work for the OMC. So we decided to drop it, even though we tried to make
a contribution when it was absolutely essential.[174]

---

[168] *Ibid.*   [169] Interview with DG Social Affairs, July 2007.
[170] Interview, June 2007.   [171] *Ibid.*
[172] The High Level Group is made up of senior Member State representatives
      (with other stakeholders contributing on relevant subjects).
[173] Cross-border healthcare purchasing and provision; health professionals;
      centres of reference; health technology assessment; information and
      e-health; health impact assessment and health systems; and patient safety.
[174] Interview with DG SANCO, October 2007.

The High Level Group reports annually to the Health Council.[175]

As announced in the above-mentioned G10 Medicines Group (see section three), the Commission set up a Pharmaceutical Forum in 2005 to take the process further around three key themes: pricing policy, relative effectiveness and information to patients on pharmaceuticals. The latter issue was one of the most controversial issues in the Pharmaceutical Review, since the Commission wanted to ease existing legislative restrictions on direct-to-consumer advertising.[176] Since this proposal was dropped at the first reading[177] (after having been rejected by a vast majority in the European Parliament), the internal market players brought the discussion back to the EU agenda through the Pharmaceutical Forum in an attempt to influence future legislation. The Forum, which meets annually, brings together health ministers (with all Member States now being invited), representatives of the European Parliament, the pharmaceutical industry and stakeholder organizations (health care professionals, patients and insurance funds). Two of the latter – namely, the European Social Insurance Partners (ESIP) and the Association Internationale de la Mutualité (AIM) – have strong concerns about the lack of transparency in the Forum, and particularly in the Working Group.[178] Other tensions are apparent: even though the Enterprise and Health Commissioners (Günter Verheugen and Markos Kyprianou, respectively) co-chair the Forum, their relationship seems rather tense (for instance, each has

---

[175] European Council, 'High Level Group on Health Services and Medical Care – information from the Commission', Doc. No. 15190/04, Brussels, 1 December 2004; European Commission, 'Work of the High Level Group on Health Services and Medical Care during 2005', HLG/2005/16, 18 November 2005; European Commission, 'Work of the High Level Group in 2006', HLG/2006/8, 10 October 2006, p. 16.

[176] Articles 86–100, European Parliament and Council Directive 2001/83/ EC on the Community code relating to medicinal products for human use, OJ 2001 No. L311/67, pp. 91–5; European Commission, 'Proposal for a European Parliament and Council Directive amending Directive 2001/83/ EC on the Community code relating to medicinal products for human use', COM (2001) 404 final, 26 November 2001; OJ 2001 No. C75/216.

[177] European Commission, 'Amended proposal for a European Parliament and Council Directive amending Directive 2001/83/EC on the Community code relating to medicinal products for human use', COM (2003) 163 final, 3 April 2003.

[178] European Social Insurance Platform and Association Internationale de la Mutualité (Joint ESIP and AIM), 'Position statement on information to patients on diseases and treatment options', Brussels, 20 June 2007, p. 1.

his own Pharmaceutical Forum web site[179] and, more importantly, each held their own public consultation on health-related information to patients). It will come as no surprise, in view of these tensions, that the second Pharmaceutical Forum (26 June 2007) only noted 'some progress'.[180]

As far as the High Level Group on Health Services and Medical Care is concerned, it was relatively active between 2004 and 2006, but then its work intensity dropped (almost completely) after September 2006. As Greer and Vanhercke note in Chapter 4 of this volume, the Group indicated that the Commission's intention to bring forward proposals to develop a Community framework for safe, high quality and efficient health services in 2007, on the basis of a consultation beginning in 2006 'will have an impact on the future work of the High Level Group'.[181] In retrospect, this sentence seems to have been the announcement of the demise (at least for the time being) of the Group. Arguably, this development is also related to the structural limitations of the Group, which was established by a Commission Decision, and not constitutionalized (in contrast to the Social Protection Committee). As a consequence, it is not accountable to the Council, which obviously limits its capacity to conduct genuine political debates. Also consider that the Commission holds both the presidency of the Group as well as its secretariat, which several Member States, and the Commission, find uncomfortable. Hence, the Council decided to launch a 'senior level committee', in which more 'political debates could take place' (notably about the proposal for a services directive). And, yet, in practice:

[T]he Group is a very clear example unfortunately of the fact that if you do not have an executive that actually does things, things do not happen. And therefore the Senior Level Group has not followed-up on most of its discussions. There is one important exception: the statement on the core values and shared principles of health systems that was prepared by the

---

[179] DG Industry's web site: http://ec.europa.eu/enterprise/phabiocom/comp_pf_En.htm; DG SANCO's web site: http://ec.europa.eu/health/ph_overview/other_policies/pharma_forum_En.htm.

[180] 'Pharmaceutical Forum Introduction', DG Health and Consumer Protection web site: http://ec.europa.eu/health/ph_overview/other_policies/pharma_forum_En.htm.

[181] European Commission, 'Work of the High Level Group', above n.175, pp. 15–6.

Senior Level Group, and adopted by the Council in 2005, was a genuinely useful exercise.[182]

The European Commission, in September 2006, launched a public consultation on how to ensure legal certainty regarding cross-border health care under Community law, and announced proposals for later in 2007.[183] Questions were asked, for example, about what areas require greater legal certainty and what tools would be appropriate to tackle these different issues at EU level – whether binding legal instruments (a regulation or a directive), 'soft law' (e.g., an interpretative communication) or other means. The Commission stated that while '[a]ny or all of these different types of instruments could be combined in an overall package of Community action ... ensuring legal certainty seems likely to require at least some elements being dealt with through legislative action'.[184]

Arguably, the increased activities of the Commission – especially DG MARKT, but also ECOFIN, which issued a new report on the impact of ageing populations on public spending[185] – inspired the Member States to try to 'guide' the Commission while it was developing its announced framework for safe, high quality and efficient health services. In June 2006, the twenty-five health ministers endorsed a statement on common values (universality, access to good quality care, equity and solidarity) and principles (quality, safety, care that is based on evidence and ethics, patient involvement, redress, and privacy and confidentiality). Crucially, ministers invited the European Commission 'to ensure that common values and principles contained in the Statement are respected when drafting specific proposals concerning health services'.[186] Since ministers 'strongly believe that developments in this area should result from political consensus, and not

[182] Interview with DG SANCO, October 2007.
[183] European Commission, 'Consultation regarding Community action on health services', SEC (2006) 1195/4, 26 September 2006.
[184] *Ibid.*, p. 11.
[185] Economic Policy Committee, 'Summary report: impact of ageing populations on public spending on pensions, health and long-term care, education and unemployment benefits for the elderly', Doc. No. ECFIN/EPC(2006)REP/238, 6 February 2006.
[186] Council Conclusions on common values and principles in EU health systems, Employment, Social Policy, Health and Consumer Affairs Council Meeting, Doc No. 9658/06 (Press 148), Luxembourg, 1–2 June 2006, p. 33.

solely from case law',[187] they invited the institutions of the European Union more generally (read, the European Court of Justice) 'to ensure that common values and principles contained in the Statement are respected in their work'.[188]

Finally, summarizing some 270 responses[189] to the above-mentioned public consultation regarding 'Community action on health services',[190] the Commission concluded in the spring of 2007 that a majority view of contributors felt that 'a combination of both "supportive" tools (such as practical cooperation, or the "open method of coordination") and legally binding measures' (either through changes within the existing regulations on the coordination of social security systems, or by means of a new specific directive on health services) would be best.[191] In other words, law and governance were expected to complement each other. The majority of national governments and many other stakeholders expressed the wish that any Community action should be based on the Council's 'common values and principles of EU health systems'.[192]

Some of the views from the public consultation were taken forward by the (informal meeting of) health ministers in Aachen, which debated cross-border care based on a number of very explicit questions, and even addressed the specific content of a health services directive (including its recitals, objective, definitions and the content of different chapters) and an 'options paper' dealing (very explicitly) with the '[c]onsequences when excluding planned health care services from Regulation 883/04'. In a paper issued after the informal Council meeting, the three successive German, Portuguese and Slovenian Presidencies[193] 'strongly suggest that the Commission presents a broad

---

[187] *Ibid.*, p. 34.   [188] *Ibid.*, p. 33.

[189] 276 responses were received from national governments, regional authorities, international and national umbrella organizations, social security institutions, universities, industry and individual citizens.

[190] European Commission, 'Summary report of the responses to the consultation regarding "Community action on health services"', SEC (2006) 1195/4, 20 April 2007.

[191] *Ibid.*, p. 34.   [192] *Ibid.*, p. 33.

[193] Germany held the EU Presidency during the first half of 2007. It was followed by Portugal on 1 July 2007 and Slovenia on 1 January 2008. The three successive presidencies have developed a joint 'Trio Presidency' eighteen-month programme of Council activities, which is designed to increase continuity in the Council's work.

framework on all of the above-mentioned issues, not just on patient mobility'.[194]

Was the Commission able and willing to capitalize on this political willingness for a 'broad framework'? It seems not immediately. The Commission proposals on health care services took a long time to appear. A proposal expected at the end of 2007[195] was delayed at the last instant due to protests among Member States and lobbying from MEPs, some of whom feared that the debate about this piece of legislation could undermine the ratification of the EU's new Treaty. Arguably, for the same reason, the publication of a watered-down version of the proposal was delayed, for the second time, in February 2008. The proposal eventually appeared in July 2008, as part of the 'Social Agenda'.[196]

The emerging governance framework of EU-level health care policy described here will be underpinned by its partial 'constitutionalization' in the Lisbon Treaty (if it is ratified by all the Member States). The Lisbon Treaty will amend Article 152 EC, to further enhance (or possibly constrain) the Commission's competence to encourage cooperation between the Member States in the public health field, which will include 'preventing physical and mental illness and diseases'. This Commission-sponsored cooperation is to include, 'in particular, initiatives aiming at the establishment of guidelines and indicators, the organisation of exchange of best practice, and the preparation of the necessary elements for periodic monitoring and evaluation'.[197] The list of areas within which the EU may adopt 'incentive measures' (in other words, financial support through various programmes, particularly the public health programmes

---

[194] Trio Presidency, 'Health care across Europe: striving for added value', Notes of the Trio Presidency, Aachen, 20 April 2007, p. 5.

[195] In its Annual Policy Strategy for 2007, the Commission announced that it would 'develop a Community framework for safe, high quality and efficient health services, by reinforcing cooperation between Member States and providing certainty over the application of Community law to health services and healthcare'. European Commission, 'Annual policy strategy for 2007: boosting trust through action', COM (2006) 122 final, 14 March 2006, p. 11.

[196] Proposal for a Directive on the application of patients' rights in cross-border healthcare COM (2008) 414 final.

[197] See Article 168(2), Treaty on the Functioning of the European Union, Consolidated Versions of the Treaty on European Union and the Treaty on the Functioning of the European Union, OJ 2008 No. C115/1.

discussed above) also is further specified.[198] Moreover, the role of the European Parliament as a recipient of information is made explicit in the Lisbon revisions.[199]

5. Conclusions

Health is and will continue to be an area within which the competence of the EU institutions is highly constrained. This has been reconfirmed by the Treaty of Lisbon.[200] At the same time, however, health is no longer a 'non-topic' for the EU, and neither the EU institutions, nor the governments of the Member States, can now retreat from that position, for how could the EU not be 'for' health and health care?

We have described EU health care law, policy and governance as a double patchwork. The limitations of: (a) the political incapacity to adopt 'positive' legislation; (b) a longstanding but increasing impact of EU law on national health care systems; and (c) a divided policy space, have triggered 'political spillovers pushing consecutive rounds of EU policy initiatives, pressed for by domestic policy-makers, to deal with the unintended consequences'.[201] More particularly, those responsible for health care at the national levels have responded, feeding into the EU's use of the 'governance tool kit' in health care fields. No less than five sets of actors, which we have labelled as 'public health', 'social affairs', 'internal market', 'enterprise' and 'economic', have crowded the EU health care governance space and have established different

---

[198] The revised provision (new Article 152(5)) will give the European Parliament and the Council competence to adopt 'incentive measures designed to protect and improve human health and in particular to combat the major cross-border health scourges, measures concerning monitoring, early warning of and combating serious cross-border threats to health, and measures which have as their direct objective the protection of public health regarding tobacco and the abuse of alcohol, excluding any harmonisation of the laws and regulations of the Member States'.

[199] The new Article 152(2) will state that 'the European Parliament shall be kept fully informed' of Commission-sponsored coordination between the Member States.

[200] See Article 168(7), Treaty on the Functioning of the European Union: 'Union action shall respect the responsibilities of the Member States for the definition of their health policy and for the organisation and delivery of health services and medical care. The responsibilities of the Member States shall include the management of health services and medical care and the allocation of the resources assigned to them'.

[201] Hemerijck, *Revisiting productive welfare*, above n.90, p. 25.

(as opposed to integrated) and largely uncoordinated responses, all of which, at least, have the potential to have an impact at the domestic level. So far, law and governance have existed largely in parallel, with governance processes 'in the shadow' of legislation.

We have seen that, within each of these sets of players, the European Commission, often from a very early stage, set the terms of the debate, including in processes such as the patient mobility processes and the OMC. In other words, governance does not seem to significantly destabilize the independent agency, or even hegemony, of the Commission as the lynch pin of Community law and policy-making. However, there are strong indications that now that the different health care processes are 'up and running', the Commission's internal divisions may allow the Council and national governments to reassert control. One should recall in this context that, under the United Kingdom Presidency, the Council (daringly) asked for 'more leadership' in the European health care debate. A clear message addressed to the Commission, it seems. And yet, one key actor is quite sceptical:

DG Social Affairs has the legal instruments (legal base), but it does not have the legitimate constituency at national level. DG SANCO has privileged relationships with national actors, but it does not have the legal instruments. Result: we have to find a compromise, but for the moment it is a real conflict, a battle for power. Of which we do not see the end yet.[202]

Another clear feature of the double EU health care governance patchwork is that public consultations are increasingly used by the European Commission as a tool to legitimize further initiatives and to create ownership of the final proposal among stakeholders. Examples include consultations on the draft strategic guidelines for the new programming period of the Structural Funds, on freeing Europe from exposure to environmental tobacco smoke, on the follow-up to the Court's jurisprudence relating to the reimbursement of medical expenses incurred in another Member State, on health-related information for patients, on how to ensure legal certainty regarding cross-border health care, and David Byrne's electronic Reflection Process in 2004 on the Commission's new EU health strategy. These consultations seem to help to depoliticize debates (which are sometimes even said to

[202] Interview with DG Social Affairs, July 2007.

be too technical to be discussed among politicians) and thus remain relatively isolated from high profile media or other public scrutiny. And yet, as we have shown, in most cases their effect is significant, as in the case of the Pharmaceutical Forum, which was instrumental in bypassing issues which were rejected in the Pharmaceutical Review.

Another feature of the new EU health care governance patchwork is an increasing interlinking between classical EU law-making and governance processes. Examples of this linkage include the High Level Process of Reflection, which played a key role in pressing the Commission to propose legislation on health services in the internal market. They include the networked governance processes of 'Europe against Cancer' feeding into tobacco legislation. They also include the High Level Group on Health Services and Medical Care, which organized pressure to increase EU funding for health care infrastructure through the Structural Funds, and promoted coordination of national health care policies and adopted soft law measures such as the 2005 'EU Guidelines for Purchase of Treatment Abroad', effectively bypassing the lack of legislative guidance from the EU on this issue. Other examples include the Transparency Committee (set up under Directive 89/105/ EEC),[203] which was reactivated because of the information requirements of the Pharmaceutical Forum, and which spilled over into new kinds of cooperation. Thus, new Member States are using the (formal and especially informal) exchanges of information between Committee members (e.g., on the therapeutic value-added of new medicines) 'to arm themselves against the invasion of new pharmaceutical products on their markets'.[204] Another example is the data protection regulation (covered by Directive 95/46/EC),[205] for which the Commission offers 'to work with the Member States ... to raise awareness' of the provisions of the Directive that apply to the health care sector. This governance approach presumably sits alongside more classical modes of implementation and enforcement of EU legislation by the Commission envisaged by the Treaty. Taking all these examples together, it will come

---

[203] Council Directive 89/105/EEC relating to the transparency of measures regulating the prices of medicinal products for human use and their inclusion in the scope of national health insurance systems, OJ 1989 No. L40/8.

[204] Interview with member of High Level Group, September 2007.

[205] European Parliament and Council Directive 95/46/EC on the protection of individuals with regard to the processing of personal data and on the free movement of such data, OJ 1995 No. L281/31.

as no surprise, then, that non-binding measures are far from being per-ceived as irrelevant by the Member States and that the decision-making process leading to their adoption involves hard politics.

In sum, the cross-fertilization between law and governance seems to point towards the future development of 'hybrid' policy instru-ments: far from abandoning legislative responses, the EU institutions are keen to pursue them *alongside* the array of governance mechanisms now available to them. A case in point of such 'instrument hybridity'[206] is the interlinking between the OMC and the ESF. The scope of the ESF was redirected in 1999, so that the Fund could support, during the 2000–6 programming period, the newly launched 'European employ-ment strategy', another EU governance process launched in 1997.[207] Even more important in the context of this chapter is that the new ESF Regulation, which determines the tasks of the ESF, the scope of its assistance and the eligibility criteria for the 2007–13 programming period, explicitly refers to the 'open method of coordination on social protection and social inclusion',[208] of which the health care OMC is now one particular strand. Consequently, there is no reason why in the near future certain elements of the health care OMC would not be taken into account by the Commission, de jure or de facto, to deter-mine whether expenditure is eligible for assistance under the Fund.[209]

What will happen in the future? Most importantly, EU health law and governance will be increasingly interlinked. At first glance, it would seem that we are unlikely to see significant additions to the legislative landscape, in terms of EU law that *directly* treats the pro-vision of health care in the internal market or competition law. Even if the Commission's proposal for a directive on health care services

---

[206] D. Trubek and L. Trubek, 'New governance and legal regulation: complementarity, rivalry or transformation', *Columbia Journal of European Law* 13 (2007), 539–64. See also T. Hervey and L. Trubek, 'Freedom to provide health care services within the EU: an opportunity for hybrid governance', *Columbia Journal of European Law* 13 (2007), 623–49.

[207] European Parliament and Council Regulation 1784/1999/EC on the European Social Fund, OJ 1999 No. L213/5. More particularly, the Regulation stipulated in Article 1 that 'the Fund shall contribute to the actions undertaken in pursuance of the European Employment Strategy and the Annual Guidelines on Employment'.

[208] Article 4(3), European Parliament and Council Regulation 1081/2006/EC, above n.22, p. 16.

[209] Interview with DG Social Affairs, February 2007.

in the internal market does emerge, it will not significantly change the current position. However, this may be too hasty a conclusion, since support for further legislation may be spurred by the information and new understandings generated through the learning mechanisms of governance procedures, such as the OMC, other forms of policy coordination, and information generation and dissemination drawing on EU funding opportunities. Furthermore, legislation in other fields of EU law that *indirectly* affects health care systems will continue to be adopted, but the 'health care mainstreaming' obligation, which will be further embedded in the Treaty following the Lisbon amendments,[210] will be applied more seriously due to the increased visibility of health in the Commission's vista, and because of Member States' increased willingness to discuss health care at the EU level, at least in the context of governance processes. Finally, consistent with the 'constitutional asymmetry' thesis, the 'negative integration' and destabilizing dynamic of litigation before the Court will continue. But this will only be at the margins and, arguably, because the Court is no more blind to governance measures than it is to legislation – and proposed legislation – it will increasingly be inspired by the outcomes of the governance process in its judgements (e.g., perhaps when interpreting 'undue delays', 'solidarity' or a definition of 'public interest' in the context of cross-border health care services; or an agreed list of justifications for non-discriminatory restrictions on the free movement to provide services, freedom of establishment or free movement of persons).

Non-hierarchical, networked methods of governance, based on shared learning, information collection and dissemination, benchmarking, and so on, are likely to continue to be important, since the EU is likely to continue to use information, influence and incentives, rather than hierarchical law-making and regulation in health care fields. The challenges of non-hierarchical governance that apply in any field will apply perforce in the health care governance arena. How will the relevant actors be included, each with an 'equal voice' at the table? At present, EU health care governance remains largely a 'closed shop' of high level civil servants, EU officials and experts, and many governance practices are particularly poorly integrated into domestic policy processes. Consequently, (European and domestic) parliamentary overview remains poorly developed. What about Member States

---

[210] See Article 9, Treaty on the Functioning of the European Union.

where human capacity is scarce, so participation in these processes is more limited than in those better endowed with human capacity? How will the processes be protected from 'capture' by powerful interests, be they in the pharmaceutical, tobacco or private health insurance industries? These questions are not only questions for non-hierarchical governance structures – they apply equally in the context of more traditional hierarchical law-making and regulatory processes.

Some empirical evidence of longer-standing governance processes suggests that they are being used as an increasingly important trigger for ambitious domestic welfare state reform.[211] It seems that Frank Vandenbroucke was right when he said that:

Open co-ordination can and should be a creative process, because it will enable us to translate the much discussed but often unspecified "European social model" into a tangible set of agreed objectives, to be entrenched in European co-operation. … Efficient EU co-operation can help identify and prepare the legislative work [at] both a national and EU level.[212]

The synergies offered by such an integration of law and governance provide the EU with an opportunity to take health care policy forward, while balancing the interests of the internal market and competition, alongside those of 'social Europe'.

In the final analysis, neither positive nor negative integration in the classical senses will be the dominant mode for EU law or policy-making in the health care context. Rather, we can expect an interaction, or set of interactions, between legislative and governance processes. And, although the story we tell in this chapter may be read to imply that the law and policy patchwork is becoming increasingly 'joined up', for all the reasons explained here, it will never become a single all-encompassing woven tapestry.

---

[211] M.-P. Hamel and B. Vanhercke, 'The OMC and domestic social policymaking in Belgium and France: window dressing, one-way impact, or reciprocal influence?', in M. Heidenreich and J. Zeitlin (eds.), *Changing European employment and welfare regimes: the influence of the open method of coordination on national labour market and social welfare reforms* (London: Routledge, 2009).

[212] F. Vandenbroucke, 'European integration and national health care systems: a challenge for social policy', Speech at the Ghent Conference on 'European Integration and National Health Care Systems: a Challenge for Social Policy', Ghent, 7–8 December 2001, p. 5.

3 | EU regulatory agencies and health protection

GOVIN PERMANAND AND ELLEN VOS

1. Introduction

The challenges involved in the governance of the European Union's (EU) internal market, as well as the need for closer collaboration between Member States, have seen EU policy-makers increasingly turn to executive or regulatory agencies outside the Commission structure.[1] These agencies are entrusted to execute a wide range of tasks from simple information collection and dissemination, to the adoption of decisions that are binding on all Member States.[2] Seen within the context of the need for reform of the Commission and the general striving of the Community institutions for better law-making based on principles of good governance, it is not surprising that, in the new millennium, the resort to European-level agencies is more popular than ever. Moreover, as the EU's competences in social affairs continue to develop, the Commission's use of agencies has further spread into health-related areas. We have thus witnessed a mushrooming of agencies such as the European Medicines Agency,

We would like to thank Rita Baeten, Irene Glinos, Tamara Hervey and Elias Mossialos for their helpful feedback on an earlier version of this chapter.

[1] Although the European Community represents the first pillar of the European Union's Treaty structure, for simplicity's sake we use the terms EU and Community interchangeably in this Chapter.

[2] See, in general, E. Chiti, 'The emergence of a Community administration: the case of European agencies', *Common Market Law Review* 37 (2000), 309–43; E. Vos, 'Reforming the European Commission: what role to play for EU agencies?', *Common Market Law Review* 37 (2000), 1113–34; M. Everson et al., 'The role of specialised agencies in decentralising EU governance', Report presented to the Commission (2000), http://ec.europa. eu/governance/areas/group6/contribution_En.pdf; S. Frank, *A new model for European medical device regulation – a comparative legal analysis in the EU and the USA* (Groningen: Europa Law, 2003); D. Geradin and N. Petit, 'The development of agencies at EU and national levels: conceptual analysis and proposals for reform', Jean Monnet Working Paper No. 01/04 (2004).

the European Agency for Safety and Health at Work, the European Monitoring Centre for Drugs and Drug Addiction, the European Food Safety Authority, the European Aviation Safety Agency, the European Maritime Agency, the European Centre for Disease Prevention and Control and, most recently, the European Chemicals Agency. These agencies do not work to similar remits and do not exercise the same degrees of authority. But many have an impact on the way the Community protects the health of its citizens, and they shift the coordination of specialized, technical and scientific expertise to the European level.

More recently, agencies have been seen as a constitutive element within the so-called 'new modes of governance' (NMG) approach to the making and enforcing of rules at EU level. The NMG debate focuses on the shift away from the traditional 'Community method' of regulation to embrace softer, more responsive and reflexive modes, with the incremental and consensus-generating approach of the open method of coordination (OMC) best conforming to this ideal.[3] But the increase in agency numbers, even if seen from this softer perspective, raises a number of concerns. As the European agencies are, for the most part, decentralized networks of variegated national level players and answerable to the Commission, they are neither sufficiently independent nor powerful to act as regulators in the traditional sense. At the same time, with agencies created to bolster better governance in the EU, to address areas of collective action, as well as to provide scientific guidance, it is clear that their sphere(s) of influence are growing. Moreover, the Commission's relationship to them is often one of dependence. This, in turn, raises questions about agency accountability, their relationship with the Member States, and the extent to which further discretionary powers could be given to them, were the Treaties or secondary legislation to allow this.

This chapter examines two agencies with a particularly important role to play in human health and safety protection, and thus impacting on Member State health care systems: the European Medicines Agency (EMEA) and the European Food Safety Authority

---

[3] See D. Trubek and L. Trubek, 'Hard and soft law in the construction of social Europe: the role of the open method of co-ordination', *European Law Journal* 11 (2005), 343–64. See also Chapter 4 in this volume.

(EFSA).[4] Another agency that would be relevant for the study of health (care) is the European Centre for Disease Prevention and Control (ECDC). However, given our focus on policy and regulation (and primarily as they apply to the single European market (SEM)), rather than public health per se, the ECDC falls outside our coverage here.[5]

These medicines and foodstuffs agencies are particularly interesting as they are examples par excellence of softer, more responsive and reflexive modes of governance, and may be indicative of, if not instructive for, the development of new governance patterns for health protection in the EU. Moreover, because of the decisive role they play in the re-regulation of health issues at the EU level – as will be shown – and foremost in the context of the internal market, both agencies have an impact on national health systems, even if not an immediate or ostensibly direct one.

To this end, the chapter first looks at the development of European agencies in general, in order to understand the reasons behind and rationale for their proliferation. It then briefly profiles the development of EU competences in health, and the extensive activities of European legislators to regulate the pharmaceuticals and food safety arenas on health grounds, although as part of the EU's internal market policy. These activities have been undertaken particularly in response to the potential threats to health (and health care) that the deregulatory initiatives of the 1980s may otherwise have had.[6] We see that, in both domains, therefore, the EU has extensive legislative powers to determine which products or substances may be considered 'safe' and may obtain a marketing authorization within the SEM.[7] In this, the European Commission relies to a great extent on the technical and scientific expertise of the agencies to serve both its health protection and internal market goals, which in turn affects Member State health care systems. The chapter thus examines the roles of both agencies and addresses specific questions relating to their risk assessment mandates, composition, independence and accountability, and the extent of their influence. Some observations on the use of European agencies in general, and with regard to the EMEA and

---

[4] Although the EMEA is also responsible for veterinary medicinal products, and the EFSA also for animal health, we consider their roles only in respect of human health protection.
[5] See Chapter 5 in this volume.
[6] See Chapter 5 in this volume.
[7] The 'regulatory pathway', as Leigh Hancher puts it. See Chapter 15 in this volume.

EFSA specifically, and their potential impact on health protection and national health systems, are provided by way of conclusion.

2. European agencies as a new mode of governance

Agencies have been created within the Community's institutional framework since the 1970s. A strong Commission push saw many agencies set up during the 1990s given the single market programme, and in the 2000s we observe renewed interest (also as part of the NMG approach). This latter wave can in large part be put down to the bovine spongiform encephalopathy (BSE) crisis of 1996 and the subsequent need to regain the trust of the general public, stakeholders and regulators in EU decision-making involving health protection. Inquests into the BSE crisis and its handling made it clear that the Commission had been ill-equipped to deal with the various elements involved in regulating the foodstuffs sector, and that it lacked the expertise and organizational infrastructure to deal with highly technical questions and/or crises more generally. It was felt that independent (scientific) expertise and authority was needed to inform policy-making – for instance, in terms of divesting the science from the politics – and to enable proper risk analysis activities. There was also much domestic level interest in specialized agencies at the time, and a growing confidence in this decentralized approach based on the American tradition of independent statutory agencies.[8]

A. Delegating to European agencies

Stemming from this, there is now a considerable (and growing) literature on the emergence and operation of agencies in the European national and Community frames. While we are unable to review this here, it is noteworthy, even if only in passing, that principal–agent analysis[9]

[8] M. Thatcher, 'Delegation to independent regulatory agencies: pressures, functions and contextual mediation', *West European Politics* 25 (2002), 125–47.
[9] See, for example, M. Thatcher and A. Stone Sweet, 'Theory and practice of delegation to non-majoritarian institutions', *West European Politics* 25 (2002), 1–22; P. Magnette, 'The politics of regulation in the European Union', in D. Geradin, R. Muñoz and N. Petit (eds.), *Regulation through agencies in the EU: a new paradigm of European governance* (Cheltenham: Edward Elgar, 2005).

(including a multi-principals view),[10] and historical institutionalism[11] are widely used as explanatory approaches in the political science literature. They generally focus on the 'why' from the Community macro perspective, while additional meso-level considerations on the part of policy-makers are often concerned with ensuring the credibility of decision-making (and decision-makers),[12] promoting market efficiency and fairness, addressing the delegation problem,[13] and serving the public interest more widely. Agencies also have been seen as a progression of the wider 'privatisation, liberalisation, welfare reform and deregulation' agenda of European governments since the late 1970s.[14]

Notwithstanding the validity of the different theoretical lenses – which we cannot explore here – in practical terms, the EU agencies have been created on numerous grounds, but mainly in response to an increased demand for information, expert advice and coordination at the Community level, as well as the need to lessen the Commission's workload and its search for more efficient and effective decision-making. Further, the resort to agencies is generally favoured by the Member States. First, they perceive benefits from collective action in given policy domains, along with improved governance, but are at the same time unwilling to strengthen the Commission. Second, the EU agencies are generally networks functioning to a 'hub and spoke' model,[15] which directly involves national level counterparts.

[10] R. Dehousse, 'Delegation of powers in the European Union: the need for a multi-principals model'. Draft Discussion Paper Connex 2–3, Centre d'études européennes de Sciences Po, 12 November 2006, www.arena.uio.no/events/LondonPapers06/DEHOUSSE.pdf.

[11] See, for example, T. Christensen and P. Lægreid, 'Regulatory agencies – the challenge of balancing agency autonomy and political control', *Governance: An International Journal of Policy, Administration and Institutions* 20 (2001), 499–520; S. Krapohl, 'Thalidomide, BSE and the single market: an historical-institutionalist approach to regulatory regimes in the European Union', *European Journal of Political Research* 46 (2007), 25–46.

[12] See, for example, S. Krapohl, 'Credible commitment in non-independent regulatory agencies: a comparative analysis of the European agencies for pharmaceuticals and foodstuffs', *European Law Journal* 10 (2004), 518–38.

[13] See, for example, G. Majone, 'Delegation of regulatory powers in a mixed polity', *European Law Journal* 8 (2002), 319–39.

[14] G. Majone, 'The agency model: the growth of regulation and regulatory institutions in the European Union', *European Institute of Public Administration (EIPAScope)* 3 (1997), 1–6.

[15] R. Dehousse, 'Regulation by networks in the European Community: the role of European agencies', *Journal of European Public Policy* 4 (1997), 246–61.

While not having a single designation (e.g., 'agency', 'office', 'centre', 'authority' or 'foundation'), the European agencies can at their simplest be defined as bodies that, in addition to the European institutions, operate within the EC or EU realm in order to fulfil specific tasks, and which have an independent administrative structure.[16] Other characteristics depend on the type of body and policy domain. They are often based on existing (scientific) committees and, in some cases, have been designed to replace this comitology structure. The agencies generally support the Community institutions and national authorities in identifying, preparing and evaluating specific policy measures and guidelines. Only a handful have been given any concrete decision-making powers,[17] however, and, particularly for legal and political science analysts, even these do not amount to independent regulatory agencies in the traditional sense. Numerous typologies of agencies have been attempted[18] – and the Commission has often changed its own categories – but a simple classification of the agencies can be based on the following factors: the pillars of the EU; the legal basis for establishing the agency; their organizational structure; and the functions and nature of the agencies' powers.

B. *Classification according to function*

European agencies are thus situated across policy domains and, at the time of writing, there are currently twenty-eight spanning the three pillars of the EU (including one undergoing final preparations). There are twenty-two agencies in the first pillar (European Communities) – including the EMEA and EFSA – three within the second pillar (Common Foreign and Security Policy), and three set up under the third pillar (Police and Judicial Cooperation in Criminal Matters). A listing of all the European agencies within the three pillars, and a brief outline of their purpose, can be found in Table 3.1. Listing these agencies helps to convey a sense of the scope of agency work in the EU, not to mention their proliferation since early 2000. Furthermore, it is clear that

---

[16] European Commission, 'Operating framework for the European agencies', COM (2002) 718 final, 11 December 2002.

[17] That the agencies can be granted strictly circumscribed executive powers subject to Commission-imposed constraints is a result of the 'Meroni doctrine' based on the ECJ's ruling in Case 9/56, *Meroni* v. *High Authority* [1958] ECR 133.

[18] See, for instance, Geradin and Petit, 'The development of agencies', above n.2.

many of these will, even if indirectly, have an impact on health matters within the EU frame, as well as on the Member States' health care systems and policy-making priorities. The (growing) number of the agencies also suggests their acceptance among the Member States within the context of less top-down and more NMG-oriented approaches at EU level. Agencies are regarded as softer modes of regulatory governance than the use of hard law, and their envisaged independence fosters a sense of credibility.

Towards externalizing management tasks, there is a fourth category of agency outside the pillars.[19] Governed by a separate legal framework,[20] 'executive agencies' are established to execute certain tasks relating to the management of one or more Community programmes. They are established for a fixed period and are located within the Commission, either in Brussels or Luxembourg. There are currently six such offices: the Education, Audiovisual and Culture Executive Agency; the European Research Council Executive Agency; the Executive Agency for Competitiveness and Innovation; The Research Executive Agency; the Trans-European Transport Network Executive Agency; and the Executive Agency for Health and Consumers (EAHC). The latter was set up in 2005 under the auspices of the Commission's Directorate-General for Health and Consumer Protection (DG SANCO) to manage the EU's multi-annual public health programmes (1 January 2003 to 31 December 2007[21] and 1 January 2008 to 31 December 2013), and its mandate expires in December 2015.[22] As an executive rather than a regulatory agency, a detailed discussion of the EAHC falls outside the scope of this chapter.

---

[19] Since 2009, there is an additional separate category of two agencies relating to the European Atomic Energy Community Treaty (EURATOM).

[20] Council Regulation 58/2003/EC laying down the statute for executive agencies to be entrusted with certain tasks in the management of Community programmes, OJ 2003 No. L11/1.

[21] European Parliament and Council Decision 1786/2002/EC adopting a programme of Community action in the field of public health (2003–2008), OJ 2002 No. L271/1. European Parliament and Council Decision establishing a second programme of Community action in the field of health (2008–2013), OJ 2007 No. L301/3. The programmes focus on health information, health threats and health determinants. The agency was initially called the Public Health Executive Agency.

[22] Commission Decision 2008/544/EC amending Decision 2004/858/EC in order to transform the Executive Agency for the Public Health Programme into the Executive Agency for Health and Consumers, OJ 2008 No. L173/27, Article 1 (2).

Table 3.1. *Agencies of the EU*

Agencies of the first pillar: Community agencies

Name	Acronym	Established*	Location	Profile	Web site
European Centre for the Development of Vocational Training	Cedefop	1975[23]	Thessaloniki, Greece	Cedefop is the European Union's reference centre for vocational education and training and supports vocational training of professionals and the development and improvement of vocational training measures throughout Europe.	www.cedefop. europea.eu
European Foundation for the Improvement of Living and Working Conditions	EUROFOUND	1975[24]	Dublin, Ireland	EUROFOUND analyses living and working conditions and issues guidelines and recommendations for social policy decision-makers.	www. eurofound. europa.eu
European Training Foundation	ETF	1990[25]	Turin, Italy	The ETF supports vocational training reform in the partner countries and translates EU policy into practical training and labour market instruments for non-EU countries.	www.etf. europa.eu

Table 3.1. (*cont.*)

Agencies of the first pillar: Community agencies

Name	Acronym	Established*	Location	Profile	Web site
European Medicines Agency	EMEA	1993[26]	London, United Kingdom	The EMEA's main responsibility is the protection of human and animal health; it endeavours to ensure optimum evaluation and supervision of medicines in Europe.	www.emea. europa.eu
Office for Harmonization in the Internal Market (Trade Marks and Designs)	OHIM	1993[27]	Alicante, Spain	OHIM administers Community trade-marks and designs, which guarantee their owners uniform legal protection applicable in all Member States of the European Union.	http://oami. europa.eu
European Environment Agency	EEA	1994[28]	Copenhagen, Denmark	The EEA provides information on the state of Europe's environment. It is also open to non-EU countries with similar aims.	www.eea. europa.eu
European Agency for Safety and Health at Work	EU-OSHA	1994[29]	Bilbao, Spain	EU-OSHA acts as a catalyst for developing, collecting, analysing and disseminating information	www.osha. europa.eu

that is intended to make workplaces in Europe safer, healthier and more productive.

Name	Abbreviation	Year	Location	Description	Website
Translation Centre for the Bodies of the European Union	CdT	1994[30]	Luxembourg	CdT meets the translation needs of the decentralized Community agencies.	www.cdt.europa.eu
Community Plant Variety Office	CPVO	1995[31]	Angers, France	CPVO grants industrial property rights for plant varieties that apply throughout the Community.	www.cpvo.europa.eu
European Monitoring Centre for Drugs and Drug Addiction	EMCDDA	1995[32]	Lisbon, Portugal	The EMCDDA collects and disseminates 'objective, reliable and comparable information' on drugs and drug addiction in Europe.	www.emcdda.europa.eu
European Food Safety Authority	EFSA	2002[33]	Parma, Italy	EFSA provides independent scientific advice and clear communication on existing and emerging risks in the field of food and feed safety.	www.efsa.europa.eu
European Aviation Safety Agency	EASA	2002[34]	Cologne, Germany	EASA's task is to create uniform safety standards for the safety of aviation.	www.easa.europa.eu

Table 3.1. (*cont.*)

Agencies of the first pillar: Community agencies

Name	Acronym	Established*	Location	Profile	Web site
European Maritime Safety Agency	EMSA	2003[35]	Lisbon, Portugal	EMSA provides technical and scientific advice to the Commission in the field of maritime safety and prevention of pollution by ships, and provides support in developing new legislation.	www.emsa.europa.eu
European Network and Information Security Agency	ENISA	2004[36]	Heraklion, Greece	ENISA's task is to support and advise the Commission and Member States in matters of information security.	www.enisa.europa.eu
European Centre for Disease Prevention and Control	ECDC	2004[37]	Solna, Sweden	ECDC's task is to coordinate action to monitor and combat epidemics at the European level.	www.ecdc.europa.eu
European Railway Agency	ERA	2004[38]	Valenciennes and Lille, France	The ERA reinforces railway safety and interoperability throughout Europe.	www.era.europa.eu

European Agency for the Management of Operational Cooperation at the External Borders of the Member States of the European Union	Frontex	2004[39]	Warsaw, Poland	Frontex coordinates the Member States' operational management in ensuring the security of the EU's external borders. It provides assistance in training border guards, conducts risk analyses, monitors relevant research and, if necessary, assists Member States in circumstances requiring increased technical and operational assistance at borders.	www.frontex. europa.eu
European Global Navigation Satellite Systems Supervisory Authority	GSA	2004[40]	Brussels, Belgium	GSA took over from the Galileo Joint Undertakings, and manages all public interests related to European global satellite navigation system programmes. Objectives include laying of foundations for a fully sustainable and economically viable Galileo system.	www.gsa. europa.eu
Community Fisheries Control Agency	CFCA	2005[41]	Vigo, Spain	CFCA organizes the operational coordination of fi sheries control and inspection activities by the Member States, and assists them in complying with the Common	www. cfca. europa.eu

Table 3.1. (*cont.*)

Agencies of the first pillar: Community agencies

Name	Acronym	Established*	Location	Profile	Web site
				EU Fisheries Policy in order to ensure its effective and uniform application.	
European Chemicals Agency	ECHA	2006[42]	Helsinki, Finland	ECHA manages the registration, evaluation, authorization and restriction processes for chemical substances, in order to ensure consistency across the European Union.	www. echa. europa.eu
European Fundamental Rights Agency	FRA	2007[43]	Vienna, Austria	FRA builds on the European Monitoring Centre on Racism and Xenophobia and provides assistance and expertise on fundamental rights when implementing community law, and supports the EU institutions and Member States in taking measures and formulating appropriate courses of action	www. fra. europa.eu

Name	Acronym	Established*	Location	Profile	Web site
European Institute for Gender Equality	EIGE	2007[44]	Vilnius, Lithuania	EIGE aims to strengthen the promotion of gender equality, including gender mainstreaming in all Community and resulting national policies, to fight against gender discrimination and to raise awareness of gender equality through technical assistance to the Community institutions and national authorities.	http://ec. europa.eu/social/ main.jsp? catId=732 &langId=en

Agencies of the second pillar: Common Foreign and Security Policy (CFSP)

Name	Acronym	Established*	Location	Profile	Web site
European Union Satellite Centre	EUSC	2001[45]	Torrejón de Ardoz, Spain	The EUSC analyses information from satellite imagery in support of Union decision-making in the field of the CFSP. It thereby strengthens both the CFSP and the European Security and Defence Policy, particularly with regard to crisis monitoring and conflict prevention. The Centre also conducts research and development projects.	www.eusc. europa.eu

Table 3.1. (*cont.*)

Agencies of the second pillar: Common Foreign and Security Policy (CFSP)

Name	Acronym	Established*	Location	Profile	Web site
European Union Institute for Security Studies	ISS	2002[46]	Paris, France	ISS promotes the EU's security interests. It contributes to the CFSP through research and debate on security and defence issues, forward-looking analysis for the Council and High Representative of the EU, and the development of a transatlantic dialogue on all security issues with the EU, the United States and Canada.	www. iss.europa.eu
European Defence Agency	EDA	2004[47]	Brussels, Belgium	The EDA's task is to improve defence and crisis management capabilities under the European Security and Defence Policy.	www.eda. europa.eu

Agencies of the third pillar: police and judicial cooperation in criminal matters

Name	Acronym	Established*	Location	Profile	Web site
				task of facilitating effective, close cooperation between the Member States in preventing and combating international organized crime.	
European Police College	Cepol	2000[48]	Hook, United Kingdom	Cepol organizes training for police officers to provide information on different police systems and cross-border police work. Its aim is to support the national police forces, particularly in the fight against cross-border crime. From 2006 onwards, Cepol has become an EU agency having separate legal personality.	www.cepol. europa. eu

| European Union's Judicial Cooperation Unit | Eurojust | 2002[49] | The Hague, the Netherlands | Eurojust assists the Member States, in particular, with the investigation and prosecution of serious cross-border and organized crime. Emphasis is placed on improving the competent authorities' coordination of cooperation and fostering cooperation in criminal justice throughout Europe. | www.eurojust.europa.eu |

---

* Year of establishment under legislation, not date of first operations.

[23] Council Regulation 337/75/EEC establishing a European Centre for the Development of Vocational Training, OJ 1975 No. L39/1.

[24] Council Regulation 1365/75/EEC on the creation of a European foundation for the improvement of living and working conditions, OJ 1975 No. L139/1.

[25] Council Regulation 1360/90/EEC establishing a European Training Foundation, OJ 1990 No. L131/1, as amended by Council Regulation 2063/94/EC amending Regulation 1360/90/EEC establishing a European Training Foundation, OJ 1994 No. L216/9; Council Regulation 1572/98/EC amending Regulation 1360/90/EEC establishing a European Training Foundation, OJ 1998 No. L206/1; and Council Regulation 2666/00/EC on assistance for Albania, Bosnia and Herzegovina, Croatia, the Federal Republic of Yugoslavia and the Former Yugoslav Republic of Macedonia, repealing Regulation 1628/96/EC and amending Regulations 3906/89/EEC and 1360/90/EEC and Decisions 97/256/EC and 1999/311/EC, OJ 2000 No. L306/1.

26 Council Regulation 2309/93/EEC laying down Community procedures for the authorisation and supervision of medicinal products for human and veterinary use and establishing a European Agency for the Evaluation of Medicinal Products, OJ 1993 No. L214/1.

27 Council Regulation 40/94/EC on the Community trade mark, OJ 1994 No. L11/1.

28 Council Regulation 2062/94/EC establishing a European Agency for Safety and Health at Work, OJ 1994 No. L216/1; Council Regulation 1643/95/EC amending Regulation 2062/94/EC establishing a European Agency for Safety and Health at Work, OJ 1995 No. L156/1.

30 Council Regulation 2965/94/EC setting up a Translation Centre for bodies of the European Union, OJ 1994 No. L314/1; Council Regulation 2610/95/EC amending Regulation 2965/94/EC setting up a Translation Centre for bodies of the European Union, OJ 1995 No. L268/1.

31 Council Regulation 2100/94/EC on Community plant variety rights, OJ 1994 No. L227/1; Council Regulation 2506/95/EC amending Regulation 2100/94/EC on Community plant variety rights, OJ 1995 No. L258/3.

32 Council Regulation 302/93/EEC on the establishment of a European Monitoring Centre for Drugs and Drug Addiction, OJ 1993 No. L36/1; Council Regulation 3294/94/EC amending Regulation 302/93/EEC on the establishment of the European Monitoring Centre for Drugs and Drug Addiction, OJ 1994 No. L341/7.

33 European Parliament and Council Regulation 178/2002/EC laying down the general principles and requirements of food law, establishing the European Food Safety Authority and laying down procedures in matters of food safety, OJ 2002 No. L031/1.

34 European Parliament and Council Regulation 1592/2002/EC on common rules in the field of civil aviation and establishing a European Aviation Safety Agency, OJ 2002 No. L240/1.

35 European Parliament and Council Regulation 1406/2002/EC establishing a European Maritime Safety Agency, OJ 2002 No. L208/1.

36 European Parliament and Council Regulation 460/2004/EC establishing the European Network and Information Security Agency, OJ 2004 No. L77/1.

37 European Parliament and Council Regulation 851/2004/EC establishing a European Centre for Disease Prevention and Control, OJ 2004 No. L142/1.

38 European Parliament and Council Regulation 881/2004/EC establishing a European Railway Agency (Agency Regulation), OJ 2004 No. L220/3.

39 Council Regulation 2007/2004/EC establishing a European Agency for the Management of Operational Cooperation at the External Borders of the Member States of the European Union, OJ 2004 No. L349/1; European Parliament and Council

Notes to Table 3.1. (cont.)

Regulation 863/2007/EC establishing a mechanism for the creation of Rapid Border Intervention Teams and amending Council Regulation 2007/2004/EC as regards that mechanism and regulating the tasks and powers of guest officers, OJ 2007 No. L199/30.

[40] Council Regulation 1321/2004/EC on the establishment of structures for the management of the European satellite radionavigation programmes, OJ 2004 No. L246/1.

[41] Council Regulation 768/2005/EC establishing a Community Fisheries Control Agency and amending Regulation 2847/93/EEC establishing a control system applicable to the common fisheries policy, OJ 2005 No. L128/1.

[42] European Parliament and Council Regulation 1907/2006/EC concerning the Registration, Evaluation, Authorisation and Restriction of Chemicals (REACH), establishing a European Chemicals Agency, amending Directive 1999/45/EC and repealing Council Regulation 793/93/EEC and Commission Regulation 1488/94/EC as well as Council Directive 76/769/EEC and Commission Directives 91/155/EEC, 93/67/EEC, 93/105/EC and 2000/21/EC, OJ 2006 No. L396/1.

[43] Council Regulation 168/2007/EC establishing a European Union Agency for Fundamental Rights, OJ 2007 No. L53/1.

[44] European Parliament and Council Regulation 1922/2006/EC on establishing a European Institute for Gender Equality, OJ 2006 No. L403/9.

[45] Council Joint Action 2001/555/CSFP on the establishment of a European Union Satellite Centre, OJ 2001 No. L200/5.

[46] Council Joint Action 2001/554/CSFP on the establishment of a European Union Institute for Security Studies, OJ 2001 No. L200/1.

[47] Council Joint Action 2004/551/CFSP on the establishment of the European Defence Agency, OJ 2004 No. L245/17.

[48] Council Act drawing up the Convention based on Article K.3 of the Treaty on European Union, on the establishment of a European Police Office (Europol Convention), OJ 1995 No. C 316/1.

[49] Council Decision 2002/187/JHA setting up Eurojust with a view to reinforcing the fight against serious crime, OJ 2002 No. L63/1.

For the purpose of this chapter, we regard regulatory agencies as broader than in the American sense, and consider them to be independent legal entities created by secondary legislation in order to help regulate a particular sector at the European level, and to help implement a particular Community policy regime. These agencies thus play an active role in exercising executive powers at the EU level. We thus closely link to the usage that is common in the 'Brussels circuit'.[50] A regulatory agency in the EU context has the following characteristics: it is created by a (European Parliament and) Council act; it has its own domestic legal personality; it comprises autonomous management bodies; it exercises financial independence; and it operates to a set of well-defined missions and tasks.[51]

Most of the agencies are mandated to collect and disseminate information and otherwise have merely advisory powers. This is also true of the health-oriented agencies: the European Drugs and Drug Addiction Monitoring Centre, which has the provision and supervision of information, along with creating and coordinating relevant networks, as its main tasks; the European Medicines Agency, which issues expert opinions on the market access of new drugs in the EU and monitors their post-approval safety; and the European Food Safety Authority, which is mandated to collate data and information and to provide well-informed, independent scientific opinions on food safety issues. Indeed, the EMEA and EFSA, which are otherwise regarded as strong agencies because of their risk analysis and recommendation-issuing

---

[50] See European Commission, 'Draft interinstitutional agreement on the operating framework for the European regulatory agencies', COM (2005) 59 final, 25 February 2005, p. 5; European Commission, 'European agencies – the way forward', COM (2008) 135 final; and SEC (2008) 323, 11 March 2008.

[51] A conceptualization proposal was tabled by the Commission's Legal Service, SEC (2001) 340, cited in A. Quero, 'Report by the working group 3a. Establishing a framework for decisionmaking regulatory agencies', SG/8597/01EN, Preparation of the White Paper on Governance Work – Improving the Exercise of Executive Responsibilities, June 2001. The EU's web site has a dedicated 'Agencies of the EU' page (http://europa.eu/agencies/index_En.htm), which defines a Community agency as 'a body governed by European public law; it is distinct from the Community Institutions (Council, Parliament, Commission, etc.) and has its own legal personality. It is set up by an act of secondary legislation in order to accomplish a very specific technical, scientific or managerial task, in the framework of the European Union's "first pillar".'

roles in sensitive and often highly technical policy domains (versus the more information gathering and dissemination roles of other agencies) – not to mention their underlying aim to protect the public from harm – do not take legally binding decisions. Both provide scientific advice to the Commission on the basis of which it then adopts and delivers a decision.

It is a function of the Commission's lack of technical and specialized expertise, as well as its inability to keep pace across a multitude of policy areas, that EU regulatory agencies are being developed in such numbers. Given public interest concerns, and the often scientific nature of policies involving health considerations, it is perhaps unsurprising that European agencies exist in the medicines and foodstuffs domains. On the other hand, with health policy a comparatively weak area of Community competence, and one that the Member States are especially sensitive about, perhaps it is a surprise that the EU has been able to set up agencies for medicine control and food safety. In order to help us understand why the two agencies were created and what they mean for health protection and national health systems in general, a brief overview of the 'Europeanization' of health protection is provided in the next section.

3. Europeanization of health protection and the emergence of 'health agencies'

Social concerns – and health-specific issues in particular – were not among the initial designs in respect of the original 1951 Treaty of Paris.[52] But, in establishing the European Atomic Energy Community, the 1957 Treaty of Rome included a specific chapter on health and safety at work. This, in turn, led to initial European worker safety standards for protection against ionizing radiation and was subsequently extended to the wider population. The Treaty also established the European Economic Community, which aimed to promote economic growth, develop closer ties and raise living standards among the signatory countries. It was recognized that the Community's common economic interests would be served by improved social interests

[52] Article 55 of the 1951 Treaty of Paris made allowances for Member States' research and cooperation over the health and safety of workers in the coal and steel industries.

as well. This unintentional – or at least unspecified – spread of Community competence from one policy domain to another (in this case, from economic to social affairs), primarily via the need to serve the requirements of the internal market, has been dubbed 'spillover' in the European political science literature.

Chapter 5 of this volume considers the history and scope of EU public health competences in detail. But it is worth highlighting here several important developments that contributed to the thinking on, and eventual emergence of, health protection as an area for agency authority.

A. *Health protection and the treaties*

The 1986 Single European Act (SEA) set out progress towards a 'single European market' by 1992 as an institutional corollary of the Commission's 1985 programme on a new approach to technical harmonization and standards, which in essence announced a de-regulatory operation.[53] Spillover meant that health matters would now be pursued within this broader and primarily economic, market-serving context, despite it already being accepted that a single market would directly impact on a range of health (care) issues.[54] Even if it was not as explicit as some might have hoped,[55] the SEA thus established the legal basis for the single market to take consumer health protection requirements into consideration.

The 1992 Maastricht Treaty then sought to formally entrench public health protection as a constituent element in all areas of Community policy under a new Article 129.[56] The Treaty also

[53] European Commission, 'Technical harmonisation and standards, a new approach', COM (85) 19 final, 31 January 1985; European Commission, 'Completion of the internal market', White Paper, COM (85) 310 final, 14 June 1986.

[54] See M. Cadreau, 'An economic analysis of the impacts of the health systems of the European single market', in J. Kyriopoulos, A. Sissouras and J. Philalithes (eds.), *Health systems and the challenge of Europe after 1992* (Athens: Lambrakis Press, 1991); C. Altenstetter, 'Health care in the European Community', in G. Hermans, A. F. Casparie and J. H. Paelinck (eds.), *Health care in Europe after 1992* (Leiden: Dartmouth, 1992).

[55] See, for instance, G. Robertson, 'A social Europe: progress through partnership', *European Business Journal* 4 (1992), 10–6; P. Curwen, 'Social policy in the European Community in light of the Maastricht Treaty', *European Business Journal* 4 (1992), 17–26.

[56] The rhetoric proved stronger than the implementation, and Article 129 EC was criticized for being a simple statement of an objective, and one that was

introduced Article 3(b), the subsidiarity provision, whereby policy decisions were to be taken at the level most appropriate to their implementation. The aim was to ensure a transparent legislative process, which ensured that not all policy would be set in Brussels, but it in essence meant a Treaty-based veto on Commission involvement in those affairs over which the Member States wished to retain autonomy. Yet, while health is generally considered to be such an area, and health care and health services (provision, financing, organization) particularly so, subsidiarity has not in fact impeded the Commission from gradually acquiring a greater health protection role than envisaged. Viewed from a broad perspective, therefore, the Community has actually developed itself into a 'leader' with regard to ensuring product safety (especially in medicines and foodstuffs), albeit mainly driven by its internal market aspirations.

The revision of Article 129, which was replaced by Article 152 in the 1997 Treaty of Amsterdam, meant that a high level of human health protection was now to be ensured in the definition and implementation of all Community policies and activities. As this was defined primarily in terms of 'the fight against the major health scourges' (and in the immediate aftermath of the BSE crisis), it was, however, seen as a missed opportunity to consolidate public health within the Community's competences.

Further Europeanization has come in large part via rulings of the European Court of Justice (ECJ), and specifically in relation to free movement issues.[57] We see this not only in respect of free movement of persons, such as patient mobility, health insurance and the reimbursement of medical costs, but also in respect of free movement of goods, such as product safety. By allowing Member States to create or maintain barriers to trade that were justified to protect public health, the Court forced the Community institutions to undertake Community action on these issues to remove trade barriers. While it is clear, therefore, that the EU's shift into the health domain was largely driven by the development of economic interests, spillover cannot on its own

ill-defined in practical terms, as no details or measures on how to achieve it were set out.

[57] See, for instance, E. Mossialos and M. McKee, 'Is a European health care policy emerging?', *British Medical Journal* 323 (2001), 248; M. McKee and E. Mossialos, 'Health policy and European law: closing the gaps', *Public Health* 120 (2006), Supp: 16–20; T. Hervey, 'EU law and national health policies: problem or opportunity?', *Health Economics, Policy and Law* 2 (2007), 1–6, who also question the direction EU of health care competences.

explain the Community's – in particular, the Commission's – involvement in medicines and food safety and the creation of the EMEA and EFSA.[58] For that, we observe that both agencies can trace their origins to a crisis in the respective policy domain.

B. The 'European' dimension to health protection in pharmaceuticals and foodstuffs

The thalidomide tragedy of the 1950s was the sharpest possible wake-up call regarding the need to regulate medicines. In Europe, this was heightened given the transnational dimension of an emerging free market. The result was the establishment of strict regulatory measures and regimes at the national and Community levels, both with regard to the grounds for granting a medicine market access and for post-approval follow-up. It was a similar situation for foodstuffs. Despite a host of food scares during the 1980s and 1990s (e.g., e-coli, salmonella, dioxins), it was not until the BSE crisis in 1996 that the Commission recognized the need for an integrated and systematic approach to regulating foodstuffs and food safety within the EU, ultimately leading to the creation of EFSA. That said, food issues have been on the EU agenda since the 1960s in respect of cross-border agricultural trade and a 'European trading environment that fostered transnational society in the production, distribution and consumption of food'.[59] Without detailing the histories of European medicines and foodstuffs/food safety regulation, a few milestones are noteworthy in respect of our interest in the EU's risk analysis role and eventual establishment of the EMEA and EFSA.[60]

---

[58] For a discussion on the merits and failings of a neo-functionalist explanation of how health became an area of Community competence, see E. Mossialos and G. Permanand, 'Public health in the European Union: making it relevant', London School of Economics (LSE) Health Discussion Paper 17 (2000).

[59] E. Randall, 'Not that soft or informal: a response to Eberlein and Grande's account of regulatory governance in the EU with special reference to the European Food Safety Authority (EFSA)', *Journal of European Public Policy* 13 (2006), 402–19.

[60] For detailed reviews of these histories see, respectively, G. Permanand, *EU pharmaceutical regulation: the politics of policy-making* (Manchester: Manchester University Press, 2006); and E. Vos and F. Wendler, 'Food safety regulation at the EU level', in E. Vos and F. Wendler (eds.), *Food safety regulation in Europe* (Antwerp: Intersentia, 2006).

For the pharmaceutical sector, the first milestone came in the aftermath of the thalidomide tragedy, when, in keeping with the proliferation of national medicine laws and regulations, the European Economic Community instituted its own legislation in 1965.[61] The first piece of Community legislation in the pharmaceuticals field, Directive 65/65/EEC, defined a medicinal product within the European market context and stipulated rules regarding the development and manufacture of medicines in the Community, along with initial guidelines for post-market monitoring. Importantly, it established safety, efficacy and therapeutic benefit as the sole grounds for marketing approval. These criteria form the basis of the EMEA's mandate today.

A second milestone was the 1975 establishment of a 'mutual recognition' procedure[62] and the Committee for Proprietary Medicinal Products (CPMP).[63] With the Commission's attention on removing trade barriers between Member States, the aim was to speed up marketing applications for new medicines and to alleviate the burden of applications being made separately to each national authority. The Committee was to act as the single authorization and arbitration body for the Community market. The mutual recognition idea was perhaps good in theory but not in practice. The Member States remained unmoved by the procedure and turned to the public health exception in the free movement rules (formerly Article 36 EC, now Article 30 EC) to object to medicines being made available in their markets without their own assessment. In an effort to address such failings, the Commission introduced the 'multistate' procedure in 1983.[64] This saw the minimum number of countries to which authorization could be extended drop from five to two. While the number of applications submitted via the

---

[61] Council Directive 65/65/EEC on the approximation of provisions laid down by law, regulation or administrative action relating to proprietary medicinal products, OJ 1965 No. L22/369.

[62] Council Directive 75/318/EEC on the approximation of the laws of Member States relating to analytical, pharmacotoxicological and clinical standards and protocols in respect of the testing of medicinal products, OJ 1975 No. L147/1.

[63] Second Council Directive 75/319/EEC on the approximation of provisions laid down by law, regulation or administrative action relating to medicinal products, OJ 1975 No. L147/13.

[64] Council Directive 83/570/EEC amending Directives 65/65/EEC, 75/318/EEC and 75/319/EEC on the approximation of provisions laid down by law, regulation or administrative action relating to proprietary medicinal products, OJ 1983 No. L332/1.

new procedure was higher than for mutual recognition, it proved cumbersome and was not favoured by the industry. Companies preferred the national route as being easier to negotiate and often for reasons related to the marketing and pricing of their medicines.

The 1986 SEA and the vision of a single market by 1992 is a third milestone. For, as part of this direction, the Commission introduced the 'concertation' procedure in 1987.[65] This applied only to biotechnologically-developed and other high technology products, but again with a view to speeding up the authorization process. Additionally, the so-called 'Transparency Directive', which obliged the Member States to adopt verifiable criteria vis-à-vis their pricing of medicines and their inclusion in national health insurance systems, was agreed in 1989.[66] Further legislation pertaining to, *inter alia,* good manufacturing practice, labelling, patent protection, advertising and sales promotion, and wholesale distribution[67] all followed within this free movement context.

In 1993 came the fourth milestone, with legislation creating the European Agency for the Evaluation of Medicinal Products (now the European Medicines Agency). Opened in 1995, and subsuming the CPMP, the EMEA was to provide scientific advice on all applications for marketing authorization within the Community, and

---

[65] Council Directive 87/22/EEC on the approximation of national measures relating to the placing on the market of high-technology medicinal products, particularly those derived from biotechnology, OJ 1987 No. L15/38.

[66] Council Directive 89/105/EEC of 21 December 1988 relating to the transparency of measures regulating the pricing of medicinal products for human use and their inclusion within the scope of national health insurance systems, OJ 1989 No. L40/8.

[67] Commission Directive 91/356/EEC laying down the principles and guidelines of good manufacturing practice for medicinal products for human use, OJ 1991 No. L193/30; Council Directive 92/27/EEC on the labelling of medicinal products for human use and on package leaflets, OJ 1992 No. L113/8; Council Regulation 1768/92/EEC concerning the creation of a supplementary protection certificate for medicinal products, OJ 1992 No. L182/1; Council Directive 92/26/EEC concerning the classification for the supply of medicinal products for human use, OJ 1992 No. L113/5; Council Directive 92/25/EEC on the wholesale distribution of medicinal products for human use, OJ 1992 No. L113/1. See, further, L. Hancher, *Regulating for competition. government, law, and the pharmaceutical industry in the United Kingdom and France* (Oxford: Clarendon Press, 1990); L. Hancher, 'The European pharmaceutical market: problems of partial harmonisation', *European Law Review* 15 (1990), 9–33; and L. Hancher, 'Creating the internal market for pharmaceutical medicines – an Echternach jumping procession?', *Common Market Law Review* 28 (1991), 821–53.

was empowered with a new centralized procedure[68] under which all applications were made directly to the agency, but with the Commission still adopting the final and binding decision. Importantly, the new regime was not intended to affect the powers of the Member States to set the prices of medicines or to include them in the scope of national health systems or social security schemes.[69] This remains the case today. The EMEA is nonetheless regarded as a success in having minimized the administrative burden of new applications and expedited the authorization of new medicines in the EU, even if it is not clear that this has translated into quicker access for patients. Revised legislation strengthening the operations of the agency, which came into force in 2005,[70] has since sought to build on this success.

In the food sector too, we can discern several milestones in the Europeanization process. Until the 1986 BSE crisis, the Commission had used its comitology structure to reconcile tensions between food safety issues and sensitivities at the national level, and free trade and market harmonization goals at the European level. Rules and policies were created on a piecemeal basis, and sometimes via jurisprudence through the ECJ. From 1974, the Commission had a risk assessment body to which it could turn for advice on public health concerns in the area of food consumption: the Scientific Committee for Food (SCF).[71] More importantly than the Commission simply having a consultative body is that the SCF was able to raise issues with the Commission on its own accord. In matters of risk management, the Commission had already created the Standing Committee on Foodstuffs (StCF) in 1969, and it considered all foodstuffs-related questions that fell within the Commission's competences. Not only could the StCF raise issues itself, but the Member States could themselves seek advice from the Committee directly. To deal specifically with crises, the Commission established a rapid-response unit within the Directorate-General for Agriculture and Rural Development (DG Agriculture) in 1984.

[68] Council Directive 93/39/EEC amending Directives 65/65/EEC, 75/318/EEC and 75/319/EEC in respect of medicinal products, OJ 1993 No. L214/22.
[69] Article 1, European Parliament and Council Regulation 726/2004/EC laying down Community procedures for the authorization and supervision of medicinal products for human and veterinary use and establishing a European Medicines Agency, OJ 2004 No. L136/1.
[70] *Ibid.*
[71] The Scientific Veterinary Committee (SVC) was also established.

The Commission and the Member States were satisfied with this committee arrangement until the BSE crisis exposed its failings. BSE was not simply an 'accident', but rather the consequence of intensive farming practices exacerbated by poor institutional management and regulation. Given that StCF discussions had perhaps become more collegial than rigorous,[72] and British interests – which had dominated the relevant scientific committee, the Scientific Veterinary Committee – had downplayed the risks of BSE for humans,[73] the need for a structured and systematic approach was a recommendation of the European Parliament's 1997 Medina Ortega report into the handling of the crisis.[74] The scientific committees were thus combined and absorbed within the Consumer Affairs Directorate-General of the Commission (now the Directorate General for Health and Consumers, DG SANCO). At the same time, the Food and Veterinary Office (FVO) was set up as part of DG SANCO, though located in Ireland, and a broader intersectoral and intrasectoral integration of food safety policy resulted.[75] As the Medina Ortega report had concluded that public health interests had been subverted in favour of producer and economic interests, public health protection in respect of foodstuffs was now high on the Commission agenda and on its way to becoming a European, rather than Member State, matter.[76]

In the following years, a recipe for a new Community approach was designed.[77] The so-called 'from farm to fork' precept (i.e., introducing

[72] Vos and Wendler, *Food safety regulation*, above n.60.

[73] Krapohl, 'Thalidomide, BSE and the single market', above n.12.

[74] European Parliament, 'Report on the alleged contraventions or maladministration in the implementation of Community law in relation to BSE, without prejudice to the jurisdiction of the Community and the national courts', A4–0020/97/a, PE 220.544/Fin/A, 7 February 1997.

[75] T. Ugland and F. Veggeland, 'Experiments in food safety policy integration in the European Union', *Journal of Common Market Studies* 44 (2006), 607–24.

[76] The BSE crisis is also seen as having promoted European health ministers into a 'knee jerk' political revision of (old) Article 129 EC, resulting in the somewhat rushed (current) Article 152 EC. Health ministers were under pressure to show not only how such a crisis could be prevented in the long term, but also how it would be addressed in the short term. See, for instance, H. Stein, 'The Treaty of Amsterdam and Article 129: a second chance for public health in Europe?', *Eurohealth* 3 (1997), 4–8.

[77] European Commission, 'General principles of food law in the European Union', Green Paper, COM (97) 176 final, 30 April 1997; European Commission, 'Food safety', White Paper, COM (99) 719 final, 12 January 2000.

traceability) became a key plank in the efforts to re-establish consumer confidence. In turn, it resulted in 2002 in the adoption of the 'General Food Law'.[78] This sought to address safety concerns in tandem with internal market requirements, and with risk analysis at its heart – thus going beyond public health protection to covering wider consumer issues as well (e.g., labelling). Procedures and standards for ensuring safe foods within the EU were also set down. These paved the way for the eventual creation of EFSA as a centralized body, and one which would work in a transparent and accountable fashion towards rebuilding confidence and protecting public health. This, at least, is the view of those involved, for not all commentators would agree. Giandomenico Majone, who has long championed the regulatory agency model at EU level, said of the White Paper on food safety's vision for a food agency: 'once more bureaucratic inertia and vested interests, at national and European levels, have prevented the emergence of much needed institutional innovation'.[79] Others have simply summed up the creation of EFSA as a 'political, rather than science-based solution',[80] since the final agency model did not include any regulatory powers (only risk assessment and risk communication), and would not therefore help in streamlining approvals and market authorization as many industry leaders and policy-makers had hoped.

C. Balancing single market priorities

Despite the attention paid to health protection, it remains clear that the role of the single market in both domains should not be understated. In pharmaceuticals, the Commission, since its first piece of legislation in 1965, has sought to achieve some harmonization of Member State markets, and there is now a raft of legislation.[81] Nevertheless, the Member States have consistently blocked Commission initiatives

---

[78] European Parliament and Council Regulation 178/2002/EC laying down the principles and requirements of food law, establishing the European Food Safety Authority and laying down procedures in matters of food safety, OJ 2002 No. L31/1.

[79] G. Majone, 'The politics of regulation and European regulatory institutions', in J. Hayward and A. Menon (eds.), *Governing Europe* (Oxford: Oxford University Press, 2003).

[80] L. Buoninno, S. Zablotney and R. Keefer, 'Politics versus science in the making of a new regulatory regime for food in Europe', *European Integration Online Papers* 5 (2001), 1.

[81] For a full listing, see EudraLex Volume 1, http://ec.europa.eu/enterprise/pharmaceuticals/eudralex/homev1.htm.

towards market integration, often turning to the subsidiarity principle. We see this primarily in respect of pricing and reimbursement, where, after accepting the impossibility of top-down harmonization, the Commission has sought greater alignment of Member State policies. The Commission's view is that a more harmonized market is in the interests of both consumers and producers (not to mention Member States and the EU as well). But the prospect of harmonized prices and loss of Member State autonomy in respect of health care spending under a single market remain taboo to many national policy-makers. Yet, we have the EMEA, which, in issuing recommendations on marketing authorizations, is not only one of the EU's most powerful agencies, but has a direct impact on national health care decisions.

A similar situation exists for foodstuffs. Although the market is perhaps more harmonized than for medicines, it still does not represent a single market per se. And, while the health complexities of pharmaceutical regulation were recognized from the outset, for foodstuffs this recognition became clearer only as more legislation was introduced. This includes both horizontal and vertical legislation, such as that relating to additives or food agents, or specific food categories such as chocolate and honey. As with medicines, the number of individual legislative instruments for foodstuffs is considerable. However, unlike for drugs, where internal market imperatives followed the need to regulate on health grounds, initial foodstuffs regulation was concerned with overcoming barriers to trade and promoting the free movement of products, with the health protection element developing later in the wake of a number of food scares. It is something of an irony that, at the time EU pharmaceutical regulation was being consolidated, EU foodstuffs regulation was subject to a complete re-assessment.

Their respective health protection impetuses notwithstanding, the Commission clearly views EFSA and the EMEA as instruments of the internal market. The Commission has often regarded national food safety provisions as barriers to trade, and has seen various harmonization initiatives be rejected by Member States. We see this even in respect of the BSE crisis, which revealed that some Member States may have been taking advantage of the EU's pre-existing administrative (cum regulatory) structure to forward their own interests.[82]

---

[82] See G. Majone, 'The credibility crisis of Community regulation', *Journal of Common Market Studies* 38 (2000), 273–302.

Additionally, a number of Member States that had opposed earlier Commission efforts to promote harmonization within the sector simply banned British beef outright.[83] The same applies for pharmaceuticals pre-EMEA. The Member States did not otherwise accept the mutual recognition concept in practice, and generally cited public health concerns as grounds for not accepting other countries' medicines in their own markets. That this was actually in order to protect domestic industry or to discriminate against the reimbursement of imported products is generally acknowledged. So, although each has a health crisis as its spur, the end result for both agencies is that their mandates cover not just health protection via the application of strict regulatory criteria in accordance with scientific expertise, but also ensuring that the free movement of products in their respective sectors is enabled to the highest degree possible.

4. Health (care), the European Medicines Agency and the European Food Safety Authority

Comparing the regulation of medicines and foodstuffs in the EU necessarily highlights some differences, but there are certain similarities to consider in view of the aims and functions of EMEA and EFSA.

In both arenas, not only must the products be accessible and safe to consume, but consumers can expect to be informed where this is not the case and protected when it is. This implies a commitment to risk analysis, comprising the distinct elements of risk assessment, risk communication and risk management (see Figure 3.1). There are also informational asymmetries that characterize both sectors, and that regulators can help to mitigate through improved communication and greater operational transparency. At the EU level, regulation is also concerned with standard policies and guidelines within the single market.

A background point to be borne in mind is that one of the main differences between the two sectors lies in the timing of regulatory intervention. For medicines, notwithstanding that most national agencies have a role in pharmacovigilance, the emphasis is on pre-market regulation. Since Directive 65/65/EEC, quality, safety and efficacy are

---

[83] When it became clear just how considerable the spread (and threat) of BSE was – not to mention the lack of accountability that was revealed – a consensus emerged that common European policies were in the Member States' interest, in turn contributing to consensus over the formation of EFSA.

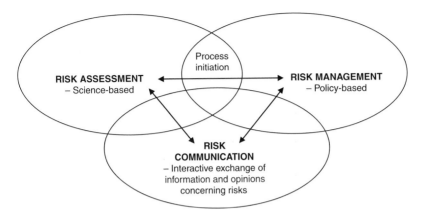

Figure 3.1 Risk analysis
Source: www.who.int/foodsafety/micro/riskanalysis/en/

the sole approval criteria for new medicines, with the assessment of applications representing the main element of the EMEA's work. For foodstuffs, the considerable fragmentation of the market precludes much ex ante testing and the focus is thus post-market. While pharmaceutical regulation has involved public authorities, foodstuffs have generally relied on self-regulation by producers and retailers; governments are usually involved in setting content requirements, limits and labelling laws. As the growing number of national food safety agencies in Europe shows, this is changing – in part because of food scares, but also because of increasing levels of production, high technology approaches to farming, the considerable use of additives and chemicals in food, along with the potential opportunities and threats raised by globalization. We thus see an increasing trend towards pre-market control and the setting into place of authorization procedures.

A. *Core functions and the politics of scientific advice*

The EMEA began operations in 1995, replacing the Community's earlier approval mechanisms. The crux of its role lies in assessing marketing authorization applications for new medicinal products via either a centralized or decentralized procedure. The former represents the mandatory application route for certain products[84] and involves the

---

[84] Centralized approval is required for biotechnology-derived products, orphan drugs, products containing a new active substance not previously authorized

relevant committee delivering an opinion. There is a Committee for Medicinal Products for Human Use (CHMP), a Committee for Orphan Medicinal Products (COMP), a Committee on Herbal Medicinal Products (HMPC) and, since 2007, a Paediatric Committee (PDCO). Following a committee opinion, the Commission then issues a formal EU-wide decision (the Standing Committee on Medicinal Products for Human Use has an important say on behalf of the Member States). Applications are subject to two assessments undertaken by Member State medicines agencies acting as rapporteurs. The latter, essentially a mutual recognition procedure, involves one Member State granting a product a licence, after which multiple national authorizations can be issued without the need for separate applications. This is the process for conventional products and allows Member States to register a formal objection.[85] Should a manufacturer seek to launch a product in only one Member State, the application is simply made to the national agency concerned (the relevant EMEA committee is called upon only if adjudication becomes necessary).

Among other tasks, the EMEA provides scientific advice and incentives to help stimulate the development of new medicines, and works towards developing best practice for medicines evaluation and supervision in Europe. Pharmacovigilance is part of the agency's mandate and, since 2005, it has maintained the public access 'Eudravigilance' database, which is a network and management system for reporting and evaluating suspected adverse reactions during the development and post-approval phases of medicines (it also operates a Europe-wide clinical trials database). The agency has a role in undertaking inspections, either through its own capacity or by coordinating Member State activities in this direction. With national medicines agencies directly involved in the EMEA regime – the above-

in the EU, and medicines for the treatment of HIV/AIDS, cancer, diabetes or neurodegenerative disorders. By 2009, this will be extended to antiretrovirals and medicines designed to treat autoimmune and other immunological diseases. It is voluntary for other 'innovative' products. The definition of 'innovative' is not clear, but will cover drugs 'of major interest from the point of view of public health and in particular from the point of view of therapeutic innovation'. See Article 14(9), European Parliament and Council Regulation 726/2004/EC laying down Community procedures for the authorisation and supervision of medicinal products for human and veterinary use and establishing a European Medicines Agency, OJ 2004 No. L136/1.

[85] Member States may object and appeal on public health grounds, and the EMEA has a protocol in place to consider such instances.

mentioned 'hub and spoke' model – the regulation of medicines thus remains a joint EU–Member State competence.

EFSA opened its doors in 2002 and, similarly to the EMEA, was designed to integrate and replace the Community's existing regulatory functions, which had failed over the BSE crisis. It may therefore be argued that it was a political rather than health crisis that led to the creation of EFSA,[86] but we may also differentiate the initial health crisis from the subsequent political scandal. EFSA's primary tasks are four-fold: the provision of scientific advice and information, including issuing expert opinions and carrying out safety or risk assessments, along with technical support to the Community in respect of policy and legislation; collating and analysing information and data towards risk characterization and monitoring; to promote and facilitate the development of shared risk assessment approaches in the EU; and communicating risks in respect of the various elements of its mandate. The communication element of EFSA's role is paramount given the agency's origins in the BSE crisis and the need to engender confidence among consumers. EFSA is thus mandated to communicate directly to the public.

Comparable to the EMEA's committees, EFSA has a series of area-specific scientific panels that undertake the risk assessments behind its opinions.[87] These opinions are forwarded to the Commission, which adopts a decision after receiving a favourable opinion from the Standing Committee on the Food Chain and Animal Health, composed of Member States representatives.[88] A further similarity is that EFSA does not supplant national agencies, although it does engage with them more directly than the EMEA. Both the EMEA and EFSA rely on national agencies for the scientific work behind their

---

[86] C. Clergeau, 'European food safety policies: between a single market and a political crisis', in M. Steffen (ed.), *Health governance in Europe: issues, challenges and theories* (London: Routledge, 2005).

[87] There are nine scientific panels: (a) additives, flavourings, processing aids and materials in contact with food; (b) animal health and welfare; (c) biological hazards; (d) contaminants in the food chain; (e) additives and products used in animal feed; (f) genetically modified organisms; (g) dietetic products, nutrition and allergies; (h) plant protection products or substances and their residues; and (i) plant health. At the time of writing, preparations are underway to split the first panel into two separate units.

[88] Should an unfavourable opinion be delivered, or in the absence of an opinion, the Commission's draft decision is sent to the Council, which may adopt a decision.

evaluations. EFSA's role here has been seen as that of *primus inter pares*, as it coordinates national agencies' efforts, often in specific areas.[89] However, in view of its dependence on the national agencies as built into its organizational structure through its Advisory Forum, and partly due to a lack of resources, the importance of the Member States' agencies for EFSA's scientific work is likely to increase. It is important to note that, given its strong communication focus, just like the EMEA, EFSA does not assume responsibility for Community or Member State food safety legislation. Moreover, it is not in charge of labelling, inspections or other food safety controls. Risk assessment and communication are the core of EFSA's mandate; risk management falls to the Commission and Member States.

The question of agenda-setting (and marketing authorization) is one where the two agencies differ. Unlike the EMEA, which requires an applicant product to begin its scientific evaluation and risk assessment work, EFSA is dependent on the Commission to essentially 'invite' it into a particular policy issue. Yet, the agency can also initiate an opinion on its own initiative, and thereby try to put the issue on the EU's decision-making agenda. In identifying the policy issues and controlling the policy space, the Commission thus remains the agenda-setter in the foodstuffs arena. This is not the case for medicines, where the Commission is not involved until the EMEA opinion has been sent.

Both agencies are committed to delivering the 'best possible' scientific advice, the former in respect of the safety, quality and efficacy of medicines, the latter in terms of risk assessments vis-à-vis foodstuffs. This shifting of the risk assessment function away from the Member States to the relevant scientific committee or panel represents a Europeanization of the science in both sectors and a commensurate depoliticization of the health protection function. That said, both sectors remain highly political, and foodstuffs especially so. It is therefore interesting to observe that, due to the increasing importance of science in these sectors, and the 'scientification' of politics, there is again high potential for a politicization of the science. This was the case in the pre-BSE food regulation era and, ironically perhaps, a phenomenon that post-BSE legislation and EFSA have sought to combat.

For instance, in 2006, EFSA's Deputy Executive Director stated that the agency feels the influence of national politics, and that it

---

[89] Vos and Wendler, *Food safety regulation*, above n.60.

has 'sometimes [come] under pressure from the Commission to make or give a decision in a certain way'.[90] This is due to the fact that EFSA opinions form the basis of Commission decisions and are thus discussed by the college of Commissioners and, at times, put to a vote in the Council of Ministers. The politics of the Commission's discussions is evident in the case of two genetically modified (GM) maize lines, Bt11 and 1507.[91] Despite EFSA's view that they were safe, then Agriculture Commissioner Stavros Dimas opposed their approval in 2007. Other Commissioners were in favour and discussions – irrespective of the science – thus continued. As for EFSA's exposure to national politics, with qualified majority voting required in the Council, the Member States can effectively block one another. Moreover, it means under comitology procedures that they can collectively impede the Commission's draft decisions despite these being based on EFSA's scientific opinion, as has occurred in many cases of GM authorizations. At the same time, it is interesting to observe that the Member States may in fact use scientific arguments during the comitology process in their attempts to block the Commission's draft authorizations, which are based on EFSA's opinions. Faced with a request to look at these arguments, EFSA has often declined to do so in detail, and considers these arguments to be often more political than scientific. It is something of a paradox, then, that as EFSA seeks to keep scientific risk evaluation independent, by separating assessment from management, the science itself is becoming politicized as the health protection function is taken away from Member States.

For the EMEA, the politics are perhaps less immediate, but the fact that the opinions delivered by the CHMP are generally accepted by the Commission leads to two lines of thinking. First, that this may be an indication of the strength of the science (and/or the Commission's lack of capacity to validate it). Indeed, the Committee's opinions are delivered as finished documents in the expectation that the Commission can issue them as they are and without undue delay. Second, that this reflects the acceptability of the position to the Member States. For, unlike in the case of EFSA's opinions, where the (panels of the)

---

[90] H. Koeter, as interviewed in A. El Amin, 'EU's food agency battles attempts to hijack science', *Food Quality News*, 21 September 2006, www.foodqualitynews.com/news/ng.asp?id=70720-efsa-health-claims-antibiotics.

[91] GMOs are authorized at the EU level based on EFSA's risk evaluation, although no GM crops have been approved in the EU since 1998.

Standing Committee on the Food Chain and Animal Health convenes to discuss every proposal, the Medicines Standing Committee is given thirty days to respond in writing to an opinion, with the proposal accepted if no response is received. The Committee's members are, in the main, from the same regulatory authority as the CHMP (or other evaluation committee) members. Ellen Vos thus ascribes the Commission's general policy of endorsement to the fact that a normative or 'nationally-flavoured' element is taken to be implicit within the assessments delivered by the Committee (and the Commission would rather not contradict the Member States).[92] This contributes to the contention that the Member States view the EMEA's opinions as more credible than those of EFSA and that, as a result, the latter will not become as strong or successful as the former.[93] In this manner, we can interpret the reinforcement of the role of Member States within and around EFSA as the Commission's and EFSA's attempt to overcome the decisional deadlock on matters surrounding genetically modified organisms (GMOs).

The fact that neither agency has the executive power to regulate in the manner of an independent regulatory agency such as the United States Food and Drug Administration (FDA) is in large part due to the political and institutional constraints surrounding the comparative roles and interests of the Commission and Member States in the health (care) arena, and the policy-making architecture of the EU polity itself.[94] Furthermore, the political interests at the national and supranational levels, far less the strength of producer interests within both policy domains, have also helped to ensured that power remains fractured. For EFSA, there are thus calls for increased centralization in order to decrease uncertainties, foster efficiency and increase consumer confidence.[95]

---

[92] E. Vos, 'European administrative reform and agencies', European University Institute Working Papers No. RSC 2000/31 (2000).

[93] Krapohl, 'Credible commitment', above n.12 .

[94] This relates to the imbalance or constitutional asymmetry between the Commission's economic and social policy competences, and has been shown to have had an effect on the EMEA's mandate and wider EU regime for pharmaceutical regulation. See G. Permanand and E. Mossialos, 'Constitutional asymmetry and pharmaceutical policy-making in the European Union', *Journal of European Public Policy* 12 (2005), 687–709.

[95] L. Caduff and T. Bernauer, 'Managing risk and regulation in European food safety governance', *Review of Policy Research* 23 (2006), 153–67.

B. Good governance

Given the increasing public health impact of their roles, their aims to ensure public confidence and their impact on national health care priorities, it is therefore essential that EFSA and EMEA be independent, accountable and transparent in exercising (regulatory) authority. Furthermore, given the softer approach to regulation and policy-making espoused by new modes of governance thinking, a participatory approach – in so far as is possible – is also deemed to be a positive element. These are among the EU's own principles of good governance,[96] and tie into the Commission's Communication on the operating framework for the European agencies.[97] However, while these are stated objectives, questions remain over both agencies' commitment to these considerations.

Independence

(Independent) regulatory agencies are to be above any interference from government or producers – or indeed from any other interested party. And while this may be the optimal view, in theory if not in practice, Scott notes that the Commission 'formula for the EU regulatory agencies' does not actually even aspire towards this: '[it] appears to represent, simultaneously, an embracing of the agency model, and a rejection of its development along the lines of the independent regulatory agency'.[98] Indeed, it may be argued that, given their various aspects of direct involvement in the agencies' work, the Commission, the European Parliament, the Member States and the industry all have some degree of influence.

All agencies are linked to the Commission via the relevant Directorate-General. For EFSA, this is DG SANCO (responsible for health and consumer protection); for the EMEA, it is the Directorate-General for Enterprise and Industry (responsible for industrial policy). Although the EMEA's institutional setting stems from its origins in the single market programme, it may legitimately be asked why the

---

[96] European Commission, 'European governance', White Paper, COM (2001) 428 final, 25 July 2001.
[97] European Commission, 'Operating framework', above n.16.
[98] C. Scott, 'Agencies for European regulatory governance: a regimes approach', in Geradin, Muñoz and Petit (eds.), *Regulation through agencies*, above n.9.

agency is linked to the 'business' arm of the Commission rather than the 'health' arm. This is especially the case in view of the concerns over the intertwining of business and health interests as raised by the Medina Ortega report on the BSE crisis. Indeed, several commentators, including several Members of the European Parliament (MEP), have raised queries in this direction.[99] That said, it should equally be acknowledged that a lack of expertise and capacity regarding the medicines sector more widely (e.g., industrial policy concerns or pricing and reimbursement issues) would seem to preclude DG SANCO from being solely responsible. This duality is in fact expressed in the composition of EMEA's management board, which has two Commission members, Heinz Zourek, acting Director-General of DG Industry, and Andrzej Ryś, Director of Public Health and Risk Assessment in DG SANCO. For EFSA, the Commission has one representative on the Board, the current Director-General of DG SANCO, Robert Madelin.

The Commission's links to the agencies via its representatives in the management boards are important, as these bodies oversee activities and are charged with the important tasks of agreeing the budget and choosing the executive director. It is noteworthy that, while both agencies are supposed to work at arm's length from the Commission, separating risk assessment from risk management, it is clear that there is a strong interface between the agencies and the Commission. In the case of EFSA, there is a 'grey zone' between the agency and the Commission in which they closely interact and where the separation is, in practice, not upheld in a clear-cut way. Moreover, several specific legislative acts assign the Commission the competence to review EFSA acts (e.g., regarding pesticides residues and GM food and feed). Furthermore, we can note how, by arguing that their acts are not mentioned in Article 230 EC, both agencies try to avoid such reviews by hiding behind the Commission. For instance, in a recent case where the EMEA had rejected an application for a variation to a marketing authorization, the Court of First Instance dismissed the applicant's appeal (directed against EMEA itself) on the basis that the EMEA

---

[99]   See, for instance, S. Garattini and V. Bertele, 'Adjusting Europe's drug regulation to public health needs', *Lancet* 358 (2001), 64–7; and selected MEPs' letter to European Parliament in February 2002, www.haiweb.org/campaign/DTCA/MariaNegristatementDTCA_files/lettertoeu.htm.

was not listed among the institutions mentioned in Article 230 EC. However, it ruled that, as the EMEA had only been endowed with advisory powers, the EMEA's refusal must be deemed as emanating from the Commission itself and would hence be reviewable.[100] This kind of case-law may lead to the strange situation of the Commission being held responsible for acts[101] for which the legislator had clearly conferred responsibility on EMEA.[102]

The influence of Member States on the agencies' activities is clearer in the case of EMEA, given that its management board comprises one representative from each Member State. While such national representation does not, at first sight, seem compatible with an agency whose science is supposed to be above national interests, it is of course not the board that adopts EMEA's scientific opinions. That

---

[100] Case T-133/03, *Schering-Plough Ltd* v. *Commission and EMEA* (Order of CFI of 05.12.2007). The Court ruled that '[i]n so far as Regulation EC No. 2309/93 [laying down Community procedures for the authorisation and supervision of medicinal products for human and veterinary use and establishing a European Agency for the Evaluation of Medicinal Products, OJ 1993 No. L214/1] provides for only advisory powers for the EMEA, the refusal referred to in Article 5(4) of Commission Regulation EC No. 542/95 [concerning the examination of variations to the terms of a marketing authorization falling within the scope of Council Regulation 2309/93/EEC, OJ 1995 No. L55/15] must be deemed to emanate from the Commission itself. Since the contested measure is imputable to the Commission, it may be the subject of an action directed against that institution. It follows that the action must be dismissed as inadmissible in so far as it is directed against the EMEA'. See paras. 22 and 23. See also Case T-123/00, *Thomae* v. *Commission* [2002] ECR II-5193.

[101] In the case at stake, Case T-133/03, *Schering-Plough*, above n.100, the CFI nevertheless ruled that there was no longer any need to adjudicate on the action in so far as it was directed against the Commission.

[102] In Case T-133/03, *Schering-Plough*, above n.100, for example, the relevant provision was Article 5(4) of Regulation 542/95: '[w]here the Agency is of the opinion that the application cannot be accepted, it shall send a notification to that effect to the holder of the marketing authorisation within the period referred to in paragraph 1, stating the objective grounds on which its opinion is based:

(a) within 30 days of receipt of the said notification, the marketing authorisation holder may amend the application in a way which takes due account of the grounds set out in the notification. In that case the provisions of paragraphs 1, 2 and 3 shall apply to the amended application;

(b) if the marketing authorisation holder does not amend the application as provided for in (a) above, this application shall be deemed to have been rejected.'

said, members of the agency's scientific committees do represent the competent authorities of the Member States and are also appointed by the Member States, even if they are mandated to act in a non-partisan manner. EFSA, meanwhile, does not have Member State representatives on its management board – a fact that is unique among the European agencies[103] – and has independent scientific experts on its scientific committees who do not represent the competent authorities of the Member States. Nevertheless, a lack of resources and capacity (especially when compared with the United States FDA), as well as the above-mentioned decisional deadlock in GM cases, might lead EFSA to seek to strengthen its cooperation with national authorities, perhaps even to include them in its organizational structure.

The role of the European Parliament in respect of the agencies, although primarily institutional, is important. The Parliament sets the budget and the annual discharge, which affords it considerable influence. In the case of the EMEA, the Parliament also has two representatives (national experts appointed as impartial individuals) on the management board. The Commission has criticized this representation,[104] but the Parliament has insisted on having representatives as long as the Member States are also represented, pointing to the fact that it is not MEPs who are on the board but merely representatives of the Parliament.

The Parliament's power of budgetary oversight raises questions regarding the agencies' financial independence more generally. In the case of EMEA, of a total budget of €173 307 000 for the year 2008, the agency received 72.9% from applicant fees and 21.9% from the Commission. The remaining 5.2% came from other sources. Since the agency's establishment, the ratio of fees to direct Commission funding has continued to rise. This financial dependence on its clients has been criticized on several grounds, most important of which is perhaps that speed rather than quality of assessment will become the EMEA's focus.[105] Although the dangers of this type of fee-for-service arrangement are clear, it should not be forgotten that many national

[103] An advisory forum comprising Member State representatives responsible for risk assessment was created within EFSA as compensation.

[104] European Commission, 'Draft interinstitutional agreement', above n.50.

[105] See, for instance, J. Abraham and G. Lewis, *Regulating medicines in Europe: competition, expertise and public health* (London: Routledge, 2000); Garattini and Bertele, 'Adjusting Europe's drug regulation', above n.99.

medicines agencies in Europe are also heavily dependent on applicant fees (the United States FDA is also funded by user fees, amounting to almost one-fifth of its budget, which also reflects a rising amount). EFSA, on the other hand, derived its entire €66.4 million budget for 2008 from the EU budget, and the August 2007 findings of a DG SANCO consultation on the possibility of introducing applicant fees found support for the idea in only a limited set of cases.[106] This arrangement poses its own potential failings, for not only is EFSA institutionally to some extent linked to DG SANCO, but so too is it financially dependent on the Commission as well.[107]

We perhaps see this reflected in elements of EFSA's science-making, where it would appear that the agency's commitment to hard science is to be balanced with its principal's interests. Randall uses the example of the agency's position on genetically-modified organisms (GMOs):

Accepting a wide-ranging precautionary approach, leaving virtually all GM issues in a state of regulatory suspension, was anathema not only to the United States Government and American agribusiness, but also to EFSA, its exchequer (the Commission) ... EFSA chose to do what its most important customer, the Commission, expected it to.[108]

With the exception of the maize crops referred to earlier, the Commission has adopted all EFSA opinions in the GM arena.

As the aim of both agencies is to provide quality and objective information, this begins with the scientists. So what of the independence of the individual experts involved in the EMEA committees and EFSA panels? The 'older' medicines agency committees (e.g., the CHMP) are comprised of experts nominated by the Member States. The 'newer' ones (e.g., the HMPC) have members from the Commission, patient organizations and some agency nominations. All are required to sign declaration of interest forms, with EMEA members demonstrating that they have no ties to industry. The need for this was highlighted by the 'Poggiolini affair' of the early 1990s,

---

[106] DG SANCO, 'Summary of the comments received on the consultation paper on the advisability and feasibility of establishing fees for EFSA', August 2007, http://ec.europa.eu/food/consultations/sum_cons_Efsa_fees_En.pdf.

[107] The fact that both agencies are mentioned under the Commission's budget line also implies a certain dependence on the Commission.

[108] Randall, 'Not that soft', above n.59.

where Dulio Poggiolini, then head of both the former Committee for Proprietary Medicinal Products (CPMP, now CHMP) and the Italian drug agency, was accused of taking bribes and gifts from the industry.[109] In contrast, members of the scientific committee and panels of EFSA are selected on the basis of their scientific excellence after an open competition and nominated by the management board. Nevertheless, EFSA has experienced some controversies over conflicting interests as well. For instance, several members of its GMO panel had evaluated some products on behalf of their national agencies as well as for EFSA. Abstention over a conflict of interest is possible, although for the GMO panel it was decided that only where the representative was involved in the risk management element at home – not the scientific assessment – was there a conflict.[110] The committee and panel members' declarations are available on the respective web sites (for EFSA, they are renewed annually) and a register of names is publicly available – this was not initially the case when the EMEA first commenced operations. Meanwhile, EFSA has further sharpened its rules on declarations of interests.[111]

Accountability

Accountability is, in general, a contentious subject in the supranational context. The unelected nature of the Commission and the ECJ in particular has led to a wide-spread notion of a 'democratic deficit' in the EU. Nevertheless, it is generally accepted that being accountable at the EU level means being accountable to the European Parliament, which comprises directly-elected representatives and exercises budgetary control. The Parliament's representation on the EMEA management board may help serve this accountability function, but, as these representatives have little direct contact with the Parliament, it appears more cosmetic than substantial.[112]

[109] See G. Permanand, *EU pharmaceutical regulation*, above n.60, p. 129.
[110] L. Levidow and S. Carr, 'Europeanising advisory expertise: the role of "independent, objective and transparent" scientific advice in agri-biotech regulation', *Environment and Planning C: Government and Politics* 25 (2007), 880–95.
[111] EFSA, 32nd Meeting of the Management Board, Bucharest, 11 September 2007.
[112] E. Vos, 'Independence, accountability and transparency', in Geradin, Muñoz and Petit (eds.), *Regulation through agencies*, above n.9.

What of public accountability more widely? Since the 2005 legislation was introduced, the EMEA management board has included two consumers' and one doctors' representatives. These representatives are appointed by the Council in consultation with the Parliament from a list chosen by the Commission. Patient representation may be seen as a key step towards improving accountability, and it followed concerted lobbying by consumer-oriented groups. But the Commission's nominations will need to be carefully scrutinized to ensure that no conflicts of interest arise (such as industry sponsorship). EFSA's management board comprises, in addition to the one Commission representative, fourteen independent experts (appointed by the Council in consultation with the Parliament, but on the basis of a Commission nomination), four of whom have experience with organizations promoting consumer or patient interests within the food chain. There is, however, no requirement that these experts be completely free of industry links, even if they are not permitted to receive payments. That said, failures to declare conflicts of interest have been noted in the case of the GMO panel.[113] It is not clear, therefore, that the current management board constellation of either agency really serves the interests of accountability. In fact, the argument could be made that the Commission, the European Parliament and the Member States (in the case of the EMEA), can all exert some control over the agency via their representatives.[114]

Transparency

Related to independence and accountability is transparency. If a regulator is going to be successful in securing public trust, it needs to be as open and forthcoming as possible in respect of its activities generally, and of (scientific) decision-making specifically. Among other things, this means 'reason giving' – making decisions and dissenting views available, delivering timely responses, granting access to documentation and involving stakeholders. In the EU context, transparency most often means accessibility of documents, and, in this regard, both EFSA and the EMEA are subject to the EU's legislation

---

[113] Friends of the Earth, 'Throwing caution to the wind – a review of the European Food Safety Authority and its work on genetically modified foods and crops', November 2007, www.foeeurope.org/GMOs/publications/EFSAreport.pdf.

[114] *Ibid.*

on public access to European institutions' documents.[115] Their web sites therefore post a considerable amount of information, covering both the science and the administration and operations of the agencies. At the same time, they fall short in certain areas.

For instance, although it is potentially able to publish minority opinions, EFSA has, to date, not done so. The agency is obliged to look out for potential scientific divergences between various bodies and, in such cases, actively try to ensure agreement among the scientists. In instances where EFSA and another EU or Member State scientific authority may disagree, Article 30 of the 'General Food Law'[116] requires the two to try to resolve the disagreement between them. It is only where this is not possible that a (joint) document explaining the discrepancies is made public. More specifically, EFSA's GMO panel has been accused of 'selectively "front-stag[ing]" the most internally consensual and scientifically defensible arguments, thus selectively enacting transparency'.[117] So, while EFSA's advice is held up to be transparent on the basis of consent, the process of reaching the consensus is not necessarily made available. Moreover, it is not clear that the agency adequately states the scientific uncertainties in its opinions, and perhaps takes too black and white a view.[118] Addressing uncertainties might help risk management (by the Commission and Member States) in the public interest, but, on the other hand, it may also give the impression of poor science.

EMEA has a similar role as watchdog, looking out for potential scientific conflicts with a similar 'conflict clause',[119] and the transparency issue is one it has fought since its inception. The agency may want to be as open as possible, but commercial secrecy is a major concern in the pharmaceutical sector and the industry represents a strong actor. It is, therefore, understandable that sensitive information and data needs to be suppressed. However, if companies are able to anonymously withdraw products where a negative assessment is suspected, and the minutes of meetings to discuss marketing applications, the names of rejected

---

[115] European Parliament and Council Regulation 1049/2001/EC regarding public access to European Parliament, Council and Commission documents, OJ 2001 No. L145/43.

[116] Regulation 178/2002/EC, above n.78.

[117] Levidow and Carr, 'Europeanising advisory expertise', above n.110.

[118] M. Van Asselt, E. Vos and B. Rooijackers, 'Science, knowledge and uncertainty in EU risk regulation', in M. Everson and E. Vos (eds.), *Uncertain risks regulated* (London: Routledge-Cavendish, 2009).

[119] Article 59, Regulation 726/2004/EC, above n.69.

products and the reasons for rejection, not to mention the names of with-drawn products and the withdrawing companies, are not made available in the public domain, it is perhaps then unsurprising that the EMEA has in the past been heavily criticized for paying only lip-service to the idea of transparency. Most of this has changed under the 2005 legislation,[120] and reflects just how important (risk) communication is in terms of ensuring confidence in the regulator and in the sector more widely. It remains the case, however, that research information on clinical and preclinical tri-als, or information on evaluations, are not released (the FDA makes both available), while much of the material that is made public remains quite technical and inaccessible to the lay user.

Participation

Related to transparency is the issue of wider participation and how public health concerns are taken on board in the agencies' assess-ments. In this regard, a 2003 Court of First Instance ruling vis-à-vis an EMEA opinion is instructive. In Case T-326/99,[121] Nancy Olivieri, a former clinical investigator of the active ingredient deferiprone, which had been given a favourable first opinion by the EMEA, pre-sented new information in respect of the drug's potential toxicity and inefficacy in the treatment of thalassemia. After an initial suspension, the CPMP revisited the application at the Commission's request – though did not involve Dr Olivieri in the deliberations – and issued a revised, still favourable, opinion upon which the Commssion issued an authorization of the drug Ferriprox. Dr Olivieri sought to have the Commission decision and the underlying EMEA revised opinion overturned. However, her demand was rejected, as the Court of First Instance held that she did not have an interest in bringing the pro-ceedings in order to protect public health or in order to defend her professional reputation, and the complaint was declared inadmissible. An important element in this case was the Court's decision that, while third parties can be consulted with respect to scientific input, and can have special access when doing so on public health grounds, they do

[120] See, for example, G. Permanand, E. Mossialos and M. McKee, 'Regulating medicines in Europe: the European Medicines Agency, marketing authorisation, transparency and pharmacovigilance', *Clinical Medicine* 6 (2006), 87–90.

[121] Case T-326/99, Olivieri v. *Commission and European Agency for the Evaluation of Medicinal Products* [2003] ECR II-06053.

not have an automatic right to participate or be heard. Only when the Commission deems it 'indispensable in order to safeguard public health' can persons other than the marketing authorization holder be invited to share their observations.

The EU does nonetheless seek broader involvement of stakeholders, in particular civil society groups, as part of its good governance policy. Participation is a key tenet of the Commission's good governance criteria, and both agencies could do more in this respect. The EMEA has a Patients' and Consumers' Working Party, which provides recommendations to the EMEA and its human scientific committees on all matters of direct or indirect interest to patients in relation to medicinal products, but does not grant patients nearly the same degree of access to the evaluators as it does the industry. Meanwhile, EFSA, through its recently-established Stakeholders Platform, seeks to ensure a higher degree of stakeholder involvement in agenda-setting.

The role of industry

Although not the focus of this chapter, a final element worthy of consideration – given that it impacts on their adherence to principles of good governance – is the agencies' relationship to industry. The EMEA's role includes providing applicants with scientific advice up to six years in advance of their filing an application. This is in order to work with companies towards their products fulfilling the approval criteria, and is clearly a function of the agency's single market duties. The extent of this cooperation is not always clear – what, in practice, is the line between helping applicants understand what is needed to meet the requirements of a successful application for their product, and actually instructing them on what they need to do to 'get a pass'? It also goes considerably further than that undertaken at national level or by the FDA.

If not so explicit, EFSA would seem to have a similar mandate and design in respect of the single market, where 'the agency's institutional architecture has therefore been framed by the imperative to construct an authority capable of restoring market confidence without threatening the habit of those multinational companies which occupy this arena'.[122] More specifically, a 2004 report by Friends of

[122] G. Taylor and M. Millar, "The appliance of science': the politics of European food regulation and reform', *Public Policy and Administration* 17 (2002), 125–46.

the Earth highlighted a pro-biotechnology industry bias in the work of the GMOs panel, not just in terms of favourable opinions, but also in the selective use of evidence in reaching those opinions.[123] These relations tie into the question of agency independence more widely, and echo broader views that the agencies may be too close to the industry.

C. *EMEA, EFSA and Member State health systems*

With respect to their impact on national health systems, the agencies were not designed to affect Member State priorities and policy competences. In this regard, the constitutional asymmetry noted in Chapter 1 of this volume, between the EU's comparatively well-developed economic policy (single market) versus poorer social policy (including health) functions, is reflected in the agencies' mandates. It is clear, for instance, that the EMEA's centralized authorization system for pharmaceuticals does not affect the powers of the Member States to set prices or to include medicines in the scope of national health systems or social security schemes. In EFSA's case, the agency's inability to put specific issues on the political agenda, as well as its susceptibility to Member State politicking, suggests that its immediate impact on national health care systems is limited. On the other hand, EFSA can decide to issue an opinion on its own initiative, thereby indirectly influencing the political agenda. At the same time, the EMEA's authorizations do establish what medicines can and cannot (and by extension could or should) be available within national markets and health systems. Meanwhile, EFSA's expert advice on safe food and foodstuffs has the potential to affect countries' health care strategies to improve nutrition and combat diet-related diseases and obesity. These types of indirect or potential impacts, especially in view of a policy environment that promotes comparative best (or good) practice learning, are important and should be stressed. And given both agencies' commitment to strong communication activities to apprise and update stakeholders (especially consumers), they may be able to implicitly influence agendas more than is generally thought.

Despite an explicit impact not being envisaged, it is also clear that both agencies will increasingly serve as contact points for Member States

[123] Friends of the Earth, 'Throwing caution to the wind', above n.113.

and stakeholders, such as health care professionals, industry, patient and consumer organizations, and other nongovernmental organizations. The EMEA is, for example, obliged to assist Member States in the communication of health risks and to help them in the provision of information to health care professionals and the general public about those medicinal products evaluated by the agency.[124] Furthermore, the agency closely cooperates with the Member States' competent authorities in pharmacoviligance and post-marketing authorization tracking. It is also required to develop contacts with the relevant stakeholders.[125] EFSA too needs to closely collaborate with the competent authorities of the Member States. Moreover, it has developed contacts with the stakeholders through its Consultative Stakeholder Platform. In view of its increasing profile and importance – both because of its expanding role as assigned to it by EU legislation and its proactive attitude – EFSA increasingly seems to be growing into the above-mentioned *primus inter pares* of interdependent and deliberative networks of national authorities. We see this through its Advisory Forum and the networks of organizations that are active in the relevant technical areas. Further, due to their design and embedding of national authorities and experts within their structures and operations, and in having only a modest number of staff (the EMEA has approximately 500 core staff, and EFSA has 350),[126] both agencies are heavily dependent on decentralized networks of national authorities.

In this manner, both agencies can be viewed as constituent elements within a new, emerging architecture of experimentalist governance in the EU,[127] and would appear to be impacting decision-making within national health care systems, even if not as markedly as hard law.

5. Conclusion

This chapter has served to outline the role of European agencies in general, and the EMEA and EFSA in particular. It has sought to

---

[124] Article 57, Regulation 726/2004/EC, above n.69.
[125] Article 78, Regulation 726/2004/EC, above n.69.
[126] By comparison, and covering a much smaller population, the FDA has altogether some 9000 individuals employed in the two areas.
[127] C. Sabel and J. Zeitlin, 'Learning from difference: the new architecture of experimentalist governance in the EU', *European Law Journal* 14 (2008), 271–327.

examine their respective roles in relation to health protection and their (real and potential) impacts on national health systems, in terms of scientific evaluation, recommendation/opinion-giving, and the involvement of national counterparts and authorities. The discussion has outlined the emergence of both agencies and examined their mandates in health protection, along with factors that impact on how they execute their functions. By way of conclusion, we briefly revisit some of the main points in respect of the agencies' roles as protectors of health.

Understanding the reasons for the delegation of authority to EU-level agencies in the fields of medicines and foodstuffs means understanding national and EU-level policy-makers' aims in respect of: securing political commitments for long-term goals; increasing credibility at the same time as disassociating policy-making from science; increasing efficiency in highly technical areas; serving the aims of the single market; and harmonizing/standardizing national measures to the greatest extent possible. Additionally, the uncertainties surrounding risk analysis – such as where experts disagree on a given issue (e.g., the unknown long-term effects of a given medicine or the applicability of the precautionary principle to GMOs) – mean that policy-makers are often keen to derogate the science in order not to suffer the political costs of bad decisions or mistakes. The potential for such blame-shifting is likely to have contributed to the creation of both agencies, and EFSA in particular (not to mention the number of national food safety authorities that sprang up throughout Europe following the BSE crisis).

In the wakes of the thalidomide and BSE crises, we have seen that the need to ensure patient safety and (re-)establish consumer confidence has resulted in (further) centralization in both the pharmaceutical and foodstuffs sectors. Indeed, the fact that Community involvement in health and safety regulation may be considered to be spillover from the market integration objective may in turn explain why the Community has not been well-equipped to face these and other difficulties. The EU's response, in the main, has been to 'Europeanize' the science, with expert committees being established or consolidated at the EU level. In turn, these committees have evolved into regulatory agencies, each with considerable authority.

Considering the EMEA as a 'protector of health', it serves this function primarily through its evaluations. By allowing only those medicines that have passed the 'public health test' and demonstrated their quality, safety and efficacy onto the European market, Member States and consumers can have a high degree of trust in the medicines they use. As with any regulatory regime, it is not perfect. The recent withdrawals and issuance of 'black-box' warnings on several high profile drugs highlight the need to be vigilant and to have good pharmacovigilance, as well as risk analysis structures and procedures, in place. Additionally, the changes introduced by the 2005 legislation have shored up and strengthened the EMEA's role in key areas. Yet it remains the case that the agency's mandate is heavily oriented towards serving the interests of the single market and the industry, and that there are numerous measures that could be made available to the agency towards better serving public health interests, or at least serving them more directly. In many respects, the same can be said of EFSA. The agency clearly has serving the public interest through communicating the findings from good science as its primary aim, while also striving to arrive at better science in order to ensure human health. Yet we have seen that both the risk assessment and risk communication exercises can still be highly political. Moreover, the division between risk assessment and risk management is not so easy in practice.

It is clear that more than thirty years after the thalidomide tragedy and more than ten years after the BSE crisis, many improvements have been made in order to ensure consumers' health and trust. These reform initiatives were led primarily by the desire of the European institutions to regain trust in their science-based decision-making, while also ensuring health protection and the free movement of medicines and foods. Both the EMEA and EFSA have played an important part in this. While neither agency has the executive power to regulate in the manner of an independent regulatory agency such as the FDA, they both play a decisive role in the context of the internal market policy in the re-regulation of health issues at the EU level. As such, they have an influence on national health systems. We observed that their design and structure, which rely heavily upon (and to some extent absorb) national competent authorities, mean that they are likely to become true reference points for health-related questions. In this manner, both agencies – indeed, the proliferation of European agencies in general – can be seen as elements of the emergent architecture of experimentalist governance in the EU.[128]

---

[128] *Ibid.*

Although both agencies still have gaps as regards accountability and transparency, they may serve as examples for the 'new EU health care governance patchwork',[129] highlighting the resort to more 'soft' mechanisms for deliberation and networking with the various actors involved.

[129] See Chapter 2 in this volume.

4 | *The hard politics of soft law: the case of health*

SCOTT L. GREER AND BART VANHERCKE

1. Introduction

Talk of networked 'new governance' is everywhere. It elicits strong reactions – from scorn to extreme enthusiasm and from unthinking participation in new fora to excited applications of recondite social philosophy. Familiarity with the phenomenon also varies. Some forms of new governance are often found in health, but they are not necessarily known as such, while others have long histories outside health but are largely unknown within.

This chapter discusses new governance in EU health policies, examining the mechanisms and frameworks that EU institutions and Member States have introduced into health policy-making. These mechanisms promise to induce law-like behaviour by creating norms and networks (whether they will have that effect, or are intended to have that effect, varies). There are four obvious questions about any new policy development including 'new governance', and we answer them in the next three sections. What is it? How did it get started? Why is it happening? And what effect might it have?

A fifth question, naturally, is what has it done? Unfortunately, we cannot reasonably ask that question. For better or for worse, there is not much impact to study. Most new governance processes in health care became operational after 2005, or even later. Furthermore, many of the effects will be on process rather than outcomes – the direct effects will be on the networks and worldviews of policy-makers. The effects on infant mortality or leukemia deaths will often have to be

The research carried out for this chapter benefited from funding by the 'Shifts in Governance' programme of the Dutch Science Foundation (NWO), the Nuffield Trust (UK), a National Science Foundation (US) grant and the 'Society and Future' programme, implemented and financed by the Belgian Science Policy Office. We would like to thank the editors for their comments and Simone Rauscher for her assistance.

inferred from those process changes. In this chapter, we introduce some of the definitional issues involved in the discussion of new governance and soft law; the EU's versions of new governance, including the open method of coordination (OMC); the mechanisms by which new governance might work; and the possible future for new governance mechanisms in EU health policy.

We first explain what new governance is, highlighting the conceptual difficulties and uncertain status that it occupies in the academic literature and practical politics. New governance is built on networks rather than hierarchies, but networks are not new and hierarchies have not vanished. As a result, defining it is always difficult. The second section asks why it started. It explains the history of new governance, highlighting the extent to which it is a tool of some groups (whom we call 'social') in a multisided contest to frame the questions of EU health policy and define its agenda. The third section asks why it is happening. It examines new governance in the EU, working with the open method of coordination as our case study, and identifying the effects it has in light of broader theories of new governance. The European Union has few forms of new governance that are unique to health. Most of its policy instruments, including Member State groups, networks of specialists or the OMC, are policy tools that it uses in many sectors and has also generalized to the health sector. We find that it can be popular because it strengthens networks among officials and advocates, and it potentially will interact with, channel and shape 'harder' law made by the Court or internal market law.[1]

The fourth section, then, asks what it might do, inferring its effects from activities to date and the experience of new governance in other EU policy areas. New governance in health is often dominated by the European Commission, and will continue to be a feature of EU health politics. This is partly because networks will always exist, but it is mostly because the learning and networking function it provides can be attractive to a good number of Member State and Commission officials. The conclusion argues that it will continue to exist because it is a tool for Member States to enter into 'dialogues' with the Court and Commission – even if learning or policy influence does not matter, it is possible that the Court and Commission will be warned off health

---

[1] See Chapter 2 in this volume.

systems policy by clear statements from the Member States. Given its relatively low cost, that should be enough to sustain it. It will matter more, though, if some new governance mechanism can become the framework for EU health policy. In other words, it will matter most if it displaces the Court and internal market law as the key norm entrepreneur in this policy area. The data used in this chapter comes from 170 interviews conducted since 2004 among lobbyists and officials in the EU, reviewed in Greer,[2] and Hamel and Vanhercke,[3] as well as an analysis of official documents (national governments and EU institutions).

2. New governance and soft law

The scope of government has never been as great as the scope of ordered social activity. The writ of states has always been supplemented by a wide variety of networks, coalitions, professions and groups with shared ideas. That fact is the basis for the conversation about new governance: new governance is governance that takes place outside 'traditional' hierarchical, legal mechanisms such as the 'Community method' of legislation taught in EU textbooks.[4] It is also the basis for some of the conceptual confusion surrounding 'new governance', 'soft law', 'experimentalist governance' and other such concepts. We know better what they are *not* than what they *are*. And if it is hard to say what 'new governance' is, then it is also hard to say if it is actually new, or if it actually governs anything.[5] Nor is it easy to work out what it means in practice. Jordan and Schout, for example, observe that the 'EU governance literature still has not fully explored

---

[2] S. L. Greer, *The politics of European Union health policies* (Buckingham: Open University Press, forthcoming 2009).

[3] M. -P. Hamel and B. Vanhercke, 'The OMC and domestic social policymaking in Belgium and France: window dressing, one-way impact, or reciprocal influence?', in M. Heidenreich and J. Zeitlin (eds.), *Changing European employment and welfare regimes: the influence of the open method of coordination on national labour market and social welfare reforms* (London: Routledge, 2009).

[4] G. Majone, *Dilemmas of European integration: the ambiguities and pitfalls of integration by stealth* (Oxford: Oxford University Press, 2005), p. 59.

[5] An overview by Treib, Bähr and Falkner avoids 'the fashionable labels of "old" and "new" modes of governance. ... Whether a given mode of governance is "new" or "old" is an empirical rather than an analytical question. ... Should we consider a mode of governance new if it emerged

what governance *actually* means in terms of implementation ... In fact, academics are still struggling to agree common definitions of ... terms like the "open method of coordination (OMC)".[6]

A. Why discuss 'new governance'?

New governance involves 'a shift in emphasis away from command-and-control in favour of "regulatory" approaches, which are less rigid, less prescriptive, less committed to uniform approaches, and less hierarchical in nature'. The idea of new (or experimental, or soft) governance 'places considerable emphasis upon the accommodation and promotion of diversity, on the importance of provisionality and reversibility ... and on the goal of policy learning'.[7] In practice, EU policy often fits these criteria. It is increasingly: (a) deliberative (consensus is often regarded as provisional); (b) multilevel (connecting different levels of government – crucially, this means that it is not strongly hierarchical, or hierarchical at all); (c) a departure from norms of representative democracy (accountability is defined in terms of transparency and scrutiny by peers); (d) a combination of framework goals set from above combined with considerable autonomy for lower-level units and agents to redefine the objectives in light of learning; and (e) built on reporting (on their performance) and participation in peer review (in which results are compared with those pursuing other means to the same general ends).[8]

---

within the last five or ten years, within the last two or three decades, or within the last century? ... Moreover, the question of whether a given mode of governance should be considered "old" or "new" also depends on the specific policy area one is focusing on'. Many supposedly innovative forms of governance that occurred rather recently in one particular field of study 'may turn out to be quite old in other contexts'. O. Treib, H. Bähr and G. Falkner, 'Modes of governance: towards conceptual clarification', *Journal of European Public Policy* 14 (2007), 1–20.

[6] A. Jordan and A. Schout, *The coordination of the European Union: exploring the capacities of networked governance* (Oxford: Oxford University Press, 2006).

[7] G. de Búrca and J. Scott, 'Introduction: new governance, law and constitutionalism', in G. de Búrca and J. Scott (eds.), *New governance and constitutionalism in Europe and the US* (Oxford: Hart, 2006), pp. 2–3.

[8] C. Sabel and J. Zeitlin, 'Learning from difference: the new architecture of experimentalist governance in the European Union', *European Law Journal* 14 (2008), 271–327.

The intellectual and political history of the concept explains why these definitions might seem vague. The newness of new governance in the EU (and elsewhere) is partly intellectual. Theorists of new governance are often reacting against needlessly reductive theories that ascribed far too much dominance to states and formal public bureaucracies.[9] A health ministry will often share power over health care with organized professions; therefore, accounts that focused on the ministry would have been incomplete. Even more difficult to grasp, however, are the networks only partially captured by the organized profession. Academic, professional and other networks allocate resources and shape outcomes without having any formal power or even existence. 'New governance', intellectually speaking, is part of a family of theories that incorporates these forms of governance into social sciences and legal doctrines that often pay too little attention to actors outside the formal, legal state.

Practical efforts to develop new governance, or at least the more theorized ones, emerge from the same source. Frustration with the various incapacities of states, public bureaucracies or the EU institutions combines with a practical sense of what networks can do – and the result is a series of attempts to harness networks as tools of public action.

The development of new governance in the EU reflects both of these roots. Just as scholars began to speak of governance, a diverse group inside and outside the EU institutions began to seek ways to address policy problems in ways that are foreign to the EU's traditional approach. The specific 'problems' that the EU institutions face are all clear from the Treaties. First, the 'Community method' of legislation is slow, rigid, sometimes difficult to meaningfully enforce, and capable of producing some strange outcomes when implemented in complex situations. Its very representativeness and concern for consensus means that it can frustrate policy advocates. Second, the EU is constrained by its Treaty bases. Its powers in health are very limited, and in health care its specific competences are negligible. This does not mean that it is restricted to those areas in which Member States

---

[9] For examples from international relations, see A.-M. Slaughter, *A new world order* (Princeton: Princeton University Press, 2004). For a discussion of the concept in EU politics, see L. Hooghe and G. Marks, *Multi-level governance and European integration* (Lanham: Rowman and Littlefield, 2001).

have seen fit to allocate it a competence. It does mean, however, that its engagement with those areas (such as health services) does not just lack democratic legitimacy or an obvious useful purpose; it is also badly distorted by the requirement that it operate on the basis of internal market, social security or other Treaty bases.

The formal institutions of the EU, if they are to operate according to the Community method, must regard health care not as health care but as something else (probably the single internal market). Many see that as unsatisfactory: it does not recognize the specificity of health, it could create vast transition costs as well as damage solidarity, and it is difficult to see how it allows the EU to address some of the issues, such as health inequalities, where many Member States are interested in sharing experiences and learning at an EU level. Note, for example, that the first ever peer review on health care issues in the context of the OMC was held (with nine peer countries, stakeholder representatives and the European Commission) with a view to developing 'a European perspective on access to health care and the reduction of health inequality'.[10] If the EU is to have a role in health services, many believe it is better that it be channelled in a coherent direction that improves health care.

B. Defining new governance in EU health policy

Discussion of new governance in EU health policies suffers from the basic definitional problem of all discussions of new governance: the tension between definitions that rely on intention (i.e., whether something is intended to be new governance), definitions that rely on mechanisms (standard-setting, norms, credentialing) and definitions that rely on identifiable impact. If we define new governance based on the intention of members, then every committee that sets out to define standards or promote convergence counts, even if nobody notices it. If we define new governance by mechanisms, then almost any decent international conference qualifies. And if we define it by impact, then we cannot identify new governance other than by tracing an event

---

[10] C. Masseria, 'Access to care and health status inequalities in a context of healthcare reform', Synthesis Report, Peer Review and Assessment in Social Inclusion, Hungary, 17–18 January 2007, p. 3, http://ec.europa.eu/ employment_social/spsi/docs/social_inclusion/2007/pr_hu_En.pdf.

backwards and finding something other than hierarchical law-making by states. Given this problem, it is not surprising that new governance is often defined by its negative.

To avoid the problem, we take advantage of the fact that the EU is one of the great producers of explicit new governance mechanisms. It is relatively rare among formal political institutions in its formal, declared use of new governance.[11] As a result, we choose to take the EU at its word and focus on the intention, ignore other (unintended) examples of the mechanisms at work, and discuss ways to identify their impact. In other words, new governance instruments are those that are intended by their creators to work through norms and networks rather than hierarchies and traditional legal instruments. If they work, they start to authoritatively allocate resources and change behaviour, and if they are successful they might even have advantages (flexibility, experimentation) that traditional, democratically legitimated legislative procedures do not have.

Linda Senden has built a set of definitions on the intentions of EU institutions. She divides EU new governance into three broad categories. A first, rather general, category is 'soft governance', which Senden designates as 'preparatory and informative instruments'. This means green papers, white papers, action programmes and informative communications. These instruments are adopted with a view to preparing further Community law and policy and/or providing information on Community action. As such, they can also be regarded as fulfilling a pre-law function.[12] As we will see further on, this category also includes preparatory documents and recommendations of expert groups. 'Interpretative and decisional instruments' are instruments that:

[A]im at providing guidance as to the interpretation and application of existing Community law. ... The decisional instruments go further than mere interpretation by indicating in what way a Community institution – usually the Commission – will apply Community law provisions in individual cases when it has implementing and discretionary powers. To this category belong notably the Commission's communications and notices

---

[11] European Commission, 'European governance', White Paper, COM (2001) 428 final, 25 July 2001.

[12] L. Senden, 'Soft law, self-regulation and co-regulation in European law: where do they meet?', *Electronic Journal of Comparative Law* 9 (2005), 18–9.

and also certain guidelines, codes and frameworks frequently adopted in the areas of competition law and state aid. ... As such, they can be considered to fulfill primarily a post-law function.[13]

A nice example of such an instrument is the 'Altmark package' discussed in Chapter 9.[14]

In this chapter, we concentrate on a third category of soft law instruments. These are 'steering instruments'. Box 4.1 lists some of the main such mechanisms at work in the EU health policy sector. These aim at establishing or giving further effect to Community objectives and policy or related policy areas. Sometimes, this means declarations and conclusions, but it can also mean other efforts to create closer cooperation or even harmonization through recommendations, resolutions and codes of conduct, which are 'used as alternatives to legislation and, in view of this, they can often be said to fulfill a para-law function'.[15]

The most widely known of these policy coordination mechanisms is, without doubt, the open method of coordination (OMC). We use it as our main case study because OMC has become, as we will illustrate, a template for soft governance in the EU, and also because it is well researched.

C. *New governance at work: the OMC*

The OMC, described in Box 4.1, has attracted considerable – and according to some – unduly favourable scholarly as well as political attention since its inauguration by the European Council at the Lisbon Summit.[16] Since there is no legal definition of the OMC in the Treaty or other binding texts, it is reasonable to rely on the Presidency Conclusions of this Lisbon Summit. They introduce it as 'the means of spreading best practice and achieving greater convergence towards the main EU goals'. According to the Conclusions, this involves: fixing *guidelines* (with specific timetables); establishing quantitative and qualitative *indicators* and *benchmarks* (against the best in the world);

---

[13] *Ibid.*   [14] See Chapter 9 in this volume.
[15] Senden, 'Soft law', above n.13, 19.
[16] European Council, 'Presidency Conclusions', 23 and 24 March 2000, para. 7, www.consilium.europa.eu/ueDocs/cms_Data/docs/pressData/en/ec/00100-r1.en0.htm.

Box 4.1   Varieties of new governance in health

The Platform on diet, nutrition and physical activity

The Platform as it exists today was established in March 2005. It reflects the politics of that year – the new Barroso Commission's focus on economic competitiveness; a shift to the right in the European Parliament, which made Community-method legislation less likely; and personnel changes in the Directorate-General for Health and Consumer Protection (DG SANCO) that made it more dynamic. Interested in addressing the interlocking problems of diet and activity that lead to obesity, the Commission brought together a wide variety of interested parties to produce the Platform. The process was simple enough: participants, including NGOs and private firms, as well as Member States, were invited to make commitments that would contribute to healthy eating and physical activity. They report annually on their progress. At the same time, the Platform and its subgroups were the venues for debates about improving health in Europe. These debates brought firms, civil society and others together, and gave the Commission a useful way to gauge reactions and test support for the policies that emerged as the Barroso Commission and the European Parliament became less liberal. It was a major contributor to the May 2007 Strategy on Nutrition, Overweight and Obesity-related Health Issues.[17]

The High Level Group on Health Services and Medical Care

The High Level Group on Health Care is the oldest of the EU new governance tools in health care, and its ancestry is certainly the longest. It is the successor to the High Level Process of Reflection, which was an initial effort to map out the consequences of (especially) internal market law for health services. The Process concluded in 2003 with a call for a more permanent structure, and the Group, that structure, was formed in 2004. While the Process that gave rise to it had a wide membership, putting nongovernmental organizations and Member States side by side, the Group itself is made up of officials from the Member States. It is serviced by DG SANCO. It was quite active between 2004 and 2006,

---

[17] European Commission, 'A strategy for Europe on nutrition, overweight and obesity related health issues', White Paper, COM (2007) 279, 30 May 2007.

but became very quiet after September 2006. This should not have come as a surprise: in its 2006 report, the Group indicated that the Commission's intention to bring forward proposals to develop a Community framework for safe, high quality and efficient health services in 2007, on the basis of consultation beginning in 2006 'will have an impact on the future work of the High Level Group'.[18] In retrospect, this sentence seems to have been the announcement that the Group would be stifled and replaced with something more amenable to Commission control. It was then reborn, rather dramatically, in 2008. According to Member State interviewees, this was because the delays to the proposed health services directive had left DG SANCO with no effective forum. The DG remedied that problem by resuming the Group's meetings.

The open method of coordination (OMC)

The OMC for health and long-term care was formally launched in 2004 and is administered by the Social Protection Committee (SPC). It became operational in 2006, when the Council merged the three social OMC processes (for pensions, social inclusion, and health and long-term care). The health care strand of the 'streamlined' Social Protection and Social Inclusion OMC involves:

- Common objectives, political priorities agreed by the Member States and subject to a variety of influences within Member States and in Brussels.
- The three shared objectives of the SPC in all subfields are: (a) social cohesion, equality and opportunities; (b) effective interaction between the Lisbon objectives; and (c) good governance (see Box 4.2). They were agreed in March 2006.
- The streamlining of the social OMCs did not change the older health objectives (agreed by the Council at Nice in 2000) of high-quality, financially sustainable health systems with access for all.
- Indicators developed by Member States to assess their progress towards reaching the common objectives (see Box 4.4). So far, progress in developing harmonized (EU) health indicators has been rather slow, and no targets (quantified objectives) have been set, even though the Commission is building up pressure on

---

[18] European Commission, 'Work of the High Level Group in 2006', HLG/2006/8, 10 October 2006, pp. 15–6.

Box 4.1 (*cont.*)

Member States that provide long-term care in a devolved context to set national targets.[19]

- Peer review. The purpose of learning within the OMC is not just to oblige Member States to provide information in a transparent and consistent way. The Organisation for Economic Co-operation and Development and World Health Organization, among others, already do that. The OMC is designed to go beyond this by promoting genuine peer review – asking Member State officials, and outsiders from civil society, to participate in a structured and contextualized exchange of information. Multiple interviewees in the Commission commented that in order to have real exchanges of practical knowledge, the important thing is to send line officials responsible for specific policy areas, rather than the international division of health ministries.
- National reporting obligations. These give the peer reviewers something to review, and take two forms:
  - National reports on strategies, initially, present the status of the country and its current strategies; Member States report on what they see as national 'best practices', some of which are then retained in the joint reports (see below).
  - The subsequent reports respond to both changes in the indicators and to the advice of OMC peers, reporting on both the evolution of the policy approaches and the changes in outcomes.

The European Commission (in the form of the Directorate-General for Employment, Social Affairs and Equal Opportunities) also participates in peer review, taking advantage of its ability to muster expert views and its position as a hub of the OMC process. Thus, the health care section of the 2007 Joint Report highlighted challenges and planned strategies with regard to (inequities in) access to health care, including those resulting from decentralization; the

---

[19] European Commission, 'Joint report on social protection and social inclusion 2008: social inclusion, pensions, healthcare and long-term care', Directorate-General for Employment, Social Affairs and Equal Opportunities (2008), p. 90, http://ec.europa.eu/employment_social/spsi/docs/social_inclusion/2008/joint_report_En.pdf.

insufficiency of current long-term care and the priority given to home care services; coordination between primary, outpatient and inpatient secondary and tertiary care and between medical, nursing, social and palliative care; the striking differences in expenditure and personnel employed and the need to control costs; problems with regard to retention and supply of medical staff; and, finally, the search for win–win strategies, where Member States recognize the interlinkages between access, quality and financial sustainability.[20]

national and regional *targets*; and periodic *monitoring*, evaluation and *peer review* organized as *mutual learning processes*.[21] It is a common EU policy tool; it was applied firstly and most prominently to economic policies (1992) and employment (1997), and more recently to social inclusion (2000), pensions (2001) and health care (2004). According to Metz, a dozen OMCs are up and running,[22] and more are coming. In the field of health, the European Commission is thinking out loud about starting new applications of OMC-type processes to areas such as organ donation and transplantation,[23] as well as nanosciences and nanotechnologies.[24] Others would like to see the method applied to obesity and cancer screening, or to e-health.[25]

We focus on the OMC because it is the most clearly defined and well researched process, with its roots traced and effects studied.[26] To

[20] European Commission, 'Joint report on social protection and social inclusion 2007: social inclusion, pensions, healthcare and long-term care', Directorate-General for Employment, Social Affairs and Equal Opportunities (2007), pp. 10–2, http://ec.europa.eu/employment_social/spsi/docs/social_inclusion/2007/joint_report_En.pdf.

[21] *Ibid.*, para. 37.

[22] A. Metz, 'Innovation in governance? Six proposals for taming open co-ordination', Center for Applied Policy Research (C.A.P.) Working Papers Policy Analysis No. 1 (2005), p. 7.

[23] European Commission, 'Organ donation and transplantation: policy actions at EU level', COM (2007) 275 final, 30 May 2007, p. 10.

[24] European Commission, 'Nanosciences and nanotechnologies: an action plan for Europe 2005–2009', COM (2005) 243 final, 7 June 2005, p. 4.

[25] European Commission, 'Making healthcare better for European citizens: an action plan for a European e-health area', COM (2004) 356 final, 30 April 2004, p. 16. Interview with DG SANCO.

[26] See the citations in V. Hatzopoulos, 'Why the open method of coordination is bad for you: a letter to the EU', *European Law Journal* 13 (2007), 309–42.

a great extent, we know what an OMC process is. It is a framework, recognizable to its participants, that fits the definition given in the Lisbon Council's Conclusions. It has been further discussed in the Commission's White Paper on governance,[27] as well as a host of academic publications.

Furthermore, it has already been applied in a variety of other areas. This means that we can draw on large-scale studies of its effects elsewhere for indicators and expectations.[28] This does not mean that the OMC is the oldest or only network in health; if anything, the Directorate General for Health and Consumer Affairs (DG SANCO) is one of the leading Directorates-General in creating new forums for civil society dialogue beyond traditional forms of EU comitology.[29] Nor does it mean that new governance, in at least its weakest forms, is wholly new or unique to the EU. If anything, the World Health Organization (WHO) 'Health for All' programme is the pioneer for structured comparisons of programmes.

3. The development of new governance in EU health policy

There is no single reason why health care emerged on the EU agenda. A few determined individuals and groups had advocated, since the 1980s, for EU health action on issues as diverse as cancer care and professional mobility, while the Commission, Parliament and Court, in their different ways, were receptive to proposals for the extension of EU competences. EU activity triggered more EU activity; each action provoked others to 'come to Brussels' to advance or just defend their positions in the new arena.[30] The EU health care agenda

---

[27] European Commission, 'European governance', above n.12.

[28] Heidenreich and Zeitlin (eds.), *Changing European employment*, above n.3; R. Dehousse (ed.), *L'Europe sans Bruxelles?: Une analyse de la méthode ouverte de coordination* (Paris: L'Harmattan, 2004); J. Zeitlin and P. Pochet (eds.), *The open method of co-ordination in action: the European employment and social inclusion strategies* (Brussels: PIE-Peter Lang, 2005); J. Zeitlin and D. Trubek (eds.), *Governing work and welfare in a new economy* (Oxford: Oxford University Press, 2003).

[29] A. Slob and F. Smakman, *Evaluation of the civil society dialogue at DG Trade: assessment of relevance, effectiveness and efficiency of CSD policy and procedures* (Rotterdam: ECORYS for DG Trade, 2006).

[30] S. L. Greer, 'Uninvited Europeanization: neofunctionalism and the EU in health policy', *Journal of European Public Policy* 13 (2006).

is a mixture of arguments over competences and substantive policies, with protagonists often switching emphases between their substantive goals and their views of the legitimate distribution of responsibility for health care. This section traces the role played by new governance mechanisms and their advocates in the history of the EU's health policy role.

The key point is that new governance mechanisms are like anything else in politics: intensely political. They do not transcend the strategies and calculations of EU institutions, states and interest groups. Rather, new governance mechanisms and their products are deeply affected by those interplays. Explaining the life of the two main new governance mechanisms – the OMC and the High Level Group on Health Services and Medical Care – requires an understanding of the cleavages between three groups. Each has a different interpretation of the 'problem' that EU health policy might solve, and a different overall vision and set of biases. We call them the 'economic' group, organized around the Directorate-General for the Internal Market and Services (DG MARKT), compatible with much European Court of Justice (ECJ) jurisprudence, and focused on the internal market; the 'social' group, organized around Directorate-General for Employment, Social Affairs and Equal Opportunities (DG Social Affairs) and labour or social affairs ministries, and sponsor of both the OMC and much of the rhetoric about a European Social Model; and the youngest, the 'health' group, which is organized around DG SANCO and the health ministries and experts of the Member States.

A. Health care appears on the agenda

What brought social protection (including health care) firmly to the European political agenda, then?[31] An important push factor was the fact that the finance ministers (through the Economic and Financial Affairs Council (ECOFIN) and its main advisory body, the Economic Policy Committee (EPC)), were starting to raise their voice in the health care debate at the dawn of the new millennium – for example, by issuing reports on the necessity to curb health care spending in order to be able to cope with the financial burden on welfare spending

---

[31] For a detailed account of the slow move of health care to the EU agenda from the beginning of the 1990s onwards, see Chapter 2 in this volume.

of the ageing population (see Chapter 2 for more details). Clearly, Court rulings such as the *Kohll* and *Decker* cases[32] were an important trigger as well, as were a number of other landmark cases during the second half of the 1990s, notably with regard to the application of competition law to pension funds.[33] Taken together, these cases made it clear to the Member States that social welfare services may fall under internal market rules.

'Framing' EU health policy would not just mean defining the problem; it would also mean defining the Treaty bases for future action, 'ownership' of health policy by different DGs and the policy mechanisms at work.[34] The direction of jurisprudence after *Kohll* and *Decker* suggested that health would be defined as one more service, or service of general interest, in the internal market. That galvanized proponents of alternative framings.

One group focuses on health as part of a broader social model. While the EU has a strong bias towards market-making policies built on its 'four freedoms',[35] there are other contending views of the EU's meaning. For example, it could be seen as the defender and exponent of a 'European Social Model' (ESM).[36] Advocates view health policy as part of a range of social policies that mark out a distinctive, shared, European approach to social policy and welfare. Proponents of this

---

[32] See Chapters 11 and 12 in this volume.

[33] Case C-67/96, *Albany International* v. *Stichting Bedrijfspensioenfonds Textielindustrie* [1999] ECR I-05751; Joined Cases C-115–117/97, *Brentjens* v. *Stichting Bedrijfspensioenfonds* [1999] ECR I-06025; Case C-219/97, *Drijvende Bokken* [1999] ECR I-06121.

[34] S. L. Greer, 'Choosing paths in European Union health policy: a political analysis of a critical juncture', *Journal of European Social Policy* 18 (2008), 219–31; B. Vanhercke, 'Is the OMC growing teeth? The governance turn in EU social policy co-ordination', Second Year Paper, University of Amsterdam (2007).

[35] F. Scharpf, *Governing in Europe: effective and democratic?* (Oxford: Oxford University Press, 1999); S. Greer, 'Power struggle: the politics and policy consequences of patient mobility in Europe', *OSE Policy Paper* 2 (2008).

[36] J. Kvist and J. Saari (eds.), *The Europeanisation of social protection* (Bristol: Policy Press, 2007); M. Jepsen and A. Serrano Pascual, 'The concept of ESM and supranational legitimacy-building', in M. Jepsen and A. Serrano Pascual (eds.), *Unwrapping the European social model* (Bristol: Policy Press, 2006); S. L. Greer, 'Ever closer union: devolution, the European Union, and social citizenship rights', in S. L. Greer (ed.), *Devolution and social citizenship in the United Kingdom* (Bristol: Policy Press, 2009).

'social' framing generally include trade unions, many Member States' ministries of labour and social affairs, some Member States (often France and Belgium), intellectuals concerned with the definition of the 'ESM'[37] and, crucially, DG Social Affairs within the Commission. Note that the latter now has to compete with the Commission's Bureau of European Policy Advisors (BEPA), which works directly with the Commission president and has taken a very active stance in this debate lately.[38] Advocates of this 'social' framing would seek to incorporate health into the overall policy goal of reinforcing the social model, vest concomitant responsibilities in DG Social Affairs and use mechanisms linked to DG Social Affairs, such as the OMC.

Another approach to health issues draws its intellectual reference from the traditional complexity and autonomy of health policy. These 'health' advocates generally call for recognition of the specificity of health services and have their institutional bases in established health policy communities, including health academia, ministries of health, professions and some EU-level health groups, such as the European Health Management Association, EuroHealthNet and the European Public Health Alliance (EPHA). Their affinity is with DG SANCO – a young and relatively weak DG that has had incentive to seek them out.

The prospect of an EU competence governed entirely by internal market law and the priorities of ECOFIN galvanized proponents of these alternative framings. The 'social' group, which would aim to incorporate health into an expansive 'European Social Model', moved through DG Social Affairs within the European Commission. It published, in July 1999, a Communication in which it proposed a 'concerted strategy for modernising social protection'.[39] The ministers for social affairs followed the Commission's lead and identified 'high quality and sustainable health care' as a key objective that should be pursued at the EU level.[40]

---

[37] Such as A. Giddens, P. Diamond and R. Liddle (eds.), *Global Europe, social Europe* (Cambridge: Polity, 2006).

[38] R. Liddle and F. Lerais, 'Europe's social reality', Consultation Paper, Bureau of European Policy Advisors (2007).

[39] European Commission, 'A concerted strategy for modernising social protection', COM (99) 347 final, 14 July 1999.

[40] Council Conclusions on the strengthening of cooperation for modernizing and improving social protection, OJ 2000 No. C8/7.

That same year, DG SANCO led a parallel initiative with its roots in the 'health' groups. The High Level Committee on Health,[41] which is an advisory body of the Commission's Directorate-General for Health and Consumer Protection, received a mandate to analyse the consequences of the above-mentioned *Kohll* and *Decker* ECJ rulings, and the impact of Community provisions on health systems. Note that the request to discuss the consequences of these judgements in political terms came from the health (and not the social affairs) formation of the Council.

B. *New governance mechanisms in the developing EU health policy sector*

By 1999–2000, therefore, there were already three different groups trying to define EU health policy. Using our shorthand, they are the 'economic', 'social' and 'health' advocates. The 'economic' actors, such as the ECJ, DG MARKT and ECOFIN, were defined by their focus on the place of health care in the internal market and government budgets. 'Social' actors, led by DG Social Affairs, were more concerned with incorporating health into a European Social Model. The newest were the 'health' actors, led by DG SANCO, the ministers in the Health Council, and the experts and lobbyists of the embryonic EU health policy community, who were trying to mark out a distinctive health policy arena and debate by calling for recognition of the 'specificity' of health services.[42]

The presence of three different sets of actors with different agendas and understandings of health policies in an area with unclear EU powers and little basic agreement did not speed up policy-making. But it did create the framework within which new governance was created and operates. New governance mechanisms are favoured by the 'social' advocates, in the case of the OMC, and by incumbent health actors, in the case of the High Level Group. From the point of view of a Member State that wishes to maintain its health policy

---

[41] The High Level Committee on Health is composed of senior civil servants from the health ministries of the Member States. It meets two to three times a year and operates with a number of working groups. See http://ec.europa.eu/health/ph_overview/co_operation/high_level/high_level_En.htm.

[42] Greer, 'Choosing paths', above n.34; Vanhercke, 'Is the OMC growing teeth?', above n.34.

autonomy, the new governance of health within the EU is worse than the pre-1998 status quo of no health policy at all, but it is better than the 'economic' option of governing health through internal market law and the strictures of the Stability and Growth Pact. That is because the new governance mechanisms, by definition, are more subject to alteration, permit more divergence, are harder to enforce legally and are set up to be more responsive to the concerns of health ministries. New governance mechanisms, therefore, became attractive to Member States at approximately the same time that they realized that the alternative was health policy made by the ECJ, DG MARKT and possibly ECOFIN. The new governance mechanisms that the Commission offered were the OMC, associated with DG Social Affairs, and the High Level Process of Reflection and, later, the High Level Group.

They were originally presented, in spite of Member States' reluctance to admit that there is an EU health care debate, by DG SANCO and DG Social Affairs, in April 2004. In fact, since there was no agreement on who was to take the lead in an overall strategy, this was done through two separate (announced as 'complementary') communications, published on the same day. One responded to the final report of the High Level Process of Reflection on Patient Mobility, which had been set up in 2002.[43] The other proposed an extension of OMC to health care and long-term care.[44] The latter initiative was rather surprising in view of the fact that the European Commission had tried (but failed) to obtain a mandate in this area from the March 2004 Spring European Council. Indeed, in its annual 'spring report', the Commission asked the European Council to '[e]xtend the open method of coordination in the social protection field to the modernisation of healthcare schemes'.[45] Significantly, the 2004 Spring European Council did *not* adopt the proposal.

---

[43] European Commission, 'Follow-up to the High Level Reflection Process on Patient Mobility and Healthcare Developments in the European Union', COM (2004) 301 final, 20 April 2004. See Chapter 2 in this volume for more details.

[44] European Commission, 'Modernising social protection for the development of high-quality, accessible and sustainable health care and long-term care: support for national strategies using the 'open method of coordination', COM (2004) 304 final, 20 April 2004.

[45] European Commission, 'Report from the Commission to the Spring European Council, delivering Lisbon. Reforms for the enlarged Union', COM (2004) 29 final, 20 February 2004, p. 26.

So, why did the Commission propose an OMC on health care to the Member States again within two months?[46] And why did the Health Council, after years of refusal to accept an EU role in health care, agree with the Commission's proposal to set up a permanent 'High Level Group on Health Services and Medical Care'[47] (see Box 4.1) to take forward the recommendations of the High Level Process of Reflection on Patient Mobility?

Even if the European Parliament's request to the Council in March 2004 'to adopt as a matter of principle the application of the open coordination method' in the field of health care[48] may have had *some* influence, there were three catalytic events. One was the implementation of the Working Time Directive against the background of the *Jaeger* and *SiMAP* decisions; few Member States had prepared adequately for the Directive's implementation, and the Court's decisions made that implementation more expensive. This concentrated attention on the EU. The second factor, highlighted by many national and European actors in this area, and which opened up new possibilities and galvanized many health actors, was the publication of the draft proposal for a 'Services Directive'.[49] Finally, it can be argued that the right balance between the Commission's 'social' and 'health' DGs could only be found after DG SANCO found sufficient legitimacy in the recommendations of the aforementioned High Level Process of Reflection to claim part of the territory. So the Council formally launched the health care OMC in October 2004.[50]

There are three signs that Member States meant the soft governance of health care – the OMC and the High Level Group alike – to be their instrument, rather than a new platform for an ambitious Commission. First, this OMC was launched with a provisional

---

[46] European Commission, 'Modernising social protection', above n.44.
[47] European Commission, 'Commission decision setting up a High Level Group on Health Services and Medical Care', C (2004) 1501, 20 April 2004.
[48] European Parliament Resolution on the Communication from the Commission – Proposal for a joint report on 'health care and care for the elderly: supporting national strategies for ensuring a high level of social protection', Doc. No. A5–0098/2004, 24 February 2004, para.7.
[49] European Commission, 'Proposal for a Directive of the European Parliament and of the Council on services in the internal market', COM (2004) 2 final, 5 March 2004. See, further, Chapters 11 and 12 in this volume.
[50] Council Meeting on Employment, Social Policy, Health and Consumer Affairs, Council Press Release Doc. No. 12400/04, 4 October 2004.

institutional architecture (provisional common objectives, no common set of indicators, preliminary reports instead of action plans, etc.).[51] Second, the Council was very clear about its lack of enthusiasm. The Social Affairs Council not only stressed that this OMC should be introduced 'in a progressive and flexible manner, while placing a strong emphasis on added value',[52] but also decided it should:

[B]e subject to the following conditions: it should not impose an excessive administrative burden; health ministries should be directly involved in the OMC process; overlaps with the follow-up of the high level reflection on patient mobility should be avoided; coherence of views should be ensured within the single EU Council formation of ministers of health and social policy; the joint working with the Economic Policy Committee should continue.[53]

This is not the prose of the newly enamoured.

Third, the ministers for health opted to vest control of the European health care agenda in the Council. In 2005, health ministers agreed to draw up a statement on the core values and shared principles that unite the health systems of the Member States. Significantly, these values and principles were not elaborated by the High Level Group on Health Services and Medical Care. Instead, this work was done by a Committee of Senior Officials on Public Health (CSOPH), which is, in fact, a special gathering of the regular Council Working Party on Public Health and which was set up at exactly the same time as the High Level Group.[54] Arguably, Member States felt the need to be able to undertake discussions in a setting that would not be limited in its deliberations to public health and consumer issues and would be controlled by the Member States – and, more particularly, the EU presidencies and the Council Secretariat, rather than by the European Commission.

Even after its official kick-off, the political level remained prudent: the 2005 Spring European Council did not confirm the

[51] Vanhercke, 'Is the OMC growing teeth?', above n.34.
[52] European Commission, 'Council High Level Group on Health Services and Medical Care – information from the Commission', Doc. No. 15190/04, 1 December 2004, p. 9.
[53] Council Press Release, above n.50, p. 9.
[54] Council Public Health Working Party Meeting at Senior Level, 'Report from the Presidency', Doc. No. 15281/05 SAN 204, 2 December 2005.

launch of the health care OMC. This clearly did not stop cooperation taking off at the administrative level: responding to the Council's request, Member States submitted preliminary national reports on health care and long term care. The reports identified a wide variety of issues for further work.[55] In fact, a senior civil servant in the Commission claimed that 'after all this hesitation, the Member States now "discovered" the OMC. If we were to follow all the issues they proposed, it would completely flood the Social Protection agenda for years to come.'

Perhaps most importantly, the initial reports helped, in the words of a Belgian senior civil servant, to 'occupy the health care territory vis-à-vis the Economic Policy Committee and the High Level group on Health Services and Medical Care' – in other words, to support the 'social' agenda of DG Social Affairs and its network over the alternative 'economic' and 'health' frameworks and networks.

The national preliminary reports also inspired the European Commission's 'streamlining' proposal of late 2005, in which it proposed to integrate the social inclusion, pensions and health care OMCs into one single framework – i.e., the social protection and social inclusion OMC.[56] Since the adoption of this 'streamlining' reorganization by the 2006 Spring European Council, the health care OMC now has become one of the 'strands' of the social protection and social inclusion OMC. In practice, it is managed by the Social Protection Committee (SPC), a group of high-level officials that was established in 2000, as well as by its Sub-Group on Indicators (created in February 2001). The SPC is an advisory body to the Employment, Social Policy, Health and Consumer Affairs Council (EPSCO) of the EU and is composed of two delegates from each Member State and the Commission, which provides the secretariat. Every three years, in a 'national report on strategies for social protection and social inclusion' (which includes a section on health and long-term care), Member States explain the progress made in reaching a number of policy objectives (priorities) specific to social inclusion, pensions and

---

[55] Social Protection Committee, 'Review of preliminary national policy statements on health care and long-term care', Memorandum of the Social Protection Committee, November 2005.

[56] European Commission, 'Working together, working better: a new framework for the open coordination of social protection and inclusion policies in the European Union', COM (2005) 706 final, 22 December 2005.

Box 4.2 Common objectives with regard to health care

Member States should provide accessible, high-quality and sustainable health care and long-term care by ensuring:

(a) access for all to adequate health and long-term care; that the need for care does not lead to poverty and financial dependency; and that inequities in access to care and in health outcomes are addressed;

(b) quality in health and long-term care, and the adaptation of care, including developing preventive care, to the changing needs and preferences of society and individuals, notably by developing quality standards reflecting best international practice and by strengthening the responsibility of health professionals and of patients and care recipients; and

(c) that adequate and high-quality health and long-term care remains affordable and financially sustainable by promoting a rational use of resources, notably through appropriate incentives for users and providers, good governance and coordination between care systems and public and private institutions. Long-term sustainability and quality require the promotion of healthy and active life styles and good human resources for the care sector.

Source: European Commission.[57]

---

health care policies (see Box 4.2 for the full set of common objectives with regard to health care and long-term care).

Member States subscribed to three 'overarching objectives', which apply to the three strands of the streamlined OMC. For example, with the third overarching objective, Member States commit themselves to promote 'good governance, transparency and the involvement of stakeholders in the design, implementation and monitoring'[58] of their social inclusion, pensions, and health care and long-term

---

[57] European Commission, 'Joint report on social protection and social inclusion 2007: social inclusion, pensions, healthcare and long-term care', Directorate-General for Employment, Social Affairs and Equal Opportunities (2007), p. 83, http://ec.europa.eu/employment_social/spsi/docs/social_inclusion/2007/joint_report_En.pdf.

[58] *Ibid.*

Box 4.3 Overarching objectives covering the three strands of the open method of coordination for social protection and social inclusion

Promote:

(a) social cohesion, equality between men and women and equal opportunities for all through adequate, accessible, financially sustainable, adaptable and efficient social protection systems and social inclusion policies;

(b) effective and mutual interaction between the Lisbon objectives of greater economic growth, more and better jobs, and greater social cohesion, and with the EU's sustainable development strategy; and

(c) good governance, transparency and the involvement of stake-holders in the design, implementation and monitoring of policy.

Source: European Commission.[59]

care policies (see the full list of overarching objectives in Box 4.3). Once the Commission (DG Social Affairs) has received all the national strategy reports, it analyses and assesses Member States' progress towards the common objectives with the help of national and European indicators. The assessment is then published in a joint report, which is adopted by the Commission and the Council and submitted, every year, to the (Spring) European Council to inform heads of state and government on the progress in the area of social protection and social inclusion.

As far as indicators are concerned, work within the health care strand is clearly less advanced than in the areas of pensions and (especially) social inclusion, for which there is an agreement on a full battery of commonly agreed *EU* indicators (i.e., harmonized at EU level). In contrast, for health, a 'preliminary portfolio' of

---

[59] European Commission, 'Working together, working better: a new framework for the open coordination of social protection and inclusion policies in the European Union', COM (2005) 706, 22 December 2005.

mostly *national* health care indicators was adopted in June 2006 (see Box 4.4 for more details).[60] At the time of writing, the full list of indicators and their meanings have not been agreed upon; difficulties in data collection and handling, as well as political risks, have all slowed down the work on indicators (even though it continued throughout 2007 and 2008), and therefore the health care OMC as a whole.

Consider, by way of illustration, the fact that the European Scrutiny Committee of the House of Commons in the United Kingdom refused to scrutinize the afore-mentioned Commission's Communication through which it proposed to extend the OMC to health care.[61] The Committee in fact wondered 'why such exchanges of views as are required could not be achieved by other, less intrusive, means (the Minister refers, for example, to the existing or proposed Commission and Council groups on health services and medical care)'.[62] In his response to the Committee, the Minister said that he detected no wish by Member States to use the OMC as a means to devise 'new legislation or new targets or new EU indicators' and that 'we are not having [new] targets foisted upon us by anyone'.[63] Apparently, this convinced the Committee: in March 2005, the Committee explained that it had assuaged its concerns when the Minister 'told us repeatedly that the application of the method would not lead to the imposition on the United Kingdom of new targets and indicators'.[64] And yet it warned the government: the Committee looks 'forward to receiving the progress reports the Minister has offered to provide. We shall scrutinize them, in particular, to see if they include any targets or indicators for Member States.'[65] In other words, the OMC might look 'soft' but, in some cases, it feels quite hard to those who are touched by it.

[60] European Commission, 'Portfolio of overarching indicators and streamlined social inclusion, pensions, and health portfolios, social and demography analysis', 7 June 2006, pp. 40–50, http://ec.europa.eu/employment_social/social_inclusion/docs/2006/indicators_En.pdf.

[61] European Commission, 'Modernising social protection', above n.44.

[62] UK Parliament, House of Commons, European Scrutiny Committee, Health care and long-term care, 32nd Report, 9 DOH (25576), 2004, para. 9.9.

[63] UK Parliament, House of Commons, European Scrutiny Committee, 11th Report of Session 2004–05, 2005, para. 9.12.

[64] *Ibid.*, para. 9.14.   [65] *Ibid.*, para. 9.15.

Box 4.4 Preliminary portfolio of indicators in the health care open method of coordination

1. Health-related 'Overarching' Indicators

Key dimension	Name/source
Health outcome, inequality in health	Healthy life expectancy (NAT).* Source: Eurostat
Financial sustainability of social protection systems	Projected total public social expenditures (NAT). Source: EPC/AWG
Inequalities in access to health care	Unmet need for care.** Source: EU-SILC

2. Indicators Reflecting Each of the Common Objectives in the Area of Health and Long-term Care

Key dimension	Name/source
Access and inequalities in outcomes (Common Objective 1)	Self-reported unmet need for medical care.** Source: EU-SILC Self-reported unmet need for dental care.** Source: EU-SILC Infant mortality (EU).*** Source: Eurostat Life expectancy (EU). Source: Eurostat Healthy life years (NAT). Source: Eurostat The proportion of the population covered by health insurance (NAT). Sources: OECD and national data Self-perceived limitations in daily activities (NAT). Source: EU-SILC Self-reported unmet need for medical examination (NAT). Source: EU-SILC

	Self-reported unmet need for dental care (NAT). Source: EU-SILC
	Acute care beds (NAT). Sources: Eurostat, OECD, WHO
	Physicians (NAT). Sources: Eurostat, OECD, WHO
	Nurses and midwives (NAT). Sources: Eurostat, WHO, OECD
	Self-perceived health (NAT). Source: EU-SILC
Quality (Common Objective 2)	Prevention measures: vaccination (NAT). Source: OECD
Sustainability (Common Objective 3)	Total health expenditure per capita (EU). Source: SHA
	Total health expenditure as a percentage of GDP (EU). Source: SHA-OECD
	General government expenditure on health as a percentage of total health expenditure (EU). Source: NHA
	Private health expenditure as a percentage of total health expenditure (EU). Source: NHA
	Total expenditure on main types of care (EU). Source: SHA-OECD
	Projections of public expenditure on health care as a percentage of GDP (NAT). Source: EPC/AWG
	Projection of public expenditure on long-term care as a percentage of GDP (NAT). Source: EPC/AWG

Box 4.4 (*cont.*)

[*] NAT: Commonly agreed national indicator[66]
^{**} Use, definition and breakdown to be agreed upon once data is available for all countries
^{***} EU: Commonly agreed EU indicator
EU-SILC: European Union Statistics on Income and Living Conditions; SHA-OECD: System of Health Accounts of the Organisation for Economic Co-operation and Development; NHA: National Health Accounts of the World Health Organization; EPC/AWG: Economic Policy Committee/Ageing Working Group.
Source: European Commission 2006;[67] European Commission 2007.[68]

At the beginning of this section, we asked why the OMC and other soft law instruments were developed in EU health care policy. It has become clear by now that the emergence of soft law with regard to health care did not just come 'out of the blue': it is the result of bargaining between different sets of strategic actors who have specific, sometimes conflicting, interests.

4. The ambiguity of new governance instruments

'Soft' processes have also been an instrument to increase the political weight of social affairs players vis-à-vis 'economic' players such as the Economic Policy Committee and the ECOFIN Council.[69] Both the health and social affairs players had (and still have) a case to defend

---

[66] Commonly agreed national indicators based on commonly agreed definitions and assumptions that provide key information to assess the progress of Member States in relation to certain objectives, while not allowing for a direct cross-country comparison, and not necessarily having a clear normative interpretation.

[67] European Commission, 'Portfolio of overarching indicators and streamlined social inclusion, pensions, and health portfolios', D (2006), 7 June 2006, pp. 7–13, 40–50.

[68] European Commission, 'Joint report on social protection and social inclusion 2007: social inclusion, pensions, healthcare and long-term care', Directorate-General for Employment, Social Affairs and Equal Opportunities (2007), p. 412, http://ec.europa.eu/employment_social/spsi/docs/social_inclusion/2007/joint_report_En.pdf.

[69] B. Vanhercke, 'Political spill-over, changing advocacy coalition, path dependency or domestic politics? Theorizing the emergence of the social

against economic players, all of which have tried to shape the terms of the EU health care debate, and expand their influence in it. Together, they have created a very crowded political debate and some political instruments whose purpose and seriousness are ambiguous and mean different things to different people.

Although the evidence is rather limited, some have illustrated the use of soft law to ensure compliance with Court rulings (soft law as a tool to implement hard law).[70] Others claim the exact opposite: that soft law is being used to avoid specific legislation on health care by 'keeping the Commission busy'.[71] In this view, Member States strategically accept soft law to prevent any further surrender of formal national competences to the European level.[72] Among our interviewees, some see it as a way for the Commission to keep the Member States busy, and divert them into a process that the Commission controls more closely than the High Level Group, while soaking up time and energy that Member States could spend blocking EU policy.[73] Others saw it as a way to reinforce the position of DG SANCO or DG Social Affairs within the Commission,[74] while at least one of its founding fathers considers the EU to be an appropriate venue in which to find and tackle (at least superficially shared) 'highly similar challenges'.[75] Governments have used 'soft' European processes as a way to blame Europe for tough decisions at home.[76]

protection OMC's', Paper presented at the Conference on 'Governing Work and Welfare in an Enlarged Europe', University of Wisconsin, Madison, 19–20 May 2006.

[70] H. Gribnau, 'Soft law and taxation: the case of the Netherlands', *Legisprudence* 1 (2008), 291–326; J. B. Skjærseth, O.S. Stokke and J. Wettestad, 'Soft law, hard law, and effective implementation of international environmental norms', *Global Environmental Politics* 6 (2006), pp. 104–20.

[71] Interview with Belgian Civil Servant.

[72] R. De Ruiter, 'To prevent a shift of competences? Developing the open method of coordination: education, research and development, social inclusion and e-Europe', PhD Thesis, European University Institute (2007).

[73] Interviews with French and German officials.

[74] Interview with European Commission, November 2007.

[75] F. Vandenbroucke, 'Open co-ordination and the European pension debate', Speech at the International Conference 'Open Co-ordination and Retirement Provision', Berlin, 9–10 November 2001.

[76] M. Ferrera and E. Gualmini, *Rescued by Europe? Social and labour market reforms in Italy from Maastricht to Berlusconi* (Amsterdam: Amsterdam University Press, 2004), p. 208.

Most EU soft law processes are just as ambiguous in their intent as Member States' calls for frameworks and legal certainty. Member States can declare that they seek good health care and a framework for EU policy and mean that they would like restraints on the activities of the Court and Commission. Anti-obesity advocates can see the Platform on Diet, Nutrition and Physcial Activity as a way to undermine junk food companies, while those companies can see it as a way to deflect regulatory threats and charges of bad corporate citizenship. The OMC process can be a way to channel Commission and Court pressures for European-level activities into a relatively harmless, ameliorative direction. Nobody, after all, will declare that they want bad, inegalitarian health care financed by a 'Ponzi scheme'.[77] Few would say that they cannot learn from other EU Member States (they can also, of course, learn from non-EU Member States. In many ways, the best comparator for the Netherlands, with its similar population size, is the equally urban Australia, notwithstanding its non-EU membership and its location eight time zones away.)

Ambiguous words are useful when there is no fundamental agreement: a combination of vagueness and homiletics will satisfy everybody around the table, defer the real arguments, diffuse them into different fora and possibly change their grounds. In retrospect, ambivalence can be seen as creating openings for new EU competences, but at the time it might look equally as if it were blocking them off. Extending this logic, instruments such as the OMC or the Platform are ambiguous processes. There would have been more efforts to block them if it had been clear what they were supposed to do.

This ambiguity means that it can be seen as increasing or decreasing the EU's competences, democracy and the 'quality' of policy debate.[78] An abundant literature has emerged over the last few years calling the OMC – and perhaps all new governance – 'weak and ineffective' and thus a 'paper tiger'. The 'delivery gap' of the OMC, which is often referred to, is predictable in view of the 'weakness of the

---

[77] 'Ponzi' schemes are a type of illegal pyramid selling scheme named for Charles Ponzi, who duped thousands of New England residents into investing in a postage stamp speculation scheme back in the 1920s. See US Securities and Exchange Commission, www.sec.gov/answers/ponzi.htm.

[78] J. Zeitlin, 'Introduction: the open method of co-ordination in question', in Zeitlin and Pochet (eds.), *The open method of co-ordination*, above n.28, pp. 22–4.

peer pressure system'[79] and, more generally, the 'design flaws' of the process. Coordination processes are therefore dismissed as 'rhetoric and cheap talk', which appear 'remote and irrelevant'. Or, worse, the OMC may even be a 'fashionable red herring', which distracts attention from other, more relevant issues. Some scholars have noticed the irony of the term 'open' method of coordination, which is perceived as being much more closed than the Community method.[80] Thus, due to its 'lack of transparency and pluralism', the OMC should instead be labelled a 'closed method of coordination' or even an 'open method of centralization'.[81]

This is certainly a challenge. How do we reconcile these negative reviews with the volume of activity and the expectations that the OMC and other new governance strategies matter? One way is to identify the necessary conditions for successful new governance. One major study does just this. It identifies three principal conditions for new governance to work. They are simple. The first two are enough to create learning mechanisms and processes, discussed in the next section. The first condition is uncertainty. The solution should not be clear. In health, this is obviously the case – much of the time, the problem is not clear either. The second condition is a 'distribution of power in which no single actor has the capacity to impose her own preferred solution'.[82] If we assume that Bulgaria, Austria, Sweden and Ireland are indeed facing the same policy questions, or at least form a useful natural experiment, then health easily fulfils those criteria. The third criterion is something entirely different – namely, a penalty for failure. We discuss this later.

A. *The OMC as learning*

Meeting the first two criteria of uncertainty and relative equality of actors means that the OMC can have an influence by letting Member

[79] S. Collignon *et al.*, 'The Lisbon strategy and the open method of co-ordination. 12 recommendations for an effective multi-level strategy', Notre Europe Policy Paper No. 12 (2005).

[80] K. Jacobson and A. Vifell, 'Integration by deliberation? On the role of committees in the OMC', Paper prepared for the Workshop 'Forging Deliberative Supranationalism in the EU', Florence, 7–8 February 2003, p. 23.

[81] S. Smismans, 'EU employment policy: decentralisation or centralisation through the open method of coordination?', European University Institute Working Paper LAW No. 2004/1, p. 15.

[82] Sabel and Zeitlin, 'Learning from difference', above n.8, p. 13.

States learn from each other. This entails discussion between different Member States that allows them to draw lessons. Going beyond this idea requires abandoning the idea of states as unitary actors and, instead, disaggregating then. Talk of state 'peer pressure' is a metaphor rather than a theory or a mechanism. States are not unitary actors, and the complex mixes of public, para-public and private organizations that form health systems still less so. So identifying the impact of any form of new governance involves understanding who engages. That is initially a dispiriting exercise for partisans of new governance, but paying more attention to networks and less attention to mythical unitary states is ultimately a better way to identify or promote the policy consequences of the OMC or similar mechanisms.

Member States have very different ways of dealing with EU matters, and health ministries have been under less pressure than most to adapt to Europe (the EU might have been important for a long time in issues such as tobacco, medical products and pharmaceuticals regulation, professional qualifications and food safety, but most health ministries are overwhelmingly focused on the organization and delivery of health services and effectively delegate the other policy areas to their specialists).

The interaction of states with the health OMC is explained by some basic characteristics of EU affairs that we can paint with a broad brush. The default setting for any Member State when presented with a new EU policy task is to handle it through its established bureaucratic mechanisms.[83] This typically involves some combination of work by the Brussels permanent representation, in a coordinating or simply a servicing role, and a role for central coordinating agencies, whose power ranges from crucial in the United Kingdom (the Cabinet Office European Secretariat) and France (the *Secretariat Général des Affaires Européennes*) to relatively weak in Germany. Most of these officials are European specialists, generalists or delegated officials from ministries with such a wide range of responsibilities that they are close to being generalists.[84]

---

[83] H. Kassim *et al.* (eds.), *The national co-ordination of EU policy: the European level* (Oxford: Oxford University Press, 2001); H. Kassim, B. G. Peters and V. Wright (eds.), *The national co-ordination of EU policy: the domestic level* (Oxford: Oxford University Press, 2000); Jordan and Schout, *The coordination of the European Union*, above n.6.

[84] Greer, *The politics of European Union health policies*, above n.2.

The complexity of the policy issues means that every Member State relies on line officials from the functional ministries involved for information and opinions – ultimately, the process is one of circulating EU papers, draft positions or policy responses among the relevant divisions and seeing who is interested and has an opinion. If politicians do not have strong opinions (as they did, for example, on tobacco control), this puts a great deal of influence in the hands of the relevant parts of the health ministries. It also explains, for example, the wide diversity of issues raised by the Member States for the SPC to consider, as these are the issues raised by the different units of all the different health departments.

Typically, ministries of labour or social affairs lead on the 'streamlined' SPC processes, and health ministries, if they are different, contribute the health section and comment on the overall statement. Every EU state's health ministry has an international division responsible for following, coordinating and allocating responsibilities for EU policy issues; these, in turn, rely on functional units that understand concrete policy when they need to prepare positions or interpret EU policy. Some countries also have strong regional governments, whose role in policy ranges from full involvement and a credible veto threat (Germany) to a legal requirement for consultation (the United Kingdom), to consultation as a hard-won victory for regional governments (Spain). Their engagement with the OMC varies: a delegate chosen from the German *Lander* shadows the federal representative at every step, while the United Kingdom Department of Health simply asked Northern Ireland, Scotland and Wales to fill out their own sections of the OMC questionnaire. At every stage, something can go wrong, and tradeoffs must be made, and there is a small subfield of political scientists who study the different ways Member States organize this process.

The OMC, like anything else, fitted into this process. International divisions of health ministries are typically charged with participating, as they know who has the data and are practiced at writing suitable statements of national policy. The problem, from the point of view of improving learning, is that international divisions do not design pharmaceutical co-payments or programmes for the reduction of iatrogenic infections. Increasing the technical complexity of a process is one way to engage line officials; international divisions, which tend to be very small in health departments, will happily cede responsibility to different parts of the bureaucracy and might appreciate the opportunity to interest them in EU affairs. As a result, the health ministries tend to be the dominant actors in working meetings such as the OMC; even in highly centralized countries such as France and the United Kingdom, the high-level coordinators usually engage only when the state as a whole is adopting a position.

From the point of view of Member States, this is highly efficient. From the point of view of the EU institutions, it is also highly efficient; Member States act as peak-level aggregators of information and opinion. Furthermore, it does not preclude exploiting somebody else's internal tensions. But, from a learning point of view, it is not particularly satisfactory. In so far as habit and bureaucratic rationality keep it in the hands of the international divisions, it is likely to remain a limited form of learning because the wrong people will do the learning (i.e., not the line officials).

In other words, new governance matters when it escapes international units and strengthens transversal specialist networks that share worldviews or policy goals (political scientists have many names for these: epistemic communities and policy advocacy coalitions are the two most common).[85] The Platform on Diet, Nutrition and Physical Activity is a notable example; it increases legitimacy and resources for some groups that were previously weak at home and absent in Brussels, while apparently empowering the 'corporate social responsibility' arms of big food companies.[86]

EU networks, such as those required by the Blood Directive, the EMEA or the European Centre for Disease Prevention and Control, bind together Member State agencies – and thereby homogenize and sometimes create those agencies.[87] They socialize blood,

---

[85] P. M. Haas, 'Introduction: epistemic communities and international policy coordination', *International Organization* 46 (1992), 1–35; H. C. Jenkins-Smith and P. Sabatier, 'Evaluating the advocacy coalition framework', *Journal of Public Policy* 14 (1994), 175–203.

[86] Cf. C. J. Martin, 'Nature or nurture? Sources of firm preference for national health reform', *American Political Science Review* 89 (1995), 898–913.

[87] J.-C. Faber, 'The European Blood Directive: a new era of blood regulation has begun', *Transfusion Medicine* 14 (2004), 257–73; A.-M. Farrell, 'The emergence of EU governance in public health: the case of blood policy and regulation', in M. Steffen (ed.), *Health governance in Europe* (London: Routledge, 2005), pp. 134–51; B. Hauray, *L'Europe du médicament: politique- expertise- intérêts privés* (Paris: Presses de Sciences Po, 2006); D. Rowland, *Mapping communicable disease control administration in the UK* (London: Nuffield Trust, 2006).

pharmaceutical and communicable disease experts to work together and legitimate a European model in each of those sectors.[88] In the area of regulating blood supplies, for example, it was necessary in many Member States to create a responsible agency that would conform to the Blood Directive.[89] The Commission organized networks that would bring together experts from existing Member State agencies and the officials responsible for organizing new ones. The result was much more homogeneity than the Directive required, as the information came from these mechanisms and the Commission's networks legitimated certain forms of organization. This European model served a reference point when the experts proposed new organizations or more resources in their home governments. It is one thing to mishandle blood supplies if they are handled on a largely domestic basis. This can be an oversight in an area that is usually low salience. Experience also shows that it can often be covered up for a short period, and, while the political consequences can be painful, they are also unpredictable. It is another thing to gather comparable data, make it public and then fail to meet EU obligations as defined by one's own experts. The latter situation makes failure more visible and failing countries are more likely to be shamed into action; at the same time, it empowers experts who promise to bring the network up to EU norms.

This mechanism can be powerful, but is highly variable. In so far as new governance penetrates within states, it is capable of strengthening and giving direction to networks that cross-cut them. These networks can become more capable of pursuing their own goals with the added ideas, legitimacy and technical support of being part of an established kind of European network. Its efficacy, therefore, depends on the extent to which it finds allies and to which they are in a position to effect policy change. Many policy instruments depend on finding allies on the ground – empowering people who already agreed with you or giving extra leverage to networks.[90] The newly empowered

---

[88] See Chapter 3 in this volume.

[89] European Parliament and Council Directive 2002/98/EC setting standards of quality and safety for the collection, testing, processing, storage and distribution of human blood and blood components and amending Directive 2001/83/EC, OJ 2003 No. L33/30. Interview with DG SANCO, autumn 2005.

[90] C. Erhel, L. Mandin and B. Palier, 'The leverage effect. The open method of co-ordination in France', in Zeitlin and Pochet (eds.), *The open method*

members of transversal networks have to be in a position to have an impact. A Member State's agreement to health targets is worthless if its regional governments or para-statal organizations pursue different goals. Box 4.5 illustrates how target setting in the context of OMC can work in practice.

These two conditions – lack of hierarchy and lack of an agreed solution (or problem) – create an environment where new governance has been shown to work. Detailed analyses of the effectiveness of OMCs that have been operational for a longer period of time – for example, in the field of social inclusion, pensions and employment – show that European soft governance increasingly is used as 'leverage' by a variety of actors, particularly through mechanisms such as: (a) rationalization of policies (e.g., initiating a culture of assessment and monitoring); (b) horizontal coordination (e.g., between and within administrations); (c) vertical coordination (e.g., strengthening of cooperation between national and subnational levels of government, and exchange of experience between them); (d) legitimation (e.g., to underpin bargaining arguments and new policy priorities, indicators and targets being key to this process); and (e) participation (e.g., increased involvement of grass-root organizations and trade unions).[91]

New governance of health care also might work under such conditions as learning and a consensus might influence priorities and policies. In fact, the Commission is already encouraging Member States that provide long-term care in a *devolved* context to adopt the kind of *national* targets that were illustrated in Box 4.5: '[n]ational guidelines and targets can ensure uniform provision across the wide spectrum of service providers and the different levels of government involved in

of co-ordination, above n.28; J. Visser, 'The OMC as selective amplifier for national strategies of reform. What the Netherlands want to learn from Europe', in Zeitlin and Pochet (eds.), *The open method of co-ordination*, above n.28.

[91] Hamel and Vanhercke, 'The OMC and domestic social policymaking', above n.3; and M. van Gerven and M. Beckers, 'Unemployment protection reform in Belgium, Finland, the Netherlands and the UK. Policy learning through OMC?', in Heidenreich and Zeitlin (eds.), *Changing European employment*, above n.3; M. Lopez-Santana, 'Soft Europeanization? The differential influences of European soft law on employment policies, processes, and institutional configurations in EU Member States', PhD thesis, University of Michigan (2006).

Box 4.5 Target setting in the framework of the open method of coordination

The Belgian National Action Plan on Social Inclusion(NAP/ Inclusion) 2006–8 proposes to increase the proportion of (subsidized) social housing for rent as a percentage of the total number of private households according to the following timeline:

2003	2004	2008	2010
6.2%	6.3%	7%	8%

Importantly, these are (national) 'Belgian' targets, whereas housing is mainly a subnational (regional) competence in this country. Hamel and Vanhercke have identified a number of effects of setting national targets for subnational competencies, which:

- puts pressure on increased coordination of regional policies (if the regions do not perform well, the national targets may be missed as well);
- strengthens the demand for coordination at the national level since some kind of institution has to do the job (even if the subnational level has the bulk of the competencies in a given issue area);
- increases the visibility and legitimacy of the issues at stake, which are, as a consequence, picked up by a wider range of stakeholders; and
- puts pressure on the strengthening of national statistical capacity, as well as of tools for monitoring and evaluating social policies (without these, there is no way to check whether targets have been met).

Source: Hamel and Vanhercke.[92]

---

[92] M.-P. Hamel and B. Vanhercke, 'The OMC and domestic social policymaking in Belgium and France: window dressing, one-way impact, or reciprocal influence?', in M. Heidenreich and J. Zeitlin (eds.), *Changing European employment and welfare regimes: the influence of the open method of coordination on national labour market and social welfare reforms* (London: Routledge, forthcoming 2009).

the management and financing of long-term care services'.[93] There is no *a priori* reason why such targets could not be extended later on to, say, drug prescriptions for general practitioners or other health related issues. The operation of other soft law mechanisms (economic policies, employment, social inclusion) has made it very clear that once target setting has become an accepted instrument of a given OMC, the pressure to establish national or even EU-wide targets is hard to ignore for any Member State.[94] This will create serious new questions for regional governments that value their autonomy, as well as important new opportunities for those who prefer shared standards.

But it need not work. It will work principally if the learning mechanisms create or empower transversal health networks within Member States.

B. *The OMC as soft law*

Learning can be good, but any process with no hierarchy and no agreed solutions can degenerate into a conference. Sabel and Zeitlin add, therefore, that experimental governance will be most powerful when there is an unattractive 'default penalty' – i.e., something worse that will happen if the experimental governance fails. This can include a 'destabilization regime', in which the direction of policy creates a search for alternatives 'by in effect terrorizing them into undertaking a search for novel solutions'.[95]

The history of health care policy clearly has such a feature – the penalty for lack of action is progressive submission to internal market law as extended in an unpredictable, case-by-case manner. So far, this destabilization has terrorized interest groups and states alike into paying much more attention to EU health care policy (the High Level Process of Reflection on Patient Mobility is the instrument most clearly intended to head off the Court, and the initial Services Directive proposal contains the most clearly 'terrifying' default penalty). The ultimate question is whether any of the soft law instruments

[93] European Commission, 'Joint report on social protection and social inclusion 2008: social inclusion, pensions, healthcare and long-term care', Directorate-General for Employment, Social Affairs and Equal Opportunities (2008), p. 90, http://ec.europa.eu/employment_social/spsi/docs/social_inclusion/2008/joint_report_En.pdf.

[94] Hamel and Vanhercke, 'The OMC and domestic social policymaking', above n.3.

[95] Sabel and Zeitlin, 'Learning from difference', above n.8, p. 39.

will prevent the default penalty. Will a properly functioning OMC, or High Level Group, or something else, slow or stop Article 49 juris-prudence, state aid and competition cases that are assimilating health into the internal market? Will participation in these new governance processes increase the Member States' willingness to accept new ('positive') EU legislation in this politically sensitive area?

There is, of course, no textbook reason why the ECJ should listen to the OMC or the conclusions of other new governance mechanisms such as the Platform or the High Level Groups. So the analytically conserva-tive answer is that new governance is irrelevant. But that is not the way that courts in general or the ECJ in particular work. Courts engage in dialogue, more or less formally, with other institutions, and rarely make decisions that frontally attack a strong consensus. Consider the health decisions alone: they began with almost comically small issues (orthodontia and spectacles in Luxembourg), constantly reiterated that Member States are responsible for their health services, and neverthe-less created a large and novel jurisprudence of health care.

If that is the case, then the statements of consensus from new governance can head off the Court by allowing certain DGs, inter-est groups and Member States to take a unified stance. There have been legal and political science studies of the Court that specifically ask how it tends to take sides in its decisions. It shows no favours to Member States and is neutral towards the European Parliament, but the strongest finding is that it generally defers to the positions of the European Commission.[96] When it evaluates a policy, it engages in 'majoritarian activism': it sides with a majority of Member States, hammering down the ones that stick out.[97]

This argument is to some extent conjecture. There are no studies of the specific effects of the OMC on the Court's decisions because there are not enough decisions and the mechanisms would be methodo-logically difficult to find, but the Court has been shown to participate in these dialogues – or, as political scientists would have it, be sensi-tive to the political consequences of its decisions. It also means that

---

[96] J. Jupille, *Procedural politics: issues, influence and institutional choice in the European Union* (Cambridge: Cambridge University Press, 2004); A. Stone Sweet, 'Judicial authority and market integration in Europe', in T. Ginsburg and R. A. Kagan (eds.), *Institutions and public law: comparative approaches* (Frankfurt: PIE-Peter Lang, 2005).

[97] M. Poiares Maduro, *We the Court: the European Court of Justice and the European economic constitution* (Oxford: Hart, 1998).

new governance need not actually change any health policy; its ability to make consensus statements that deter the Court from further advancing internal market law is independent of its ability to change or improve health systems. Of course, a block on the Court's liberalizing direction in policy (and future legislation such as the Services Directive), and the option of learning and policy change, is what the 'social' and 'health' groups seek.

5. New governance in EU health policy: what future?

We began by pointing out that new governance instruments in EU health policy share the burden of confusion that has always surrounded the concept. That confusion is not surprising, given that 'new governance' mechanisms are not new and do not always produce governance. But they are obviously rife in the EU as a whole, and the EU has done us the service of making them explicit and giving them names such as OMC and High Level Group. We found an answer to the question of what new EU governance is in the 'steering mechanisms' of Senden's typology.

Second, we asked why new governance has developed in EU health care. The answer was a political story of a competition to frame EU health policy as an economic (internal market), social or health policy issue. That framing would determine the debates and possible responses. The new governance mechanisms emerged as a reaction of those focused on social and health policies to the development of EU law – principally, decisions by the ECJ but also the pressures of European Monetary Union. The direction of ECJ decisions both created an EU competence and gave it a concrete form – the internal market (patient mobility), state aids, competition and public procurement law. That form did not reflect the priorities, values or expertise found in health systems. Consequently, health ministries and health interest groups were at least grudgingly receptive to the Commission when it proposed new governance mechanisms; the OMC and the High Level Group (and the later Platforms).

Third, we asked what might be the effect now that the new governance mechanisms have been created. In health, they are both recent and still provisional, as reflected by the recent emergence of EU health policy issues and the reluctance of Member States to permit even this relatively unthreatening expansion of EU competence. But there are conditions, identified in studies of the most-researched mechanisms (the OMCs for other policy areas), that allow us to judge the likelihood of an effect. We found that there are two conditions that health easily satisfies: lack of hierarchy and lack of agreed solutions. Those are both fertile ground for networks, but not necessarily learning or the development of binding norms. Learning and norms depend on the extent to which Member States' officials and interest groups engage and use new governance mechanisms as leverage. The third condition that new governance mechanisms generally satisfy (if they are effective) is an unattractive default penalty. While the unattractiveness of the default penalty – market-oriented policy-making by the ECJ – is clear, the extent to which new governance would prevent it is not clear. Nor is it clear that new governance mechanisms would have to actually affect health systems or policies in order to 'head off' the Court. New governance might affect policy without staving off the expansion of internal market law, and it might equally deter the Court and DG MARKT without affecting a single doctor or patient, and it might achieve almost nothing.

What, then, is the likely future of new governance in health policy? Understanding the likely influences requires understanding its practical and institutional context. This means understanding that new governance mechanisms compete for time and political attention with other health policy issues – and that they are tools of political actors with distinct interests. We identify the basic problem, which is that new governance tools are both competitive with each other (time spent on the OMC might be time subtracted from time spent on the Platform) and are at this point part of a contest over the nature and priorities of EU health policy. So, they might be abandoned if Member States do not get adequate use out of them. Furthermore, they might be abandoned if one or more EU institution dislikes their consequences.

The following subsections identify the cost that new governance imposes on EU institutions and Member States in relation to the benefits. We think them sufficient to keep new governance mechanisms alive, even if they might not be sufficient to shape policy or carry the day for a social or health framing of EU health policy.

A. Using scarce resources

One obvious conclusion from the step-by-step retracing of the emergence and development of EU soft law on health care is that this is a very crowded place, even if we have simplified by leaving a number of processes and groups – and the whole structure of comitology – out of this chapter.[98] Different combinations of interest groups, Member States, Commission DGs and individual entrepreneurs have created, in a remarkably short time span, (multiple) networks, (high level) committees, groups, reflection processes, forums and the like, each of them with the aim of influencing, through 'soft' (as opposed to legal) tools such as deliberation, some aspect of Member States' health care policies. As we have shown, this influence of soft law is by no means 'automatic' or the isolated work of 'experts and bureaucrats', but is shaped through 'hardboiled' politics in the national and EU arenas.

In real life, the same people (high-level civil servants and political advisors) are in charge of following several (if not all) of these health care processes, and they must decide how much to invest in them, and what they can draw from them. Their time is scarce. This finding concurs with the fact that many contributors (in particular, several national governments) to the Commission's consultation on a Community action on health care services were 'concerned about division or duplication of work on health care between different bodies at European level, and argued for a rationalization of activities and resources concerning health care at Community level'.[99] More pragmatically, three interviewees (one in Germany, two in Spain) asked, at the end of an interview, why the OMC was such a focus of academic attention instead of more important health issues. But it also crosscuts the logic of learning – while the processes can look duplicative to an international department of a ministry, a line official might only see and value (or be annoyed by) a single thread.

B. Commission ... Council, Member States ... Parliament

The second likely influence on the future is the role of the different EU institutions. Above all, this means the role of the Commission. The

---

[98] Greer, 'Choosing paths', above n.34.
[99] European Commission, 'Summary report of the responses to the consultation regarding "Community action on health services"', SEC (2006) 1195/4, , 20 April 2007, p. 32.

Commission is the key actor in any of these processes; for instance, by framing the same issue differently in different contexts to persuade the Member States, by creating new allies from scratch (for example, by inventing the European Health Forum or European patient groups), but also with regard to the timing of releasing, or putting on hold, communications, reports, etc. Thereby, the Commission, from a very early stage, set the terms of the debate, brought along the Member States when they dragged their feet, and made different new governance mechanisms operational in an incremental way.

The Commission naturally has its own preferences: the High Level Working Group's on-again, off-again history is in large part due to those preferences. The Group is largely an intergovernmental body that writes its own reports – and has a far higher degree of autonomy from the Commission than that enjoyed by other consultative groups. This naturally makes it the Commission's least favorite group. It is moribund now, and the Commission helped make it so. One simple way to do this is to avoid calling Working Group meetings. Another is to avoid making its documents public. Working Groups met in 2006 and 2007, but less and less often. The Commission's (Europa) web site, which most researchers take as a complete record of EU activities, did not post all of the results of the Group's meetings; an official showed one of us dozens of emails asking the Commission to post the minutes of Working Group meetings. Those minutes never did appear on Europa, and the best that Member State officials could do was insert obscure references in the 2006 annual report.[100] This combination of laggardly secretarial work and bad web management might have been a reflection of Commission priorities (which do not include helping out with intergovernmental policy forums) and might have been strategic, knocking off a competitor to the Commission's chosen fora. Either way, they helped smother the High Level Group. It gained a reprieve, then, from the delays to the proposed directive on health services. DG SANCO made moves to revive it in early 2008 when the directive faced troubles and the DG needed some ongoing forum in which to develop health policy.

This is not to say that Member States do not play an important role in all this. Both individual Member States (e.g., the Belgian

[100] European Commission, 'Work of the High Level Group in 2006', HLG/2006/8, 10 October 2006.

and Spanish Presidencies in 2001 and 2002) and small groups of Member States do have an important influence on the debates, especially when they manage to set up networks that include national and European civil servants, academics and politicians. Now that Member States have discovered the potential of this OMC, they have circularized their health departments, which predictably has flooded the agenda (see also section three above). The real meaning of the OMC remains in dispute, and Member States' attitudes vary. In late 2007, one French interviewee became very irritated when one of us suggested that his country supports the OMC, arguing that it was a waste of time and diverted Member State attention from the real Commission agenda. British officials agreed in less pungent terms.

The one actor that is largely absent from this story, however, is the European Parliament. In that sense, one can understand why it recently complained about the institutional and legal (read, democratic) implications of the use of 'soft law' instruments.[101] This is hardly surprising: many efforts to increase the legitimacy of EU policy, including these, rely on interest representation, rather than procedural democracy.[102]

These factors point to more new governance in the future. The Commission is the most active EU institution, and its fragmentation and internal competition generally enhance its entrepreneurialism. As a result, it is likely to continue offering new governance mechanisms in much the same way that it offered the High Level Group to health policy communities and the OMC to more socially engaged groups.

C. Persistence and usefulness

Against the context of scarce resources and elective affinities with the Commission, what is the future likely to be for new governance? Above all, it is clear that soft law and new governance in

---

[101] European Parliament, 'Draft report on institutional and legal implications of the use of "soft law" instruments', Doc. No. 2007/2028(INI), 15 March 2007.

[102] S. L. Greer, E. M. da Fonseca and C. Adolph, 'Mobilizing bias in Europe: lobbies, democracy, and EU health policymaking', *European Union Politics* 9 (2008), 403–33.

the field of health care exist in the shadow of hard law. The legal debates require intellectual energy and time, and the OMC is seen as a 'luxury' by many actors involved, who will invest time in it if they have it.

There are some strong indications, however, that formal recognition and use of new governance in EU health policy is here to stay. The Barroso Commission, no special advocate of social models or new governance, 'has continued to propose new OMC processes when faced with the perceived need for joint action in politically sensitive institutionally diverse policy fields'.[103] And in spite of all the skepticism (especially from academics), many (if not all) of the 'other' Commission-led new governance processes on health care (including the European Health Policy Forum, the High Level Committee on Health and the High Level Process of Reflection on Patient Mobility) sooner or later refer to the OMC as a 'goal to attain'.[104] Thus, the OMC seems to have become a 'template' for EU soft law mechanisms, and we have illustrated that, even within the limited field of health care, new proposals for launching OMC processes arise on a regular basis.

New governance might do better than survive. If new governance seems likely to prevent the 'default penalty' of internal market law, then it will be favoured by many more actors. The default penalty, or destabilization regime, is incorporation into the single internal market. That prospect helped explain the emergence of the High Level Group and the OMC in health. The problem is that the default penalty is administered by the European Court of Justice interacting with Member State courts and, intermittently, by allies in the Commission. If the Court responds to the OMC (or other fora), then the OMC will gain importance as a form of soft law that becomes intertwined with, and may eventually even head off, hard law. If the OMC turns out to

---

[103] Sabel and Zeitlin, 'Learning from difference', above n.8, p. 25.
[104] EU Health Policy Forum (EHPF), *Recommendations on EU Social Policy* (Brussels: EHPF, 2003), p. 7; European Commission, 'The internal market and health services', Report of the High Level Committee on Health, 17 December 2001, p. 26, http://ec.europa.eu/health/ph_overview/Documents/key06_En.pdf; European Commission, 'Minutes of the meeting of the High Level Process on Patient Mobility and Healthcare Developments in the European Union', HLPR/2003/2 REV 1, 3 February 2003, p. 5; M. Kyprianou, 'The new European healthcare agenda', Speech at the European Voice Conference 'Healthcare: Is Europe Getting Better?', Brussels, 20 January 2005, p. 6.

be a way to run academic health policy colloquia while the Court is rewriting the fundamental rules of the game, it would be legitimate for states to lose interest. Member State officials lack tools to influence the European Court of Justice; they do not lack opportunities to attend international conferences.

Obviously, there may be different reasons why the OMC or other groups are supported by those who play a role in it. And that is the case for soft law and new governance in general. It is very easy to argue that they are irrelevant, and perhaps non-existent. But they keep reappearing, in policy as well as in theory. The different mechanisms we enumerated provide the reasons why. Even if they never replace the Community method, and fail as the countermove to ECJ jurisprudence, the different groups fulfil multiple functions. Strengthening networks, opening up new possible EU competencies, contributing to epistemic Europeanization and shaping political consensus are all evanescent activities that lack consistent, visible, empirical outcomes – but which matter. And the staying power of EU new governance in health policy is evidence of its multiple functions. Even if a process fails to change policy, it might be a useful learning opportunity for officials or lobbies. By making trade-offs, such as balancing the competition and social protection objectives of health care systems, increasing transparency and discussing varying solutions to solve problems among Member States, the OMC can provide policy-makers with equipment to tackle such difficult issues. If this is indeed the case, the OMC increasingly will be perceived by the actors involved as a useful tool in the domestic policy-making tool kit. Feedback mechanisms will further ensure its continuation. In other words, new governance in EU health care is here to stay – because it serves the different purposes of many actors and is often a simple recognition of networks that exist already. The challenge will be working out when, how and why it matters.

5 | Public health policies

MARTIN MCKEE, TAMARA HERVEY AND
ANNA GILMORE

1. Introduction

This chapter considers how the European Union (EU) has discharged its obligations to develop and implement public health policy, obligations that arise primarily from its competences granted by Article 152 EC and Article 95 EC on the creation of the EU's internal market.

In doing so, the EU confronts four important tensions. The first concerns the relationship between those matters that are national and those that are international. Throughout history, threats to public health have transcended national borders, initially in the form of infectious diseases and more recently in the form of trade in dangerous goods, such as tobacco. Yet, reflecting the absence of an appropriate international architecture, responses have largely been developed and implemented at a national level. This only began to change in the latter part of the nineteenth century, when a series of international sanitary conferences began a process that would, in time, lead to the creation of the World Health Organization. However, even now, international public health remains a state-based model, involving interactions among state-defined actors, albeit through institutions established in international law.[1]

The nub of this tension is that the EU is neither an international public health organization nor a state. The EU lacks the public health expertise, resources and experience of international bodies such as the World Health Organization, the World Bank or UNICEF. It also lacks the capacity – in particular, the financial and human resources – of a state, which would enable it to deliver public health policies. Neither a state nor an ordinary international organization, the EU is often termed a 'supranational' body. However, 'supranational public

---

[1] K. Lee, K. Buse and S. Fustukian, *Health policy in a globalising world* (Cambridge: Cambridge University Press, 2002), p. 5.

health' is not a developed or recognized concept. How, then, does the EU respond to the requirement to develop public health policy? As we will see through the case studies discussed in this chapter, in some respects the EU acts, or attempts to act, as if it were an international public health organization. In other respects, the EU acts, or attempts to act, as if it were a state. Overall, it is not possible to discern a distinctive all-encompassing 'supranational' public health model that would apply to the EU. Rather, what emerges is a series of partially connected EU laws and policies that have various effects on public health.

A second tension concerns the concept of subsidiarity.[2] The EC Treaty has established a set of obligations for the EU institutions concerning the protection and promotion of public health but also makes clear that the organization and delivery of health care services is the responsibility of the Member States and not of the EU.[3] Yet, while public health and health care are discrete policy domains in EU law, in practice they are inextricably interlinked. Public health measures can reduce the burden of disease falling on health care systems, exemplified by the spectacular fall in smoking-related diseases in many countries in the past decade, while health promotion is a core function of a health care system. In practical terms, this can make it difficult to ascertain what is or is not within the scope of EU law.

The third tension is between the imperative to promote public health and the consequences of the EU's own legal system, especially those elements designed to create the internal market, within which the 'factors of production' move freely. Free trade within the internal market is the keystone of the EU's legal order, on which the processes of European integration rely. Supreme and directly effective provisions of EU (internal market) law make it possible for restrictions on free movement of goods and people within the EU to be challenged before national courts.[4] Yet, from its inception, it was recognized that

---

[2] See Article 5(2) EC: '[i]n areas which do not fall within its exclusive competence, the Community shall take action, in accordance with the principle of subsidiarity, only if and insofar as the objectives of the proposed action cannot be sufficiently achieved by the Member States, and can therefore, by reason of the scale or effects of the proposed action, be better achieved by the Community'.

[3] Article 152(5) EC.

[4] See Chapter 2 in this volume.

the free trade on which the then European Economic Community was built would inevitably have to incorporate measures to address public health risks.

Microorganisms have taken advantage of trade routes from the earliest days, exemplified by the spread throughout Europe of the Black Death in 1348. Throughout history, the speed with which an infectious disease epidemic spread was limited only by the means of transport available at the time. Horses and sailing ships have given way to aircraft, so that, as the outbreak of SARS in 2002 showed, infections can now traverse the globe in a few hours. From at least the time of the Venetian Republic, which introduced the system known as quarantine, whereby ships would wait outside ports for forty days to ensure they were free from disease,[5] governments have struggled to balance the benefits of free trade against the risks of epidemics. In the EU, this balancing act takes place within laws on the internal market. But, as we will see, the EU has also used its explicit public health competences to develop elements of public health policy that cut across the four freedoms.

The fourth tension arises from the situation within the European Commission whereby one Directorate-General (the Directorate-General for Health and Consumer Protection (DG SANCO)) has a specific responsibility for public health, but many policies that might be considered to be directly relevant to public health are located elsewhere, often reflecting other priorities and underpinned by different values. For example, although drug dependence was the only one of the 'major health scourges' to be specified in Article 129 of the Treaty of Maastricht, EU policy on illicit drugs has been developed within its policy on 'freedom, security and justice'.[6]

Although the creation of a separate Directorate-General with responsibility for public health was, in part, a response to the Commission's failure to ensure food safety following the emergence of bovine spongiform encephalopathy (BSE), responsibility for food safety now resides with the European Food Safety Agency in Parma.

Health and safety, which also might be expected to fall within the remit of a Directorate-General with responsibility for health, is instead covered by the Directorate-General for Employment, Social

[5] L. O. Gostin, *Public health law: power, duty, restraint* (Berkeley: University of California Press, 2000).
[6] EC Treaty, Title IV.

Affairs and Equal Opportunities (DG Social Affairs), with extensive involvement by the European Agency for Health and Safety at Work, located in Bilbao, and the European Foundation for the Improvement of Living and Working Conditions, located in Dublin.

Moreover, the EU has a long-standing environmental policy, with a significant body of environmental law involving matters such as air and water quality, waste disposal and noise pollution,[7] all of which have direct consequences for public health and yet are under the auspices of the Directorate-General for Environment, Nuclear Safety and Civil Protection (DG Environment).

Public health research, of which the European Union is now a major funder, is the responsibility of the Directorate-General for Science, Research and Development (DG Research), while consistent Europe-wide information on health and its determinants is collected by EUROSTAT.[8] Responsibility for the European Union's borders, a vital defence against smuggling of narcotics and tobacco, resides with the Directorate-General for Justice, Freedom and Security (DG Justice).

The EU's Common Agricultural Policy exerts a major influence on the diet – and thus on the health – of Europeans,[9] encouraging the consumption of meat and dairy products rather than fruit and vegetables as a result of incentives developed initially when the problem facing Europe was one of possible starvation rather than oversupply. Yet even though the share of the European workforce engaged in agriculture is a fraction of what it once was, agricultural policy remains focused on meeting the needs of providers rather than consumers, under the leadership of the Directorate-General for Agriculture and Rural Development (DG Agriculture).

---

[7] See, for instance, Council Directive 96/62/EC on ambient air quality assessment and management, OJ 1996 No. L296/1; European Parliament and Council Directive 2000/60/EC establishing a framework for Community action in the field of water policy, OJ 2000 No. L327/1; European Parliament and Council Directive 2006/12/EC on waste, OJ 2006 No. L114/1; European Parliament and Council Directive 2002/49/EC relating to the assessment and management of environmental noise, OJ 2002 No. L189/1.

[8] M. McKee and J. Ryan, 'Monitoring health in Europe: opportunities, challenges and progress', *European Journal of Public Health* 13 (2003), Supp: 1–4.

[9] Faculty of Public Health, *A CAP on health: the impact of the EU Common Agricultural Policy on public health* (London: Faculty of Public Health, 2007).

The provisions of the internal market also exert a major influence on public health, not only in relation to tobacco, which is discussed in detail below, but through influencing the trade in other products that impact on health. For example, internal market regulations forced Finland, when it joined the EU, to dismantle elements of its state alcohol monopoly and, not long afterwards, following Estonia's accession, it reduced domestic prices as a consequence of its inability to block imports of cheap drinks from nearby Estonia. As predicted, there has been a steep rise in deaths from alcohol-related disorders.[10] Thus, as even this brief overview shows, responsibility for the factors that influence the health of Europe's population is dispersed widely within the Commission.

Given the scope of public health at the level of the EU, it is necessary to be selective. This chapter begins by setting out the legal framework for the EU's competence in public health, discussing the Treaty provisions and the regulations governing the EU's public health programmes. It then examines the challenges faced by the EU in developing public health policy through two case studies: communicable diseases and tobacco. The case studies reflect a range of different types of EU activity, including both 'hard law' and 'soft law' responses, as well as the development of EU-level policies in these fields. The two examples selected also represent areas of significant political and social impact, where the EU's involvement has enjoyed a relatively high profile. The chapter concludes with a summary of the key interactions between EU law and policy in the area of public health, and some thoughts on its future trajectory.

2. The EU's competence in public health

A. *The Treaty*

Although Article 100A(3) of the 1987 Single European Act required the Commission when taking harmonizing measures to take as a base for its proposals a high level of health protection, it was not until the Treaty of Maastricht entered into force in 1993 that the EU had

---

[10] A. Koski, R. Sirén, E. Vuori and K. Poikolainen, 'Alcohol tax cuts and increase in alcohol-positive sudden deaths: a time-series intervention analysis', *Addiction* 102 (2007), 362–8.

explicit competence in the field of public health. Amendments to the EC Treaty in the Maastricht Treaty, Articles 3(o) and 129, stipulated that the Community should contribute to the attainment of a high level of health protection and identified two areas for Community action: disease prevention and health protection. This stipulation was strengthened in the 1997 Amsterdam Treaty through Article 152 EC. Article 152(1) EC requires the EU to 'mainstream' health protection, by 'ensur[ing] a high level of human health protection' in all its policies and activities. This confers upon the Commission – and, specifically, DG SANCO – a responsibility to ensure that this is the case, implying a duty to conduct health impact assessments of EU policies. However, DG SANCO's capacity to do so is extremely limited and commentators have noted how some EU policies clearly do not ensure a high level of human health protection, most notably subsidies for tobacco production,[11] which will only be phased out by 2010.

The EU's action complements national policies. It must 'be directed towards improving public health, preventing human illness and diseases, and obviating sources of danger to human health'. It must tackle 'the major health scourges, by promoting research into their causes, their transmission and their prevention, as well as health information and education'. In 1999, when the Treaty of Amsterdam entered into force, this part of Article 152 EC was significantly expanded from the Maastricht mandate, in response to the BSE crisis.[12]

Article 152(2) sets out the division of powers between the Member States and the EU institutions in the field of public health. Member States are obliged to coordinate their public health policies and programmes, in liaison with the Commission. The provision makes it clear that, in accordance with the principle of subsidiarity, the main responsibility for public health remains firmly with the Member States. This is emphasized by sub-paragraph 5, which provides that 'Community action in the field of public health shall fully respect the responsibilities of the Member States for the organization and

---

[11] L. Joossens and M. Raw, 'Are tobacco subsidies a misuse of public funds?', *British Medical Journal* 30 (1996), 832–5.

[12] T. Hervey, 'The legal basis of European Community public health policy', in M. McKee, E. Mossialos and R. Baeten (eds.), *The impact of EU law on health care systems* (Brussels: PIE-Peter Lang, 2002); T. Hervey and J. McHale, *Health law and the European Union* (Cambridge: Cambridge University Press, 2004).

delivery of health services and medical care'. Presumably, the main concern of the Member States in agreeing this part of Article 152 was the preservation of national competence over the financing of national health systems, a matter of ongoing (at the time of writing) debate within and beyond the Commission.[13]

Article 152(4) sets out the procedures by which the EU institutions may act in the health field, and delimits the types of measures that may be enacted. Two types of legislation are envisaged: 'measures' and 'incentive measures'. The 'incentive measures' of Article 152(4)(c) are the basis for the various European Commission-funded public health programmes, discussed below. In addition, the EU institutions may adopt binding regulatory measures on the safety of human blood and organs and public health measures in the veterinary and phytosanitary fields. Some of these provisions, especially those in Article 152(4)(b), are not an extension of Community competence, as they refer to areas of well-established EU policy – in particular, the Common Agricultural Policy. Their specific inclusion in Article 152 is apparently due to failings such as those exposed by the BSE crisis.[14] Significantly, a different legislative procedure (co-decision, which involves the European Parliament and qualified majority voting in the Council, rather than the old procedure of Article 37 EC) is to be used for such measures that are directly concerned with protecting public health.[15] However, the worldwide ban on sales of British beef in 1996, and thus prior to the Treaty of Amsterdam, was imposed by the Commission on the basis of a directive enacted under Article 43 of the Treaty, which allows it to take immediate action where there is a risk to human or animal health.[16]

Other provisions in Article 152(4)(a) are more obviously an extension of the power of the EU institutions. Their presence in the Treaty

---

[13] D. Cohen, 'EU residents may be able to travel to any member state for care from 2010', *British Medical Journal* 335 (2007), 1115.

[14] A. P. Van der Mei and L. Waddington, 'Public health and the Treaty of Amsterdam', *European Journal of Health Law* 5 (1998), 129–54.

[15] Although the Council is to act by qualified majority under Article 37 EC, the role of the European Parliament is consultative only, in contrast to the co-decision role envisaged in Article 152 EC.

[16] Council Directive 90/425/EEC concerning veterinary and zootechnical checks applicable in intra- Community trade in certain live animals and products with a view to the completion of the internal market, OJ 1990 No. L224/29; M. McKee and E. Steyger, 'When can the European Union restrict trade on grounds of public health?', *Journal of Public Health Medicine* 19 (1997), 85–6.

may be explained by various health scandals concerning blood and human organs, such as the distribution and transfusion of HIV-infected blood and blood products.[17] It may also be relevant that an embryonic 'market' in human blood, organs and other substances is emerging in the EU. Using ordinary internal market law to regulate this 'market' is politically and ethically sensitive in many Member States, as these substances are neither conceptualized as 'goods' nor the object of ordinary commerce or consumption. However, 'consumers' of these 'goods' do need to be protected within the EU's legal framework. Article 152 EC gives power to the Council to enact the necessary protective regulations as public health measures. Such measures may be modelled on existing consumer protection regula-tion based on internal market provisions, in which EU law sets only a 'minimum floor' of regulatory protection and Member States are free to enact higher standards if they wish. Again, the subsidiarity principle is invoked, with a specific exclusion in sub-paragraph 5 for 'national provisions on the donation or medical use of organs and blood'. This refers to the significant differences in the Member States' legal systems concerning donor consent.[18]

Article 152(4)(a) has been used as the legal basis for the Blood Safety Directive,[19] which provides that only duly accredited, authorized or licensed national blood establishments may collect and test human blood, and sets various inspection requirements and quality control systems with respect to such establishments. It is also the legal basis for the Human Tissue Directive,[20] which requires Member States to establish a regulatory framework for the 'donation, procurement, testing, processing, preservation, storage and distribution of human

[17] H. Roscam Abbing, 'Human tissue and consumer protection from a European perspective', *European Journal of Health Law* 2 (1995), 298–304; Van der Mei and Waddington, 'Public health', above n.14; J. Abraham and G. Lewis, *Regulating medicines in Europe: competition, expertise, and public health* (London: Routledge, 2000).

[18] Roscam Abbing, 'Human tissue', above n.17.

[19] The 'Blood Safety' Directive, European Parliament and Council Directive 2002/98/EC on setting standards of quality and safety for the collection, testing, processing, storage and distribution of human blood and blood components and amending Directive 2001/83/EC, OJ 2003 No. L33/30.

[20] European Parliament and Council Directive 2004/23/EC on setting standards of quality and safety for the donation, procurement, testing, processing, preservation, storage and distribution of human tissues and cells, OJ 2004 No. L102/48.

tissues and cells intended for human applications and of manufactured products derived from human tissues and cells intended for human applications'.[21] This Directive applies to all human tissues and cells, including haematopoietic peripheral blood, umbilical-cord and bone-marrow stem cells, reproductive cells (eggs, sperm), foetal tissues and cells and adult and embryonic stem cells. However, it excludes from its scope of application those tissues and cells that are used as an autologous[22] graft in the same surgical procedure, blood and blood products (these are already covered by the Blood Safety Directive), and 'organs, or parts of organs if their function is to be used for the same person as the entire organ on or in the human body'.[23]

What is perhaps most significant about Article 152 EC is that it gathers together powers and activities of the EU institutions in the public health field in a much more coherent and logical manner than in the pre-1999 Treaty provisions. If one considered the Treaty texts alone, one might conclude that the EU can now be said to have its own public health policy, which interacts with those at the national level in the Member States, albeit one that is somewhat more modest than in areas such as environmental policy. To some extent, the details of that policy are a matter for elaboration among the institutions of the European Union. In this respect, therefore, the EU can be said to be acting more like a state than a conventional international organization in the development of its public health policy.

The Treaty of Lisbon does envisage the further 'mainstreaming' of public health, with a new Article 9 TFEU,[24] which reiterates the obligation on the EU to take into account 'protection of human health' in defining and implementing its other policies. Although this provision was already present in the EC Treaty post-Maastricht, its position in the post-Lisbon Treaties suggests greater legal weight. Yet the Europeanization of public health is far from complete, and is unlikely ever to be so given the significant constraints on EU competence that

---

[21] Article 2(1), Directive 2004/23/EC, above n.20.
[22] This means 'cells or tissues removed from and applied back to the same person'. Article 3(q), Directive 2004/23/EC, above n.20.
[23] Article 2(2)(c), Directive 2004/23/EC, above n.20.
[24] Under the Lisbon Treaty amendments, the EC and EU Treaties are replaced by the Treaty on European Union and Treaty on the Functioning of the European Union (TFEU).

are embedded in the pre-Lisbon EC Treaty and repeated in other provisions of the Treaty of Lisbon,[25] as well as the practical reality of there being political opposition to transferring further responsibility for public health policy to the EU level.

B. *The public health programmes*

Article 152 provided the legal basis for the first EU-level integrated public health framework programme. Before 2003, the EU had adopted a range of smaller programmes in various high profile public health areas, such as 'Europe against Cancer'[26] and 'Europe against AIDS'.[27] In each case, they were the result of exceptional circumstances. Thus, Europe against Cancer, initiated in 1987, arose from a proposal by President François Mitterand of France (advised by Professor Maurice Tubiana) and Prime Minister Bettino Craxi of Italy (advised by Professor Umberto Varonese), shortly after the former had been diagnosed with prostate cancer.[28] The establishment of a programme to combat cancer, even if it involved stretching the scope of European law, set an important precedent when the AIDS epidemic emerged.

The Amsterdam revisions gave the Commission a new impetus and, in 1998, under the leadership of Commissioner David Byrne, the Commission launched a debate on a new direction for EU public health policy.[29] A fundamental revision was proposed, envisaging an integrated EU public health strategy with three strands:

[25] Under the amendments introduced by the Treaty of Lisbon, Article 152 EC is replaced by Article 168(7) TFEU. This elaborates the previous Article 152(5) EC to include the sentence: '[t]he responsibilities of the Member States shall include the management of health services and medical care and the allocation of the resources assigned to them'.

[26] Resolution of Council and the Representatives of the Governments of the Member States on a programme of action of the European Communities against cancer, OJ 1986 No. C184/19.

[27] Decision of the Council and Ministers of Health for the Member States 91/317/EEC adopting a plan of action in the framework of the 1991 to 1993 'Europe against AIDS' programme, OJ 1991 No. L175/26.

[28] A. Gilmore and M. McKee, 'Tobacco policy in the European Union', in E. A. Feldman and R. Bayer (eds.), *Unfiltered: conflicts over tobacco policy and public health* (Cambridge, MA: Harvard University Press, 2004), p. 394.

[29] European Commission, 'Communication from the Commission to the Council, the European Parliament, the Economic and Social Committee and the Committee of the Regions on the development of public health policy in the European Community', COM (98) 230 final, 15 April 1998.

- improving information for the development of health
- reacting rapidly to threats to health
- tackling health determinants through health promotion and disease prevention.

The basic principles underpinning this proposed strategy remain in place today and concentrate on a limited number of priorities: to emphasize the improvement of health; to be sufficiently flexible to respond to new developments; and to be credible and convincing from the point of view of the citizens of the EU.

The first Public Health Framework Programme (2003–8) was based on those three priorities, which were set out as the programme's general objectives in Article 2 of its enabling instrument, Council and Parliament Decision 1786/2002/EC.[30] Each general objective was to be pursued by 'actions' from among those listed in the Annex of the Decision, organized by reference to the three general objectives of Article 2 of the Decision. The detail here reflects topical concerns of the health systems of the Member States at the time, at least those related to 'public' health elements on disease prevention and health promotion. For instance, 'rapid reaction to health threats' includes exchange of information on strategies to counter health threats from physical, chemical or biological sources in emergency situations, including those relating to terrorist acts.[31] Other examples include developing strategies for reducing antibiotic resistance, implementing strategies on life-style related health determinants, and exchanging information on genetic determinants of health and the use of genetic screening.

The 'actions' are implemented by EU-level support for 'activities', in cooperation with the Member States. 'Activities' may implement all or part of an action, and may be combined. The complex arrangement of 'objectives', 'actions' and 'activities' reflects a compromise position between those legislative actors who wished to place more constraints on the funding of the EU public health programme and those who valued flexibility. Broadly speaking, the European Parliament sought greater flexibility, while the Council sought to impose constraints on

---

[30] European Parliament and Council Decision 1786/2002/EC adopting a programme of Community action in the field of public health (2003–2008) – Commission Statements, OJ 2002 No. L271/1.

[31] Decision 1786/2002/EC, above n.30, Annex, 2.4.

the disbursement of EU finances for the public health programme. 'Activities' fall into four categories, related to:

- monitoring and rapid reaction systems
- health determinants
- legislation
- consultation, knowledge and information.

The last category includes matters such as developing and maintaining networks for exchange of information on best practice in public health and the effectiveness of health policies.[32] Since 1 January 2005, the implementation of the public health programme has been carried out by an executive agency, on behalf of the Commission.[33]

DG SANCO, under the leadership of Markos Kyprianou, Commissioner from 2004, commenced negotiations on the second Public Health Programme (though the word 'public' has now disappeared from its title) in April 2005.[34] The Commission's bold proposal aimed to merge 'public health' and 'consumer protection' into one joint programme, and the text of the proposal tied this explicitly to 'what citizens want'.[35] The Commission proposed three core objectives for the programme. The programme would:

[P]rotect citizens from risks and threats which are beyond the control of individuals, and that cannot be effectively tackled by individual Member States alone; increase the ability of citizens to take better decisions about

[32] Article 3(d)(v), Decision 1786/2002/EC, above n.30.

[33] Commission Decision setting up an executive agency, the 'Executive Agency for the Public Health Programme', for the management of Community action in the field of public health – pursuant to Council Regulation 58/2003/EC, OJ 2004 No. L369/73. The Executive Agency for the Public Health Programme has now been renamed the Executive Agency for Health and Consumers, see Commission Decision 2008/544/EC of 18 June 2008 amending Decision 2006/415/EC concerning certain protection measures in relation to highly pathogenic avian influenza of the subtype H5N1 in poultry in the Community, OJ 2008 No. L173/27. See also http://ec.europa.eu/eahc/index.html; and Chapter 4 in this volume.

[34] European Commission, 'Proposal for a European Parliament and Council Decision establishing a programme of Community action in the field of health and consumer protection 2007–13', COM (2005) 115 final, 6 April 2005.

[35] 'EU citizens want to live healthily and safely wherever and whoever they are and to have confidence in the products and services they consume. They also want a say in the decisions that affect their health and consumer interests. The EU, national and regional authorities, businesses and civil society must play a part to respond to these concerns, but there are common health and consumer policy challenges that only EU level action can tackle.' *Ibid.*, 2.

their health and consumer interests; and it would mainstream health and consumer policy objectives across all Community policies in order to put health and consumer issues at the centre of policy-making.

Had these objectives, especially the third, been adopted, there would have been a marked change from the first Public Health Programme, giving DG SANCO a position within broader EU policy-making that it does not currently enjoy. The objectives were to be met by six 'strands' of the programme: the existing three of health information, health threats and health determinants, and three new ones – response to threats, disease prevention and cooperation between health systems. The proposed financial framework was €1203 million.

The integration of health and consumer protection did not survive long. The Conference of Presidents[36] decided on 30 June 2005 to split the proposal into two programmes.[37] The European Parliament proposed eight objectives for the health programme. These included improving efficiency and effectiveness in health systems, tackling health inequality and empowering citizens by facilitating patient mobility and increasing transparency between the various countries' health systems, all of which would again have suggested a significant change of focus from the current programme. The latter objective arose from the activity of various EU institutions and actors[38] following the *Kohll* litigation on free movement of patients.[39] The Parliament proposed a budget – solely for the health programme strand and excluding the consumer protection elements of the original proposal – of €1500 million.

Following the inter-institutional agreement on the EU's future financial framework for 2007–13,[40] in May 2006 the Commission amended

---

[36] The Conference of Presidents consists of the President of the European Parliament and the chairpersons of the political groups within Parliament. It is responsible, *inter alia*, for relations between the European Parliament and other EU institutions.

[37] Draft European Parliament legislative resolution on the proposal for a European Parliament and Council Decision on a programme of Community action in the field of health and consumer protection (2007–2013) – health aspects, OJ 2006 No. C291E/372.

[38] Such as the High Level Group on Health Care and Medical Systems.

[39] T. Hervey, 'The European Union and the governance of health care', in G. de Búrca and J. Scott (eds.), *New governance and constitutionalism in Europe and the US* (Oxford, Portland: Hart, 2006), pp. 179–210.

[40] Interinstitutional Agreement between the European Parliament, the Council and the Commission on budgetary discipline and sound financial management – Declarations, OJ 2006 No. C139/1.

its original proposal, taking account of the new reality that, by virtue of the new financial settlement, the budget available for health was about one third of that originally envisaged. The Commission accordingly focused its proposal more tightly, around three objectives:

- improving citizens' health security
- promoting health for prosperity and solidarity
- generating and disseminating health knowledge.

The proposed budget was €365.6 million. The Commission added new foci on health inequalities, promoting healthy ageing and addressing children's health and gender questions, some of which reflect the European Parliament's proposed amendments.[41] The Council reached political agreement (unanimously) on a common position[42] that endorsed this budget and these three objectives[43] in November 2006.

A few further changes were made at the Parliament's second reading, in July 2007.[44] By this stage, it was obvious that the programme could not begin until January 2008. Parliament sought to bring health inequalities further to the fore, by including this explicitly within the second objective, which then read 'to promote health, including in the

---

[41] European Commission, 'Communication from the Commission pursuant to the second subparagraph of Article 251(2) of the EC Treaty concerning the common position of the Council on the adoption of a European Parliament and Council Decision establishing a second Programme of Community action in the field of Health (2007–2013)', COM (2007) 150 final, 23 March 2007.

[42] European Council, 'Common position adopted by the Council with a view to the adoption of a European Parliament and Council Decision establishing a second programme of Community action in the field of health (2007–13)', 16369/06, Interinstitutional File 2005/0042 A (COD).

[43] Article 2, Decision 1786/2002/EC, above n.30: '1. The Programme shall complement, support and add value to the policies of the Member States and contribute to increased solidarity and prosperity in the European Union by protecting and promoting human health and safety and improving public health. 2. The objectives to be pursued through the actions set out in the Annex shall be:

– to improve citizens' health security,
– to promote health,
– to generate and disseminate health information and knowledge.

The actions referred to in the first subparagraph shall, where appropriate, support the prevention of major diseases and contribute to reducing their incidence as well as the morbidity and mortality caused by them.'

[44] European Parliament Resolution on the Council common position for adopting a European Parliament and Council Decision establishing a

---

Box 5.1 Resources available under the Public Health Programme 2008–13

Operational Objective 1: Citizen's Health Security – €97.572 million

- Action 1: protect citizens against health threats – €65.048 million.
- Action 2: improve citizen's safety – €32.524 million.

Operational Objective 2: Promote Health – €113.834 million

- Action 1: foster healthy, active ageing and help bridge inequalities – €42.281 million.
- Action 2: promote healthier ways of living by tackling health determinants – €71.553 million.

Operational Objective 3: Generate and Disseminate Health Knowledge – €113.82 million

- Action 1: exchange knowledge and best practice – €48.78 million.
- Action 2: collect, analyse and disseminate health information – €65.04 million.

---

reduction of health inequalities'. The financial envelope was reduced to reflect the reduction in running time of the programme to €321.5 million. Both of these changes are reflected in the final legislative text.[45]

The EU's first Public Health Programme attracted considerable interest. Many more applications for funding were received than the available funding could support, with applications from all Member States. The EU was able to fund some projects under all the 'actions' and 'activities' envisaged.[46] However, it is not easy to assess the overall impact of the programme, as it lacked specific goals against

---

second programme of Community action in the field of health (2008–2013), 16369/2/2006 – C6–0100/2007 – 2005/0042A(COD).

[45] European Parliament and Council Decision 1350/2007/EC establishing a second programme of Community action in the field of health (2008–13), OJ 2007 No. L301/3.

[46] W. J. Oortwijn *et al.*, *Interim evaluation of the public health programme 2003–2008* (Santa Monica: RAND Corporation, 2007), pp. 100–1.

which its success (as opposed to that of individual projects) could be measured. Moreover, as we have seen, priorities for the EU's public health programmes are determined within the EU's normal legislative processes. There are many criteria that can inform the process of priority setting in public health, based on considerations such as the contribution to the burden of disease, the cost–effectiveness of intervention or the magnitude of future risk. The extent to which such considerations have informed the development of the EU's public health programmes – and thus what they seek to achieve – is unclear.

Concerns have been voiced about the emphasis placed on different types of projects within the public health programme. A focus on 'innovation' may mean that relatively simple pilot projects tend to be favoured over longer term or more complex activities. The competitive tendering process and the need to put together EU-wide partnerships and to secure co-funding mean that applications are likely to be conservative rather than ground-breaking. The same can be said for the selection of projects for funding. It is not always clear what the criterion of 'EU added value' means in practice.

The extent to which the results of projects are subsequently embedded into national practices is also unclear. The lack of any requirement for a 'legacy plan' in applications means that opportunities may be missed to ensure that the benefits of successful activities will be sustained into the future. Neither is it clear how the results of the public health programme can be fed into EU law and policy-making where this might be appropriate.

There is little evidence of horizontal coordination between the Public Health Programme and other Commission activities. An independent report[47] found strained relationships with the Directorates-General for Employment and Social Affairs; Environment, Nuclear Safety and Civil Protection; Regional Policy; and Development, although it did find good relationships with DG Research. In some cases (the Directorate-General for Competition, DG MARKT), it seems that relationships may be virtually non-existent. Finally, although the Commission has established working relationships with WHO and the Organisation for Economic Co-operation and Development (OECD) (as well as other international organizations), these relationships also pose problems of coordination, perhaps because the programme's

[47] *Ibid.*, pp. 106–7.

complexity makes the multiple relationships involved impossible to manage in practice.

Yet, as already noted, the EU's Public Health Programme represents only one of the means by which the EU fulfils its obligation to improve public health, prevent human illness and diseases, and obviate sources of danger to human health.[48] In order to illuminate some of the others, this chapter now turns to examine in more detail how all of these developments impact on one of the key areas of public health: the control of communicable disease.

3. The detection and control of communicable diseases

The primary legal framework on communicable disease control within which the EU and its Member States operate is governed by international law and, specifically, the International Health Regulations. These originated in the International Sanitary Regulations, agreed by governments meeting in Paris in 1851. In due course, responsibility for the Regulations passed to the World Health Organization, which, in 1969, consolidated and updated them, creating the International Health Regulations (IHR). By the end of the twentieth century, it was apparent that they had failed to keep pace with changing circumstances. Specifically, they focused on a limited number of diseases (plague, yellow fever, cholera and, initially, smallpox, until it was eradicated), they depended on timely and accurate notification by government (despite growing evidence that some governments suppressed information to protect tourism and other economic interests), and they failed to address the need for rapid transmission of information. The 2005 revision of the regulations addresses all of these concerns. Instead of verified cases of the three diseases, states are required to notify WHO of any 'public health emergency of international concern'.[49] This is an event that constitutes a risk to other states and that may require a coordinated international response. Criteria for notification include the seriousness of the event, how unusual it is, the potential to spread internationally and the possibility that restrictions on trade or travel may result. The IHR encompass not only communicable diseases but also

[48] Article 152(1) EC.
[49] World Health Organization, *International Health Regulations* (Geneva: WHO, 2005).

toxic and other hazardous exposures. Linked to the implementation of the IHR, a Global Outbreak Alert and Response Network has been established, with its secretariat based within WHO. It links a number of other networks, including the Global Public Health Intelligence Network, a web crawler that monitors emerging evidence suggestive of disease outbreaks. As with the earlier Regulations, governments are limited in the actions they may take to impede trade and travel. Any action that 'significantly interfere(s)' with international traffic, defined as refusing it or delaying it for 24 hours, must be justified on scientific grounds, as must any medical checks on potential travellers.

The revised IHR came into force on 15 June 2007 and 194 states are parties to them. They allow WHO to make recommendations, including restrictions on travel and trade, but they incorporate no enforcement mechanism. There is, instead, a dispute resolution procedure. Prior to the coming into force of the IHR, it was possible for governments to register reservations. No EU Member State did so.

The EU itself is not a party to the IHR,[50] but all of its Member States are. Although the Commission claims that some matters within the IHR are matters of exclusive Community competence,[51] an alternative interpretation is that these are matters of shared competence between the EU and its Member States.[52] Article 57 of the IHR requires that '[s]tates parties that are members of a regional economic integration organization shall apply in their mutual relations common rules in force in that regional economic integration organization'. Thus, should WHO recommend a restriction on trade or travel, the EU would have to act collectively, following an initiative from the Commission. The European Commission has published a communication setting out the interrelationships between the IHRs and EU law and has proposed a series of working practices, with a 'memorandum of understanding' to clarify relationships and to ensure coordinated responses.[53] Consequently, the remainder of this section

[50] This reflects the EU's constrained competence in the field of health.
[51] For example, Article 26 of the International Health Regulations, above n.49, on protection of personal data. See European Commission, 'International health regulations', COM (2006) 552 final, 26 September 2006, on the International Health Regulations.
[52] See Article 4 TFEU, to enter into force if the Treaty of Lisbon is ratified by all the Member States.
[53] European Commission, 'International Health Regulations', above n.49.

should be interpreted in the light of the Member States' international obligations under the IHR.

The progressive dismantling of borders within Europe – most recently, the expansion of the border-free 'Schengen area' to include twenty-eight states[54] – with the resultant increase in mobility of people and goods, has greatly increased the opportunity for the spread of infectious diseases. There are, however, various safeguards in the Treaties that have been developed in subsequent legislation. In particular, although outside the scope of this chapter, there is an extensive body of law linked to monitoring and compliance mechanisms to ensure the safety of agricultural products.[55] Here, discussion will be confined to the basic principles determining when a Member State can act to restrict the movement of goods and people on the grounds of public health.

A. Restrictions on movements of goods

Articles 28 and 29 EC prohibit any quantitative restrictions on imports and exports between Member States, *or any measures having equivalent effect.* The meaning of 'equivalent effect' was established in *Dassonville,*[56] which stated that '[a]ll trading rules enacted by Member States which are capable of hindering, directly or indirectly, actually or potentially, intra-Community trade are to be considered as measures having an equivalent effect to quantitative restrictions'. The key point is the focus on the effect of the measure, and not its intention. However, Article 30 EC does make provision for prohibitions or restrictions on imports, exports or goods in transit justified on grounds of 'public morality, public policy or public security; the protection of health and life of humans, animals or plants … Such prohibitions or restrictions shall not, however, constitute a means of arbitrary discrimination or a disguised restriction on trade between Member States.'

The interpretation of these provisions follows from the *Cassis de Dijon* case,[57] which addressed the refusal by German authorities, on grounds of public health, to allow the sale of a French liqueur on the

---

[54] Belgium, France, Germany, Italy, Luxembourg, the Netherlands, Denmark, Greece, Portugal, Spain, Austria, Finland, Sweden, Cyprus, the Czech Republic, Estonia, Hungary, Latvia, Lithuania, Malta, Poland, Slovakia, Slovenia, Bulgaria, Romania, Iceland, Norway and Switzerland.

[55] R. O'Rourke, *European food law* (London: Sweet and Maxwell, 2005).

[56] Case C-8/74, *Procureur du Roi v. Dassonville* [1974] ECR 837.

[57] Case 120/78, *Cassis de Dijon* [1979] ECR 649.

basis of its alcohol content. The European Court of Justice ruled, first, that there was a presumption that a good lawfully marketed in one Member State should be admitted into any other Member State without restriction and, second, if a restriction was imposed to achieve a legitimate public health goal, it must be proportionate to the goal it pursues and it must use the least restrictive means to achieve it. For example, a restriction on imports would not be permitted if safety could be assured by enhanced labelling.[58] Consequently, the principle of proportionality is now accepted as applying to actions affecting the fundamental freedoms by the EU and by Member States. Such actions must be suitable and necessary to achieve the desired end and must not impose a burden on the individual that is excessive in relation to the objective to be achieved.

The Court has been willing to permit restrictions not only where there is a clear case for action, but also where there is genuine doubt about the risk to health. This was apparent when it upheld the decision by authorities in the Netherlands to ban the import of processed cheeses containing nisin, even though other countries believed it to be safe.[59] In contrast, it has rejected restrictions viewed primarily as obstacles to trade, even when they might possibly be justified on grounds of public health. An example was its rejection of a British ban on poultry imports just before Christmas in 1981,[60] ostensibly because of a fear of importing Newcastle disease, but viewed by many as an attempt to stop imports of French turkeys and to protect the British turkey market.

B. Restrictions on movements of people

The Treaties also make provision for restrictions on the movement of people between Member States on grounds of public health, although the circumstances in which this may be done are extremely limited. The earliest European legislation setting out the basis for restricting movement was Directive 64/221/EEC,[61] which covered individuals suffering from certain conditions. These included the diseases specified in the International Health Regulations, active or latent

---

[58] *Ibid.*
[59] Case 53/80, *Koninklijke Kassfabriek Eyssen BV* [1981] ECR 409.
[60] Case 40/82, *Commission* v. *United Kingdom (Turkeys)* [1982] ECR 2793.
[61] Council Directive 64/221/EEC on the co-ordination of special measures concerning the movement and residence of foreign nationals which are

tuberculosis, syphilis, and other infectious or contagious parasitic diseases if they were subject to provisions that applied to nationals in the country concerned. They also included certain diseases and disabilities 'which might threaten public policy or public security'. These were drug addiction and profound mental disturbance.

Directive 64/221/EEC has since been repealed by Directive 2004/38/EC.[62] This substantially narrows the conditions that may lead to restrictions to those considered by WHO to have epidemic potential or where restrictions are also being applied to citizens of the Member State concerned. Furthermore, action to remove someone so affected cannot be taken if they have been in the country for over three months.

C. A European surveillance and response system

Formal legal powers to inhibit the movement of goods or people are, of course, only one element of a comprehensive response to communicable disease. As noted above, the 1992 Treaty of Maastricht gave the EU not only power, but also responsibility, to act in the field of public health. What is now Article 152 EC provided the legal basis for the EU's subsequent actions in establishing proactive mechanisms to combat communicable disease.

Since the early 1990s, the European Commission had supported the development of various networks linking national authorities responsible for communicable disease surveillance and control. These were very successful and there are numerous examples of outbreaks that were only detected because of effective communication within the networks. For instance, the linking of outbreaks of *Legionella* infection across Europe back to a resort where individuals from various Member States were staying, but who only became ill when they returned to their home country, enabled identification of the source of the infection in circumstances where only a few cases might be detected in a particular country, and thus the source would not

justified on grounds of public policy, public security or public health, OJ 1964 No. 56/850

[62] European Parliament and Council Directive 2004/38/EC on the right of citizens of the Union and their family members to move and reside freely within the territory of the Member States amending Regulation 1612/68/EEC and repealing Directives 64/221/EEC, 68/360/EEC, 72/194/EEC, 73/148/EEC, 75/34/EEC, 75/35/EEC, 90/364/EEC, 90/365/EEC and 93/96/EEC, OJ 2004 No. L158/77.

otherwise have been found.[63] In other cases, serotyping allowed what would otherwise seem like isolated episodes of food-borne infection to be traced to a factory supplying small quantities of products across Europe. Yet this system was far from perfect. The networks depended to a large extent on the enthusiasm of committed individuals. Geographical coverage was often extremely patchy. There was no sustainable funding and networks had to rebid for resources regularly, with no certainty that the work they were doing would be seen as important.

An evaluation of Europe's ability to respond to outbreaks that crossed borders was undertaken in 1999.[64] It reviewed a series of outbreaks involving meningococcal disease, salmonella and shigella food poisoning, legionella, and influenza, and found numerous problems. International surveillance is critically dependent on well-functioning national systems, but, in some Member States, these were extremely weak. Even when outbreaks were detected, they were sometimes not notified to neighbouring countries. The study of influenza revealed a low level of preparedness in several Member States. Funding for investigations of outbreaks was often extremely fragile and it was often impossible to identify resources in the short time scales involved. One outbreak investigation that was studied required the coordination of funds from seven different sources. There was a particular problem when resources were required to conduct investigations in third countries. Communication mechanisms were often weak, exemplified by failures to transmit information on outbreaks of *Legionella* infection to the travel industry. Finally, there were few opportunities for shared learning between national authorities and others.

This evaluation strengthened the case for change. At the time, the prevailing political climate was unfavourable to the creation of a new European institution. Consequently, there was a broad consensus that the way forward was to build on, but strengthen, the existing networks (see Box 5.2). However, the discovery of anthrax in postal packages in the United States in 2001 and the emergence

---

[63] C. Joseph *et al.*, 'An international investigation of an outbreak of Legionnaires disease among UK and French tourists', *European Journal of Epidemiology* 12 (1996), 215–9.

[64] L. MacLehose *et al.*, 'Communicable disease outbreaks involving more than one country: systems approach to evaluating the response', *British Medical Journal* 323 (2001), 861–3.

of severe acute respiratory syndrome (SARS) in south-east Asia in 2002 – events with profound implications for state security and the economy, respectively – led to a rethink. In 2004, the EU established a new European Centre for Disease Prevention and Control (ECDC).[65] Based in Stockholm, the ECDC is designed to provide a structured, systematic response to the threat from communicable diseases and other serious health threats in Europe. It complements but does not replace existing national centres for disease control and European networks. Its main tasks, and some examples of how it undertakes them, are as follows:

- Surveillance: ECDC supports epidemiological surveillance activities at the European level. This involves actions by the ECDC itself, by the various networks or by national centres of excellence. ECDC coordinates the work of the European Disease Surveillance Networks.
- Scientific advice: ECDC convenes expert groups drawing on its EU-wide networks and ad hoc scientific panels.
- Identification of emerging health threats ('epidemic intelligence'): a web-based notification system provides the means for 24-hour access to specialists in communicable diseases and dissemination of information in real time to Member States. Responsibility for action remains with Member States and the Commission.
- Training: the European Programme for Intervention Epidemiology Training (EPIET) has made a major contribution to training communicable disease epidemiologists in Europe. It enables epidemiologists to undergo training at a national public health institute in another Member State.
- Health communications: ECDC publishes Eurosurveillance, a bulletin on disease surveillance and prevention circulated rapidly within the European public health community.
- Providing technical assistance: ECDC supports networks of reference laboratories, taking measures to enhance their quality and expertise. It has a rapid reaction capacity that extends beyond the EU. It can also support the Commission in the area of humanitarian aid and assistance in responding to outbreaks in developing countries.

---

[65] European Parliament and Council Regulation 851/2004/EC establishing a European Centre for disease prevention and control, OJ 2004 No. L142/1.

Box 5.2 European networks involved in surveillance and control of communicable diseases[66]

General surveillance

BSN   Basic Surveillance Network

Sexually transmitted/blood-borne diseases
Euro-HIV   European Centre for the
                                       Epidemiological Monitoring of
                                       AIDS

ESSTI   European Surveillance of Sexually
                                       Transmitted Infections

Vaccine preventable diseases
ESEN   European Seroepidemiology Network
ELWGD   European Laboratory Working
                                       Group on Diphtheria
EUVAC-NET   Surveillance Community Network
                                       for Vaccine Preventable Infectious
                                       Diseases
EU IBIS   European Union Invasive Bacterial
                                       Infections Surveillance

Zoonoses/food-borne diseases
Enternet   International Surveillance Network
                                       for the Enteric Infections
                                       Salmonella and VTEC
DIVINE-NET   Prevention of emerging (food-borne)
                                       enteric viral infections: diagnosis,
                                       viability testing, networking and
                                       epidemiology

Respiratory diseases
Euro-TB   European Surveillance of
                                       Tuberculosis
EISS   European Influenza Surveillance
                                       Scheme

---

[66] R. Reintjes, 'International and European responses to the threat of communicable disease', in R. Coker, R. Atun and M. McKee (eds.), *Health systems and the challenge of communicable disease: experiences from Europe and Latin America* (Buckingham: McGraw Hill, 2008), pp. 141–53.

Box 5.2 (*cont.*)

| EWGLINet | European Working Group for Legionella Infections |

Antibiotic resistance/nosocomial infections

EARSS	European Antimicrobial Resistance Surveillance Consumption
ESAC	European Surveillance of Antimicrobial Consumption
HELICS	Hospitals in Europe Link for Infection Control through Surveillance

Others

| ENIVD | European Network for Imported Viral Diseases |
| EUNID | European Network of Infectious Diseases Physicians |

The ECDC has been moving forward on many fronts. Several networks have been integrated into the ECDC's activities, such as the European Influenza Surveillance Scheme (EISS), the Early Warning and Response System (EWRS) and the European Centre for the Epidemiological Monitoring of AIDS (EuroHIV). In April 2008, it increased consistency with WHO reporting requirements.[67] The ECDC is also working to strengthen links with the broader public health community, including by hosting a meeting with twenty-one European scientific societies representing a wide range of disciplines related to public health in February 2007, which was designed to facilitate networking and collaboration. In June 2007, it presented the first comprehensive report on communicable disease in the EU.[68]

The ECDC has achieved a great deal in a very short time, but now stands at a crossroads. Its role is very limited compared with,

[67] Commission Decision 2008/351/EC amending Decision 2000/57/EC as regards events to be reported within the early warning and response system for the prevention and control of communicable diseases, OJ 2008 No. L117/40.

[68] A. Amato-Gauci and A. Ammon, 'Annual epidemiological report on communicable diseases in Europe', Report on the status of communicable diseases in the EU and EEA/EFTA countries, Stockholm, European Centre for Disease Prevention and Control (2007).

for example, the American Centers for Disease Control, and its relationships with national surveillance authorities are not fully defined. An external evaluation published in summer 2008 identified potential for ECDC to extend its work into other health threats that cross borders, including environmental pollution, its involvement in health surveillance, especially in the area of non-communicable disease, supporting national systems where these are weak, and facilitating consistent definitions and reporting mechanisms, or development of benchmarks for national disease surveillance systems. However, it proposed that no decision be taken until 2013. A recent study analysing seven European surveillance systems suggested that such benchmarks could be an effective tool for comparing systems and identifying priorities for improvement.[69]

D. *Communicable diseases: a summary*

In summary, the provisions of EU law and policy discussed in this section show how the EU has navigated the tension between the free movement implied by internal market law and the potential threats to public health arising from the greater ease with which communicable diseases might spread within a single European market. Public health protection can no longer serve as a guise for national trade protectionism. International health regulations provide a neutral basis for genuinely necessary restrictions on free movement.

The EU response to the control of communicable disease has evolved rapidly since 2000. At its centre is the ECDC, which has grown quickly to become a major international player. The legal basis in the Treaty has been used to develop a secure institutional infrastructure at the EU level, and to sustain EU funding for communicable disease control. In these respects, the EU is acting increasingly like a state. However, the ECDC acts in partnership with national authorities, with whom it shares competences. Moreover, the EU does not sit at the same table as the states parties in the international public health organizations that negotiate key legal instruments such as the IHR.

---

[69] R. Reintjes *et al.*, 'Benchmarking national surveillance systems: a new tool for the comparison of communicable disease surveillance and control in Europe', *The European Journal of Public Health* 17 (2007), 375–80.

Instead, the EU tends to work alongside the international institutions, especially the WHO Regional Office for Europe.

We turn now to consider our second case study: the EU's control of tobacco. Again, we are interested in the roles of EU legislation, especially internal market law, alongside soft law, and also the use of EU-funded projects to create and disseminate information that is subsequently used in legislative processes to promote public health.

4. Tobacco control

For many years, the European Commission took almost no action to counter the health threat posed by tobacco. An attempt, under occupational health provisions, to include action against smoking in the 1983 Asbestos Directive[70] received little support from Member States, so that the most that could be achieved was a requirement to display 'no smoking' signs in work-places where asbestos was being used. Another opportunity to take action arose in 1985, during discussions on harmonizing excise duties. However, advice was obtained from a Dutch academic later discovered to be reporting to the tobacco firm Philip Morris, and little was achieved.

The establishment, in 1987, of the 'Europe against Cancer' programme (EACP) at last placed tobacco control firmly on the agenda. The EACP initially functioned as a relatively independent unit reporting directly to the Directorate-General of Social Affairs and was supported by an influential expert committee. Its first 'action plan to combat cancer' (1987–9)[71] identified tackling smoking as a priority and, in 1988, it began to develop legislative proposals. By the late 1980s, the introduction of qualified majority voting, coupled with new provisions in the Single European Act on health and safety (designed to balance some of the consequences of the internal market) made legislation possible. Between 1989 and 1992, seven directives and one non-binding resolution on tobacco were adopted. These measures represented a considerable improvement

---

[70] Council Directive 83/477/EEC on the protection of workers from the risks related to exposure to asbestos at work (second individual Directive within the meaning of Article 8 of Directive 80/1107/EEC), OJ 1983 No. L263/25.

[71] Council and Government Representatives of the Member States resolution on a programme of action of the European Communities against cancer, OJ 1986 No. C184/19.

on what had existed in some countries, such as the Netherlands and Greece, where there had been almost no tobacco-control legislation. Elsewhere, as in the United Kingdom, legislation supplanted ineffective voluntary agreements. The comparative EU-wide data generated by EACP assisted in marshalling sufficient support for legislation at the EU level.[72]

After 1992, although tobacco control remained on the agenda, the development of legislation appeared to slow, with new directives only enacted in the field of tobacco taxation throughout the rest of the 1990s (see Table 5.1). One reason was the tortuous negotiation of, and subsequent challenge to, the Advertising Directive, as detailed below. However, other factors also played a part. The Danish decision to reject the Maastricht Treaty, and evidence of waning support for the EU elsewhere, served to caution against expanding the scope of European legislation generally. The recently-introduced principle of subsidiarity also discouraged legislation.[73]

More specifically, while the Treaty of Maastricht did confer a public health competence on the EU, the creation of eight new public health programmes diverted attention from tobacco control. Simultaneously, internal disagreements within the Commission led, in 1992, to the EACP being subsumed within the Commission's public health unit and the role of its expert committee being undermined. Key staff left and the programme was left substantially weakened by what many saw as a deliberate ploy. This was compounded a few years later by the termination of the contract of the Bureau for Action on Smoking Prevention, which had supported the Commission's work on tobacco, perhaps because Commission staff felt that it was too vociferous in its calls for action.[74] This decision was supported by the Governments of Germany, the Netherlands and the United Kingdom,[75] as well as

---

[72] See L. Trubek, M. Nance and T. Hervey, 'The construction of a healthier Europe: lessons from the fight against cancer', 26 *Wisconsin International Law Journal* (2008) 804–43.

[73] L. Joossens, 'Comments on Commission report COM (95) 285 final, on the approximation of taxes on cigarettes', International Union Against Cancer, September 1996.

[74] L. Doyle, 'Brussels stubs out cash for anti-smoking group', *Guardian*, 10 October 1996.

[75] I. I. Gabara, 'Why the EU's tobacco policy is up in smoke', *Wall Street Journal Europe*, 10 October 1996.

Table 5.1. *Major EU tobacco control directives*[76]

Labelling and product regulation

Labelling Directive 1989	89/622/EEC	Tar and nicotine yield to be printed on the side and health warnings on the front of each pack. Each warning to cover 4% of the appropriate surface, 6% for countries with two official languages and 8% for countries with three official languages.
Smokeless Tobacco Directive 1992	92/41/EEC	Amended Directive 89/662/ EEC by introducing warnings for packaging of tobacco products other than cigarettes and banning the marketing of certain tobacco products for oral use.
Tar Yield Directive 1990	90/239/EEC	Sets a maximum tar yield of 15 mg per cigarette by 31 December 1992 and 12 mg per cigarette from 31 December 1997.
Tobacco Products Directive 2001 (replaces Directives 89/662/EEC, 92/41/EEC and 90/239/EEC)	2001/37/EC	Specifies a reduction in tar yield from 12 mg to 10 mg, sets nicotine and carbon monoxide limits, health warnings to cover 30% of the pack front, additive and ingredient disclosure, a ban on misleading product descriptors such as 'light' and 'mild'. Derogations on tar yield for Bulgaria until January 2011.

---

[76] Note that some of the earlier directives have been replaced by later directives, as indicated in the table.

Table 5.1. (*cont.*)

Taxation

Tax Directives 1992, 1995, 1999 and 2002	92/78/EEC 92/79/EEC 92/80/EEC 95/59/EEC	Set minimum levels of duty on cigarettes and tobacco.
(1999 and 2002 Directives amend earlier Directives)	99/81/EC	
	2002/10/EC	Requires an overall excise duty (specific and ad valorem combined) of at least 57% of the final retail selling price of the price category most in demand, plus a VAT rate of 13.04%. Introduces a fixed minimum amount of taxation expressed in euros by requiring that the minimum excise rates outlined above shall be at least €64 per 1000 cigarettes for the price category most in demand.

Advertising and sponsorship

Television Broadcasting Directive 1989 (amendments made by Directives 97/36/EC and 2007/65/EC in response to new technology)	89/552/EEC	Bans all forms of television broadcast and on-demand audiovisual media service advertising for tobacco products.
Tobacco Advertising and Sponsorship Directive 1998. Annulled October 2000	98/43/EC	A comprehensive ban on tobacco advertising and sponsorship.
Tobacco Advertising Directive	2003/33/EC	Bans cross-border sponsorship, advertising in printed publications, on the Internet and radio.

the Agriculture Directorate-General,[77] all known to be sympathetic to tobacco producers.

An additional key factor restraining the adoption of further EU law from the mid-1990s was the development of the tobacco industry lobby. Although ever present, previous work[78] suggests that it was not until this point that the industry became seriously engaged in the European legislative scene. The Confederation of European Community Cigarette Manufacturers (CECCM), established in the late 1980s, assumed a greater lobbying role, working with national lobbyists to influence governments such as that of the United Kingdom, described as 'a key ally of the tobacco industry in the European Community'.[79] As elsewhere, the industry used 'favourable contacts'[80] to enhance its lobbying position. The Philip Morris Institute for Public Policy Research was established in 1993 as 'a non-profit organisation which aims to stimulate debate by publishing discussion papers that address major policy issues confronting today's European decision-makers'. Links were built with libertarian organizations throughout Europe, with employers (especially in the hospitality and advertising industries) and with trade unions (especially those representing tobacco workers and growers). Individuals on influential EC committees – such as the European Confederation of Employers and of Unions[81] and the European Trade Unions Confederation – were targeted assiduously.

In spite of these various obstacles, the EU has developed an array of legal measures concerning tobacco control. It has also played a key role in promoting tobacco-free life-styles, including the funding of two major media campaigns – the 'Feel Free to Say No' campaign (2001–4) and 'HELP: For a Life without Tobacco' (2005–8) – and has played a key role in the negotiation of WHO's Framework Convention on Tobacco Control (FCTC). The following sections provide a brief review of these measures.

---

[77] R. Watson, 'European antismoking group loses grant', *British Medical Journal* 311 (1995), 10.
[78] Gilmore and McKee, 'Tobacco policy', above n.28, p. 394.
[79] D. Martin and D. B. Martin, 'Why Philip Morris needs the United Kingdom', Memorandum to Gerard Wirz, Philip Morris, Bates Nos. 2501207805–09 (1992).
[80] P. Morris, 'Smoking restrictions 3-year plan', Phillip Morris Corporate Affairs Europe (undated).
[81] *Ibid.*

It must be noted that since Article 129 (now 152) EC expressly excludes the ability to take harmonizing measures for public health purposes, all EU tobacco control directives (other than the Taxation Directives), have been enacted as internal market measures under Article 100a (now 95) EC. Measures adopted under Article 95 EC must be proportionate (i.e., they must not go further than necessary in achieving the aim of ensuring the smooth functioning of the internal market). This has left them open to challenge by the tobacco industry and its allies, who have now challenged all the major Tobacco Control Directives enacted since 1989, as described in detail below.[82]

A. Advertising ban

Bans on tobacco advertising are a proven means of reducing smoking, a finding that is hardly surprising given the tobacco industry's willingness to spend many millions of euros promoting its products. Yet, for many years, the industry maintained the fiction that advertising was only undertaken to encourage people to switch brands.

In 1989, the European Union banned tobacco advertising on television. This ban was contained within a broader directive regulating trans-border television services, Directive 89/552/EEC.[83] The same year, a comprehensive advertising and sponsorship ban was proposed and, following amendment, was approved by the Parliament in 1992, in the face of concerted tobacco industry opposition. It then became stuck in the Council of Ministers for many years, with Germany, the Netherlands and the United Kingdom consistently blocking it. The German Government, during its Presidency in 1995, sought to introduce a weakened compromise proposal, now confirmed to have been developed by the industry,[84] but it failed to gain sufficient support. The crucial change was the election of a Labour Government

---

[82] ASPECT Consortium, *Tobacco or health in the European Union: past, present and future*, The ASPECT Report (Brussels: European Communities, 2004).

[83] Council Directive 89/552/EEC on the coordination of certain provisions laid down by Law, Regulation or Administrative Action in Member States concerning the pursuit of television broadcasting activities, OJ 1989 No. L298/23.

[84] M. Neuman, A. Bitton and S. Glantz, 'Tobacco industry strategies for influencing European Community tobacco advertising legislation', *Lancet* 359 (2002), 1323–30.

in the United Kingdom in 1997, with a manifesto commitment to reverse the stance of the outgoing Conservative Government, members of which had strong financial links with the tobacco industry. There was, however, a delay, as the new government was discovered to have weakened its support, allowing an exemption for Formula One motor racing, a move that coincided with the acceptance of a large donation from a leading figure in motor racing.[85] Denials of a link provoked wide-spread public disbelief. However, the new stance by the United Kingdom Government did make a compromise agreement possible, although Germany and Austria remained opposed. Soon afterwards, however, Germany and four British tobacco companies mounted a legal challenge, arguing that the new Directive 98/43/EC was illegal, violated several elements of the Treaty and was a misuse of the EU's legislative power.[86]

As explained above, in the absence of a legislative basis in public health, the Directive was enacted as an internal market measure under Article 95 EC on the basis that it intended to standardize the market in tobacco advertising across the EU. The industry claimed that, because the Directive's principal aim was public health protection, the EU was not competent to act, and the Directive was therefore a misuse of power. The Court, following its Advocate General, rejected this particular line of reasoning, but did rule against the Directive on the grounds that it was not properly enacted on the legal basis of Article 95 EC.[87] The Court accepted that obstacles to the free movement of goods and services could arise from differences between national laws on the advertising of tobacco products. In the case of press products, for instance, different restrictions in different Member States on the advertising of tobacco products in the printed press was likely to give rise to obstacles to the free movement of the printed media or advertising services. But this does not apply to all types of products in, on or through which tobacco products are advertised. To prohibit advertising tobacco on posters, parasols, ashtrays and so on, which do not cross borders,

---

[85] J. Warden, 'UK adheres to Formula One exemption', *British Medical Journal* 315 (1997), 1397–402.

[86] Case C-376/98, *Germany v. European Parliament and Council (Tobacco Advertising)* [2000] ECR I-8419; Joined Cases T-172/98 and T-175/98 to T-177/98, *Salamander* [2000] ECR II-2487 (these latter cases were held to be inadmissible by the Court of First Instance).

[87] Case C-376/98, *Germany v. European Parliament*, above n.86, paras. 98–9, 101, 105, 111, 114, 116.

or in advertising spots in cinemas in no way facilitates trade in those products. Thus, the Directive exceeded its legal basis as an internal market measure because, instead of facilitating, or removing barriers to, trade, in the case of some advertising products, the Directive prohibited it altogether. This was disproportionate to what was needed to ensure the proper functioning of the internal market. The Court also noted that the Directive neither harmonized national rules nor removed distortions of competition, either in the market for tobacco *advertising* products or services, or in the market for tobacco products themselves. The Directive was therefore annulled by the Court. This result highlights the difficulty of enacting effective public health legislation in the absence of a specific legal basis within the EC Treaty. It illustrates the limitations on the EU's ability to determine 'state-like' public health policy, especially where a specific act of public health protection is politically contentious, and therefore cannot be easily justified as necessary within the imperatives of internal market law.

Following the Court's ruling, the Commission proposed a revised directive,[88] limited to measures that the Commission considered to be the minimum needed to achieve the proper functioning of the internal market. It was confined to cross-border advertising (in print media and on the radio and Internet) and sponsorship. It also excluded a ban on indirect advertising, which the Advocate General considered as having an unproven impact on consumption.[89] The new Directive on Tobacco Advertising entered into force in August 2005. A further attempt by the German Government to mount a legal challenge to it was unsuccessful.[90] The Court found that this new Directive did eliminate obstacles to trade in advertising products

---

[88] European Commission, 'Proposal for a Directive of the European Parliament and of the Council on the approximation of the laws, regulations and administrative provisions of the Member States relating to the advertising and sponsorship of tobacco products', COM (2001) 283 final, 30 May 2001. European Parliament and Council Directive 2003/33/EC on the approximation of the laws, regulations and administrative provisions of the Member States relating to the advertising and sponsorship of tobacco products, OJ 2003 No. L152/16.

[89] AG Opinion, Case C-376/98, *Germany* v. *European Parliament*, above n.86, paras. 159–63; F. Kling, 'Ban on tobacco advertising not legal', *Tobacco Journal International* 4 (2000), 58.

[90] Case C-380/03, *Germany* v. *European Parliament and Council* [2006] ECR I-11573.

and services. The Court also dismissed pleas that the Directive circumvented Article 152(4)(c) EC, that insufficient evidence of distortions to trade was given, procedural irregularities existed and there was a breach of proportionality.

While this new partial advertising ban, focused on cross-border issues, was being finalized, the Council issued a recommendation[91] concerning aspects of tobacco control that are considered to be the responsibility of Member States. This non-binding act recommended, *inter alia*, that Member States adopt measures to restrict methods of tobacco advertising that have no cross-border effects. The 2002 recommendation is an example of an instance in which the EU's competence to adopt hard law was limited, but the EU institutions turned to soft law. As such measures are not binding or enforceable in the courts, they may have little or no practical effect. However, such soft law can sometimes be a precursor to future hard law measures, when the legal and political climate allows.[92]

B. *Product regulation and labelling*

In the late 1980s and early 1990s, the EU implemented a series of directives on labelling and tar yield, again based on the argument that the laws of Member States should be harmonized in order to ensure free trade.[93] Packs were required to display tar and nicotine yields, and include a small health warning. It soon became apparent that the industry was exploiting weaknesses in the legislation. Although Directive 89/622/EEC[94] stipulated that health warnings should be clearly legible and printed on a contrasting background,

---

[91] Council Recommendation on the prevention of smoking and on initiatives to improve tobacco control, OJ 2003 No. L22/31.

[92] An example in the health field is the 'Blood Safety' Directive, Directive 2002/98/EC, above n.19, which refers to a Commission communication and three Council resolutions in its preamble. For further examples, see L. Senden, *Soft law in European Community law* (Oxford: Hart, 2004).

[93] European Parliament and Council Directive 2001/37/EC on the approximation of the laws, regulations and administrative provisions of the Member States concerning the manufacture, presentation and sale of tobacco products, OJ 2001 No. L194/26.

[94] Council Directive 89/622/EEC on the approximation of the laws, regulations and administrative provisions of the Member States concerning the labelling of tobacco products, OJ 1989 No. L359/1.

a 1993 evaluation revealed that most had gold lettering that, being reflective, offered only minimum contrast.[95] Furthermore, manufacturers were using additives to increase the addictive effect of nicotine and to make cigarettes more attractive to first-time users.[96] This led to moves to consolidate and strengthen existing legislation in the form of a new Tobacco Products Directive drafted in November 1999 and, after much negotiation, agreed in 2001.[97] The Directive: (a) reduced the maximum tar yield from 12 to 10 milligrams and established for the first time maximum nicotine and carbon monoxide yields; (b) specified an increase in the size (to 30% of the front and 40% of the back of cigarette packs for countries with one official language) and improvement in the specification of health warnings; (c) required the disclosure of ingredients and additives, along with reasons for their use and evidence of their safety; (d) established a ban on misleading product descriptions such as 'light' or 'mild'; and (e) specified a prohibition on the marketing of non-compliant tobacco products (in terms of maximum yields and descriptors) outside the EU, a manufacturing restriction that was described by the tobacco industry as a 'de facto export ban'.[98] In addition, Member States were enabled to use pictures and graphics as part of the health warnings.

The passage of the Directive was difficult. The industry and its trade union allies argued that it would lead to job losses in European manufacturing plants and queried its legal basis in light of the ruling of the Court on the Tobacco Advertising Directive. The Parliament, however, voted to strengthen the Directive, for example, by increasing the size of the health warnings, although the Council twice rejected most of these amendments.[99] The final result, due largely to the skill

---

[95] R. Watson, 'Europe gets tougher on tobacco', *British Medical Journal* 309 (1994), 1037–8.

[96] C. Bates, G. Connolly and M. Jarvis, *Tobacco additives: cigarette engineering and nicotine addiction* (London: Action on Smoking and Health, 1999).

[97] Directive 2001/37/EC, above n.93.

[98] M. Bevers, 'Rationale behind new strategy', British American Tobacco, Bates No. 325123195–325123196 (2000).

[99] European Parliament, 'Report on the proposal for a European Parliament and Council Directive on the approximation of the laws, regulations and administrative provisions of the Member States concerning the manufacture, presentation and sale of tobacco products (recast version)', COM(1999) 594 – C5–0016/2000 – 1999/0244(COD); European Parliament, 'Recommendation

of the Parliament's rapporteur, was a compromise that went well beyond earlier legislation.

The Directive was, however, subject to a series of legal challenges by the industry, which, although centred on the validity of its legal basis in the Treaty, also invoked international agreements on trade-mark and intellectual property rights. The first case was lodged in 2000 by British American Tobacco (BAT) while the proposed Directive was proceeding through the EU legislative bodies. BAT filed an access case for Commission documents concerning preparatory work relating to the Directive proposal. This case was dismissed by the European Court of First Instance, which upheld the Commission's argument that it could not accede to an access request when the documents requested did not exist.[100] Within a few months of the Directive passing into EU law, British American Tobacco, Imperial Tobacco and Japan Tobacco International (JTI) initiated legal proceedings. They focused on the inadequacy of Article 95 as the legal basis of the Directive, claiming it was a public health measure being introduced as an internal market measure. Infringement of the principles of proportionality and subsidiarity were also cited.

In addition, the claimants maintained that the labelling provisions for yields and larger health warnings (Article 5 of the Directive) and the ban on misleading text (Article 7 of the Directive) would breach trade-mark and intellectual property rights (Article 295 EC, the fundamental right to property, and/or Article 20 of the Agreement on the Trade-related Aspects of Intellectual Property Rights). Japan Tobacco made a specific submission under this banner to protect the use of its 'Mild Seven' trade-mark for cigarettes.

The European Court of Justice declared the Directive valid in 2002.[101] However, the Court did rule that the ban on the use of

for second reading on the common position adopted by the Council with a view to adopting a directive of the European Parliament and of the Council on the approximation of the laws, regulations and administrative provisions of the Member States concerning the manufacture, presentation and sale of tobacco products', COM(1999) 594 – C5–0431/2000 – 1999/0244(COD). R. Watson, 'MEPS back tougher health warnings on cigarette packets', *British Medical Journal* 322 (2001), 7.

[100] Case T-311/00, *British American Tobacco (Investments) Ltd* v. *Commission* [2002] ECR II-2781.
[101] Case C-491/01, *R* v. *Secretary of State for Health, ex parte British American Tobacco and Imperial Tobacco Ltd* [2002] ECR I -11453.

descriptors such as 'lights' and 'mild' should not apply to products manufactured for export outside of the EU.

A further legal challenge came in 2003, when seven tobacco companies, including BAT, Philip Morris, JTI and Imperial, filed separate challenges against the Dutch Government's ingredient disclosure regulations (a transposition into national law of the Tobacco Products' Directive), whereby tobacco companies were required to submit for publication ingredients and their quantity by brand. The industry claimed the by-brand information requested constituted trade secrets that competitors and counterfeiters would profit from if disclosed. In its judgement in 2005, the District Court of The Hague acknowledged this claim but ruled that trade secrets did not themselves enjoy absolute protection, and so the challenges were rejected.[102] Imperial Tobacco and others lodged an appeal in March 2006, which has yet to reach the Dutch courts.

The final challenge concerned the Directive's ban on sales of certain types of oral tobacco – namely, snuff – first introduced in the 1992 Directive in all EU countries other than Sweden, and maintained in the 2001 Tobacco Products Directive. Challenges, brought by Match, a Swedish manufacturer of snuff, along with a German wholesaler, were rejected by the European Court of Justice in 2004.[103] Tobacco industry pressure for the ban to be lifted has continued. However, a subsequent review of the health effects of smokeless tobacco products by the Scientific Committee on Emerging and Newly Identified Health Risks, which recognized both the addictive nature and the health risks of smokeless tobacco, makes it unlikely the ban will be lifted in the near future.[104] This is, however, an area that is likely to be revisited for a variety of reasons. The industry's interest in smokeless tobacco appears to be heightened by the spread of smoke-free legislation in Europe, which is encouraging people

[102] Case Nos. 207634, 207638, 207762 and 207765, *British American Tobacco v. Netherlands*, District Court of the Hague, 21 December 2005, http://nl.vlex.com/vid/39426261.

[103] Case C-210/03, *Swedish Match AB* [2004] ECR I-11893; Case C-434/02, *André v. Landrat des Kreises Herford* [2004] ECR I- 11825.

[104] Scientific Committee on Emerging and Newly Identified Health Risks (SCENIHR), 'Health Effects of Smokeless Tobacco Products', Health and Consumer Protection Directorate-General, SCENIHR, February 2008, http://ec.europa.eu/health/ph_risk/committees/04_scenihr/docs/scenihr_o_013.pdf.

to quit smoking, accelerating the decline in cigarette sales. They anticipate that if smokers were able to use smokeless tobacco in environments where they are unable to smoke, it would help maintain their nicotine addiction and thus reduce the likelihood of their quitting as a result of smoke-free legislation.[105] But public health experts have also suggested that smokeless tobacco, which has a significantly lower health risk profile than smoked tobacco, could play a key role in tobacco control strategies by acting as a lower risk source of nicotine for addicted smokers unable to quit using conventional means.[106]

C. Environmental tobacco smoke

As early as 1986, authoritative bodies in Europe[107] concluded that involuntary smoking was a cause of disease, including lung cancer. There is now incontrovertible evidence that exposure to other peoples' smoke is a cause of cancer, heart disease and other conditions.[108] It is also clear from industry documents – in particular, those concerning a secret testing plant in Germany operated by Philip Morris – that the industry has long been aware of the risks, yet has assiduously sought to confuse public

---

[105] M. McKee and A. Gilmore, 'Smokeless tobacco: seeing the whole picture', *International Journal of Epidemiology* 36 (2007), 805–8.

[106] Tobacco Advisory Group of the Royal College of Physicians, *Harm reduction in nicotine addiction: helping people who can't quit* (London: Royal College of Physicians, 2007).

[107] International Agency for Research on Cancer (IARC), *Monographs on the evaluation of the carcinogenic risk of chemicals to humans: tobacco smoking* (Lyon: World Health Organization, 1986); Scientific Committee on Tobacco and Health, *Report of the Scientific Committee on Tobacco and Health* (London: Stationery Office, 1998).

[108] K. Hackshaw, M. R. Law and N. J. Wald, 'The accumulated evidence on lung cancer and environmental tobacco smoke', *British Medical Journal* 315 (1997), 980–8; M. R. Law, J. K. Morris and N. J. Wald, 'Environmental tobacco smoke exposure and ischaemic heart disease: an evaluation of the evidence', *British Medical Journal* 315 (1997), 973–80; P. Boffetta *et al.*, 'Multicenter case-control study of exposure to environmental tobacco smoke and lung cancer in Europe', *Journal of National Cancer Institute* 90 (1998), 1440–50; Scientific Committee on Tobacco and Health, *Report of the Scientific Committee, ibid.*; National Cancer Institute, *Health effects of exposure to environmental tobacco smoke: the report of the California Environmental Protection Agency* (Bethesda: US Department of Health and Human Services, Public Health Service, National Institutes of Health, National Cancer Institute, 1999).

understanding and deter policy action in this area.[109] In the mid-1990s, for example, the industry undertook a major media campaign suggesting, misleadingly, that the risk of lung cancer from passive smoking was similar to that from everyday activities such as eating biscuits or drinking milk.[110] In parallel, it established a front organization, the 'European Working Group on Environmental Tobacco Smoke and Lung Cancer', which sought to discredit the evidence of risk by focusing, often misleadingly, on methodological issues.[111] Other challenges to the evidence were written by scientists who, as later revealed, were funded by the tobacco industry. A particularly notorious example was the industry's attempt to undermine a major study by the International Agency for Research on Cancer (IARC). The industry waged a three-pronged attack, spending more than twice that spent by IARC on the original study.[112] First, it commissioned research, directed by firms of lawyers, that would either contradict the findings or confuse the picture.[113] Second, it selectively leaked the IARC study, allowing the industry to present its own interpretation when the study was still undergoing peer review, so as to prevent the authors from responding. When the report was finally published, it was 'old news'. Third, the industry engaged in extensive political lobbying to counteract the report's findings, even managing to get the Commission to sponsor a seminar organized by an industry consultant that attacked the basis of the report.[114]

In its efforts to prevent legislation on smoke-free environments, the industry's key messages have been the promotion of cooperation and

---

[109] P. A. Diethelm, J. C. Rielle and M. McKee, 'The whole truth and nothing but the truth? The research that Philip Morris did not want you to see', *Lancet* 366 (2005), 86–92.

[110] G. Davey Smith and A. N. Phillips, 'Passive smoking and health: should we believe Philip Morris's "experts"?', *British Medical Journal* 313 (1996), 929–33; C. Colin and H. Maisonneuve, 'Misleading information on environmental tobacco smoke in the French lay press', *International Journal of Epidemiology* 26 (1997), 240–1.

[111] Davey Smith and Phillips, 'Passive smoking', *ibid.*

[112] E. K. Ong and S. A. Glantz, 'Tobacco industry efforts subverting International Agency for Research on Cancer's second-hand smoke study', *Lancet* 355 (2000), 1253–9.

[113] D. E. Barnes and L. A. Bero, 'Industry-funded research and conflict of interest: an analysis of research sponsored by the tobacco industry through the Center for Indoor Air Research', *Journal of Health Politics, Policy and Law* 21 (1996), 515–42.

[114] Ong and Glantz, 'Tobacco industry efforts', above n.112.

tolerance between smokers and non-smokers (to help maintain the social acceptability of smoking), and the use of ventilation as an alternative means of reducing exposure to environmental tobacco smoke, even though this is known to be ineffective.[115] The industry, largely through its front organizations, has consistently represented freedom to smoke as something accepted by most people, even non-smokers. Yet, even in 1995, a survey of EU citizens found that approximately 80% favoured legislation to prohibit smoking in places open to the public, including public transport. A similar percentage supported work-place bans.[116] The industry's own data showed not only that 79% supported bans and 60% supported legislative restrictions, but that 86% believed environmental tobacco smoke to be harmful.[117]

Although the EU lacks the legal competence to legislate on smoking in public places (other than those that are also work-places), it does have the authority, under the rubric of health and safety at work, to legislate against smoking in the work-place. Thus Directive 89/654/ EEC[118] required that 'in rest rooms and rest areas appropriate measures must be introduced for the protection of non-smokers against the discomfort caused by tobacco smoke'. It has also combined such binding measures with non-binding resolutions and recommendations. In 1989, the Council of Ministers issued a resolution that invited Member States to implement policies on smoking in public places, using legislation or other methods.[119] In 1992 and 1996,[120] the Commission reviewed the measures taken by Member States, linking measures by a number of

---

[115] P. Pilkington and A. B. Gilmore, 'The Living Tomorrow Project: how Philip Morris has used a Belgian tourist attraction to promote ventilation approaches to the control of second hand smoke', *Tobacco Control* 13 (2004), 375–8.

[116] European Commission, 'European survey: Strong support for anti-smoking measures', *Prevention* 2 (1997), 14–5.

[117] Morris, 'Smoking restrictions', above n.80.

[118] Council Directive 89/654/EEC concerning the minimum safety and health requirements for the work-place (first individual directive within the meaning of Article 16(1) of Directive 89/391/EEC), OJ 1989 No. L393/1.

[119] Council and Ministers for Health of the Member States Resolution on banning smoking in places open to the public, OJ 1989 No. C189/1.

[120] European Commission, 'Report from the Commission to the Council, the European Parliament, the Economic and Social Committee and the Committee on the response to the Resolution of the Council and the Ministers for Health and the Member States meeting on banning smoking in places open to the public', COM (96) 573 final, 14 November 1996.

Member States to the resolution, but conceding that it was not possible to attribute changes to it directly. In 2002, the Council once again reiterated the need for Member States to take action on smoke-free workplaces, public places and transport through the 2002 Recommendation described above.[121] In 2007, the Commission issued a Green Paper entitled 'Towards a Europe free of tobacco smoke', which aimed to explore the best way to tackle involuntary smoke exposure in the EU.[122] Responses indicated that the vast majority supported the Commission's view that only a comprehensive ban on smoking in enclosed places offers adequate protection and that strengthened action at both Member State and EU level is required to achieve this, prompting the Commission to launch a follow-up initiative by the end of 2008.

Thus, despite the limitations on EU competence in this area, smoke-free policies have developed considerably in recent years, as, one after another, Member States are acting on their own initiative to implement smoke-free public places.[123] Even in Germany, which has traditionally opposed any action against smoking, there are signs of change,[124] although in others, such as Austria, where the formerly state-owned monopoly, Austria Tabac, remains highly influential, little has happened. Inevitably, the industry has worked hard to oppose such policies, arguing in particular that they will have an adverse impact on the hospitality industry, a claim that is without foundation. In all cases where bans have been implemented, they have been successful and have been associated with an increase in support for them, including among existing smokers. While it is not possible to ascribe a causative effect to EU soft law measures, it is possible that the accretion of EU resolutions, recommendations, green papers, consultations and the like do have some impact on changes at national level. They may also eventually build towards EU legislation, in situations where legal competence exists and the necessary political allegiances can be formed within the EU's legislative processes.

---

[121] Council Recommendation on the prevention of smoking and on initiatives to improve tobacco control, OJ 2003 No. L22/31.
[122] European Commission, 'Towards a Europe free of tobacco smoke: policy options at EU level', Green Paper, COM (2007) 27 final, 30 January 2007.
[123] S. Chapman, 'The future of smoke-free legislation', *British Medical Journal* 335 (2007), 521–2.
[124] T. Gruning and A. Gilmore, 'Germany: tobacco industry still dictates policy', *Tobacco Control* 16 (2007), 2.

D. Price and taxation

In 1992, the EU adopted three directives, effective from 1 January 1993, designed to harmonize tobacco taxation across its Member States.[125] These directives relate to the three principal forms of taxation on cigarettes: value-added tax (VAT), fixed specific excise duty (imposed as a fixed amount per 1000 pieces or grams) and variable or *ad valorem* excise duty (proportional to the final retail price). The *ad valorem* tax leads to price differentials between cheaper and more expensive brands that increase as the percentage level of the tax itself increases – the so-called 'multiplier effect'. A system based largely on *ad valorem* tax therefore allows more affordable cigarettes to exist on the market, but has the advantage of automatically taking account of inflation. In contrast, since specific duties (by adding a fixed price to every cigarette regardless of its baseline price) do not have this multiplier effect, they reduce price differentials and lead very cheap brands to be withdrawn from the market. These duties have to be increased regularly to allow for inflation.

The three directives introduced in October 1992 were a compromise between those in favour of *ad valorem* taxation (generally, the southern European tobacco-growing Member States seeking to keep the cheaper cigarettes containing home-grown tobacco on the market) and those in favour of specific taxation (generally, the northern European tobacco-manufacturing Member States). The directives stipulate that each Member State should apply an *overall* excise duty (specific and *ad valorem* combined) of at least 57% of the final retail selling price of the price category most in demand. In addition, the minimum specified VAT rate was set at 13.04%, meaning that the minimum overall level of taxation on cigarettes was required to be 70%. Countries were free to set the balance between *ad valorem* and specific taxation – on the condition that the latter falls in the range of 5–55%, as previously agreed in the *acquis communautaire*. As a result, while leading

---

[125] Council Directive 92/80/EEC on the approximation of taxes on manufactured tobacco other than cigarettes, OJ 1992 No. L316/10; Council Directive 92/78/EEC amending Directives 72/464/EEC and 79/32/EEC on taxes other than turnover taxes which are levied on the consumption of manufactured tobacco, OJ 1992 No. L316/1; Council Directive 92/41/EEC amending Directive 89/622/EEC on the approximation of the laws, regulations and administrative provisions of the Member States concerning the labelling of tobacco products, OJ 1992 No. L158/30.

to price increases in a number of countries, these directives did not eliminate large price differentials. By the same token, very cheap cigarettes continued to be produced, distributed and sold.

In 1995, a Commission review raised two major concerns: that the 57% rule had widened price differences between Member States, which was not in the interest of the internal market, and that an increase in manufacturers' prices would lead to an increase in retail prices, which might result in the overall excise falling below the 57% minimum. It later became apparent that these concerns had been fuelled by the tobacco industry's lobbying effort, which had succeeded in confusing the Commission.[126] Unable to agree on a way forward, the Commission held an excise conference in July 1995. One health organization and forty-two industry representatives attended. The industry journal *Tobacco International* described the meeting as a 'triumph for the national industries'. It noted that, while Member States generally intervene or respond only after the Commission has formulated a proposal, the industry intervened earlier in this case: 'while the Commission was in the process of formulating its proposals the industry could, and did, intervene – this time successfully'.[127] As a result of the lobbying – and despite the reduction in price differences from 623% in January 1992 to 372% in September 1996[128] – the Commission revised the Taxation Directive in 1999. This change gave Member States greater flexibility in setting taxes but did little to reduce the price differentials within Europe.[129]

The Commission expressed a desire to further harmonize minimum taxation levels in order to respond to public health concerns,[130]

---

[126] Joossens, 'Comments on Commission report', above n.73.

[127] R. Garran, 'Setback for RYO: EU tobacco tax harmonisation', *Tobacco International* (1995), 43–5.

[128] In April 2001, the price differential was just under 400%, the cost of a pack of 20 varying from a maximum of £4.33 in the United Kingdom to a minimum of £1.10 in Spain. See www.the-tma.org.uk/statistics/eu_facts_figures_98.htm.

[129] Council Directive 1999/81/EC amending Directive 92/79/EEC on the approximation of taxes on cigarettes, Directive 92/80/EEC on the approximation of taxes on manufactured tobacco other than cigarettes and Directive 95/59/EC on taxes other than turnover taxes which affect the consumption of manufactured tobacco, OJ 1999 No. L211/47.

[130] European Commission, 'Progress achieved in relation to public health protection from the harmful effects of tobacco consumption', COM (99) 407 final, 8 September 1999.

and issued a new directive designed to reduce price differentials and drive very cheap brands from the market. Adopted in February 2002, Directive 2002/10/EC[131] supplements the 57% rule with the requirement that the minimum total excise rate must be at least €60 per 1000 cigarettes (and €64 per 1000 by July 2006).[132] Alternatively, countries can be exempted from the 57% requirement if they have a minimum total excise duty of €95 per 1000 cigarettes (and €101 per 1000 by July 2006). A number of northern European countries currently fall under that provision.[133]

Unfortunately, however, the new Member States, despite moving towards tax harmonization since the 1990s, were allowed inordinately long delays before having to implement the full EU cigarette excise rates. This has resulted not only in a fall in real prices in most new Member States, but also led to wider price differentials within the EU.[134] Moreover, in 2009 the Court heard a claim brought by the Commission against three Western Member States, to the effect that national rules setting minimum prices for tobacco products (to prevent using tobacco as a loss leader), breached the terms of the directive.[135]

E. Industry lobbies, tobacco regulation and EU law

It is apparent that the tobacco industry has played a key role in subverting European tobacco-control policy, acting at all levels of European policy-making. Some of its activities have involved overt lobbying, but it has also engaged in extremely influential covert methods. It created 'grass roots' smoking-rights groups such as FOREST in the United Kingdom or Hen-Ry ('courteous smokers') in Scandinavia.[136] It also used a variety

[131] Council Directive 2002/10/EC of 12 February 2002 amending Directives 92/79/EEC, 92/80/EEC and 95/59/EC as regards the structure and rates of excise duty applied on manufactured tobacco, OJ 1992 No. L46/26.

[132] ASPECT Consortium, *Tobacco or health*, above n.82; A. Gilmore *et al.*, 'Free trade versus the protection of health: the examples of alcohol and tobacco', in M. McKee, L. MacLehose and E. Nolte (eds.), *Health policy and European Union enlargement* (Maidenhead: Open University Press, 2004), pp. 22–42.

[133] Gilmore *et al.*, 'Free trade', in *ibid.*

[134] ASPECT Consortium, *Tobacco or health*, above n.82.

[135] Cases C-197–8 and 221/08 *Commission* v. *France, Austria* and *Ireland*, Opinion of the AG (Kokott) 22 October 2009.

[136] S. Carlson, 'World Congress of Smokers Rights Groups (SRG's)', Philip Morris, Bates No. 2500041706–9 (1982); P. Morris,

of front groups, such as ostensible hospitality associations, to oppose smoke-free environments.[137] Other organizations were used to present industry arguments and distort scientific evidence. One tactic that has had considerable success is the industry's support for libertarian arguments, stressing freedom to smoke, and engaging human rights or civil liberties rhetoric and law. This has been used with particular effect to oppose bans on smoking in public places, with calls to non-smokers to show 'tolerance', and labeling those opposed to smoking as 'health fascists' or 'nico-Nazis',[138] with the latter exploiting a distorted version of the situation during the Third Reich.[139] It is now apparent that many libertarian organizations and commentators, such as the philosopher Roger Scruton, whose attacks on WHO's Framework Convention are widely cited,[140] were funded by tobacco companies.

The unsteady progress of legislation to tackle tobacco within the EU is of interest not just because of its implications for public health. National politicians have often criticized what they portray as the democratic deficit in the EU, arguing that Members of the European Parliament are remote from their constituents, and that the EU legislative procedures, involving the Commission, Council and the European Parliament, lack legitimacy.[141] However, in the

'Communication – smokers' organizations', *Infotopics: summaries of public information* 6 (1987), 39; T. V. Dineson, 'Interim report on the Hen-Ry promotion campaign', Philip Morris, Bates No. 2023270359–60 (1989); D. S. Harris, 'Memo on public relations effort being conducted by Hen-Ry', Philip Morris, Bates No. 2023270361–2 (1989).

[137] J. V. Dearlove, S. A. Bialous and S. A. Glantz, 'Tobacco industry manipulation of the hospitality industry to maintain smoking in public places', *Tobacco Control* 11 (2002), 94–104.

[138] J. E. Cohen *et al.*, 'Political ideology and tobacco control', *Tobacco Control* 9 (2000), 263–7.

[139] E. Bachinger and M. McKee, 'Tobacco policies in Austria during the Third Reich', *International Journal of Tuberculosis and Lung Disease* 11 (2007), 1033–7.

[140] A. Ferriman, 'Vilified for attacking tobacco', *British Medical Journal* 320 (2000), 1482.

[141] See, for example, J. Weiler, *The constitution of Europe* (Cambridge: Cambridge University Press, 1999); P. Craig and C. Harlow (eds.), *Lawmaking in the European Union* (Deventer: Kluwer, 1998); P. Craig, 'The nature of the Community: integration, democracy and legitimacy', in P. Craig and G. de Búrca (eds.), *The evolution of EU law* (Oxford: Oxford University Press, 1999). For an excellent summary, see P. Craig and G. de Búrca, *EU law* (Oxford: Oxford University Press, 2008), pp. 133–42.

debate about tobacco, it is the Parliament, debating in public, that has consistently reflected the views of European citizens, expressed through opinion polls. In contrast, it is the Council of Ministers, meeting in secret, that has often sided with the tobacco industry and against the interests of citizens. Further efforts to ensure transparency and wider public involvement in the EU's public health law and policy-making processes might therefore benefit the quest for effective tobacco regulation.

Our account of the development of EU tobacco law also exposes an aspect of the legislative process that is often hidden – the sometimes powerful role of lobbyists. In some cases, the lobbying is targeted directly at the EU institutions. In others, it is somewhat more insidious, taking place within Member States and hidden far from view. The opening of tobacco industry archives under court orders in the United States has shed some light on this process. An example is the exposure of long-standing industry funding for a number of eminent and highly influential epidemiologists and public health specialists in Germany, a factor that cannot be ignored when seeking to understand the persistent opposition by successive German Governments to effective tobacco control.[142] It is, however, extremely unlikely that lobbying and related tactics such as have been exposed in relation to tobacco are not taking place in other areas of importance for public health.

5. Looking forward

The policies of the EU impact on health in many different ways, from the environment in which its citizens live, the jobs that they do and the food that they eat. Only a fraction of these lie within the remit of what might be described as a public health policy, and, in some cases, decisions are made on other grounds that impact adversely on health. This is despite the provisions of Article 152 EC that '[a] high level of human health protection shall be ensured in the definition and implementation of all Community policies and activities'.

---

[142] T. Gruning, A. B. Gilmore and M. McKee, 'Tobacco industry influence on science and scientists in Germany', *American Journal of Public Health* 96 (2006), 20–32.

Given the limited resources that have been available to DG SANCO, which has formal responsibility for health, it can be understood, but not justified, why, so far, it has failed to assess the health impacts of policies in other areas. However, in the medium term, this situation does not seem tenable, and its failure may even be open to legal challenge.[143] Such assessments could have a major influence on EU policy, although they would also be extremely controversial.

Turning to the areas more usually considered to fall within the remit of public health, the case studies explored in this chapter show that a wide spectrum of different roles for EU law and policy are at play. The EU institutions have used a range of different regulatory techniques, sometimes blending a variety of different techniques within a particular policy field. The spectrum of roles for EU law ranges from regulation through the provisions of internal market law, through to soft law and the use of information to exercise control and effect change.

At the more 'regulatory' end of the spectrum, restrictions on the free movement of persons and goods in pursuit of protection of public health are permitted within internal market law, although they are subject to scrutiny by reference to the proportionality principle. There is EU-level regulation of the contents and labelling of products that involve or may involve a public health risk (the example we have discussed here is tobacco products; other examples include toys,[144] products made from genetically modified organisms[145] and food for which health claims are made).[146] This is not problematic from the point of view of EU law, since these matters are regulated in order to ensure that the goods can be lawfully marketed across the EU. However, as this chapter has shown, as the setting in which legislation is enacted has moved to the EU, so the industry lobby has followed.

[143] For instance, under Article 232 EC, action for 'failure to act', perhaps brought by the European Parliament.

[144] Council Directive 88/378/EEC on the approximation of the laws of the Member States concerning the safety of toys, OJ 1988 No. L187/1.

[145] European Parliament and Council Directive 2008/27/EC amending Directive 2001/18/EC on the deliberate release into the environment of genetically modified organisms, as regards the implementing powers conferred on the Commission, OJ 2008 No. L81/45.

[146] European Parliament and Council Regulation 1924/2006/EC of the European Parliament and of the Council on nutrition and health claims made on foods (corrected version), OJ 2006 No. L44/1.

More controversially, the regulation of *advertisements* for products involving or potentially involving public health risks has also been taken up at the EU level. Part of the reason for the controversy is the lack of 'fit' between this regulation and its legal basis in EU law, that of the internal market. As we have seen, the tobacco advertising litigation, in particular at the suit of Germany and various tobacco industry litigants, has to some extent impeded the EU institutions from effecting change in public health policy. The EU's regulation of taxation of tobacco products shows a similar lack of 'fit' between EU legal bases and the public health aims behind taxation of tobacco products, which essentially aim to discourage people from taking up smoking and to encourage smokers to quit. The Court's rulings in both *Tobacco Advertising* cases make it clear that the EU may not lawfully use internal market law simply to achieve public health goals.

At the other end of the spectrum, there are areas, such as that of environmental tobacco smoke, where policy changes in the Member States cannot be attributed directly to any formal Europeanization processes. However, it is widely believed that much greater interaction between members of the public health community, supported by the EU, has played a role in the diffusion of such ideas. In this way, convergence of national policies has taken place without any direct (or possibly even indirect) involvement of the EU institutions.

This chapter began by identifying a series of tensions at the heart of European public health policy. Until these can be resolved, if this is possible, the EU institutions, with their limited resources, will find it very difficult to develop a comprehensive public health policy. Instead, they must select particular legal and policy niches where they have the legislative competence, the political support and the relevant evidence to act.

Given the constraints that they face, one area that is open to them is what Terence Daintith has called 'government by dominium'[147] – that is, using the wealth of governing institutions to achieve policy aims. Of course, the EU's available funds are relatively small, but they have been used judiciously, in carefully selected policy areas. As the EU's activities in communicable disease control illustrate, very small scale beginnings, with only short term funding, have led, through their own

---

[147] T. Daintith, 'The techniques of government', in D. Oliver and J. L. Jowell (eds.), *The changing constitution* (Oxford: Clarendon Press, 1994), p. 470.

successes and also external pressures, to large scale, more integrated sets of policy-making tools and institutions, supported by a long term financial framework. The EU has exercised influence through information collection, dissemination, development of best practice and networking. The roles of formal, hard law in this respect are minimal (e.g., extending only to obligations to report information in particular formats). Yet the overall influence on policy may be more significant than the formal legal position implies.

Fundamentally, however, those who are developing public health policy at a European level must work within the framework established by EU law. EU internal market law, although based on free trade, which can pose challenges for public health, does allow for restrictions on free movement necessitated by public health protection. Several components of internal market legislation, especially those that address consumer protection, promote public health. Examples include measures in the area of food law. However, the need to frame such legislation within the parameters of Article 95 EC leaves scope for legal challenges if the legislation is too restrictive of free movement, even if this would best protect or promote public health interests. We have seen this in the context of tobacco regulation: similar processes could be imagined were the EU to take forward legislation on the sale and marketing of alcohol, an action that would be justified on the basis of the consequences for health of existing EU internal market policies.[148]

While Article 152 EC explicitly prohibits the adoption of binding EU-level laws designed to protect and improve human health and that set harmonized EU standards, the legal basis of Article 152 EC has allowed the EU to develop the Public Health Programmes. There is also specific EU legislation on some public health areas where the EU and its Member States cooperate within existing international public health structures.

6. Conclusion

Faced with the responsibility of developing public health policy, in the context of insufficient resources and competences to develop the full

---

[148] M. McKee, 'A European alcohol strategy: will the opportunity be missed?', *British Medical Journal* 333 (2006), 871–2.

range of policies and practices that make up national public health and insufficient expertise and experience to become an international public health actor, the EU has adopted a piecemeal approach, based on the 'art of the possible'. What we have examined in this chapter are some of the pockets of public health activity undertaken by the EU. Any attempt to assess the EU's *overall* approach to public health as if it were responsible for either a state-like or a supranational public health policy would conclude that the EU has not been successful in developing an all-encompassing approach to promoting and embedding public health matters within all its policies and practices. Nor can it be said that the EU has made a demonstrable contribution to the improvement of public health, generally speaking, across all of its territory. Equally, the EU cannot possibly develop equivalent competence in international public health to that of specialist international organizations dealing with public health, such as WHO. Where the EU has been successful, as our case studies show, is in directing its meagre public health resources into 'niche' areas of activity, where there are obvious contributions to be made through acting at the EU rather than the national or international levels. EU public health activities have been more successful where the EU institutions are relatively open to contributions from all stakeholders, rather than subject to lobbying from only certain stakeholders. We therefore suggest that a valuable future direction for the EU's public health policy would be to continue to focus on specific areas of activity and to develop sharper and more precise priorities, through transparent processes, informed by evidence on the burden of disease and the effectiveness of policies.

6 | Fundamental rights and health care

JEAN MCHALE

1. Introduction

The Charter of Fundamental Rights of the European Union (EU Charter) has caused much debate and controversy since it was proclaimed in Nice in December 2000.[1] For health care lawyers, the potential impact of the EU Charter on law and policy in the EU Member States is particularly intriguing. While there is a long history of engagement with litigation concerning human rights and health care in many European jurisdictions, what is notable is the considerable diversity of approaches to fundamental human rights that relate to health. The EU has shown increasing involvement with health care law and health policy over the last fifteen years.[2] It is also increasingly concerned with human rights.[3] What is perhaps not yet so clear is how the two will relate to each other. In other words, how will enhanced engagement with human rights at the EU level impact upon health law? And will one consequence of the EU Charter be that a particularly 'EU' approach to human rights in health and health care develops?

[1] See T. Hervey and J. Kenner (eds.), *Economic and social rights under the EU Charter of Fundamental Rights: a legal perspective* (Oxford: Hart 2003); S. Peers and A. Ward, *The EU Charter of Fundamental Rights; politics, law and policy* (Oxford: Hart, 2004). The Treaty of Lisbon changes the position of the Charter from that of soft law to being legally enforceable.

[2] See, for example, T. Hervey and J. McHale, *Health law and the European Union* (Cambridge: Cambridge University Press, 2004): M. McKee, E. Mossialos and R. Baeten (eds.), *The impact of EU law on health care systems* (Brussels: PIE-Peter Lang, 2002). This chapter takes an expansive interpretation of the terms 'health care law' and 'health law', following the approach taken in Hervey and McHale.

[3] Most recently, with the establishment of the European Fundamental Rights Agency, which commenced its first work programme in 2008. See Council Decision 2008/203/EC implementing Regulation 168/2007/EC as regards the adoption of a multi-annual framework for the European Union Agency for Fundamental Rights for 2007–2012, OJ 2008 No. L63/14.

Section two of this chapter explores the relationship between human rights and the regulation of health and health care. It considers various human rights principles with relevance in health contexts, as developed at the international and Council of Europe level. By reference to selected examples, it explores some of the ways in which human rights have affected health and health care at the Member State level. Diverse national approaches to controversial ethical questions may give rise to particular challenges for the EU in attempting to construct health and health care law and policy in the light of human rights principles in the future.

The third section of the chapter focuses upon the impact of human rights principles upon the EU itself. That is, in the formulation of health law and health policy in the light of the EU Charter and the recent creation of the European Union Agency for Fundamental Rights. The chapter considers how such fundamental rights principles may be utilized in developing law and policy in this area in the future. It explores whether the EU Charter will really provide radical change or whether, ultimately, the EU Charter is likely to operate more at a rhetorical level, with limited practical effects.

2. Fundamental human rights and health care law

The discourse of human rights has pervaded the regulation of health care across jurisdictions.[4] This has been particularly the case following the Nuremberg trials and the development of the Universal Declaration of Human Rights. Human rights can be loosely divided into 'negative' and 'positive' rights. Negative rights are typically contained in traditional so-called civil and political statements of human rights. These rights statements have been in existence for considerable periods of time – in some cases, several hundred years, as in the case of the United States Bill of Rights. Such rights include

---

[4] See, for example, J. Mann *et al.* (eds.), *Health and human rights: a reader* (London: Routledge, 1999); E. Wicks, *Human rights and health care* (Oxford: Hart, 2006); A. Hendriks, 'The right to health', *European Journal of Health Law* 5 (1998), 389; J. McHale, 'Enforcing health care rights in the English courts', in R. Burchill, D. Harris and A. Owers (eds.), *Economic, social and cultural rights: their implementation in UK law* (Nottingham: University of Nottingham Human Rights Centre, 1999); B. Tobes, *The right to health as a human right in international law* (Antwerp: Intersentia Publishers, 1999).

the right to life and rights to privacy of home and family life. They do not usually involve expenditure of public resources. In contrast, positive rights are to be found in more modern, frequently termed 'socioeconomic', human rights statements. Examples include the right to health and right to education. Positive rights typically involve expenditure of public money and tend to be characteristic of more affluent societies.

Several international human rights documents refer to rights applicable in the context of health law and health policy. A right to health was first explicitly stated in the Preamble of the World Health Organization (WHO) Constitution in 1946. Some United Nations human rights documents directly address health, such as the right to a standard of living adequate for health and well-being,[5] or the need for recognition of the highest attainable standard of physical and mental health.[6] International rights declarations refer to health in the work-place.[7] Other provisions contained in international statements of human rights, while not referring directly to health, may be seen as relevant to claims for rights to particular treatments.[8] Right to life claims may be used in disputes concerning the law on abortion or end of life decision-making, while rights on non-discrimination and privacy may also apply to those with particular medical conditions and their right not to be required to disclose this. Rights declarations also commonly contain prohibitions on torture and inhuman and degrading treatment, seen as a fundamental non-derogable right,[9] and prohibitions on unjustified detention. These may apply in health contexts, for instance where restrictions or limitations are placed upon persons with HIV/AIDS.[10] They may

---

[5] Article 25, Universal Declaration of Human Rights, adopted 10 December 1948 under General Assembly Resoultion 217 A (III), UN Doc. A/810, 71.
[6] *Article 12(1), International Covenant on Economic, Social and Cultural Rights, New York, 19 December 1966, in force 3 January 1976, 993 UNTS 3; 6 ILM 360.*
[7] Article 6, Universal Declaration of Human Rights, above n.5.
[8] See Article 3, Universal Declaration of Human Rights, above n.5; and Article 1, International Covenant on Civil and Political Rights, New York, 19 December 1966, in force 23 March 1976, 999 UNTS 171; 6 ILM 368.
[9] Article 5, Universal Declaration of Human Rights, above n.5.
[10] See, for example, *Enhorn* v. *Sweden* (2005) 41 EHRR 633.

also apply in a situation in which a severely incapacitated person is denied access to euthanasia.[11]

The perceived importance in Europe of recognizing human rights in the context of health care is illustrated by the Council of Europe's Convention on Human Rights and Biomedicine.[12] Article 1 of the Biomedicine Convention states that its purpose and object is to safeguard the dignity and identity of all human beings and respect their integrity and other fundamental rights and freedoms. The Convention refers to several rights that are central in health care settings, such as those concerning: consent to treatment;[13] private life and the right to information;[14] controls on genetics and the prohibition of discrimination;[15] research;[16] and the removal of organs and tissue from living donors for transplantation purposes.[17] The Council of Europe has also produced additional protocols on cloning,[18] transplantation[19] and biomedical research.[20] While the Convention and its related protocols are influential, a number of European countries, including Austria, Belgium, France, Germany,

---

[11] *Pretty* v. *UK* (2002) 35 EHRR 1.

[12] Council of Europe Convention for the Protection of Human Rights and Dignity of the Human Being with Regard to Biology and Medicine: Convention on Human Rights and Biomedicine, Oviedo, 4 April 1997, in force 1 December 1999, ETS No. 164, http://conventions.coe.int/treaty/en/treaties/html/164.htm. See P. Zilgavis, 'The European Convention on Biomedicine: its past, present and future', in A. Garwood-Gowers, J. Tingle and T. Lewis (eds.), *Healthcare law: the impact of the Human Rights Act 1998* (London: Cavendish, 2001).

[13] Articles 5–9, Biomedicine Convention, above n.12.

[14] Article 12, Biomedicine Convention, above n.12.

[15] Articles 11–3, Biomedicine Convention, above n.12.

[16] Articles 15–8, Biomedicine Convention, above n.12.

[17] Articles 21–2, Biomedicine Convention, above n.12.

[18] Council of Europe Additional Protocol to the Convention for the Protection of Human Rights and Dignity of the Human Being with Regard to Biology and Medicine on the Prohibition of Cloning Human Beings, Paris, 12 January 1998, in force 1 March 2001, ETS No. 168, http://conventions.coe.int/treaty/en/treaties/html/168.htm.

[19] Council of Europe Additional Protocol to the Convention on Human Rights and Biomedicine, on Transplantation of Organs and Tissues of Human Origin, Strasbourg, 24 January 2002, in force 1 May 2006, ETS No. 186, http://conventions.coe.int/treaty/en/treaties/html/186.htm.

[20] Council of Europe Additional Protocol to the Convention on Human Rights and Biomedicine, on Biomedical Research, Strasbourg, 25 January 2005, in force 1 September 2007, ETS No. 195, http://conventions.coe.int/treaty/en/treaties/html/195.htm.

Ireland, Luxembourg, Malta, the Netherlands, Poland, Sweden and the United Kingdom, have not ratified – or, in some cases, even become signatories to – the Convention. Of more significance, therefore, are the Council of Europe's general human rights instruments: the European Convention for the Protection of Human Rights and Fundamental Freedoms and the European Social Charter.[21]

A. *The European Convention on Human Rights*

The Council of Europe's 1950 Convention for the Protection of Human Rights and Fundamental Freedoms (ECHR) has been particularly influential in framing human rights discourse across Europe. All Member States of the EU are also members of the Council of Europe. The ECHR is a traditional statement of civil and political rights. Many Member States who are subject to the Convention have signed protocols enabling individual citizens to bring cases before the European Court of Human Rights. Over the years, a considerable number of actions brought before the European Court of Human Rights have concerned health and health care. For example, the right to life in Article 2 ECHR has been used in claims concerning the status of the fetus and abortion,[22] resource allocation in health care systems[23] and the 'right to die'.[24] Article 5 ECHR on the right to liberty and security of the person has been used extensively in the context of mental health.[25] Article 8 on the right to privacy has been used in claims concerning reproductive rights[26] (and may also have relevance to people with learning disabilities or mental illness), as has Article 12 ECHR on the right to marry and found a family.[27]

---

[21] Council of Europe Convention for the Protection of Human Rights and Fundamental Freedoms, Rome, 4 November 1950, in force 3 September 1953, ETS No. 5, http://conventions.coe.int/treaty/en/treaties/html/5.htm; Council of Europe European Social Charter, Turin, 18 October 1961, in force 26 February 1965, ETS No. 35, http://conventions.coe.int/treaty/en/treaties/html/35.htm.

[22] *H* v. *Norway* (1992) 73 DR 155: *Open Door and Dublin Well Woman* v. *Ireland* (1992) 15 EHRR 244; *Paton* v. *UK* (1981) 3 EHRR 408.

[23] *Osman* v. *UK* (1998) 29 EHRR 245; *Scialaqua* v. *Italy* (1998) 26 EHRR 164.

[24] *Pretty* v. *UK*, above n.11.

[25] See, for example, *Winterwerp* v. *The Netherlands* (1992) 15 EHRR 437; *Aerts* v. *Belgium* (2000) 29 EHRR 50.

[26] *Evans* v. *UK* (2007) 43 EHRR 21.   [27] *Dickson* v. *UK* (2006) 46 EHRR 419.

The jurisprudence of the European Court of Human Rights has had an impact on the development of health care rights across Europe. Nonetheless, the approach taken by the Court to certain controversial issues where there are wide differences in religious and ethical perspectives across states illustrates the difficulty in utilizing a human rights approach in developing health law and health policy across the EU. This is particularly notable, for example, in the context of reproductive rights. In some Member States, specific legal status is given to the embryo and fetus, which leads to consequent limitations on women's claims to reproductive rights. For example, in the Republic of Ireland, Article 40(3)(3) of the Irish Constitution provides that: '[t]he State acknowledges the right to life of the unborn, and with due regard to the equal right to life of the mother, guarantees in its laws to respect, and as far as practicable by its laws to defend and vindicate that right'. This provision is regarded as so fundamental in the Irish Republic that it led to Protocol 17 being annexed to the Treaty on European Union.[28] This states that: '[n]othing in the Treaty on European Union or in the Treaties establishing the European Communities or in the Treaties or Acts modifying or supplementing those Treaties, shall affect the application in Ireland of Article 40.3.3. of the Constitution of Ireland'.

Poland also has restrictive abortion laws. The Polish Family Planning (Protection of the Human Fetus and Conditions Permitting Pregnancy Termination) Act 1993 provides that abortion may be undertaken only where a woman's health is at serious risk, where the fetus is irreparably damaged or if the pregnancy was the result of rape or incest.[29] In contrast, other Member States have comparatively broad abortion legislation. In England and Wales for example, while abortion itself still remains a criminal offence,[30] the fetus is not recognized as having separate legal personality[31] and the current grounds for abortion contained in the Abortion Act 1967 apply

---

[28] Indeed, public distrust of the EU and its potential effect on this provision of the Irish Constitution may partially account for the 'no' vote in the Irish referendum on the Treaty of Lisbon, June 2008.

[29] The operation of this provision was recently challenged successfully at the ECtHR in *Tysiac* v. *Poland* (2007) 45 EHRR 42, and in September 2007 the ECtHR said that it would not review this judgement.

[30] Sections 58 and 59, Offences Against the Person Act 1861.

[31] *Paton* v. *BPAS* [1978] 2 All ER 987.

particularly where women seek an abortion in the first twenty-four
weeks of pregnancy.[32]

Another example is that of the disparate approaches taken to the
regulation of modern reproductive technology across Europe. In some
Member States, there is statutory regulation of modern reproductive technologies. So, for example, in the United Kingdom, modern
reproductive technology is regulated through the Human Fertilisation
and Embryology Act 1990 and a regulatory authority established
under that Act, the Human Fertilisation and Embryology Authority
(HFEA). There are certain statutory prohibitions on some controversial technologies, such as reproductive cloning.[33] The HFEA also prohibits clinics undertaking certain techniques such as sex selection for
social purposes.[34] Nonetheless, it remains the case that clinics providing modern reproductive services are given considerable discretion in
selecting patients and the legislation allows the storage of gametes and
embryos for research and treatment purposes. While there are some
limitations on the conduct of embryo research (for example, research
cannot be undertaken on the embryo fourteen days after creation) the
embryo has no recognition as having legal personality.[35] Likewise, in
Belgium, where the law was reformed in 2007 with the introduction
of the Law on Medically Assisted Reproduction and the Disposition
of Supernumerary Embryos and Gametes, there is a liberal scheme
of regulation.[36] Considerable discretion is given to physicians and in
vitro fertilization (IVF) centres in determining both which treatments
should be provided and who should have access to those treatments.
So, for example, although there is a ban on eugenic selection and sex-
selection for nonmedical purposes, IVF centres appear to be free to
decide where pre-implantation genetic diagnosis can be used.

A contrasting regulatory approach is that of Italy, a Member State
notable in the past for its limited regulation of modern reproductive

---

[32] Abortion Act 1967, as amended by the Human Fertilisation and Embryology
Act 1990.

[33] Human Reproductive Cloning Act 2001.

[34] Human Fertilisation and Embryology Authority, *Code of Practice*, 7th ed.
(London: Human Fertilisation and Embryology Authority, 2007), para.
1.13.11.

[35] Section 3, Human Fertilisation and Embryology Act 1990.

[36] See G. Pennings, 'Belgian law on medically assisted reproduction and the
disposition of supernumerary embryos and gametes', *European Journal of
Health Law* 14 (2007), p. 251.

technology. The legal position in Italy changed radically in 2004 when the new law imposed a much more restrictive regime.[37] Embryos are now equated in their legal status with neonates. The Italian law prohibits embryo screening, freezing of pre-implanted embryos, sperm and egg donation, surrogacy and embryo research.

Given such disparities in the approaches, it is unsurprising that the Council of Europe institutions have afforded a wide margin of appreciation to states where the issues that come before it are acutely and ethically controversial in nature.[38] The margin of appreciation doctrine allows discretion to individual states to interpret Convention provisions, taking into account their particular national circumstances and traditions, such as cultural practices or religious or historic traditions. So, for example, in *Paton v. United Kingdom*,[39] a married man sought, unsuccessfully, to stop his wife from having an abortion. It was alleged that not preventing the abortion constituted an infringement of the right to life of the fetus. The European Court of Human Rights rejected this claim, emphasizing the relationship between woman and fetus. It was noted that, were Article 2 on the right to life to apply to the fetus, then this would have the consequence that abortions would be unavailable even in a situation in which further continuation with pregnancy constituted a risk to the woman's life. Subsequently, in *Vo v. France*,[40] the European Court of Human Rights recognized that there were widely divergent views across Europe as to the status of the fetus, whether it was a 'person' and when life began. The Court also noted that this issue was left unclear in the Council of Europe Convention on Human Rights and Biomedicine, and took the approach that: 'it is neither desirable, nor even possible as matters stand, to answer in the abstract the question whether the unborn child is a person for purposes of the Article of the

---

[37] See J. A. Robertson, 'Protecting embryos and burdening women: assisted reproduction in Italy', *Human Reproduction* 19 (2004), 1693; R. Fenton, 'Catholic law versus women's reproductive rights', *Medical Law Review* 14 (2005), 73.

[38] See Y. Arai-Takahashi, *The margin of appreciation doctrine and the principle of proportionality* (New York: Intersentia Publishers, 2002).

[39] *Paton v. UK* (1980) 3 EHRR 408.

[40] *Vo v. France* (2005) 40 EHRR 12. See also K. O. Donovan, 'Taking a neutral stance on the legal protection of the fetus', *Medical Law Review* 14 (2006), 115. See confirmation that the embryo has no right to life under *Evans v. UK*, above n.26, p. 200.

Convention'. Instead, the Court afforded a margin of appreciation to the state on this issue.[41]

B. *The European Social Charter*

The European Convention on Human Rights is largely a traditional civil/political statement of ('negative') rights. Nonetheless, there has been some engagement with socioeconomic ('positive') rights at the Council of Europe, notably through the 1961 European Social Charter (revised 1996).[42] Like the ECHR, the European Social Charter operates through international law, binding the states that are signatories to it, which include all the Member States of the EU. Article 11 of the European Social Charter refers to the right to the protection of health:

With a view to ensuring the effective exercise of the right to protection of health, the Contracting Parties undertake, either directly or in co-operation with public or private organizations, to take appropriate measures designed, *inter alia:*

1. to remove as far as possible the causes of ill-health;
2. to provide advisory and educational facilities for the promotion of health and the encouragement of individual responsibility in matters of health; and
3. to prevent as far as possible epidemic, endemic and other diseases as well as accidents.

The European Social Charter is overseen by the European Committee of Social Rights, which 'makes a legal assessment of the conformity of national situations with the European Social Charter ... and adopts conclusions in the framework of the reporting procedure'.[43] According

---

[41] There were dissenting judgements. Two judges took the approach that Article 2 was applicable but not violated. See also *Evans* v. *UK*, above n.26; *RH* v. *Norway* (1992) 73 DR 155; *Boso* v. *Italy* [2002] ECHR-VII.

[42] European Social Charter, above n.21; Council of Europe European Social Charter (revised), Strasbourg, 3 May 1996, in force 1 July 1999, http://conventions.coe.int/Treaty/en/Treaties/Html/163.htm. See T. Hervey, 'We don't see a connection: "the right to health" in the EU Charter and European Social Charter', in G. de Búrca and B. de Witte (eds.), *Social rights in Europe* (Oxford: Oxford University Press, 2005).

[43] Rules of the European Committee of Social Rights, March 2004. See R. Brillat, 'The supervisory machinery of the ESC: recent developments and their impact', in *ibid.*

to the Committee's Conclusions, under the European Social Charter states must provide evidence of compliance with six aspects of the right to health. These are, first, a health care system including public health arrangements providing for generally available 'medical and para-medical practitioners and adequate equipment consistent with meeting its main health problems ensuring a proper medical care for the whole population'. Second, it requires the provision of special measures safeguarding health and health care access for vulnerable groups. Third, public health protection measures, preventing air and water pollution, noise abatement, food control and environmental hygiene, must be provided. Fourth, there is a requirement to provide health education. Fifth, in order to prevent epidemics, measures providing vaccination, disinfection and control of epidemics are required. A sixth aspect, although, as noted by Hervey,[44] not explicitly stated as such, is that there shall be 'the bearing by collective bodies of all, or at least a part of, the cost of health services'.[45]

The Committee has in the past been critical of health care provision by several Member States of the EU. For example, in 2001, the Committee expressed concern that there were increased waiting list times in the United Kingdom and they stated that, in light of the data, they considered that 'the organization of health care in the United Kingdom is manifestly not adapted to ensure the right to health for everyone'.[46] Regarding the sixth aspect of Article 11 of the Revised European Social Charter, the efficacy of this provision, however, is limited in that considerable discretion is given to states to determine its ambit.[47] In addition, although collective complaints can be brought by specific international nongovernmental organizations

---

[44] Hervey, 'We don't see a connection', above n.42.
[45] Council of Europe, *Case Law on the European Social Charter* (Strasbourg: Council of Europe, 1982), Conclusions I, at 59.
[46] See Doc. c-15–2-en2, discussed in T. Hervey, 'The right to health in European Union law', in Hervey and Kenner (eds.), *Economic and social rights*, above n.1, p. 208. The Committee has also cited Greece as not properly fulfilling its obligations under Article 2(4) in granting compensatory measures to workers exposed to occupational health risks. See Council of Europe European Social Charter, Turin, 18 October, 1961, in force 26 February 1965, ETS No. 35, http://conventions.coe.int/treaty/en/treaties/html/195.htm, European Committee of Social Rights, General Introduction – Conclusions XVIII-2.
[47] Hervey, 'We don't see a connection', above n.42.

enjoying participatory status with the Council of Europe, in contrast to the ECHR, the European Social Charter does not have a mechanism enabling individuals to bring specific claims before the European Committee of Social Rights.[48]

C. Health, human rights and Member States

In addition to the recognition given to human rights principles applicable in health care at the international and Council of Europe level, notable protection is given to human rights principles in general and, in certain cases, specifically to rights in the context of health care law at individual Member State level. All EU Member States have their own human rights legislation and, in many cases, this has been utilized in the context of health care. The United Kingdom, for example, has the Human Rights Act 1998, which has the effect of incorporating certain of the provisions of the ECHR into English law. Legislation and case-law must be interpreted in a manner that is compatible with the ECHR.[49] While the legislation does not enable the courts to strike down primary legislation, they may issue what is known as a 'declaration of incompatibility',[50] which places considerable pressure upon the United Kingdom Government to amend the law accordingly. However, in practice, the impact of human rights principles upon health care law in the United Kingdom since the Act came into force on 1 October 2001 has been somewhat muted. Mirroring the position at ECHR level, the national courts have afforded a wide margin of appreciation in ethically controversial cases.[51] The main exception is a willingness to intervene in mental health cases, where the European Commission and Court of Human Rights have a long history of judicial intervention.

Many EU Member States have enacted specific patients' rights legislation, although before the 1994 Amsterdam Declaration only Finland

[48] See further discussion in P. Alston, 'Assessing the strengths and weaknesses of the European Social Charter's advisory system', in de Búrca and de Witte (eds.), *Social rights in Europe*, above n.42.

[49] Sections 2 and 3, Human Rights Act 1998.

[50] Section 4, Human Rights Act 1998.

[51] For example, see in relation to assisted suicide, *R (on the application of Pretty)* v. *DPP* [2001] 1 All ER 1; *NHS Trust A* v. *M* [2001] Fam 348, on withdrawal of artificial nutrition/hydration from adults lacking mental capacity.

had its own specific patients' rights legislation as separate from more general health legislation. The Amsterdam Declaration, which followed the European Consultation on the Rights of Patients held in Amsterdam on 28–30 March 1994 (organized by the WHO Regional Office for Europe and hosted by the Government of the Netherlands), endorsed a document entitled 'The principles of the rights of patients in Europe: a common framework'.[52] Patients' rights legislation followed in a range of Member States.[53] The Danish Patients' Rights Act 1998, for instance, makes specific provision for the protection of the rights to dignity, integrity and autonomy.[54] In other European states, patients' rights continue to be included as part of general health legislation.[55] Rights to health are also found in the constitutions of several Member States.[56] It is perhaps interesting to note that in Germany, while the right to health is included in the constitutions of several *Bundesländer*, it is not part of the Federal Constitution. The closest provision here is the 'right to life and physical integrity'.[57]

At the international, European and national levels, there is considerable engagement with human rights in health and health care. But what is striking is that, while there is a commonality of

---

[52] Declaration of the World Health Organization's European Member States on the Promotion of Patients' Rights in Europe, European Consultation on the Rights of Patients, Amsterdam, 28–30 March 1994, Doc No. ICP/HLE 121, 28 June 1994, Annex, www.who.int/genomics/public/eu_declaration1994.pdf.

[53] For example, Belgium, Patients Rights Act 2002; Romania, Law of Patients Rights 2003; Lithuania, Law on Patients' Rights and Compensation of Damage to their Health 2005. For a discussion, see L. Fallsberg, 'Patients' rights in Europe', *European Journal of Health Law* 10 (2003), 5.

[54] L. Fallsberg, 'Patients' rights in the Nordic countries', *European Journal of Health Law* 7 (2000), 123.

[55] For example, Bulgarian Health Care Reform and Health Care Act 2004. See, further, S. Aleksandrova, 'The Bulgarian health care reform and Health Care Act 2004', *Medicine and Law* 26 (2007), 1.

[56] See, for example, Article 23 of the Belgian Constitution; Article 31 of the Constitution of the Czech Republic; Article 28 of the Estonian Constitution; Chapter 2, Section 19(3) of the Finnish Constitution; Article 70D of the Hungarian Constitution; Article 32 of the Italian Constitution; Article 111 of the Lithuanian Constitution; Article 11(5) of the Luxembourg Constitution; Article 22(1) of the Netherlands Constitution; Article 64(1) of the Portuguese Constitution; Article 40 of the Slovak Constitution; Article 43 of the Spanish Constitution.

[57] Article 2 (Personal Freedoms) of the German Constitution.

approaches across many jurisdictions in *general* rights statements, the interpretation and *specific* regulatory responses to such rights can be considerably different. This is particularly notable in the ethical controversies around the boundaries of life and death, such as abortion and euthanasia. However, it can also be observed in different responses to respect for principles of autonomy in matters which, on their face, would appear to attract less controversy, such as consent to treatment. Such diversity may result in regulatory challenges as the EU develops its health law and policy in light of increasing engagement with human rights.

3. Human rights, health law and the EU

The international and Council of Europe statements, along with the developments at national level outlined so far, provide the backdrop to the current position of the EU. The EU has itself affirmed recognition of principles of fundamental rights. The European Court of Justice has long recognized fundamental rights as part of EU law.[58] It has confirmed that those rights included in the ECHR are part of EU law and has further noted that the ECHR is of special significance when formulating fundamental rights in EU law.[59] When implementing EU law[60] or in derogating from Treaty obligations,[61] Member States must respect fundamental rights as general principles of EU law. However, historically, the EU has followed a 'negative' approach to the protection of fundamental rights. De Schutter comments that these have operated as limitations on EU institutions or the authority of Member States in the application of EU law.[62] They do not, in general, provide 'positive' entitlements against national authorities, which remain the main bodies that might infringe an individual's human rights in health care settings or elsewhere. Moreover, the European Court of Justice has ruled that

---

[58] Case 11/70, *International Handelsgesellschaft mbH* v. *Einfuhr* [1970] ECR 1125.
[59] Case 36/75, *Rutili* [1975] ECR 1219; Case 44/79, *Hauer* [1979] ECR 321; Case C-274/99, *Connolly* v. *Commission* [2001] ECR I-1611; Opinion 2/94 on Accession by the Community to the ECHR [1996] ECR-I-1759, para. 33.
[60] Case 5/88, *Wachauf* [1989] ECR 2609.
[61] Case C-260/89, *ERT* [1991] ECR-I-2925.
[62] O. De Schutter, 'Fundamental rights and the transformation of governance in the European Union', Reflexive Governance in the Public Interest Programme Working Paper REFGOV-FR-13 (2007).

the EU institutions do not enjoy general powers to enact human rights rules or to conclude international human rights conventions.[63] The Treaty on European Union states that the EU rests on principles of 'liberty, democracy, respect for human rights and fundamental freedoms and the rule of law'.[64] The European Court of Justice has the power to ensure that these principles are respected by the European institutions.[65] The Treaty on European Union also provides in Article 6(2) that:

The Union shall respect fundamental rights as these are guaranteed by the European Convention for the Protection of Human Rights and Fundamental Freedoms signed in Rome on 4 November 1950 and as they result from the constitutional traditions common to Member States, as general principles of Community law.

In addition, the Council has power under Article 7 TEU to take actions in relation to actual or threatened breaches of principles, which are set out in Article 6(1) TEU. There is also specific provision in Article 13 of the EC Treaty for the Council to act against 'discrimination based on sex, racial or ethnic origin, religion or belief, disability, age or sexual orientation'.

A major development in the EU's human rights agenda is undoubtedly the adoption of the 2000 EU Charter of Fundamental Rights. This section of the chapter focuses upon the EU Charter in the light of the Lisbon Treaty.[66] Although ratification of the Lisbon Treaty has been stalled by the Irish 'no' referendum vote on 12 June 2008, the EU Charter remains a validly adopted measure of EU 'soft law'. The EU Charter draws upon the Treaty of the European Union, the EC Treaty, the ECHR, the European Social Charter and also the case-law of the European Court of Justice and the European Court of Human Rights. The EU Charter thus has considerable symbolic significance. As Kenner has stated: '[p]ut simply, the objective is to make the process of

---

[63] Accession of the European Commission to the European Convention for the Protection of Fundamental Freedoms. Opinion 2/94, above n.59, paras. 27 and 34.

[64] Article 6(1) TEU.   [65] Article 46 TEU.

[66] Charter of Fundamental Rights of the European Union, Nice, 7 December 2000, not yet in force; an adapted version was proclaimed in Strasbourg on 12 December 2007.

European integration more open and legitimate by furnishing it with a layer of rights embodying values with which intrinsically most people can readily identify'.[67] So, although currently a matter of 'soft' law, as Hervey comments, the provisions may still be relevant. For instance, Article 51(1) of the EU Charter, which is addressed to the 'institutions and bodies of the Union', considered alongside Article 6(2) TEU, 'suggests a positive obligation on the institutions to take full account of the EU Charter when performing their legislative tasks'.[68] It also raises the question as to whether the EU Charter may become the basis of judicial review of actions by EU institutions. In addition, as she notes, there is the prospect that courts may consider the related jurisprudence of the European Committee of Social Rights.

Recent developments now suggest that, in the future, the EU Charter may play a much more visible role in health law and health policy issues in the EU.[69] The Treaty of Lisbon will, if it comes into force, change the EU Charter's legal status.[70] A new Article 6(1) will be inserted into the Treaty of the European Union, which provides that the Charter will have the same 'legal value' as the Treaties. The new Article 6(1) also explicitly states that it does not extend the competences of the Union. The impact of this provision is that the Charter provisions will become 'general principles' of EU law. This means that both EU and Member States, when implementing EU law, will need to comply with the EU Charter. The Charter does not itself expand the competence of the EU; rather, principles of EU law can be utilized in areas where there is already competence. Thus, individual EU citizens will be able to challenge decisions made by EU institutions or by Member States in relation to an issue within EU competence. However, if an issue arises outside the scope of EU law, then a human rights challenge would, as before, have to be brought before national courts, or, if possible, the European Court of Human Rights. In addition, the European Commission will have the power to challenge Member States if it takes the view that the Charter is being violated.

---

[67] J. Kenner, 'Economic and social rights in the EU legal order: the mirage of indivisibility in economic and social rights in the EU legal order', in Hervey and Kenner (eds.), *Economic and social rights*, above n.1.

[68] T. Hervey, 'We don't see a connection', above n.42.

[69] See, for instance, Hervey and McHale, *Health law*, above n.2.

[70] Treaty of Lisbon, Conference of the Representatives of the Governments of the Member States, C16 14/07, Brussels, 3 December 2007.

Reference is also made in the Treaty to the relationship with the ECHR. The new Article 6 of the Treaty of the European Union as inserted by the Treaty of Lisbon now also states in an important development that:

2. The Union shall accede to the European Convention for the Protection of Fundamental Rights and Freedoms. Such accession shall not affect the Union's competences as defined in the Treaties.
3. Fundamental rights, as guaranteed by the European Convention for the Protection of Fundamental Rights and Fundamental Freedoms and as they result from the constitutional traditions common to the Member States, shall constitute general principles of the Union's law.

This is to be subject to the arrangements set out in the Protocol Relating to Article 6(2) of the Treaty on European Union, which includes that there will be specific provisions in relation to preserving Union law, and for participation of the Union in the control bodies of the European Convention. In addition, mechanisms are to be established to ensure that proceedings regarding non-Member States and individuals are correctly dealt with by Member States and/or the Union where appropriate. Here the focus is on the EU Charter, but the relationship with the Council of Europe institutions will undoubtedly prove to be important and it remains to be seen how the new mechanisms will be developed and will operate.

It is possible that the change to the legal status of the EU Charter may result in more litigation constructed in the form of fundamental rights language.[71] There may also be attempts by individuals to use the EU Charter when bringing litigation at the national level, for example, in respect of seeking access to health care (explored further below).[72] The prospect of such expanded use of the EU Charter led to concerns being expressed during the drafting of the Lisbon Treaty by the United Kingdom and Poland. Polish concerns were that certain provisions of the Charter on moral and family issues would conflict with Polish law. In particular, concerns were expressed regarding same sex marriages. While a new Polish Government

---

[71] See, further, Hervey and McHale, *Health law*, above n.2, p. 407.
[72] See, further, *ibid.*, p. 408.

took office in November 2007, it indicated that, although it did not share this objection, the opt-out would remain because the governing party needed the support of opposition parties to carry the vote on the Lisbon Treaty.[73] The United Kingdom expressed concerns as to the impact of a legally-binding Charter of Fundamental Rights and Freedoms on British labour law. These two Member States have negotiated a Protocol that provides that the Charter will not extend to enabling the European Court of Justice to find that United Kingdom or Polish law is inconsistent with fundamental rights. Article 1(2) of the Protocol goes on to provide that: 'nothing in Title IV of the Charter creates justiciable rights applicable to Poland or the UK except in so far that Poland or the United Kingdom has provided for such rights in its national law'.[74]

The most fundamental 'opt out' from Lisbon was the Irish 'no' vote in its referendum on the Lisbon Treaty. Among the various issues of concern to the Irish population, it seems that the idea that the Lisbon Treaty would challenge current Irish constitutional law on abortion was part of the rationale for this vote.

A. *The impact of the Charter on health law*

How then will the EU Charter apply to health law and health policy? The EU Charter's seven titles are: dignity, freedoms, equality, solidarity, citizens' rights, justice and general provisions involving interpretation and application. The EU Charter differs from documents such as the ECHR in that the rights are very much phrased in absolute terms. Nonetheless, those rights that are included in the EU Charter are likely to be qualified in practice when they are interpreted and applied.[75] In addition, the EU Charter's Preamble distinguishes between 'rights, freedoms and principles'. Some of the EU Charter's articles are certainly written in a manner that indicates that they may be regarded as aspirational ('principles') rather than necessarily effectively justiciable ('rights' or 'freedoms').[76]

---

[73] BBC, 'No EU rights charter for Poland', *BBC News*, 23 November 2007, http://news.bbc.co.uk/1/hi/world/europe/7109528.stm.
[74] Protocol No. 7, Treaty of Lisbon.
[75] See, for example, Article 52(1), EU Charter, discussed above and below.
[76] See Lord Goldsmith, 'A charter of rights, freedoms and principles', *Common Market Law Review* 38 (2001), 1201.

Several EU Charter provisions are relevant to health law. Chapter I is headed 'Dignity'. Article 1 refers to the fundamental principle of human dignity. There is considerable debate as to what precisely constitutes respect for human dignity.[77] Within this title, as in many international statements of human rights, Article 2 makes explicit reference to the right to life. This, as noted above, is of relevance to the position of the fetus and in end-of-life decision-making. It is also possible that Article 2, combined with Article 35 (discussed below) on the right to health care, may be used in a situation in which access to health care has been denied on the basis that resources are limited. This argument has been utilized in the context of the ECHR.[78] However, more recent cases suggest that its utility in resource allocation challenges may be limited due to the fact that Article 2 ECHR 'must be interpreted in a way which does not impose an impossible or disproportionate burden on the authorities'.[79]

In addition, Article 3 refers to the integrity of the person. The drafting of this provision echoes that of the Council of Europe Convention on Human Rights and Biomedicine. Reference to the integrity of the person is also to be found in the constitutions of a number of EU Member States.[80] Article 3 states that:

2. In the fields of medicine and biology the following must be respected;
   (a) The free and informed consent of the person concerned according to the procedures laid down by law;
   (b) The prohibition of eugenic practices, in particular those aiming at the selection of persons;
   (c) The prohibition on making the human body and its parts as such a source of financial gain;
   (d) The prohibition of the reproductive cloning of human beings.

---

[77] See, for example, the discussion in. D. Beyleveld and R. Brownsword, *Human dignity in bioethics and biolaw* (Oxford: Oxford University Press, 2001); H. Biggs, *Euthanasia, death with dignity and the law* (Oxford: Hart, 2001).

[78] *Scialacqua* v. *Italy* (1998) 26 EHRR 164.

[79] *Osman* v. *UK*, above n.23.

[80] Article 2, Basic Law of the Federal Republic of Germany: '[e]veryone has the right to life and to physical integrity'; Article 15, Constitution of the Kingdom of Spain: '[e]veryone has a right to life and physical and moral integrity'; Article 25, Constitution of the Portuguese Republic: '[t]he moral and physical integrity of the person is inviolable'.

The provision on informed consent leaves a considerable degree of discretion to Member States and thus implicitly recognizes the prospect for a wide range of different approaches as to what informed consent means and who can give that consent. The prohibition on eugenic practices and selection of persons may prove controversial and lead to challenges if Member States sanction sex selection using modern reproductive technology. The prohibition on making the human body and its parts a source of financial gain also draws upon Article 21 of the Council of Europe Convention on Human Rights and Biomedicine. This principle is already recognized in the EU's Blood Safety Directive[81] and Tissue and Cells Directive.[82] So, for example, the Blood Safety Directive states in Article 20 that: 'Member States shall take the necessary measures to encourage voluntary and unpaid blood donations with a view to ensuring that blood and blood components are in so far as possible provided from such donations'. The same principle is also now to be found in the Commission's Communication on organ transplantation.[83] This provision could potentially be used in the future as a means of challenges to any proposed legislation facilitating patenting of human genetic material.[84]

Article 4 of the Charter concerns the prohibition on the infliction of torture and inhuman and degrading treatment or punishment. This is a fundamental and universally-recognized civil and political right. Its use in the health care context is a little more problematic. It could be coupled with other rights to challenge provisions that undermine decision-making autonomy. It could perhaps be utilized to claim that failure to make available health care resources resulting in denial of treatment constitutes inhuman or degrading treatment, although in

---

[81] European Parliament and Council Directive 2002/98/EC setting standards of quality and safety for the collection, testing, processing, storage and distribution of human blood and blood components and amending Directive 2001/83/EC, OJ 2003 No. L33/30.

[82] European Parliament and Council Directive 2004/23/EC setting standards of quality and safety for the donation, procurement, testing, processing, preservation, storage and distribution of human tissues and cells, OJ 2004 No. L102/48.

[83] European Commission, 'Organ donation and transplantation: policy actions at EU level', COM (2007) 275 final, 30 May 2007, para. 3.3; and see also World Health Organization Resolution WHA 42.5 condemning the sale and purchase of organs of human origin.

[84] See Hervey and McHale, *Health law*, above n.2, p. 408.

practice this may be difficult to establish, as the experience of the ECHR illustrates.[85] Article 7 in Chapter II, entitled 'Freedoms', covers the right to private life. This provision has been interpreted in the ECHR context as not only being applicable to the privacy of personal information but, in addition, as conferring respect for individual decision-making autonomy and requiring consent to any medical activity that involves an assault on the physical or psychological integrity of a person. Thus, 'a compulsory medical intervention [without the consent of the person being treated or examined], even if it is of minor importance, constitutes an interference with this right'.[86] Article 7 could, for example, be used in the context of a challenge to national implementation of the Clinical Trials Directive, which concerns the regulation of clinical trials concerning medicinal products in relation to adults lacking mental capacity, on the basis that the Member State had insufficiently protected the rights of the trial subject.[87] It could perhaps be used in a challenge to the faulty implementation of EU environmental law, on the basis that failure to properly assess environmental health risks can constitute a breach of the right to private life.[88]

Also under the title of 'Freedoms', Article 8 provides specific protection for personal data. This is relevant in protection of personal health records. The EU has already addressed the need for safeguards of the privacy of personal data through the Data Protection Directive, which

[85] See, for example, an unsuccessful attempt to utilize Article 3 of the ECHR in relation to resource allocation in the UK context in the Court of Appeal in *R v. North West Lancashire HA ex parte A* [2000] 1 WLR 977.

[86] *Y F v. Turkey* (2004) 39 EHRR 34. See also *X v. Austria* (1980) 18 DR 154, p. 155; and *Acmanne and Others v. Belgium* (1984) 40 DR 251, p. 254.

[87] European Parliament and Council Directive 2001/20/EC on the approximation of the laws, regulations and administrative provisions of the Member States relating to the implementation of good clinical practice in the conduct of clinical trials on medicinal products for human use, OJ 2001 No. L121/34; and Hervey and McHale, *Health law*, above n.2, p. 408.

[88] See *Fadeyeva v. Russia* (2007) 45 EHRR 10, in which, in spite of the wide margin of discretion available to states under Article 8 ECHR, the ECtHR found violation of Article 8 ECHR (right to private life) in a situation where threats to health arose from a steel plant. The Court found that, although the 'situation around the plant called for a special treatment of those living within the zone, the State did not offer the applicant any effective solution to help her move away from the dangerous area. Furthermore, although the polluting plant in issue operated in breach of domestic environmental standards, there is no indication that the State designed or applied effective measures which would take into account the interests of the local population,

provides controls regarding the processing of personal data.[89] The EU
Charter reinforces the EU's commitment to informational privacy.[90]
Article 9, the right to marry and found a family, is a right whose ECHR
equivalent, Article 12 of the ECHR, as was noted above, has been used
in reproductive rights claims. Article 10, which safeguards freedom of
thought, conscience and religion, may be utilized by those who believe
that the law should take into account principles of individual faith and
belief when formulating health law and health policy. The right to
freedom of expression and information contained in Article 11 may be
pertinent both in relation to public health measures that limit advertising and also potentially to those health care professionals who wish to
blow the whistle on poor standards of clinical practice.

Chapter III of the EU Charter concerns 'Equality'. Article 20 states
that all people are equal before the law. Article 21 includes the prohibition of discrimination on grounds of sex, race, colour, ethnic or
social origin, genetic features, language, religion or belief. Article
24 concerns the rights of the child and provides that children should
have the ability to freely express their views and that these should
be taken into account in accordance with their age and maturity.
Provision is made for the rights of the elderly in Article 25, which
include their right to lead a life of dignity and independence, and
Article 26 calls for the integration of persons with disabilities into
the life of the community on several levels (e.g., political, social).
While these three groups containing vulnerable persons are subject to special protection, there is no specific provision safeguarding the rights of those adults who lack mental capacity. Here, the
EU Charter stands in contrast to, for example, the EU's approach to
the regulation of clinical research, where in the regulation of trials
concerning medicinal products, the Clinical Trials Directive contains
special controls on research involving both children and adults lacking mental capacity.[91]

affected by the pollution, and which would be capable of reducing the
industrial pollution to acceptable levels.'
[89] See Chapter 13 in this volume.
[90] European Parliament and Council Directive 95/46/EC on the protection of
individuals with regard to the processing of personal data and on the free
movement of such data, OJ 1995 No. L281/31. See, further, Hervey and
McHale, *Health law*, above n.2, Chapter 5.
[91] Directive 2001/20/EC, above n.87. See A. Baeyens, 'Implementation of the
Clinical Trials Directive: pitfalls and benefits', *European Journal of Health*

One notable aspect of the EU Charter contained in Chapter IV, 'Solidarity', is that specific provision is made for a right to health care in Article 35, a provision that is in turn based on Article 11 of the European Social Charter, discussed above. Article 35 provides that:

Everyone has the right of access to preventive health care and the right to benefit from medical treatment under the conditions established by national laws and practices. A high level of human health protection shall be ensured by the definition and implementation of all Union policies and activities.

As Hervey notes, there are two elements to this Article.[92] The first is that there is an expression of individual entitlement to health care. The second is that of the repetition of the mainstreaming provision in Article 152 EC. She suggests that '[t]his element of the Charter may be seen as a kind of 'super-mainstreaming' expression of the values that should underpin EU law and policy'.[93] Article 35 may be (although has not so far been) used in free movement claims in the context of an individual who travels to another Member State to receive treatment and then claims reimbursement of the cost of that treatment. Such free movement claims have already been the subject of considerable jurisprudence over many years before the European Court of Justice.[94] The impact of these cases in arguably constructing a 'right to health care', through the application of 'economic' free movement principles rather than human rights principles in situations where individuals were subject to undue delay in their home Member States, has led to concerns at the national level as to their impact on resource allocation and to proposed new policy developments at the EU level. In July 2008, the Commission proposed

---

Law 8 (2001), 293; and Hervey and McHale, *Health law*, above n.2, pp. 248–59.

[92] Opinion 2/94, above n.59, para. 33.

[93] Hervey, 'The right to health', above n.46, p. 202.

[94] See Case C-158/96, *Kohll* v. *Union des Caisses de Maladie* [1998] ECR-I-1935; Case C-157/99, *Geraet Smits and Peerbooms* [2001] ECR I-05473; Case C-368/98, *Vanbraekel* [2001] ECR-I-5363; Case C-385/99, *Muller Faure* [2003] ECR I-4509; Case C-56/01, *Inizan* [2003] ECR I-12403; Case C-372/04, *Watts* [2006] ECR I-4325; R. (*Watts*) v. *Bedford Primary Care Trust and Another* [2006] QB 667.

a directive on the application of patients' rights in cross-border health care.[95] This is in keeping with the Court's jurisprudence, in that it constructs patients' 'rights' largely as internal market entitlements.[96] In its explanatory memorandum, the Commission states that the proposal 'respects the fundamental rights and observes the principles recognized in particular by the [EU Charter]'.[97] However, this is expressed simply in terms of the need to implement it with 'due respect for ... the principle of non-discrimination'. Will Article 35 make a practical difference in terms of litigation in the future? Hervey has argued that, while:

[A] 'right to health' might make a difference in terms of the discourse available to judicial bodies to resolve what are effectively matters of resource allocation ... [but] in the final analysis would be unlikely to make a difference in the substantive outcome of any litigation.[98]

Interestingly, however, recent reference was made to the Charter in the opinion of the Advocate General in *Aikaterini Stamatelaki* v. *NPDD Organismos Asfaliseos Eleftheron Epangelmation*.[99] Here, the Advocate General commented that:

[A]lthough the case-law takes as the main point of reference the fundamental freedoms established in the Treaty, there is another aspect which is becoming more and more important in the Community sphere, namely the right of citizens to health care, proclaimed in Article 35 of the Charter of Fundamental Rights of the European Union since "being a fundamental asset health cannot be considered solely in terms of social expenditure and latent economic difficulties. This right is perceived as a personal entitlement unconnected to a person's relationship with social security and the Court of Justice cannot overlook that aspect."[100]

---

[95] European Commission, 'Proposal for a European Parliament and Council Directive on the application of patients' rights in cross-border healthcare', COM (2008) 414 final, 2 July 2008. See also European Commission, 'Consultation Regarding Community action on Health Services', SEC (2006) 1195/4, 26 September 2006.

[96] This is reflected, *inter alia*, in the legal basis of the proposed Directive, Article 95 EC, concerning the creation of the internal market.

[97] European Commission, 'Proposal for a European Parliament and Council Directive', above n.95, p. 12.

[98] Hervey, 'The right to health', above n.46, p. 210.

[99] AG Opinion, Case C-444/05, *Stamatelaki* [2007] ECR I-3185.

[100] *Ibid.*, para. 40.

It remains to be seen to what extent such statements will be reflected in a reframing of jurisprudence in this area. They certainly do not seem to be significant in terms of the Commission's agenda here.

A further problem is that respecting a right to health care combined with other aspects of EU law may sit uneasily with respect for fundamental rights at the national level. So, for example, respect for the free movement principles in the EU Treaty may undermine individual Member States' approaches to issues such as abortion and regulation of reproduction because individuals are able to travel to other jurisdictions to receive services not allowed in their home Member State.[101]

While the provisions in the EU Charter are, on the surface, phrased very much in absolute terms, some limitations are set out in its final chapter. Article 52(1) provides that:

Any limitation on the exercise of the rights and freedoms recognised by this Charter must be provided by law and respect the essence of those rights and freedoms. Subject to the principle of proportionality, limitations may be made only if they are necessary and genuinely meet objectives of general interest recognised by the Union or the need to protect the rights and freedoms of others.

This is a very broad statement and also illustrates a further problem with human rights-based analysis – namely, how can a conflict between one person's rights and the rights and interests of others be effectively resolved? Put bluntly, are some rights more 'valuable' and thus of greater weight in any balancing calculation than others? As Hervey has commented, recognizing the right to health care of one individual is likely to have the effect of diverting resources from another person. She suggests that if an Article 35 right to health care becomes the subject of litigation, the claim of one individual seeking treatment may be denied on the basis that the rights of other persons to health care are respected in such a situation and the decision

---

[101] See, further, *R* v. *Human Fertilisation and Embryology Authority, ex parte Blood* [1997] 2 All ER 687; T. Hervey, 'Buy baby: the European Union and regulation of human reproduction', *Oxford Journal of Legal Studies* 18 (1998), 207; R. Lee and D. Morgan, 'In the name of the father? Ex parte Blood: dealing with novelty and anomaly', *Modern Law Review* 60 (1997), 840; Case C-159/90, *Grogan* [1991] ECR I-04685; and see also Hervey and McHale, *Health law*, above n.2, pp. 144–58.

to deny treatment was not disproportionate.[102] In addition, claims
to human rights may prove problematic in public health – a matter
clearly within the competence of the EU under Article 152 EC – where
calculations are made that it is necessary to limit individual human
rights in the interest of the community as a whole – for example, to
contain the spread of disease.

Article 52(3) states that, where rights included in the EU Charter
correspond to those contained in the ECHR, then the meaning and
the scope of those rights is treated as the same. This highlights the
importance of the ECHR jurisprudence and, in addition, illustrates
the limitations of the EU Charter. As noted above, the ECHR has its
limitations – in particular, that states are afforded a clear margin of
appreciation. It is further stated that the provisions of the EU Charter
do not prevent EU law from providing more extensive protection to
fundamental rights than that provided by the ECHR. Furthermore,
Article 53 provides that the EU Charter is not to be interpreted as
restricting human rights provisions that are contained in EU law,
international law or international agreements to which the Member
States are parties. These provisions thus position the EU Charter as
a basic level of protection, while recognizing that human rights protection may be enhanced by the EU. Moreover, they reflect a strong
statement that subsidiarity remains very much in force. Article 51(2)
states explicitly that the EU Charter 'does not establish any new power
or task for the Community or the Union, or modify powers and tasks
as defined by the Treaties'.

Currently, reference is certainly being made to the EU Charter in
health policy documents produced by the European Union, such as
those on organ transplantation. There is certainly the prospect that the
use of the EU Charter may facilitate dialogue across the EU as to what
is meant by certain fundamental principles, such as what constitutes
'informed consent'. However, whether the EU Charter will itself make a
considerable difference over the long term in relation to the development
of health law and health policy in the EU is uncertain. Human rights
concepts can be exceedingly fluid, and those set out in the EU Charter
are no exception. Take, for example, the concept of respect for human
dignity in Article 1 of the EU Charter. This concept is notoriously uncertain and capable of different interpretations. It has been the subject of

---

[102] See Hervey, 'The right to health', above n.46.

considerable jurisprudence in some jurisdictions, such as France, and yet is not included at all as a legal principle within other jurisdictions.[103] Or take a principle far more generally accepted across the international community, that of the right to life. Nys has commented:

There undoubtedly are certain vexed themes in medical law – such as abortion and euthanasia – where the ideas of the various Member States (but also within states) are so far apart due to religious, philosophical, ethical and other reasons that a common European regulation would be simply unthinkable.[104]

As noted above in the discussion of the ECHR on controversial issues such as abortion, there can be radical differences at the national level as to what constitute fundamental human rights and how such rights shall be protected. States that respect the principle of the sanctity of life may reach very different conclusions as to whether to sanction assisted death – as illustrated by the comparison between Belgium[105] and the Netherlands, where assisted dying is legally sanctioned,[106] and the United Kingdom, where it is a criminal offence.[107]

How might other challenges using the EU Charter operate? As noted previously, a proposed directive concerning stem cell research using fetal material could be subject to challenge under Article 1 (the need to respect human dignity), Article 2 (the right to life) and Article 3 (integrity of the person).[108] Nonetheless, the uncertainty regarding the interpretation of such provisions, along with the considerable discretion given to Member States in relation to issues such as the

---

[103] Beyleveld and Brownsword, *Human dignity*, above n.77; Biggs, *Euthanasia*, above n.77.

[104] H. Nys, 'Comparative health law and the harmonization of patients' rights in Europe', *European Journal of Health Law* 8 (2001), 317–331, at 317, 325.

[105] Belgium, Euthanasia Act 2002. See also M. Adams and H. Nys, 'Comparative reflections on the Belgium Euthanasia Act 2002', *Medical Law Review* 11 (2003), 353.

[106] Termination of Life on Request and Assisted Review Procedure Act 2001. See also H. Nys, 'Physician involvement in a patient's death: a continental European perspective', *Medical Law Review* 7 (1999), 208; J. de Haan, 'The new Dutch law on euthanasia', *Medical Law Review* 10 (2002), 57.

[107] Section 2, Suicide Act 1961; *R (on the application of Pretty)* v. *DPP*, above n.51.

[108] Hervey and McHale, *Health law*, above n.2, p. 407.

status or legal position of the fetus suggests that, in practice, such a challenge would be at best problematic and probably unsuccessful. There is the prospect that the EU Charter could have an impact at the national level through Article 51, which provides that the provisions within the Charter are applicable to Member States when implementing EU law.

The EU's continuing engagement with mental health may prove a more fertile area for engagement with human rights, given the extensive EHCR jurisprudence on this issue in the past.[109] The prospect of evolving European standards in the area of mental health is something that is effectively realizable. Here, there is the prospect that the EU may work with and build upon the work of the World Health Organization in the area of mental health.[110] Moreover, many of the issues that arise in mental health, as noted above in the context of the ECHR jurisprudence, relate to more traditional civil and political rights, such as privacy, 'negative' rights that may be less likely to prove controversial in that they usually will not explicitly involve resource allocation questions, nor usually will they involve particularly contentious ethical issues.

B. Health rights and the EU Agency for Fundamental Rights

In addition to the developments mentioned above, in 2007 the EU also established the European Union Agency for Fundamental Rights.[111] This replaces an earlier organization, the European Monitoring Centre for Racism and Xenophobia. The Agency has three roles. First,

---

[109] See, for example, European Commission, 'Promoting the mental health of the population: towards a strategy on mental health for the European Union', Green Paper, COM (2005) 484 final, 14 October 2005; European Commission, 'Together for health: a strategic approach for the EU 2008–2013', White Paper, COM (2007) 630 final, 23 October 2007. At the meeting of the EPSCO Council on 6 December 2007, Commissioner Markos Kypriano explained to Member States that he intended to organize a High Level Conference on Mental Health. See also Hervey and McHale, *Health law*, above n.2, pp. 435–6; B. Kelly, 'The emerging mental health strategy of the European Union. A multi-level work in progress', *Health Policy* 85(1) (2008) 60–70.

[110] See, for example, World Health Organization, 'Framework on human rights mental health and legislation', www.who.int/mental_health/policy/fact_sheet_mnh_hr_leg_2105.pdf.

[111] Council Regulation 168/2007/EC establishing a European Union Agency for Fundamental Rights, OJ 2007 No. L53/1.

it has the task of collating information and data regarding the effects of fundamental rights action taken by the EU and of good practice regarding the promotion of these rights. Second, it provides advice to the EU and its Member States. As part of this role, it undertakes scientific research and preparatory studies, and also formulates and publishes conclusions on specific thematic topics. Third, the Agency promotes dialogue within civil society, to raise awareness of fundamental human rights. This is effected through a cooperative network (a 'Fundamental Rights Platform'), which facilitates exchange of information between the Agency and key stakeholders.

However, the role of the Agency does not extend to systematic, permanent monitoring of human rights in the Member States for the purposes of Article 7 TEU.[112] It is not empowered to examine individual complaints brought by individuals. Neither is the Agency concerned with the legality of EU legislative acts within Article 230 EC. Rather, the Agency will have the task of cooperating with other bodies, such as governments of Member States, national human rights organizations and also other Community and Union agencies. These powers of the Agency suggest that it will fundamentally operate in an expert role, as opposed to that of a traditional supervisory body in international human rights law.

The Agency operates through nine thematic areas, which are determined through a five-year multi-annual framework. The current framework was adopted on 28 February 2008 by the Justice and Home Affairs Council of the European Union.[113] There is no explicit reference to the right to health – or indeed to any social or economic rights – although three areas may be relevant to health. These are: first, discrimination based on sex, race or ethnic origin, religion or belief, disability, age or sexual orientation and against persons belonging to minorities and any combination of these grounds; second, the rights of the child; and, third, the information society and, in particular, respect for private life and protection of personal data.[114] It is intended that the framework will be implemented in a

---

[112] The Council has stated that it may seek the assistance of the Agency as an independent person during a possible procedure under Article 7 TEU, but will not use the Agency for systematic monitoring for this purpose.

[113] Council Decision 2008/203/EC, above n.3.

[114] Two further thematic areas may also have some relevance to health, even if not as directly. These relate to the 'compensation of victims', which may

manner complementary to the work of other EU bodies, the Council of Europe and also international organizations operating in the area of human rights.

Thus far, the work of the Agency of relevance to health rights has been focused in the area of non-discrimination. Health was added as a 'thematic area' of investigation for the first time in the 2007 Annual Report, following evidence from the country reports of the interconnected nature of discrimination against minorities in health and other fields of social life.[115] In particular, work on the most vulnerable in European society – for instance, illegally resident third-country nationals, rejected asylum seekers and members of Roma communities, especially Romani women – has highlighted inequalities (in the form of indirect discrimination) in their access to basic health care, a core component of the right to health care.[116] The work of the Agency builds on earlier work by the European Commission[117] and the European Monitoring Centre on Racism and Xenophobia, which recommends action at the national and local levels, such as establishing a legal duty on public authorities to promote equality; adopting special measures to ensure equality in practice, where cultural attitudes may impede full participation of women in health care decision-making; and a 'multisectoral' approach of inclusion in health, education and housing.[118] A consultative meeting in July 2008 set the Agency's future strategy on Roma communities.

apply to occupational health in respect of claims stemming from injuries in the work-place; and to 'asylum and immigration' where the rights (including in regard to health care) of illegal immigrants and asylum seekers is often a source of debate/controversy in the Member States. This is particularly the case where such individuals have not sought asylum via the correct channels and are held in detention pending a decision.

[115] European Union Agency for Fundamental Rights (FRA), 'Annual Report 2007', http://fra.europa.eu/fra/material/pub/ar08/ar-activity_En.pdf.

[116] See FRA, 'Annual report 2008', http://fra.europa.eu/fra/material/pub/ar08/ar08-memo_en.pdf.

[117] See P. Mladovsky, 'To what extent are Roma disadvantaged in terms of health and access to health care? What policies have been introduced to foster health and social inclusion?', Research Note for the European Commission, DG Employment and Social Affairs (2007), http://ec.europa.eu/employment_social/spsi/docs/social_situation/rn_roma_health.pdf.

[118] Council of Europe, *Breaking the barriers – Romani women and access to public health care* (Luxembourg: European Monitoring Centre on Racism and Xenophobia, 2003).

The Agency's 2008 Annual Report[119] highlighted patchy implementation of the EU's anti-discrimination legislation. It also highlighted examples of good practice in tackling racism and discrimination in various areas of public service provision, including health care. Indeed, the 2008 Annual Report included a separate chapter on health care specifically as a new thematic area. Health care is treated as an 'important area of social life', and the report bases its inclusion and analysis on Article 152 of the Treaties along with the 2006 Council of Health Ministers' adoption of common values vis-à-vis health systems towards minimizing health inequalities.[120] The Agency thus adopts a broad view of health, but focuses primarily on issues surrounding discrimination and exclusion, and barriers to access to health care, especially those faced by migrants and minorities. Without going into the Report's findings in detail, noting huge variation in reported ethnic discrimination in health between Member States (both self-reported and reported by health professionals as witnesses to colleagues' behaviour), it highlights formal complaints of discrimination in health care access or treatment in some ten countries: Austria, Bulgaria, the Czech Republic, Cyprus, Finland, Germany, Latvia, Lithuania, the Netherlands and Sweden. At the same time, it points to examples in many countries (including in some of those listed above) of proactive 'good practice' measures taken by national authorities to reduce such inequalities. For instance, strategic plans aimed at those disadvantaged in national health care systems in Bulgaria, Germany, Spain, Hungary, Italy, Ireland, Poland, Portugal, Finland and the United Kingdom were commended.[121] In conclusion, the Agency's specific opinion is that 'Member States and the EU should encourage culturally sensitive training of the health workforce. Staff development and training programmes in the health care system should include components related to Roma-specific needs in health status.'[122] While the Agency's opinions are, of course, not legally enforceable, they may add to the weight of evidence where Member States are failing to guarantee access to health care in a way that discriminates on grounds of race, which may feed into challenges at the

---

[119] FRA, 'Annual report 2008', above n.116.
[120] Council Conclusions on common values and principles in European Union health systems, OJ 2006 No. C146/1.
[121] FRA, 'Annual report 2008', above n.116, pp. 91–4.
[122] FRA, 'Annual report 2008', above n.116, p. 118.

national level. The Report specifically highlights lack of awareness of potential avenues of legal redress as one of the reasons for low levels of complaints.[123] Awareness raising activities, carried out by national and international human rights NGOs, may lead to litigation based on non-discrimination entitlements, which may change the legal landscape over time. Moreover, the addition of a separate section on health care to the report, assuming that it remains a key thematic area for the future, has the potential to highlight divergences between Member States in the application of Council of Europe provisions concerning health rights, but also the intermeshing between human rights and health care in the EU in general.

4. Conclusions

The EU is becoming increasingly engaged with both health care and with fundamental human rights. It seems likely that, in the future, respect for human rights will be further embedded into the EU with a movement towards rights that are enforceable, rather than operating as 'soft law'. But, while the discourse of fundamental human rights may be used at a general level, in practice it seems unlikely that this will have a radical impact on health law and policy. Respect for fundamental human rights in health care contexts is given practical effect through national laws, policies and practices. The ECHR and the Council of Europe's Social Charter also have had some impact on the development of health law and policy. The EU's Charter of Fundamental Rights and the Fundamental Rights Agency provide mechanisms for enhancing the respect given to fundamental rights in health law and policy in the EU. The Fundamental Rights Agency may play a role, but it is too soon to truly ascertain what its impact might be. In practice, use of the EU Charter, whether in developing health policy or in litigation, is likely to prove problematic for at least four reasons. First, the fluidity or breadth of certain concepts, such as dignity, or positive rights, such as the right to health care, makes them particularly difficult to enforce. Second, the differing religious, cultural and ethical perspectives regarding certain fundamental rights questions make it difficult to develop a truly distinctive EU dimension to fundamental human rights, which would

---

[123] FRA, 'Annual report 2008', above n.116, p. 107.

require the EU to resolve a wide range of differing religious and cultural approaches across Member States. Respect for equality and diversity of cultural and religious viewpoints does not sit easily with a single 'EU' approach to fundamental human rights in health care. This is notably illustrated by Poland's recent opt-out protocol to the Lisbon Treaty. Third, the EU Charter shares with other human rights instruments an ambiguity about situations where human rights conflict, and does not make it clear how to prioritize one 'fundamental' right against another. Fourth, the scope of the Charter, in itself, is constrained by the competence of the EU. In addition, the enforceability of rights is likely to operate against EU institutions rather than more generally against national authorities, which are the main providers of health care. Furthermore, it is questionable whether the European Court of Justice will utilize the EU Charter as a mechanism for developing a distinctive rights jurisprudence. As Freedman has argued:

The record of the Court of Justice shows that it does not see rights as weapons used to "trump" legislation in the way in which the US Supreme Court does. In fact it has only extremely rarely struck down any provision of EU law for violation of human rights. Instead the Charter is likely to "function as a source of values and norms ... to influence the interpretation of EU legislative and other measures and to feed into policy-making and into EU activities more generally".[124]

It is as yet uncertain whether a discernable EU-specific dimension to fundamental human rights in the context of health care will effectively evolve or whether that is at all possible in practice. Indeed, and relating to the impact of the Charter on domestic policy more generally, a question here is how Articles 51–3 – which appear to be reaffirmations of subsidiarity and the status quo regarding no interference with national laws, constitutions and practices – will be interpreted in practice, for a strong emphasis given to specific rights that are to be ensured and administered by the Member States, such as in respect of social security and health care, would be meaningless if no tangible impact on the Member States were envisaged.

---

[124] See S. Freedman, 'Transformation or dilution: fundamental rights in the EU social space', *European Law Journal* 12 (2006), 41–60, at 41, 57.

Thus, while fundamental human rights may raise awareness and may provide a means of framing debate, it is questionable whether the assertion of fundamental rights claims in the future will necessarily provide definitive 'solutions' in many areas of health and health care law and policy in the EU. Nonetheless, that does not mean that fundamental rights should be seen as redundant. Indeed, the conflicts between them, and the different perspectives that rights analysis brings, may be invaluable in structuring policy formulation. The provisions of the EU Charter, elaborated through the work of the EU Agency for Fundamental Rights, may place EU institutions and Member States in a better position to develop law and policy in the future. As has been suggested by Freedman, the EU Charter can in the long term, perhaps, be seen as valuable in terms of the use of new forms of governance in the context of health care, such as mainstreaming and the open method of coordination.[125] As the recent work of the Fundamental Rights Agency suggests, the principle of non-discrimination may also provide a rich source of legal claims in health fields that has as yet been underexploited.

[125] *Ibid.*, 41.

7 | *EU competition law and public services*

TONY PROSSER

1. Introduction

The treatment of health care by European competition law encapsulates more clearly than almost any other public service a key dilemma: to what extent are public services subject to the norms of competition law and the internal market, or are they characterized by quite different principles of solidarity and citizenship, which make the application of market and competition principles inappropriate? As we shall see, neither the European courts nor the Commission has so far provided a completely clear set of answers to these questions, although important guidance recently has been apparent in case-law and Commission policy statements. In this chapter, I shall concentrate on the applicability of competition law to public services, and the extent to which they can be made subject to partial exemption from its rules because of their distinctive role.[1] I shall only refer in passing to the law relating to state aids and public procurement; these are of crucial importance and are inextricably related to competition law, but are the subject of a separate chapter.

2. Markets and social solidarity

Of course, an important theme of European Union policy has been to create a single internal market characterized by open competition, and a major element in this has been the development of a system of

I am grateful to Leigh Hancher for very useful comments on an earlier draft of this chapter, and to Wouter Gekiere for information on the Reform Treaty.

[1] A more detailed account of these and related issues can be found in T. Prosser, *The limits of competition law: markets and public services* (Oxford: Oxford University Press, 2005); see also W. Sauter, 'Services of general economic interest and universal service obligations as an EU law framework for curative health care', TILEC Discussion Paper 29, Tilburg University (2007).

competition law. The most important Treaty articles for this purpose are Articles 81 and 82 (there are also complex provisions dealing with mergers, but so far these have had limited importance in the health care field and so will not be covered in this chapter). Article 81 prohibits agreements between undertakings and concerted practices that have as their object or effect the prevention, restriction or distortion of competition within the common market (although exemptions may be granted under Article 81(3)), and Article 82 prohibits abuse of a dominant position by one or more undertakings. It is not difficult to see that these provisions may have a potentially important role in the health care field; examples will be given in the discussion of the case-law below, and more details will be provided in the following chapter. Essentially, they are likely to make it difficult for a market participant to attempt to coordinate activities with other participants, or to attempt to exploit its monopoly position, for example, to exclude potential competitors or to impose unfair terms on those with whom they contract. In this area, Article 86 is also of considerable importance. The first part of the Article is addressed to Member States, stating that, in the case of public undertakings or undertakings given exclusive or special rights, Member States must not make or maintain in force measures contrary to Treaty rules, notably those mentioned above in relation to competition. A particular concern has arisen where competition has been limited by law in order to prevent new competitors 'cream skimming' – in other words, seeking only the most profitable business while leaving only an unprofitable rump to the provider of a public service required to be available to all. The second part of Article 86, by contrast, permits limited relaxation of the competition rules in relation to some public services (or 'services of general economic interest', as they are termed in the Treaty). Thus, it provides a form of 'safe haven' for services that are not wholly suited for provision under competitive conditions.[2]

The law on all these questions is highly complex, being developed in detail both through the case-law of the European courts and through rule-making and guidance by the Commission.[3] Enforcement in the past has been a matter for the Commission, subject to review by

---

[2] Sauter, 'Services of general economic interest', above n.1, p. 31.
[3] For an excellent account, see A. Jones and B. Sufrin, *EC competition law*, 3rd ed. (Oxford: Oxford University Press, 2007).

the Court of First Instance and, on appeal, the European Court of Justice. However, since 2004, this system has been decentralized by giving the primary enforcement role to national competition authorities in each Member State and national courts before which private actions can be brought. As we shall see in a moment, this may be significant given the fundamental divergences in attitudes to the treatment of public services between different Member States; on the one hand, decentralization could be seen as promoting greater responsiveness to national sensitivities but, on the other, it makes a consistent approach more difficult given the major differences in national approaches. However, the basic point to be made at this stage is a simple one: the underlying purpose of the competition provisions is based on that of competitive markets as the best means of achieving two objectives. The first is that of maximizing economic efficiency through ensuring that goods are allocated to those who are prepared to pay most for them and that goods are produced at the lowest possible cost. The second is that of maximizing consumer choice through encouraging the entry into the market of competing suppliers.

The other relevant principle – and one particularly characteristic of health care – is that of social solidarity.[4] This has been noted in a number of areas of European law, and is based on a commitment to equality, notably to equal access to services irrespective of ability to pay. In this sense, the principle is based on an ideal of citizenship: that all public services are based on our inclusion in a community, not on our financial resources.[5] It is not difficult to see that this principle may come into conflict with market-based principles. Thus, a government may wish to coordinate a health service in order to guarantee equal treatment for all, rather than enhancing consumer choice, which may further promote inequalities. It may

---

[4] For detailed discussion of this theme and, in particular, the relationship between national and European Union versions of solidarity, see M. Ferrera, *The boundaries of welfare: European integration and the new spatial politics of social protection* (Oxford: Oxford University Press, 2005).

[5] For discussions of the role of citizenship in European Union law, see T. Hervey, 'Social solidarity: a buttress against internal market law?', in J. Shaw (ed.), *Social law and policy in an evolving European Union* (Oxford: Hart, 2000), pp. 31–47; and C. Barnard, 'EU citizenship and the principle of solidarity', in E. Spavanta and M. Dougan (eds.), *Social welfare and EU law* (Oxford: Hart, 2005), pp. 157–79.

wish to ensure that services are provided free or at prices that do not reflect underlying costs; again, this will be incompatible with the free play of markets, one of the aims of which is to distribute goods and services on the basis of willingness (and ability) to pay for the costs involved. As we shall see later, there is nothing in European law that prevents national governments from organizing health care systems on a basis of solidarity. However, where governments attempt to mix markets and solidarity-based provision, this is where difficulties may arise with competition law.

The highly political nature of these different principles complicates matters further, not only in the obvious sense that they represent fundamental choices about social organization, but also because they have been associated with the approaches of different Member States of the Union. Thus (to simplify a complex picture), the markets-based approach is often characterized as 'Anglo-Saxon' and associated with the United Kingdom, which is seen as almost a Trojan horse, bringing to the Union support for the unfettered market principles of the United States. By contrast, the solidarity approach is associated in particular with France, and can be seen both as reflecting its strong republican values of equal citizenship rights and as protecting a large and influential public sector. This conflict of views was seen, for example, in the European Council meeting of June 2007 designed to rescue parts of the draft Constitutional Treaty rejected by referendums in France and the Netherlands. The French prime minister achieved what was perceived as the major coup of removing the draft Treaty's inclusion of free and undistorted competition as an objective of the Union. This reflected a concern that the French referendum result was partly the outcome of a perception that the new Treaty was too 'Anglo-Saxon' and threatened public services based on citizenship. The removal was greeted with outrage in the United Kingdom and by some competition lawyers; however, this outrage tended to ignore the fact that competition is not currently one of the objectives set out in Article 2 of the Treaty – it only appears in Article 3 as an activity for achieving those goals. The main point is that both market-based principles and those of solidarity appear in Community law and the balance between them is highly contested and potentially politically incendiary. Once this background has been understood, we can now proceed to consider what role competition law plays in determining the scope of the two types of principle.

3. The scope of European Union Competition Law

Before considering in any detail the substantive provisions of competition law, the essential preliminary question is to determine its scope. To what bodies, carrying out what activities, will it apply? Unfortunately, this is a question to which no precise answer can be given, though the European Court of Justice has given some indications of possible answers in recent decisions.

The basic principle is that, in order to be covered by European Union competition law, the entity in question must be an undertaking. This term is not defined in the Treaty, but it is clear from the case-law that it does not matter whether the entity is public or private, or profit-making or non-profit; what is important is whether it is engaged in an economic activity.[6] The focus will be on the activity in question rather than the nature of the institution itself; thus, it is perfectly possible for an entity to be covered by competition law in relation to some of its activities but not others. The concept of an economic activity will exclude a number of fields of action of importance for health care. These include:

[M]atters which are intrinsically prerogatives of the State, services such as national education and compulsory basic social security schemes, and a number of activities conducted by organizations performing largely social functions, which are not meant to engage in industrial or commercial activity.[7]

For example, in the case of *Humbel*, the Court held that courses provided under a national education system were not 'services provided for remuneration' as 'the state is not seeking to engage in gainful activity but is fulfilling its duties towards its own population in the social, cultural and educational fields'.[8] The concept may also exclude non-economic regulatory activities – for example, the control and supervision of airspace on safety grounds in *Eurocontrol* and anti-pollution surveillance services in *Cali*.[9]

---

[6] See Case C-41/90, *Höfner and Elser* [1991] ECR I-1979.
[7] European Commission, 'Services of general interest', Green Paper, COM (2003) 270 final, 21 May 2003, para. 45.
[8] Case 263/86, *Humbel* [1988] ECR 5365.
[9] Case C-364/92, *Eurocontrol* [1994] ECR I-43; Case C-343/95, *Cali* [1997] EC I-1588.

The most important exclusion from the concept of economic activities in relation to health care is that of organization on the basis of social solidarity.[10] This has arisen in a number of cases concerned with social security schemes where membership was compulsory. Thus, in the case of *Poucet and Pistre*,[11] the Court considered such a scheme in France, membership of which was compulsory, which provided a basic pension regardless of the financial status and health of the contributor, and which used the contributions of active members directly to finance the pensions of retired members, thus containing a central distributive element. According to the Court, the scheme fulfilled an exclusively social function; its activity was based on the principle of national solidarity and benefits paid bore no relation to contributions. More recently, the Court decided that Germany's state-run sickness funds, in which contributions are not related to risks and payments not related to contributions, did not constitute undertakings subject to competition law. They performed an exclusively social function, founded on the principle of national solidarity, and which was entirely non-profit-making. There was also equalization of costs and risks between different funds and no competition between them in relation to their basic activity of granting obligatory state benefits (although a degree of competition had been introduced between them in relation to contributions). The emphasis in this case was thus on the underlying purpose of the activity in question.[12] Not all funds will fall outside competition law, however. For example, in *Albany*, a Netherlands pension fund was found to be an undertaking as membership was optional, benefits were proportional to contributions, the same principle of capitalization was applied as that in private funds and there was competition with the private sector.[13]

It will be most helpful to illuminate the current law by contrasting two recent cases. The first, that of *BetterCare Ltd* v. *Director General of Fair Trading*,[14] was decided not by the European courts but by

---

[10] For detailed treatment, see Ferrera, *The boundaries of welfare*, above n.4, Chapter 4, in particular.

[11] Joined Cases C-159/91 and 160/91, *Poucet and Pistre* [1993] ECR I-637.

[12] Joined Cases C-264/01, C-306/01 and C-355/01, *AOK Bundesverband* [2004] ECR I-2493.

[13] Case C-67/96, *Albany International* v. *Stichting Bedrijfspensioenfonds Textielindustrie* [1999] ECR I-5751.

[14] *BetterCare Ltd* v. *Director General of Fair Trading* [2002] CAT 7.

the United Kingdom Competition Appeal Tribunal. Nevertheless, it includes detailed analysis of the relevant European law and provides a vivid illustration of the issues. The Competition Act 1998 includes a similar prohibition of abuse of a dominant position to that in the European Treaty. BetterCare ran private care homes and complained to the Office of Fair Trading that the local health and social services trust in Northern Ireland, its main customer, was abusing a dominant position through offering unfairly low prices and unfair terms in its purchases from BetterCare of residential and nursing care. The trust also provided its own care directly, and so could be seen as being in competition with the private provider. The Director General rejected the complaint on the basis that the trust was not acting as an undertaking in purchasing care for the disadvantaged funded by taxation. The United Kingdom Competition Appeal Tribunal allowed BetterCare's appeal. It rejected the argument that the trust was carrying out social functions, as this was not relevant to its position as an undertaking This was distinguished from, for example, taking a regulatory decision on whether or not to register a residential home, which would have been outside the scope of the competition rules as 'the exercise of official authority'. The tribunal also rejected the Director General's view that the functions of the trust were based on the principle of solidarity. In doing so, it concentrated on the role of the trust in contracting:

[A]lthough the *funding* which [the trust] provides has a social purpose, the way in which [the trust] carries out or *delivers* its functions is *by using business methods* ... the contracts in question take place within a business setting and are as much commercial transactions from the trust's point of view as they are from the point of view of the independent providers.[15]

The European cases referred to above were distinguished as referring only to 'internal' solidarity between participants in the schemes, rather than 'external' solidarity between the trust and its independent providers.

This decision thus suggested that European competition law will apply to any entity that participates in markets, even if the purpose is a social one and even if the market is highly regulated. Indeed, it

---

[15] *Ibid.*, para. 234 (emphasis in original).

is difficult to think of any public institution – apart from one limited to policy-making – at least some of whose activities would not fall within the scope of competition law. There is an interesting postscript to the case: the Office of Fair Trading, on retaking the decision, concluded that there had been no breach of competition law by the trust, as it was not responsible for setting the prices paid to BetterCare. These were set by the relevant health board and Northern Ireland Government department, which were not undertakings when doing so, as they were not offering goods or services in a market but rather allocating public funds in order to discharge social functions.

This decision is to be contrasted with that of the European Court of Justice in the more recent *FENIN* case.[16] The Federación Española de Empresas de Tecnología Sanitaria (FENIN) is an association of the majority of companies that market medical goods and equipment to Spanish hospitals. It complained to the Commission that the organizations managing the Spanish health service were abusing their dominant position by delaying payment of their debts. The Commission dismissed the complaint on the grounds that the health organizations were not acting as undertakings when carrying out purchasing activities. This decision was upheld by the Court of First Instance on the grounds that what was important was not the purchasing as such, but the purpose to which the goods are put; in this case, this was the provision of services free of charge on the basis of universal cover, and so fell within the principle of solidarity. In the Court of Justice, the Advocate General, who analyses the facts and case-law and provides a preliminary opinion, agreed that the relevant issue was not the purchasing but the activities for which the purchases were to be used that mattered in determining whether competition law applied; he recommended that further findings be made to determine whether the activities of the health organizations were in fact economic in nature or based on the principle of solidarity. For example, the extent to which they competed with private organizations needed to be established.

The Court of Justice delivered a brief and somewhat cryptic judgement to the effect that:

[T]here is no need to dissociate the activity of purchasing goods from the subsequent use to which they are put in order to determine the nature of

[16] Case C-205/03, *FENIN* [2006] ECR I-6295.

that purchasing activity, and that the nature of the purchasing activity must be determined according to whether or not the subsequent use of the purchased goods amounts to an economic activity.[17]

If that use consisted of offering goods and services on a market, it would constitute an economic activity; in the case in question, FENIN had not suggested until the appeal stage that provision of treatment by the health service organizations itself constituted an economic activity, and so the Court had to accept that it did not.

At first sight, this decision seems to mark a major change from the *BetterCare* decision in that it is not the activity of participation in markets through purchasing that matters, but the purpose for which the goods and services are to be used. It may be possible, however, to distinguish the two cases in a way that would result in compatible principles. It should be remembered that, in *BetterCare*, the trust that was purchasing services from the private provider itself provided care services; thus, it was in competition with the provider in the market for care services, not just for purchasing. Therefore, the trust was engaged in an economic activity – not just in purchasing, but also in the provision of services themselves. This was the understanding of the *FENIN* decision subsequently adopted by the Office of Fair Trading in the United Kingdom, which announced that it would close cases alleging infringements of competition law concerning public bodies that were only engaged in purchasing in a particular market and not engaged in the direct provisions of goods and services in that market.[18]

At first sight, this complex case-law may appear to have led to an appropriate conclusion. If a Member State chooses to operate a health service predominantly on the basis of social solidarity, decisions of the bodies comprising it will not be covered by competition law. If, however, a Member State decides to introduce competition into the system – for example, by contracting services out to competing suppliers of health care provision or by creating a competitive internal market – then competition law will apply, as the various bodies involved will be acting as undertakings. This effective delegation of the applicability

---

[17] *Ibid.*, para. 26.
[18] Office of Fair Trading, 'The Competition Act 1998 and public bodies', Policy Note 1/2004.

of competition law to national authorities is in line with both the principle of subsidiarity, according to which no Community action should be taken where objectives can better be achieved by Member States, and the vesting of the primary responsibility for the organization and delivery of health care and medical care in Member States under Article 152 of the Treaty. It is also in line with the law relating to public procurement, which is likely to apply as services are opened up to competition.[19] The basic principle is also sound; as stated by the Advocate General in *FENIN*, it is that:

The power of the State which is exercised in the political sphere is subject to democratic control. A different type of control is imposed on economic operators acting on a market: their conduct is governed by competition law. But there is no justification when the State is acting as an economic operator, for relieving its actions of all control.[20]

The choice of system is up to the national authorities, but they must accept the consequences of their decisions.

However, there are two reasons why this division of responsibilities is not as neat as it may seem at first sight. The first is that it is unclear just how much competition needs to be introduced into a national system to make activities subject to competition law. After all, there are markets and markets, some highly regulated and others operating more freely; for example, the United Kingdom health service internal market, introduced by the Conservative Government in the 1980s, looked very different from the textbook competitive market for consumer products.[21] As Sauter has put it, the simple distinction between solidarity- and competition-based systems 'complicates efforts to introduce competition gradually or partially, while doing so is frequently not only a political necessity but also desirable ... (e.g. to offer an adjustment period or transition phase, or to experiment with greater and smaller degrees of market freedom)'.[22] The case-law offers little guidance on how much competition is necessary

---

[19] See N. Timmins, 'European law looms over NHS contracts', *Financial Times*, 15 January 2007; and Chapter 9 in this volume.

[20] AG Opinion, Case C-205/03, *FENIN*, above n.16, para. 26.

[21] See, for example, A. C. L. Davies, *Accountability: a public law analysis of government by contract* (Oxford: Oxford University Press, 2001).

[22] Sauter, 'Services of general economic interest', above n.2, p. 3.

to make the Treaty provisions applicable, and in this respect it is unfortunate that procedural reasons in *FENIN* prevented further analysis of the extent to which provision of services was competitive, as proposed by the Advocate General. No guidance on this matter was provided by the Court of Justice in that case, although in the earlier *AOK-Bundesverband* case, the Court stated that 'some competition' (presumably of a limited extent) did not in itself make competition law applicable to activities otherwise based on principles of solidarity.[23]

The second complication in the apparently neat division of responsibilities between Member States and the competition authorities lies in the fact that, even if activities are covered by competition law, there is provision in the Treaty for the special treatment of public services. This brings us to our next important theme: the role of Article 86(2) of the Treaty in relation to services of general economic interest.

4. Article 86(2) and services of general economic interest

This article is of sufficient importance to be worth quoting at some length:

> Undertakings entrusted with the operation of services of general economic interest ... shall be subject to the rules contained in this Treaty, in particular to the rules on competition, insofar as the application of such rules does not obstruct the performance, in law or in fact, of the particular tasks assigned to them. The development of trade must not be affected to such an extent as would be contrary to the interests of the Community.

This provision is clearly of enormous potential importance in the area of health care, permitting as it does partial exemption from the competition rules for some undertakings. The first question is, of course, that of what constitutes a service of general economic interest? This is primarily a matter for Member States themselves to determine. However, they are not entirely free in doing so: the European authorities can reject a decision based on a 'manifest error', and the Commission has made it clear that the public service mission of the

---

[23] Joined Cases C-264/01, C-306/01 and C-355/01, *AOK Bundesverband*, above n.13, para. 56.

undertaking must be clearly defined and 'explicitly entrusted through an act of public authority'.[24] The last requirement does not oblige the use of statute; a contract would be sufficient. Such a clear definition is also necessary for state aids law. A relevant example of a service of general economic interest in the health care area, which will be examined in detail later, is that of the provision of ambulance services.

In applying the test of whether the rules of competition law would obstruct the performance of the tasks assigned to the undertaking, the test is one of proportionality. Thus, the Commission and Court will ask whether an exception to the rules is necessary for the undertaking to perform its task, and this question has been the source of considerable controversy. Key questions have been whether some other means of achieving the same goals might be available that is less restrictive of competition, and what the effect of failure to apply the exception would be.[25]

In early cases, the Court took a highly restrictive approach to this test, holding in effect that, for an exception to the competition rules to be justified, it must otherwise be completely impossible to perform the general interest mission.[26] Thus, only restrictions that were *indispensable* could be allowed, and if other means of performing the general interest tasks were available, Article 86(2) could not be used. This restrictive approach was particularly associated with the task of building a single internal market, and concerned markets where competition was feasible, such as telecommunications and civil aviation. The case that represented the first important application of a more generous approach was that of *Corbeau* in 1993.[27] Corbeau had set up a private postal service in competition with the Belgian postal service; the latter had been given exclusive rights to provide postal services, so he was prosecuted in the Belgian courts. The exclusive rights were justified on the need to provide a basic postal service at a uniform rate throughout Belgium, a classic example of a public service requirement accompanied by restrictions on competition aimed at avoiding 'cream skimming'. The Court of Justice asked whether the restriction

---

[24] European Commission, 'Services of general interest in Europe', COM (2000) 580 final, 20 September 2000.
[25] For a more detailed discussion of different approaches to applying the test, see Sauter, 'Services of general economic interest', above n.1, pp. 24–6.
[26] See, for example, Case C-18/88, *RTT* [1991] ECR I-5941, para. 22.
[27] Case C-320/91, *Paul Corbeau* [1993] ECR I-2533.

on competition was necessary to permit the holder of the exclusive right to perform its task of general interest in economically acceptable conditions. On this basis, it accepted the legitimacy of the argument that the exclusive rights were necessary to avoid 'cream skimming' so long as competition would compromise the economic equilibrium of the service of economic interest. Thus, the test was now not whether the public service task would be impossible if competition rules were fully applied, but whether doing so would undermine the economic equilibrium of the undertaking. The court did not ask whether alternative means existed that were more compatible with free competition, such as the establishment of a universal service fund available to all operators of unprofitable services.

This less restrictive approach is also apparent in a number of later cases. For example, in *Almelo*[28] – a case concerning exclusive purchasing and sales contracts between electricity companies required to provide a universal, uninterrupted service at uniform national rates in the Netherlands – the Court, in determining whether restrictions on competition must be allowed to permit the undertakings to perform their general interest task, took into consideration the costs the undertakings had to bear, as well as legislation, particularly that concerning the environment, to which they were subject. In cases concerning gas and electricity monopolies, it was also stated explicitly that it would not be necessary to show that the survival of the undertaking would be threatened by the application of the competition rules, nor that there was no other conceivable means of achieving the public interest goals.[29] This greater openness to the use of the exception from the competition rules in Article 86(2) was accompanied by a new provision in the Treaty of Amsterdam in 1997, introducing a new Article 16 to the EC Treaty. This Article, 'given the place occupied by services of general economic interest in the shared values of the Union as well as their role in promoting social and territorial cohesion', required the Community and Member States to take care that services of general interest 'operate on the basis of principles and conditions which enable them to fulfil their missions'. Though the meaning of this provision remains obscure, it was likely to have encouraged a greater awareness of the importance of

[28] Case C-393/92, *Almelo v. NV Energiebedrijf Ijsselmij* [1994] ECR I-1477.
[29] See, for example, Case C-157/94, *Commission v. Netherlands* [1997] ECR I-5699, paras. 43, 58.

such services in both administrative decisions by the Commission and the case-law.[30]

A useful illustration of this approach can be found in a case drawn from the field of health care. *Abulanz Glöckner* concerned an application by a private ambulance service for an authorization to provide non-emergency ambulance services.[31] It had previously held an authorization, but new legislation by the German *Länder* had provided that an authorization was to be refused if granting it would be likely to have an adverse effect on the general interest in the operation of an effective public ambulance service. This restriction had previously only applied to emergency ambulance services, but now covered non-emergency services too. Renewal of the authorization was thus refused on the grounds that the public ambulance service (run by medical aid organizations such as the Red Cross and which provided both emergency and non-emergency services) was operating below capacity because of the need to provide universal geographical coverage around the clock, including in remote areas, and rapid response times in emergencies. In effect, granting an authorization would permit a form of 'cream skimming', as the costs of expensive emergency coverage were in part offset by revenue from non-emergency services. The private firm argued that there was an abuse of a dominant position on the part of the public ambulance services and that the conferral on them of what was in effect an exclusive right to provide services was in breach of Article 86(1). The public authorities argued that, even if there was such a breach, Article 86(2) would apply as it was necessary to protect the public ambulance service against operators who would provide their services only at profitable peak hours in densely populated and easily accessible areas. In other words, if competition were to be introduced, 'there is thus a serious risk that the inevitable losses of the public ambulance service are socialized, whilst its potential profits are privatized'.[32]

The Court of Justice held that the public ambulance services were undertakings to which competition law applied, and that they had been

---

[30] For analysis of Article 16, see M. Ross, 'Article 16 EC and services of general interest: from derogation to obligation?', *European Law Review* 25 (2000), 22–38.

[31] Case C-475/99, *Abulanz Glöckner* [2001] ECR I-8089.

[32] AG Opinion, *ibid.*, para. 182.

given exclusive rights to provide services that could lead to abuse of a dominant position. However, the provision of emergency ambulance services with universal round-the-clock availability was incontestably a service of general economic interest, so it was necessary to determine whether the restriction on competition was necessary for the public service to operate in conditions of economic equilibrium. The provision of emergency and of non-emergency ambulance services were so closely linked that they both fell within the concept of a service of general economic interest, and:

The extension of the medical aid organisations' exclusive rights to the non-emergency transport sector does indeed enable them to discharge their general-interest task of providing emergency transport in conditions of economic equilibrium. The possibility which would be open to private operators to concentrate, in the non-emergency sector, on more profitable journeys, could affect the degree of economic viability of the service provided by the medical aid organisations and, consequently, jeopardise the quality and reliability of that service.[33]

Only if it could be established that the public services could not meet demand at all times would the general interest argument for restricting the entry of competitors to the market not apply.

What is apparent in this case is thus a less restrictive approach to the need to justify the necessity of restrictions on competition for the proper performance of services of general economic interest. Although the Court used the test that the restrictions must be necessary to permit the service to operate in conditions of economic equilibrium, it emphasized in doing so that the 'quality and reliability' of the service must not be jeopardized. Thus, there does seem to be a recognition of the importance of the provision of high-quality and universal public services here. What is important, though, is that the public authorities must be prepared to justify such provision through positive arguments showing why restrictions on competition are justified. In effect, here we see a requirement of transparency rather than direct hostility to non-market forms of provision. Such a move towards requiring transparency is also apparent in recent developments in the approach by the other Community institutions in this area.

---

[33] *Ibid.*, para. 61.

5. The European Commission and political reform

Of course, the European courts are not the only important institutions in the European Union; the Commission also has made important statements and decisions on competition law and public services, and the Council and (to a much lesser degree) the Parliament have had major roles in reform. After the Maastricht Treaty of 1992, the political conflict between different Member States became particularly strong, especially as it had added to the EC Treaty a new Article 4 stating, *inter alia*, that the activities of the Member States and the Community shall include 'the adoption of an economic policy which ... is conducted in accordance with the principle of an open market economy with free competition'. This was perceived by some Member States as a threat to their distinctive traditions of public service. One outcome was the publication by the Commission of a Communication on services of general interest in 1996 – note that the term 'services of general interest' covers both the services of general economic interest discussed above and non-market services not subject to competition law.[34] This summarized the existing law and covered sectoral liberalization and the development of universal service obligations. It then summarized the Commission's future objectives, including introducing evaluation tools to assess the operation, performance and competence of services of general interest on a sector-by-sector basis and greater openness on policy in this area. However, the Commission rejected demands for amendment of what is now Article 86 to provide greater protection for services of general interest. Although there was recognition of the value of services of general interest, they were placed firmly within a single market context and their legitimate role appeared limited to cases of market failure.

As mentioned above, the Amsterdam Treaty in 1997 introduced a new Article 16 to the Treaty, which required the Community and Member States to take care that services of general economic interest 'operate on the basis of principles and conditions which enable them to fulfil their missions'. It also included a declaration that these provisions should be implemented 'with full respect for the jurisprudence of the Court of Justice, *inter alia* as regards the principles of equality of treatment, quality and continuity of such services' and an important protocol on

[34] European Commission, 'Communication on services of general interest in Europe', COM (96) 443 final, 11 September 1996.

public broadcasting. Although the meaning of these provisions was unclear, it did seem to result in a more positive approach to services of general interest in later statements of policy. The Commission produced a further Communication on services of general interest in 2000, which emphasized more clearly the importance of ensuring the good functioning of such services rather than seeing them simply as unwelcome impediments to a single internal market.[35] A particularly important theme was that of the need for transparency. Thus:

[I]n order to fulfil their mission, it is necessary for the relevant public authorities to act in full transparency, by stipulating with some precision the needs of users for which services of general interest are being established, who is in charge of setting up and enforcing the relevant obligations and how these obligations are going to be fulfilled.[36]

The Commission also called for recognition of the link between 'the special place of services of general economic interest in the shared values of the Union' and European citizenship.[37] This was to some extent forthcoming in Article 36 of the Charter of Fundamental Rights adopted in 2000, entitled 'Access to Services of General Economic Interest':

The Union recognizes and respects access to services of general economic interest as provided for in national laws and practices, in accordance with the Treaty establishing the European community, in order to promote the social and territorial cohesion of the Union.

The importance of this provision should not be exaggerated; legally, it is not directly enforceable, and the potential impact of a commitment to 'recognize and respect' is unclear. In comparison with more market-based rights and freedoms, including those of free movement, the practical effects of the provision are limited. Nevertheless, in conjunction with Article 16 it does represent a more positive recognition of the importance of social rights and social cohesion.[38]

---

[35] European Commission, 'Services of general interest, above n.24.
[36] *Ibid.*, para. 9.   [37] *Ibid.*, para. 64.
[38] See M. Ross, 'Promoting solidarity: from public services to a European model of competition', *Common Market Law Review* 44 (2007), 1057–80, at 1063–4, in particular.

The Communication also suggested drafting a framework directive setting out consolidated principles for the treatment of services of general economic interest. This was supported by the Parliament, and the Barcelona Summit in 2002 asked the Commission to undertake more work on this; the result was the Green Paper of 2003.[39] The Green Paper also took a positive approach to services of general interest, considering them to be 'a pillar of European citizenship, forming some of the rights enjoyed by European citizens and providing an opportunity for dialogue with public authorities within the context of good governance'.[40] A major focus was on developing principles of good governance that could be applied to services, derived from experience in the liberalized sectors of telecommunications, energy and postal services, from Article 16 and from the Commission's own White Paper on governance.[41] Examples of principles drawn from liberalized sectors were those of universal service, continuity, quality of service, affordability and user and consumer protection; these could be used to characterize a Community concept of services of general economic interest. In discussing principles of good governance, the Commission emphasized the need for the proper and transparent specification of public service requirements and the need for a transparent selection process for providers; it also built on earlier work on the means of evaluating the performance of services of general interest.

A theme was thus becoming very clear from the Commission's work. Rather than focusing on services of general interest as obstructions to the creation of a single market, the emphasis was on the need for transparency, especially in the definition of public service requirements and the choice of the organization providing the service, and on good governance. However, the later White Paper, issued by the Commission after consultation, was much more qualified and cautious.[42] Although the consultation had shown a consensus on the importance of services of general interest as a pillar of the European model of society and on the importance of universal service for social and territorial cohesion, it was also necessary to respect the diversity

---

[39] European Commission, 'Services of general interest', above n.7.
[40] *Ibid.*, para. 2.
[41] European Commission, 'European governance', White Paper, COM (2001) 428 final, 25 July 2001.
[42] European Commission, 'Services of general interest', White Paper, COM (2004) 374 final, 12 May 2004.

of different types of service – for example, the difference between social and health services and network industries such as telecommunications and energy. The proposals were almost entirely for soft law rather than a binding framework directive, and the need for the latter would be reconsidered after the coming into effect of the proposed Constitutional Treaty. In terms of later developments, important documents were issued on state aids and on procurement in 2005 and 2006; these will be considered in Chapter 9. The draft Constitutional Treaty produced by the European Convention in 2003 proposed only relatively minor changes to the provisions relating to services of general interest, notably an amendment to Article 16 providing for a new framework directive to define the principles and conditions that would enable services of general economic interest to fulfil their missions.

As is well known, the Constitutional Treaty was rejected in referendums held in France and the Netherlands, in the former case apparently in part because of concerns about possible threats to Continental traditions of public service by what was perceived as an 'Anglo-Saxon', pro-competition approach contained in it. The Lisbon Treaty agreed in October 2007 includes two relevant amendments. It would amend Article 16 to permit the Parliament and the Council to establish (by means of regulations) principles and conditions, particularly economic and financial conditions, enabling services of general economic interest to fulfil their missions. Thus, these institutions, especially the Parliament, would potentially have a greater role in rule-making, and this could include, for example, setting out requirements for good governance.[43] However, the Lisbon Treaty also includes a protocol on services of general interest attempting to clarify Article 16 by stating that the shared values of the Union include, in particular:

- the essential role and wide discretion of national, regional and local authorities in providing, commissioning and organizing services of general economic interest as closely as possible to the needs of the users;

[43] See Sauter, 'Services of general economic interest', above n.1, pp. 5–6; and, for a discussion of some of the difficult issues involved, M. Krajewski, 'Providing legal clarity and securing policy space for public services through a legal framework for services of general economic interest: squaring the circle?', *European Public Law* 14 (2008), 377–98.

- the diversity between various services of general economic interest and the differences in the needs and preferences of users that may result from different geographical, social or culture situations; and
- a high level of quality, safety and affordability, equal treatment and the promotion of universal service and of user rights.

The protocol also states that the provisions of the Treaties 'do not affect in any way the competence of Member States to provide, commission and organize non-economic services of general interest'. This latter provision would seriously limit any attempt to extend Community action into non-economic services of general interest, as had been suggested in the Green Paper.

What seems now to be apparent, then, is a further shift of emphasis. Rather than stressing the role of the Commission and European law in promoting public service values and good governance in services of general interest, the emphasis is now on the role of Member States and the diversity of different types of services of general interest. This is in keeping both with the concerns of Member States that a European model of public services might undermine their own distinctive traditions, and the less optimistic European vision after the setbacks to the Constitutional Treaty. Nevertheless, there will continue to be Community action in these areas; in a new Communication on services of general interest, the Commission states that it envisages such action as taking the form of providing legal guidance on cross-cutting issues such as the state aid rules, developing further the sector-specific policies in fields such as energy and transport, and monitoring and evaluating services on a sector-by-sector basis.[44]

6. Conclusions

Despite the complexity of the law described above, it is possible to reach some conclusions about the application of competition law to public services, including those in the health sector. In an earlier discussion of social solidarity in European law, Hervey concluded that this concept 'has the potential to be an adequate means of protection

---

[44] European Commission, 'Services of general interest, including social services of general interest: a new European commitment', COM (2007) 725 final, 20 November 2007.

for the "European social model"; a buttress against internal market law'.[45] There are two reasons why this may remain true at the level of principle in the area of competition law. The first is that the basic choice for the organization of health services on the basis of social solidarity or of competition lies with the Member States; if they choose the former, competition law will not apply. The second is that the special treatment of services of general economic interest is now well recognized and does, in principle, respect the special needs of public services to provide a universal service at uniform rates, inevitably limiting opportunities for competition. Moreover, assuming that the proposed new protocol to the Treaty is adopted, this provision will probably reinforce the degree to which Member States are permitted autonomy in organizing public services and will confirm that competition law is not applicable to non-economic services of general interest. The stress in recent case-law and other legal provisions has been on the need for transparency in the organization of public services through the proper definition of the tasks of general economic interest rather than treating them as unacceptable limits to the working of the internal market.

However, when one looks at the practical implications of the current state of the law, the position is much less clear. The first problem is that, in practice, there is not likely to be a clear distinction between a service based on social solidarity and one based on markets and competition. Health provision increasingly takes the form of a mixed economy, and the Court of Justice has not made it clear just how much competition in provision is necessary to bring the system within the scope of competition law. The second problem lies not in competition law itself but in its interaction with other areas of European law. Thus, it is artificial to separate competition law from the law of state aids and public procurement, as all are closely intertwined and share the objective of a freely operating internal market.

To some extent, recent developments in these two areas do reinforce the autonomy of Member States. Thus, the 2005 Commission decision on state aids exempts public service compensation granted to hospitals carrying out services of general economic interest from the scope of those state aids that require notification; the state aid rules,

---

[45] Hervey, 'Social solidarity', above n.5, p. 33; and Ferrera, *The boundaries of welfare*, above n.5, pp. 252–3.

of course, do not apply to non-economic services based on solidarity for the reasons set out above.[46] However, important conditions of transparency are a prerequisite for the exemption, including advance specification of the public service obligations in question and the parameters for calculating compensation. These were derived from the decision by the Court of Justice in the *Altmark* case, which set out the general position on state aids and public service compensation.[47] One implication of the case was that, although allocation of public service tasks through competitive tendering was not necessary, adopting this procedure would simplify compliance with the conditions. Secondly, health and social services procurement contracts are exempted from the full public procurement procedures. However, more limited requirements exist for advertising and impartial procedures for contracts outside the scope of the full procurement rules. These will be discussed in more detail in Chapter 9, but, given the uncertainty about the scope of competition law, and doubts as to the precise circumstances in which state aid and procurement rules will apply, the temptation for Member States may be to adopt a full process of competitive tendering for services to avoid future challenges. This in itself has well-documented problems, including disruption to the provision of services due to periodic tendering, and a 'race to the bottom' in staff terms and conditions in an effort to be the successful tenderer. As a matter of principle, European competition law respects the autonomy of Member States to determine how public services should be organized, but once a Member State departs from a model predominantly based on solidarity, the uncertainty of the law may make it difficult to avoid rapid changes towards a much more consistently market-based system, despite the potential role of the exception for services of general economic interest in creating a 'safe haven' from the competition rules.

---

[46] Commission Decision on the application of Article 86(2) of the EC Treaty to state aid in the form of public service compensation granted to certain undertakings entrusted with the operation of services of general economic interest, OJ 2005 No. L312/67.

[47] Case C-280/00, *Altmark Trans GmbH* [2003] ECR I-7747.

8 | EU competition law and health policy

JULIA LEAR, ELIAS MOSSIALOS AND
BEATRIX KARL

1. Introduction

Competition law has been an essential tool in the establishment of
the single European market (SEM) and the European Community.
The EC Treaty reflects the Community's evolution from an economic
organization with extensive competence to regulate the SEM. Social
policy, on the other hand, reflects the diversity of Member States'
social systems and remains primarily the jurisdiction of national governments. EU policies reflect a balance between European welfare
state principles of universal access to public services and social solidarity, and the competition law principles of market integration and
economic freedom.

The enforcement of EC competition law by the European Court of
Justice (ECJ) and national courts has been a significant driver pushing
health policy onto the European Union agenda.[1] Community competition rules prohibit undertakings from participating in anti-competitive activities, such as agreements to set prices or abuse of dominant
position.[2] Since the definition of an 'undertaking' focuses on the function of the organization rather than its status,[3] it has been applied
to both private and public health care services.[4] Article 152(5) EC
leaves health provision and financing squarely under the jurisdiction

The authors would like to acknowledge and express their appreciation for the
assistance of Giorgio Monti, Vassilis Hatzopoulos and Tamara Hervey for their
extensive comments on drafts of this chapter.

[1] M. McKee, E. Mossialos and R. Baeten, *The impact of EU law on health care
systems* (Brussels: PIE-Peter Lang, 2002).
[2] Articles 81 and 82 EC.
[3] Joined Cases C-159/91 and 160/91, *Poucet and Pistre* [1993] ECR I-637.
[4] Case C-205/03, *Federacion National de Empresas de Instrumentacion
Cientifica Medica Tecnica y Dental (FENIN)* v. *Commission of the European
Communities* [2006] ECR I-6295; Case T-289/03, *British United Provident
Association Ltd (BUPA) and Others* v. *Commission* [2008] ECR II-81.

of Member States, as long as other EU laws, including competition rules, are followed.

Chapter 7 in this volume presented the context of this debate by analysing competition law and public services. This chapter will present specific cases where competition laws have been applied to the health sector, providing a basis for analysis of the current state of EU law and the indications for the road ahead. The most important Treaty provisions governing competition law are Articles 81, 82 and 86 EC, found in Section 1 of Title VI.[5] Chapter 9 in this volume focuses on Section 2 of Title VI of the Treaty, which includes Articles 87–9 EC governing state aid and public procurement.

To determine whether competition law applies and whether there is a justification for state regulation restricting competition under Article 86 EC requires detailed case-by-case analysis. The jurisprudence has created legal uncertainty regarding the application of EU law to national health systems and raised questions as to the Community's role in further developing a European health policy. In 2006, the Commission conducted a consultation exploring Community action on health services.[6] The two primary issues of concern were the legal uncertainty created by ECJ rulings and how the Community could support Member States in the health services sector. In response to the process, Member States expressed an interest in receiving clarification on cross-border care, but emphasized a preference for national control of health systems under the subsidiarity principle.[7] Thus, the tension between competing interests has been building. Member States would prefer to protect national health systems from external interference, while the Commission tries to raise its profile and influence through the publication of consultations and Communications that attempt to clarify the EU's role in health policy. Meanwhile, the ECJ and national courts continue their case-by-case analysis, defining few general rules for national policy-makers to follow.

The EU is at a legal crossroads, where economic policy and social policy collide. The case-law of the European Court of Justice is at the centre of the conflict, since it has applied competition law to

---

[5] Articles 83 through 85 EC detail the duties of the Council and the Commission, as well as the entry into force of the provisions.
[6] European Commission, 'Consultation regarding Community action on health services', SEC (2006) 1195/4, 26 September 2006.
[7] *Ibid.*

the health sector in several cases.[8] The imbalance between strictly delineated economic laws and nationally-defined social policy goals has been characterized as 'constitutional asymmetry' by Scharpf.[9] Traditionally, European governments have regulated the health care sector to ensure quality, efficiency and equity in health care provision and financing. Health system reforms have decentralized decision-making, encouraged greater competition on price and quality, and forced many European patients to exercise choice as consumers. The question arises, if Member States' health systems incorporate market-based reforms, to what extent will competition law apply?

It is also important to note that EU laws apply uniformly across the Community regardless of domestic health care system structures.[10] No two Member States share the same mechanisms for planning, financing and providing health services. European national health systems have evolved based on the unique political and economic development of each Member State. It is also irrelevant whether the patient pays for services and is later reimbursed by the state, or if the services are free at the point of use. Depending upon the degree to which Member States employ market-based mechanisms to finance, manage and provide health services, the impact of competition law will vary. This diversity further complicates any attempt to harmonize EU health policy legislation.

Since health care has the potential to be both commercial and international, it is a test case for the conflict between EU economic policy and the expansion of EU social policy into new areas, including health care financing and provision. This chapter will first explain the circumstances when EU competition law applies, and will introduce some of the complexities of defining undertakings caused by recent policy developments moving health services towards market competition. The following section considers Articles 81 and 82 EC, which prohibit undertakings from forming anti-competitive cartels and abusing a dominant position. Next, Article 86 EC will be introduced in order to discuss the limitations on Member State regulation

---

[8] Case C-205/03, *FENIN*, above n.4; Case T-289/03, *BUPA*, above n.4, Case C-372-/04, *Watts* [2006] ECR I-4325.

[9] F. Scharpf, 'The European social model: coping with the challenges of diversity', *Journal of Common Market Studies* 40 (2002), 645–70.

[10] Case C-385/99, *Müller-Fauré* v. *Onderlinge Waarborgmaatschappij OZ Zorgverzekeringen* [2003] ECR I-4509.

and the potential to use the 'services of general economic interest' exception to permit restriction of competition when providing health services. Lastly, the chapter reviews EU competition enforcement mechanisms that have increased scrutiny of health-related cases as a result of decentralized enforcement delegated to national competition authorities (NCAs). Where possible, examples from a wide sample of European countries are provided; however, this chapter is not a comprehensive analysis of the current state of affairs in all twenty-seven EU Member States.

2. When does competition law apply?

Article 81(1) EC prohibits *undertakings* from practices 'which may affect trade between Member States and which have as their object or effect the prevention, restriction or distortion of competition within the common market'. As explained in greater detail in Chapter 7 in this volume, the concept of undertakings is not defined in the Treaty but by a series of ECJ cases. Undertakings are classified not by their structure but by their actions, the context in which they act, and the purpose and effect of their actions.[11] The definition evolves from the Court's attempt to distinguish between government functions and the private sector. Activities that are an exercise of sovereign power or are social activities based on solidarity are exempted from competition law.[12] Undertakings engaged in economic activities are subject to competition law, unless the 'services of general interest' exemption applies.[13]

Since the 1980s, reforms intended to improve efficiency in the health sector have encouraged greater privatization of public services. The gradual introduction of market forces to particular health services makes the delineation of undertakings dependent upon the specific nature of the activities, the context in which the services are provided, as well as a consideration of how the services will be paid for and by whom. It is possible that a government-owned hospital could engage in economic activities as an undertaking by providing services

---

[11] Joined Cases C-159/91 and 160/91, *Poucet and Pistre*, above n.3.
[12] Case C-364/92, *SAT Fluggesellschaft* v. *Eurocontrol* [1994] ECR I-43.
[13] Case C-475/99, *Ambulanz Glockner* v. *Landreis Sudwetpflaz (Glockner)* [2001] ECR I-8089; Case T-289/03, *BUPA*, above n.4.

to private patients. Similarly, a private clinic could be entrusted by the government to provide certain health services that would be protected from competition law as a social activity based on the principle of solidarity.

Competition law does not apply to governments exercising sovereign powers under the principle of *imperium*.[14] Acts emanating from the state's *imperium* are unique to sovereign governments and include defence, environmental surveillance or granting a licence.[15] By analogy, it could be argued that a ministry of health exercises sovereign authority when setting public health priorities, defining the scope of practice for health professionals and setting tariff rates for public health services. Each of these non-economic activities is exempted from competition law, even though they have an impact on the health care market. However, this is not a blanket exception. If the state engages in economic activity, such as trading in products or services, alongside private undertakings, the sovereign exemption does not apply.[16] In order to determine whether the state is exercising public powers or carrying on economic activities, it is necessary to conduct a case-by-case analysis.[17] For example, the municipality granting a license to sell tobacco is acting in its public authority capacity,[18] while a public clinic selling flu shots is engaged in an economic activity.

Entities are not undertakings if the services provided meet the criteria for social activities set out by the ECJ in the *Poucet and Pistre* case[19] and its progeny. In this case, the plaintiffs challenged the monopoly rights of two social security schemes in France. The schemes were based on the principle of solidarity, since membership was compulsory; contributions were calculated based on income regardless of the member's state of health; and all members received the same benefits. As such, these schemes were fulfilling an exclusively social function in the discharge of their legally defined duties. Similarly, in *INAIL*, the Court found that a compulsory scheme providing workers'

---

[14] Case C-343/95, *Cali & Figli* v. *Servizi Ecologici Porto di Genova (Cali)* [1997] ECR I-1580.
[15] A. Winterstein, 'Nailing the jellyfish: social security and competition law', *European Competition Law Review* 6 (1999), 324–33; *ibid.*
[16] Case C-41/90, *Hofner and Elser* [1991] ECR 1979.
[17] Case 118/85, *Commission* v. *Italy* [1987] ECR 2599.
[18] Case C-387/93, *Banchero* [1995] ECR I-4663.
[19] Joined Cases C-159/91 and 160/91, *Poucet and Pistre*, above n.3.

compensation insurance operated on the principle of solidarity, since the benefits and contribution levels were defined by law.[20] Therefore, this state-regulated insurance fulfilled a purely social purpose and was not an economic activity.

The Court has reviewed the activities of both health insurers and health providers to determine whether their activities violate competition law. In Germany, sickness funds jointly set maximum fixed amounts payable for some prescription medications, known as reference pricing. Pharmaceutical companies complained that the sickness funds were colluding to fix prices. In *AOK*,[21] the ECJ held that the sickness funds were not undertakings, since they were organized under the solidarity principle and performed a purely social function. Employees are obliged to be insured by the statutorily regulated sickness funds. The fact that the funds compete to attract members did not override the social nature of the insurance schemes. The Court also found that setting reimbursement rates was an integral part of limiting costs for state-mandated benefits.

In the process of performing social functions, health care providers must naturally engage in some economic activities. In the *FENIN* case, an association of businesses complained that hospitals in the Spanish national health service were in violation of competition laws by delaying to pay invoices, and that this was an abuse of their dominant position. The Court of First Instance found that the hospitals were not undertakings, as they are funded through social security contributions and provide health services free of charge based on the solidarity principle. The ECJ then upheld the reasoning of the lower court, concluding that the purchasing activity was not economic, since the goods purchased would be used to provide public services and would not be resold in the market. It follows that, where the purchasing function is part of the process to provide social services, it should not be judged as an economic activity merely because the goods must be purchased from the market.[22] Thus, even though an organization does engage in some economic activities, competition law may not apply to its social activities based on the solidarity principle.

---

[20] Case C-218/00, *INAIL* [2002] ECR I-691.
[21] Joined Cases C-264/01, 301/01, 354/01 and 355/01, *AOK Bundesverband* v. *Ichthyol-Gesellschaft Cordes (AOK)* [2004] ECR I-2493.
[22] Case C-205/03, *FENIN*, above n.4.

On the other hand, the Court applied competition law in a case where social insurance institutions performed additional economic activities in competition with private insurance companies. It took this view in *Fédération francaise des sociétés d'assurance (FFSA)*,[23] involving a monopoly in the voluntary supplementary pension insurance sector. Even though the undertaking employed some elements of solidarity, the economic characteristics of the optional retirement scheme led to a finding that FFSA was an undertaking. The Court also deemed the insurance activity of compulsory, supplementary pension insurance funds to be economic in several cases, including *Albany*,[24] *Brentjens*,[25] *Bokken*[26] and *Pavlov*.[27] In each of these cases, the Court emphasized the fact that all these systems were financed according to the capitalization principle, whereby an explicit contribution to the budget is allocated to each member of the plan regardless of need.[28] Where the Court finds limited evidence of the solidarity principle due to the voluntary nature of the insurance scheme, competition law will apply.

It is difficult to derive a clear test from these cases. Determining the status of an undertaking and whether its activity is social or economic requires detailed analysis of the specific health programme and the circumstances of its operation. When competition law applies to a challenged activity, the Court will first decide whether the government is involved and the activity is exempted under the *imperium* principle. Then the Court will determine whether the actor is an undertaking engaged in an economic or social activity. The definition of undertakings that can be pieced together through the relevant ECJ judgments is an imprecise case-by-case approach that weighs several criteria. The most significant factors include: (a) whether the scheme is organized under principles of social solidarity, including legally standardized contribution and benefit levels free from risk selection; (b) whether membership in the system is compulsory; (c) whether the

---

[23] Case C-244/94, *FFSA* [1995] ECR I-4019, para. 17.
[24] Case C-67/96, *Albany* [1999] ECR I-5751, paras. 81 *et seq.*
[25] Case C-115/97, *Brentjens* [1999] ECR I-6025, paras. 81 *et seq.*
[26] Case C-219/97, *Bokken* [1999] ECR I-6121, paras. 71 *et seq.*
[27] Joined Cases C-180/98 to C-184/98, *Pavlov* [2000] ECR I-6451, paras. 114 *et seq.*
[28] N. Rice and P. Smith, 'Strategic resource allocation and funding decisions', in E. Mossialos *et al.* (eds.), *Funding healthcare: options for Europe* (Maidenhead: Open University, 2002).

scheme directly competes in the market with undertakings; and (d) whether the entity exercises independent discretion in providing services for profit or is following a delegated state mandate to provide public services. The Court will then analyse the nature of the activity itself, and whether it interferes with competition within the single market to the extent that it violates competition laws.[29]

Applying the definition of undertakings to European health systems is complicated by the complex relationships between the public and private sectors. For example, if a municipality has contracted with a private service provider to manage a publicly-owned and funded facility that exclusively serves public patients, does that part of the provider's business qualify as a social activity exempted from competition laws? Alternatively, an organization that usually provides social services, such as a government-owned and operated public hospital, could engage in economic activity by providing services to private patients who pay directly for the treatments received. Reforms resulting in organizations that have mixed public and private funding and provide services to both public and private patients require detailed analysis to determine whether competition law applies. These situations also raise questions about state aid.[30] The important point here is that where the public entities are engaged in public–private partnerships, there is a risk that state aid prohibitions may be triggered.

To illustrate the complexity of the public–private and payer–provider relationships, one can consider the experiment with a general practitioner (GP) 'fundholding scheme' in the United Kingdom. GPs working as self-employed businesses consistently were recognized as undertakings providing medical services. The 1990 National Health Services and Community Care Act created a limited number of fundholding contracts between the National Health Service (NHS) and GPs for a range of medical services. These fundholders would then either provide the services themselves or contract with other providers for services not included in their practice, the idea being that the

---

[29] For further discussion on the topic of undertakings, see also Chapters 7 and 9 in this volume.

[30] The Treaty limits the granting of state aid to undertakings that distort competition in Article 87 EC. These issues are addressed in detail in Chapter 9 in this volume. The important point here is that where the public entities are engaged in public–private partnerships, there is a risk that state aid prohibitions may be triggered.

GPs would become price sensitive and more efficient. The question of whether to apply competition law is complicated by the type of contracts used between the NHS and the fundholders. While these contracts were legally enforceable, the subcontracts between the fundholders and NHS providers for additional services were 'NHS contracts', which are treated as public-service, intra-corporate agreements between a parent and its subsidiaries and therefore not legally enforceable and not covered by EU law.[31] For the purposes of this discussion, the important point is that the fundholding system blurred the definition of GP practices. On the one hand, GP practices were private undertakings providing services as an economic activity. On the other hand, GPs were also treated as public contracting authorities purchasing social services for public patients on the basis of solidarity, an action that would be considered a social activity exempted from competition law. Since the scheme was short-lived, the courts never had the opportunity to scrutinize whether competition law would apply to the fundholding system, but it remains an interesting legal puzzle.

Another mixed public–private case arising in the United Kingdom was recently considered by the United Kingdom national competition authority, the Office of Fair Trading (OFT). The Bettercare Group complained that the North and West Trust was abusing its dominant position by purchasing services at an excessively low price. Trusts are organizations that are part of the NHS in each of the four nations of the United Kingdom. They purchase – and in some cases provide – primary health care and residential care services for patients within a defined geographical area.[32] The North and West Trust provides residential care, and also contracts with the Bettercare Group to supply additional services. Thus, residents were offered a choice between publicly and privately provided services. It was this dual payer–provider function, creating competition between public and private facilities, that tipped the analysis towards the trust acting as an undertaking. On appeal, the Competition Appeal Tribunal (CAT) found that the

---

[31] For more detailed analysis of the nature of these contracts, refer to P. Cohen, 'The separation of purchaser from provider in health care systems and European Community law: the case of the British National Health Service', LSE Discussion Paper No.1 (1994).

[32] A. Talbot-Smith and A. Pollock, *The new NHS, a guide* (New York: Routledge, 2006).

Trust was an undertaking engaged in economic activities by providing services in the market, and sent the case back to the OFT to rule on the merits of the case. On remission, the OFT found that the Trust had not engaged in any abuse of dominance, since they did not have discretion to set prices. Further, the government bodies that set prices were not undertakings.[33] The fact that all of the services funded by the Trust were public services made the case difficult to reconcile with the ECJ ruling in *FENIN*. The OFT recognized that the application of the undertaking analysis may lead to a different result depending upon whether the entity also provides services in the market or merely purchases services.[34]

The *Bettercare* case highlights the question of how the central government enforces EU obligations in a decentralized health system. Since the case was specific to a trust in Northern Ireland, applying the ruling to the other nations of the United Kingdom is difficult, as there are variations in the health system structure and the degree of private sector involvement. There are several different types of trusts in the United Kingdom health system that could be engaged in economic activities. The CAT held that the trust in the *Bettercare* case was an undertaking engaged in economic activities as a provider of services in the market. Most trusts, like primary care trusts (PCTs), fall within the NHS hierarchy and are managed by NHS employees. Some trusts function exclusively as payers contracting for services. Foundation Trusts (FTs) are hospitals that have been granted special status due to superior performance, placing them outside the NHS governance structure. FTs are public benefit corporations, ultimately accountable to the parliament, not the Secretary of State for Health. Both organizations contract with either NHS or private providers for services. FTs provide services to PCTs based on legal contracts, not public-service contracts. They have the discretion to set priorities, to dispose of property, to borrow funds from the private sector and to provide services to private patients.[35]

Analysis regarding how competition law could apply to trusts in England's NHS is an open question worth further study. Initially,

---

[33] *BetterCare Group Ltd* v. *Director General of Fair Trade* (2002) 229 CAT 7.
[34] Office of Fair Trading (OFT), 'The Competition Act 1998 and public bodies', Policy Note 1/2004, OFT 443, August 2004.
[35] Talbot-Smith and Pollock, *The new NHS*, above n.32.

looking at the four part test for social activity detailed above, all NHS trusts are organized on the basis of social solidarity and provide services to all United Kingdom residents. However, there could be cases where the second two parts of the test may not be met. As discussed above, the Court would also consider whether the organization provides services that compete in the market and whether the organization's activities are narrowly defined by statute or if they enjoy independent discretion. FTs enjoy independent discretion to define business plans, to invest or dispose of assets and to enter into joint ventures with for-profit corporations for the sale of both NHS and non-NHS health care services, including private insurance.[36] On the other hand, they will be subject to government regulation, not within the NHS accountability framework like PCTs, but by an independent regulator.[37] Thus, whether the FT's activities were economic or social would depend on close scrutiny of the specific activities alleged to be anti-competitive.

Similarly, the Finnish Competition Authority (FCA) has investigated public hospitals for their expansion into private health services at below market rates. The Pirkanmaa Hospital District's Public Laboratory Enterprise was considered to be an undertaking with a dominant position in the market. The FCA warned the hospital district that 'when public production is marketized, the authorities should ensure that private players are provided with equal opportunities to compete in the field that used to be completely the responsibility of the public sector'.[38]

Some statutory reforms adopted by national health systems also create new opportunities for challenges under competition law. For example, the privatization of hospitals could lead to the application of competition law. Germany, Austria and some new Member States have experimented with new forms of hospital ownership and management that establish complex public–private relationships. A study

---

[36] S. Boyle, 'What foundation trusts mean for the NHS', Report for the Overview and Scrutiny Committee of the Royal Borough of Kensington and Chelsea, January 2004, www.rbkc.gov.uk/howwegovern/yourcouncil/oscreport_foundationtrusts.pdf.

[37] Part 1, Section 2, The Health and Social Care (Community Health and Standards) Act 2003.

[38] Finnish Competition Authority, '2003 yearbook', www.kilpailuvirasto.fi/tiedostot/vuosikirja_2003_Englanti.pdf.

funded by the European Commission discovered that there were several reasons for public owners to privatize hospitals in Germany. Fiscal reasons included the need to reduce public debts and to be free of the responsibility to balance the financial deficits of hospitals, since the German financing system no longer guarantees full cost compensation. There is also external pressure from EU economic policies limiting public budget deficits. Public authorities following restrictive fiscal policies increasingly rely on privatizations to solve budget problems. These policies have led to both an increase in the number of private hospitals and a new type of hybrid, publicly-owned hospital with independent private status.[39] Whether these hybrid semipublic hospitals engage in social or economic activities must depend on the details of individual cases. These changes have also resulted in closer scrutiny by the German Competition Authority (GCA). The GCA has recently denied mergers in several cases where private hospitals have sought to acquire public facilities that could achieve excessive dominance in local hospital markets.[40] Similarly, in Austria, hospital reform has created publicly-owned but privately-managed hospitals. These reforms also have the goal of giving hospitals greater flexibility and independence from local political influence. Private managers outsource a larger portion of non-clinical services and establish public–private partnerships.[41] This level of discretion and freedom to work with private patients could be characterized as economic activities subject to competition law.

Post-communist new Member States have gone through waves of health system reforms that also raise complex unanswered questions. Communist-era health systems were vertically integrated, and strictly

---

[39] Wirtschafts- und Sozialwissenschaftlisches Institut (WSI), 'Liberalization, privatization and regulation in the German Healthcare Sector/ Hospitals', November 2006.

[40] German Competition Authority (GCA), Press Releases, 17 January 2008, www.bundeskartellamt.de/wEnglisch/News/2008_01_17. php; 29 April 2005, www.bundeskartellamt.de/wEnglisch/News/ Archiv/ArchivNews2005/2005_04_29.php; 11 September 2006, www. bundeskartellamt.de/wEnglisch/News/Archiv/ArchivNews2006/2006_09_11. php; and 8 November 2006, www.bundeskartellamt.de/wEnglisch/News/ Archiv/ArchivNews2006/2006_11_08.php.

[41] A. Fidler et al., 'Incorporation of public hospitals: a 'silver bullet' against overcapacity, managerial bottlenecks and resource constraints? Case studies from Austria and Estonia', Health Policy 81 (2007), 328–38.

state controlled. After the fall of the communist governments, the health systems required significant capital investment to facilitate reorganization and modernization. However, these reforms were further frustrated by high demand for services as was customary under the old system, and a lack of public confidence caused by corruption. Within this context, new Member States also experimented with reforms opening up public health services to the private sector, especially in the case of hospitals. In Estonia, hospital reforms from 1994 to 2001 altered the legal status of many hospitals under private law, leaving their status ambiguous and their public service mandate unclear.[42] In Lithuania, hospitals underwent similar periodic reforms following the collapse of the former Soviet Union. Since 1996, the health care system as a whole has been moving towards using contracts, as many health care institutions have been redefined as public not-for-profit entities with independent boards.[43] Recently, public–private partnerships (PPPs) have become increasingly popular. Many municipalities have new responsibilities to manage health services provision within newly decentralized health system reforms. The local governments have struggled with a lack of capacity or authority to manage health clinics owned by the Ministry of Health. Complexities over the tendering and contract management processes have required the passage of new legislation to facilitate the new arrangements.[44] The resulting lack of oversight and coordination in these cases opens questions about whether the provision of care in these quasi-public facilities should be characterized as economic or social activities. In the health sector, there are many examples of health system reforms that could dilute the social aspect of public services towards more market-based provision of health services. This shift towards emphasizing economic activities could lead to more health care organizations being designated as undertakings and, consequently, additional legal scrutiny under EU law.[45]

---

[42] T. Palu and R. Kadakmaa, 'Estonian hospital sector in transition', *Eurohealth* 7 (2001), 3.

[43] Z. Logminiene, 'Hospital sector reform in Lithuania', *Eurohealth* 7 (2001), 3.

[44] K. Kerschbaumer, 'Public-private partnerships in Eastern Europe', *Eurohealth* 13 (2007), 7–10.

[45] As undertakings, they may also be subject to additional financial reporting requirements. Directive 2005/81/EC on the transparency of financial relations between Member States and undertakings, OJ 2005 No. L312/47, further clarified the specifics of reporting requirements. For any of the health

3. Prohibited conduct under competition law

Once competition rules apply, there are extensive rules protecting the neutral playing field of the internal market stemming from the EC Treaty and secondary legislation. Consistent with the principles of economic freedom, EU competition laws prohibit cartels and the abuse of a dominant position from negatively affecting competition within the single market. Here, the discussion will focus on the rules and cases most relevant to the health care sector.

A. Cartels

Unlawful cartels are formed by agreements between undertakings that 'may affect trade between Member States and which have as their object or effect the prevention, restriction or distortion of competition within the common market' (Article 81 EC). In other words, any form of collusion with the potential to negatively interfere with competition is prohibited. Article 81 EC continues with a brief list of some examples of prohibitive conduct, including price fixing, limiting production or sources of supply, or requiring supplementary contract terms extraneous to the essential agreement.

Traditionally, cases in this area involve markets for goods rather than service provision. In the health care sector, several cases have been heard in national courts concerning anti-competitive cartels dealing in pharmaceuticals, medical devices or related services.[46] In 1999, there was a case in Italy against two pharmaceutical companies for colluding to fix prices and coordinate market share.[47] Recently, in Germany, four pharmaceutical wholesalers engaged in a 'discount battle' after Andreae-Noris Zahn AG (Anzag) increased its discounts to expand its market share. After Anzag decided to end this price war, the wholesalers exchanged information about customer pharmacies and

---

organizations that could be engaging in economic activities as undertakings, the administrative burden alone of establishing separate accounting procedures will be extremely costly and time consuming. However, it is unclear when financial reporting rules apply, how they should be enforced and the extent of penalties for violations.

[46] For further analysis of the pharmaceuticals market, see Chapter 15 in this volume.

[47] Italian Antitrust Authority (IAA), Press Release, 22 July 1999, www.agcm.it/eng/index.htm.

monthly turnovers to redistribute the pre-existing market share. The German Competition Authority found that there was an intentional agreement constituting a quota cartel bordering on a price-fixing cartel and fined all four companies, as well as seven executives personally.[48] In France, the Competition Council fined two companies for colluding to share the market for medical devices during a public tender and reached a settlement with four pharmaceutical groups for anti-competitive agreements in the distribution of pharmaceuticals.[49] In Latvia, the Competition Council fined a medical gas monopolist for price discrimination ranging from 54% to 281%.[50] Similarly, in Italy, four medical device companies refused to present tenders in the colostomy device market for two years in an effort to drive up prices, demonstrating an anti-competitive agreement.[51] In Hungary, the Hungarian Competition Council (HCC) found that three corporations cooperated in violation of competition laws to win contracts managing information systems for university hospitals. On appeal, the municipal court of Budapest concurred with the finding that the companies had entered into an anti-competitive agreement, but disagreed on the extent of the infringement upon competition and reduced the fines by 10%.[52] More recently, the HCC fined a medical equipment distributor for establishing an exclusive distribution scheme.

The Danish Competition Appeals Tribunal overruled a decision by the Danish Competition Council deciding that a vertical agreement between pharmaceutical wholesalers and insolvent retail pharmacies was insufficient to unlawfully infringe upon competition. The Danish Pharmaceutical Association entered into an agreement with wholesalers to help insolvent retail pharmacies with special

[48] German Competition Authority (GCA), Press Release, 19 April 2007, www.bundeskartellamt.de/wEnglisch/News/Archiv/ArchivNews2007/2007_04_19.php.

[49] French Conseil de la Concurrence (FCC), Press Releases, 30 October 2007, www.conseil-concurrence.fr/pdf/avis/07d22.pdf; 20 January 2003, www.conseil-concurrence.fr/user/standard.php?id_rub=127&id_article=243.

[50] A. Rubene, 'The Latvian Competition Council fines the medical gas monopolist for the application of an unfair and discriminating price', *e-Competitions Law Bulletin* No. 16460 (2006).

[51] Italian Antitrust Authority (IAA), Press Release, 8 August 2007, www.agcm.it/eng/index.htm.

[52] Hungarian Competition Council, Press Release, 21 February 2007, www.gvh.hu/gvh/alpha?do=2&st=2&pg=137&m166_act=3.

credit terms. Once a retailer entered into such an arrangement, the agreement prohibited the retailers from switching between suppliers. The Competition Council ruled that the insolvency scheme violated Article 81 EC as an anti-competitive agreement. While the Appeals Tribunal agreed with the Council, it extended the analysis to consider that the Danish pharmaceutical market was highly regulated and the wholesalers were limited to competing on service and cost-based discounts. The facts further demonstrated that the Pharmaceutical Association had forced the arrangement on the wholesalers, rather than the wholesalers having exploited the retailers' weak bargaining position. Thus, the Appeals Tribunal found that the agreement was anti-competitive on its face, but that the evidence did not prove that the agreement restricted competition in violation of Article 81 EC.[53] This case is of particular interest because the language of Article 81 does not require a finding of serious infringement, only that it may affect trade. The Appeal Tribunal could have ruled based on the second requirement of Article 81(1) – that the object of the agreement was not to distort competition but to prevent market consolidation. However, the Tribunal instead limited the scope of the article, increasing the burden of proof to include a showing of serious infringement.

In the area of health services, agreements among providers or professional associations could be construed as anti-competitive cartels. NCAs and national courts in several Member States have found cases of unlawful price fixing agreements made by professional associations. As early as 1992, the Finnish Competition Council found that the Finnish Medical Association and Dental Associations had violated the price cartel prohibition by recommending prices to members.[54] The Austrian Federal Supreme Court found that an association of pharmacists had violated competition law by producing and distributing a

---

[53] Danish Competition Authority, 'Decision by the Danish Competition Appeals Tribunal, the insolvency scheme of the pharmaceutical sector', Press Release, 8 June 2007, www.ks.dk/english/competition/national-judgments/national-judgments-2007/2007–06–08-decision-by-the-danish-competition-appeals-tribunal-the-insolvency-scheme-of-the-pharmaceutical-sector/.

[54] Finnish Competition Authority (FCA), Press Releases, 3 November 1992 and 29 October 1993, www.kilpailuvirasto.fi/cgi-bin/english.cgi?sivu=cartels.

list of selling prices for pharmaceuticals and accessories.[55] Similarly, the Czech, Greek, Hungarian, Italian and Portuguese competition authorities each fined professional health associations for anti-competitive practices setting fees.[56] The Irish Competition Authority has settled collusion cases against the Dental Association, the Hospital Consultant Association and the Medical Organization prior to the Irish High Court reaching a judgment. All three of these cases involved the associations encouraging their members to threaten withholding services if their demands were not met.[57] The prevalence of cases against professional associations may be further evidence of the erroneous assumption that EU laws do not apply to the health sector.

In 1994, German and French national courts each considered cases involving cartels of health professionals. The German Federal Supreme Court found that the Bremen Chemist Association included an anti-competitive restriction in their membership rules. The chemists' professional code of conduct included a provision restricting the advertising and sale of product samples, while other retailers are not similarly restricted. When the association discovered that a chemist was selling samples for a nominal fee, the association threatened to take legal action against him. The Court found that both the section of the professional code at issue and the threat of legal action violated German competition rules.[58] The French Constitutional Court was asked to strike down a French law that established a monopoly for

---

[55] Case 16 Ok 14/97, *Apotheker*, Austrian Federal Supreme Court, 23 June 1997, www.kartellrecht.at/OGH14–97.html.

[56] Czech Office for the Protection of Competition, Press Release, 17 February 2003, www.compet.cz/en/information-centre/press-releases/competition/czech-medical-chamber-fined-450000-czk/; Greece Competition Authority, 'Annual report on competition policy in Greece 2005', www.epant.gr/img/x2/news/news16_1_1190293793.pdf; Hungarian Competition Authority, 'Annual report on competition law and policy developments in Hungary 2005', www.gvh.hu/domain2/files/modules/module25/pdf/GVH2005AnnualReport.pdf; Italian Antitrust Authority, '2000 Annual Report', www.agcm.it/eng/index.htm; and Law Business Research, 'Portuguese Competition Authority fines professional associations', *Global Competition Review* 8 (2005), 45.

[57] Irish Health Insurance Authority, Press Releases, 28 April 2005, www.tca.ie/NewsPublications/NewsReleases/NewsReleases.aspx?selected_item=43; 28 September 2005, www.tca.ie/NewsPublications/NewsReleases/NewsReleases.aspx?selected_item=31; and 28 May 2007, www.tca.ie/NewsPublications/NewsReleases/NewsReleases.aspx?selected_item=196.

[58] *Re A Pharmacist's Sale of Stock*, [1994] ECC 275.

licensed opticians as anti-competitive. A distributor of contact lenses complained that the French law requiring that suppliers of optical care appliances be managed by qualified opticians enforced by the optician's trade association constituted either a concerted practice or an abuse of a dominant position violating Articles 81 and 82 of the EC Treaty. The French court rejected the argument and held that the sale of contact lenses may be restricted with the aim of protecting public health. The court also explained that professional persons or trade associations, such as the opticians, joining together to enforce the observance of laws favourable to them cannot, in the absence of specific allegations of discrimination, constitute a violation of competition laws.[59] These rulings demonstrate that national courts have permitted specific restrictions on competition as justified by public health concerns so long as the national court or ECJ finds that the means used to protect public health are proportional to the limit on trade.

More recently, the Belgium Supreme Court heard an appeal filed by a pharmacist who was sanctioned for violating a regulation of the local association of pharmacists by opening his pharmacy on a Saturday afternoon. The pharmacist argued that he was exercising his right to freely practice his profession and that the regulation prohibiting shops from opening during scheduled on-call service violated the Belgian Competition Act. The Court agreed – as an undertaking, the Order of Pharmacists should use on-call service to guarantee regular and normal administration of health care but must also be consistent with the Competition Act. The Court sent the case back to the Appeals Council to determine whether the opening of a pharmacy beyond normal opening hours 'disrupts or threatens the continuity of the administration of health care'.[60] Each of these cases found that domestic regulation of pharmacists was in conflict with competition law prohibiting anti-competitive collusion by cartels, as found in Article 81 EC.

The more complex cases for professional associations are agreements that raise barriers to entry. Professional associations often serve dual public and private functions. States may delegate the regulation of the profession to peer organizations that must maintain

---

[59] *Laboratoire de Prothèses oculaires* v. *Union nationale des syndicats d'opticiens de France* [1994] ECC 457.
[60] Joris Ballet, 'The Belgian Supreme Court held that obligatory opening and closing hours for pharmacists violate the Competition Act', *e-Competitions Law Bulletin* No. 15370 (2006).

minimum quality standards to protect the public from unskilled or inexperienced practitioners. These associations may also advocate for the business interests of their members who are undertakings, which could violate either the cartel restrictions or abuse of dominant position discussed below. Unfortunately, the case-law to date is thin on this complex topic.

Exclusions

The prohibition against anti-competitive cartels is inapplicable where the undertaking's actions are restricted by law. The cartel prohibition applies only to anti-competitive conduct displayed by undertakings on their own initiative.[61] If the state has regulated the economy in the interests of public policy – by setting official prices, for example – the participation of an association in the scheme does not violate Article 81 EC.[62] Notwithstanding the absence of a prohibited cartel agreement, the ECJ considered whether a Member State deprived any of its own regulations of their state character by delegating the responsibility for decisions affecting the economic sphere to private undertakings.[63] The association concerned cannot be accused of concluding an agreement in violation of Article 81 EC where the Member State transfers the responsibility for intervening in economic processes to the association. Consequently, the Member State is not allowed to delegate sovereign powers of economic regulation to an association.[64] In the *Reiff* and *Delta* cases, the Court found that, where the competent public authorities were experts in the field and were not bound to follow industry or association recommendations, and where the

---

[61] Joined Cases C-359/95 P and C-379/95 P, *Ladbroke Racing* [1997] ECR I-6265, para. 33.

[62] Case C-38/97, *Librandi* [1998] ECR I-5955, paras. 30 and 34; Case C-185/91, *Reiff* [1993] ECR I-5801, paras. 15–9; Case C-153/93, *Delta* [1994] ECR I-2517, paras. 15–8; Case C-96/94, *Centro Servizi Spediporto* [1995] ECR I-2883, paras. 22–5.

[63] Case C-38/97, *Librandi*, above n.62, para. 26; Case 267/86, *Van Eycke* [1988] ECR 4769, para. 16; Case C-185/91, *Reiff*, above n.62, para. 14; Case C-153/93, *Delta*, above n.62, para. 14; Case C-96/94, *Centro Servizi Spediporto*, above n.62, para. 21.

[64] H. Schröter, 'Kommentierung der Artikel 81–83 EGV', in H. von der Groeben and J. Schwarze (eds.), *Kommentar zum Vertrag über die Europäische Union und zur Gründung der europäischen Gemeinschaft*, Vol. 2, 6th ed. (Baden Baden: Nomos Verlag, 2003); see Case C-38/97, *Librandi*, above n.62, para. 26; Case 267/86, *Van Eycke*, above n.63, para. 16; Case

ministry retained final approval of the decision, the Member State had not delegated its authority.[65] In the *Centro Servizi Spediporto* and *Librandi* cases, the Court based its decisions on the fact that the competent public authorities sought the opinions of other public and private institutions prior to their approval of proposals, or even fixed the tariffs ex officio.[66] Similarly, an undertaking cannot be penalized for violation of Article 81(1) EC where the conduct was required by national legislation.[67] In *CIF*,[68] the Italian NCA was obliged to disapply national law that hindered competition by establishing an anticompetitive cartel. Although there are few cases arising from health sector regulation, these public transport cases are analogous.

Employing the principle of proportionality, the Court permits restrictions on competition to protect a legitimate national interest. Although the *Wouters* case concerns the Dutch bar association, the Court's analysis could easily be applied to the regulation of medical professions as well. Lawyers challenged the bar association rule prohibiting multidisciplinary partnerships between lawyers and accountants as a restriction of the creation of a new form of business in violation of competition law. The Court held that Article 81(1) EC does not apply, since the bar association was entrusted to ensure the proper practice of the legal profession and a multidisciplinary practice could create conflicts of interest for the lawyers' clients. The Court determined that national interests took priority over the limited restriction of competition, by applying a proportionality test.[69] Thus, the Court could strike a similar balance between narrow restrictions on competition law and specific categories of public service policies. In the health sector, there arises a similar conflict of interest where doctors are paid by private insurance for some patients and public insurance for others. Where the doctors have different incentives for

---

C-185/91, *Reiff*, above n.62, para. 14; Case C-153/93, *Delta*, above n.62, para. 14; Case C-96/94, *Centro Servizi Spediporto*, above n.63, para. 21.

[65] Case C-185/91, *Reiff*, above n.62, paras. 21–3; Case C-153/93, *Delta*, above n.62, paras. 20–2.

[66] Case C-96/94, *Centro Servizi Spediporto*, above n.62, paras. 27–30; Case C-38/97, *Librandi*, above n.62, paras. 31 and 35.

[67] Case C-198/01, *Consorzio Industrie Fiammiferi (CIF) Autorita Garante della Concorrenza e del Mercato* [2003] ECR I-8055.

[68] *Ibid.*

[69] Case C-309/99, *J. C. J. Wouters et al v. Algemene Raad van de Nederlandse Orde van Advocaten (Wouters)* [2002] ECR I-1577.

providing different treatments, conflicts could easily arise where the private patients could receive treatment earlier but at a higher cost, causing a welfare loss to the health market.

Though rare, the Court has also carved out an exception for one specific type of agreement relevant to the health care sector. Collective bargaining agreements between labour and management are not subject to competition law. The Court found that social policy concerns would be significantly compromised if management and labour were subject to Article 81(1) EC when negotiating and implementing changes to working conditions.[70] Scholars have argued that *Albany's* rationale is unique, in that the Court rarely singles out a narrowly specified type of agreement for special exceptions. Since this ruling is so narrowly tailored and the revised Article 152 EC on public health does not reference any analogous consideration, it is unlikely that the Court would choose to exclude a particular type of health sector agreement from competition law.[71] But the ruling is relevant for health policy-makers to keep in mind when considering system reforms that may have an effect upon labour relations.

The Dutch Competition Authority (DCA) also found that agreements do not violate Article 81 where collective purchasing of goods or services enhances consumer welfare by containing costs while restricting competition. The DCA preliminarily ruled that an agreement between five Dutch health insurers designating preferred suppliers distorted competition between the insurers. The DCA was asked to provide an informal opinion regarding the pilot pricing policy. The policy focused on three groups of medicines and defined the maximum price for reimbursement. Since these health insurers compete with one another, the DCA reviewed the agreement to determine whether competition among the insurers was restricted. The DCA concluded that competition was not compromised since the scope of the programme was narrowly limited and policy holders would benefit from the savings.[72] Unfortunately, the DCA has not reported any

---

[70] Case C-67/96, *Albany International* v. *Stichting Bedrijfspensioenfonds Textielindustrie* [1999] ECR I-5751.
[71] P. J. Slot, 'Applying the competition rules in the healthcare sector', *European Competition Law Review* 24 (2003), 580–93.
[72] Dutch Competition Authority (DCA), 'Permitted pharmaceutical preference pricing policy for health insurers', Press Release, 22 June 2005,

subsequent analysis evaluating the policy or indicating whether the policy has been extended beyond the pilot phase.

B. *Abuse of dominant position*

The EC Treaty prohibits an undertaking with a dominant position from exploiting its market power to distort or restrict competition. When the Commission seeks to establish an infringement of Article 82 EC, it must show the following: that an undertaking is dominant in a given market; that it has abused its dominant position; that the abuse has an effect on trade between Member States; and that there is no objective justification for the abuse. There are issues for health systems at several points in this legal analysis.

First, the market must be defined in terms of product, geographic area and time frame. Although abuse must affect trade between states, there is no requirement that the geographical area must include more than one state. The Court has considered the port of Genoa to be a market sufficient for these purposes, because of its role in trade throughout the EU.[73] Defining the market could be as straightforward as utilizing the specifications for a medical device under an anti-competitive exclusive distribution agreement. In the area of pharmaceuticals, defining the market is particularly challenging, given that several arguments similar to those made for patent protection could distinguish between products, such as method of delivery, treatment pathway or mode of action.[74] Defining markets in health services cases can be particularly challenging. Patients select providers based on a number of objective and subjective factors. Due to the high set-up and labour costs, it is difficult for hospitals to adjust their product mix when competition is introduced. A recent analysis of the partially-privatized Dutch hospital market found that both traditional and new economic approaches to defining markets were inappropriate for the Dutch health care system. Both the unique relationships

---

www.nmanet.nl/engels/home/News_and_publications/News_and_press_releases/2005/05_21.asp.

[73] Case C-179/90, *Merci convenzionali Porto di Genova* [1991] ECR I-589, para. 15; and P. J. Slot and A. Johnston, *An introduction to competition law* (Oxford, Portland: Hart, 2006).

[74] See Chapter 15 in this volume for a more detailed discussion of the pharmaceuticals market.

between health insurance contracts and hospitals, as well as the difficulty of mapping patient preferences, influence how markets could be defined in the Dutch health system.[75]

The next step in the analysis is an assessment of the undertaking's dominance in the market. Thus, the first two steps in the analysis are closely linked. As the definition of the market narrows, it is easier to show that the undertaking is dominant in that market. In the past, the Commission was criticized for blurring these issues by tailoring the definition of the market to facilitate a finding of dominance.[76] In response, the Commission adopted the 'market definition notice' approach, based on economic theory, and thus formalized its methodology.[77] The market definition notice approach analyses whether there is sufficient demand and supply substitutability so that no undertaking influences the price of the goods or services in question.[78] Once it has been established that the undertaking is dominant in the market, the question then turns to whether it has infringed competition by abusing its dominance. Abuse is often categorized as either exploitative or exclusionary. Exploitative abuse includes monopolistic behaviours, including price fixing, selective contracting, reductions in quantity or quality, and refusal to modernize production or service provision. Exclusionary abuse raises barriers to entry, limiting competitors' participation in the market, such as in cases of refusal to deal.

As an example of exclusionary abuse, the Dutch Competition Authority investigated a case where a group of pharmacies shared considerable market power as a result of their joint participation in an electronic filing system that included patient information. Rather than focusing on the issue of whether this was an anti-competitive cartel, the DCA found that the electronic system promoted efficiency for the health system and improved services for patients. The anti-competitive

---

[75] M. Varkevisser *et al.*, 'Defining hospital markets for antitrust enforcement: new approaches and their applicability to the Netherlands', *Health Economics Policy and Law* 3 (2008), 7–29.

[76] L. Gyselen and N. Kyriazis, 'Article 86: the monopoly power measurement issue revisited', *European Law Review* 11 (1986), 134; S. Baker and L. Wu, 'Applying the market definition guidelines of the EC Commission', *European Competition Law Review* 19 (1998), 273–81.

[77] European Commission, 'Notice on the definition of relevant market for the purposes of Community competition law', OJ 1997 No. C372/5.

[78] For a more in depth discussion of these legal issues, see G. Monti, *EC competition law* (Cambridge: Cambridge University Press, 2007), Chapter 5.

behaviour was found to be an abuse of dominant position for the arbitrary exclusion of new pharmacies. Initially, the decision on whether to admit a pharmacy to the system was conducted by a vote among the participating members, without objective and transparent criteria or any procedure for appeal. This exclusion functioned as a barrier to entry into the market. As a result of the DCA's investigation and statement of objections, the pharmacists voluntarily adapted their admission rules. The DCA was sufficiently satisfied with the changes in the admission procedures to close the file.[79]

Predatory pricing is another form of exclusionary abuse. As with all cases, the first step requires defining the market. In pharmaceutical markets, there are several possible approaches to defining markets, such as arguments made for patent protection or in pricing policies, distinguishing factors such as treatment pathways and modes of action. A recent case before the French Competition Council demonstrates how far the competition authority may stretch the market definition analysis when it is concerned about anti-competitive activities. The French NCA found that GlaxoSmithKline France (GSK) was liable for abuse of dominant position through predatory pricing in a market where Glaxo was not dominant. The Council's investigation determined that GSK sold Zinnat, an injectable antibiotic 'at a price below costs so as to deter generic drug manufacturers from effectively entering the hospital market'.[80] The Council also found that GSK was dominant in the market for injectable aciclovir (an antiviral drug) sold to hospitals. Rather than finding that there were associative links between the two markets, the Council found abuse of dominance because the predatory pricing was part of a global intimidation strategy to discourage generic manufacturers from entering other GSK hospital markets.[81]

In another predatory pricing case, an English firm, Napp, used market segmentation to become super-dominant in the supply of

---

[79] Dutch Competition Authority, Press Release, 6 June 2003, www.nmanet.nl/engels/home/News_and_Publications/News_and_press_releases/2003/03_22.asp.

[80] See also Chapter 15 in this volume. French Conseil de la Concurrence (FCC), Press Release, 14 March 2007, www.conseil-concurrence.fr/user/standard.php?id_rub=211&id_article=695.

[81] A. Schulz and J. de Douhet, 'French Competition Council vs. GSK France: who is the predator?', eSapience Centre for Competition Policy, June 2007.

morphine tablets and capsules. Napp offered prices below costs to the hospital segment of the market, capturing more than 90% of the hospital market. Although the hospital segment is only 10–4% of the total market, it has greater strategic importance than the community segment, since it is the access point for new patients. The United Kingdom OFT found that Napp's pricing policy had foreclosed the hospital market, excluding competitors from entry into both market segments.[82] Similarly, the OFT awarded damages to Healthcare at Home, an in-home care provider, against the pharmaceutical company Genzyme, for abuse of dominant position for bundling the price for Cerezyme services to include the cost of providing home delivery.[83]

In another example, the DCA reviewed a complaint of exploitative abuse filed by physiotherapists and GPs against Dutch health insurers. The health providers alleged that the insurers abused their dominant position by refusing to negotiate the terms of the contract and to increase the fees paid to the professionals. The DCA found that there is no duty to negotiate, so long as the procurement procedures were objective, transparent and non-discriminatory. These findings were further supported by the problem that there was an oversupply of physiotherapists, undermining their request for increased fees.[84]

In some cases, selective contracting could be another example of exploitative abuse that could lead to an anti-competitive complaint. In some social health insurance systems, insurance funds are monopolists with a dominant position in the market to contract with providers. If the funds are engaged in economic activity warranting an application of the status of an undertaking, then they could be at risk of abuse of dominant position. When there is an insufficient supply of doctors or hospitals, the funds can contract with all providers available. The funds may have significant leverage as monopolists in defining contract terms, which could lead to an abuse of a dominant position. Alternatively, where there is an oversupply of providers and the funds must restrict the number of contracts or the number of

---

[82] *Napp Pharmaceutical Holdings Ltd* v. *Director General of Fair Trading* [2002] Comp. AR 13.
[83] Case No. 1016/1/03, *Genzyme Limited* v. *Office of Fair Trading* [2004] CAT 4.
[84] Dutch Competition Authority, Press Release, 27 May 2005, www.nmanet.nl/engels/home/News_and_publications/News_and_press_releases/2005/05_16.asp.

procedures to contain costs, a question arises as to the process used to select providers. There could be another risk of abuse of dominant position through a refusal to contract with particular providers if decisions are made subjectively or arbitrarily. Payers should use transparent criteria for contract selection, such as national standards of minimum quality, or maximum prices. A question as to whether physicians or hospitals should have due process rights to appeal cases terminating or rejecting their contracts could also arise. Ultimately, the social health insurance fund may not be held responsible for abuse of dominant position if their activities are justified as a service of general economic interest (discussed in the next section).

C. State regulation and services of general economic interest

While Articles 81 and 82 EC define the rules to limit an undertaking's anti-competitive behaviour, Article 86 EC applies when Member States interfere with a market by granting exclusive rights (Article 86(1)), or by entrusting an undertaking with the operation of a service of general economic interest (SGEI) (Article 86(2)). The liberalization of state monopolies is encouraged in Article 86(1). Decisions of the European Court of Justice that provide interpretations of this provision show the development of criteria to test whether a state monopoly is lawful.[85] In short, firms must meet efficiency standards and the state must limit grants to avoid awarding excess monopoly power that could have additional anti-competitive consequences. One such case arose in Germany, where the *Land* of Rheinland-Pfalz granted an undertaking (Ambulanz Glockner) the exclusive right to provide ambulance services in a rural area, giving the company a dominant position in the market. In *Glockner*, the ECJ was asked whether the provision of services under the grant abused its dominant position or was justified by public policy concerns under the SGEI exception found in Article 86(2).[86] Although there is no precise regulatory definition of SGEI, the Courts and the

---

[85] Case C-41/90, *Hofner and Elser* v. *Macrotron* [1991] ECR I-1979; Case C-179/90, *Merci Convencionali Porto di Genova* v. *Siderugica Gabrielli* [1991] ECR I-5889; Case C-475/99, *Glockner* [2001] ECR I-8089; Case C-18/88, *Regi des telegrapes et des telephones (RTT)* v. *GB-Inno-BM SA* [1991] ECR-5941; and Case C-320/91, *Corbeau* [1993] ECR I-2533.

[86] Case C-475/99, *Ambulanz Glockner* v. *Landreis Sudwetpflaz (Glockner)* [2001] ECR I-8089.

Commission have specified that, for Article 86(2) to apply, the public service mission must be clearly defined and explicitly entrusted through an act of public authority.[87] A series of Court cases have interpreted this section in detail. First, the service must be 'entrusted through an act of public authority', including legislative regulations, 'non-exclusive licences' or ministerial orders. Second, the SGEI must be widely available to the community and it cannot be concerned with private interests, such as copyrights.[88] Beyond these basic characteristics, Member States have discretion to define the services that would not be satisfactorily provided by the market, also within Article 16 EC.[89] This exception should not be seen as a free pass to violate competition laws. Similarly to the analysis in *Wouters*, the Court applies a proportionality test. The restriction on competition must be necessary and proportionate for the undertaking to perform its task. If there is a less restrictive means to achieve the same public interest goals, then the exception would not apply.[90]

Traditionally, the Court would narrowly apply the SGEI exception to cases where the economic conditions in which the undertaking operates necessitate an exception from competition laws. In *Almelo*, the Court decided that it was permissible for a regional distribution company to have exclusive purchasing and sales contracts for electricity. The suspension of competition rules was necessary for financial stability; if competition were permitted, it would be impossible for the undertaking to perform its public service task.[91] The Court then expanded the SGEI exception to also consider non-economic factors. In *Glockner*, the Court found that the company was an undertaking

[87] European Commission, 'Communication from the Commission, accompanying the Communication on "a single market for 21st century Europe" services of general interest including social services of general interest a new European commitment', COM (2007) 725 final, 20 November 2007; and Case C-280/00, *Altmark Trans GmbH* [2003] ECR I-7747.

[88] Case C-127/73, *Belgishe Radio en Televisie et Societe Belge des Auteurs, Compositeurs et Editeurs v. SV SABAM et NV Fonior* [1974] ECR 313; and Case C-66/86, *Ahmed Saeed Flugreisen and Silver Line Reiseburo BmbJ v. Zentrale sur Bekampfung unlaurteren Wettbewerbs e V* [1989] ECR 803.

[89] Communication from the Commission – services of general interest in Europe, OJ 2001 No. C17/4.

[90] D. Chalmers *et al.*, *European Union law* (Cambridge: Cambridge University Press, 2006), p. 1138.

[91] Case C-393/92, *Municipality of Almelo and Others v. NV Energiebedrift Ijsselmij* [1994] ECR I-1477.

since ambulance facilities had not always been provided by public authorities. The *Land* argued that the grant of exclusive rights was necessary to ensure ambulance services were available, since it was otherwise unprofitable to offer emergency transport. Although the grant of exclusive rights put the company at risk of abusing its dominant position, the restriction on competition did not violate competition rules. First, the Court found that the grant of exclusive rights was justified, since the service would not be economically viable without the restriction on competition. Thus, the grant of exclusive rights served as a cross-subsidy to other parts of the business to make the company more economically viable.[92] The Court went on to reason that the SGEI exception was also necessary to ensure the quality and reliability of the ambulance services.[93]

The Court's analysis and judgment in the *Glockner* case recognizes the reality of public service financing and the state's need to balance a number of factors when making health policy decisions. Prosser (Chapter 7 in this volume) sees this case as an expansion of the Court's analysis to include broader public values, in addition to economic benchmarks to judge whether the SGEI exception applies.[94] If the quality and reliability of public services should be considered when carving out exceptions to competition law, one might ask whether these factors should carry equal or greater weight than the economic factors, especially in the context of health services. It could be argued that health services are unique among public services on economic grounds due to the complexity and difficulty of overcoming market failures, and on public interest grounds due to the fundamental importance of health care.

States may delegate important public services to independent agencies that could result in anti-competitive activities. For example, a case of abuse of dominant position arose where the Government of Malta entrusted the National Blood Transfusion Centre (NBTC) with the collection and management of sensitive materials such as blood products. Under regulations enacted in 2003, the NBTC also was required to commercialize the distribution of its products, in addition to its traditional function as the official regulator of blood products.

---

[92] T. Prosser, *The limits of competition law* (Oxford: Oxford University Press, 2005), p. 288.
[93] Case C-475/99, *Ambulanz Glockner* v. *Landreis Sudwetpflaz (Glockner)* [2001] ECR I-8089.
[94] Prosser, *The limits*, above n.92.

The NCA in Malta, the Maltese Commission for Fair Trading (CFT), found that the NBTC conducted activities as a government regulator and as an undertaking. By capitalizing on this dual role, the NBTC was restricting or distorting competition in the health care market, since patients faced a choice of either opting for a private hospital and paying for the blood products, or going to a public hospital where they would not be charged for blood.[95] Articles 82 and 86 EC preclude Member States from granting undertakings the power to regulate or set standards in a market where they also compete.[96]

In the most recent case, *BUPA*, the Court of First Instance upheld the Irish Government's regulation of the health insurance market, using a risk equalization scheme, under Article 86(2).[97] This case and other issues of private health insurance are addressed in more detail in the chapter by Thomson and Mossialos (Chapter 10). It is worth mentioning here that the Court applied the *Altmark* test to determine whether the Commission was accurate in its conclusion that the risk equalization scheme was not a grant of state aid, finding that there was an act of public authority entrusting the entity with an SGEI mission and the universal and compulsory nature of that mission. The Court also found that the Commission was correct in its assessment that the regulation of the market was necessary and proportionate to the goal of providing all Irish residents access to a minimum level of private health insurance services at the same price.[98] Finally, it should be mentioned that the Court affirmed that Member States have wide discretion to define what they regard as SGEIs and that the definition of such services by a Member State can be questioned by the Commission only in the event of manifest error.[99]

In November 2007, the Commission published its views on the proposed Protocol on Services of General Interest, annexed to the Treaty of Lisbon, with specific analysis of the particular situation of health services.[100] The Communication essentially summarizes the existing

---

[95] European Competition Law Review, 'Malta, Abuse of Dominant Position – Blood', Case Comment, *European Competition Law Review* 28 (2007), 120–1.
[96] Case C-18/88, *Régie des télégraphes et des téléphones (RTT)* v. *GB-Inno-BM SA* [1991] ECR-5941.
[97] Case T-289/03, *BUPA*, above n.4.   [98] *Ibid.*
[99] Case T-289/03, *BUPA*, above n.4, para. 166.
[100] European Commission, 'Services of general interest, including social services of general interest: a new European commitment', COM (2007) 724 final, 20 November 2007.

jurisprudence of the European Court of Justice interpreting Article 86 EC. In a specific section on health services, the Commission reiterates the balancing of Member States' responsibilities with its own interest in setting out a framework for safe, high-quality and efficient cross-border health care services. Thus, in the area of health care in particular, Member States can continue to regulate health services as long as they also meet the requirements of Article 86(2) as interpreted by the Court, especially the proportionality principle.

Efficient operator

If Member States were to declare that all health services qualified as SGEI, would health systems enjoy a blanket exemption from competition law? Thus far, the Court has not provided a clear answer. Under the *Altmark* decision, the Court requires that in cases where the public service obligation has not been chosen by competitive tender, the level of compensation defined by the contract should depend upon an analysis of the costs of a 'typical, well-run undertaking'. Thus, the Court would look for a measure of efficiency, to draw a comparison with an 'efficient operator'.[101] As discussed at length in the *BUPA* case, the Commission was satisfied that the compensation paid to some insurers and not others as a result of the risk adjustment scheme did not create the possibility of offsetting costs that might result from inefficiencies on the part of an insurer subject to the scheme. The Commission appropriately found that the scheme took into account the costs of an insurer's average claim, so that insurers were not allowed to keep the benefit of their own inefficiencies.[102]

This efficiency requirement indicates a preference for some type of tender process that rewards a firm that could provide the public service obligation efficiently. Once a firm provides SGEI, the state may have an ongoing responsibility to monitor the SGEI to determine whether the provider continues to supply services efficiently over time. This standard would require a significant administrative burden on the Member State. In the *BUPA* case, the Court of First Instance focused on whether the Commission satisfied its burden to identify whether the scheme resulted in a grant of state aid. It is unclear whether the Irish Government is required to review the insurers to determine whether

[101] Case C-280/00, *Altmark Trans GmbH* [2003] ECR I-7747.
[102] Case T-289/03, *BUPA*, above n.4.

they provide the SGEI efficiently. The *Altmark* efficient operator principle could be one of the hurdles used to raise the level of scrutiny of Member State SGEI awards in an area where the Commission otherwise would have to respect their wide discretion.

4. Enforcement of competition law

Enforcement of EU competition law is diffused among EU institutions, national courts and national competition authorities. Prior to the modernization of the competition law enforcement system in 2004, the Commission was unable to address the growing number of complaints of anti-competitive behaviour. Council Regulation 1/2003/EC delegates authority to investigate, regulate and enforce competition law to NCAs. Since enactment of the reforms, the number of cases in the health care sector has increased substantially, due to the NCAs' proximity and familiarity with domestic legislation and policies, and the Commission's focus has shifted to sector-wide investigations and coordination of NCAs. Several NCAs, including those of Finland, Germany, Italy, the Netherlands and the United Kingdom, have paid special attention to the health care sector. However, NCAs will only be effective if they have adequate financial resources, staff expertise and independence. Consequently, the level of NCA scrutiny of competition in the health sector varies widely.

In addition to the national court enforcement discussed above, supranational enforcement by the Commission under Article 85 (now Article 81) EC was originally set out in Regulation 17/62/EEC, following the German rules-based tradition. Various attempts to improve efficiency or to shift more cases to national systems were unsuccessful. For example, the Commission set *de minimis* rules to prioritize only significant violations of Article 81 EC. The modernization of competition enforcement defined by Council Regulation 1/2003/EEC came into effect in May 2004.[103] The Commission's new role includes setting priorities, enforcing state aid rules and ensuring consistent enforcement throughout the EU. The newly-established European Competition Network (ECN) is a framework for cooperation among

[103] Council and European Parliament Regulation 1/2003/EC on the implementation of the rules on competition laid down in Articles 81 and 82 of the Treaty, OJ 2003 No. L1/1.

the NCAs, but has no independent legal authority. The Commission further controls the NCAs by reviewing all decisions prior to formal publication. At this point, the Commission may comment on the decision or override the relevant NCA's jurisdiction and open its own proceedings.[104] Although these mechanisms encourage uniform application of competition law, the potential for inconsistencies persists.

Post-decentralization, the volume of cases has increased and there are greater opportunities for variation in enforcement, despite the best efforts of the ECN. For example, the Latvian Competition Council was established in 1998, but only heard five cases of abuse of dominance in 2005 and eleven in 2006. The Council wants to continue to double the number of cases each year, at least through 2009.[105] Differences in resource allocation, experience and expertise among NCAs mean that there is wide variation in the level of enforcement within Member States. Some NCAs have relatively few staff and limited budgets, and may feel pressure to take only high profile cases that will result in significant fines generating revenue for their government. The European Bank for Reconstruction and Development has funded several projects in former communist countries to encourage the enactment of competition law and the development of institutions. Their indicators reflect that the new Member States' enforcement of competition law is improving and has encouraged actual market competition. However, one area of concern is the lack of effectiveness of the appeals process.[106] One researcher also argued that the appellate institutions' personnel lack sufficient training to reverse decisions of the NCAs.[107]

Since Regulation 1/2003/EC came into force in May 2004, there has only been limited independent analysis of the implementation of the new enforcement scheme. It is clear, however, that a number of

---

[104] Monti, *EC competition law*, above n.78.
[105] Latvian Competition Council, 'Annual Report 2005'; Latvian Competition Council, 'Annual Report 2006', www.kp.gov.lv/?object_id=618; and A. Rubene, 'The Latvian Competition Council fines the medical gas monopolist for the application of an unfair and discriminating price', *e-Competitions Bulletin* No. 12435 (2006).
[106] See M. Vagliasindi and L. Campbell, 'The EBRD: promoting transition through competition', *Law in Transition* (2004), 35–45, at 41, Chart 6, www.ebrd.com/pubs/legal/lit041g.pdf.
[107] J. Rossi, 'Competition law enforcement mechanisms', *Law in Transition* (2004), 78–84, www.ebrd.com/pubs/legal/lit041m.pdf.

risks and uncertainties arise, leaving the full impact on both economic and social policy an open question. Wilks points out that there are a number of risks related to variation in a decentralized system where 'variations in application may be deliberate, inadvertent, or opportunistic as the regimes respond to differing sets of pressures'.[108] Concerns over accountability, forum shopping, vulnerability to lobbying and lack of competence all jeopardize the implementation and integrity of the new system. Wilks argues further that the Commission's successful centralizing and the increasing juridification of competition law result in economic policy enjoying excessive power and potentially 'becom[ing] a destructive force in the regulation of the European economy ... The law may require competition authorities to act in ways incompatible with national interests in employment, [and] social welfare.'[109] Overly rigid, legalistic rules that fail to take social policy priorities into account could undermine the solidarity principles inherent in national health policies.

Applying Wilks' analysis to the health sector, it is easy to imagine how NCAs could also be subject to both political and economic pressures. The health care sector is important politically and economically, features influential pharmaceutical industry lobbies, as well as being a sensitive election issue. The Italian NCA has adjudicated several cases against the pharmaceutical industry, commented on proposed financing legislation and criticized variations in regional health systems since the 1990s. By contrast, the Estonian NCA's annual reports and decisions are diplomatically constructed to avoid findings of anti-competitive behaviour in the health sector.[110] Even though the United Kingdom Office of Fair Trading has dealt with a number of health-related cases, it has thus far refrained from challenging English National Health Service reforms – such as the economic activities of

---

[108] S. Wilks, 'Agency escape: decentralization or dominance of the European Commission in the modernization of competition policy?', *Governance: An International Journal of Policy, Administration, and Institutions* 18 (2005), 431–52.

[109] *Ibid.*, 449–50.

[110] In the 2004, 2005 and 2006 annual reports from the Estonian NCA pharmacies, health insurance funds and a pharmaceutical cartel were investigated for anti-competitive activities, but none were held liable. Estonian Competition Board, 'Annual Report 2004'; Estonian Competition Board, 'Annual Report 2005'; Estonian Competition Board, 'Annual Report 2006', www.konkurentsiamet.ee/?id=11591.

foundation trusts – that have introduced market elements but have arguably not gone far enough to establish a competitively neutral environment for private providers.

In addition to variations in the level of enforcement, national governments differ in terms of designation of authority to NCAs. Many NCAs have multiple functional areas, including complaint investigation, consumer protection, enforcement and regulation. In some countries, such as Ireland, Finland, Denmark and Sweden, the NCA has an executive enforcement role, where it conducts research, provides recommendations, monitors transactions and, in some cases, files complaints. The NCAs of each of these countries have produced reports providing recommendations on how to improve competition in particular segments of the health services sector, such as the private insurance market in Ireland discussed earlier. Only the national courts in these countries have the jurisdiction to rule on competition cases. The separation of authority gives the Irish NCA, for example, more latitude to advise health officials. In other countries, such as the United Kingdom, the Netherlands, Portugal, Italy, Germany and France, the NCA plays both an adjudicatory and an advisory role. National courts are bound by the findings of the competition authority in some jurisdictions, such as the United Kingdom and Germany.[111] For example, in the United Kingdom, the OFT adjudicates violations of the Competition Act, in addition to its advisory role. If the NHS presented difficult competition issues to the OFT for advice it could potentially expose itself to litigation.

NCAs in some countries have commented on proposed or enacted health legislation or have advocated in favour of improving competition in the organization of national health systems. Health system reforms that have decentralized authority and decision-making to the regional or local level weaken the central government's control over specific health policies. In Italy, the NCA has commented on the anti-competitive aspects of proposed health legislation and of the implementation health policies. As early as 1998, the Italian Antitrust Authority (IAA) reported to government and parliament on local health boards' dual payer–provider function, creating an anti-competitive conflict of interest. Responding to a number of complaints by clinics, labs and patients regarding selective contracting

---

[111] Monti, *EC competition law*, above n.78, p. 435.

by local health boards, the IAA found that several regions had implemented the same health policies inconsistently and that the inconsistencies resulted in anti-competitive markets. Some local health boards focused on the patients' freedom to choose providers, while others focused on the planning of services, limiting choice in an attempt to contain costs, but failed to include incentives for efficiency. In 2005, the IAA again focused on local health boards that had individually interpreted national regulations, resulting in problems with accreditation of private providers and leading to selective contracting.

The Finnish Competition Authority supported legislative reforms that were enacted in 2002 requiring generic substitution of medicines, unless a physician specifically forbids the replacement. The FCA argued that the reform would encourage competition and control the increase of medicines expenditures, and went further in proposing additional amendments to the legislation to enhance economic incentives.[112] The Hungarian Competition Authority has weighed in on the health reform debates in Hungary, arguing that a balance should be found between a wholly state-run health sector and that of a fully competitive health market run by private insurance companies. The HCA presented a discussion paper that considers the areas for competition, why competition cannot solve existing regulatory problems and provides suggestions on where competition should be stronger.[113]

Similarly, the Swedish Competition Authority (SCA) has identified several local government policies that interfere with competition. In Sweden, county councils and municipalities are entrusted with health care provision and financing. Local governments plan for services based on local needs, and also regulate the private practitioners' market by approving the establishment and public reimbursement of local practices. Moreover, county councils own and operate most health care facilities.[114] The diversity of local regulations makes it difficult for providers to expand into neighbouring markets. The SCA published a market analysis, which found that

[112] Finnish Competition Authority, '2003 yearbook', above n.38.
[113] Hungarian Competition Council, Press Release, 13 April 2007, www.gvh. hu/gvh/alpha?do=2&st=2&pg=133&m5_doc=4521.
[114] Health Systems in Transition (HiT) Summary, Sweden, 2005, www.euro. who.int/Document/E88669sum.pdf.

the tight regulation of the establishment of new local practices had resulted in a decline in the number of new doctors entering private practice, and that this barrier to entry in the market had significantly limited health services supply.[115] Arbitrary local regulations infringe upon competitive neutrality. The SCA has argued that municipalities that simultaneously define health care budgets and provide health services substantially hinder price competition.[116] With decentralized health systems, the question then becomes: what should the central government do to prevent local policies from interfering with competition? Could the benefits of decentralization, such as increased accountability and responsiveness, ever outweigh the benefits of competitive markets? Health policy-makers, national courts and the European Court of Justice may each find different answers to these questions.

Thus far, the Netherlands has gone the furthest among EU Member States towards incorporating competition policy when implementing health system reforms. In 2006, the Dutch Healthcare Authority (DHA) was established to implement health system reforms, paving the way for market forces to operate in the health care services sector. The DHA supervises both health care providers and insurers in the curative and long-term care markets. The Healthcare Inspectorate will monitor quality, while the DHA encourages competition based on quality.[117] In preparation for this system-wide reform, the Dutch Government negotiated with the EU Commission for the authorization of a €15 billion grant of state aid for private health insurers to cover start-up costs. Pre-existing sickness funds were permitted to roll-over financial reserves as start-up capital while they transform into private insurers.[118] It is still too soon to assess the successes and

---

[115] Swedish Competition Authority (SCA), 'Assessment for improving consumer welfare in health and elderly care', English Summary (2007), www.kkv.se/upload/Filer/ENG/Publications/rap_2007–3_summary.pdf.

[116] Swedish Competition Authority (SCA), 'Business as usual? Clearer demarcation between authorities and markets', English Summary (2004), www.kkv.se/upload/Filer/ENG/Publications/rap_%202004_4summary.pdf.

[117] Dutch Health Authority, 'Strategy of the Dutch Health Authority', October 2006, www.nza.nl/7113/10118/NZA_Strategy-internet.pdf.

[118] European Commission, 'State aid: Commission endorses €15 billion public funding for new Dutch health insurance system', Press Release No. IP/05/531, Brussels, 3 May 2005.

failures of this transformation. Other Member States should perhaps note that the Commission's support for Dutch market reforms may be a sign of its preference for comprehensive market reforms.

The rising cost of pharmaceuticals has increased pressure on Member States to define regulations that will improve efficiency and competition on the price of medicines. NCAs in several countries have weighed in on the debates in addition to strictly enforcing competition law against the pharmaceutical industry. NCAs in Denmark, Estonia, Finland, Italy and Sweden have conducted investigations into improving competition in this market, concluding that regulations of the distribution and location of retail outlets should be reformed. NCAs in Poland and Latvia have articulated concerns that the retail pharmacy market is becoming more concentrated.[119] The Danish NCA advocated for greater price competition by setting maximum prices for reimbursement, rather than fixed prices.[120] The Italian authorities recommend the deregulation of retail pharmacy ownership and that automated over-the-counter (OTC) machines be allowed outside pharmacies.[121] The Slovak NCA also found that restrictions in the Slovak Chamber of Pharmacists Code of Ethics contained limitations on the geographic location of pharmacies, unlawfully restricting competition.[122] In the United Kingdom, the OFT has published a report with extensive recommendations for reforming the Pharmaceutical Price Regulation Scheme by replacing it with a value-based approach to pricing.[123]

---

[119] Polish Office for Competition and Consumer Protection, 'Pharmaceutical products market in Poland', Press Release, 7 December 2006, www.uokik. gov.pl/en/press_office/press_releases/art66.html; Latvian Competition Council, 'Annual Report 2005', www.kp.gov.lv/uploaded_files/KP%20 parskats%202005%20En%20Final.pdf.

[120] Danish Competition Authority, '2005 Annual Report', Chapter 6, 'Pharmacies', English Summary, www.ks.dk/english/publications/ publications-2005/2005–06–08-competition-report-2005/chapter-6-pharmacies/.

[121] IAA, Press Release, 23 September 2005, www.agcm.it/eng/index.htm.

[122] Slovak Competition Authority, 'Decision of the Association of Entrepreneurs – Slovak Chamber of Pharmacists', Press Release, 2002, www.antimon.gov.sk/eng/article.aspx?c=394&a=2129.

[123] Office of Fair Trading, 'The pharmaceutical price regulation scheme', February 2007, www.oft.gov.uk/shared_oft/reports/comp_policy/oft885. pdf.

Finally, the EU's new decentralized enforcement scheme allows for the possibility of damages claims, creating incentives for privately-filed actions. Even though the Court has affirmed the right of victims to compensation,[124] these cases are rare. Private litigation could serve to protect plaintiffs' rights and, by extension, consumer welfare, as well as to deter future anti-competitive behaviour. Unlike the Commission, victims may not be discouraged from filing claims simply to avoid politically sensitive issues. Naturally, there are a number of procedural challenges to private actions, such as the burden of proving both that the defendants' acts restrict competition and that the plaintiff has personally suffered a loss as a result. Variations in national civil procedures, available remedies and judicial expertise in competition law will lead to differences in the outcomes of competition law cases. But the Commission sees benefits in the filing of both 'follow on' claims after a competition authority has found a violation of competition law, and 'stand alone' cases where the private actor initiates proceedings in a fresh case, as was articulated in the 2005 Green Paper.[125] Refusal to deal with cases could be raised by undertakings that have tried to expand operations into markets dominated by the public sector and that have been slow to modernize in the wake of health system reforms. Similarly, competitors may raise an abuse of dominance claim in cases where mixed public–private funding and provision of care restrict market entry. If health care markets become more broadly European – and even global – plaintiffs may be persuaded to file claims against foreign companies operating in Europe as well. However, the political implications of filing against a national health service may discourage current contractors from raising controversial issues. But corporations seeking entry into closed markets could be expected to consider private actions to encourage the adoption of competitively neutral policies. In this light, *Bettercare* may not be seen as an anomaly, but as only one of the first attempts. So far, only ten of the twenty-seven Member States have had any private anti-trust cases, and in those courts litigation is still rare.[126]

---

[124] Case C-453/99, *Courage and Crehan* [2001] ECR I-6297; and Joined Cases C-295/04 to 298/04, *Manfredi* [2006] ECR I-6619.

[125] Monti, *EC competition law*, above n.78.

[126] Centre for European Policy Studies, 'Making antitrust damages actions more effective in the EU: welfare impact and potential scenarios', Report for

The United Kingdom High Court recently ruled on the type of damages that are available to private plaintiffs filing 'follow on' claims under EU competition law in the United Kingdom.[127] The Commission fined several firms in the vitamins industry for anti-competitive agreements in setting prices and sales quotas. A group of purchasers filed 'follow on' actions requesting several types of damages, including compensatory, exemplary and restitutionary damages.[128] The High Court's ruling limiting the remedy to only compensatory damages may discourage future claimants from bringing private claims in England.

On 2 April 2008, the Commission published a White Paper on damages actions for breach of the EC antitrust rules.[129] These long awaited proposals seek to protect the right of victims to full compensation for all damage suffered as a result of a breach of competition law. Other stated purposes include deterrence of future infringements and the preservation of public enforcement mechanisms.[130] One of the prohibitive hurdles in filing stand-alone, private anti-trust litigation is the difficulty of obtaining the relevant evidence to prove that unlawful activity has occurred and that the plaintiff has suffered harm. The Commission suggests some minimum *inter partes* discovery rules to facilitate the production of documents and prevent wholesale abuse. However, Member States have little incentive to enact a whole raft of discovery procedures that narrowly apply to competition litigation. The Commission also emphasizes the need for a 'European approach', implying that, although inspired by the United States enforcement record, the EU will find its own more balanced approach to private litigation. Thus, two complementary mechanisms for collective redress are proposed, adopted from the effectiveness of United States class action law suits. On the other hand, the proposal limits damages to compensatory awards, as in the recent United Kingdom case. Lack of harmonization on discovery, damage awards and attribution

---

the European Commission (2008), http://ec.europa.eu/comm/competition/ antitrust/actionsdamages/files_white_paper/impact_study.pdf.

[127] *Devenish Nutrition Limited & Others* v. *Sanofi-Aventis SA (France) & Others* [2007] EWHC 2394 (Ch).

[128] *Ibid.*

[129] European Commission, 'Damages actions for breach of the EC antitrust rules', White Paper, COM (2008) 165 final, 2 April 2008.

[130] *Ibid.*

of court costs will inevitably lead to forum shopping and could result in inconsistent enforcement.

Although the Commission seems to have worthy objectives, the implementation of these changes appears unlikely. Civil procedure rules evolve within domestic jurisprudence and typically apply broadly to many, if not all, types of civil cases. To revise discovery rules exclusively for private competition litigation could open a legislative can of worms that could have unintended political consequences that legislators would prefer to avoid. Worse yet, even if implemented, the proposals fall short of providing sufficient incentive to encourage private litigation. In the United States, the possibility of recovering damages of up to three times the amount of the overcharge is the golden carrot that motivates anti-trust litigation. The Commission's 'European approach' to private litigation will need further development if it is to achieve its goals of encouraging victims to seek compensation for harm inflicted by anti-competitive activities.

5. Conclusions

Despite the EU's lack of explicit competence in the area of health, Member States' domestic health care systems do not enjoy immunity from the application of EU competition law. Even incremental reforms to improve efficiency based on market competition may open the door for competition laws to apply. This creates a tension between the EU's explicit goals to promote both economic and social progress, and legal uncertainty for health policy-makers. EU competition law governs the actions of undertakings and Member States. The complexity of the relationship between public and private funding and provision of health care services is but one example demonstrating how undertakings participate in the health services sector. Professional associations can no longer protect members by negotiating fees or disseminating price information without risking being fined as anti-competitive cartels – as has already occurred in at least nine Member States. The privatization of hospital ownership or management may expose health providers to the application of competition law. Similarly, large health organizations run the risk of abuse of dominant position charges if their expansion threatens price competition, as evidenced by the rise in the number of health sector merger cases investigated by NCAs. However, this chapter is not an exhaustive analysis of the wide range of issues on the subject occurring in all EU Member States. The analysis presented merely outlines the depth and breadth of the issues beginning to surface.

Naturally, the majority of published cases originate from the pre-1995 Member States. What remains to be analysed in detail is how the newer Members States will address these issues and whether the Commission will use its scarce enforcement resources to encourage or coerce compliance with EU laws. Since the eastern European Member States' health systems were highly centralized under communism, the only direction for the reforms to go was towards increased competition, decentralization and privatization. These health systems have been under significant pressure to modernize quickly within constrained budgets. Whether their policies have been sensitive to European competition law prohibitions is yet another topic for further study.

Despite the fact that some national health officials still believe that health is a protected domestic issue,[131] NCAs have focused on the economic aspects of health care, allowing greater EU involvement in health system organization despite the protection of Article 152(5) EC. NCAs are not charged with enforcing the Treaty as a whole, only competition laws. Therefore, the decentralization of enforcement has strengthened economic policy priorities to the detriment of social policy objectives. Many NCAs have limited financial resources and staff experienced in health sector issues. National autonomy on issues such as civil court procedures, the types of remedy available and political risks will limit the prevalence of private actions. Concerns over the accountability and independence of NCAs also have been raised. Thus, both the definition and the enforcement of competition laws when applied to health sectors is an evolving subject worthy of further consideration.

The only thing that is clear, based on the law presented here, is that each case must be analysed in detail. There are few bright distinctions between economic and social functions in mixed public and private health systems. Competition law will not necessarily apply, while the services of general interest exception will not always provide a

---

[131] S. Greer, 'Choosing paths in European Union health policy: a political analysis of a critical juncture', *Journal of European Social Policy* 18 (2008), 219–31.

safe haven, allowing Member States to distort or restrict competition when regulating health services. The Commission continues to pursue legal clarity through attempts to develop a coherent European framework for health care. However, Member States have demonstrated little political will to support any European health policy that will interfere with their domestic policies.

9 | Public procurement and state aid in national health care systems

VASSILIS HATZOPOULOS

1. Introduction

The recognition by the European Court of Justice (ECJ) that health care services are services within the meaning of the EC Treaty has very important legal implications, most of which are still to materialize. Free movement of patients, recognized in *Kohll, Geraets-Smits and Peerbooms* and their progeny,[1] is just the tip of the iceberg. Much more crucial than accommodating the few thousands of 'peripatetic'

I would like to express my gratitude to the editors for their confidence and to Rita Baeten and Irene Glinos for their limitless help both in substantive and in coordination matters; without their help, this chapter would have been much poorer. I also want to acknowledge help from all those who worked for the national case-studies. In the United Kingdom, Julia Lear; Hungary, Zoltan Szabo; Italy, Chiara Miglioli; the Netherlands, Tom De Gans, Bert Hermans, Rita Baeten and Irene A. Glinos; Belgium, Rita Baeten and Irene A. Glinos.

[1] Case C-158/96, *Kohll* v. *Union des Caisses de Maladie* [1998] ECR I-1931; Case C-157/99, *Geraets Smits and Peerbooms* [2001] ECR I-5473. For these cases and their progeny, see V. Hatzopoulos, 'Killing national health and insurance systems but healing patients? The European market for health care services after the judgements of the ECJ in *Vanbraekel* and *Peerbooms*', *Common Market Law Review* (2002), 683–729; and, more recently, V. Hatzopoulos, 'Health law and policy, the impact of the EU', in G. de Búrca (ed.), *EU law and the welfare state: in search of solidarity* (Oxford: Oxford University Press, European University Institute, 2005), pp. 123–60. See also G. Davies, 'Welfare as a service', *Legal Issues of European Integration* (2002), 27–40; P. Cabral, 'The internal market and the right to cross-border medical care', *European Law Review* (2004), 673–85; and A. P. van der Mei, 'Cross-border access to health care within the EU: some reflections on *Geraets-Smits and Peerbooms* and *Vanbraekel*', *Medical Law* (2002), 189–213; and A. P. van der Mei, 'Cross-border access to medical care: non-hospital care and waiting lists', *Legal Issues of European Integration* (2006), 167–82; A. Kaczorowska, 'A review of the creation by the ECJ of the right to effective and speedy medical treatment and its outcomes', *European Law Journal* (2006), 345–70. For a full account of the relationships between the EU and health law, see T. Hervey and J. McHale, *Health law and the European Union* (Cambridge: Cambridge University Press, 2004).

patients moving from one state to another[2] is the issue of financing high performing health care systems that have universal coverage.

Financing health care and securing universal coverage tradition-ally have been tasks attributed to the state. Indeed, even in 'an era of contractualized governance in the delivery of public services',[3] where the 'providential state' gives way to the 'regulatory state'[4] and where the containment of public spending is an absolute value, nobody in Europe seriously questions the need for the public fund-ing of health care.[5] However, once it is established that health care services are 'services' within the meaning of the Treaty and that there is a 'market' for health care, public money cannot reach this market in an arbitrary way. It has rightly been pointed out that 'while in the 1990s the debate concerned anti-competitive prac-tices and Article 82 EC ... since the beginning of the current mil-lennium, the main question has shifted to the means of financing public services and to state aid'.[6] Hence, public funds have either to be disbursed following a competitive tender based on objective and transparent criteria, or to be individually evaluated under the Treaty rules on state aid.

The aim of this chapter is to examine (and to some extent to speculate upon) the ways in which the rules on public procurement and on state aid may affect the organization of public health care systems of Member States. In order to better illustrate the resulting questions, we shall try to base the various findings on the national systems of six Member States.

---

[2] See Chapter 12 in this volume.
[3] C. Bovis, 'Financing services of general interest in the EU: how do public procurement and state aids interact to demarcate between market forces and protection?', *European Law Journal* 90 (2005), 79–109.
[4] See G. Majone, 'The rise of the regulatory state in Europe', *West European Politics* 17 (1994), 77–101; F. McGowan and H. Wallace, 'Towards a European regulatory state', *Journal of European Policy* 3 (1996), 560–76.
[5] Even in the most pro-competitive economies, where provision is increasingly secured through private means, such as in the United Kingdom or the Netherlands, private finance initiatives are perceived as complementary – not an alternative – to public funding; see below.
[6] L. Idot, 'Les services d'intérêt général économique et les règles de concurrence', in J. V. Louis and S. Rodriguez (eds.), *Les services d'intérêt économique général et l'UE* (Belgium: Bruylant, 2006), p. 41, unofficial translation.

For the sake of clarity, the structure followed is simplistic and resembles that of a judgment: first, the legal framework needs to be reviewed in order to account for several recent developments that have upset the legal scenery (section two), then the law will be applied to the facts, in order to obtain a more precise idea of the ways in which the various health care systems are (or may be) affected by EC rules on state aid and public procurement (section three). Some conclusions will follow (section four).

2. Public procurement and state aid

Despite the fact that the relevant rules appear in different sections of the EC Treaty, public procurement and state aid are linked in many ways.[7]

A. *Logical links between state aid and public procurement*

First, there is a logical link between state aid and public procurements. When public authorities wish to favour specific players in a given market, they can do so in two ways: directly, by giving them public subsidies, or indirectly, by awarding them public contracts. Hence, both sets of rules are designed to prevent public authorities from unduly meddling with markets. The rules on state aid (Articles 87–9 EC) prohibit such money infusions, unless they are specifically 'declared compatible' by the Commission, following a notification procedure.[8] The rules on public procurement, on the other hand, set in Directives 2004/17/EC and 2004/18/EC (the Public Procurement Directives),[9] require that public contracts be awarded following

---

[7] For a more complete account of the relationship between the two series of rules, see A. Bartosch, 'The relationship of public procurement and state aid surveillance – the toughest standard applies?', *Common Market Law Review* 35 (2002); and, more recently, Bovis, 'Financing services', above n.3.

[8] For a recent and comprehensive account of the Court's case law concerning state aids, see J.-D. Braun and J. Kuehling, 'Article 87 and the Community courts: from revolution to evolution', 45 *Common Market Law Review* (2008), 465–98.

[9] European Parliament and Council Directive 2004/17/EC coordinating the procurement procedures of entities operating in the water, energy, transport and postal services sectors, OJ 2004 No. L134/1; the 'General' Procurement Directive, European Parliament and Council Directive 2004/18/EC on the

stringent requirements of publicity, transparency, mutual recognition and non-discrimination. Adherence to these requirements is overseen by national jurisdictions, which have been awarded extraordinary powers to that effect by the so-called 'Procedures' Directives.[10]

Second, a logical conclusion stems from the above. Since both sets of rules pursue the same objectives, they must not apply simultaneously, but alternatively. Indeed, one of the conditions for the application of the rules on state aid is that the recipient of the aid must be an undertaking – and thus money transfers between public bodies or in favour of non-commercial entities are not caught. On the other hand, public procurement rules are deemed to apply to so-called 'public markets' (*marches publics*), 'where the state and its organs enter in pursuit of the public interest' and not for profit maximization.[11] Hence, 'contracting entities' in the sense of the Public Procurement Directives are the state, regional and local authorities and 'bodies governed by public law'. The latter's legal form (public scheme, company, etc.) is irrelevant,[12] as long as three conditions are met: they need (a) to have legal personality; (b) to be financed or controlled by the state (or an emanation thereof); and (c) to have been 'established for the specific purpose of meeting needs in the general interest, not having an industrial or commercial character'. The Court has made it clear that these are cumulative conditions.[13] Member States have been invited to enumerate in Annex I of

---

coordination of procedures for the award of public works contracts, public supply contracts and public service contracts, OJ 2004 No. L134/114.

[10] Directive 89/665/EEC of the Council of 21 December 1989 on the coordination of the laws, regulations and administrative provisions relating to the application of review procedures to the award of public supply and public works contracts, OJ 1989 No. L395/33; and Directive 92/13/EEC of 25 February 1992 coordinating the laws, regulations and administrative provisions relating to the application of Community rules on the procurement procedures of entities operating in the water, energy, transport and telecommunications sectors, OJ 1992 No. L76/14. Both Directives have recently been amended by Directive 2007/66/EC of the European Parliament and the Council of 11 December 2007, OJ 2007 No. L335/31.

[11] See Bovis, 'Financing services', above n.3; C. Bovis, 'Recent case law relating to public procurement: a beacon for the integration of public markets', *Common Market Law Review* 39 (2002), 1025–56; and C. Bovis, 'The regulation of public procurement as a key element of European economic law', *Europeal Law Journal* 4 (1998), 220–42.

[12] Case C-360/96, *BFI Holding* [1998] ECR I-6821, para. 53.

[13] See, for example, Case C-44/96, *Mannesmann Anlangebau Austria* [1998] ECR I-73; and Case C-360/96, *Gemeente Arnhem* [1998] ECR I-6821.

Directive 93/37/EC,[14] now replaced by Annex III of Directive 2004/18/ EC, national 'bodies' that fall into the above category.

However, this enumeration is not exhaustive, and the Court has been called upon on several occasions to interpret the above three conditions. Unsurprisingly, the most controversial condition has been the one related to the distinction between activities in the pursuance of general interest and activities of an industrial or commercial character. Following the judgements of the Court in the *Mannesmann*, *BFI Holding* and, more recently, *Agora and Excelsior* cases,[15] two series of conclusions may be drawn.

First, the fact that some activity serves the general interest does not, in itself, exclude the industrial or commercial character of that very activity. Or, to use the Court's wording, there is 'a distinction between needs in the general interest not having an industrial or commercial character and needs in the general interest having an industrial or commercial character'.[16]

Second, in order to ascertain into which of the above categories an activity falls, the Court uses a set of criteria (*faisceau d'indices*), which may be summarized as follows: (a) the absence of considerable competition in providing the same activity; (b) the existence of decisive state control over the said activity;[17] (c) the pursuance of the activity and the satisfaction of the relevant needs in a way that is different from what is offered in the market place; and (d) the absence of financial risk. These are all factors that point towards an absence of industrial and commercial character.[18]

These criteria are very similar to the ones used by the Court to ascertain whether an entity is to be viewed as an 'undertaking'.[19] Therefore,

---

[14] Council Directive 93/37/EEC concerning the coordination of procedures for the award of public works contracts, OJ 1993 No. L199/54.

[15] Case C-360/96, *BFI Holding*, above n.13; Case C-44/96, *Mannesmann*, above n.14; see also Joined Cases C-223/99 and C-260/99, *Agora and Excelsior* [2001] ECR I-3605.

[16] Joined Cases C-223/99 and C-260/99, *Agora and Excelsior*, ibid., para. 32.

[17] Not the entity providing it; this is a distinct condition directly enumerated in the Directives, see above.

[18] See C. Bovis, *EC public procurement: case law and regulation* (Oxford: Oxford University Press, 2006), Chapter 7; S. Arrowsmith, *The law of public and utilities procurement* (London: Sweet & Maxwell, 2005), Chapter 5.

[19] For these criteria, see below; for more detail on the health care sector, see Hatzopoulos, 'Health law', above n.1, pp. 123–60, 149–55. Bovis, 'Financing services', above n.3, takes up the same point at p. 84.

it would seem that, to the extent that the two series of criteria are applied consistently, an entity that is not an undertaking will, more often than not, be considered to be a contracting entity. Hence, any given entity will be subject either to the competition and state aid rules or to the ones on public procurement, but not both.[20] This viewpoint also finds support in the very text of the Utilities Procurement Directive, both in its previous version (Article 8(1), Directive 93/38/EC)[21] and in its current version (Article 30, Directive 2004/17/EC), where it is stated that 'contracts ... shall not be subject to this Directive if, in the Member State in which it is performed, the activity is directly exposed to competition on markets to which access is not restricted'.

B. Formal links between state aid and public procurement

This logical link has been turned into a formal one in the Court's judgement in *Altmark*[22] and the Commission's 'Altmark package'.[23] In this case, the Court reversed previous case-law, where it followed a 'state aid' approach, in favour of a 'compensation' approach.[24] Before *Altmark*, any subsidy given to an undertaking for the accomplishment of some service of general interest would qualify as a state aid. Such aid could be upheld, by virtue of Article 86(2) EC, provided it were duly notified under Article 88 EC.[25] In *Altmark*, the Court held that

---

[20] See also Arrowsmith, *The law of public and utilities procurement*, above n.19, p. 265, taking up this point. The fact that the same entity may qualify as an undertaking for several activities and as a public authority for others (see Chapter 7 in this volume) does not alter the analysis; for any given activity, only one set of rules should be applicable.

[21] Council Directive 93/38/EC coordinating the procurement procedures of entities operating in the water, energy, transport and telecommunications sectors, OJ 1993 No. L82/39; Article 8(1) of this Directive was interpreted by the Court in Case C-392/93, *R v. HM Treasury ex parte British Telecommunications PLC* [1996] ECR I-1631.

[22] Case C-280/00, *Altmark Trans GmbH* [2003] ECR I-7747; for this case, see M. Merola and C. Medina, 'De l'arrêt Ferring à l'arrêt Altmark: continuité ou revirement dans l'approche du financement des services publics', *Cahiers de Droit Européen* (2003), 639–94.

[23] For which, see below, in the following paragraphs.

[24] See Bovis, 'Financing services', above n.3; J. Y. Chérot, 'Financement des obligations de service public et aides d'état', *Revue Europe* (2005), 5.

[25] See, for instance, Case C-387/92, *Banco Exterior de Espana* [1994] ECR I-877; Case T-106/95, *FFSA v. Commission* [1997] ECR II-229; and, on appeal, Case C-174/97, *P* [1998] ECR I-1303.

such financial support may not constitute a state aid at all, provided four conditions are met, cumulatively:

First, the recipient undertaking must actually have public service obligations to discharge, and the obligations must be clearly defined. Second, the parameters on the basis of which the compensation is calculated must be established in advance in an objective and transparent manner. Third, the compensation cannot exceed what is necessary to cover all or part of the costs incurred in the discharge of the public service obligations, taking into account the relevant receipts and a reasonable profit. Finally, where the undertaking which is to discharge public service obligations, in a specific case, is not chosen pursuant to a public procurement procedure which would allow for the selection of a tenderer capable of providing those services at the least cost to the community, the level of compensation needed must be determined on the basis of an analysis of the costs which a typical undertaking, well run and adequately provided with means of transport, would have incurred.[26]

From the very wording of the fourth condition, it follows that the default setting for the attribution and financing of some public service obligation is through public procurement. Only in the exceptional circumstances where this is not the case should prices be determined according to hypothetical market conditions.

More than the wording, the substantive content of this fourth condition suggests that the application of the procurement rules will be the means to avoid the applicability of the state aid rules. For one thing, it will be very difficult to prove what the costs of 'a typical undertaking, well run and adequately provided with means of transport' would have been in a hypothetical market – for example, what are 'adequate' means of transport? Most importantly, for most services of general interest there is no market other than the one emerging under the impulse of EC law. Hence, it will be virtually impossible to simulate such conditions in order to ascertain what the cost structure of a 'well run typical undertaking' would be.[27] The only way to benefit from the Court's judgment in *Altmark* and evade the application of the rules on

---

[26] The excerpt reproduced here summarizes paragraphs 89–93 of the Court's judgement and is taken from the Commission's *Altmark* decision, para. 4, for which see the following paragraphs.

[27] See, further, for the difficulties of these conditions, Idot, 'Les services', above n.6.

state aid would be to attribute public service contracts and the related funding to public procurement procedures.[28]

What is more, the first three conditions of the *Altmark* test are also certain to be fulfilled by the award of public service contracts through public tenders – although they do not necessarily require such tenders. The award contract will fulfil the formal requirement of condition number one. The content of the tender documents will satisfy conditions two and three.[29]

The Court's judgement in *Altmark* has been followed by the so-called 'Altmark package', also known as the 'Monti-Kroes package'. This consists of three documents: one directive, one decision and one communication.

- Directive 2005/81/EC[30] modifies Directive 80/723/EEC[31] and requires any undertaking that 'receives public service compensation in any form whatsoever in relation to such service and that carries

---

[28] Since the fourth condition is the hardest to fulfil, national authorities often start the examination of any given measure from this condition and immediately dismiss the applicability of the *Altmark* criteria; see for example Bulgarian Commission for the Protection of Competition, Case K3K-175/2006, *Elena Avtotransport*, 2 November 2006, para. 346, reported and briefly commented upon by D. Fessenko, 'The Bulgarian NCA clears state aid in the form of compensation for public transportation services under national state aid rules (*Elena Avtotransport*)', *e-Competitions Law Bulletin* No. 13146 (2007).

[29] It may be that the Court in *Altmark* was inspired by European Commission, 'Draft proposal for a European Parliament and Council Regulation on action by Member States concerning public service requirements and the award of public service contracts in passenger transport by rail, road and inland waterway', COM (2002) 107 final, 21 February 2002, which provided for the award of public service contracts following competitive and transparent tenders. This proposal, however, has been the object of intense negotiations between the European Parliament and the Council, and is currently on the verge of being adopted on the basis of a substantially modified draft, see European Commission, 'Communication from the Commission to the European Parliament pursuant to the second subparagraph of Article 251(2) of the EC Treaty concerning the common position adopted by the Council with a view to the adoption of a Regulation of the European Parliament and of the Council on public passenger transport services by rail and by road', COM (2006) 805 final, 12 December 2006.

[30] Commission Directive 2005/81/EC of 28 November 2005 amending Directive 80/723/EEC on the transparency of financial relations between Member States and public undertakings as well as on financial transparency within certain undertakings, OJ 2005 No. L312/47.

[31] Commission Directive 80/723/EEC on the transparency of financial relations between Member States and public undertakings, OJ 1980 No. L195/35.

on other activities' to undertake a separation of accounts of activities for which it receives compensation from its other activities.

- More importantly, Commission Decision 2005/842/EC,[32] adopted on the basis of Article 86(3), provides for some kind of 'block exemption' from the state aid rules where the *Altmark* conditions are not met. This 'block exemption'[33] covers three categories of service providers: (a) any service provider of small size (turnover of under €100 million during the last two years) receiving a limited amount of compensation (up to €30 million annually); (b) transport serving up to a certain number of passengers; and (c) hospitals and social housing undertakings, without any limitation. This text offers important information concerning the way in which the Commission will apply the four *Altmark* criteria – especially that concerning 'just' compensation. Subsidies falling within the scope of the Decision qualify as state aid (according to *Altmark*) but are deemed compatible with the internal market and need not be notified to the Commission.
- Finally, the 'Community framework for state aid in the form of public service compensation'[34] sets the Commission's position in respect of those subsidies that do not fall either under the *Altmark* judgement (and hence, do not constitute aid) or under the 'Altmark Decision' (and constitute aid that is automatically authorized by the Commission) and need to be notified in order to obtain an individual declaration of compatibility.

The Altmark package was further complemented by two texts of (ultra) soft law, in the form of Commission staff working documents, attached to the latest Commission Communication on 'services of

---

[32] Commission Decision 2005/842/EC on the application of Article 86(2) of the EC Treaty to state aid in the form of public service compensation granted to certain undertakings entrusted with the operation of services of general economic interest, OJ 2005 No. L312/67.

[33] The term 'block exemption' is used here in a generic manner. This Decision based on Article 86(3) EC should not be confused with the five state aid 'block exemptions' adopted by the Commission by virtue of the authorization given to it by Council Regulation 994/98/EC on the application of Articles 92 and 93 of the EC Treaty to certain categories of horizontal aid, OJ 1998 No. L142/1, based on Article 89 EC, a state aid legal basis.

[34] Community Framework for state aid in the form of public service compensation, OJ 2005 No. C297/4. In a different context, it would make sense to enquire what a 'Community Framework' is and how this is different from a Communication, if at all.

general interest, including social services of general interest'.[35] Each of these working documents contains a list of frequently asked questions (FAQs) and answers thereto. The first working document answers questions concerning the application of public procurement rules to social services of general interest,[36] while the second (and longest) provides an interpretative tool for the 'Altmark' Decision 2005/842/EC.[37] The very fact that the two working documents are attached to the same Commission Communication clearly shows the direct links between public procurement and state aid.[38]

In light of the above texts, there is no doubt that, despite other approaches previously followed by the Court,[39] the so-called 'compensation' approach currently prevails in determining whether public

[35] European Commission, 'Communication from the Commission to the European Parliament, the Council, the European Economic and Social Committee and the Committee of the Regions accompanying the Communication on "a single market for 21st century Europe" – services of general interest, including social services of general interest: a new European commitment', COM (2007) 725 final, 20 November 2007.

[36] European Commission, 'Frequently asked questions concerning the application of public procurement rules to social services of general interest', Commission Staff Working Document, SEC (2007) 1514, 20 November 2007.

[37] European Commission, 'Frequently asked questions in relation to Commission Decision of 28 November 2005 on the application of Article 86(2) of the EC Treaty to state aid in the form of public service compensation granted to certain undertakings entrusted with the operation of services of general economic interest, and of the Community Framework for state aid in the form of public service compensation', Commission Staff Working Document, SEC (2007) 1516, 20 November 2007.

[38] While these drafts were being proofread, the *Altmark* orthodoxy received an important blow from the Court of First Instance's (CFI's) judgement in Case T-289/03, *BUPA* v. *Commission* [2008] ECR II-81. In this judgment, the CFI held that, at least in the field of health, Member States enjoy a wide scope of discretion when defining the scope of services of general interest. Therefore: (a) the content of services of general interest need not be defined in any 'excruciating' detail – hence *Altmark* conditions one and two (clear definition of the subsidized service and transparent calculation of its cost) become more of a theoretical requirement; and (b) conditions three and four (no overcompensation, compared to a normally efficient undertaking) are only controlled by the Commission and Court for manifest error – therefore shifting the burden of proof to the party claiming overcompensation or inefficiencies. It is not clear how this judgment will be received and applied in the future, but this author would be tempted to view a political judgement as being unlikely to reverse the stricter *Altmark* logic.

[39] For which, see C. Bovis, 'Financing services', above n.3, who distinguishes: (a) the state aid approach; (b) the compensation approach; and (c) the quid pro quo approach.

funds given out for the accomplishment of services of general interest constitute an aid. Under this approach, the rules on public procurement play a pivotal role in two ways: (a) *externally*, as a means of defining the scope of application of the state aid rules (an entity charged with some mission of general interest that qualifies as a contracting entity is unlikely to be an undertaking and therefore may receive public funds without being constrained by the rules on state aid); and (b) *internally*, as the main means for the application of Article 86(2) EC in the field of state aid, according to the *Altmark* test.

Thus, in practice, any entity receiving public money should answer the following questions in order to position itself in respect of the state aid rules:

(a) Is it an undertaking or not? If it is itself a contracting entity then the most likely answer is negative. If, however, the answer is positive then:

(b) Does the undertaking fall into any of the categories contemplated by the 'Altmark' Decision (small size, transport, hospital), in which case the aid is deemed lawful, without notification being necessary? If the answer is negative, then:

(c) Is the money received compensation for some public service within the meaning of the *Altmark* judgement? If the undertaking in question has not been chosen following a public tender procedure, the likely answer is negative and the moneys received will constitute an aid; then:

(d) How can the terms and conditions attached to the aid be formulated in order for it to be individually declared lawful by the Commission, according to its 'Framework' Communication?

C. Procurement principles as a means of regulating the internal market

The importance of the public procurement rules and principles as a means of regulating the flow of public funds in the Member States has been stressed a great deal by both the Court and the Commission during the last few years.[40] In fact, the relevant case-law, together with the *Altmark*

---

[40] See C. Bovis, 'Developing public procurement regulation: jurisprudence and its influence on law making', *Common Market Law Review* 43 (2006), 461–95.

judgments discussed above, constitute the two main developments of economic law in the Court's case-law. The Court has handed down two series of judgements in this respect.

First, the Court has held that, next to the specific and technical rules of the Public Procurement Directives, a series of general principles apply in all circumstances where public money is put into the market – that is, on top of, or outside the scope of, the Procurement Directives. The Court began by holding, in *Commission v. France, Nord Pas de Calais*,[41] that, on top of the Directive's technical rules, a general principle of non-discrimination should also be respected in any award procedure. More importantly, in a series of judgments starting with *Telaustria*,[42] a case concerning a concession in the field of tel-ecommunications, the Court held that the same principle also applies to concession contracts (and presumably any other type of contract that involves public funding and is not covered by the Procurement Directives). *Coname*[43] concerned the direct award, in Italy, of a contract for the service covering the maintenance, operation and monitoring of the methane gas network. In its judgment, the Court further explained that the above requirement of non-discrimination carries with it a further requirement of transparency, satisfied by adequate publicity. This trend was further pursued some months later in *Parking Brixen*,[44] another Italian case concerning the construction and management of a public swimming pool. The Court found that 'a complete lack of any call for competition in the case of the award of a public service concession does not comply with the requirements of Articles 43 EC and 49 EC *any more than with the principles of equal treatment, non-discrimination and transparency*'.[45] The same was confirmed some days later in *Contse*,[46] which concerned the award of a contract for the supply of home oxygen equipment in Spain.

Picking up on the momentum created by these judgments, the Commission has come up with an interpretative Communication on the Community law applicable to contract awards not or not fully subject to the provisions of the public procurement directives (the so-called '*de*

---

[41] Case C-225/98, *Commission v. France* [2000] ECR I-7445.
[42] Case C-324/98, *Telaustria* [2000] ECR I-745.
[43] Case C-231/03, *Coname* [2005] ECR I-7287.
[44] Case C-458/03, *Parking Brixen* [2005] ECR I-8612.
[45] *Ibid.*, para. 48 (emphasis added).
[46] Case 234/03, *Contse* [2005] ECR I-9315.

minimis Communication').[47] This Communication covers: (a) contracts below the thresholds for the application of the Procurement Directives; and (b) contracts that are covered by the Directives but are listed in Annex IIB of the General Procurement Directive and in Annex XVIIB of the Utilities Directive and are, thus, excluded from the technical procurement rules. Concession contracts and public–private partnerships (PPPs) are not covered by this Communication, as a larger consultation process was initiated by the Commission's White Paper of 2004, followed by a Communication of November 2005;[48] the outcome of the process was the 2008 Interpretative Commission Communication.[49] The *de minimis* Communication basically explains the way in which the principles set out in the Court's jurisprudence should be put to work. The four principles pursued are: (a) non-discrimination (based on nationality) and equal treatment (also in purely national situations); (b) transparency; (c) proportionality; and (d) mutual recognition (hereinafter, the 'procurement principles'). According to the Communication, the obligations accruing to contracting entities under the general Treaty rules are proportionate to the interest that the contract at stake presents for parties in other Member States. Four aspects of the award procedure are taken up by the Commission: advertising prior to the tender, content of the tender documents, publicity of the award decision and judicial protection.

Without entering into the details of this Communication, it is worth making two points. First, from the four aspects treated by the Communication, all but the one relating to pre-contractual publicity are already regulated by the Public Procurement Directives for those service contracts (above the thresholds) that are included in Annex IIB (and XVIIB of the Utilities Directive): the Procurement Directives themselves set minimal requirements concerning the technical specifications

---

[47] European Commission, 'Interpretative Communication on the Community law applicable to contract awards not or not fully subject to the provisions of the public procurement directives', OJ 2006 No. C179/2.

[48] European Commission, 'Communication from the Commission to the European Parliament, the Council, the European Economic and Social Committee and the Committee of the Regions on public-private partnerships and community law on public procurement and concessions', COM (2005) 569 final, 15 November 2005.

[49] European Commission, 'Interpretative Communication on the application of Community law on public procurement and concessions to institutionalized public-private partnerships (IPPP)', C (2007) 6661, 5 February 2008. See http://ec.europa.eu/internal_market/publicprocurement/ppp_En.htm.

used in the tenders, as well as the publicity of the contract's award, while the 'Procedures Directive' is fully applicable to these services. This first point leads to the second: since the legislator specifically decided to treat services included in Annex IIB (and XVIIB of the Utilities Directive) in a given way, is it politically admissible and legally sound for the Commission to impose more stringent obligations through a text of soft law?

The Court has shown its great attachment to the general principles linked to public procurement in a second series of cases, *a priori* entirely foreign to award procedures. The most recent and most striking example is to be found in the Court's judgement in *Placanica*, a case concerning bet collection in Italy.[50] According to the Italian legislation, this activity required a government licence, from which undertakings quoted in the stock market (mostly non-Italian) were altogether excluded. The Court did not restrict itself to finding that such a blanket exclusion was disproportionate to the objective of protecting consumers. It further stated that, whenever operators have been unlawfully excluded from the award of licences (which were determinate in number), 'it is for the national legal order to lay down detailed procedural rules to ensure the protection of the rights which those operators derive by direct effect of Community law' and that 'appropriate courses of action could be the revocation and redistribution of the old licences or the award by *public tender* of an adequate number of new licences'.[51] This reflects an idea that is being implemented in the regulated industries (telecommunications, energy, etc.) and that had been put forward by the Commission (but never taken up) on a more general scale, concerning access to essential facilities:[52] whenever some scarce resource is to be distributed between competitors, the way to do it is through public tendering procedures.

Hence, not only do the basic procurement principles (i.e., non-discrimination and equal treatment, transparency, proportionality

---

[50] Joined Cases C-338/04, C-359/04 and C-360/04, *Placanica* [2007] ECR I-01891.

[51] *Ibid.*, para. 63 (emphasis added).

[52] Organisation for Economic Co-operation and Development, 'The essential facilities concept', OECD/GD(96)113 (1996), Contribution of the European Commission, pp. 93–108, at 102, www.olis.oecd.org/olis/1996doc.nsf/ LinkTo/OCDE-GD(96)113.

and mutual recognition) apply to all tenders involving public money,[53] but also public tenders should be held in order for other (non-financial) valuable resources to be put into the market; of course, these tenders also should abide by the basic principles governing public procurement. Hence, if a *limited* number of hospitals were to be accredited into a national health care system or a *limited* number of insurance funds admitted to participate in a national insurance system, they should be chosen according to the above principles.[54]

Therefore, according to the latest case-law of the Court, the basic principles governing public procurement (i.e., non-discrimination and equal treatment, transparency, proportionality and mutual recognition) become key components of the regulatory framework of the internal market.

3. Applying the EC rules to national health care

Against this background, the question arises: if, how and to what extent do the rules – or, indeed, the principles – on public procurement and those on state aid affect – or should affect – the provision of health care in the Member States?[55]

The organization of health care in all Member States constitutes an expression of social solidarity.[56] As such, it shares some basic characteristics: it is intended to have universal coverage, it is publicly funded

---

[53] It is interesting to note in this respect that, following the judgement of the Court in Case C-507/03 *Commission* v. *Ireland*, An Post [2007] ECR I-9777 and Case C-119/06, *Commission* v. *Italy, Ambulance services* [2007] ECR I-168 (for which see below), it became clear that while the Directive rules apply to all awards above the thresholds, the general procurement principles require that the affectation of the internal market be positively established.

[54] The situation is different if an indeterminate number of entities (hospitals, funds, etc.) that fulfil specific requirements fixed in advance are admitted into the system; a different question still arises when Member States decide to run their health care/insurance systems relying exclusively on purely public bodies.

[55] For the first (and latest) official position on this issue see European Commission, 'Communication from the Commission', above n.35. This Communication comes with two 'working documents': European Commission, 'Frequently asked questions', above n.36; and European Commission, 'Frequently asked questions', above n.37.

[56] Newdick puts forward the idea that social solidarity thus organized is placed in danger by the negative integration measures pursued by the ECJ. See C. Newdick, 'Citizenship, free movement and health care: cementing individual rights by corroding social solidarity', *Common Market Law Review* 43 (2006),

and entails cross-subsidization of risks (good risks financing bad ones) and patients (young and healthy patients financing the elderly and sick). These main characteristics apart, health care systems in the Member States are organized in a great variety of ways. In view of this great diversification, it is impossible to determine in an all-encompassing manner the way in which the EC rules on public procurement and on state aid affect the organization of health care in Member States. For this reason, it will be useful to ground the present inquiry on specific Member State case-studies and offer illustrations based upon these.[57]

Since the rules on state aid, on the one hand, and on public procurement, on the other, are so closely related and their application rests on the same sets of criteria,[58] in the analysis that follows we shall examine each individual criterion rather than the two sets of rules separately.

A. Where is the service of general interest?

The pursuance of general interest is a key criterion for qualifying a body as a 'contracting entity' in the sense of the Public Procurement Directives. At the same time, it is the main condition for the application of the 'compensation' logic inaugurated with the Court's judgment in *Altmark*.

There is no doubt that providing health care for an entire population constitutes a service of general interest. This general assertion, however, is pregnant with ambiguities. Assuming that universal coverage of the population is an absolute aim (and, hence, that the personal scope of the system is inelastic), there remain at least three variables in defining the scope of 'general interest' in the field of health care:

(a) the kinds of treatments (and pharmaceuticals) provided by the system vary from one state to the other, according to religious, moral, scientific and other perceptions: cosmetic surgery, sex

---

1645–68; see also R. Houtepen and R. ter Meulen, 'New types of solidarity in the European welfare state', *Health Care Analysis* 8 (2000), 329–40.

[57] Thanks to the valuable help of researchers and colleagues from the London School of Economics, the Observatoire social européen and other research institutes, some aspects of the healthcare systems of the following six member states are being discussed: England, the Netherlands, Belgium, Italy, Hungary and Greece.

[58] See above section 2 subsections A and B of the present C.

modification, pain treatment and abortions are just some examples where divergences exist between the various Member States;

(b) the quality of medical treatments provided may vary as a result of: (i) the qualification level of health professionals; (ii) the number of health professionals; (iii) the medical infrastructure of the hospitals (number and quality); (iv) waiting time to have access to the system; (v) waiting time to receive any given treatment, etc.; and

(c) the quality of nonmedical services, such as accommodation, catering, cleaning, etc.

In most Member States, the level of health care that should be provided is described in one or more legislative acts (see, for example, the 1987 Hospital Act in Belgium, the 1977 NHS Act in the United Kingdom, etc.) or some other regulatory act (see, for example, the 2001 Agreement between the Government, the Regions and the Provinces of Trento and Bolzano for the Application of Legislative Decree 502/1992 in Italy). In some states, a general provision securing a high level of health care to the population is also to be found in the Constitution (see, for example, Article 70(D) of the Hungarian Constitution and, in less compelling formulations, Article 22 of the Dutch Constitution, Article 23 of the Italian Constitution, Article 23(2) of the Belgian Constitution or Article 21(3) of the Greek Constitution).[59]

These norms, however, even when they go beyond mere principles, very rarely provide a detailed description of the above variables and, hence, fail to define the precise scope of general interest in health care. Next to these general rules, very specific and complex rules are

---

[59] It is worth noting that, even in Hungary, the Constitution sets high requirements for the protection of health. Article 70(D): '(1) People living within the territory of the Republic of Hungary have the right to the highest possible level of physical and mental health. (2) The Republic of Hungary implements this right through arrangements for labour safety, with health institutions and medical care, through ensuring the possibility for regular physical training, and through the protection of the built-in natural environment.' The Constitutional Court of this country has decided that this is not an absolute and static right, but should be interpreted within the economic and social context at any given moment. See in general about constitutionalism and social rights in Hungary, J.-J. Dethier and T. Shapiro, 'Constitutional rights and the reform of social entitlements', in L. Bokros and J.-J. Dethier (eds.), *Public finance reform during the transition. The experience of Hungary* (Washington, DC: World Bank, 1988).

to be found concerning the calculation of various treatment units, the funding of the various parts of hospital budgets, etc.[60] Usually, however, these technical rules relate to the cost of specific activities and treatments and do not represent the entire cost of services of general interest in health care.

Therefore, it would seem that the application of EC law would require the introduction, in the field of health care, of the concept of 'service of general interest' or 'public service' and a precise definition of its content. This would be necessary both for identifying with precision which entities are likely to qualify as 'contracting entities' and for applying the *Altmark* test. This should be done in a way that is more detailed than in the general constitutional or even legislative texts, but less technical than in the financial/accounting instruments. Four questions arise in this respect.

First, how detailed is detailed enough for the requirements of *Altmark* and the 'Altmark Decision' to apply? In this respect, the Belgian experience is interesting, yet by no means conclusive. After the 'Altmark Decision', the Belgian Parliament added, in December 2006, a general clause to Article 2 of the general 'Hospital Act' (loi du 7 août 1987). This clause formally states that 'hospitals perform a task of general interest', in order for them to qualify for the funding possibilities opened up by the 'Altmark' Decision. In its Consultative Opinion No. 41.594/3, the Belgian Council of State inquired whether such a simple modification could bring all hospitals within the scope of the 'compensation approach', since the other elements of the *Altmark* test were not specified: nature and duration of the services, territory concerned, calculation and justification of the charge required for the accomplishment of services of general interest. The Belgian Parliament, nonetheless, considered that all these elements could be adequately inferred from the legislation already in place and adopted the above modification.[61]

Second, the *Altmark* ruling entails a logical shift: while the national logic is one of defining the scope of a health care *system*, the EC logic is to define a *set of* health care *services* of general interest. This, in turn, may entail re-assessing some of the assumptions concerning

---

[60] For which see below.
[61] See the explanatory memorandum of the proposal in the Belgian Chamber of Representatives, www.dekamer.be/FLWB/pdf/51/2760/51K2760001.pdf.

the provision of health care. For instance, all hospitals, public and private, offer various categories of hotel amenities. If rooms with three or more patients may reasonably qualify as services of general interest, the same may not be true for single or even double rooms, except where this is justified by medical reasons.[62]

Third, and in direct relationship with the previous point, are Member States free to fix the outer limits of 'services of general interest'? The Commission in its 'Altmark' package states that it will only interfere in cases of 'manifest error'.[63] This view finds support in the case-law of the Court. In this respect, it may be useful to compare the judgments of the Court concerning ambulance services. In the Austrian *Tögel* case,[64] the Court reasoned that any award of ambulance transport contracts should be made according to the 'Services' Directive 92/50/EEC, provided that this text had become binding at the relevant date (which was not the case for Austria). Taking this point further, in *Commission v. Italy, Ambulance Services*,[65] the Court made clear that the obligation to abide by the public procurement rules (or, depending on the circumstances, principles) remains even if the intention of the authority is to award the contract to a non-profit organization (such as the Red Cross) using personnel working on a volunteer basis.[66]

In the German *Glöckner* case,[67] on the other hand, the Court admitted that ambulance contracts could be awarded on the basis of a prior authorization, with no tendering procedure. This was so because: (a) reasonably priced urgent services with a large territorial coverage constituted a service of general interest; and (b) other transport services,

---

[62] In some states, such a distinction is already made – for example, in Belgium, both hospitals and practitioners may charge supplements to patients staying in single or double rooms; for occupants of double rooms, there is a cap on the supplements charged, while for those living in single rooms there is no cap, either for 'hotel' or for medical services.

[63] See Commission Decision 2005/842/EC, above n.32, Recital 7; and Community Framework, above n.34, Recital 9.

[64] Case C-76/97, *Tögel* [1998] ECR-5357.

[65] Case C-119/06, *Commission v. Italy*, above n.53.

[66] In this specific case, however, the Court dismissed the Commission's action, because the Commission had failed to prove: (a) that the total amount of the contract was above the thresholds for Council Directive 92/50 to be applicable; and (b) that the contract did present some trans-border interest for the general Treaty rules to become applicable.

[67] Case C-475/99, *Glöckner* [2001] ECR I-8089.

although not directly linked with the general interest, served to finance the former. Hence, in *Glöckner*, despite the precedent set by *Tögel*, the Court was not willing to interfere with the German definition of services of general interest and the way they are financed. The same non-interventionist stance was followed by the Court more recently in *Commission v. Ireland, Ambulance Services*.[68] In this case, the Court found no contractual relationship – and hence no award – to exist between the Health Authority and the Dublin City Council, which provided ambulance services, each one of them being empowered by law to provide emergency ambulance services. Finally, it should be remembered that, in the *Commission v. Italy, Ambulance Services* cases discussed above,[69] the Court, despite its broad statements in favour of the applicability of the procurement principles, allowed the Member State to pursue its system of contract award.

If Member States enjoy a wide discretion in extending the scope of services of general interest, the same is not true when it comes to lowering the standards of care – although the limits to their discretion are of an indirect nature. Therefore, in *Geraets-Smits and Peerbooms*,[70] the Court held that the authorities of a Member State, if they do not offer a treatment themselves, may not refuse to refund it only by reference to national standards and practices, if it is obtained in another Member State. Similarly, in *Müller-Fauré*,[71] the Court held that if national waiting lists are far too long for the medical condition of any individual patient, then he/she should be entitled to receive treatment in another Member State.

Fourth, a more radical idea may be put forward:[72] it may be that hospitals do not offer public services at all. According to this analysis, the service of general interest resides in assuring universal coverage and adequate funding for health care – health care itself may be purchased at any time, at the right price. In such a scenario, only the sickness insurance funds would be performing some task of general economic interest. However, in view of the preceding paragraphs and

---

[68] Case C-532/03, *Commission v. Ireland*, above n.53.
[69] Case C-119/06, *Commission v. Italy*, above n.54.
[70] Case C-157/99, *Geraets Smits and Peerbooms*, above n.2.
[71] Case C-385/99, *Müller-Fauré* [2003] ECR I-4509.
[72] See, for example, G. Chavrier, 'Etablissement public de santé, logique économique et droit de la concurrence', *Revue du Droit de la Sécurité Sociale* (2006), 274–87.

of the fact that the 'Altmark Decision' holds legitimate any aid given to hospitals for the fulfilment of public service obligations, this radical analysis is not likely to be widely followed any time soon.

B. How is it financed?

The definition of the scope of health care services of general interest is intrinsically linked to the question of financing these same services. In this respect, several points should be made.

Distinguishing capital costs from exploitation costs

In most Member States (all those studied in this chapter), there is a more or less clear distinction between, on the one hand, capital investment, infrastructure, etc., and, on the other hand, exploitation costs, directly linked to the number of units produced (patients/treatments administered).[73] Two points should be made in this respect.

First, this dissociation, spontaneously made by Member States, corresponds to the model chosen by the EC legislature for the development of another field where infrastructure occupies a very important role: rail transport.[74] This distinction, however, has proven difficult to implement in the rail sector, even where clear rules of accounting unbundling did exist. This has led the EC legislator in the field of rail transport to require the organic separation of entities dealing with infrastructure from those offering services.[75] Hence, it remains to be ascertained, at a state-by-state level, how this distinction works for health care. Furthermore, an important difference exists between rail and hospital infrastructure, both developed with public money: the former may be hired out to competitors of its holder, while the same is not true for the latter. Therefore, the direct financing of infrastructure by the public purse may affect competition both at the level of

---

[73] In the Netherlands, however, this has changed as of 2008; the system whereby capital costs were not included in the total sum hospitals could claim from the contracted health insurers has been replaced by one whereby part of capital costs are negotiable (between hospitals and insurers) and included in DRGs.

[74] See Article 6, Council Directive 91/440/EEC for the development of community rail, OJ 1991 No. L237/25.

[75] See Article 6(2), European Parliament and Council Directive 2001/12/EC modifying Directive 91/440, OJ 2001 No. L75/1.

hospitals (public/private or between Member States) and at the level of insurance funds. The Belgian experience is instructive in this respect. In Belgium, hospital infrastructure is financed at 40% by the Federal Ministry of Health, while the remaining 60% is funded by the Communities. When Belgian hospitals conclude contracts with Dutch health insurers, they charge the same tariffs to them as they do to the Belgian health insurance system. This means that the investment cost for hospitals is only charged at 40%. Some Dutch hospitals do perceive this to be a distortion of competition and a Dutch organization of hospitals stated that they consider this to be non-permissible state aid in favour of Belgian hospitals.[76] It is difficult, however, to see how such a distortion could be remedied. The 40:60 funding ratio, linked to the federal structure of the state and embodying important political choices, may not be put directly into question by the rules on state aid (provided that transparency is ensured). On the other hand, it does not seem possible for Belgian hospitals to charge insurers differently, depending on their state of establishment.

Second, infrastructure and other fixed costs traditionally have been financed directly by the public purse, but, in recent years, some states have tried to attract private investment. The Private Funding Initiative (PFI) in the United Kingdom has set the pace, and other countries have followed suit. The emergence of new contractual forms, such as public–private partnerships (PPPs) and concessions offer further means of bringing in private funds. These will not be examined in the present chapter, but one remark should, nonetheless, be made: the choice of private investors who will participate in contributing capital to public hospitals (like in other public infrastructure) may only be made following the 'public procurement principles'.[77]

Calculating the cost of public service

Hospitals' budgets have very complicated structures and vary from one state to another. A point in common is that, next to capital investment costs (see above) they distinguish: (a) fixed costs, such as maintenance, heating, personnel, etc.; and (b) variable costs, directly linked to the volume of their activity. The way to calculate this latter segment

---

[76] I. Glinos, N. Boffin and R. Baeten, *Cross-border care in Belgian hospitals: an analysis of Belgian, Dutch and English stakeholder perspectives* (Brussels: Observatoire social européen, 2005), p. 66.
[77] See above, section 2, subsections B and C.

of expenses has been reviewed in most Member States during the last few years. In order to create incentives to contain cost and rationalize treatments, three main directions have been followed: (a) advance payments through prospective budgets based on average costs of hospitals in the same category; (b) calculation of the average costs on the basis of diagnosis-related group (DRG) or equivalent measuring unit,[78] only occasionally completed or adjusted by the application of fee-for-service or length-of-stay criteria; and (c) the possibility of efficient hospitals keeping any surplus. Not only do these measures force the hospitals to pursue a sounder management of financial resources, they also dramatically increase transparency. By the same token, the *Altmark* requirement of calculating the precise cost of public service is likely to be satisfied.

Transparency and cost calculation is also served by the fact that, in all of the Member States examined herein, practitioners are mainly self-employed (with the exception of Hungary, where the only considerable category of self-employed practitioners are family doctors) and enter into contracts with hospitals or funds. An issue here is the way that physicians' fees are fixed: it would seem that a system of public tendering like the Italian one would be preferable to, say, the Belgian system, where fees are fixed under the auspices of the public fund (National Institute for Health and Disability Insurance (NIHDI)) and may or may not be adhered to by each individual physician.[79] There are three reasons for this: first, because price fixing by public authorities and/or professional

---

[78] Diagnoses Related Groups (DRGs) or equivalent measuring units (Diagnose Behandelings Combianties (DBCs) in the Netherlands, Healthcare Resource Groups (HRGs) in England). DRGs are predefined pairs, whereby each specific medical condition is matched up with a determined treatment and/or length of stay.

[79] The Court is not particularly keen on price fixing by professional associations and other bodies. See recently Joined Cases C-94/04 and C-202/04, *Cipolla e.a.* [2006] ECR I-11421. See also, at the national level, a settlement reached before the Irish Competition Authority on 25 May 2007, whereby the Irish Medical Organisation, an association of GPs in Ireland, has undertaken not to take action in relation to prices in respect of several of their activities; the settlement is reported and briefly commented upon by O. Lynskey, 'The Irish Competition Authority settles price-fixing proceedings in the health insurance sector', *e-Competitions Law Bulletin* No. 14004 (2007); and by C. Hatton and S. A. Kauranen, 'The Irish Competition Authority settles an alleged price-fixing dispute in the health

organizations may fall foul of either the competition or the internal
market rules, or both; second, because the prices obtained through
public tendering are more likely to reflect the market price in any
given geographic area; and, third, because if the award criterion
is not only price but also quality, then better qualified physicians
would obtain better contracts. A different – but linked – issue is the
price public hospitals should charge practitioners for use of hospital
infrastructure in order to offer 'fee-for-service' health care services
outside the health system. In this respect, a recent judgment of the
French Council of State clearly illustrates the strain public health
systems are going through:[80] in the face of well-established legislation and jurisprudence that allowed only for the payment of a flat
'occupancy fee' for facilities, the Council of State admitted that
the actual economic value of the service may be mirrored in the
fee the practitioner is made to pay to the hospital. This evolution
under French law reflects the divergences existing in other Member
States: in England, practitioners retain a portion of the revenues
realized privately before feeding the rest back to the NHS, while, in
Belgium, the situation is closer to the one traditionally prevailing in
France, whereby a mere *'droit d'usage'* is charged.

A further point in assessing the transparency of the way the cost
of public service is calculated relates to the number of intermedi-
aries involved. The more diverse the routes for public monies to
reach hospitals and/or funds, the less transparency there will be. An
illustration may be offered by the Hungarian system, where public
hospitals: (a) receive funding for their infrastructure directly from
the Ministry of Health; (b) receive money for their services from the
health insurance fund, which (money), however, is mediated either
through (large) municipalities or through local governments, or
both. Moreover, the mediation of the health insurance fund's money

sector relating to medical examination reports to life insurance companies',
e-Competitions Law Bulletin No. 13967 (2007).

[80] Case No. 293229, *Syndicat National de Défense de l'Exercice Libéral de la
Médecine à l'Hôpital*, Conseil d'Etat, 16 July 2007, www.legifrance.gouv.fr/
affichJuriAdmin.do?oldAction=rechJuriAdmin&idTexte=CETATEXT0000
18006881&fastReqId=620987082&fastPos=1; for this case, see, briefly, B.
du Marais and A. Sakon, 'According to the French State Council, the tariff
that public hospitals levy on private activities of medical doctors employed as
civil servants can partly be related to a market price', *Concurrences* (2007),
148–50.

through local authorities, both in Hungary and in Italy, may result in political choices altering knowledgeable economic calculations. Hence, the calculation of the cost of public service may be flawed, thus making the application of the public procurement and/or state aid law more likely.

Funding the cost of services of general interest

According to the 'Altmark Decision' 2005/842/EC of the Commission, state aid given to hospitals for the accomplishment of public service obligations entrusted to them is exempt from notification and automatically legal, irrespective of the amount. Aid awarded to hospitals, however, needs to be strictly measured on the accomplishment of a public service. Several questions arise in this respect.

First, it is not clear what should happen if hospitals fail to accomplish their mission of general interest and who would be qualified to ascertain such failure – it may be that some system of monitoring should be set up as a consequence of the *Altmark* requirements.[81] Indeed, second, such a monitoring system seems to be required in order to control overcompensation. Third, under the Decision, overcompensation is explicitly ruled out and needs to be paid back, subject to a margin of 10%, which may be carried forward to the next year. Hence, the system of efficient hospitals 'keeping the surplus' of their annual budget introduced in some states as an incitement for efficient management[82] should be revised in light of the above. Fourth, while the 'Altmark package' allows for some reasonable profit to be made by the provider of services of general interest, it is not clear whether and how this should materialize in the hospital sector.

---

[81] It would seem that Commission Decision 2005/842/EC, above n.32, does require some monitoring, especially to oversee overcompensation; see Article 4(d).

[82] Such a system was introduced, for example, in Belgium in 2001: the overall available budget is divided into five groups of hospitals on the basis of percentage shares, which are determined *a priori* for the different types of costs and hospital groups. Each hospital is allocated the same average cost per work unit of the group to which it belongs. Objectively observable and justifiable cost differences, such as labour costs, are taken into account. Hospitals that manage their communal services more efficiently than the group average are allowed to release financial resources that can be used for other purposes. In England, a funding scheme adopted in 2002 but gradually phased in between 2004 and 2009 follows a similar pattern: the Department of Health (DoH) sets national tariffs for Healthcare Resource

The above considerations apply to monies given to hospitals directly by the state budget (e.g., in England),[83] or by public insurance funds or funds where membership is compulsory (e.g., in Italy, Hungary, Belgium and Greece).[84] It is unclear whether the same principles apply to a system like the Dutch one, where private insurers compete with one another for patients (but are under an obligation to admit everyone), and hospitals compete for contracts with as many insurers as possible. In other words, it is not clear whether 'public' monies are involved. On the one hand, the presence of market forces and freely negotiated contracts would point to a negative answer. On the other hand, the fact that membership of some fund is compulsory may lead to a positive answer.[85] If the former solution were retained and no 'public' monies were involved, then payments from health funds to hospitals would not qualify as state aid at all and could only be scrutinized under Articles 81 and 82 EC. If, on the other hand, funds did qualify as 'public', then the Dutch system would be no different from the other Member States examined.

C. *Who is a contracting entity and who is an undertaking?*

In the analysis above, it has been put forward that any given entity should qualify either as a contracting entity or as an undertaking and that the two qualifications should be mutually exclusive. The criterion for determining when an entity qualifies as an undertaking is as

Groups (HRGs), similar to DRGs. The national tariff is adjusted by a market forces factor to account for unavoidable differences in costs across regions. Providers who deliver services at a cost below the tariff prices will retain the surplus. However, the new funding scheme is intended to create competition on quality of services and efficiency (waiting times) rather than price.

[83] The Department of Health (DoH) gives tax money to the primary care trusts (PCTs), which in turn contract with public and private hospitals and general practitioners (GPs).

[84] See, for an example where a state aid was given by the Belgian pension fund ONSS (which is the NIHDI equivalent in the field of pensions) to a private undertaking, in the form of payment facilities, Case C-256/97, *Déménagements-Manutention Transport SA (DMT)* [1999] ECR I-3913; see also Case C-75/97, *Maribel* [1999] ECR I-3671.

[85] It should be noted that in another context, in Case C-75/97, *Maribel, ibid.*, para. 23, as well as in Case C-200/97, *Ecotrade* [1998] ECR I-7907, para. 34, the Court has held that 'measures which, in various forms, mitigate the charges which are normally included in the budget of an undertaking and which, without therefore being subsidies in the strict meaning of the word, are similar in character and have the same effect are considered to constitute aid'.

broad as 'the exercise of an economic activity'.[86] On the one hand, a contracting entity is one that 'does not pursue an activity of an economic or commercial nature'.[87] What is more, one of the fundamental principles of a market economy is that operators may contract with whomever they wish:[88] any given entity may not be subject simultaneously to free competition and to the restrictive and time-consuming rules of public procurement.[89] However, this is not necessarily true in a hybrid economic sector, such as the provision of health care. Possibly more controversial than the technical issues above is the more general question of whether health care provision should be subject to the procurement rules at all. In this respect, some of the arguments put forward against the general application of public procurement rules to the core of health care provision include: (a) the lack of flexibility of the procurement rules, especially in respect of the role of non-profit social organizations; (b) the transformation of partnership relationships into competitive ones; (c) the restriction of cooperation between local authorities, resulting from the restrictive concept of 'in-house contracting' followed by the EC; (d) the negative effect on establishing long-term trust relationships with suppliers and other partners; (e) the possible disruption of the continuity of public service; (f) increased transaction costs; and (g) delays.[90] Most of these concerns are being dealt with – although not really answered – by the Commission in its most recent Communication on services of general interest and the

[86] See also Chapters 7 and 8 in this volume. For a more thorough analysis of the concept of 'economic activity', see O. Odudu, *The boundaries of EC competition law* (Oxford: Oxford University Press, 2006), pp. 26–45.
[87] See Arrowsmith, *The law of public and utilities procurement*, above n.18; and Bovis, *EC public procurement*, above n.18.
[88] This 'freedom to deal' is known in competition law as the 'Colgate doctrine' from the US Supreme Court's judgment in *United States* v. *Colgate & Co.*, 250 US 300 (1919).
[89] See above section 2, subsections B and C.
[90] See, for example, European Commission, 'Social services of general interest: feedback report to the 2006 questionnaire of the Social Protection Committee', pp. 10–2, http://ec.europa.eu/employment_social/social_protection/docs/feedback_report_en.pdf. See also (on an earlier set of replies from the Member States) M. Maucher, 'Analysis of the replies of all European Union Member States' governments to the questionnaire of the Social Protection Committee preparing the Communication on Social and Health Services of General Interest', Observatory for the Development of Social Services in Europe, 16 September 2005, www.soziale-dienste-in-europa.de/Anlage25573/auswertung-antworten-ms-mitteilung-sgdai-ed.pdf.

accompanying documents.[91] In these texts, the Commission confirms its attachment to the application of the public procurement rules and principles in the area of health care.

Contracting entities: some certainty?

In Annex III of Directive 2004/18 member states have enumerated, in a non-exhaustive manner, the entities which they deem subject to the procurement rules.[92]

- Belgium considers three hospital centres owned by the central government to be contracting authorities.[93] The fact that the remaining 63 public hospitals (run by the Communities) are not included in the annex only means that their qualification as a contracting entity is not automatic. Until the last revision of the Annex, in effect from January 1, 2009, the NIHDI was also included, but has been taken off the list ever since. Several other funds, mostly pension ones, are also included in the list.

- Italy enumerates indistinctively all bodies administering compulsory social security and welfare schemes and a general category of 'organizations providing services in the public interest'. This presumably covers hospitals owned by the Local Health Authorities (ASLs) as well as public hospitals. It is less clear whether hospitals having the status of trust are also covered, although the most likely answer is positive.

- Greece gives only general definitions which clearly encompass all public healthcare funds and all hospitals where the state owns more than 51% stock or finances at least 50% of the annual budget (=all public hospitals); also in Annex XII (Central government authorities) two public hospitals are expressly enumerated.

- The Netherlands lists the university hospitals, within the meaning of the Law on Higher Education and Scientific Research and

---

[91] See European Commission, 'Communication from the Commission', above n.35; and the accompanying 'working document', European Commission, 'Frequently asked questions', above n.36.

[92] This annex has been modified for the last time by Commission Decision 2008/963/EC of 9 December 2008 [2008] OJ L 349/1, with effect as of 1 January, 2009.

[93] The majority of hospitals in Belgium are private hospitals (151 out of 215, equal to 70%, in 2005). Most private hospitals are owned by

several bodies involved in the management of hospital facilities, accreditation of health providers, etc.

- The UK enumerates the NHS Strategic Health Authorities (SHAs), who are the entities responsible for the attainment of the health targets decided by the Secretary of State for Health. However, under the current design of the NHS the largest part of contracting is not done by the SHAs but by the Primary Care Trusts (PCTs). In 2000 the NHS Purchasing and Supply Agency (PASA) was set up as an executive agency of the Department of Health and was entrusted to centralize and carry out procurement on behalf of all NHS entities.
- Hungary gives general definitions broadly in the same sense as Greece.

From the above list, it becomes clear that, even in public procurement, an area where substantial harmonization has been taking place for over twenty years and where Member States are supposed to be on the same wavelength, common solutions are non-existent. It also becomes clear that Member States have no shared views on the role the various entities play in their respective health care systems.

Undertakings everywhere?

There is no doubt that self-employed physicians, even when they are contracted in a national health care scheme or in a hospital, are undertakings.[94] In contrast, doctors who are public employees (for instance, as is the case for the vast majority in Hungary) are not.

The position of insurance funds is more complex. A very broad distinction may be drawn between funds where membership is compulsory and those offering complementary cover: the former would not

religious charitable orders, while the remainder are owned by universities or sickness funds. Public hospitals are for the most part owned by a municipality, a province, a community or an inter-municipal association (which is a legal form of association that groups together local authorities, public welfare centres and, in some cases, the provincial government or private shareholders). Both private and public hospitals are non-profit organizations. Hospital legislation and financing mechanisms are the same for both the public and private sectors.

[94] Joined Cases C-180/98 to 184/98, *Pavlov a.o.* [2000] ECR I-6451.

qualify as undertakings, while the latter would. The reason is that, in the former, the state's intervention in order to secure the objective of 'universal minimum cover' may be such that the commercial freedom of these entities may be jeopardized. Hence, for example, regulatory measures in Germany and (prior to 2006)[95] in the Netherlands imposed on private insurers:

[T]he provision of lifetime cover, the introduction of policies with mandatory pooling, standardized minimum benefits, guaranteed prices and the establishment of direct or indirect cross subsidies from those with private to those with statutory coverage. In contrast, regulation of most markets for complementary and supplementary cover tends to focus on *ex post* scrutiny of financial returns on business to ensure that insurers remain solvent.[96]

However, this is a simplistic distinction and may be misleading: private funds offering 'complementary' cover account for an increasing portion of the market (10–20% of total health expenditure in the EU) and tend to be increasingly regulated by Member States, in a way that their qualification as 'undertakings' may be called into question.

There is no hard and fast rule for determining whether an insurance fund qualifies as an undertaking. Rather, as noted above, the Court refers to a set of criteria (*faisceau d'indices*). From a relatively long series of judgments,[97] it follows that elements that would point to a

[95] For details on the recent modification of the Dutch health insurance system, see the contributions by G. J. Hamilton, 'A new private universal Dutch health insurance in the Netherlands'; E. Steyger, 'The proposed Dutch health insurance system in the light of European Law'; and J. van der Gronden, 'Is a Member State entitled to introduce regulated competition into the health care sector under EC law? Reaction to the contribution of Prof. E. Steyger', in A. den Exter (ed.), *Competitive social health insurance yearbook 2004* (Rotterdam: Erasmus University Press, 2005).

[96] For this excerpt and for the critique that follows, see S. Thomson and E. Mossialos 'Regulating private health insurance in the EU: the implications of single market legislation and competition policy', *European Integration* 29 (2007), 89–107, at 93–4.

[97] See Case C-238/94, *FFSA* [1995] ECR I-4013; Case C-70/905 *Sodemare* [1997] ECR I-3395; Case C-67/96, *Albany International* v. *Stichting Bedrijfspensioenfonds Textielindustrie* [1999] ECR I-5751; Joined Cases C-155/97 and C-157/97, *Brentjens* [1999] ECR I-6025; and Case C-219/97, *Drijvende* [1999] ECR I-6121, respectively. On these three cases, see L. Idot, 'Droit social et droit de la concurrence: confrontation ou cohabitation

non-market entity include:[98] (a) the social objective pursued; (b) the compulsory nature of the scheme; (c) contributions paid being related to the income of the insured person, not to the nature of the risk covered; (d) benefits accruing to insured persons not being directly linked to contributions paid by them; (e) benefits and contributions being determined under the control or the supervision of the state; (f) strong overall state control; (g) the fact that funds collected are not capitalized and/or invested, but merely redistributed among participants in the scheme; (h) cross-subsidization between different schemes; and (i) the non-existence of competitive schemes offered by private operators.[99]

In this respect, the judgment in *FENIN* should be singled out,[100] not least because the Court, in appeal proceedings from the Court of First Instance, confirmed that an entity that purchases goods (or services) not in order to resell them in the market, but in view of accomplishing some essentially social task, is not an undertaking.[101] This, however, has not prevented the Polish Office for Competition and Consumer Protection, in a decision of March 2007,[102] from censuring the National Health Fund, whose task is to ensure health services to insured persons (a traditional public authority task), for abusing its dominant position (!) by fixing below-cost contracting prices for dentists.

(à propos de quelques développements récents)', *Europe* (1999), Chron. 11; Case C-218/00, *Batistello* [2002] ECR I-691; Case T-319/99, *FENIN* v. *Commission* [2003] ECR II-357; upheld by the Court in Case C-205/03 P, *FENIN* [2006] ECR I-6295; Case C-355/00, *Freskot* v. *Elliniko Dimosio* [2003] ECR I-5263; Joined Cases C-264/01, C-306/01, C-354/01 and C-355/01, *AOK Bundesverband* [2004] I-2493.

[98] Note that these are broadly the same considerations – but from the opposite perspective – as the ones used to identify contracting entities, see above n.19 and the relevant text.

[99] For a more detailed analysis of those criteria, see Hatzopoulos, 'Health law and policy', above n.1, pp. 123–60. For a critical view of the Court's meddling with social funds, see F. Kessler, 'Droit de la concurrence et régimes de protection sociale: un bilan provisoire', in R. Kovar and D. Simon (eds.), *Service public et Communauté Européenne: entre l'intérêt général et le marché*, Vol. I (Paris: La documentation française, 1998), pp. 421 and 430, where there is reference to other critical commentators.

[100] Case C-205/03 P, *FENIN*, above n.97.

[101] See M. Krajewski and M. Farley, 'Non-economic activities in upstream markets and the scope of competition law after *FENIN*', *European Law Review* 32 (2007), 111–24.

[102] Decision No. DOK 28/2007 of 7 March 2007 concerning the practices of the National Health Fund, reported and commented upon by J. Farrugia and by M. Tomaszefska, 'The Polish Office for Competition and Consumer

At the other end of the spectrum, on the basis of the *FENIN* reasoning, it would seem that public hospitals securing adequate treatment to individual patients, typically free of charge, do not qualify as undertakings. This logic, however, is being called into question by at least two developments. First, in its 'Altmark' Decision, the Commission admits that monies given to hospitals (irrespective of ownership) for fulfilling their public service obligations qualify as aid, albeit justified aid. This, in turn, implies that hospitals are undertakings. Second, the German *Bundeskartellamt* (possibly the most influential national competition authority in the EU), in a decision of March 2005, blocked a merger between two public hospitals; hence, it considered them to be undertakings subject to merger control.[103] Although this decision of the German competition authority is in line with its previous law concerning utilities,[104] one may object that the utilities sector has been heavily regulated for more than twenty years, both at the level of procurement and at the level of deregulation/re-regulation, and that comparing health care with the utilities sector, at this stage of Community law, is materially inappropriate and legally inconclusive. The trend of holding public hospitals as subject to competition (and therefore to competition rules) has been confirmed in the 2007 *Amphia* judgment of the Dutch Supreme Court, whereby it held that public hospitals are subject to enough competition so as not to qualify as 'contracting authorities'.[105]

It is, therefore, difficult to foresee when a public hospital will be held to constitute an undertaking. It would seem that criteria such as: (a) an independent board of directors; (b) a relative flexibility in the execution of the budget; (c) contractual freedom; and (d) a relatively developed side activity of a commercial nature, etc., are likely to

---

Protection holds that the National Health Fund has imposed its dominant position by imposing low purchase prices of health services (Narodowy Fundusz Zdrowia)', *e-Competitions Law Bulletin* No. 13674 (2007).

[103] Decision B10–123/04, *Rhön-Klinikum AG, Landkreis Rhön-Grabfeld*, Bundeskartellamt, 23 March 2005, reported and commented upon by H. Bergmann and F. Röhling, 'The German Federal Cartel Office vetoes a merger of two public hospitals *(Greifswald University Hospital/ Wolgast Hospital)*', *e-Competitions Law Bulletin* No. 12733 (2006).

[104] According to the above commentary.

[105] For this case see V. Hatzopoulos & H. Stergiou 'Public procurement law and health care: From theory to practice' in Can de Gronden, J., Krajewski, M., Neergaard, U., & Szyszczak, E., *Health Care and EU Law* (The Hague: Asser Press, forthcoming).

make a public hospital qualify as an undertaking.[106] Hence, hospitals having the form of a trust, for example, in England and in Italy, are likely to qualify as undertakings.

Undertakings subject to the procurement rules?

From the two previous paragraphs, it becomes clear that: (a) it is very difficult to know which entities in the field of health care qualify as contracting entities; and (b) entities that some years ago were thought of as completely evading the market rules are increasingly being treated as undertakings at the EU and at the national levels. What is more, these imprecise categories often overlap. We saw that many Member States (such as Belgium, Greece and Italy) have included in Annex III of the Procurement Directive health care funds, many of which would qualify as undertakings under the criteria set by the Court. At the same time, most public hospitals do currently follow some procurement rules, at least for purchasing goods (this is the case, for example, in England, through PASA, and in Greece and Hungary).[107] In Belgium, even private hospitals are subject to public procurement rules (at least for construction and heavy equipment), since they receive 60% of their capital investment budget from the Communities. At the same time, private hospitals, and probably many public ones, would qualify as undertakings. This is not a satisfying situation, for the reasons explained above in section two, subsections B and C. As will be explained in section three, subsection D, below, for an entity involved in health care, it is much less constraining to be qualified as a contracting entity rather than as an undertaking. The latter qualification becomes even more problematic in view of the recent 'decentralization' of the application of EC competition law introduced by Regulation 1/2003/EC,[108] as it may lead to very divergent solutions, especially concerning borderline hospitals. In this respect, Decision 2005/842/

---

[106] This may be counter-productive, to the extent that Member States may be inclined to resist any of the above economically sound measures just in view of evading the EC Treaty competition rules.

[107] Greece has had an infringement procedure initiated against it by the Commission for the technical specifications used in several tendering documents for the supply of medical devices, see Case C-489/06, *Commission* v. *Greece* (not yet reported).

[108] Council Regulation 1/2003/EC on the implementation of the rules on competition laid down in Articles 81 and 82 of the EC Treaty OJ 2003 No. L1/1.

EC (the 'Altmark' Decision) is a positive step, since it clears hospitals, irrespective of their qualification as undertakings, from the application of the state aid rules. It may be that a similar 'block exemption' could also clarify the position of hospitals under Article 81 EC. However, no advance clearance from the application of Article 82[109] may be given and, indeed, the invocation of abuses against hospitals is a likely scenario. A possible solution to this problem could lie in adapting the system of the Utilities Procurement Directive (2004/17/EC) in the health care field – that is, to require Member States to provide a complete list of all the entities that are considered to be contracting entities (thus evading their being qualified as undertakings) and to implement a mechanism for the regular revision of this list, similar to Article 30 of the Directive, accounting for market developments and the introduction of competition.

D. What kind of award procedures should be followed?

When an entity in the field of health care qualifies as a 'contracting authority' in the sense of the Procurement Directives, its obligation to run competitive tenders is not an absolute one. There are limitations stemming both from the nature of the award (completely closed or completely open) and from the nature of services (health care, included in Annex III of the Procurement Directive). Four cases may be distinguished.

No contractual relationship

In some health care systems, the public authorities responsible for delivering care establish and run their own treatment facilities, in the form of treatment centres, small hospitals or clinics. Such is the case, for example, of the ASLs in Italy or the PCTs in England, and some funds in Greece do the same. The Court has held that an award procedure is only necessary when a *contract* is to be entered into – and that no entity can contract with itself. If services are provided between two bodies belonging to the same public entity, we are in the presence of 'in-house provision' of services.[110] In-house provision applies to any service offered between bodies with no separate legal personality. In the

---

[109] For further discussion of Articles 81 and 82 EC, see Chapters 7 and 8 in this volume.

[110] See, in general, Arrowsmith, *The law of public and utilities procurement*, above n.18, paras. 6.196–6.193. See also M. Giorello, 'Gestions *in house,*

presence of distinct legal entities, in-house provision only exists where two conditions are fulfilled, in a cumulative manner:[111] (a) the procuring entity should exercise over the supplying entity 'a control which is similar to that which it exercises over its own departments'; and (b) the supplying entity should carry out 'the essential part of its activities' with the procuring entity. While the latter condition will rarely be a problem in the case of hospitals, etc., created by public authorities or funds, the former may prove problematic and counter-productive in the future. In a highly contested judgement, in *Teckal*,[112] the Court has held that private participation in the shareholding of a public company, even at a percentage of 0.02%, may disturb the 'similar control' of the local authority that controls the remaining 99.98%, unless such an authority holds special privileges by virtue of the company's constitution. This may discourage public hospitals from seeking private investors or, conversely, investors from giving money to entities in which the public authorities have privileges.[113] Both in England and in Italy, private funding initiatives for public hospitals are under way. Hence, in-house provision will be increasingly unlikely. If, notwithstanding, the relationship is found to be 'in-house', then no award procedure is necessary. The same is true for health care systems like the Hungarian and the Greek systems, where all public hospitals cooperate, by law, with all public funds. In all these cases, the qualification of a body as a contracting authority has legal consequences only when the entities concerned purchase extra capacity, outside their own 'production'.

Closed awards

In some cases, Member States may wish to confer an exclusive or special right to one or several undertakings. Instituting such rights is not forbidden by the Treaty rules, especially if such rights are linked to the provision of some service of general interest. This link may be direct (i.e., the service over which a special right is conferred is itself a service of general interest) or indirect (i.e., the service over which

entreprises publiques et marchés publics: la CJCE au croisement des chemins du marché intérieur et des services d'intérêt économique général', *Révue du Droit de l'Union Européenne* (2006), 23–50.

[111] Case C-107/98, *Teckal* [1999] ECR I-8121. [112] *Ibid.*

[113] In this respect, the 'golden shares' case-law becomes relevant, where the Court condemned Member States for instituting shares with increased voting (or other rights) while opening up their utilities companies to private markets. See, for example, Case C-367/98, *Commission* v. *Portugal* [2002]

a special right is conferred is used to finance a contiguous service of general interest).[114] The Procurement Directives are not applicable to the award of such contracts,[115] but the general Treaty rules are. This means that, as the law stands at present, if new rights were to be awarded, this should be done according to the 'procurement principles' highlighted above in section two, subsection C. If, however, the new award is only necessary in order to extend pre-existing exclusive or special rights, it may be that the selection may operate without a public tender. This outcome seems to stem from the Court's judgment in *Glöckner*,[116] where the Court admitted that extending the duration of previous special rights for ambulance and transport services did not require a tendering procedure. This part of the Court's judgement, however, is very laconic and obscure, and may have been overturned by the more recent and more peremptory judgement in *Placanica*.[117] It should be noted that, in this case, the Court held that even the revocation and redistribution by public tender of authorizations may be required in order to make up for the violation of the Treaty rules. Hence, it is not clear whether 'closed processes' are allowed and under what circumstances.

Open awards

In contrast, on many occasions Member States award contracts not on the basis of a competitive tender but upon the fulfilment of several criteria set in advance. In the field of health care, this practice is quite wide-spread, since in many Member States all physicians and/or all hospitals that fulfil several criteria may be contracted into the public health care system. This is true for physicians in Belgium, Hungary, Greece, the United Kingdom and also (subject to advance planning) for hospitals in Belgium.

In this case, the award procedure has the characteristics of the delivery of an administrative authorization, since everyone who fulfils

ECR I-4731; Case C-483/99, *Commission* v. *France* [2002] ECR I-4781; Case C-503/99, *Commission* v. *Belgium* [2002] ECR I-4809; Case 463/00, *Commission* v. *Spain* [2003] ECR I-4581.

[114] See Case C-320/91, *Corbeau* [1993] ECR I-2562; Case C-393/92, *Almelo* [1994] ECR I-1477; Case C-475/99, *Glöckner*, above n.67.

[115] Article 18, European Parliament and Council Directive 2004/18/EC, above n.9.

[116] Case C-475/99, *Glöckner*, above n.67.

[117] Joined Cases C-338/04, C-359/04 and C-360/04, *Placanica*, above n.50.

the conditions set in advance should be awarded a contract. Hence, the case-law of the Court on the delivery of authorizations becomes relevant: the conditions for their delivery should be objective, transparent and non-discriminatory, and known in advance, while the procedure should take a reasonable time and be subject to judicial review.[118]

Competitive awards

Finally, there are cases where a proper competitive tender is to be held. This is what should happen in Italy, the United Kingdom, Hungary and Greece when the relevant public authorities or trusts need to contract with hospitals and doctors – on top of the ones directly run and/ or financed by them.

In this case, the Public Procurement Directive (2004/18/EC) should be applied. It should be noted that 'health and social services' are enumerated in Annex IIB of the Directive and are only subject to a partial application of its rules. The only Directive provisions that are applicable to the Annex IIB services are Article 23, on the technical specifications to be used in the tender documents, and Article 35(4), on the publication of an award notice.[119] For the rest, the contracting entity is free to follow the award procedure of its choice, provided this satisfies the general 'procurement criteria' recognized by the Court: non-discrimination and equal treatment, transparency, proportionality and mutual recognition. Therefore, the freedom left by the EC legislature in favour of entities operating, *inter alia*, in the health sector is seriously circumscribed by the recent case-law of the Court. As explained above, this requires adequate publicity, extended mutual recognition and, most importantly, does not allow for clauses that would exclude, directly or indirectly, operators from other Member States. The Commission's 'Framework' Communication of the 'Altmark package' clarifies the above requirements and further restricts the freedom of action of the contracting entities. The doubts expressed above as to whether

---

[118] See, among many, Case C-157/99, *Geraets Smits and Peerbooms*, above n.1.; C-368/98, *Vanbraekel* [2001] ECR-I-5363.

[119] Article 21, European Parliament and Council Directive 2004/18/EC, above n.9. Mixed contracts (which involve the provision of both health care and other Annex II A services) should be awarded on the basis of the contract having the most important value. See Article 22, Directive 2004/18/EC. See also the Court's judgment in Case C-475/99, *Glöckner*, above n.67.

this 'Framework' could and should affect the procurement practices of health care entities remain to be tested before the national courts and, ultimately, the ECJ.

4. Conclusion

National health care systems embody the principle of solidarity and require public monies, alone or together with private investment. In either case, and depending on the public–private mix, these resources may not reach the 'market' for health care services in an arbitrary way, but should be channelled through the Treaty rules on state aid and/or on public procurement.

Health care systems in most Member States are in a transition, whereby public and private coexist: private investors are increasingly involved as state funding becomes scarce. In the meantime, hospitals are developing advanced accounting methods and managerial independence. This transition, pregnant with political, economic and legal uncertainties, explains the malaise in applying the EC rules. Rules that are designed to regulate different situations and that, according to the recent case-law of the Court, are linked through a logic of mutual exclusion, are tangled into unforeseen legal combinations. Qualifying entities involved in the provision of health care as undertakings and/ or as contracting entities is an exercise where legal sophistication and imagination go hand in hand. The current situation is far from securing legal certainty, or even predictability.

In a previous article, I had put forward the idea that 'entities caught by the rules on competition should unequivocally be exempted from observance of the rules on public procurement, while some guidelines should be drawn in order to avoid a rigid and counter-productive application of the rules on state aid on the organization and functioning of national health care systems'.[120] After some hesitation, the Court in *Altmark* and the Commission in the 'Altmark package' have tried to disentangle some of the skein by exempting hospitals from the rules on state aid, under given circumstances. However, the *Altmark* conditions are too demanding and, in practice, are very rarely fulfilled. Further action may be required by the Commission in the form of a block exemption regulation from Article 81 EC for health care

---

[120] Hatzopoulos 'Health law and policy', above n.1, p. 168.

providers. Member States could themselves ease the application of the Treaty rules by setting out clearly which of the entities involved in the provision of health care they deem to be undertakings and which ones are contracting entities; this list should be regularly updated. Even if all this were to happen, the legal situation would still be complicated, reflecting the material differences of the national health care systems.

How deeply the EC rules on public procurement and on state aid are going to affect the organization of national health systems cannot be determined at this stage. This will depend both on the regulatory technique used and on the positions adopted by the various actors.[121]

Concerning regulatory technique, in policy fields where hard law (the harder you can get: state aid is run on a daily basis and public procurement is regularly monitored by the Commission) has a strong-hold, softer means of regulation could seem inappropriate. This view, however, should not overlook two factors. First, that the Commission itself has regularly had recourse to soft law in the field of state aid and, recently, also in the field of public procurement (see, for example, the *de minimis* Communication on procurement).[122] Second, that under pressure from technological development, economic realities and EC law, Member States are aware of the fact that inertia is not a policy option in the field of health care. Dynamism thus inflicted could be steered towards a convergence model through some kind of soft cooperation, 'in particular initiatives aiming at the establishment of guidelines and indicators, the organization of exchange of best practice, and the preparation of the necessary elements for periodic monitoring and evaluation'.[123] The fact that the part of the sentence in quotation marks is directly copied from the Lisbon Treaty provision dealing with 'Public Health' clearly indicates that this is a road that will be taken.

From the point of view of the actors involved, it has to be observed that the process has been led by private litigators supported by the ECJ. The Commission, on the contrary, has been notably absent. This pattern is likely to continue in the foreseeable future. Even if

[121] See a first assessment by G. Davies, 'The process and side-effects of harmonisation of European welfare states', Jean Monnet Working Paper No. 02/06 (2006), pp. 1–64.

[122] European Commission, 'Interpretative Communication', above n.47. On the use of soft law in the field of health care in general, see Chapter 4 in this volume.

[123] Article 168(2), Consolidated Version of the Treaty on the Functioning of the European Union, OJ 2008 No. C115/1.

the Commission decided to assume a more active stance, it could be 'silenced' by Member States and their parliaments. Indeed, Article 192(7) of the Treaty on the Functioning of the European Union provides, in similar, but perhaps stronger, terms to those of Article 152(5) EC, that 'Union action in the field of public health shall fully respect the responsibilities of the Member States for the definition of their health policy and for the organization and delivery of health services and medical care, and the allocation of resources assigned to them'. Moreover, according to Article 12 of the EU Treaty and the Protocols 'on the role of national parliaments' and 'on the application of the principles of subsidiarity and proportionality', the Commission's initiatives are subject to strong scrutiny.

The use of soft law and soft coordination, combined with the absence of strong steering from the Commission, make the impact of the EU rules on national health care systems very difficult to foresee. For this reason, retrospective analysis of the impact of the former on the latter becomes all the more important.

10 | *Private health insurance and the internal market*

SARAH THOMSON AND ELIAS MOSSIALOS

1. Introduction

In 1992, the legislative institutions of the European Union (EU) adopted regulatory measures in the field of health insurance.[1] The mechanism affirming the free movement of health insurance services – the Third Non-life Insurance Directive[2] – does not apply to health insurance that forms part of a social security system. But all other forms of health insurance, which we refer to as 'private health insurance', fall within the Directive's scope. This chapter examines the implications of the Directive, and some aspects of EU competition law, for the regulation of private health insurance in the European Union. The EU-level regulatory framework created by the Directive imposes restrictions on the way in which governments can intervene in markets for health insurance. However, there are areas of uncertainty in interpreting the Directive, particularly with regard to when and how governments may intervene to promote public interests. As in most spheres of EU legislation, interpretation largely rests on European Court of Justice (ECJ) case-law, so clarity may come at a high cost and after considerable delay.

The chapter also questions the Directive's capacity to promote consumer and social protection in health insurance markets. In many ways, the Directive reflects the health system norms of the late 1980s and early 1990s, a time when boundaries between 'social security' and 'normal economic activity' were still relatively well defined

---

[1] This is an extensively revised and updated version of an article that originally appeared as S. Thomson and E. Mossialos, 'Regulating private health insurance in the European Union: the implications of single market legislation and competition policy', *Journal of European Integration* 29 (2007), 89–107. The authors are grateful to Rita Baeten, Tamara Hervey and Willy Palm for their comments on an earlier draft of the chapter.

[2] The third 'Non-life Insurance' Directive, Council Directive 92/49/EEC on the coordination of laws, regulations and administrative provisions relating to direct insurance other than life assurance, OJ 1992 No. L228/23. From here on we refer to this as 'the Directive'.

in most Member States.[3] Today, these boundaries are increasingly blurred – the new health insurance system in the Netherlands is a case in point. As governments look to private health insurance to ease pressure on public budgets or to expand consumer choice, uncertainty about the scope of the Directive and concerns about its restrictions on regulation are likely to grow.

We base our analysis on discussion of private health insurance-related ECJ rulings and cases of infringement of the Directive or other EU rules. Where actual examples are lacking, the analysis is, inevitably, more speculative. In the following sections, we provide a brief introduction to private health insurance in the European Union; summarize the main changes brought about by the Directive and its initial impact on regulation of private health insurance in EU Member States; examine uncertainty as to when and how governments can intervene in health insurance markets; and conclude with a summary of key points.

2. Private health insurance in the European Union

Private health insurance is often defined as insurance that is taken up voluntarily and paid for privately, either by individuals or by employers on behalf of individuals.[4] This definition recognizes that private health insurance may be sold by a wide range of entities, both public and private in nature. Organizations involved in providing private health insurance in the European Union include statutory 'sickness funds', non-profit mutual or provident associations and commercial for-profit insurance companies. In practice, however, the distinction between statutory and voluntary coverage is not always useful in determining what counts as private health insurance. Three examples illustrate this point. In 2006, the Netherlands introduced a universal health insurance scheme that is both statutory (it is compulsory for all residents) and private (operated by private insurers and governed by private law). The universal scheme replaced a system in which higher earners were excluded from statutory cover and could only obtain cover from private insurers. Conversely, higher-earning

---

[3] R. White, *EC social security law* (Harlow: Longman, 1999).
[4] E. Mossialos and S. Thomson, 'Voluntary health insurance in the European Union: a critical assessment', *International Journal of Health Services* 32 (2002), 19–88.

employees in Germany can join the statutory health insurance scheme on a voluntary basis – making them voluntarily but publicly insured – or choose to be covered by a private insurer. In Belgium, a mutual association recently began to provide what was traditionally seen as voluntary cover (of non-publicly-reimbursed hospital costs) on a compulsory basis. By extending this form of cover to all its members, it was able to offer it at a cheaper rate.

These developments stretch standard definitions of private health insurance. It may therefore be more constructive to focus on the role private health insurance plays in relation to public – or statutory – health coverage. Understanding this relationship is also important in light of the Third Non-life Insurance Directive, as we discuss below. Most EU Member States provide universal or near universal public coverage for health as part of a wider system of 'social protection'. Due to the dominance of public coverage, private health insurance generally plays a modest role. For example, many Member States have a market for private health insurance that supplements public coverage by giving people greater choice of provider – often access to care in the private sector – and enabling them to bypass public waiting lists (see Table 10.1). This form of 'supplementary' private health insurance tends to be purchased by wealthier and better-educated people.[5] Because it covers individuals and services already covered by the statutory health system, it rarely contributes to social protection.[6]

There are contexts in which private health insurance plays a more significant role. For example, 'complementary' private health insurance can cover services that are excluded from the statutory benefits package (outpatient visits, occupational therapy, dental care, etc.), as in Ireland, where it is combined with supplementary insurance and covers about

---

[5] E. Mossialos and S. Thomson, *Voluntary health insurance in the European Union* (Copenhagen: World Health Organization, 2004).

[6] It could be argued that supplementary private health insurance contributes to social protection if those who rely on private insurance do not make use of publicly-financed health care, freeing up public resources to be spent on those without private cover. However, there is little evidence in support of this argument. There is more evidence to suggest that supplementary private health insurance can actually distort public resource allocation in favour of richer groups – for example, where doctors are allowed to work in the public and the private sector and can generate waiting lists for publicly-financed care in order to boost their private activity. See J. Yates, *Private eye, heart and hip* (Edinburgh: Churchill Livingstone, 1995).

Table 10.1. *Functional classification of private health insurance markets*

Market role	Driver of market development	Nature of cover	EU examples
Substitutive	Public system inclusiveness (the proportion of the population to which coverage is extended)	Covers population groups excluded from or allowed to opt out of the public system	Germany, the Netherlands (prior to 2006)
Complementary (services)	Scope of benefits covered by the public system	Covers services excluded from the public system	Belgium
Complementary (user charges)	Depth of public coverage (the proportion of the benefit cost met by the public system)	Covers statutory user charges imposed in the public system	France, Slovenia, Denmark
Supplementary	Consumer satisfaction (perceptions about the quality of publicly-financed care)	Covers faster access and enhanced consumer choice	United Kingdom

Source: adapted from E. Mossialos and S. Thomson, 'Voluntary health insurance in the European Union: a critical assessment', *International Journal of Health Services* 32 (2002), 19–88; and T. Foubister *et al.*, *Private medical insurance in the United Kingdom* (Copenhagen: World Health Organization, 2006).

50% of the population.[7] Or it may reimburse the costs of statutory user charges, as in Slovenia[8] and France,[9] where it covers over 70% and 92% of the population, respectively. In other Member States, private health insurance provides 'substitutive' cover for people excluded from some aspects of the statutory health system. This was the case for higher-earning households in the Netherlands prior to the introduction of statutory universal coverage in 2006. The 2006 reforms effectively abolished substitutive private health insurance in the Netherlands (or extended it to cover the whole population, depending on your perspective). Self-employed people in Belgium were also excluded from statutory cover of outpatient care prior to 2008, and wealthier households in Ireland were excluded from publicly-financed hospital care prior to the introduction of universal hospital cover. In addition, substitutive private health insurance may cover people who are allowed to opt into and out of the statutory scheme, such as higher-earning employees in Germany.

Differences in market role are reflected in the contribution private health insurance makes to spending on health care – both total levels of expenditure and levels of private expenditure. Table 10.2 shows how this contribution is very small in most Member States, only exceeding 5% of total spending and 20% of private spending in Austria, France, Germany, the Netherlands (prior to 2006) and Slovenia. However, spending through private health insurance has grown over time in many countries, particularly in the newer Member States of central and eastern Europe, where health insurance markets were more or less non-existent in the early to mid-1990s.[10]

3. Regulation and the Third Non-life Insurance Directive

Health insurance attempts to alleviate some of the uncertainty around ill health. We do not usually know if or when we might fall ill; nor

---

[7] The Competition Authority, *Competition in the private health insurance market* (Dublin: The Competition Authority, 2007).
[8] *Ibid.*
[9] I. Durand-Zaleski, *The health system in France* (New York: The Commonwealth Fund, 2008).
[10] S. Thomson, 'What role for voluntary health insurance?', in J. Kutzin, C. Cashin and M. Jakab (eds.), *Implementing health financing reform: lessons from countries in transition* (Copenhagen: WHO Regional Office for Europe on behalf of the European Observatory on Health Systems and Policies, 2009).

Table 10.2. *Private health insurance (PHI) in the EU: contribution to total and private expenditure on health, 1996 and 2005*

Country	PHI as a percentage of total expenditure on health		PHI as a percentage of private expenditure on health	
	1996	2005	1996	2005
Austria	9.0	8.2	19.9	21.3
Belgium	1.8	3.5	8.5	12.1
Bulgaria	0.0	0.1	0.0	0.3
Cyprus	1.7	4.3	2.6	7.6
Czech Republic	0.0	0.2	0.0	2.1
Denmark	1.4	1.6	7.7	9.2
Estonia	0.0	0.1	0.0	0.3
Finland	2.4	2.3	9.9	10.2
France	12.4	12.8	51.7	61.1
Germany	7.5	9.1	42.1	39.7
Greece	2.0	2.1	4.3	4.3
Hungary	0.0	0.9	0.2	3.4
Ireland	9.2	6.4	32.1	33.0
Italy	1.0	0.9	3.6	3.8
Latvia	0.7	0.8	1.8	1.7
Lithuania	0.0	0.4	0.1	1.1
Luxembourg	0.7	1.6	10.1	17.6
Malta	1.1	2.1	3.7	9.8
Netherlands*	19.5	20.1	57.7	58.5
Poland	0.0	0.6	0.0	2.1
Portugal	1.3	3.8	4.0	13.8
Romania	0.0	4.5	0.0	18.2
Slovakia	0.0	0.0	0.0	0.0
Slovenia	12.3	12.7	55.3	51.3
Spain	3.5	4.7	12.8	15.8
Sweden	0.0	0.3	n/a	2.0
United Kingdom	3.3	1.0	19.2	7.9

* Figures supplied for the Netherlands refer to the period prior to the reforms introduced in 2006. Private expenditure on health is usually made up of PHI and out-of-pocket payments (including user charges).
Source: World Health Organization, *World Health Statistics 2007* (Geneva: World Health Organization, 2007).

do we always know how severe an illness will be or how much it will cost to treat it. By pooling health risks (across groups of people) and resources (over time), health insurance provides protection from the financial risk associated with ill health. In this way, it makes a valuable contribution to social welfare. However, markets for health insurance require regulation to protect consumers and insurers from the potentially negative effects of market failures, such as adverse selection and risk selection.[11] Without government intervention to correct market failures, health insurance would not be easily access-ible to people at high risk of ill health, people already in ill health and people with low incomes. Governments in most high-income countries therefore ensure that health insurance is compulsory for the whole population, that contributions are based on income, and that publicly-financed 'insurers' (whether sickness funds, private insurers or a national health service) cannot deny cover to any individual.

In contrast to the rules applied to statutory health insurance, the principles of which are broadly convergent across the European Union, there is considerable variation in the regulation of private health insur-ance. Prior to the introduction of the Third Non-life Insurance Directive in 1992, the extent to which EU governments intervened in markets for health insurance was largely determined by the role private cover played in the health system (see Table 10.1). Thus, substitutive private health insurance in Germany and the Netherlands tended to be rela-tively heavily regulated,[12] mainly to ensure access to private cover for older people and people in poor health, but also to protect the finances of the statutory health insurance scheme, which in both cases covered a disproportionate amount of higher-risk households.[13] The extent of regulation was also influenced by aspects of market structure, such as the number and mix of insurers in operation – particularly, markets dominated by mutual associations – and political ideology.

[11] N. Barr, *The economics of the welfare state*, 3rd ed. (Oxford: Oxford University Press, 1998).

[12] S. Thomson and E. Mossialos, 'Choice of public or private health insurance: learning from the experience of Germany and the Netherlands', *Journal of European Social Policy* 16 (2006), 315–27.

[13] This is partly due to the way in which these systems are (were, in the Dutch case) designed and regulated. For example, in Germany, the statutory health insurance scheme is attractive to families because it covers dependants for free, whereas private insurers charge separate premiums for all family members. It is also due to risk selection by private insurers.

Two broad approaches to regulation prevailed: minimal financial or prudential regulation focusing on solvency levels, or material regulation emphasizing control of prices and products. While both approaches aimed to protect consumers from insurer insolvency,[14] material regulation also endeavoured to ensure access to health care through access to health insurance. Under the subsidiarity principle – established in EU law through the European Community Treaty (Article 5 EC) – governments were free to decide on the appropriate form of regulation required in a given context. Over the last thirty years, the EU legislature has restricted this freedom by introducing a series of directives aimed at creating an internal market in insurance services.[15] Grounded in the principle of the free movement of services (enshrined in Articles 43 49 and 50 EC), the internal market in insurance services was intended to enhance competition and consumer choice. EU competence in this area comes from the fact that insurance is considered to be an economic activity.

The Third Non-life Insurance Directive created, for the first time, an EU-level framework for regulating health insurance. The first and second generation of insurance directives had been limited to the cover of 'large risks' of a commercial nature, such as aviation or marine insurance and reinsurance (which were considered small enough, in relation to the size or status of their policy holders, not to require special protection).[16] 'Mass risks' involving individuals and small businesses were excluded on the grounds that they required special protection because their policy holders would not normally have the ability to judge all the complexities of the obligation they undertook in

---

[14] Financial or prudential regulation focuses on ex post scrutiny of an insurer's financial returns on business. Material or contract regulation involves ex ante scrutiny of an insurer's policy conditions and premium rates on the grounds that this eliminates the potential for insolvency.

[15] First Council Directive 73/239/EEC on the coordination of laws, regulations and administrative provisions relating to the taking-up and pursuit of the business of direct insurance other than life assurance, OJ 1973 No. L228/3; Second Council Directive 88/357/EEC on the coordination of laws, regulations and administrative provisions relating to direct insurance other than life assurance and laying down provisions to facilitate the effective exercise of freedom to provide services and amending Directive 73/239/EEC, OJ 1988 No. L172/1; Council Directive 92/49/EEC, above n.2.

[16] R. Merkin and A. Rodger, *EC insurance law* (London: Longman, 1997); D. Mabbett, 'Social regulation and the social dimension in Europe: the example of insurance', *European Journal of Social Security* 2 (1997), 241–57.

an insurance contract.[17] The third generation of insurance directives extended the application of internal market legislation to all types of risks, including mass risks such as health insurance.

As a result of the Directive, insurers have full freedom to provide services throughout the European Union, with or without a branch presence. The mechanisms facilitating free movement are 'home country control' (Article 9), a single system for the authorization and financial supervision of an insurance undertaking by the Member State in which the undertaking has its head office; the mutual recognition of systems of authorization and financial supervision; and the harmonization of minimum solvency standards (Article 17). ECJ case-law confirms that insurance activities fall under the scope of the Directive (Article 2) when they are carried out by insurance undertakings at their own risk, following insurance techniques, and on the basis of contractual relationships governed by private law.[18] ECJ case-law more broadly (not relating to the Directive) also suggests that activities with an exclusively social purpose involving solidarity are beyond the scope of internal market and competition rules.[19]

To protect the freedoms outlined above and to prevent barriers to competition, the Directive brought about two key changes for private health insurance. First, the Directive accords primacy to the financial approach to regulation: the requirement for governments to abolish existing product and price controls (Articles 6(3), 29 and 39) renders material regulation redundant and, in some cases, illegal. Second, it requires governments to open markets for private health insurance to competition at the national and EU levels (Article 3).

Material regulation in the form of national rules requiring the prior approval or systematic notification of policy conditions, premium rates, proposed increases in premium rates and printed documents insurers use in their dealings with policy holders are no longer permitted (Articles 6(3), 29 and 39). Such rules played an important regulatory function in several countries – notably, France, Germany and Italy. However, most

---

[17] K. Nemeth, 'European insurance law: a single insurance market?', EUI Working Paper LAW No. 2001/4 (2001).

[18] Case C-238/94, *José García* [1996] ECR I-1673; Case C-296/98, *Commission* v. *France* [2000] ECR I-3025.

[19] Joined Cases C-159/91 and C-160/91, *Poucet and Pistre* [1993] ECR I-637; Joined Cases C-264/01, C-306/01, C-354/01 and C-355/01, *AOK Bundesverband* [2004] ECR I-2493.

Member States amended existing laws or passed new laws to comply with the Directive. Legislative changes generally involved the introduction of tighter solvency controls. Some also resulted in the loosening or outright abolition of prior approval and systematic notification. France proved to be the exception in this respect, contravening the Directive by continuing to insist that insurers notify the supervisory authority when they launched a new product.[20] The European Court of Justice ruled against the French Government in May 2000.[21]

Although the Directive prevents governments from introducing regulatory measures that go beyond solvency requirements, Member States do retain limited residual powers to protect policy holders. For example, if the home supervisory authority fails to prevent an insurer from infringing the host country's domestic law, the host supervisory authority may take action (Article 40(5)). More importantly, the host supervisory authority may impose specific measures in the form of restrictions on insurance contracts, in the interest of the 'general good', where contracts covering health risks 'may serve as a partial or complete alternative to health cover provided by the statutory social security system' (Article 54(1)). Where this is the case, the government can require private insurers to 'comply with the specific legal provisions adopted by that Member State to protect the general good in that class of insurance' (Article 54(1)).

Article 54(2) and recitals to the Directive list the types of legal provisions that may be introduced if private cover provides a partial or complete alternative to statutory cover: open enrolment, community rating, lifetime cover, policies standardized in line with the cover provided by the statutory health insurance scheme at a premium rate at or below a prescribed maximum, participation in risk equalization schemes (referred to as 'loss compensation schemes') and the operation of private health insurance on a technical basis similar to life insurance. Measures taken to protect the general good must be shown to be necessary and proportionate to this aim, not unduly restrict the right of establishment or the freedom to provide services, and apply in an identical manner to all insurers operating within a Member State.

---

[20] European Commission, 'Insurance: Commission launches new infringement proceedings against France concerning mutual benefit companies', Press Release IP/00/466, Brussels, 2000.

[21] Case C-296/98, *Commission v. France*, above n.18.

The German Government has used Article 54(1) to justify intervention in its substitutive market, where risk selection by private insurers has prevented some older people and people with chronic illnesses from buying an adequate and affordable level of private cover.[22] Regulatory measures include the provision of lifetime cover, the introduction of policies with mandatory pooling, standardized minimum benefits and guaranteed prices, and the establishment of indirect cross subsidies from those with private to those with public coverage. The same regulatory measures were also present in the Dutch substitutive market prior to 2006. Private insurers in the German substitutive market are subject to further regulation concerning the way in which they fund cover (on a similar basis to life insurance) and the provision of information to potential and existing policy holders.

In contrast, regulation of many markets for complementary and supplementary cover has tended to focus on ex post scrutiny of financial returns on business to ensure that insurers remain solvent. Insurers are often permitted to reject applications for cover, exclude cover of, or charge higher premiums for individuals with pre-existing conditions, rate premiums according to risk, provide nonstandardized benefit packages and offer annual contracts, while benefits are usually provided in cash rather than in kind. However, there are some notable exceptions – many of them recent – particularly where complementary private health insurance is concerned. Relatively heavily regulated markets for complementary cover can be found in Belgium, France, Ireland and Slovenia. It is no coincidence that these are also the countries in which regulation of private health insurance has been most problematic from an EU law perspective (see below).

4. Implications for government intervention in health insurance markets

At first sight, the Directive appears to give governments significant scope for regulating private health insurance under the general good

---

[22] J. Wasem, 'Regulating private health insurance markets', Paper prepared for the Four Country Conference on 'Health Care Reforms and Health Care Policies in the United States, Canada, Germany and the Netherlands', Ministry of Health, Welfare and Sport, Amsterdam, 23–25 February 1995; F. Rupprecht, B. Tissot and F. Chatel, 'German health care system: promoting greater responsibility among all system players', INSEE Studies No. 42 (2000), pp.1–23.

principle, which broadly refers to any legislation aimed at protecting consumers (in any sector, not just the insurance sector). But, on closer examination, interpretation of the principle is shown to be problematic in two areas: first, the issue of what is meant by complete or partial alternative to statutory health insurance; and, second, what types of intervention are necessary and proportionate. These problems arise because there is no agreed definition of the general good; interpretation relies on ECJ case-law. Following complaints about the absence of a definition, the European Commission[23] tried to clarify when and how the general good might be invoked in the insurance sector, but its Interpretive Communication failed to provide new information.[24] Calls for further clarification persist on the grounds that the lack of a definition creates legal uncertainty, while the process of testing questionable use of the general good through the courts is prohibitively lengthy and expensive.[25] We discuss interpretation of the general good in relation to when and how governments can intervene in markets for private health insurance.

A. When can governments intervene?

There is uncertainty about when the general good can be invoked to justify material regulation, mainly because the Directive does not define what it means by partial or complete alternative to statutory health insurance. How then can we distinguish between private cover that falls into this category and private cover that does not? Circumstantial factors suggest that the distinction may hinge on whether or not private health insurance plays a substitutive role. For example, Article 54 was inserted during negotiations prior to the drafting of the Directive at the instigation of the German, Dutch and Irish Governments.[26] Perhaps as a result of lobbying by Member States with substitutive markets, the regulatory measures outlined in Article 54(2) are an exact match of

---

[23] From here on we refer to the European Commission as 'the Commission'.
[24] European Commission, 'Interpretative Communication on the freedom to provide services and the general good in the insurance sector', OJ 2002 No. C43/5.
[25] Mossialos and Thomson, 'Voluntary health insurance', above n.5.
[26] Association Internationale de la Mutualité (AIMS), 'Towards a fourth generation of European insurance directives?', Newsletter No. 5 (1999), pp. 1–3.

those that were in place in Germany, Ireland and the Netherlands when the Directive was being negotiated. To date, the regulations applied to private insurers in these three countries have not been challenged by the Commission.[27] In addition, a summary of the Directive dating from 2006 and available on the Commission's web site refers to the Directive having 'specific rules for health cover serving as a *substitute* for that provided by statutory social security systems'.[28]

Recent policy developments in the Netherlands shed further light on how we might make this distinction. Dissatisfaction with the dual system of statutory cover for lower earners and voluntary private cover for higher earners had led successive Dutch governments to consider the introduction of a single, universal system of health insurance. Some governments favoured a public system, others preferred private options, in spite of concerns about the applicability of internal market rules to a private system.[29] In 2006, a universal and compulsory privately-operated system governed under private law came into force. Regulatory measures under the new system include open enrolment, lifetime cover, government-set income-based contributions deducted at source, additional community-rated premiums set by each insurer, a package of minimum benefits in kind or cash defined by the government and a risk equalization scheme.[30]

Prior to the introduction of the new system, the Dutch Government asked the Commission to clarify whether or not Article 54 could be relied on to justify such extensive regulation.[31] The Commission's response came in the form of a letter to the Dutch Minister of

---

[27] Although some aspects of the regulatory environment in Ireland have recently been questioned by the Commission (see below).

[28] Council Directive 92/49/EEC, above n.2; European Commission, 'Financial services: insurance', Activities of the European Union: Summaries of Legislation (2006), http://europa.eu/scadplus/leg/en/s08012.htm (emphasis added).

[29] H. Maarse, 'Health insurance reform (again) in the Netherlands: will it succeed?', *Euro Observer* 4 (2002), 1–3.

[30] G. J. Hamilton, 'Private insurance for all in the Dutch health care system?', *European Journal of Health Law* 10 (2003), 53–61. Ministry of Health Welfare and Sport, 'Do you have compulsory or private health insurance? A single new-style health insurance for everybody as of 1 January 2006'. Brochure of the Ministry of Health, Welfare and Sport (2005).

[31] H. Hoogervorst, 'Letter from the Dutch Minister of Health, Welfare and Sport to the European Commissioner for the Internal Market', Ministry of Health, Welfare and Sport, 8 October 2003.

Health from the (then) Commissioner for the Internal Market Frits Bolkestein.[32] In the letter,[33] Bolkestein states that the privately-operated system falls within the scope of the Directive, even though it is compulsory, because the insurers involved are carrying out 'an insurance activity'. However, he notes that the regulatory measures can be justified under Article 54 for two reasons: first, the system, though private, can be construed as constituting a 'complete alternative' to statutory health insurance; and, second, the regulations (with some caveats, see below) 'appear necessary to ensure legitimate objectives pursued by the Dutch government'.[34] The Commission supported this position in response to written questions put forward by Members of the European Parliament in 2005.[35] It also stated that the new Dutch system was 'to be considered as a statutory sickness insurance scheme'.[36]

Bolkestein's letter goes on to point out that it would not be proportionate to apply the proposed regulatory measures to 'any *complementary* insurance cover offered by private insurers *which goes beyond the basic social security package of cover* laid down by the legislation'.[37] The letter therefore suggests that 'partial or complete alternative' can be understood in terms of the benefits provided by a particular insurance scheme. Substitutive private health insurance constitutes an alternative to statutory cover because it replaces statutory benefits for those who are excluded from some aspects of the statutory system (higher earners in the Netherlands prior to 2006 and Ireland) or those who are allowed to choose statutory or private cover (higher earners in Germany). Whether the substitutive cover is a partial or

---

[32] F. Bolkestein, 'Letter from the European Commission to the Dutch Minister of Health, Welfare and Sport', European Commission, 25 November 2003.

[33] The legal status of Bolkestein's letter is not clear.

[34] Bolkestein, 'Letter from the European Commission', above n.32, p. 2.

[35] C. McCreevy, 'Answer given by Mr McCreevey on behalf of the Commission', European Parliament, Doc. No. E-3829/05EN, 12 December 2005; C. McCreevy, 'Answer given by Mr McCreevey on behalf of the Commission', European Parliament, Doc. No. E-3828/05EN, 5 January 2006; C. McCreevy, 'Answer given by Mr McCreevey on behalf of the Commission', European Parliament, Doc. No. E-3830/05EN, 24 January 2006.

[36] V. Špidla, 'Answer given by Mr Špidla on behalf of the Commission', European Parliament, Doc No. E-1274/06EN, 25 April 2006.

[37] Bolkestein, 'Letter from the European Commission', above n.32, p. 3 (emphasis added).

complete alternative depends, presumably, on whether the benefits it provides are 'partial' (for example, cover of mainly outpatient care in Ireland) or 'complete' (cover of outpatient and inpatient care in Germany and the Netherlands). Conversely, complementary and supplementary cover cannot be construed as alternatives to statutory cover because they offer benefits in addition to those offered by the statutory system.

On the basis established in Bolkestein's letter, material regulation would only be permissible where private health insurance covers the same benefits as those provided by statutory health insurance. But 'partial alternative' could be interpreted in other ways. The logic behind allowing governments to intervene in substitutive markets implies that purely financial regulation of solvency levels will suffice for the purposes of consumer protection but will not be enough to ensure social protection (access to health care). Bolkestein's letter implicitly assumes that only substitutive private health insurance provides social protection. But what if other forms of private health insurance also contribute to social protection? For example, where the statutory benefits package (the 'basic social security package of cover' mentioned by Bolkestein) is relatively narrow – and/or subject to extensive co-payments – it could be argued that individuals do not have adequate protection from the financial risk associated with ill health unless they purchase complementary private health insurance covering excluded (and effective) services and/or statutory user charges. In such cases, complementary cover provides a degree of social protection. Material regulation to prevent private insurers from selecting risks might therefore be justified. Under the Directive, however, rules to ensure affordable access to complementary private cover would be illegal.

The implications of outlawing material regulation of complementary cover depend on various factors, not least the extent to which this form of cover does, in practice, contribute to social protection. This issue may become more serious in future if markets for complementary cover develop and expand in light of constraints on public funding. For example, in recent years, policy-makers across the European Union have intensified efforts to define statutory benefits packages, often putting in place explicit criteria (including cost–effectiveness) to determine whether or not certain procedures should be publicly financed.[38] Such efforts may implicitly assume that statutory benefits packages can be complemented by voluntary take-up of private insurance covering less effective and/or non-cost-effective services. In practice, however, efforts to set priorities and measure cost–effectiveness tend to be limited by technical, financial and political considerations, making it easier for governments to exclude whole areas of service, such as primary care, outpatient drugs or dental care, than single interventions of low cost–effectiveness.[39] This means that complementary insurance often covers a range of necessary and cost-effective services. Similarly, in some countries, governments have introduced or raised statutory user charges to supplement public resources, again under the assumption that complementary cover will bridge the funding gap. Complementary cover of statutory user charges in France has grown from covering 33% of the population in 1960 to 85% in 2000.[40] It now accounts for about 13% of total expenditure on health (see Table 10.2). Complementary cover of statutory user charges introduced in Slovenia in 1993 now covers over 90% of the population eligible to pay user charges (about 70% of the total population) and accounts for over 11% of total health expenditure.[41]

However, greater reliance on complementary cover can create or exacerbate inequalities in access to health care. In France, the likelihood of having complementary cover and the quality (generosity) of that cover have been highly dependent on social class, age, employment and income levels.[42] Research from France and Spain shows that

---

[38] B. Gibis, P. Koch and J. Bultman, 'Shifting criteria for benefit decisions', in R. Saltman, R. Busse and J. Figueras (eds.), *Social health insurance systems in western Europe* (Maidenhead: Open University Press, 2004), pp. 189–206; J. Schreyögg *et al.*, 'Defining the "health benefit basket" in nine European countries: evidence from the European Union Health BASKET Project', *European Journal of Health Economics* 6 (2005), Supp: 2–10.

[39] C. Ham and G. Robert (eds.), *Reasonable rationing: international experience of priority setting in health care* (Buckingham: Open University Press, 2003).

[40] S. Sandier, V. Paris and D. Polton, *Health care systems in transition: France* (Copenhagen: WHO Regional Office for Europe on behalf of the European Observatory on Health Systems and Policies, 2004).

[41] T. Albreht *et al.*, *Health care systems in transition: Slovenia* (Copenhagen: WHO Regional Office for Europe on behalf of the European Observatory on Health Systems and Policies, 2002).

[42] N. Blanpain and J.-L. Pan Ké Shon, 'L'assurance complémentaire maladie: une diffusion encore inégale', *INSEE Première* 523 (1997); A. Bocognano *et al.*, *Which coverage for whom? Equity of access to health insurance in France* (Paris: CREDES, 2000).

those who do not have complementary cover do not consult doctors and dentists as frequently as those with cover.[43] In Slovenia, there are concerns about the affordability of complementary cover and its effect on access to publicly-financed health care.[44] Anecdotal evidence suggests that doctors may be reluctant to provide publicly-financed care to people without private cover in case they are unable to pay the necessary user charges.[45] There are also concerns for market stability, as complementary private health insurance covers a disproportionately high number of older people.

Governments in several Member States recognize that complementary cover of statutory user charges can contribute significantly to social protection. In 2000, the French Government introduced free complementary cover for people with low incomes,[46] raising the proportion of the population covered to over 92%.[47] In 2006, it extended favourable fiscal treatment to any private insurers offering open enrolment and community-rated premiums (see below). Since 2005, the Slovenian Government has required private insurers to offer open enrolment and community-rated policies accompanied by a risk equalization scheme.[48] In 2007, the Belgian Government also introduced open enrolment and other rules to ensure access to health insurance, particularly for people in poor health and disabled people.

The lack of a definitive interpretation of partial or complete alternative creates further uncertainty when we consider what happens if a particular market for health insurance changes from playing a substitutive to a complementary role. In Ireland, for example, private health insurance developed at a time when entitlement to publicly-funded inpatient and outpatient care was restricted to low and middle-income households. A significant proportion of the population could only

---

[43] P. Breuil-Genier, 'Généraliste puis spécialiste: un parcours peu fréquent', *INSEE Première* 709 (2000); L. Rajmil *et al.*, 'The quality of care and influence of double health care coverage in Catalonia (Spain)', *Archives of Disease in Childhood* 83 (2000), 211–4.

[44] Albreht *et al.*, *Health care systems in transition*, above n.41.

[45] Thomson, 'What role for voluntary health insurance?', above n.10.

[46] Through a scheme known as *Couverture Maladie Universelle-Complémentaire*.

[47] Durand-Zaleski, *The health system in France*, above n.9.

[48] A. Milenkovic Kramer, 'Health insurance in Slovenia', unpublished report (2006).

access health services by paying out of pocket or buying private cover, which may partly explain why, when the Irish market was liberalized in 1994, private insurers were subject to quite stringent regulation involving open enrolment, minimum benefits, community-rated premiums and a risk equalization scheme[49] (see below). However, the level of public benefits has gradually increased so that low-income households and all those aged seventy and over have free access to all types of care, while non-elderly higher-income households have access to services that are predominantly publicly-funded but subject to co-payments.[50] In 2006, the government further increased the number of people eligible for free primary care.[51] The regulatory framework originally justified under Article 54(1) could now be questioned on the grounds of whether or not private health insurance in Ireland still constitutes a partial or complete alternative to statutory health insurance. In other words, it is debatable whether the Irish market for private health insurance continues to play a significant role in providing social protection.

In the past, the Commission has avoided formally addressing what might or might not constitute a partial or complete alternative where the issue has not been absolutely clear cut. When it approved the Irish risk equalization scheme, for example (see below), it deliberately abstained from commenting on the compatibility of the regulatory framework with the Directive. The recent *BUPA*[52] ruling on the Irish regulatory framework did not address the issue either (see below). Informally, however, the Commission has acknowledged that there is a need for further clarification.

Beyond its potential impact on social protection, the restriction of material regulation of non-substitutive cover may have implications for consumer protection. Examples include the possibility of conditional sale and consumer detriment arising from product differentiation.

---

[49] In effect, these were the regulations already in place prior to 1994 (with the exception of the risk equalization scheme, which had not been necessary when VHI Healthcare was the only insurer).

[50] D. McDaid and M. M. Wiley, *Ireland: health system review* (Copenhagen: WHO Regional Office for Europe on behalf of the European Observatory on Health Systems and Policies, 2009).

[51] Department of Health and Children, 'Tánaiste announces increase in means test for GP Visit Card', Department of Health and Children, 26 June 2006, www.dohc.ie/press/releases/2006/20060626.html.

[52] Case T-289/03, *BUPA and Others* v. *Commission* (not yet reported).

Where voluntary cover is offered by the same entities responsible for providing statutory cover, insurers can take advantage of the absence of open enrolment or lifetime cover requirements for voluntary cover to terminate a voluntary contract when an individual moves to a rival insurer for statutory cover. This 'conditional' sale is a form of risk selection that is particularly likely to deter older people or people in poor health from switching from one statutory insurer to another, for fear that a new insurer might reject their application for cover, a new voluntary contract might be too expensive (taking into account the person's current age) and/or might exclude pre-existing conditions (that had developed since the signing of the original voluntary contract and were therefore covered by that contract). Conditional sale poses a barrier to competition among statutory health insurers. If construed as abuse of dominant position, it could breach EU competition rules. However, although there is evidence to suggest that conditional sale prevents fair competition in Belgium, Germany, the Netherlands and Switzerland,[53] we are not aware of any ECJ case-law in this area. We discuss the issue of product differentiation in the following subsection.

B. How can governments intervene?

The second area of uncertainty concerns the types of intervention that might be considered necessary and proportionate. Article 54(2) and recitals to the Directive list the legal provisions governments can introduce where private cover provides a partial or complete alternative to statutory cover. But it is not clear if the list should be understood as being exhaustive, in which case unlisted interventions would contravene the Directive. And, again, there is the problem of interpreting partial or complete alternatives. In this subsection, we discuss interventions that have been disputed under internal market or competition legislation, or that may be contentious in future.

Financial transfers (risk equalization schemes)

Risk equalization schemes are a direct form of intervention typically involving financial transfers from insurers with a lower than average

---

[53] F. Paolucci *et al.*, 'Supplementary health insurance as a tool for risk selection in mandatory basic health insurance markets: a five country comparison', *Health Economics, Policy and Law* 2 (2007), 173–92.

risk profile to insurers with a higher than average risk profile. They are an essential component of health insurance markets with open enrolment and community rating, where they are introduced to ensure access to health insurance and fair competition among insurers.[54] Risk equalization measures aim to lower insurers' incentives to compete through risk selection, and to encourage insurers to compete in terms of cost and quality. As such, they are widely applied to public or quasi-public entities involved in the provision of statutory health insurance (for example, in Germany and the Netherlands).[55] More recently, governments have applied them to private health insurers in Ireland (2006) and Slovenia (2005). Internationally, risk equalization schemes are also applied to private health insurers in Australia, Chile and South Africa. Wherever risk equalization has been introduced in the European Union, it has been subject to legal challenge by private insurers and/or infringement proceedings[56] initiated by the Commission in response to complaints.

The legal challenges in Ireland[57] and the Netherlands[58] have focused on the potential for financial transfers made under a risk equalization scheme to breach competition rules on state aid. There has been less emphasis on whether or not they breach internal market rules in the

[54] W. P. van de Ven and R. C. van Vliet, 'How can we prevent cream skimming in a competitive health insurance market? The great challenge for the 90s', in P. Zweifel and H. Frech III (eds.), *Health economics worldwide (developments in health economics and public policy)* (Amsterdam: Kluwer, 1992), pp. 23–46; J. Puig-Junoy, 'Managing risk selection incentives in health sector reforms', *International Journal of Health Planning and Management* 14 (1999), 287–311.

[55] W. P. van de Ven *et al.*, 'Risk adjustment and risk selection in Europe: six years later', *Health Policy* 83 (2007), 162–79.

[56] Infringement proceedings based on the Article 226 EC procedure are triggered by complaints to the European Commission. Following an informal process (informal contacts with the Member State concerned to provide the Commission with more information) and failure to reach a settlement, the formal process involves three stages. First, the Commission writes a letter of infringement to the Member State government asking it to submit its observations on the alleged infringements. Second, if the Commission considers that the Member State has not satisfactorily responded, it delivers a 'reasoned opinion', setting out the formal reasons why the Member State has failed to comply with its obligations under the Treaty and asking the government to redress the breach, usually within two months. Third, if the Member State does not respond satisfactorily, the Commission refers the matter to the European Court of Justice.

[57] Case T-289/03, *BUPA*, above n.52.

[58] Case T-84/06, *Azivo Algemeen Ziekenfonds De Volharding* v. *Commission* (case withdrawn from the register October 2008).

form of the Directive. An unsuccessful domestic legal challenge in Slovenia also focused on unfair competition, but did not refer either to EU competition or internal market rules.[59] However, the Commission's current infringement proceedings against the Slovenian Government do focus on breach of the Directive. One of the issues at stake seems to be whether or not the risk equalization scheme in Slovenia can be justified by Article 54. In the following paragraphs, we briefly outline the legal challenges in the three countries.

The Netherlands

Bolkestein's letter to the Dutch Minister of Health raised concerns that the Dutch Government's risk equalization scheme, part-financed from public funds, might contravene EU rules about state aid.[60] However, in 2005, the Commission issued a decision authorizing the transfer of public funds as, in its opinion, the aid did not unduly distort competition.[61] Despite further assurances from the European Commissioner for Competition,[62] Dutch analysts and politicians continued to question the legality of the risk equalization scheme, noting that the ECJ would have the final say on whether or not the scheme was both necessary and proportionate.[63] In 2006, a Dutch insurer brought a case before the ECJ, challenging the Commission's 2005 authorization of the risk equalization scheme primarily on the grounds that the scheme breached EU rules on state aid.[64] The insurer also argued that the new Dutch health insurance system was incompatible with the Directive and Articles 43

---

[59] Milenkovic Kramer, 'Health insurance', above n.48.

[60] Bolkestein, 'Letter from the European Commission', above n.32, p. 3.

[61] European Commission, 'State aid: Commission endorses €15 billion public funding for new Dutch health insurance system', Press Release No. IP/05/531, 3 May 2005. McCreevy, 'Answer', above n.35.

[62] A. Reerink and E. Rosenberg, 'Neelie Kroes over staatssteun aan nieuwe zorgstelsel', NRC Handelsblad, 5 October 2005.

[63] A. den Exter, 'Blending private and social health insurance in the Netherlands: challenges posed by the EU', in C. M. Flood, K. Roach and L. Sossin (eds.), *Access to care, access to justice: the legal debate over private health insurance in Canada* (Toronto: University of Toronto Press, 2005), pp. 257–77; E. Meijer and K. Liotard, 'Written question to the European Commission: entry into force in 2006 of a new Care Insurance Act in the Netherlands and its relationship with competition policy and the common market. II. Acceptance and equalisation', European Parliament, Doc No. E-3829/05, 11 October 2005.

[64] Case T-84/06, *Azivo Algemeen Ziekenfonds*, above n.58.

and 49 EC (on freedom of establishment and free movement of services respectively). It accused the Commission of failing to provide reasons to substantiate its view that the risk equalization scheme did not contravene either the Directive or competition rules on state aid. The CFI ordered that the case be removed from the register in October 2008.

Ireland

The risk equalization scheme in Ireland has also been challenged as breaching competition rules on state aid. In 1994, the Irish market was opened up to competition to comply with the Directive. Prior to this, private health insurance was almost exclusively provided by Vhi Healthcare, a quasi-public body under the jurisdiction of the Department of Health. By 1994, Vhi Healthcare covered about 37% of the population.[65] After the market was opened up to competition, the Irish Government relied on Article 54 to maintain the informal rules that applied to Vhi Healthcare, involving open enrolment, community-rated premiums, minimum benefits and lifetime cover. The Irish Government also passed new legislation allowing it to establish a risk equalization scheme to be activated by the government at the request of the independent Health Insurance Authority (HIA) if it became evident that private insurers were competing through risk selection rather than on the basis of administrative efficiency and quality.[66] In 2006, the government triggered the risk equalization scheme on the advice of the HIA.

In 1998, BUPA Ireland, a branch of the United Kingdom insurer BUPA that set up in Ireland in 1996, complained to the Commission that the (not yet triggered) risk equalization scheme was a form of state aid that distorted competition and discouraged cost containment in the health sector.[67] In response, the Irish Government argued that the Directive allowed Member States to exercise reasonable discretion with respect to the general good and that the scheme had particular regard for the need for proportionality.[68] Five years later, the

---

[65] Department of Health and Children, 'Private health insurance', White Paper, Department of Health and Children (1999).

[66] *Ibid.*

[67] BUPA Ireland, 'Risk equalisation', BUPA Ireland (2003), previously available from www.bupaireland.ie//whatsnew/RiskEqual.pdf.

[68] Department of Health and Children, 'Submission to the European Commission's study on voluntary health insurance in the European Union', Department of Health and Children (2001).

Commission issued a decision[69] stating that financial transfers made under the scheme would not constitute state aid for two reasons.[70] First, the scheme would legitimately compensate insurers for obligations they faced in carrying out a service of general economic interest (Article 86(2) EC). Second, the compensation was limited to what is necessary and proportionate to ensure stability in a community-rated market for private health insurance. The decision also noted that the scheme would not distort competition, penalize efficiency or create perverse incentives that might lead to cost inflation, nor was it likely to deter insurers from entering the market, as new entrants could exclude themselves from the scheme for up to three years. Even if financial transfers were to be considered a form of state aid, the Commission pointed out that this aid would not, by itself, amount to a violation of the Directive.

The Commission's decision is as noteworthy for what it abstains from commenting upon as for what it confirms. It explicitly states that it assessed the risk equalization scheme's compatibility with state aid rules 'without prejudice to the analysis of its compatibility with other relevant EU rules, and in particular with [the Directive]', emphasizing that it was made independently of any consideration as to whether the Irish market could be regarded as a partial or complete alternative to cover provided by the statutory system.[71] BUPA Ireland subsequently challenged the Commission's reluctance to consider whether the scheme infringed the Directive. Asking the ECJ to suspend the decision in 2003,[72] it accused the Commission of misapplying the public service compensation test and wrongly identifying open enrolment, community rating, minimum benefits and lifetime cover as public service obligations when they actually represent rules generally applied to all insurers offering private health insurance. It also accused the Commission of failing to consider whether these obligations imposed a financial burden on Vhi Healthcare and whether the risk equalization scheme would affect the

---

[69] Unlike Bolkestein's letter, above n.32, a Commission decision is binding and judicially reviewable at the suit of the addressee or those directly and individually concerned (Article 230 EC). Article 88(2) EC and Regulation 659/99/EC give the Commission the power to make such decisions.

[70] European Commission, 'Ireland – risk equalisation scheme in the Irish health insurance market', State Aid Decision No. 46/2003, European Commission (2003).

[71] *Ibid.*, p. 8.

[72] Case T-289/03, *BUPA*, above n.52.

development of trade contrary to the interests of the Community, and of failing to initiate a formal investigation procedure, given the complexity of the arguments and the economic analysis required. The Dutch and Irish Governments and Vhi Healthcare joined the legal proceedings in defence of the Commission. BUPA Ireland also launched a domestic challenge to the risk equalization scheme in 2006 (see below). The following year, it pulled out of the Irish market and its business was bought by Quinn Healthcare, an Irish company. Quinn Healthcare has also challenged the risk equalization scheme (within Ireland).

In 2008, the Court of First Instance (CFI) dismissed BUPA's application, finding its claim inadmissible.[73] The CFI used the criteria[74] laid down in *Altmark*,[75] finding that the Commission had been right to conclude that the risk equalization scheme did not contravene EU state aid rules. It is worth going into the CFI's decision in some detail, since the arguments involved are revealing. BUPA had argued that private health insurance in Ireland could not constitute a service of general economic interest (SGEI) since there was no obligation of general interest imposed on insurers to provide certain services and those services were not available to the whole population. Rather, they were optional – even 'luxury' – financial services and not intended to replace the public social security system. BUPA also argued that the decision of whether or not SGEIs were being carried out was a decision for European Community institutions and not to be delegated to national authorities. In contrast, the Irish Government contended that the definition of SGEIs falls primarily within the competence and discretion of the Member States and that private health insurance is 'an important instrument of the social and health policy pursued by Ireland ... and an important *supplement* to the public health insurance system, although it does not *replace* that system'.[76] It added that, because the obligations of open enrolment and community rating ensure that

---

[73] *Ibid.*
[74] These are as follows: (a) the recipient undertaking must have public service obligations to discharge and the obligations must be clearly defined; the service must also be of a universal and compulsory nature; (b) the parameters on the basis of which the compensation for carrying out the SGEI mission is calculated must be established in advance in an objective and transparent manner; (c) the necessity and proportionality of the compensation must be provided for; and (d) comparison with an efficient operator must be established.
[75] Case C-280/00, *Altmark Trans GmbH* [2003] ECR I-7747.
[76] Case T-289/03, *BUPA*, above n.52, para. 164 (emphasis added).

private health insurance is available to all, it is not necessary that it should be universal, compulsory, free of charge, economically accessible to the whole population or constitute a substitute for the public social security system.

Responding to these claims and counterclaims, the CFI confirmed that Member States have a wide discretion to define what they regard as SGEIs. Moreover, the definition of such services by a Member State can only be questioned by the Commission in the event of a manifest error.[77] It found that there had been an act of public authority creating and entrusting an SGEI mission in Ireland. It also found that the compulsory nature of the SGEI mission could lie in the obligation on insurers to offer certain services to every citizen requesting them (open enrolment) and was strengthened by other obligations, such as community rating, lifetime cover and minimum benefits.[78] According to the CFI, these obligations guarantee that the Irish population has 'wide and simple access' to private health insurance, which entitles private health insurance to be characterized as universal within the meaning of Community law.[79] The CFI went on to note:

[T]he criterion of universality does not require that the entire population should have or be capable of having recourse to it in practice … the fact that approximately 50% of the Irish population has subscribed to PMI [private medical insurance] cover indicates that, in any event, the PMI services respond to a very significant demand on the Irish PMI market and that they make a substantial contribution to the proper functioning of the social security system, in the broad sense, in Ireland.[80]

The CFI further found that the parameters used to calculate the risk equalization payments were sufficiently clearly defined and that the scheme itself was necessary and proportionate to the costs incurred. In addition, it found that insurers operating less efficiently than their competitors would not be able to gain undue advantage from the risk equalization scheme, because the scheme compensated insurers based on average costs.[81] Finally, the CFI concluded that the risk equalization scheme was necessary and proportionate for the purposes of

---

[77] *Ibid.*, para. 165.   [78] *Ibid.*, paras. 188–91.
[79] *Ibid.*, para. 201.   [80] *Ibid.*, para. 201.
[81] See Chapter 9 in this volume for further discussion of this aspect of the Court's ruling.

Article 86(2) EC. It noted that the Commission had been right to support the risk equalization scheme as a measure necessary to prevent destabilization of the community-rated Irish market caused by active risk selection on the part of Vhi Healthcare's competitors.[82]

The comments by the CFI on the nature of the Irish market are particularly revealing. Paragraph 204 states:

In the light of the foregoing, the applicant's [BUPA's] very general argument concerning the optional, complementary and 'luxury' nature of the PMI services cannot succeed. Apart from the fact that the applicants disregard, in this context, the various levels of PMI cover available, they have not submitted a detailed challenge to the argument put forward by the defendant [the Commission] and by Ireland that Irish PMI constitutes, alongside the public health insurance system, the second pillar of the Irish health system, the existence of which fulfils a mandatory objective of social cohesion and solidarity between the generations pursued by Ireland's health policy. According to the explanations provided by Ireland, PMI helps to ensure the effectiveness and profitability of the public health insurance scheme by reducing pressure on the costs which it would otherwise bear, particularly as regards care provided in public hospitals. Within the framework of the restricted control that the Community institutions are authorised to exercise in that regard, those considerations cannot be called in question either by the Commission or by the Court. Accordingly, it must be accepted that the PMI services are used by Ireland, in the general interest, as an instrument indispensable to the smooth administration of the national health system and they must be recognised, owing to the PMI obligations, as being in the nature of an SGEI.

These comments and the ruling as a whole suggest three things. First, not only do national governments have considerable discretion in deciding what is in the general interest, but the regulations in place themselves contribute to the definition of a particular service as being in the general interest. In other words, if the Irish Government defines a service as being in the general interest, regulations such as open enrolment and community rating can only strengthen the government's case, although the necessity and proportionality tests would still apply. This apparently circular argument reflects the complexity of determining what is and is not an SGEI in the absence of a central

[82] Case T-289/03, *BUPA*, above n.52, paras. 285–86.

definition, but it reinforces the significant scope for Member State autonomy in this area. Second, the Irish Government claims that, even though private health insurance in Ireland plays a supplementary rather than a substitutive role, it is an important instrument of Irish social and health policy – 'the second pillar of the Irish health system' – and helps to sustain the public health insurance scheme by relieving pressure on public hospitals. The ruling notes that these claims cannot be questioned by the Commission or the CFI. Consequently, if a government says that private health insurance is a key component of the national health strategy, the European Union's legislative institutions must accept it as being the case. Third, the CFI makes much of the fact that private health insurance in Ireland covers about half of the Irish population and takes this as evidence that it makes a 'substantial contribution to the proper functioning of the [Irish] social security system'. Thus, the degree of population coverage might bolster arguments about the contribution of private health insurance to the 'national health strategy'.

In spite of the CFI's ruling, which BUPA decided not to appeal against, the Irish regulatory framework has continued to be questioned in the domestic courts. In 2006, the Irish High Court ruled against BUPA's legal challenge to the risk equalization scheme. BUPA appealed and, in 2008, the Supreme Court upheld its appeal on procedural grounds, finding that the risk equalization scheme was based on an incorrect interpretation of the meaning of community rating in the relevant law and would therefore have to be abandoned.[83] However, the Supreme Court did not question the risk equalization scheme on other grounds, so a change in legislation may be sufficient to secure the scheme's domestic legitimacy. In the meantime, the scheme has been set aside.

Slovenia

The CFI ruling came after the Commission had initiated infringement proceedings against Belgium and Slovenia, but may have some bearing on both of these cases. In this subsection, we discuss the case against Slovenia. The case against Belgium is discussed in a subsequent subsection. In 2005, two of the three insurance companies

---

[83] *BUPA Ireland Limited and Anor v. Health Insurance Authority and Others* [2008] IESC 42.

operating in the Slovenian complementary private health insurance
market (covering statutory user charges) challenged legislation establishing a risk equalization scheme. The largest insurer, Vzajemna[84]
(a mutual association), argued that the scheme would favour the two
other (commercial) insurers and encourage risk selection, while the
larger commercial insurer, Adriatic,[85] argued that the scheme would
distort competition. Neither challenge referred to EU law, and the
Slovenian High Court ruled in the government's favour.[86] However,
in 2007, following a complaint from Vzajemna, the Commission initiated infringement proceedings against the Slovenian Government,
arguing that the risk equalization scheme could not be justified
under Article 54(1) of the Directive because complementary private
health insurance in Slovenia does not constitute a partial or complete
alternative to statutory health insurance. The Commission's letter
of formal notice, the contents of which have not been made publicly available, may also have noted that the requirement for insurers
involved in the complementary market to inform the regulator of
changes to policy conditions and premiums breaches the Directive
(Articles 6, 29 and 39) and that the requirement for insurers to put
50% of any profits generated back into the private health insurance
scheme is problematic.[87]

The Slovenian Government responded by arguing (in May 2007) that
the complementary market is a part of the broader social security system and has been defined in legislation as a service of general interest.[88]
It also drew to the Commission's attention the similarities between the
Irish market and the Slovenian market. Previously, the Commission
had rejected the government's claim that the Slovenian market represented a partial or complete alternative to compulsory health insurance,
arguing instead that the market played a supplementary role. While it

[84] Vzajemna, 'Dispute put forward to High Court regarding the new Health Care
and Health Insurance Act No. U-I-277/05', Vzajemna, 22 December 2005.

[85] Adriatic, 'Dispute put forward to High Court regarding the new Health Care
and Health Insurance Act No. U-I-282/05–1', Adriatic, 10 October 2005.

[86] S. Toplak, 'Constitutional Court failed to please Vzajemna and Adriatic',
The Finance Business Daily Newspaper, 17 September 2005, www.
finance-on.net/show.php?id=137526; Milenkovic Kramer, 'Health
insurance', above n.48.

[87] A. Rednak and T. Smrekar, 'Evropa žuga Sloveniji zaradi zdravstvenih
zavarovanja', *Finance*, 4 May 2007.

[88] Slovenia Business Week, 'Government responds to EU's warning over health
insurance', *Slovenia Business Week* 18 (2007), p. 10.

seems clear that the Slovenian Government will need to address potential breaches of the Directive's ban on systematic prior notification of policy conditions and premiums, it is less clear, following the *BUPA* ruling, whether the risk equalization scheme breaches the Directive or EU state aid rules. The CFI's rationale for upholding the Commission decision in favour of the risk equalization scheme in Ireland could apply, with even greater force, in the Slovenian case. First, there is an act of public authority creating and entrusting an SGEI mission (given in the Slovenian Health Care and Health Insurance Act), which, along *BUPA* lines, is both compulsory and universal in nature. Second, complementary private health insurance covers an even greater proportion of the population than in Ireland (70%), strengthening the government's claim that the complementary market is part of the social security system. And, third, following *BUPA*, does the Commission have the right to question the claims of the Slovenian Government? The Commission is due to respond.

In our view, both the Dutch and Slovenian cases for risk equalization seem stronger than the Irish case, in the Netherlands because the 'private' health insurance scheme *is* the statutory health insurance scheme, and in Slovenia because the complementary market makes a more significant contribution to social protection than the predominantly supplementary market in Ireland. For example, the extent of statutory cost sharing has increased in Slovenia[89] in recent years, whereas it has gone down in Ireland.[90] Reflecting this, private health insurance in Slovenia accounts for over half of all private spending on health (the second highest proportion in the European Union after France), but only a third of private health expenditure in Ireland (see Table 10.2).

Benefits

Governments can regulate the benefits offered by private insurers by specifying a minimum level or standard package of benefits and/ or requiring benefits to be provided in kind rather than in cash. The first intervention aims to facilitate price competition, while both aim to lower financial barriers and ensure access to a given range of health services.

[89] Milenkovic Kramer, 'Health insurance', above n.48.
[90] McDaid and Wiley, *Ireland: health system review*, above n.50.

Minimum or standard benefits

The question of whether or not regulators should be able to specify minimum or standard benefits – as they do in Germany, Ireland and the Netherlands (prior to 2006 and now) – has not yet been legally challenged as a form of material regulation that contravenes the Directive or as an intervention that impedes the free movement of services. Nevertheless, we raise it as an issue that has implications for consumer protection. The issue is also pertinent since a key objective underlying the introduction of the internal market in insurance was to stimulate competition among insurers, precipitating efficiency gains and bringing consumers the benefits of wider choice and lower prices.[91] The preamble to the Directive states that it is in policyholders' interest that they should have access to 'the widest possible range of insurance products available in the Community so that [they] can choose that which is best suited to [their] needs' (Recital 19).[92]

In theory, product differentiation benefits consumers by providing policies tailored to meet particular needs. It benefits insurers by allowing them to distinguish between high and low risk individuals. But, in practice, it may be detrimental to consumers in two ways. First, it gives insurers greater opportunity to select risks, leading to access problems for high risk individuals. Second, making consumers choose from a wide range of highly differentiated products restricts competition, which only operates effectively where consumers find it easy to make informed comparisons about price and quality.

To encourage competition based on price and quality (rather than risk selection), regulators can require insurers to offer a standard package of benefits, use standardized terms when marketing products, inform potential and existing policy holders of all the price and product options open to them and provide consumers with access to centralized sources of comparable information. However, the Directive specifically outlaws product and price controls, except where private health insurance constitutes a partial or complete alternative to statutory cover. Even in these circumstances, control is limited to offering benefits standardized in line with statutory benefits – that is, the primary aim is to ensure that the privately insured have access to

---

[91] European Commission, 'Liberalisation of insurance in the single market: update and questions', *Single Market News* 11 (1998), 1–8.
[92] Council Directive 92/49/EEC, above n.2.

the same services as the publicly insured, rather than to facilitate price competition. For example, governments in Germany and the Netherlands have required private insurers to offer older policy holders benefits that match statutory benefits.[93]

In the absence of product regulation, liberalization of health insurance markets in some Member States has been accompanied by rising levels of product differentiation, with evidence suggesting that consumers may be confused by the proliferation of products on offer.[94] For example, an official investigation into information problems in the market for supplementary private health insurance in the United Kingdom found that increased product complexity did not benefit consumers; rather, consumers sometimes paid more than they should and often purchased inappropriate policies.[95] An OECD study noted that as the diversity of schemes in the United Kingdom market rose, consumers faced increasing difficulty in comparing premiums and products, a concern echoed by consumer bodies in other Member States.[96]

Perhaps due to limited price competition and private insurers' limited ability to control costs, prices appear to have gone up rather than down in many Member States. Research based on data from several Member States shows that, during the 1990s, the compound annual growth rate of private health insurance premiums rose much faster than the average annual growth rate of total spending on health care.[97]

Benefits in kind

The provision of benefits in kind enhances social protection by removing financial barriers to accessing health care. Bolkestein's letter to the Dutch Minister of Health suggests that the Dutch Government's requirement for insurers to provide a basic package of benefits in kind could infringe the free movement of services by creating barriers for non-Dutch insurers entering the market and might need to be assessed for proportionality and necessity.[98] This raises concerns not only

---

[93] Mossialos and Thomson, *Voluntary health insurance*, above n.5.
[94] *Ibid.*
[95] Office of Fair Trading, 'Health insurance: a second report by the Office of Fair Trading', Office of Fair Trading (1998).
[96] Organisation for Economic Co-operation and Development, 'Private health insurance in OECD countries: compilation of national reports', OECD (2001).
[97] Mossialos and Thomson, *Voluntary health insurance*, above n.5.
[98] Bolkestein, 'Letter from the European Commission', above n.32, p. 3.

for the new Dutch system, but for statutory and substitutive private health insurance in other Member States. However, the issue has not yet been subjected to legal challenge.

Differential treatment of insurers

Under the Directive, governments can no longer influence market structure (by restricting the provision of private health insurance to a single approved insurer or to statutory health insurance funds) or discriminate against particular types of insurer. For example, Recital 25 outlaws regulations preventing non-specialist or composite insurers from providing health insurance. When the German Government transposed the Directive, it had to abolish its rule excluding non-specialist insurers from entering the private health insurance market, but used its social law to prohibit employers from contributing to policies offered by composite insurers, leading the Commission to refer Germany to the European Court of Justice.[99] Germany amended its legislation and the case was removed from the register in December 2003. Other areas in which the Directive affects differential treatment of insurers concern solvency requirements and tax treatment.

Solvency requirements

National laws often distinguish between non-profit and for-profit institutions, sometimes resulting in preferential treatment of non-profit institutions. This usually favours mutual associations, which have a long history of involvement in statutory and private health insurance in many Member States and traditionally operate in different areas of the market from commercial insurers.[100] The special status accorded to mutual associations has given rise to difficulties under the Directive. For example, French mutual associations operate under a special *Code de la Mutualité*, which means they were subject to less rigorous solvency rules than commercial insurers or provident associations.[101] In 1999, the European Court of Justice ruled against France for its failure to transpose fully the Directive with regard to mutual associations.[102] However, the French Government failed to

---

[99] Case C-298/01, *Commission v. Germany* (not yet reported).
[100] W. Palm, 'Voluntary health insurance and EU insurance directives: between solidarity and the market', in M. McKee, E. Mossialos and R. Baeten (eds.), *The impact of EU law on health care systems* (Brussels: PIE-Peter Lang, 2002).
[101] *Ibid.*   [102] Case C-239/98, *Commission v. France* [1999] ECR I-8935.

act and the Commission was forced to begin fresh infringement proceedings under Article 228 EC the following year, which eventually resulted in the adoption of a revised code tightening the solvency requirements for mutual associations and bringing French law in line with the Directive.[103]

Solvency rules have also led to controversy in Belgium and Ireland. Mutual associations in Belgium engaged in selling a mixture of complementary and supplementary private health insurance operate under separate solvency rules from commercial insurers. Both types of insurer competed to provide cover for self-employed people, who were excluded from statutory cover of outpatient care. More recently, they also began to compete to provide complementary cover of some hospital costs. For example, the Mutualité Chretienne, which is one of several statutory health insurers, also provided its members with compulsory complementary cover of all hospital costs above a deductible per inpatient stay.[104] Previously, this type of cover had been exclusively offered by commercial private insurers. In 2006, the European Commission began infringement proceedings against the Belgian Government on the grounds that differential treatment might distort the market.[105]

The issue regarding self-employed people in Belgium has been addressed by extending statutory cover of outpatient care to them from 2008. However, the issue of complementary private health insurance has been more problematic. The Belgian Government has argued that the Directive does not apply to mutual associations because the cover they provide is part of the social security system, their activity is based on solidarity rather than being economic in nature and, if the complementary cover they provide were to be viewed as an economic activity, it would be a service of general economic interest and exempt from competition rules under Article 86(2) EC. In 2008, the Commission rejected this defence and sent a

---

[103] European Commission, 'Insurance', above n.20. European Commission, 'Insurance: infringement proceedings against France concerning mutual societies and the requirement of a marketing information sheet', Press Release No. IP/00/876, 28 July 2000.

[104] Mutualité Chretienne, 'L'Hospi Solidaire, parce que l'hospitalisation ne doit pas être un luxe', www.mc.be/fr/100/campagne_hospi/index.jsp.

[105] European Commission, 'Commission scrutinises Belgian law on supplementary health insurance provided by private sickness funds', Press Release No. IP/06/1781, 13 December 2006.

reasoned opinion to Belgium, asking it to amend its national rules
so that mutual associations are no longer governed by separate solvency and supervisory rules.[106] As shown in the discussion of France
(below), the Commission is unlikely to consider this type of differential treatment of insurers to be necessary or proportionate to the
costs incurred in carrying out SGEI activities.

In the 1970s, the Irish Government had obtained a derogation from
the First Non-life Insurance Directive's solvency requirements for its
quasi-state insurer Vhi Healthcare.[107] This meant that Vhi Healthcare
was not subject to the same solvency requirements as its commercial competitors and was not regulated by the same regulatory body.
In January 2007, the Commission began infringement proceedings
against Ireland in response to a claim made by Vivas (a commercial
insurer that entered the Irish market in 2004) that Vhi Healthcare
had breached the conditions of its derogation from the Directive by
carrying out business in addition to its core health insurance activity.[108] The Irish Government subsequently brought forward plans to
change the status of Vhi Healthcare. It has announced that, by the
end of 2009 (not 2012 as originally stated), Vhi Healthcare will be a
conventional insurer authorized by the financial regulator.[109]

Some of these solvency issues may change in the future, with the
introduction of new economic risk-based solvency requirements in
2012 (the so-called 'Solvency II' framework).[110] The Commission is
proposing to move away from a 'one-model-fits-all' method of esti-
mating capital requirements to more entity-specific requirements,
which would be applied to all entities regardless of their legal status.
However, as yet, the implications of this new framework for health
insurance are not clear.

---

[106] European Commission, 'Internal market: Commission requests Belgium to
amend law on supplementary health insurance provided by private sickness
funds', Press Release No. IP/08/691, 6 May 2008.

[107] The Competition Authority, *Competition*, above n.7.

[108] European Commission, 'Insurance: Commission scrutinises exemption
of Irish Voluntary Health Insurance Board from EU rules', European
Commission (2007).

[109] Department of Health and Children, 'Government approves reform
measures for private health insurance market', Department of Health and
Children, 25 April 2007.

[110] European Commission, 'Solvency II: frequently asked questions',
MEMO/07/286, 10 July 2007.

Tax treatment

Tax incentives in France, Luxembourg and Belgium have traditionally favoured mutual or provident associations over commercial insurers. In Luxembourg, the existence of a 'gentleman's agreement' between mutual associations and commercial insurers has prevented the latter from complaining about preferential tax treatment.[111] The agreement rests on the understanding that mutual associations will not encroach on commercial insurers' dominance of the market for pensions and other types of insurance. Prior to 2008, Belgian mutual and commercial insurers competed to cover outpatient care for self-employed people. Mutual associations providing this cover benefited from state subsidies, whereas commercial insurers did not. The commercial insurers tried to challenge this in the Belgian courts, but lost their legal challenge. In 2006, the Commission began infringement proceedings against this preferential treatment, but the issue is no longer relevant, as the Belgian Government now extends statutory outpatient cover to all self-employed people.[112]

Preferential tax treatment of mutual insurers has been most problematic in France, where mutual and provident associations have been exempt from health insurance premium tax since 1945. In 1992, the French Federation of Insurance Companies (FFSA) lodged two complaints against the French Government for this discriminatory tax policy, arguing that it contravened EU rules on state aid. Their complaints were eventually upheld by a Commission decision in November 2001 and the French Government was asked either to abolish the tax exemptions in question or to ensure that the aid did not exceed the costs arising from the constraints inherent in a service of general economic interest.[113] At the same time, the Commission noted that it did not regard the provision of private health insurance by these associations to be a service of general economic interest explicitly provided for in their articles. The French Government responded

---

[111] Mossialos and Thomson, *Voluntary health insurance*, above n.5.
[112] European Commission, 'Commission scrutinises Belgian law on supplementary health insurance provided by private sickness funds', European Commission (2007); European Commission, 'Internal market', above n.106.
[113] European Commission, 'State aid: Commission calls on France to put an end to certain tax exemptions for mutual and provident societies', Press Release No. IP/01/1575, 13 November 2001.

by removing the health insurance premium tax exemption for mutual and provident associations[114] and, instead, applying it to two types of private health insurance contract: those based on 'solidarity' (*contrats solidaires*) – in this case, contracts concluded without a prior medical examination or other reference to an individual's risk of ill health – and 'responsible' contracts (*contrats responsables*), in which private health insurers agree not to cover new co-payments intended to encourage patients to obtain a referral for specialist care and to adhere to protocols for the treatment of chronic illnesses. At first, the Commission agreed that this new exemption was compatible with EU rules on state aid.[115] However, in 2007, it launched a formal investigation into the new *contrats*, to find out if they are indeed non-discriminatory and how much consumers really stand to benefit from the advantages granted to insurers.[116] The results of this investigation have not yet been published.

Some argue in favour of treating mutual associations differently on the grounds that they provide better access to health services because they generally offer open enrolment, lifetime cover and community-rated premiums, whereas commercial insurers usually restrict access by rejecting applications, excluding the cover of pre-existing conditions and risk rating premiums.[117] In a market where mutual associations and commercial insurers operate side by side, the latter may be able to undermine the former by attracting low risk individuals with lower premiums, leaving mutual associations to cover high risks. However, while the distinction between non-profit and for-profit insurers is important

---

[114] In 2006, in response to a further decision from the Commission, the French Government abolished the exemption from insurance premium tax for mutual and provident associations on non-health insurance business. European Commission, 'State aid: Commission calls on France to put an end to certain tax exemptions for mutual and provident societies', Press Release No. IP/05/243, 2 March 2005.

[115] European Commission, 'Exemption from tax on health insurance contracts', OJ 2005 No. C126/10; European Commission, 'France – éxoneration de la taxe sur les contrats d'assurance maladie', State Aid Decision No. E 46/2001, European Commission (2001).

[116] European Commission, 'State aid: Commission opens formal investigation into French plan to grant tax aid to insurers', Press Release No. IP/07/1692, 14 November 2007.

[117] M. Rocard, 'Mission mutualité et droit communautaire: rapport de fin de mission', Government of France (1999); Palm, 'Voluntary health insurance', above n.100, pp. 195–234.

in so far as an insurer's profit status determines its motivation and influences its conduct, in practice there is considerable variation in the way in which mutual associations behave; in some Member States, their conduct may be indistinguishable from the conduct of commercial insurers. As it is not possible to make assumptions about an insurer's conduct on the basis of its legal status, it would be more appropriate to discriminate on the basis of conduct, favouring insurers who offer greater access to health services or, where appropriate, penalizing those who restrict access. This was the approach taken by the French Government in 2004 and again in 2006, when it expanded the remit for exemption from insurance premium tax to any insurer agreeing to abide by specific rules intended to promote access to health care.[118]

5. Conclusions

In some ways, the EU regulatory framework established by the Directive places limits on national competence in the area of private health insurance. It relies on financial regulation to protect consumers, prohibiting material regulations such as price and product controls, except where private cover constitutes a complete or partial alternative to statutory health insurance and so long as any intervention is necessary, proportionate and non-discriminatory. We have argued that the Directive is not sufficiently clear about when governments can justify material regulation of private health insurance. This is mainly because there is no explicit consensus about the meaning of partial or complete alternative, leading to uncertainty and confusion among policy-makers, regulators and insurers. Where the Commission and, more recently, the European Court of Justice (in *BUPA*), have had opportunity to clarify this aspect of the Directive, they have tended to sidestep the issue, relying instead on rules about services of general economic interest to authorize (Ireland) or prohibit (France) government intervention. Key exceptions are Bolkestein's letter, in which he argues that Article 54(1) of the Directive should not be used to justify material regulation of complementary private health insurance, and a description of the Directive on the Commission's web site, which refers to 'substitutive' private health insurance.

---

[118] Sécurité Sociale, 'Contrat responsable', Sécurité Sociale (2008), www.securite-sociale.fr/comprendre/reformes/reformeassmal/decrets/maitrise/20050930.htm.

Bolkestein's definition of complementary cover fails to recognize that this type of private health insurance increasingly contributes to social protection for those who purchase it, operating in an unofficial partnership with statutory health insurance where it offers reimbursement of statutory user charges and/or provides access to effective health services excluded from the statutory benefits package. In particular, complementary cover of statutory user charges tends to be purchased by a relatively high proportion of the population, making it regressive in financing health care (because it is not restricted to richer groups) and creating or exacerbating inequalities in access to health care.[119] If, as we have argued, the logic underlying Article 54(1) is to permit material regulation where private health insurance fulfils a social protection function, then obliging complementary insurers to offer open enrolment, lifetime cover and community rating would be necessary to ensure equitable access to health care, while a risk equalization scheme might be needed to lower incentives to select risks and to encourage competition based on price and quality. The Irish experience highlights the complexity of the issues at stake and the difficulties caused by legal uncertainty.

The Directive has been amended several times since its introduction, most recently in 2007.[120] None of the amendments has had any direct bearing on private insurance. In 2008, the Commission circulated a proposal for an amended directive that would repeal and replace the Third Non-life Insurance Directive and several other insurance-related directives under the 'Solvency II' framework.[121] Once again, there are no major changes specifically relating to private

---

[119] A. Wagstaff *et al.*, 'Equity in the finance of health care: some further international comparisons', *Journal of Health Economics* 18 (1999), 263–90; E. van Doorslaer, C. Masseria and X. Koolman for the OECD Health Equity Research Group, 'Inequalities in access to medical care by income in developed countries', *Canadian Medical Association Journal* 174 (2006), 177.

[120] European Parliament and Council Directive 2007/44/EC 5 September 2007 amending Council Directive 92/49/EEC and Directives 2002/83/EC, 2004/39/EC, 2005/68/EC and 2006/48/EC as regards procedural rules and evaluation criteria for the prudential assessment of acquisitions and increase of holdings in the financial sector, OJ 2007 No. L247/1.

[121] European Commission, 'Amended Proposal for a Directive of the European Parliament and of the Council on the taking-up and pursuit of the business of insurance and reinsurance (SOLVENCY II)', COM (2008) 119 final, 21 April 2008.

health insurance. The only real change seems to be in the wording of Recital 58 (Recital 24 of the original Directive), which now excludes open enrolment, community rating and lifetime cover as possible measures that may be introduced to protect the general good (where private health insurance serves as a partial or complete alternative). It is not clear whether this omission has any particular significance.[122]

By maintaining the same wording as the Directive ('complete or partial alternative'; Article 204), the proposed new directive has missed a key opportunity to address legal uncertainty. The Commission's reluctance to be explicit about what the phrase means, the importance of the phrase in the infringement proceedings against Slovenia (but its seeming irrelevance in the eyes of the Court of First Instance in *BUPA*), and increasing reliance on the Treaty (Article 86(2) EC) to justify intervention in private health insurance markets (in France and Ireland) suggest that the Commission would have done better to have removed the phrase from the proposed directive. As the Court confirms, whether or not private health insurance requires material regulation to protect the general good should be a matter for national governments. We have argued that the logic underlying Article 54(1) is to ensure access to private health insurance where it contributes to social protection. However, as definitions of social protection may vary from one country to another (and even within a country, over time), deciding what does or does not contribute to social protection is, in our view, a largely political issue. It is therefore a matter best left to the discretion of national political processes.

If, as the Court states in *BUPA*, governments have relative freedom to define private health insurance as being a service of general economic interest, and regulations such as open enrolment can be construed as demonstrating SGEI obligations, then there seems little need for further elaboration of this particular issue in the form of a directive, particularly given the uncertainty created by the current and proposed wording and the fact that proportionality must still be tested, regardless of which process (Treaty or Directive) applies. It

---

[122] As before, Recital 58 of the third 'Non-life Insurance Directive', above n.2, states that standardized benefits offered at a premium rate at or below a prescribed maximum, participation in loss compensation (risk equalization) schemes, and private health insurance operated on a technical basis similar to life insurance may be introduced as measures to protect the general good.

remains to be seen whether the *BUPA* ruling will change the position of the Commission in its infringement proceedings against Slovenia (at least concerning the legality of the risk equalization scheme), since the Slovenian Government now has a good legal basis on which to defend the SGEI nature of its complementary private health insurance market. The SGEI argument is unlikely to be much help to the Belgian Government, however, because hard and soft law alike consistently reject differential treatment of insurers based on legal status. A more pragmatic (and effective) approach to influencing the conduct of insurers is to favour those who adhere to specific principles. France has led the way here, with its system of tax exemptions for insurers that uphold *contrats solidaires* or *contrats responsables*, although even this move is under investigation by the Commission.

We have also argued that there is uncertainty about what sort of government intervention in the private health insurance market might be considered to be necessary or proportionate, not just because of the Directive, but also under EU state aid rules. While it is clear that differential treatment of insurers based on legal status will not be tolerated, it is much less clear whether regulatory requirements such as open enrolment and risk equalization schemes are compatible with the Directive – particularly (but not exclusively) where non-substitutive private health insurance is concerned. For example, the Commission's decision to authorize risk equalization in the Netherlands has been challenged by a Dutch insurer,[123] even though the new Dutch health insurance system is broadly accepted as being statutory in nature. The Commission has contributed to this uncertainty by approving the risk equalization scheme in Ireland (on the grounds that private health insurance in Ireland constitutes a service of general economic interest), but accusing the Slovenian risk equalization scheme of contravening the Directive – and yet, as we have argued, the case for risk equalization might be stronger in Slovenia than in Ireland. It is possible that the *BUPA* ruling will, in practice, remove some of this uncertainty.

Finally, we have argued that the Directive's regulatory framework may not provide sufficient protection of consumers. In markets where private health insurance does not contribute to social protection, the Directive assumes that financial regulation will protect consumers. But solvency rules alone may not be adequate if health

---

[123] Case T-84/06, *Azivo Algemeen Ziekenfonds*, above n.58.

insurance products are highly differentiated. Information asymmetry exacerbated by product differentiation appears to be a growing problem in markets across the European Union and the Commission has not yet put in place mechanisms for monitoring anti-competitive behaviour by insurers. Communications from the Commission have also raised doubts about the compatibility of certain regulatory measures with competition rules – for example, the provision of benefits in kind.[124] If a requirement for insurers to provide benefits in kind were to be found to contravene competition rules, there would be implications for statutory as well as private health insurance.

The Directive reflects the regulatory norms of its time. When it was introduced in 1992, the Commission may have been convinced that it would provide ample scope for governments to protect consumers where necessary and would not jeopardize statutory arrangements. Article 54 would protect markets contributing to social protection, while, in markets regarded as purely supplementary, the benefits of deregulation (increased choice and competition resulting in lower prices) would outweigh concerns about consumer protection. These assumptions are more problematic now, partly because there is no evidence to suggest that the expected benefits of competition have, as yet, materialized. Private health insurance premiums in many Member States have risen rather than fallen in recent years, often faster than inflation in the health sector as a whole, while insurers' expansion across national borders has been limited to cross-border mergers and acquisitions, rather than genuinely new entrants to the market.[125] The new Dutch health insurance system has not yet seen any cross-border activity and the number of insurers in operation has swiftly fallen to about five.

The assumptions are also problematic due to increased blurring of the boundaries between normal economic activity and social security. On the one hand, the case-law reviewed in this chapter shows governments how they might put their health insurance arrangements beyond the scope of internal market law, either by placing them firmly within the sphere of social security or by invoking the general good defence. On the other hand, as the Dutch system shows, the trend seems to be going in the opposite direction. Consequently,

[124] Bolkestein, 'Letter from European Commission', above n.32.
[125] Mossialos and Thomson, *Voluntary health insurance*, above n.5.

social security is no longer the preserve of statutory institutions or public finance, a development likely to bring new challenges for policy-makers. Greater blurring of the public–private interface in health insurance gives rise to complexities that neither the existing Directive nor the proposed new directive seem equipped to address. In light of these complexities, only some of which we have attempted to highlight here,[126] we think it is time for a debate about how best to move forward. A priority for debate should be to find ways of thinking about private health insurance that go beyond 'partial or complete alternative' to statutory cover. These terms are unclear and do not reflect the often complicated relationship between public and private cover. At least in the European Union, private health insurance rarely offers a genuine 'alternative' to statutory cover.[127] We also emphasize that financial regulation may not be the only or best means of protecting consumers in health insurance markets. If it is not possible to reach a political consensus about re-examining the need for material regulation of private health insurance under some circumstances, then the Commission and the Member States should consider how best to improve the way in which products are marketed and the quality of the information available to consumers.

[126] There are other issues that may also be relevant – for example, the introduction of medical savings accounts as part of either private or public coverage. Medical savings accounts (MSAs) involve compulsory or voluntary contributions by individuals to personalized savings accounts earmarked for health care. They do not involve risk pooling (except in so far as they are combined with insurance). Consequently, they do not involve any form of cross-subsidy from rich to poor, healthy to unhealthy, young to old or working to non-working. The only example of MSAs in an EU context is in Hungary, where savings accounts that benefit from tax subsidies are used voluntarily to cover statutory cost sharing or to cover out of pocket payments for services obtained in the private sector.

[127] S. Thomson, T. Foubister and E. Mossialos, *Financing health care in the European Union: Challenges and Policy Responses* (Copenhagen: World Health Organization on behalf of the European Observatory on Health Systems and Policies, 2009).

11 | *Free movement of services in the EU and health care*

WOUTER GEKIERE, RITA BAETEN AND
WILLY PALM

1. Introduction

Throughout the European Union, health care systems traditionally
have been characterized by extensive regulatory intervention. National
and regional authorities intervene mainly to ensure equal access, sustainability, quality, safety, equity and efficiency of health care for the
citizens residing in their territory. Given the multitude of different
actors involved, they need to align these overall principles and objectives with the interests of stakeholders to ensure the stable cooperation
of all the players in the system.

Increasingly, this high level of public intervention has been challenged on the part of the European Community. Regulation in the
field of health care is being scrutinized with regard to its conformity with EU law, particularly Community rules on free movement (of
persons, goods and services). As different forms of mobility in the EU
increase and also extend to all sectors, including health care, national
measures and mechanisms increasingly run the risk of being seen as
unjustified obstacles to free movement, which is prohibited under the
EC Treaty.[1] This chapter will focus particularly on the impact of the
EC Treaty rules on free movement of services, which encompass both
the principles of free provision of services (Article 49–50 EC) and of
free establishment of providers (Article 43 EC).

Mainly spurred on by the jurisprudence of the European Court
of Justice (the Court) and the action undertaken by the European
Commission, the application of these two principles has gradually
made its way into national health systems and has extended far
beyond the specific cases of patient and provider mobility. This trend
is followed with suspicion by many policy-makers and actors. They
mainly fear the deregulatory effect that is likely to cripple steering

---

[1] See Chapter 2 in this volume.

instruments and may conflict with the specific objectives pursued by national health policy and its important challenges. Most policy actors also point to the legal uncertainty created by the internal market logic and its inequitable consequences. The political debate, which culminated in the exclusion of health services from the Services Directive,[2] looks at how free movement principles can be reconciled with health policy objectives, and how an acceptable balance can be found between respecting free movement principles and the need to regulate and steer the health sector. This comes at a time when there is an increased emphasis on the economic dimension of the health sector, and its potential for boosting the Lisbon agenda is acknowledged.

Very often reference is made to the specific features characterizing this sector, which warrant specific treatment and attention. Firstly, the specificity of health policy lies in the fact that health and access to health care are acknowledged as fundamental human rights by several international treaties, including the Charter of Fundamental Rights of the European Union.[3] In addition, when health care is discussed in an economic context, the existence of important market failures that could occur when health care is delivered in an unregulated setting are highlighted. Primarily, the need for government regulatory intervention follows from the asymmetry of information between health care providers and patients. Patients generally lack the necessary background knowledge to make informed decisions about the care they need, as well as the quality and effectiveness of the care they receive, whereas health care providers have the unique power to induce demand and to set prices. Moreover, health care expenditure is highly concentrated among a minority of the population, which can be identified relatively easily on the basis of risk factors such as age, education level and socioeconomic status. Even if, in the health sector, competing economic actors are involved in organizing and providing health care, it is widely accepted that their activities require regulation to bring them fully in line with the goals of public health and social policy. Others have pointed to the risk that unbridled liberalization and deregulation in health care could make health systems less

---

[2] Article 2(2)(f), European Parliament and Council Directive 2006/123/EC on services in the internal market, OJ 2006 No. L376/36.

[3] Article 36, Charter of Fundamental Rights of the European Union, OJ 2000 No. C364/1.

effective, more costly and less equitable.[4] Since health care systems in the EU are mainly publicly financed, it is also important to take into account changes in the behaviour of both patients and health care providers that result from their awareness that the full cost or a substantial part thereof is born by a third public party/financier.[5] Given the fact that, as a consequence, patients are likely to seek to receive – and providers to seek to supply – more health care, government regulatory intervention is needed to prevent publicly funded systems from suffering losses in economic efficiency, which could undermine the entire health care system's sustainability.

This chapter provides a detailed analysis of the impact of the EC Treaty provisions on free movement of services on health systems. It particularly looks into the reasoning that EU institutions – particularly the European Court of Justice and the European Commission – have developed with respect to the provision of health care. Section two deals with the scope of free movement rules and focuses on the qualification of health care services as 'economic' activities within the meaning of the EC Treaty. The qualification as economic services is important, as it implies that national regulatory measures could be regarded as unjustified restrictions to free movement and therefore open to legal challenge by discriminated parties or the European Commission. In this way, free movement rules may affect the regulatory autonomy of Member States to organize health care and related national social security systems. It also looks at the notion of barriers to free movement in the field of health care. Here we will amplify how almost any regulatory or institutional aspect of health care provision can be challenged as a potential obstacle to free movement. In section three, we will explain that these regulatory measures will have to be justified and will flesh out how the conditions under which impediments to free movement can be justified. The section illustrates that providing good evidence to justify public intervention under the free movement rules is very challenging for health authorities.

---

[4] See, for example, A. Maynard, 'European health policy challenges', *Health Economics* 14 (2005), Supp: 256.

[5] In insurance-based health care systems, or more generally in insurance markets, this phenomenon is typically referred to as 'moral hazard'. For an overview of organizational responses to 'moral hazard', see C. Donaldson, K. Gerard and S. Jan (eds.), *Economics of health care financing: the visible hand* (London: Macmillan Press, 2003), p. 38.

Finally, section four will identify the relevant policy initiatives taken at a European level, will look at how Member States are dealing with the consequences of the relevant case-law, trying to reinstate legal certainty and regain control over policy in this area. More specifically, the section will discuss the Services Directive and the attempt to develop a more adapted Community framework for health services. It will also link to the discussion on social services of general interest, as it is commonly accepted that health care would qualify under this new concept in the European policy debate on positioning public service obligations. We will try to explain the complexity of the policy process and analyse why, so far, policy initiatives have not succeeded in presenting appropriate answers to the challenges at hand.

One major area of focus in this chapter is the 'creeping' application of the rules on free movement of services. However, the chapter will not address areas where specific EU legislation already has been developed. There are different scenarios that trigger free movement rules.[6] First of all, recipients of services – patients, in the first place, but also purchasers of care – can seek and contract to receive medical care abroad. This area has been mainly pushed by the European Court of Justice case-law based on Article 49 EC, which established a series of principles governing the statutory reimbursement of costs of health care provided abroad. This issue is analysed further in Chapter 12. Cross-border provision of private health insurance services is not tackled in this chapter either, as the issues are dealt with in Chapter 10 and are mainly governed by specific EU legislation. As a second dimension, the service activity itself can move across borders when the health care service is provided at a distance from another country, at the individual request of a recipient or a commissioner of services. The legal framework applicable when this service activity is provided by electronic means will be dealt with in Chapter 13 on EU law and e-health. Finally, EC Treaty rules on free movement of services also come into play when the health care provider moves across borders to deliver health care. Health care professionals can temporarily move to another country and challenge regulatory measures as unjustified restrictions to their free movement rights on the basis of Article 49 EC. But health care providers – such as health care professionals, pharmacies, clinical

---

[6] See also European Commission, 'Communication on the consultation regarding Community action on health services', SEC (2006) 1195/4, 26 September 2006.

laboratories or hospitals – can also move to another Member State on a more permanent basis with a view to supplying health care there. On the basis of Article 43 EC, these health care providers could argue that the regulatory barriers they face in the receiving state are a *prima facie* unlawful infringement to their freedom of establishment. The specific Community framework governing the free movement of health professionals will be analysed in more detail in Chapter 14. Our chapter will thus focus on the direct application of the free movement rules of the EC Treaty, which aim to ensure that providers can freely provide services temporarily (freedom to provide services) or permanently (freedom of establishment) in another Member State without the existence of specific secondary legislation.

2. Health care as an economic activity and its consequence

A. *The economic nature of health care*

The specificity of health care has for a long time dominated the European debate on the application of free movement principles in this sector. Since the development of health and social protection systems has been largely determined by the historical, social and economic background of individual countries, and national welfare states have drawn quite some legitimacy from the organization of these systems, traditionally some reluctance can be observed when it comes to sharing this competence with other administrative levels. Moreover, in legal terms, health care has long been considered to be 'an island beyond the reach of Community rules'.[7]

However, the only determining criterion to establish whether a service falls under the scope of the fundamental principles of free establishment (Article 43 EC) or free service provision (Article 49 EC) is its economic character. Services within the meaning of the EC Treaty are defined by Article 50 EC as any activities 'where they are normally provided for remuneration, insofar as they are not governed by the provisions relating to freedom of movement for goods, capital and persons'. The qualification of 'social' – or statutorily

---

[7] See Opinion of the Advocate General Tesauro in Case C-120/95, *Decker* v. *Caisse de Maladie des Employés Privés* [1998] ECR I-1831; and Case C-158/96, *Kohll* v. *Union des Caisses de Maladie* [1998] ECR I-1931.

covered – health care[8] as services under the meaning of Article 50
EC has raised quite some discussion. The constitutive element of
remuneration is particularly contentious for services that are of a
public nature or linked to the general interest.

Long before the application of EU free movement rules to the health
care sector was put on the political agenda by the well-known cases
of *Kohll* and *Decker*, the economic nature of (private) health services
was acknowledged by the Court in the cases *Luisi and Carbone*, and
Grogan.[9] The *Kohll* and *Decker* rulings of 1998 established for the
first time the link with statutory reimbursement and social security.[10]
Even if the Court accepted the specific nature of health care that is
provided within the context of a social security scheme, it did not
agree to remove it from the ambit of the fundamental principle of free
movement.[11] In its consecutive judgements, the Court further clarified
that the specific type of statutory cover – be it reimbursement, benefit-
in-kind or national health service – nor the specific type of health service – hospital or non-hospital – does not alter the economic nature of
the health service in question.[12]

Article 49 EC applies where a patient ... receives medical services in a hospital environment for consideration in a Member State other than her State
of residence, regardless of the way in which the national system with which
that person is registered and from which reimbursement of the cost of those
services is subsequently sought operates.[13]

To challenge this reasoning, often the comparison is made with courses
under national systems of public education, which were not considered

[8] J. Nickless, 'The internal market and the social nature of health care', in
    M. McKee, E. Mossialos and R. Baeten (eds.), *The impact of EU law on
    health care systems* (Brussels: PIE-Peter Lang, 2002), p. 64.
[9] Joined Cases 286/82 and 26/83, *Luisi and Carbone* v. *Ministero del Tesoro*
    [1984] ECR 377; Case C-159/90, *The Society for the Protection of Unborn
    Children Ireland Ltd* v. *Grogan* [1991] ECR I-4685.
[10] V. G. Hatzopoulos, 'The ECJ case law on cross-border aspects of the health
    services', DG Internal Policies of the Union Briefing Note, IP/A/IMCO/
    FWC/2006–167/C3/SC1, January 2007, p. 2, www.europarl.europa.eu/
    comparl/imco/studies/0701_healthserv_Ecj_En.pdf.
[11] Case C-158/96, *Kohll*, above n.7, para. 21. See also Case 279/80, *Webb*
    [1981] ECR 3305, para. 10.
[12] Case C-157/99, *Geraets-Smits and Peerbooms* [2001] ECR I-5473, paras. 53–5;
    Case C-385/99, *Müller-Fauré and Van Riet* [2003] ECR I-4509, para. 103.
[13] Case C-372/04, *Watts* [2006] ECR I-4325, para. 90.

by the Court to be economic activities.[14] To exclude public education from the scope of the free movement of services, the Court mainly referred to the fact that: (a) the price is not agreed upon between the service provider and the recipient; (b) the state, when establishing and maintaining a national education system, is not seeking to engage in any gainful activity but is fulfilling its duties towards its own population in the social, cultural and educational fields; and (c) the service is essentially financed from the public purse.[15] Despite obvious similarities and the fact that Member States as well as the Advocate General have referred to it, the Court has never been required to test whether these conditions have been fulfilled in the health care cases. The reason why the link with the public education cases has never been made seems to lie in the fact that, in the patient mobility cases, the persons concerned have always paid directly for the treatment received from the provider established in another Member State. Only subsequently has reimbursement for the costs incurred been sought from the statutory social security system in the home state. Therefore, the patient seems to have received the treatment in a private capacity and the supplier of the service could hardly be considered to be an agent of a public health service, at least not one to which the patient was affiliated.

Remarkably, the Court has always carefully avoided qualifying as a 'service' health services provided to a patient under the health system to which he or she is affiliated. In *Watts*, the Court clearly indicated that there was 'no need in the present case to determine whether the provision of hospital treatment in the context of a national health service such as the NHS is in itself a service within the meaning of those provisions [of Article 49]'.[16] It is established case-law that the Treaty provisions on free establishment and free provision of services do not apply to purely internal situations in a Member State.[17]

---

[14] Case 263/86, *Humbel* [1988] ECR 5365; Case C-109/92, *Wirth* [1993] ECR I-6447.

[15] The Court specified that the fact that pupils or their parents partly contribute to the operating expenses of the system does not alter the nature of the service within the meaning of the EC Treaty.

[16] Case C-372/04, *Watts*, above n.13, para. 91.

[17] For instance, Joined Cases C-54/88, C-91/88 and C-14/89, *Criminal proceedings against Eleonora Nino and Others* [1990] ECR I-3537, para. 12. However, recent case-law shows that freedom of establishment within the meaning of Article 43 EC even applies in the case of rules that lack a specific cross-border element. See below.

However, looking at the competition cases related to health care, where the economic nature of the activity – and the operator engaged in it – also needs to be acknowledged, it seems as though the Court has applied a more narrow approach to statutory health services delivered to domestic patients. In the *FENIN* case, the Court confirmed the judgement of the Court of First Instance, which held that the Spanish national health service management bodies should not be considered to be undertakings when purchasing goods, since this activity should not be dissociated from the subsequent use to which the goods are put – that is, in the provision of services free of charge to its members on the basis of universal cover and according to the principle of solidarity.[18]

It seems doubtful whether this classification as a 'non-economic' health service could be extended to all situations and all health systems.[19] Moreover, as the Advocate General in this case, Poiares Maduro, highlighted, the scope of freedom of competition and that of the freedom to provide services are not identical. There is nothing to prevent a transaction involving an exchange being classified as the provision of services, even where the parties to the exchange are not undertakings for the purposes of competition law.[20]

B. Barriers to free movement of services

The fact that the provision of health care is a service activity within the meaning of the EC Treaty implies that health care providers established in one Member State are granted a 'fundamental freedom' to establish themselves or provide their services in another Member State. Originally, the rationale behind the EC Treaty free movement rules was to eliminate discriminatory provisions and guarantee that service providers, including health service providers, established in one Member State and operating in the territory of another Member State – either

---

[18] Case C-205/03, *FENIN* [2006] ECR I-6295.

[19] S. A. de Vries, 'Patiëntenzorg in Europa na *Watts*: Wiens zorg?', *SEW – Tijdschrift voor Europees en Economisch Recht* 55 (2007), 136.

[20] Opinion of Advocate General Maduro in Case C-205/03, *FENIN*, above n.18, para. 51. See also E. Szyszczak, 'Competition law and services of general economic interest', Paper presented at the ERA Conference 'European Economic Integration and National Social Protection Systems: Towards a New Form of Internal Market', Brussels, 31 May-1 June 2007, p. 2.

temporarily or more permanently through an establishment – would enjoy the same conditions as the nationals of the state in which they operate (the principle of non-discrimination or national treatment). The interpretation of what constitutes a barrier to free movement has gradually extended to measures that in themselves are not directly discriminatory.

Articles 49–50 EC set out the principle of non-discrimination or national treatment in the case of temporary cross-border service provision. However, this principle was gradually abandoned from the Court's early jurisprudence onwards.[21] Indeed, the Court has interpreted Articles 49 and 50 EC to require that the host Member State refrain from imposing on health service providers established in another Member State other or additional rules that also do not apply to providers established in the host Member State. Apart from directly discriminatory rules, under Article 49 EC the Court also scrutinizes, on a case-by-case basis, measures that apply without distinction and that, although not in themselves discriminatory, would eventually have the same effect – in that existing conditions would make it easier for domestic providers to comply with these measures (so-called 'indistinctly applicable' or 'indirectly discriminatory' measures).[22] This applies when the measures are 'liable to prohibit or otherwise impede the activities of a provider of services established in another Member State'.[23] The judgment in *Commission* v. *France* provides a perfect illustration of this. The Court considered that the French requirement to have a business seat in France in order for biomedical analysis laboratories to obtain a license and to be authorized to work under the French statutory health insurance constituted a restriction to the freedom to provide services because 'it de facto precludes laboratories established in

---

[21] See, for instance, Case 107/83, *Klopp* [1984] ECR 2971; Joined Cases 154/87 and 155/87, *Wolf* [1988] ECR 3897; Case 143/87, *Stanton* [1988] ECR 3877.

[22] See also Case 120/78, *Cassis de Dijon* [1979] ECR 649.

[23] Case C-76/90, *Säger* v. *Dennemeyer* [1991] ECR I-4221, para. 12, and confirmed in recent case-law: 'Article [49] of the Treaty requires ... the abolition of any restriction, even if it applies without distinction to national providers of services and to those of other Member States, when it is liable to prohibit or otherwise impede the activities of a provider of services established in another Member State where he lawfully provides similar services'. See also, in the framework of patient mobility, Case C-157/99, *Geraets-Smits and Peerbooms*, above n.12, para. 69.

another Member State from being able to provide services to insured persons established in France'.[24]

A typical feature of temporary cross-border service provision under Articles 49 and 50 EC is that the health service provider that operates in another Member State does not cease to be regulated by its Member State of establishment. As a consequence, under Articles 49–50 EC, as interpreted by the Court, the host Member State is not entitled to restrict cross-border entry of health service providers into its market, where this would imply that the provider faces a double regulatory burden.[25] Thus, as soon as health service providers are established in a Member State and lawfully provide services similar to the ones that they intend to provide abroad they automatically acquire a right to provide their services in other Member States.[26] This position is based on the principle of mutual recognition, which is one of the corner-stones of the single market, as it guarantees free movement without the need to harmonize Member States' legislation.[27] However, as we will discuss below, this mutual recognition principle, according to which the rules of the Member State of origin prevail, is applied in a conditional manner.

When health service providers move (or wish to move) to another Member State on a more permanent basis in order to operate there, they are caught by the principle of freedom of establishment under Article 43 EC. Given the fact that most health care providers moving to another Member State in order to provide their services there are

---

[24] Case C-496/01, *Commission v. France* [2004] ECR I-2351, para. 91. The fact that the Court recognizes that it is for the Member State in which the patient is affiliated to decide which medical treatments are covered by sickness insurance and to establish the extent to which sickness coverage is made available to its insured patients does not change this conclusion. Case C-385/99, *Müller-Fauré*, above n.12, para. 98.

[25] E. Spaventa, 'From Gebhard to Carpenter: towards a (non-)economic European Constitution', *Common Market Law Review* 41 (2004), 743–73, at 748; K. A. Armstrong, 'Mutual recognition', in C. Barnard and J. Scott (eds.), *The legal foundations of the single market* (Oxford: Hart, 2002), p. 226.

[26] V. G. Hatzopoulos, *Le principe communautaire d'équivalence et de reconnaissance mutuelle dans la libre prestation de services* (Brussels: Bruylant, 1999), p. 192.

[27] European Commission, 'Communication from the Commission to the Council and the European Parliament on mutual recognition in the context of the follow-up to the action plan for the single market', COM (1999) 299 final, 16 June 1999.

likely to require some form of establishment in that Member State, the EC Treaty provisions on freedom of establishment have a potentially greater impact on Member States' regulatory autonomy. The notion of establishment, as interpreted by the Court, can be considered to include the setting up or running of a clinical laboratory, a pharmacy, a hospital facility or even the private practice of a self-employed health care professional, provided that, in accordance with the Court's case-law, the presence of a stable and continuous participation in the economic life of the host Member State is proven.[28]

From a regulatory point of view, the situation of a health care provider operating under Article 43 EC differs from the scenario under Article 49 EC because, in the former case, the service provider ceases, for most purposes, to be governed by the Member State of previous establishment, with the result that the application of the host Member State's rules will not imply a double regulatory burden.[29] Although the text of Article 43 EC does not only target national restrictions that are discriminatory on the basis of nationality, the European Court of Justice has traditionally adopted a rather narrow approach to its interpretation. Admittedly, Article 43(2) mentions 'the conditions laid down for its own nationals', referring to the host state, but this is 'included' within the idea of freedom of establishment, not determinative of it. For instance, with regard to the refusal under the Belgian social security scheme to reimburse the services of clinical biology laboratories whose members, partners or directors are not all natural persons[30] authorized to carry out medical analyses, the Court argued that equality of treatment was still respected and that 'each Member State is, in the absence of Community rules in this area, free to lay down rules for its own territory governing the activities of laboratories providing clinical biology services'.[31] The Court concluded that the refusal was not an infringement of Article 43 EC (formerly Article 52 EC) since the measures applied without distinction to Belgian nationals and those of other states and that 'the Belgian law does not prevent doctors or pharmacists who

---

[28] See, for example, Case C-55/94, *Gebhard* [1995] ECR I-4165, para. 25; Case C-70/95, *Sodemare* [1997] ECR I-3395, para. 24.

[29] Spaventa, 'From Gebhard to Carpenter', above n.25, 748.

[30] 'Natural persons' is a legal term meaning individual human beings, as opposed to 'legal persons', which are firms, companies and so on.

[31] Case 221/85, *Commission* v. *Belgium* [1987] ECR 719, para. 9.

are nationals of other Member States from establishing themselves in Belgium and operating there a laboratory to carry out clinical analyses qualifying for reimbursement under the social security system'.[32] Moreover, in the *Sodemare* case, which concerned a Luxembourg profit-making company that was denied permission to run elderly care homes through subsidiaries in Italy because Italian legislation reserved private participation in the state social welfare system only for non-profit operators, the Court adopted a similar reasoning.[33] Contrary to the Opinion of the Advocate-General, who argued that the Italian law was indirectly discriminatory,[34] the Court suggested that the fact that profit-making companies were automatically excluded from participating in the running of a statutory social welfare system could not be regarded as a breach of the principle of freedom of establishment, as this would not place profit-making companies from other Member States in a less favourable factual or legal situation to profit-making companies from the Member State in which they are established.[35]

However, the European Court of Justice has gradually broadened the application of Article 43 EC from covering only directly discriminatory rules towards covering rules that are only liable to create discrimination (indistinctly applicable or indirectly discriminatory measures), in particular through a series of cases linked to national legislation establishing a single-practice rule, preventing health professionals from maintaining their registration or practice in one Member State when trying to establish themselves in another Member State. According to the Court, such rules are not compatible with the principle of freedom of establishment, as they constitute a restriction that is liable to create discrimination against practitioners established in another Member State or to raise obstacles to accessing the profession that go beyond what is necessary to achieve the intended objectives.[36] The Court observed that single-practice rules were applied

---

[32] *Ibid.*, para. 11.   [33] Case C-70/95, *Sodemare*, above n.28.
[34] *Ibid.*, Opinion of Advocate General Fennelly.   [35] *Ibid.*, paras. 33–4.
[36] Case C-96/85, *Commission* v. *France* [1986] ECR I-1475; Case C-351/90, *Commission* v. *Luxembourg* [1992] ECR I-3945. See also Case 107/83, *Klopp*, above n.21 (on the legal profession). V. G. Hatzopoulos, 'Killing national health and insurance systems but healing patients? The European market for health care services after the judgements of the ECJ in *Vanbraekel* and *Peerbooms*', *Common Market Law Review* 39 (2002), 683–729, at 703.

more severely to health professionals from other Member States and concluded that the measures were unduly restrictive.[37]

From 1993, the European Court of Justice progressively expanded the prohibition mentioned in Article 43 from (directly and indirectly) discriminatory rules to all 'national measures liable to hinder or make less attractive the exercise of fundamental freedoms guaranteed by the Treaty'[38] and made these measures subject to justification. In the landmark *Gebhard* case, a German lawyer, qualified as a '*Rechtsanwalt*' in Germany but working in Italy and using the title of '*avvocato*' without being registered with the local Italian bar, successfully argued before the Court that this registration requirement was an obstacle to freedom of establishment that needed justification.[39]

The impact on health care of the expansion of Article 43 towards *indistinctly applicable* measures is even more substantial than in the case of Article 49 EC. Whereas (health) service providers can challenge certain national regulatory measures as barriers to Article 49 EC because they essentially constitute a double regulatory burden, (health) service providers can now also lawfully rely upon Article 43 EC to challenge the very existence of regulatory measures, even if these measures lack any specific cross-border element.[40] This is particularly important for the field of health care, as it is characterized by a vast array of regulatory interventions, such as rules on professional behaviour, patient access, quality and effectiveness, taxation, and payments and pricing, etc., which do not specifically relate to cross-border situations.[41]

The measures that are subject to scrutiny under the principle of free movement not only include regulation directly governing access to a national health care services market; they also include regulation that governs the exercise of the health care activity itself.

---

[37] Case C-96/85, *Commission v. France*, above n.36, paras. 12–3; Case 351/90, *Commission v. Luxembourg*, above n.36, paras. 15 and 19.

[38] Case C-55/94, *Gebhard*, above n.28, para. 37.

[39] *Ibid.*, para. 37. This was confirmed in two health care cases that concerned national regulatory measures reserving the exercise of certain medical activities for doctors: Case C-8/96, *Mac Quen* [2001] ECR I-837; and Case C-294/00, *Deutsche Paracelsus Schulen v. Gräbner* [2002] ECR I-6515.

[40] Spaventa, 'From Gebhard to Carpenter', above n.25, 749.

[41] This has also been analysed by Y. Jorens and M. Coucheir 'The European legal framework in relation to provider mobility', Europe for Patients Project, Deliverable to the European Commission, WP 2, unpublished (2005), p. 74.

In addition to the purely quantitative restrictions that limit the number of health care providers entitled to provide their services in a Member State's territory (for example, territorial planning rules restricting the number of health service providers (such as pharmacies) according to the number of inhabitants and the minimum distance between them, or quota systems limiting the number of health professionals working within the statutory health system),[42] qualitative measures that limit access to a certain activity and that can even result in restricting the number of service providers can also be targeted. These categories can cover a broad range of requirements, as illustrated in the list below, which includes examples from case-law and policy documents:

- ownership rules for clinics and pharmacies;[43]
- bans on operating more than one entity;[44]
- bans on enterprises active in the distribution of medicines (or having links with companies active in this area) acquiring holdings in private pharmaceutical companies or community pharmacies;[45]
- limits on the choice of legal form for clinics or pharmacies;[46]
- bans on opening a pharmacy in areas without a doctor's surgery;[47]
- refusals under a national social security scheme to reimburse services of clinical biology laboratories whose members, partners or directors are not all natural persons authorized to carry out medical analyses;[48]

---

[42] Case C-456/05, *Commission v. Germany* [2007] ECR I-10517.

[43] Joined Cases C-171/07 and C-172/07, *Apothekerkammer des Saarlandes and Others* (not yet reported) (prohibition of foreign ownership of pharmacies); Case C-531/06, *Commission v. Italy* (not yet reported) (national rules reserving the ownership of pharmacies for pharmacists or legal entities consisting of pharmacists).

[44] European Commission's reasoned opinions to Spain (No. 2001/5261) and Austria (No. 2004/4468). See European Commission, 'Internal market: infringement proceedings concerning Italy, Austria and Spain with regard to pharmacies', Press Release No. IP/06/858, 28 June 2006, http://europa.eu/rapid/pressReleasesAction.do?reference=IP/06/858&format=HTML&aged=1&language=EN&guiLanguage=en.

[45] Case C-531/06, *Commission v. Italy*, above n.43.

[46] Case C-171/07 and C-172/07, *Apothekerkammer des Saarlandes*, above n.43.

[47] European Commission, 'Internal market', above n.44.

[48] Case C-221/85, *Commission v. Belgium* [1987] ECR 719.

- prohibitions on the enrolment in a professional register of any doctor or dental surgeon who is still enrolled or registered in another Member State;[49]
- national rules reserving the task of carrying out certain medical activities to a category of professionals holding specific qualifications, to the exclusion of health providers who are not qualified medical doctors;[50]
- requirements to obtain an authorization to set up a private outpatient clinic for dental medicine[51] or requirements to have a place of business within a national territory in order to obtain the requisite operational authorization and to work under the statutory health insurance system;[52] and
- rules on minimum staff levels.[53]

All of these elements remain subject to scrutiny under the EC Treaty provisions for as long as they are not replaced by any harmonizing, secondary EU-level rules, which would then become the only framework of judicial review,[54] as is the case, for instance, for minimum training requirements for service providers.[55]

In light of this broadened interpretation of what is to be considered an obstacle to free movement, the Court's earlier assessment of measures that were not seen as discriminatory is likely to be called into question again.

Indeed, this is what happened with the Court's judgment in the above-mentioned Belgian case regarding the refusal to reimburse for services provided by clinical biology laboratories whose members, partners or directors are not all natural persons authorized to carry

---

[49] Case C-96/85, *Commission v. France*, above n.36.

[50] Case C-108/96, *Mac Queen*, above n.39.

[51] Case C-169/07, *Hartlauer Handelsgesellschaft mbH* v. *Wiener Landesregierung and Oberösterreichische Landesregierung* (not yet reported).

[52] Case C-496/01, *Commission v. France*, above n.24.

[53] Article 15(2)(f), European Parliament and Council Directive 2006/123/EC on services in the internal market, OJ 2006 No. L376/36. The original proposal of the European Commission also applied to health and health care services, see European Commission, 'Proposal for a Directive of the European Parliament and of the Council on services in the internal market', COM (2004) 2/3 final, 5 March 2004, Article 4(1), Juncto Recital 14.

[54] Case C-37/92, *Vanacker and Lesage* [1993] ECR I-4947, para. 9; Case C-324/99, *DaimlerChrysler* [2001] ECR I-9897, para. 32; Case C-322/01, *DocMorris* [2003] ECR I-14877, para. 64.

[55] See Chapter 14 in this volume.

out medical analyses. Where the Court initially did not consider this an infringement of Article 43 EC, since the measures applied without distinction to Belgian nationals and those of other states, fifteen years later the European Commission started to question very similar rules. On 18 July 2002, a formal request was sent inviting Belgium to modify certain provisions of the Royal Decree laying down conditions in relation to clinical analysis.[56] The Commission was of the opinion that Belgium imposed conditions that were too restrictive on medical laboratories in order to qualify for reimbursement by the sickness insurance scheme. Apart from the requirement that clinical laboratories had to be run by doctors, pharmacists or chemical science graduates, these conditions also included a ban on operators running more than one laboratory within a specific geographical area and a ban preventing operators from having links with other entities active in the medical profession. Belgium subsequently modified its national legislation. On 13 December 2006, in a reasoned opinion, the European Commission requested that France modify its legislation on ownership of biological analysis laboratories. According to the Commission, the legislation restricted non-biologists from owning a stake in a firm operating biological analysis laboratories and prohibited an individual or a legal entity from owning stakes in more than two firms set up to jointly operate one or more medical biological analysis laboratories, both of which were alleged to be incompatible with Article 43 EC.[57]

Moreover, the status of the *Sodemare* landmark ruling has become more uncertain today. In that judgment, the Court took for granted that a Member State, in exercising its power to organize its social security system, may indeed consider it necessary to achieve the exclusively social aims of the system by limiting the scope of contracting to non-profit-making private operators,[58] despite the obvious restrictive nature of this rule. This almost gives the impression that the Court considered activities performed within social welfare systems to be non-economic in nature, falling outside the scope of Treaty rules on free movement altogether. However, this position would contradict

---

[56] Royal Decree No. 143 of 30 December 1982.
[57] European Commission, 'Free movement of services: infringement proceedings against France', Press Release No. IP/06/1793, 13 December 2006.
[58] Case C-70/95, *Sodemare*, above n.28, paras. 31–2.

more recent judgments.[59] The Court has always recognized Member States' sovereign powers to organize their social security systems in the absence of harmonization at EU level, as long as these powers are exercised in compliance with EU law, in particular the provision on the freedom to provide services.[60] Within these terms, the logic acknowledges the existence of differences between national regulatory regimes and accepts that public intervention may be necessary to correct for certain market failures or to guarantee certain principles and values of general interest, such as social justice.[61]

Despite the political importance of the *Sodemare* judgement, confirming the power of Member States to make strategic and value-based choices in the context of their social protection system by distinguishing between certain types of providers of social welfare services, it is clear that today this delicate balance between Member States' regulatory autonomy in the field of national health systems and the application of free movement rules will have to be implemented in the context of finding a justification for impediments. Thus, the key question focuses on whether the specific measure impeding free movement is necessary to fulfil a public interest objective and whether it is proportionate. The accepted grounds of justification and the manner in which the necessity and Proportionality Tests apply to health care will be analysed further in the following section.

3. Justified and unjustified restrictions to free movement in health care

A. From 'non-discrimination' to 'justification'

From the analysis above, it follows that the threshold for the application of EC Treaty free movement rules on health services is relatively low. Although rules on free movement of services were originally considered to target discrimination against service providers by another

---

[59] Hatzopoulos, 'Killing national health', above n.36, 721.

[60] Case C-372/04, *Watts*, above n.13, para. 92.

[61] T. K. Hervey and J. V. McHale, *Health law and the European Union* (Cambridge: Cambridge University Press, 2004), p. 46; K. Lenaerts and T. Heremans, 'Contours of a European social union in the case-law of the European Court of Justice', *European Constitutional Law Review* 2 (2006), 101–15, at 109–10.

Member State, the European Court of Justice's scrutiny now extends to measures that apply without distinction to domestic providers and providers from abroad. Consequently, almost any regulatory or institutional aspect of health care provision can be challenged as a potential obstacle to free movement.[62]

Despite the fact there is a low threshold for the application of free movement, the EC Treaty does not intend to create a completely deregulated internal market nor does it give health care providers unconditional access to a particular domestic health care market. Regarding both the freedom to provide services and the freedom of establishment, Member States are allowed to maintain barriers to free movement provided that they are justified in the public interest. The justification consists of a Necessity Test and a Proportionality Test. Along with the condition that the measure is applied in a non-discriminatory manner, Member States have to prove that it is objectively necessary for ensuring the attainment of a public interest objective (Necessity Test), and that it does not exceed what is necessary to attain the objective, nor that the same result can be achieved by a less restrictive rule (Proportionality Test).[63]

For service providers established in a Member State wishing to provide their services temporarily abroad, we highlighted in the previous section that the Court introduced the principle of mutual recognition. However, this mutual recognition principle, according to which the rules of the Member State of origin (home state) prevail, is applied in a conditional manner. It allows the Member State of destination (host state) to justify a national measure that constitutes a barrier to the freedom to provide services.[64] Hence, the main question related to Article 49 EC seems to be to what extent the host Member State will be entitled

---

[62] G. Davies, 'The process and side-effects of harmonisation of European welfare states', Jean Monnet Working Paper 02/06 (2006), www. jeanmonnetprogram.org/papers/06/060201.pdf.

[63] See cases on patient mobility: e.g., Case C-385/99, *Müller-Fauré*, above n.12, para. 68; Case C-157/99, *Geraets-Smits and Peerbooms*, above n.12, para. 75. See also Case C-76/90, *Säger*, above n.23, paras. 15–7; Case C-275/92, *Customs and Excise Commissioners* v. *Schindler and Schindler* [1994] ECR I-1039. Compare with Case C-405/98, *Gourmet International* [2001] ECR I-1795 (mutual recognition also amounts to an obligation in the home state to recognize the right of a provider established in its territory to provide services in another Member State).

[64] See also C. Barnard and S. Deakin, 'Market access and regulatory competition', in C. Barnard and J. Scott (eds.), *The legal foundations of the single European*

to impose additional requirements on health providers who are already subject to regulation in their home state.[65] Similarly, for service providers wishing to move more permanently to another Member State, the Court also gradually subjected to justification the 'national measures liable to hinder or make less attractive the exercise' of their freedom of establishment. In the *Gebhard* case, mentioned above, the Court agreed that the registration requirement was an obstacle to the freedom of establishment that needed justification: 'they must be applied in a non-discriminatory manner; they must be justified by imperative requirements in the general interest, they must be suitable for securing the attainment of the objective which they pursue; and they must not go beyond what is necessary in order to attain it'.[66] This *Gebhard* formula was later confirmed in two health care cases, *Mac Quen*[67] and *Gräbner*,[68] which dealt with national provisions reserving the exercise of certain medical activities to physicians. In both cases, the restrictions were considered justified and necessary to protect public health. We will now have a closer look at the way justification can be obtained.

B. The Necessity Test: is regulatory intervention in the field of health care imperative for the protection of a higher public interest goal?

Under the Necessity Test, Member States will have to show that it is 'not reasonably practical' to adjust their regulatory arrangements in the field of health care to allow free movement of services and that these arrangements are genuinely necessary.[69] As shown by recent case-law, the Court is well aware of the potentially devastating effects of applying free movement rules to the detriment of public health

---

market (Oxford: Hart, 2002), p. 213: once a market access test is adopted, there is a presumption in favour of market access, which can be rebutted by the Member State demonstrating an overriding national or public interest.

[65] Spaventa, 'From Gebhard to Carpenter', above n.25, 748.

[66] Case C-55/94, *Gebhard*, above n.28, para. 37.

[67] Case C-108/96, *Mac Quen*, above n.39: Belgian national rules reserve the task of carrying out certain optical examinations to a category of professionals holding specific qualifications, such as ophthalmologists, to the exclusion of opticians who are not qualified medical doctors.

[68] Case C-294/00, *Deutsche Paracelsus Schulen* v. *Gräbner*, above n.39, concerning prohibition of the exercise of the activity of 'healer' by people not qualified as doctors. See above.

[69] Davies, 'The process and side-effects', above n.62, p. 28.

or the sustainability of national health systems and related social protection.

At the heart of the Necessity Test lies the identification of a public interest objective. First of all, there is a specific Treaty-based exception in Article 46(1) EC for regulatory arrangements that protect public health.[70] Even if this exception could not permit the exclusion of the health care sector as a whole from the scope of free movement,[71] the Court accepted within this derogation that Member States could restrict the freedom to provide medical and hospital services in so far as this was deemed necessary for the objectives of maintaining a balanced medical and hospital service open to all and a treatment facility or medical competence within a national territory that is essential for the public health and even the survival of the population.[72]

Apart from the Treaty-based exception of the protection of public health, the Court has adopted the concept of the 'rule of reason' to justify non-discriminatory measures that serve the public interest. However, these rule of reason justifications can only be used for indirectly discriminatory measures, and thus not for measures that are directly discriminatory on grounds of nationality. In this respect, the Court accepts a long list of public interest objectives that need to be safeguarded in health care, such as the risk of seriously undermining the financial balance of the social security system[73] or to prevent overcapacity in the supply of medical care. In doing so, the Court's case-law recognizes the Member States' need for health care planning.[74] With regard to hospital planning, for instance,[75] the Court recognized that:

For one thing, such planning seeks to ensure that there is sufficient and permanent access to a balanced range of high-quality hospital treatment in the State concerned. For another thing, it assists in meeting a desire to control

---

[70] Article 46 EC applies equally to free establishment as to free provision of services (see Article 55 EC).

[71] Case C-158/96, *Kohll*, above n.7, para. 46.

[72] *Ibid.*, paras. 50–1.

[73] *Ibid.*, para. 41. The Court, however, recalls that aims of a purely economic nature cannot justify a barrier to the fundamental principle of freedom to provide services.

[74] Lenaerts and Heremans, 'Contours of a European social union', above n.61, 110. See also Davies, 'The process and side-effects', above n.62, p. 111.

[75] Hospital planning is said to cover 'the number of hospitals, their geographical distribution, the way in which they are organised and the

costs and to prevent, as far as possible, any wastage of financial, technical and human resources. Such wastage would be all the more damaging because it is generally recognised that the hospital care sector generates considerable costs and must satisfy increasing needs, while the financial resources which may be made available for healthcare are not unlimited, whatever the mode of funding applied.[76]

While it is established case-law that 'purely economic' reasons cannot justify restrictions,[77] it is clear that, nevertheless, the Court considers the financial impact of the exercise of the free movement right on a case-by-case basis, through the justification of any threat of financial imbalance to the social security system (mentioned above).[78] The concern over financial balance not only relates to the national systems that are funded through the collection of social security contributions. In certain Member States, the health care budget is not (or not entirely) financed by social security contributions, but partly (or even entirely) financed by tax income. Thus, it is useful to qualify the assessment of the threat of financial imbalance as an assessment of the impact on so-called 'macro-affordability', which means the affordability of the whole welfare system.[79]

Apart from identifying public interest objectives motivating any regulatory intervention that might obstruct free movement, Member States will also have to adopt strict reasoning as to why these measures

[76] facilities with which they are provided, and even the nature of the medical services which they are able to offer'. See, *inter alia*, Case C-372/04, *Watts*, above n.13, para. 108; Case C-385/99, *Müller-Fauré*, above n.12, para. 77; Case C-157/99, *Geraets-Smits and Peerbooms*, above n.12, para. 76.

[76] Case C-372/04, *Watts*, above n.13, para. 109; Case C-385/99, *Müller-Fauré*, above n.12, paras. 79–80; Case C-157/99, *Geraets-Smits and Peerbooms*, above n.12, paras. 78–9.

[77] Case C-398/95, *SETTG* [1997] ECR I-3091, para. 23; Case C-158/96, *Kohll*, above n.7, para. 41; Case C-385/99, *Müller-Fauré*, above n.12, para. 72.

[78] This overriding reason is directly linked to the justification of 'the need to preserve the cohesion of the tax system' as introduced by the European Court of Justice in the *Bachmann* case. Case C-204/90, *Bachmann* [1992] ECR I-249. See also Case C-300/90, *Commission* v. *Belgium* [1992] ECR I-305; V. G. Hatzopoulos, 'Do the rules on internal market affect national health care systems?', in M. McKee, E. Mossialos and R. Baeten (eds.), *The impact of EU laws on health care systems* (Brussels: PIE-Peter Lang, 2002), pp. 138–9.

[79] Lenaerts and Heremans, 'Contours of a European social union', above n.61, 110–1. See also Davies, 'The process and side-effects', above n.62, p. 30. Davies argues that the Court will only consider the financial impact if it is such that the stability of the entire domestic system is threatened.

are the only ones possible to ensure the public interest objective, with less restrictive measures being insufficient to attain the objective. This will be assessed through the Proportionality Test.

C. The Proportionality Test: does the obstruction of free movement go beyond what is necessary?

The core of the justification procedure lies not so much in the identification of a public interest objective as in the proof of the targeted measure's proportionality towards achieving it. Member States' ability to regulate health service providers from abroad operating in their territory – either temporarily or more permanently through an establishment – seems to become subject to a general proportionality requirement,[80] even if rules are also applicable without distinction to domestic care providers. Member States wishing to maintain obstacles to free movement as proportionate measures face a relatively high burden of proof. In addition, the Court requires that all the particular circumstances of an individual case be examined. Even if a rule, in general, is justified, this does not automatically mean that it is justified in each specific situation. This flexibility requirement is very demanding for regulation.[81] Even though the Court tends to leave a wide margin of discretion to the Member States to substantiate that national measures are not disproportionate to the 'public interest' objectives concerned, such as the protection of public health or the safeguarding of the balance of the social security system,[82] it will often be difficult for health regulators to provide evidence on the proportionality of the regulation in question.

---

[80] Jorens and Coucheir, 'European legal framework', above n.41, p. 5; Davies, 'The process and side-effects', above n.62, p. 33.

[81] Davies, 'The process and side-effects', above n.62, p. 29.

[82] See, for example, Spaventa, 'From Gebhard to Carpenter', above n.25, 764; and Y. Jorens, M. Coucheir and F. Van Overmeiren, 'Access to health care in an internal market: impact for statutory and complementary systems', *Bulletin Luxembourgeois des questions sociales* 18 (2005), 1–136, at 27. This conclusion is somewhat different in the case of harmonizing measures at EU level. See, for example, W. Sauter, 'Services of general economic interest (SGEI) and universal service obligations (USO) as an EU law framework for curative health care', TILEC Discussion Paper, DP 2007–029, Tilburg University, September 2007.

The Proportionality Test in the case of temporary provision of health care services

In cases where Member State rules target health care providers offering services temporarily in their territory, they have to take into account measures to which these providers are already subject in their home states. In order to lawfully maintain rules imposed on health care providers established in another Member State, the host state will have to provide – on a case-by-case basis – very good reasons to maintain a double regulatory burden. This means that the host Member State will have to demonstrate that the legislation of the Member State of establishment does not adequately protect the particular public interest objective.[83] The host Member State, for instance, will have to accept the quality standards and the quality checks performed in the Member State of establishment, provided that they guarantee equivalent protection. In the above-mentioned case where France required a business seat in France for biomedical analysis laboratories to obtain the necessary operating license and to be authorized to work under the French statutory health insurance, the Court concluded that it went beyond what is objectively necessary for the purpose of ensuring a high level of public health protection as required under Article 46 EC.[84] In response to the French Government's argument that the requirement allowed effective quality controls, the Court stated that the French authorities could instead require laboratories established in another Member State to prove that the controls carried out by the Member State in which they already have their place of business 'are no less strict than those applicable in France and monitor compliance with provisions which safeguard at least the same level of health protection as the French rules'.[85]

The argument that, in the absence of EU-level harmonization or bilateral agreements, it is impossible for inspectors from one Member State to carry out on-the-spot checks with health care providers in other Member States was also raised in cases dealing with patients who sought reimbursement for treatment abroad. In the *Stamatelaki* case, the Greek national social security system

---

[83] Jorens and Coucheir, 'European legal framework', above n.41, p. 56; Davies, 'The process and side-effects', above n.62, p. 28. See Case C-272/94, *Guiot* [1996] ECR I-1905.
[84] Case C-496/01, *Commission v. France*, above n.24, para. 92.
[85] Case C-496/01, *Commission v. France*, above n.24, para. 74.

excluded all reimbursement of hospital treatment to Greek citizens provided by a private hospital in another Member State (in this case, the United Kingdom), with the exception of children under fourteen. The Greek Government argued that the exclusion was justified, *inter alia*, by the fact that:

Greek social security institutions do not check the quality of treatment provided in private hospitals in another Member State and verification as to whether hospitals with which an agreement has been entered into are able to provide appropriate – identical or equivalent – medical treatment [is lacking].[86]

The Court dismissed the argument by saying that private hospitals in other Member States are also subject to quality controls and that doctors established in those states who operate in those establishments provide professional guarantees equivalent to those of doctors established in Greece, by reference to EU-level legislation on mutual recognition of professional qualifications.[87]

The argument that restrictions are justified on the basis of the need to guarantee quality of health services as part of the protection of public health was already dismissed by the Court in the *Kohll* judgement, also referring to the EU-level framework concerning the mutual recognition of professional qualifications.[88] However, such an EU-level framework does not exist for quality standards and quality controls in hospitals. Nonetheless, the Court also applied the mutual recognition principle in the *Stamatelaki* case.[89] For the attainment of the 'protection of public health' objective, the Greek Government needed to rely upon checks by the Member State of the treating hospital. However, the imposition of mutual trust in the absence of minimum rules at EU level or bilateral agreements is not a self-evident solution. As a recent European study shows, there is a wide variation between and within Member States in the way and the extent to which they have implemented programmes to ensure quality of care. In particular, there is great diversity in the quality

---

[86] Case C-444/05, *Stamatelaki* [2007] ECR I-3185, para. 36.
[87] Such as European Parliament and Council Directive 2005/36/EC on the recognition of professional qualifications, OJ 2005 No. L255/22.
[88] Case C-158/96, *Kohll*, above n.7, para. 49.
[89] Case C-444/05, *Stamatelaki*, above n.86, paras. 36–7.

of clinical care.[90] In its proposal for a health services directive, the European Commission included a provision imposing on Member States the responsibility to ensure quality and safety standards of health care, to redress this gap in EU law and to ensure quality standards to patients seeking care abroad.[91]

Another important aspect of the Proportionality Test is to assess whether there are no other measures available to the host Member State that are less restrictive to the freedom to provide services. In the French case of biomedical analysis laboratories, the Court suggested a less restrictive alternative in proposing that France might impose its level of public health protection on laboratories established in another Member State but wishing to offer services to members of the national sickness insurance scheme through an authorization scheme rather than requiring an establishment in France.[92] Similarly, in the *Stamatelaki* case, the Court concluded that excluding reimbursement of any treatment in a foreign private hospital was a disproportionate measure, because less restrictive alternative measures were available, such as the implementation of a prior authorization scheme and, if appropriate, the determination of reimbursement scales for the cost of treatment.[93] Nevertheless, the Court seems to provide Member States with 'a clear means of restricting, or at least rationalizing, "exodus" from the national welfare system towards other Member States' facilities, through the use of a prior authorization procedure'.[94] In line with the Court's rulings in the cases on reimbursements of costs for medical treatment abroad, authorization procedures must, however, 'be based on objective, non-discriminatory criteria which are known in advance'.[95]

In assessing whether the host Member State should have relied upon a less restrictive measure in a particular case, the European Court of Justice often directly refers to the presence (or the absence) of a

---

[90] H. Legido-Quigley *et al.*, *Assuring the quality of health care in the European Union* (Copenhagen: WHO Regional Office for Europe on behalf of the European Observatory on Health Systems and Policies, 2008).
[91] European Commission, 'Proposal for a Directive of the European Parliament and of the Council on the application of patients' rights in cross-border healthcare', COM (2008) 414 final, 2 July 2008.
[92] Case C-496/01, *Commission* v. *France*, above n.24, para. 93.
[93] Case C-444/05, *Stamatelaki*, above n.86, para. 35.
[94] V. Hatzopoulos and T. U. Do, 'The case law of the ECJ concerning the free provision of services: 2000–2005', *Common Market Law Review* 43 (2006), 923–991, at 941.
[95] See, for example, Case C-372/04, *Watts*, above n.13, para. 116.

particular EU-level framework. In the *Gräbner* case, which dealt with the exercise of a particular medical profession in a Member State's territory, the Court recognized that:

[T]he decision of a Member State to restrict to a group of professionals with specific qualifications, such as qualified doctors, the right to carry out medical diagnoses and prescribe treatments for illness or to alleviate physical or mental disorders may be considered to be a suitable means of achieving the objective of safeguarding public health.[96]

Faced with the question of whether a Member State could then lawfully prohibit the exercise of a medical activity by those not qualified as doctors – *in casu*, 'healers' – the Court concluded that this did 'not go beyond what is necessary to achieve the aim of safeguarding public health',[97] despite the fact that it could be argued that a less restrictive measure existed to safeguard public health. Deutsche Paracelsus Schulen submitted that the Austrian authorities could have made the exercise of the profession of '*Heilpraktiker*' subject to a certain period of practice or to an examination (of the knowledge and aptitude of the applicant) similar to that provided for by the German legislation.[98] The Court particularly referred to the fact that there was no definition at the EU level of activities that are restricted to persons with a doctor's qualification. Even though it respected the host Member State's assessment of the public health risk linked to the performance of medical acts by people without a doctor's qualification, it stressed nonetheless that this assessment was liable to change over time due to progress made on knowledge of methods and their effects on health.[99]

The analysis of the Proportionality Test in the Court's case-law clearly shows that the mutual recognition principle is applied in a conditional manner. However, under its initial proposal for a services directive, the European Commission opted for automatic mutual recognition.[100] Service providers, including health care providers, would only be subject to the national provisions of their Member State of origin and this principle would apply to all requirements applicable to access to service activities as well to the exercise thereof, regardless

---

[96] Case C-294/00, *Deutsche Paracelsus Schulen*, above n.39, para. 43.
[97] *Ibid.*, para. 50. [98] *Ibid.*, para. 45. [99] *Ibid.*, paras. 48–9.
[100] European Commission, 'Proposal for a Directive' above n.53, Article 16.

of whether they fall within an area harmonized at the EU level and regardless of the legal field to which they belong under national law.[101] At the same time, the European Commission included a detailed (limited) list of derogations to the country of origin principle for certain service activities and certain EU-level rules, including the ones on the recognition of professional qualifications.[102]

Even though mutual recognition, as proposed by the European Commission, certainly drew inspiration from the Court's case-law, it clearly went significantly further. Whereas, under the Court's case-law, host Member State rules are only side-stepped in so far as their application would give rise to unjustified restrictions to free movement, the Commission's proposal declared the mutual recognition principle to be unconditional, since it prevented the host Member State from continuing to rely upon restrictions to free movement that were not necessarily prohibited under EC Treaty rules. The European Commission introduced a specific procedure for Member States wishing to apply for an individual derogation to the country of origin principle on the basis of public order, public health and public safety. However, the Commission's list of grounds – referred to earlier – was more limited compared to the justification grounds recognized by the Court.[103]

The introduction of the country of origin principle not only caused a legal debate, it prompted many health policy stakeholders to declare that the general application of the country of origin principle was incompatible with the provision of health care, which, by its nature, required a high level of regulatory intervention from the Member State in which the health care is provided.[104] The controversy surrounding the impact of

[101] *Ibid.*, Articles 16 and 4(9), Juncto Recital 21.
[102] *Ibid.*, Articles 17 and 18.
[103] The fact that the Commission's proposal only provided very specific harmonized rules to ensure protection of the general interest – namely, in the field of information duties for service providers, professional insurance and guarantees, information on the existence of after-sale guarantees and settlement of disputes (*ibid.*, Articles 26–8 and Article 32) – also created a certain legal tension between the Commission's proposal and the EC Treaty. As indicated above, a certain 'harmonizing' Community measure only replaces the relevant EC Treaty provisions as the only framework of judicial review provided that the Community rules deal with these aspects exhaustively.
[104] European Health Policy Forum, 'Recommendations on health services and the internal market', 26 May 2005, p. 15, http://ec.europa.eu/health/ ph_overview/health_forum/docs/Recom_health_services.pdf.

the country of origin principle came to an end after health care services were excluded from the scope of the Services Directive in 2006.[105]

The Proportionality Test in cases of permanent establishment of health service providers

Instead of focusing on whether the host state has very good reasons to maintain a double regulatory burden, in cases of restrictions that are directed at health care providers operating in their territory through an establishment, the Proportionality Test focuses on whether the rule securing the attainment of the public interest objective is indeed a suitable measure for securing the attainment of a public interest objective or the least restrictive measure for free movement.

As explained above, the Proportionality Test came into play only gradually, starting with Court cases on the national single practice rules. These rules prevented health professionals from maintaining their registration or practice in a Member State when wanting to establish themselves in another Member State. Even though the Court considered that these measures were indirectly discriminatory, it also applied a modest Proportionality Test by concluding that these rules could also raise obstacles to access to the profession that go beyond what is necessary for achieving the intended objectives,[106] that they applied more severely to foreign health professionals and that, hence, they were unduly restrictive.[107] It was only after the adoption of the *Gebhard* ruling[108] and the requirement to also scrutinize measures that applied without distinction to providers from abroad that a full Proportionality Test became common ground in the scrutiny of regulatory measures under Article 43 EC. Given the fact that health service providers moving to another state and setting up an establishment there could now challenge rules for which a specific cross-border element is lacking, the burden of proof that Member States face in showing that measures are not disproportionate is increasing.

---

[105] Article 2(2)(f), European Parliament and Council Directive 2006/123/EC on services in the internal market, OJ 2007 No. L376/36–68.

[106] Case C-96/85, *Commission* v. *France*, above n.36; Case 351/90, *Commission* v. *Luxembourg*, above n.36. See also Case C-107/83, *Klopp*, above n.21; V. G. Hatzopoulos, 'Killing national health', above n.36, 703.

[107] Case C-96/85, *Commission* v. *France*, above n.36, paras. 12–3; Case C-351/90, *Commission* v. *Luxembourg*, above n.36, paras. 15 and 19.

[108] Case C-55/94, *Gebhard*, above n.28.

The justification process for national regulatory measures under Article 43 EC, even in the absence of a specific cross-border situation, bears a particular resemblance to the screening and mutual evaluation process in the much-discussed Services Directive. According to Article 15 of the Services Directive in particular, Member States have to screen their national legislation for the very existence of specific requirements that are deemed particularly restrictive for access to, and the exercise of, service activity and to verify whether these requirements are non-discriminatory, necessary and proportional. The list of these requirements includes quantitative and territorial restrictions, the obligation on a provider to take a specific legal form, price fixing mechanisms, requirements fixing a minimum amount of employees, requirements stipulating that an intermediary provider must allow access to certain specific services provided by other service-providers and an obligation on the provider to supply other specific services jointly with its service. Clearly, all these types of requirements play an important role in national and regional health policies, for example in planning facilities, setting tariffs, establishing care pathways, setting up referral systems and ensuring quality of care. Generally, Member States implement these requirements to safeguard accessibility, sustainability and quality of health care services and pharmacies in their territory. However, a systematic and pre-emptive screening of all regulation in health care was considered undesirable by many stakeholders, as it would lead to legal uncertainty; it could turn out to be difficult in some cases to sufficiently substantiate certain measures and therefore could disrupt the consistency of the health system as a whole.[109] This was one of the main reasons why the inclusion of health services in the original Commission proposal was contested and finally led to health care being excluded.

Despite the removal of health services from the scope of the Services Directive, national regulatory measures on health care nonetheless remain subject to scrutiny under Article 43 EC provided that they are brought before a court that applies Article 43 EC. This could be either a national court (which could refer to the European Court of Justice under the preliminary ruling procedure) or the European Court of Justice, in actions brought by the Commission against a Member State

---

[109] For instance, European Health Policy Forum, 'Recommendations', above n.104, pp. 14–5.

for failure to fulfil an obligation under the Treaty.[110] A clear example is *Commission* v. *Germany*,[111] where the implementation of a quota system based on the effective needs of care for psychotherapists wishing to practice under the German statutory sickness insurance scheme was declared to restrict the freedom of establishment. More particularly, the Court condemned the way transitional provisions in German law favoured psychotherapists who already had practised under the German statutory health insurance in a region of Germany in the past, as it failed to take into account comparable or similar professional experience in other Member States.[112] Even though in his Opinion the Advocate General considered the restriction to be justified and proportionate to objectives of public interest – namely, on the one hand, the protection of established rights and the legitimate expectations of the practitioners already working under the German statutory health insurance and, on the other, the prevention of overcapacity and safeguarding a uniform supply of psychotherapeutic care to statutorily insured persons in Germany[113] – the Court found that the German Government failed to prove that extending the transitional provisions to psychotherapists with comparable activity under the statutory system of other Member States during the reference period would have jeopardized these objectives.[114]

Regulatory intervention in the field of health care can also be found to be an unjustified obstacle to the freedom of establishment because the measures that it involves are not appropriate for ensuring the attainment of a particular public interest objective. In the *Hartlauer* judgement, which concerned the refusal of the *Wiener Landesregierung* and *Oberösterreichische Landesregierung* to authorize a company (Hartlauer) to set up and operate independent outpatient dental clinics, the Court clarified that this implies that the measure genuinely reflects a concern to attain that objective in a consistent and systematic manner.[115] According to the Austrian legislation, a prior authorization scheme based on an assessment of the needs of the market was required for setting up and operating independent outpatient dental

---

[110] Article 226 EC.
[111] C-456/05, *Commission* v. *Germany*, above n.42.
[112] *Ibid*., para. 54.
[113] *Ibid*., Opinion of Advocate General Mengozzi, para. 95–7.
[114] *Ibid*., para. 72.
[115] Case C-169/07, *Hartlauer Handelsgesellschaft*, above n.51, para. 55.

clinics, but not for setting up new group practices. Having clarified that group practices may have comparable features, generally offer the same medical services and are subject to the same market conditions, the Court concluded that the prior authorization scheme could not have consistently and systematically pursued the public interest objectives involved.[116] Moreover, the fact that each of the involved Austrian provinces applied different criteria for the assessment of the existence of a need for the services of the new outpatient dental clinic led the Court to believe that the authorization scheme was not based on a condition adequately circumscribing the exercise of the national authorities' discretion and therefore was not a suitable means for attaining these objectives. These judgments indicate that Member States may not have that much margin to justify territorial and quantitative restrictions relating to health care activities (hospitals, clinic laboratories, pharmacies, etc.) under Article 43 EC. Moreover, qualitative restrictions imposed on health care providers, especially clinical biology laboratories, pharmacies and opticians, have increasingly come to the attention of the European Commission and the Court. In an earlier Greek case, the Court held that the prohibition on qualified opticians from operating more than one optician's shop could be not be justified, since less restrictive measures such as 'requiring the presence of qualified, salaried opticians or associates in each optician's shop, rules concerning civil liability and rules requiring professional indemnity insurance' could equally achieve the objective of protecting public health.[117] The Court could apply the same reasoning in similar situations, such as the case of *DocMorris*, a joint-stock company based in the Netherlands, which was authorized by the German *Landesregierung* of Saarland to take over and operate an existing pharmacy in Saarbrücken, even though it contradicted the Federal Law on Pharmacies, which contains a limitation in terms of the legal form a pharmacy should take.[118] While the Advocate General – in his Opinion on the *DocMorris* case – developed the

---

[116] *Ibid.*, paras. 58–63.
[117] C-140/03, *Commission* v. *Greece* [2005] ECR I-3177, para. 35.
[118] C. Lafontaine, 'National law on pharmacies and its non-application by a Member State's public authorities – *DocMorris* again leading the way to accomplish freedom of establishment', *Zeitschrift für Europarechtliche Studien* 9 (2006), 301–40, http://archiv.jura.uni-saarland.de/projekte/Bibliothek/text.php?id=432.

argument that there would not be fundamental differences between the sale of optical products in the Greek case, on the one hand, and the sale of medicines, on the other hand,[119] the Court did not share this reasoning and concluded that Germany had not exceeded the limits of its discretionary powers in the field of health care by prescribing that only a qualified pharmacist can possess and run a pharmacy.[120] The Court adopted the same reasoning in *Commission v Italy* concerning Italian legislation reserving the operation of pharmacies to qualified pharmacists.[121] The European Commission also launched a series of infringement procedures against various other Member States – Austria, Germany and Spain – regarding their national legislation governing pharmacies.[122] In particular, these cases question the lawful character of national restrictions relating to the opening and running of pharmacies, such as discriminatory provisions for the purposes of obtaining a licence to operate a pharmacy, rules on the ownership of pharmacies, territorial planning, rules limiting the choice of legal form for a pharmacy and limitations on the number of pharmacies in a location based on the number of inhabitants and the minimum distance between them.[123] This list of requirements bears a particular resemblance to the requirements included in a European Commission report in 2004, which identified a series of regulatory restrictions in the professional services, including pharmacies, which have the biggest potential to harm competition without being objectively justified.[124] Apart from price fixing and advertising regulations, the Commission also refers to entry requirements and reserved rights, regulations governing the business structure and multidisciplinary practices. Even though the report focused on the impact of EU

---

[119] See Opinion of Advocate-General Bot in Joined Cases C-171/07 and C-172/07, *Apothekerkammer des Saarlandes and others*, above n.43, paras. 61–9.

[120] Joined Cases C-171/07 and C-172/07, *Apothekerkammer des Saarlandes and others*, above n.43, para 60.

[121] C-531/06, *Commission v. Italy*, above n.43, para 90.

[122] Eubusiness, 'European Commission targets Germany over pharmacy rules', 2 February 2008, www.eubusiness.com/news-eu/1201871822.86/; and European Commission, 'Internal market: infringement proceedings concerning Italy, Austria and Spain with regard to pharmacies', Press Release No. IP/06/858, 28 June 2006.

[123] European Commission, 'Internal market', above n.122.

[124] European Commission, 'Report on competition in professional services', COM (2004) 83 final, 9 February 2004. Medical professions are not covered by this report.

competition rules on professional regulations, it is clear that these requirements also can be considered to be obstacles to the freedom of establishment and that national governments are increasingly likely to be invited to provide sufficient justification for maintaining these requirements in the public interest.

4. Health care and free movement: the policy challenge

A. *National actors and the call for more legal certainty*

Member States, health care regulators, public authorities and concerned stakeholder groups only became aware of what is at stake in a piecemeal way.[125] Indeed, to date, most of the Court's jurisprudence has addressed the issue of statutory reimbursement of health care provided in another Member State, which in itself is only a limited phenomenon with low financial impact. Although extensive case-law has clarified the scope of Member States regulatory capacity in the case of patient mobility,[126] recent infringement procedures and pending cases address other regulatory aspects, triggered by health service providers wishing to move to other Member States to offer their services there. In fact, sometimes these complaints filed with the European Commission are instigated by domestic competitors challenging measures that limit their freedom in the market. Increasingly, internal market rules have been discovered as a useful political argument to criticize the rigidity of health care systems and to argue in favour of market-oriented reforms, enhancing free choice and opening new markets. Commercial interest groups, including international hospital chains and pharmaceutical manufacturers and wholesalers supported by free market think tanks, are using free movement as an effective tool to foster for-profit activities in the health sector. Health care systems and their governing bodies thus will increasingly

---

[125] As expressed by Davies: 'precisely because obedience to the law is relatively low or at least often delayed, it becomes possible to sneak surprisingly radical principles into the case-law. By the time Member States realize their implications – because national authorities are at last beginning to apply them, or the ECJ is using them more often and widely – they have been around long enough to seem established.' Davies, 'The process and side-effects', above n.62, p. 13.

[126] See Chapter 12 in this volume.

be challenged by external actors.[127] Member States' policies allowing more room for commercial providers can inadvertently spill over into other systems.

Member States have come a long way in acknowledging the applicability of related case-law to their respective health systems and to grasp its wider potential impact. The diversity of national health systems also means that free movement provisions affect Member States in very different ways. In addition, differences in the political composition of governments and in national approaches to the role of commercial actors in health care systems also lead to different positions. While some Member States have openly and proactively addressed the question of the EU-compatibility of their health systems and reforms, others have tended to disregard potential incompatibilities between their regulation and internal market rules, trying to 'hide' their legislation from EU institutions.[128] Within governments, the concerns of health ministers are not always shared either by their colleagues of other departments (such as economic affairs). Some policy departments, striving for increased economic growth, are in favour of supporting the export of health services. Such policies can be pushed by actors in the domestic health system hoping to benefit from increased mobility. As a result, Member States, even if they all seem to voice a similar concern, do not necessary have the same motives when dealing with patient mobility and health care issues at the EU level.

There seems to be at least a shared concern among Member States' health sector authorities and policy-makers that the internal market rules may have adverse effects on the basic objectives of their systems. This is also why, in June 2006, the EU health ministers issued a common statement to emphasize the need to protect the values and principles that underpin the health systems of the EU and to ensure that EU integration supports these values and contributes to the important challenges that lie ahead in reconciling individual needs with available finances.[129] These concerns, which have also been voiced by social and professional organizations involved in health care, centre around

---

[127] M. Ferrera, *The boundaries of welfare: European integration and the new spatial politics of social protection* (Oxford: Oxford University Press, 2005), p. 49.

[128] *Ibid.*, p. 157.

[129] Conclusions of the Health Council, 26 June 2002, http://ec.europa.eu/ health/ph_overview/Documents/mobility_council_ccl_En.pdf; Council of

the impact of free movement provisions on the social character of national health care systems, their internal cohesion and the steering capacity of public authorities. However, Member States seem less able to substantiate the concrete impact of internal market rules. To illustrate this, in their replies to the 2006 Commission consultation on cross-border care,[130] only a few Member States went beyond the issue of patient mobility to point to the deregulating effect of provisions on free movement of services.[131]

Although the Court's case-law allows for striking a balance between free movement, on the one hand, and the protection of public interest objectives, on the other, it does not provide legal certainty. It ultimately depends on the particular circumstances of each case whether a restrictive measure is actually considered necessary and reasonable under EC Treaty rules on free movement. Although political reactions after the first Court rulings focused on the conditions for reimbursing care abroad and on the necessary preconditions to allow more flexible patient mobility, the concern about the potential loss of steering capacity for health sector authorities and the call for legal certainty, not only for patients, but also for public authorities, was present from the outset.[132]

However, when it comes to determining action to address these concerns, Member States are less clear as to the kind of policy instruments to be applied. Traditionally, they are extremely reluctant to allow any intrusion on their national autonomy and try to shelter their systems from EU interference. Even if the creeping pressure from EU law made them hesitantly engage in a debate at the EU level on finding a common policy response, the Member States seem to be caught in the paradox that, in order to safeguard their steering capacity and autonomy in this domain, they would have to accept some EU interference in their

the European Union, 'Council Conclusions on common values and principles in EU health systems', 2733rd Employment, Social Policy, Health and Consumer Affairs Council Meeting, Luxembourg, 1–2 June 2006, www.eu2006.at/en/News/Council_Conclusions/0106HealthSystems.pdf.

[130] http://ec.europa.eu/health/ph_overview/co_operation/mobility/results_open_consultation_en.htm#2.

[131] These include Portugal, Luxemburg, Germany and Belgium, as well as, to some extent, France and Norway.

[132] See, for example, W. Palm *et al.*, 'Implications of recent jurisprudence on the coordination of healthcare protection systems', General report produced for the Directorate-General for Employment and Social Affairs of the European Commission (2000).

health care systems. Any EU legislative proposal will indeed entail the sharing of some powers over health care systems between the national and the EU levels. This explains why Member States, which are in principle in favour of an EU-level legislative initiative, tend to become reluctant once concrete proposals have to be discussed.

Spurred by the 'threat' of an all-encompassing screening exercise, as proposed by the Services Directive, Member States have shown some willingness to engage in the pragmatic approach of the High Level Group on Health Services and Medical Care (see below). After actively pushing for the exclusion of health services from the scope of the Services Directive, the Member States also accepted the alternative of a more adapted health services directive, which – as expressed under the German Presidency in 2007 – sought to provide a broad framework, not limited to patient mobility.[133] This position, to some extent, was inspired by an informal grouping of social democrat health ministers, involving influential Member States such as the United Kingdom, Germany and Spain.[134] This group suggested that a sector-specific directive could describe the common values and principles underpinning European health systems, outline their objectives, define the different types of instruments public authorities use to properly manage their systems (such as planning, tariff setting mechanisms, authorization schemes for providers, etc.) and identify the conditions under which the use of these instruments would be in conformity with Treaty provisions.[135] The ideas of the 'Aachen group' were presented at an informal Health Council meeting in 2006 and Belgium attached this position in a 'non-paper' to its reply on the Commission consultation.[136]

---

[133] Council of the European Union 'Health care across Europe – Community framework for health services, exchange of views / adoption of Council conclusions', Doc. No. 9540/07, 16 May 2007, http://register.consilium. europa.eu/pdf/en/07/st09/st09540.en07.pdf.

[134] The so-called 'Aachen group', named after the place they first met. The composition of this group varies over time, depending on the composition of the respective governments. Ministers that participated in the group during the elaboration of these proposals include: the United Kingdom, Germany, Luxemburg, Belgium, Portugal and, at some times during the process, Sweden, Italy and Spain.

[135] Non-paper presented at the Informal Council Meeting of the Employment, Social and Health Ministers, Helsinki, 6–8 July 2006.

[136] http://ec.europa.eu/health/ph_overview/co_operation/mobility/ results_open_consultation_en.htm#2.

B. *Searching for policy responses at the EU level*

Despite the growing awareness of the need to provide a more consistent and political solution to the problems created by the application of free movement rules to the health sector, and the pressure created by new judgments and infringement procedures, it has proven difficult to find an adequate policy response to the developments described in this chapter. Member States' differing opinions and hesitant positions, as well as the complexity of the issues at stake, the lack of a clear legal basis in the Treaty to deal with these issues and an inherent inertia towards any fundamental changes to the rules of the game, certainly play an important role. But it is also true that not all of the stakeholders involved have the same concerns and objectives.

Since 2002, several policy initiatives have been taken at the EU level in an attempt to clear the legal uncertainty and to alleviate the pressure on the regulatory powers of health authorities. Various processes have been led by different Directorates-General in the European Commission, reflecting different approaches and objectives. However, it seems that, so far, none of these policy processes has succeeded in providing adequate answers to the issues at stake.

The horizontal (internal market) approach

As the guardian of the EC Treaty and instigator of Community legislation, the European Commission is one of the most important drivers in ensuring that territorial, quantitative and qualitative requirements in the field of health care are not too restrictive in the context of free movement principles. Health services are explicitly mentioned in a Communication on the internal market as 'a new emerging sector where the benefits of the internal market have to be made tangible'.[137] More specifically, the Directorate-General for the Internal Market and Services (DG MARKT), whose central mission is to secure for the benefit of the EU's citizens and businesses ever greater European market integration, monitors Member States' compliance with EU rules on free movement. This DG is inclined to deal with health services in the

---

[137] European Commission, 'Communication from the Commission to the Council, the European Parliament, the European Economic and Social Committee and the Committee of the Regions on a single market for citizens. Interim report to the 2007 Spring European Council', COM (2007) 60 final, 21 February 2007.

same way as other economic services. It is used to being confronted, in all economic sectors, by Member States and other actors trying to justify specific rules and approaches that are considered (by DG MARKT) to be protectionist and to hinder free movement. The DG is suspicious of any initiative that attempts to emphasize the specificities of health care services in their relation to free movement provisions or to define health care as a service of general interest. Moreover, it lacks structural links with the public authorities responsible for funding and organizing health care systems.

One way for DG MARKT to further a single market in services is the possibility of launching infringement procedures against Member States to force them to remove obstacles to the free movement of services and the freedom of establishment. The Commission could also take initiatives that go beyond infringement procedures in order to ensure the application of free movement rules in particular fields. This was suggested, for instance, in a recent study on regulatory restrictions on pharmacies.[138] This study suggests that reducing these barriers would not only enhance productivity in the EU but also lead to substantial social welfare increases, after which it concludes: '[t]here seems to be a need for further policy aimed at removing obstacles to the freedom of establishment in the field of pharmacy services'.[139] In addition, in its report of July 2003 on the application of internal market rules to health services, DG MARKT concluded that the internal market in health services was not functioning satisfactorily and that different tools were being considered to ensure Member States' compliance with the Court's rulings, including the SOLVIT network[140] and the creation of an EU-level legal framework.[141]

Although launching infringement procedures are indeed a powerful tool to remove obstacles to free movement, at the same time it has its weaknesses and limitations, as it operates very slowly and in a piecemeal

---

[138] Ecorys Nederland BV, 'Study of regulatory restrictions in the field of pharmacies', Report commissioned by the European Commission, DG Internal Market and Services, 22 June 2007, http://ec.europa.eu/internal_market/services/docs/pharmacy/report_En.pdf.

[139] *Ibid.*, p. 83.

[140] SOLVIT is a network linking the national administrations of every Member State. Its task is to find rapid solutions to problems arising from the application by Member States of the rules governing the internal market.

[141] European Commission, 'Report on the application of internal market rules to health services. Implementation by the Member States of the Court's

fashion. This is also why, in January 2004, the Commission adopted a proposal for a directive on services in the internal market. This 'horizontal' directive, applying to all services falling under the scope of Articles 43 and 49 EC, was to implement free provision of services and free establishment in a more systematic manner. The inclusion of health services in its scope was mainly motivated by the fact that it would be a means of codifying the Court's jurisprudence on statutory reimbursement of cross-border health care. However, the Commission's proposal also illustrated in a very clear way how the impact of the free movement provisions on health care systems went far beyond the issue of patient mobility. Even if, after two years of fierce policy debate, health care services were finally excluded from the eventual Directive 2006/123/EC,[142] this did not eliminate the applicability of the Treaty's free movement rules to health services. The European Commission, as guardian of the Treaty, thus keeps on targeting restrictions imposed by particular Member States that are deemed to be unjustified barriers.[143] It could even be claimed that since health services were excluded from the Services Directive, the Commission has stepped up its infringement activity.

The sectoral (health systems) approach

While the purely internal market approach failed, another more pragmatic approach was simultaneously pursued. Already, in 2003, at the request of the Council,[144] a 'High Level Process of Reflection on Patient Mobility and Health Care Developments in the European Union' was set up by the European Commission. This informal process was composed of health ministers from most EU15[145] Member States (later extended to the new candidate Member States), some European stakeholder organizations and a representative from the European Parliament, and was chaired by the three EU Commissioners responsible for the internal market, health and social affairs. Its goal was to step up cooperation among Member States in the field of health care with a view to making better use of resources, improve sharing of

---

jurisprudence', Commission Staff Working Paper, SEC (2003) 900, 28 July 2003.

[142] Directive 2006/123/EC, above n.2.

[143] See section 3 above.

[144] Conclusions of the Health Council, 26 June 2002, http://ec.europa.eu/health/ph_overview/Documents/mobility_council_ccl_En.pdf.

[145] States belonging to the EU before May 2004.

information, accessibility and quality, as well as to enhance legal certainty over the application of internal market rules to health care.

This broad and consensual approach was much promoted by the Directorate-General for Health and Consumer Protection (DG SANCO), whose powers are intrinsically linked with Article 152 EC, allowing EU action to complement national policies and to encourage cooperation among Member States, provided that the responsibility of Member States to organize and deliver health services and medical care is respected. DG SANCO can be considered to be the EU counterpart of national health ministries and is thus more aware of their concerns about the impact of free movement rules. Given its responsibility with regard to consumer protection, it is also more inclined to look after the interests of the health care 'consumer' than the health care provider. Therefore, its approach is broader than just removing obstacles to free movement, and extends to ensuring that free movement can take place under conditions that are optimal for patients.

After the High Level Process – and as one of its outcomes – a High Level Group on Health Services and Medical Care (HLG) was created, with the aim of taking forward the recommendations to support European cooperation in the field of health care and to monitor the impact of the EU on health care systems. This Group, consisting of senior officials of EU Member States and chaired by the European Commission, looked for pragmatic solutions to a range of specific issues, such as defining common guidelines for cross-border contracting, establishing better information sharing on health professionals and patient safety issues, and defining the role and criteria for European reference centres. One of the subgroups developed a methodology and practical tool for systematically assessing the impact of EU policy and legislative initiatives in various fields on health systems.[146]

Although the objectives of the High Level Process also included finding ways to reconcile national health policy with European obligations, the final report did not introduce concrete proposals, but instead enumerated a full range of possible governance instruments, ranging from 'changing the Treaty' to 'initiatives by Member States

---

[146] http://ec.europa.eu/health/ph_overview/co_operation/high_level/index_En.htm.

and bilateral cooperation'.[147] It was suggested that these options could be considered in more depth once the final text of the then Constitutional Treaty was approved, in the context of which the option of a new legal basis to legislate on services of general interest, including health services, was discussed. Besides the creation of the High Level Group as a 'permanent monitoring mechanism', the only other concrete element was the integration of health care into the draft Services Directive, which was adopted only a few weeks after the High Level Process ended, and which was later presented by the Commission as one of the outcomes of this Process, although it was never presented there nor discussed.[148]

When the purely internal market approach of DG MARKT crash-landed with the removal of health care services from the Services Directive, DG SANCO took over to lead the process to develop a separate initiative in the area of health.[149] It started by organizing a broad consultation to find out what the sector's expectations were and what a 'more adapted' proposal should look like. However, from the start, it was clear that DG SANCO aimed for a broader 'Community framework for safe, high quality and efficient health services ... reinforcing cooperation between Member States and providing certainty over the application of Community law to health services and healthcare'.[150]

While it is not the intention of the Commission to encourage citizens to look for care in another Member State, it seeks to ensure that, if they do, they can be confident about the care they receive and are sufficiently informed about their rights. Next to clarifying the entitlements of citizens to statutory cover for health services provided in another Member State, this proposal for a new directive on the application of patients' rights in cross-border health care also

---

[147] European Commission, 'High Level Process on Patient Mobility and Healthcare Developments in the European Union, outcome of the reflection process', HLPR/2003/16, 9 December 2003, http://europa.eu.int/comm/health/ph_overview/Documents/key01_mobility_En.pdf.

[148] European Commission, 'Follow-up to the High Level Reflection Process on Patient Mobility and Healthcare Developments in the European Union', COM (2004) 301 final, 20 April 2004.

[149] European Commission, 'Amended Proposal for a Directive of the European Parliament and of the Council on services in the internal market', COM (2006) 160 final, 4 April 2006.

[150] European Commission, 'Consultation regarding Community action on health services', SEC (2006) 1195/4, 26 September 2006, p. 2.

addresses the question of what Member States should be responsible for in cross-border care – namely, to secure common principles, such as ensuring quality and safety standards, information, redress and liability, as well as privacy protection against unlawful processing of personal health data. Finally, the proposal sets a basis for cooperation between Member States on a range of aspects that would facilitate cross-border health care.[151]

While the consultation received a high level of response and was followed by a comprehensive impact and feasibility assessment,[152] the formal adoption of the proposal by the College of Commissioners was repeatedly postponed. This delay seems to reflect important disagreements within the Commission, also fuelled by the fear that any new dissonance might jeopardize the ratification process of the Lisbon Treaty or the reinstatement of the next EU Commission in 2009.

Despite the ambitious plans to develop an amended proposal that would include all dimensions of cross-border health care (patient mobility, provider mobility, service mobility) and that would 'also contribute to the wider challenges facing health systems, beyond the specific case of cross-border healthcare itself', the proposal mainly focuses on cross-border patient rights. The proposal does not provide any of the much needed legal certainty regarding how national health authorities can ensure the common values of their health systems, such as universality, equity and solidarity, without infringing free movement rules.

The generic (social services of general interest) approach

As it seems that neither the horizontal nor the sectoral approach can produce the required guidance on how to strike a balance between free movement principles and Member States' regulatory intervention in health care, final rescue perhaps may come from another DG, the Directorate-General for Employment, Social Affairs and Equal Opportunities (DG Social Affairs). This DG, whose mission it is to

---

[151] European Commission, 'Proposal for a Directive', above n.91. See also Chapter 12 in this volume.

[152] W. Palm, M. Wismar and K. Ernst, 'Assessing possible directions for the Community action on healthcare services: summary of the expert panels', in M. Wismar et al. (eds.), Cross-border healthcare: mapping and analysing health systems diversity (Copenhagen: WHO Regional Office for Europe on behalf of the European Observatory on Health Systems and Policies, 2009).

contribute to the development of a modern, innovative and sustainable European Social Model, has traditionally played a leading role in the debate on the social dimension of the internal market. While, for more than forty years, through the EU regulatory framework on the coordination of social security systems for persons moving within the Community,[153] it was the uncontested guardian of EU citizens' access to health care outside the state of affiliation, its role has been increasingly challenged by Court rulings on patient mobility. After it failed to integrate the ambit of the rulings fully within the scope of the modernization process of EC Regulation 1408/71/EEC, DG Social Affairs only played a secondary role in the political process of dealing with the concrete consequences of the Court's case-law. However, when it comes to addressing the wider implications of applying internal market rules to health care, it could claim back its central role through its work in developing a generic framework for social services of general interest.

Health services are indeed also part of a broader framework of services of general interest, particularly social services of general interest (SSGI).[154] The concept of services of general economic interest refers to Article 86(2) EC, according to which service providers entrusted with a mission of general interest and engaging in economic activities can be partly or even completely exempt from competition rules if these rules are liable to hinder or render the task assigned to these providers impossible. Since EU competition rules pose very similar challenges to the organization and financing of national health care systems to those challenges posed by free movement rules, the concept of services of general economic interest seems to be a valuable opportunity in the search for an appropriate EU legal framework.

In its 2004 White Paper on services of general interest, the European Commission stressed that the personal nature of many social and health services leads to requirements that are significantly different from those in networked industries.[155] It favoured a 'systematic approach

---

[153] Council Regulation 1408/71/EEC on the application of social security schemes to employed persons and their families moving within the Community OJ 1971 No. L149/2; Council Regulation 574/72/EEC fixing the procedure for implementing Regulation 1408/71/EEC on the coordination of social security schemes for persons moving within the Community OJ 1972 No. L74/1. See also Chapter 12 in this volume.

[154] See Chapter 7 in this volume.

[155] European Commission, 'Services of general interest', White Paper, COM (2004) 374 final, 12 May 2004.

in order to identify and recognise the specific characteristics of social and health services of general interest and to clarify the framework in which they operate and can be modernised' and announced a Communication on SSGI, including health services.[156] Even though the publication of this Communication, due in 2005, was postponed to await the outcome of the debate on the Services Directive, after the exclusion of health services from that Directive, the Commission also excluded them from the scope of this Communication, claiming that a specific initiative would be taken in this area, which would also cover this wider aspect.[157] Even if the European Parliament, in its first reading of the Services Directive, had advised separately that both health and social services should be excluded from the scope of the Directive, there was no real reason to lift health services out of the Communication. Although the Communication outlined the characteristics of SSGI and described specific problems they could encounter, these problems would definitely also apply to health, and in some instances, direct reference was made to health care.[158]

In spite of the fact that the issues at stake are nearly identical for both sectors, the distinction between these two policy processes is also confirmed in the Commission's most recent Communication on services of general interest, including SSGI, which was attached to its 2007 Communication on 'a single market for the 21st century'.[159] While this Communication does not really provide new elements, it mainly encourages Member States to endow services of general

---

[156] Member States contributed to the preparation of this Communication by reporting on the situation of social and health services in their countries through a questionnaire prepared in the Social Protection Committee (SPC), 'Social Services of General Interest', Questionnaire, http://ec.europa.eu/employment_social/social_protection/docs/questionnaire_En.pdf, and Member States that replied to the SSGI questionnaire, http://ec.europa.eu/employment_social/social_protection/answers_En.htm.

[157] See R. Baeten, 'Health and social services in the internal market', in C. Degryse and P. Pochet (eds.), *Social developments in the European Union 2006* (Brussels: ETUI-REHS, Observatoire social européen and Saltsa, 2007), pp. 161–85.

[158] European Commission, 'Communication from the Commission, implementing the Community Lisbon programme: social services of general interest in the European Union', COM (2006) 177 final, 26 April 2006.

[159] European Commission, 'Communication from the Commission to the European Parliament, the Council, the European Economic and Social Committee and the Committee of the Regions, accompanying the

interest with a clear mandate through official legislation and provides a further explanation on the applicable rules. The document leaves few hopes for securing the long-debated specific legislative framework for services of general interest (SGI), arguing that the Lisbon Treaty includes a protocol on services of general interest.[160] Instead, it opts for a pragmatic approach and intends to provide concrete solutions to concrete problems. One such solution was the launch of a web site providing information and answers to frequently asked questions on the application of EU law on SGI.[161] The first two working documents deal with the rules on state aid and on public procurement with regard to SSGI.[162] Strikingly, these documents do explicitly deal with health care services.[163]

In conclusion, even if it remains unclear as to whether the Commission intends to approach health services as services of general interest,[164] some may interpret the fact that the proposal for a new directive on health services is integrated into the new social agenda as an indication that the different processes in the future may at least become better aligned or even integrated.

5. Conclusions

This chapter focused on the impact of the fundamental principles of free provision of services and free establishment of service providers

Communication on "a single market for 21st century Europe", services of general interest, including social services of general interest: a new European commitment', COM (2007) 725 final, 20 November 2007.

[160] See Chapter 7 in this volume.

[161] http://ec.europa.eu/services_general_interest/index_en.htm.

[162] European Commssion, 'Frequently asked questions in relation with Commission Decision of 28 November 2005 on the application of Article 86(2) of the EC Treaty to State aid in the form of public service compensation granted to certain undertakings entrusted with the operation of services of general economic interest, and of the Community Framework for State aid in the form of public service compensation', Commission Staff Working Document, SEC (2007) 1516, 20 November 2007; and European Commission, 'Frequently asked questions concerning the application of public procurement rules to social services of general interest', Commission Staff Working Document, SEC (2007) 1514, 20 November 2007. For discussion of these documents, see Chapter 9 in this volume.

[163] See Chapter 9 in this volume.

[164] The Commission's legislative proposal on patients' rights only contains a general statement that health systems are also part of the wider framework

on health systems, as enshrined in Articles 49–50 EC and Article 43
of the EC Treaty. Besides the fact that all health systems are based
on a common set of values and objectives – as was explicitly confirmed by health ministers in their statement of June 2006[165] – they
also share the common feature of requiring a high degree of regulation to implement these underpinning values and to organize health
care that is safe, high quality and cost-effective for the whole population. However, public intervention in health care increasingly faces
challenges from an EU perspective. While the European Court of
Justice and the European Commission act as guardians over compliance with EC Treaty rules and are driven by the need to preserve non-
discrimination, free movement and choice, Member States, as well as
other actors involved in the health sector, are more concerned about
the potential crippling effect on their steering capacity over publicly-
run health systems.

In fact, the threshold for the application of rules on the free movement of services is relatively low. From the moment it is established
that health care is an economic activity provided for remuneration,
irrespective of whether it is funded publicly, any national measure
that would deter or even prevent health care providers from offering
their services, temporarily or more permanently, in another Member
State – or, inversely, citizens from applying to these providers – would
formally constitute an obstacle to free movement. In the case of providers temporarily providing services in another Member State, the
fact that they would face a double regulatory burden is already likely
to hinder free movement. Based on the principle of mutual recognition, Member States are invited to rely on each others' regulation and
assessment to accept providers entering the market. But, even more so
in the context of ensuring free establishment of providers, virtually
any regulatory or institutional aspect that health care providers have
to comply with to operate in the territory of a Member State or to
work under its statutory health insurance could be challenged, even
if at first sight it would not be linked to cross-border situations. This
can range from measures restricting the quantity of providers according to population size or catchment area, rules establishing norms

of services of general interest. See European Commission, 'Proposal for a
Directive', above n.91, Recital 4.
[165] Conclusions of the Health Council, above n.129.

on staff levels, pricing and quality, to more qualitative restrictions, such as rules on professional conduct and qualification, ownership, or legal form. All of these rules include both individual health professionals and health care facilities such as hospitals, pharmacies and clinical laboratories, even if for the latter no specific EU framework for mutual recognition of qualifications and quality standards exists.

However, the application of free movement rules in the field of health care is not unconditional. The EC Treaty provides the possibility to justify any measure hindering free movement if it proves to be necessary for protecting public health or another public interest objective, such as the health system's financial sustainability. In several instances, the European Court of Justice has recognized the need for Member States to regulate health services and providers in order to preserve the public interest. As demonstrated in this chapter, the core of the justification does not lie so much in the so-called 'necessity' test, identifying the public interest objective and proving that the targeted measure is necessary to preserve it, but rather in the 'proportionality' test, proving that the measure is an appropriate means for attaining the public interest objective, that it does not exceed what is necessary to attain this objective and that it cannot be achieved by a less restrictive measure. Member States face a relatively high burden of proof, as they need to provide sufficient evidence showing that the non-application of a restrictive measure in a particular case would jeopardize the public interest objective. Not only is it difficult to demonstrate what would happen without the measure, this leaves little room to consider the measure in its wider context and assess its coherence within the broader regulatory framework, taking into account the role of public payers and purchasers.

For this reason, the introduction of a mutual evaluation process, as proposed in Article 15 of the Services Directive, to systematically screen national regulation of health services for unjustified barriers to free movement of health services was deemed particularly risky and undermining for health systems' governance. Such a measure could lead to undesirable deregulation and force Member States to dramatically adjust the organization of their health care system, even partly retreating from it.

Being aware of this problem, policy-makers have been looking for ways to reconcile the individual right to free movement with the public objective of running an efficient health system, guaranteeing

Gekiere, Baeten and Palm

citizens equal access to health care that is affordable, safe and of high quality, and that produces the best value for money. While Member States seem to be caught in the paradox that, in order to safeguard their steering capacity and autonomy, they would have to accept some EU interference in their health care systems, the European Commission seems neither willing nor able to provide guidance, as it is torn between different currents, reflecting the different objectives and responsibilities of the respective Directorates-General. After the backlash on the inclusion of health care in the Services Directive, the Commission announced a new, flexible proposal for health services. While the adoption of this proposal has been delayed because of internal division within the College of Commissioners and the fear that a renewed uprising would be detrimental at a critical time (the ratification of the Lisbon Treaty and the ending of terms for both the European Commission and Parliament), the new proposal seems to essentially focus on establishing a framework for patients using cross-border care[166] and tries to carefully sidestep the more delicate question of clarifying the impact of EU rules on free movement on health systems at large.

Despite the fact that the Court has indeed demonstrated its awareness of important market failures occurring in health care and has accepted the need to regulate health services, a more consistent and less piecemeal solution is still needed, providing more certainty to health policy-makers. This could be done by making explicit what measures can be upheld, establishing a broader justification test or even reversing the burden of proof. Given the similar problems related to the concept of services of general economic interest under Article 86(2) EC, a combined approach for health care should be considered.

[166] See also Chapters 9 and 12 in this volume.

12 Enabling patient mobility in the EU: between free movement and coordination

WILLY PALM AND IRENE A. GLINOS

1. Introduction

Free movement of patients – or patient mobility, as it is commonly referred to – implies people accessing health care services outside their home state.[1] Although health care normally is delivered close to where people live, in some instances the need for medical care arises while away from home or patients decide to seek care elsewhere. Patients' readiness to travel for care, especially across borders,[2] is determined by a mix of factors linked to the specific situation of the patient, to the specific medical needs and to availability of care at home and abroad. Motivations for travelling abroad for care vary from the search for more timely, better quality or more affordable health care to treatment responding better to the patient's wants or needs – including when care is inexistent or even prohibited at home.[3]

While citizens in the EU, in principle, are free to seek health care wherever they want and from whatever provider available, in practice this freedom is limited by their ability to pay for it or by the conditions set out by public and private funding systems for health care. Traditionally, countries have confined statutory cover for health care delivered to their population to providers established in their territory.[4] Whereas initially, bilateral conventions derogated from this territoriality

---

[1] By 'home' state or country, we mean the country of residence, which is usually also the country where the patient is affiliated to the social security system.
[2] Patient mobility can also take place *within* countries, when, for instance, health care provision is regionalized and patients move from one region or province to another. For example, on intra-regional flows in Italy, see G. France, 'Cross-border flows of Italian patients within the European Union', *European Journal of Public Health* 7 (1997), Supp: 18–25; I. A. Glinos and R. Baeten, 'A literature review of cross-border patient mobility in the European Union', Observatoire social européen, September 2006, pp. 74–5.
[3] Glinos and Baeten, 'A literature review', above n.2, pp. 5–7.
[4] In some cases, cover is even further reduced to specific types or contracted health care professionals. See also, on the issue of access hurdles, R. Busse and E. van

principle[5] to ensure access to care for people living and working in different Member States, a more general derogation was established in the context of European integration under Article 42 EC, based on the fundamental principle of free movement of persons.[6] More recently, further steps in opening provider choice options for patients across the European Economic Area (EEA) have been made through the jurisprudence of the European Court of Justice (ECJ), based on the freedom to provide services as contained in Article 49 EC.

Although patient mobility is still a phenomenon of relatively modest scale, in terms of both overall numbers of people receiving health care in another Member State and financial impact,[7] the fact that patients are allowed to move more freely between health care systems raises a series of issues and can have consequences for the way delivery of care is organized. Certain countries and regions experience high concentrations of patient mobility, and patient flows can be considerable in some circumstances or for particular medical conditions. As numbers grow, issues relating to the quality of care, liability, responsibility and safety of care received abroad become more prominent. These developments, in combination with a decade of groundbreaking rulings by the ECJ, have placed patient mobility and cross-border health care more firmly on the political agenda in the last decade at both Member State and EU level.[8] Increasing personal mobility within the Union, its changing nature, the emerging problems and challenges occurring within national health systems, as well as the uncertainty around the impact of jurisprudence for national health care systems, have made

Ginneken, 'Access to healthcare services within and between countries of the European Union', in M. Wismar *et al.* (eds.), *Cross-border healthcare: mapping and analysing health systems diversity* (Copenhagen: WHO Regional Office for Europe on behalf of the European Observatory on Health Systems and Policies, 2009), pp. 12–50.

[5] R. Cornelissen, 'The principle of territoriality and the Community regulations on social security', *Common Market Law Review* 3 (1996), 439–471, at 464.

[6] See also A. P. van der Mei, *Free movement of persons within the European Community, cross-border access to public benefits* (Oxford: Hart, 2001).

[7] Although the available data on the extent of cross-border care is extremely patchy, it is commonly agreed that the current volume of patient mobility is relatively low, estimated at around 1% of overall public expenditure on healthcare. See European Commission, 'Consultation regarding Community action on health services', SEC (2006) 1195/4, 26 September 2006, p. 6. On the available data, see also Busse and van Ginneken, 'Cross-border healthcare data', in Wismar *et al.* (eds.), *Cross-border healthcare*, above n.4, pp. 219–58.

[8] See Chapter 4 in this volume for a detailed chronological analysis.

national policy-makers more wary of any developments that could weaken their policies to contain costs and strengthen actors' account-ability. This has led to fierce debates about the inclusion of health services in the Directive on Services in the Internal Market[9] and about the necessity of applying a more adapted approach for health care within the European policy framework.

This chapter will analyse the state of the regulatory framework in this field as well as the relevant case-law of the ECJ. In particu-lar, it will address the questions of who actually steers the policy on patient mobility and how the debate on free movement of patients has changed over time to anticipate the phenomenon's changing patterns, as well as the evolving behaviour and expectations of patients. It will also refer to the wider impact of the application of the Treaty-based principles of free movement, which is further developed in Chapter 11 in this volume (on free movement of health services).

The chapter will start by looking into the various governance aspects of patient mobility. It will do so by clarifying the conceptual, legal and policy fundamentals of the phenomenon, as well as the key actors and their roles (section two). The following section (section three) exam-ines the changing legal landscape, the requirements and motivations of the patient groups concerned with mobility, as well as the range of approaches that public authorities and health care actors have taken to channel patient flows. Section four analyses the most recent pol-icy developments in the field as national and EU-level decision-makers have tried to define the direction that patient mobility and its govern-ance should take. In the concluding section, we present a summary of the key issues and suggest which challenges possibly lie ahead.

2. The governance of patient mobility in the European Union

A. The conceptual construct of patient mobility

Before going into the governance developments on free movement of patients, we need to clarify what concepts and values lie at the heart of the policy debate. For Member States, patient mobility is rather

---

[9] European Parliament and Council Directive 2006/123/EC on services in the internal market, OJ 2006 No. L376/36.

an exception to the rule. Their main concerns are the loss of control and the equity implications it may have for their health care systems. For the EU institutions, the focus is rather on removing impediments to free movement and implementing the choice resulting from it. Inevitably, the fact that the political agenda on patient mobility differs widely between actors becomes a source of conflict.

The debate on free movement of patients is conceptually centred on the question of whether the right to health care extends to service providers outside the state of affiliation. This right to health care as a part of the European welfare state has been constructed on the notion of so-called 'positive' rights.[10] These rights are community-based; they involve the pooling of resources and redistributive allocation (from the wealthy and healthy to the poor and ill), promoting reciprocity and solidarity. By contrast, the ECJ in its rulings has regarded the right to health care as a 'negative' right – i.e., a right promoting the individual's liberty. Having defined medical activities as services falling within the scope of the fundamental freedom to provide services, it follows that people are free to seek medical care anywhere in the EU and that any hindrance to this freedom, including coming from statutory reimbursement rules, would need to be justified. Through the case-law of the ECJ, the scope for Member States to deny cover outside the national territory has reduced significantly. This logic, which effectively gives EU citizens the possibility (and the right) to obtain treatment outside their state of affiliation, might well be to the detriment of the community[11] and may carry important consequences in terms of equity. A key function of health care systems is to define priorities based on evaluations of what is beneficial to the community as a whole (the public interest). These priorities feed into decisions on planning and financing of the system. An individual patient choosing to go abroad for care (e.g., to obtain faster access) and who, based on EU law, can claim cover for it, could be considered to effectively

---

[10] The distinction between positive versus negative rights is an established one in the political philosophy literature and does not carry any value judgement. It distinguishes between rights requiring an intervention by the state (positive rights) and rights rather calling for temperance by public authority (negative rights).

[11] C. Newdick, 'Citizenship, free movement and health care: cementing individual rights by corroding social solidarity', *Common Market Law Review* 43 (2006), 1645–68.

disregard public priority-setting and divert tax-payers' money away from the national system.

What this boils down to is a tension between the four freedoms interpreted as conferring rights on the individual to health care, and the finite resources of the system, which have to be allocated in the fairest, most efficient way for the community. Moreover, free movement has equity implications because it is likely to benefit the least ill, the most literate and the wealthiest. These population groups tend to be more articulate, confident and targeted in terms of their health care needs and expectations;[12] they are likely to be more knowledgeable about their rights and more familiar with travelling abroad; and they are likely to be better able to afford the transport costs, as well as to cover medical expenses before reimbursement. Patient mobility is often sold under the banner of increased choice of provider and of treatment on a Europe-wide scale. In reality, it might well be an advantage for members of already privileged social strata.

These tensions are not just conceptual; they translate into contentious relationships between the actors involved with the free movement of patients. At the policy level, the diverging positions lead to conflicting priorities (as will be shown in this chapter). Member States are concerned with maintaining steering capacity over their systems. They inherently protect their health care systems and the principles of solidarity and collective rights they are built on. The European Commission, by its nature, promotes, and the ECJ protects, the individual rights that EU citizens derive from the Treaties. The Commission is pushing for increased choice in an integrated European market. It is supported in this by actors with a stake in the choice agenda, such as health insurers and hospitals. However, there is variation within the Commission. Different policies and different approaches are favoured by individual Directorates-General in accordance with their mission and responsibilities (see also Chapter 10). The Directorate-General for the Internal Market and Services (DG MARKT) concentrates on the effective functioning of the market for goods and services and their free circulation. The Directorate-General for Health and Consumer Protection (DG SANCO) watches over the public health and consumer issues related to free movement. The Directorate-General

---

[12] Z. Cooper and J. Le Grand, 'Choice, competition and the political left', *Eurohealth* 13 (2007), 18–20.

for Employment, Social Affairs and Equal Opportunities (DG Social Affairs) is committed to the unhindered mobility of workers and to ensuring their social security rights through the coordination mechanism that for decades has made it possible for persons moving within the Community to obtain health care. We deal with this mechanism in detail below.

B. *Social security coordination*

Since the foundation of the European Community, the policy of awarding access to health care outside the state of social security affiliation was essentially governed by secondary Community law, based upon the fundamental principle of free movement of persons enshrined in the EC Treaty. Based upon Article 42 EC, a Community framework was established to ensure the coordination of social security rights of migrant workers and their family members, including the right to statutory health care. Whereas EC Regulations 1408/71/ EEC and 574/72/EEC,[13] in the first place, were intended to establish entitlements in the (new) Member State of residence for citizens moving to another Member State, or for migrant workers and their families working and living in different Member States, Article 22 and 22-*bis* (for non-active persons) specifically address the case of access to treatment outside that 'home state'. Fundamentally, these provisions provide for conditional access to care outside the state of affiliation: either people require care that has become medically necessary during a temporary stay or they receive authorization from their competent institution to obtain treatment in another Member State. These cases will be further elaborated in the next section.

Fundamentally, the social security coordination mechanism seeks to answer three key questions: where and under what conditions is an entitlement to health care benefits in kind opened in another Member

---

[13] Council Regulation 1408/71/EEC on the application of social security schemes to employed persons and their families moving within the Community, OJ 1971 Sp.Ed. Series I, p. 416; Council Regulation 574/72/ EEC fixing the procedure for implementing Regulation 1408/71/EEC on the coordination of social security schemes for persons moving within the Community, OJ 1972 Sp.Ed. Series I, p. 159. These Regulations are regularly amended. The latest consolidated versions are available via Eur-lex, www. eur-lex.europa.eu/.

State; which legislation determines the scope and modalities of this entitlement; and who will have to cover the costs? As a general rule, people who fall under the scope of this mechanism and meet the conditions are covered as though they were insured under the statutory system of the Member State where they are treated, and this at the expense of the competent Member State – generally, the state where the person works and pays social security contributions. In practice, this means that the benefit package, tariffs and the statutory reimbursement conditions and formalities of the state in which treatment occurs apply to patients who are affiliated to another Member State.

This 'coordination route' is considered to be a sort of 'safety net',[14] a minimum guarantee to enable citizens to use their right to free movement. Through national legislation, Member States can extend the entitlements established under Community law. The European Court of Justice has stated repeatedly that Article 22 of Regulation 1408/71/EEC is in no way intended to regulate, and hence does not in any way prevent, the reimbursement by Member States, at the tariffs in force in the competent state, of costs incurred in connection with treatment provided in another Member State, even without prior authorization.[15]

Traditionally, the social security coordination policy is governed by the Directorate-General for Employment, Social Affairs and Equal Opportunities of the European Commission together with the Administrative Commission on Social Security for Migrant Workers, which is composed of Member State representatives. Their role is to deal with all administrative questions and questions of interpretation arising from the Regulation and to foster and develop cooperation between Member States in social security matters by modernizing procedures for information exchange. The actual implementation is operated by the national institutions in charge of the statutory health protection system with the help of so-called E-forms.[16]

Since 1999, the social security coordination mechanism was put under revision to better take account of societal developments, as well

---

[14] See European Commission, 'A Community framework on the application of patients' rights in cross-border healthcare', COM (2008) 415 final, 2 July 2008, p. 5.

[15] Case C-158/96, *Kohll* v. *Union des Caisses de Maladie* [1998] ECR I-1931, para. 27; Case C-56/01, *Inizan* [2003] ECR I-12403, para. 19; Case C-368/98, *Vanbraekel* [2001] ECR I-5363, para. 36.

[16] http://ec.europa.eu/employment_social/social_security_schemes/docs/eform_healthcare_En.pdf.

as to integrate new ECJ jurisprudence. Already, in 2003, its personal scope was extended to include non-EU nationals who are affiliated to a social security scheme within the EU.[17] In 2004, a new Social Security Regulation (Regulation 883/04/EC) was adopted to replace Regulation 1408/71/EEC.[18] However, this new Regulation will only enter into force after the adoption of a new implementing regulation replacing Regulation 574/72/EEC.[19]

Besides the complexity and rigidity often imputed to this framework of social security coordination, it also suffers from some practical and administrative problems (see also section three), which induce 'competition' with the more flexible Treaty-based access route as created by the case-law of the European Court of Justice. However, as is often repeated, the coordination mechanism also offers considerable advantages over the free choice model derived from the jurisprudence: patients using the well-defined procedures of Article 22 of Regulation 1408/71/EEC are better ensured that eventually their health care costs will be covered; they do not need to advance payment, as they can benefit from the third party payer system in place in the country of treatment; they have better guarantees that the level of coverage will match more closely the tariff charged by the treating provider and, in some cases, they can be covered for services that are not even included in the benefit basket of their country of affiliation. It is due to the fact that the social security coordination mechanism grants rights and advantages that citizens would not have otherwise that the ECJ has explicitly upheld the coordination route.[20]

C. *The case-law of the European Court of Justice*

Traditionally, the European Court of Justice has played an important role in defining citizens' entitlements to care outside their state of affiliation,[21] first within the context of the classical coordination route,

---

[17] Council Regulation 859/2003/EC extending the provisions of Regulation 1408/71/EEC and Regulation 574/72/EEC to nationals of third countries who are not already covered by those provisions solely on the ground of their nationality, OJ 2003 No. L124/1.

[18] European Parliament and Council Regulation 883/04/EC on the coordination of social security systems, OJ 2004 No. L166/1.

[19] A proposal was submitted by the Commission in early 2006. See www.secu.lu/legis/EURO-INT/reg_app_2004_883_prop/rapport%20gqs.pdf.

[20] Case C-56/01, *Inizan*, above n.15, para. 22.

[21] For example, Case 182/78, *Pierik* [1979] ECR 01977.

and, more recently, also by directly relying on the EC Treaty. As will become clear, this has had far-reaching implications.

Since 1998, through the case-law of the ECJ,[22] an alternative procedure for the assumption of health care delivered by a provider established in another Member State has been created.[23] Contrary to the social security coordination framework, this route is directly based on the fundamental principles of free movement of goods and services as enshrined in Articles 28 and 49 of the EC Treaty, respectively. It is settled case-law that medical activities fall within the scope of Article 50 EC, which defines what is to be considered a service under the EC Treaty, there being no need to distinguish in that regard between care provided in a hospital environment and care provided outside such an environment, or to have regard to the special nature of certain services.[24] Indeed, the Court made clear that a medical service provided in one Member State and paid for by the patient should not cease to fall within the scope of the freedom to provide services (Article 49 EC) merely because reimbursement of the costs of the treatment involved is applied for under another Member State's sickness insurance legislation, be it based on reimbursement, benefits in kind or national health service.[25]

Consequently, reimbursement for cross-border care cannot be unduly restricted. The actions brought before the ECJ were mainly inspired by the restrictive pre-authorization policies that Member States applied, refusing patients permission to obtain treatment outside the state of affiliation. Although the Court repeatedly confirmed that Community law does not detract from the powers of the Member States to organize their social security systems, at the same time it made clear that Member States nevertheless must comply with

---

[22] Case C-120/95, *Decker* v. *Caisse de Maladie des Employés Privés* [1998] ECR 1831; Case C-158/96, *Kohll*, above n.15; Case C-157/99, *Geraets-Smits and Peerbooms* [2001] ECR 5473; Case C-385/99, *Müller-Fauré* [2003] ECR 4509; Case C-372/04, *Watts* [2006] ECR I-4325; Case C-444/05, *Stamatelaki* [2007] ECR I-3185.

[23] For a detailed description of the case-law, see E. Mossialos and W. Palm, 'The European Court of Justice and the free movement of patients in the European Union', *International Social Security Review* 56 (2003), 3–29.

[24] Case C-157/99, *Geraets-Smits and Peerbooms*, above n.22, paras. 53–4.

[25] Case C-157/99, *Geraets-Smits and Peerbooms*, above n.22, para. 55; Case C-385/99, *Müller-Fauré*, above n.22, para. 103; Case C-372/04, *Watts*, above n.22, para. 89.

Community law when exercising those powers.[26] Any measure that would deter or prevent citizens from seeking treatment from foreign providers is prohibited unless it can be justified by overriding reasons of general interest and proves to be necessary, proportional and non-discriminatory.[27]

Clearly, limiting the reimbursement of health care to providers established in the Member State of affiliation would be contrary to Article 49 EC. This was made clear in a case initiated by the Commission against France in which a French provision rendering impossible the reimbursement of the costs of biomedical analyses performed by a German laboratory on the basis that it did not have a place of business in France was held to be unlawful as it could not be justified by the need to maintain a high level of health protection.[28] In addition, submitting statutory cover for care provided in another Member State to the condition of prior authorization was regarded as an obstacle to the freedom to provide services, since it would deter or even prevent people from seeking care outside their home state.[29] Even if prior authorization were required to receive coverage in the state of affiliation, it would be considered, both for patients and for foreign service providers, to be a hindrance to free movement if authorization were more difficult to obtain for treatment abroad. This reasoning was followed in the *Leichtle* case, where the statutory cover for a health care service provided outside Germany was subject to the condition that it had to be established in a report drawn up by a medical officer or medical consultant that the health care was absolutely necessary

---

[26] In the absence of harmonization at the Community level, it is for the legislation of each Member State to determine the conditions in which social security benefits are granted. However, when exercising that power, Member States must comply with Community law, in particular the provisions on the freedom to provide services. Those provisions prohibit the Member States from introducing or maintaining unjustified restrictions on the exercise of that freedom in the health care sector. Case C-158/96, *Kohll*, above n.15, paras. 17–9; Case C-157/99, *Geraets-Smits and Peerbooms*, paras. 44–6; Case C-385/99, *Müller-Fauré*, above n.22, para. 100; Case C-56/01, *Inizan*, above n.15, para. 17.

[27] See, further, Chapter 11 in this volume.

[28] Case C-496/01, *Commission v. France* [2004] ECR I-02351.

[29] Case C-158/96, *Kohll*, above n.15, para. 35; Case C-157/99, *Geraets-Smits and Peerbooms*, above n.22, para. 69; Case C-56/01, *Inizan*, above n.15, para. 54; Case C-372/04, *Watts*, above n.22, para. 98.

owing to the greatly increased prospects of success outside the Federal Republic of Germany.[30]

On the other hand, citizens cannot rely on Article 49 EC in order to claim reimbursement for a service that is not included in their home state's benefit package, provided that the list is drawn up in accordance with objective criteria, without reference to the origin of the products or services. This is why, in the case of two Dutch patients who received 'experimental treatment' in another Member State, the ECJ stated that if a Member State's legislature (i.e., the Dutch) has enacted a general rule under which the costs of medical treatment will be assumed – provided that the treatment is 'normal in the (Dutch) professional circles concerned' – only an interpretation on the basis of what is 'sufficiently tried and tested by international medical science' can be regarded as satisfying these requirements.[31]

In practice, the ECJ is of the opinion that the condition of prior authorization cannot be justified for non-hospital services. Judging the case of a Dutch insured person who preferred to obtain dental treatment from a German dentist, the Court considered that its removal would not seriously undermine the financial balance of the social security system nor jeopardize the overall level of public health protection, since it was not expected that patients would be willing to travel to other countries in large numbers for this type of care, given linguistic barriers, geographic distance, the cost of staying abroad and lack of information about the kind of care provided there.[32] Furthermore, in principle, the choice of patients to receive services in another Member State would have no or only limited financial impact, as patients would only be entitled to claim reimbursement of the cost of the treatment within the limits of the cover provided by the sickness insurance scheme in the Member State of affiliation.[33] Consequently, EU citizens should be granted reimbursement for outpatient care in another Member State under the same conditions and according to the same tariffs as applicable at home. In other words, not only is the legal base of this Treaty-based procedure different from the traditional social security coordination procedure (free movement

---

[30] Case C-8/02, *Leichtle* [2004] ECR I-02641, para. 32.

[31] C-157/99, *Geraets-Smits and Peerbooms*, above n.22, paras. 85–9 (referring to Case 238/82, *Duphar* [1984] ECR 00523) and paras. 17–21, 91–4.

[32] Case C-385/99, *Müller-Fauré*, above n.22, para. 95.   [33] *Ibid.*, para. 98.

of services and goods versus free movement of persons), it also applies a different concept of equal treatment: whereas, under social security coordination, cross-border patients are treated *as though they were insured in the country of treatment*, under the Treaty-based route they are treated *as though the treatment were provided in the country of affiliation*.

For hospital services, by contrast, the Court accepted that submitting statutory cover for services provided in another Member State to prior authorization could be justified as a necessary and reasonable measure, since its removal would jeopardize the planning of hospital services, which is considered necessary to guarantee a rationalized, stable, balanced and accessible supply of hospital services to the entire population. Also, it recognized that the hospital sector generates considerable costs and must satisfy increasing needs, while the financial resources that may be made available to health care are not unlimited, whatever the mode of funding applied. Therefore, planning, possibly through a contracting system, is also considered to be necessary in order to control costs and prevent wastage of financial, technical and human resources.[34]

Even though the ECJ accepted prior authorization for hospital services, the discretionary power of Member States to apply this condition was restricted. The ECJ underlined that prior authorization could not be used arbitrarily, as it should be based on objective, non-discriminatory criteria that are knowable in advance. Moreover, a prior administrative authorization scheme must be based on a procedural system that is easily accessible and capable of ensuring that a request for authorization will be dealt with objectively and impartially within a reasonable time, and in which refusals to grant authorization can be challenged in judicial or quasi-judicial proceedings.[35] The practical implications of this will be further elaborated in section three.

By creating a procedure for the reimbursement of health care costs generated outside the Member State of affiliation that is directly based on the EC Treaty, and concurrently maintaining the pre-authorized procedure, as included under the social security coordination regime

---

[34] Case C-157/99, *Geraets-Smits and Peerbooms*, above n.22, paras. 76–8; Case C-385/99, *Müller-Fauré*, above n.22, paras. 77–82; Case C-372/04, *Watts*, above n.22, paras. 108–12.

[35] Case C-372/04, *Watts*, above n.22, para. 116.

(see section three), the Court has created a dual system of access to cross-border care.[36] This has added to the administrative complexity and the lack of clarity of entitlements.[37]

D. *The policy response to the ECJ rulings*

Concerned by the advances of the free movement principles into national health care territory and by the ECJ's expansive approach, Member States have sought to regain control over developments by moving decision-making in this area away from the juridical sphere and into the political domain. There are two sets of motivations underlying this intervention: (a) to improve legal certainty regarding the application of free movement rules to health care; and (b) to support Member States, and foster cooperation between them, in certain fields from which patient mobility would benefit (sharing resources, ensuring quality and safety and sharing information).[38] Whereas national governments initiated the discussion on patient mobility, gradually the Commission has taken the driver's seat in steering the political process.

Following several early fruitful initiatives during the Belgian and Spanish Presidencies in the second half of 2001 and first half of 2002, which mainly served to raise awareness among Member States about the potential challenges for health care systems posed by free movement, the Council of Health Ministers agreed in June 2002 to launch a 'High Level Process of Reflection'. Intended as a forum where delegates from the Member States and the European Commission, together with stakeholder representatives and the European Parliament, could examine and discuss issues related to patient mobility and health care developments in the light of European integration, the one-year process concluded in December 2003 with a series of nineteen recommendations on how to take cooperation forward to promote the better use

---

[36] W. Palm *et al.*, 'Implications of recent jurisprudence on the coordination of healthcare protection systems', General report produced for the Directorate-General for Employment and Social Affairs of the European Commission (2000), p. 132.

[37] T. Hervey and L. Trubek, 'Freedom to provide health care services within the EU: an opportunity for a transformative directive', *Columbia Journal of European Law* 13 (2007), 623–49.

[38] European Commission, 'Consultation', above n.7.

of resources, improve the sharing of information, accessibility and quality of care, and to reconcile national health policy goals with European internal market obligations. One of these recommendations invited the European Commission 'to consider the development of a permanent mechanism at EU level to support European cooperation in the field of health care and to monitor the impact of the EU on health systems'.[39] This materialized in July 2004 in the High Level Group on Health Services and Medical Care (HLG), which was to take forward the work initiated by the High Level Process of Reflection. In the HLG, representatives from Member States together with technical experts, organized in working groups, tackle issues related to seven main areas: cross-border health care purchasing and provision, health professionals, centres of reference, health technology assessment, information and e-health, health impact assessment and health systems, and patient safety. The work and focus of the HLG reflects the attention given to cross-border health care. One of the outcomes was the production, in late 2005, of a set of non-binding guidelines for the purchasing of treatment abroad. The guidelines aim to propose a framework to enhance both (legal and financial) clarity for contracting partners and the protection of patients and health care systems.[40] Also in 2005, the working group on centres of reference commissioned an expert report on rare diseases. The report provides an overview of Member States' different approaches to rare diseases and explores the potential for establishing European networks of reference centres.

Yet Member States' (sudden) willingness to engage in political debates on health care, an area traditionally jealously guarded from EU interference, should be seen in the context of the increasing pressure on national governments to accept the application of internal market rules in national health systems. Besides the sequence of new cases before the ECJ involving different Member States, as well as different types of health systems and of health services, the European Commission also pursued its role of guarding compliance with Community law and following its pro-market agenda. In a report on the application of internal market rules to health services

---

[39] http://ec.europa.eu/health/ph_overview/Documents/key01_mobility_En.pdf.
[40] http://ec.europa.eu/health/ph_overview/co_operation/mobility/docs/highlevel_2005_017_en.pdf.

(July 2003) issued by DG MARKT, the Commission concluded that the internal market in health services was not functioning satisfactorily and European citizens were encountering unjustified or disproportionate obstacles when applying for reimbursement or authorization.[41] Whereas reference was made to the High Level Process of Reflection, the report already clearly indicated that other tools were being considered to ensure Member States' compliance with the Court's rulings, including creating a Community legal framework. Even though, since 1998, Member States had been preparing the modernization and simplification of the existing legal framework of social security coordination, which was considered to be too complex and bureaucratic and therefore not fit to absorb the changes taking place, attempts to integrate the new Treaty-based procedure into the new Social Security Coordination Regulation 883/04/EC failed.[42]

In early 2004, the Commission put forward its proposal for a directive on services in the internal market.[43] In its draft, which envisaged the realization of the internal market for services through a horizontal non-sectoral approach, health services were included in the scope of application, while a specific article (Article 23) codified the ECJ jurisprudence on the assumption of health care costs in another Member State. This provision stipulated that Member States could not make the assumption of the costs of non-hospital care in another Member State subject to the granting of an authorization where the cost of that care would have been assumed by their social security system if provided in the national territory. This should, however, not prevent Member States from maintaining conditions

---

[41] European Commission, 'Report on the application of internal market rules to health services by the European Commission', Commission Staff Working Paper, SEC (2003) 900, 28 July 2003.

[42] When the new Regulation 883/04, above n.18, was adopted, the revision of the chapter on sickness and maternity benefits was already concluded under the Danish Presidency in the second half of 2002.

[43] European Commission, 'Proposal for a European Parliament and Council Directive on services in the internal market', COM (2004) 2 final, 5 March 2004. For a complete analysis, see R. Baeten, 'The potential impact of the services directive on healthcare services', in P. Nihoul and A.-C. Simon (eds.), *L'Europe et les soins de santé* (Brussels: De Boeck/Larcier, 2005), pp. 239–62; E. Van den Abeele, 'Adoption of the Service Directive: a Community big bang or a velvet revolution?', in C. Degryse and P. Pochet (eds.), *Social developments in the European Union 2006* (Brussels: Observatoire social européen, Saltsa, 2007), pp. 127–59.

and formalities, such as a referral system, to which they make the receipt of this care subject in their territory. For hospital care provided in another Member State,[44] Article 23 requested that Member States ensure that prior authorization would not be refused where the treatment in question is among the benefits provided for by the legislation of the Member State of affiliation and where such treatment cannot be given to the patient within a time frame that is medically acceptable in light of the patient's current state of health and the probable course of the illness.[45] In any case, statutory cover for care provided in another Member State should not be lower than that provided by their social security system for similar health care services provided in the national territory.

The approach set out in Article 23 of increasing legal certainty by codifying ECJ case-law in a horizontal directive aimed at establishing an internal market for services as a whole was also confirmed by the Commission's follow-up Communication on the High Level Process.[46] However, the European Parliament, in a motion in April 2005 referring to the special nature of health care, disapproved of this approach and requested a separate Commission proposal.[47] The legislature's stance was later confirmed when the European Parliament, after months of heated debate, voted on 16 February 2006 for the exclusion of health services from the Services Directive. As a consequence, the Commission announced in its amended proposal of April 2006 that it would present a separate legal initiative covering health care services.

[44] European Commission, 'Proposal', above n.43, Article 4 defined hospital care as medical care that can be provided only within a medical infrastructure and that normally requires the accommodation therein of the person receiving the care, the name, organization and financing of that infrastructure being irrelevant for the purposes of classifying such care as hospital care.

[45] Also, European Commission, 'Proposal', above n.43, required that prior authorization for treatment provided in another Member State be in conformity with the general requirement for any authorization scheme, such as the conditions of non-discrimination, necessity, proportionality, objectivity, publicity, legal certainty and openness to legal challenge (Article 23(4)).

[46] European Commission, 'Follow-up to the High Level Reflection Process on Patient Mobility and Healthcare Developments in the European Union', COM (2004) 301 final, 20 April 2004.

[47] J. Bowis, 'European Parliament report on patient mobility and healthcare developments in the European Union', A6–0129/2005, 29 April 2005.

In a new communication published in September 2006 – this time by DG SANCO – the Commission set out a broader perspective for addressing health services at EU level.[48] The new Community framework is to ensure safe, high quality and efficient health services throughout the European Union by reinforcing cooperation between Member States and resolving legal uncertainties over the application of Community law to health services and health care. In order to gain an insight into Member States' and stakeholders' views as to how to achieve this, the Commission initiated a large public consultation process between September 2006 and February 2007.[49] The consultation confirmed the need for a broad approach, not only addressing financial aspects but also issues such as clinical oversight, continuity of care, medical liability and redress.[50] Also, the need for more and clearer information was emphasized repeatedly.[51] However, given the diversity of health systems and the variable directions and levels of developing policy in different areas, it is difficult to find consensus on the appropriate measures to take. Apart from clarifying legal issues, a bottom-up approach is generally preferred for establishing the necessary context of safe, high-quality and efficient care to be guaranteed to citizens wishing to be treated outside their home state.[52]

The Commission was expected to put forward a new legislative proposal by the end of 2007. However, internal differences within the College of Commissioners,[53] as well as political factors and considerations, such as a change of Health Commissioner, the ratification process of the Lisbon Treaty and the political fear of a new flare-up of heated discussions on the role of the EU in health care, delayed the process. Finally, on 2 July 2008, the long awaited proposal for a directive on the application of patients' rights in

---

[48] European Commission, 'Consultation', above n.7.
[49] Baeten, 'The potential impact', above n.43.
[50] European Commission, 'Summary report of the responses to the consultation regarding "Community action on health services"', Health and Consumer Protection Directorate-General, 20 April 2007.
[51] See also W. Palm, M. Wismar and K. Ernst, 'Assessing possible directions for the Community action on healthcare services: summary of the expert panels', in Wismar *et al.* (eds.), *Cross-border healthcare*, above n.4.
[52] *Ibid.*, p. 6.
[53] EurActive, 'Confusion surrounds EU's health services directive', *EurActiv*, 28 January 2008; Europolitics, 'Wallström raises objections to Kyprianou's directive', *Europolitics*, 17 December 2007.

cross-border health care was issued in the context of the renewed social agenda.[54] While taking a broader approach, including provisions for ensuring the quality and safety of cross-border care, as well as other flanking measures to support optimal conditions for treatment undertaken throughout the EU, at the same time the proposal stays faithful to the principles set out in the ECJ case-law. To some extent, this new proposal could be regarded as going even further than the former Article 23 in the Services Directive, which kept close to the wording and scope of the ECJ rulings – i.e., very much based on the distinction between hospital and non-hospital care. The relevant Chapter III in the new proposal, on the use of health care in another Member State, starts by first establishing the general principle that Member States should not prevent their insured citizens from receiving health care that is included in their own benefit baskets in another Member State (Article 6(1)). For that reason, it stipulates that health care provided in another Member State should be statutorily reimbursed up to the same level as 'had the same or similar healthcare been provided in the Member State of affiliation, without exceeding the actual costs of healthcare received' (Article 6(2)). That reimbursement – at least for the costs of non-hospital care – shall not be made subject to prior authorization (Article 7). For hospital care,[55] the proposal accepts that Member States, under certain conditions, may uphold a system of prior authorization (Article 8(3)). This is the case when the treatment would have been assumed by the Member State's social security system had it been provided in its territory and when the purpose of the system is to address the outflow of patients if it seriously undermines (or at least is likely to undermine) the financial balance of a Member State's social security system and/or the planning and rationalization carried out in the hospital sector in order to ensure

---

[54] European Commission, 'Proposal for a European Parliament and Council Directive on the application of patients' rights in cross-border healthcare', COM (2008) 414 final, 2 July 2008.

[55] Hospital care in *ibid.*, is defined as health care that requires overnight accommodation of the patient of at least one night (Article 8(1)(a)), while leaving the possibility to extend this to out-patient healthcare to be included on a specific list set up and regularly updated by the Commission, which either require the use of highly specialized and cost-intensive medical infrastructure or medical equipment or involve treatments that present a particular risk for the patient or the population (Article 8(1)(b)).

'the maintenance of a balanced medical and hospital service open to all or the maintenance of treatment capacity or medical competence on the territory of the concerned Member State' by avoiding hospital overcapacity, imbalance in supply and wastage.

Clearly, the acceptance of a system of prior authorization for hospital care is no longer taken for granted but made subject to conditions that may be difficult to prove. Even though the specific wording of Article 8(3) may lead us to believe that Member States are not required to prove the actual undermining effect of a generalized implementation of the Directive, but only demonstrate that the prior authorization system is put in place with the purpose of preventing any distortion, Article 8(4) unambiguously states that the prior authorization system must be limited to what is necessary and proportionate to avoid such an impact. Along the same lines, while the proposal, in principle, accepts that the Member State of affiliation can impose on the patient using cross-border care the same conditions, criteria of eligibility and regulatory and administrative formalities as would apply at home (Article 6(3)), at the same time these conditions, criteria and formalities, as well as the reimbursement procedures and criteria for health care in another Member State, need to meet the non-discrimination test, as well as the Necessity and Proportionality Test (Article 9(1)).[56] In other words, the proposal is not likely to reassure Member States as to their control over patient flows and the financial implications, since it sheds more doubt in terms of the applicable benefit package ('same or similar health care'), the use of prior authorization for hospital treatment in another Member State, and on the conformity of conditions and formalities to which statutory reimbursement can be made subject.[57]

---

[56] See Chapter 10 in this volume on the justification of obstacles to free movement of health services in the EU.

[57] Whilst finalizing this book, the Council of the European Union was in the process of substantially amending the proposal and the European Parliament adopted a legislative resolution amending the proposal in first reading. See Council of the European Union, 'Proposal for a Directive of the European Parliament and of the Council on the application of patients' rights in cross-border healthcare', Progress Report, Document 16514/08, Brussels, 11 December 2008; European Parliament Legislative Resolution of 23 April 2009 on the proposal for a Directive of the European Parliament and of the Council on the application of patients' rights in cross-border healthcare (COM(2008)0414 – C6–0257/2008 – 2008/0142(COD)).

E. Cooperation initiatives and contractual arrangements in the field

Actors in the field and public authorities, either national or regional, have not awaited guidance or consensus from the European level to seek more adapted solutions to enable and coordinate patient mobility. Already in the early 1990s, cross-border projects emerged, especially in intra-Community border regions, with the purpose of relaxing access to health service providers across the border or stimulating exchange and cooperation between administrations and other actors. Since then, cross-border cooperation has consolidated and matured in many places.[58]

As a more tailor-made solution, patient mobility can be arranged through direct cross-border contractual agreements involving at least two cooperating partners in different Member States setting up a contract to allow for patient flows. This can be between health care providers (private or public), insurers (private or public) and/or public bodies (at the local, regional or national levels).[59] These contracts generally determine the scope of the specific arrangement (both personal and material), specify the financial conditions and address other organizational aspects, such as transportation to and from the foreign hospital, the planning of after-care, etc. While arrangements involving statutory bodies generally follow the conditions and financial rules as determined in the social security coordination mechanism (see above), contractual arrangements (with no official involvement) often deviate from the coordination mechanism, as signing parties define different procedures and rules. This means that new elements and practices may enter a health care system via the cross-border contracting route.[60]

---

[58] I. Glinos, 'Cross-border collaboration', in Wismar *et al.* (eds.), *Cross-border healthcare*, above n.4.

[59] I. A. Glinos, R. Baeten and N. Boffin, 'Cross-border contracted care in Belgian hospitals', in M. Rosenmöller, M. McKee and R. Baeten (eds.), *Patient mobility in the European Union: learning from experience* (Copenhagen: WHO Regional Office for Europe on behalf of the European Observatory on Health Systems and Policies, 2006), pp. 97–119; T. Nebling and H.-W. Schemken, 'Cross-border contracting: the German experience', in M. Rosenmöller, M. McKee and R. Baeten (eds.), *Patient mobility in the European Union: learning from experience* (Copenhagen: WHO Regional Office for Europe on behalf of the European Observatory on Health Systems and Policies, 2006), pp. 137–56.

[60] See below.

3. Types of patient mobility and related arrangements for access

Within the broad spectrum of possible patient movements between Member States, different patient mobility types can be distinguished.[61] The most obvious distinction is between persons *needing* medical assistance while abroad (they first move, then need care) and persons *seeking* medical care abroad (they first need care, then move). Furthermore, two special categories can be identified: people living in border regions and pensioners settling in another Member State. Although these two groups represent specific features and particularities in their own right, both in terms of needs for cross-border care, as well as in terms of arrangements through which patient mobility takes place, they will be examined in the context of the two main categories above.

By 'arrangements', we mean the financial and organizational mechanisms in place to enable cross-border consumption of care and financial cover for treatment in another Member State. These arrangements constitute patient mobility 'routes', which have different origins and legal bases. As set out above, we can distinguish between three main types: the traditional coordination route, the Treaty-based route established by the ECJ case-law and the contractual route initiated bilaterally between actors in the field. The three types of arrangements differ noticeably, not just in practical and financial terms, but also in terms of which actor leads the mobility process. While the first type is a typical statutory arrangement led by public authorities, the second type is mainly driven by individual citizens (who can afford to pay up-front, as well as to cover travel and accommodation costs). In the third type, decision-making is in the hands of contracting partners. The arrangements that are relevant for each of the different patient types will be explained in greater detail below.

A. People seeking treatment abroad

In the context of the internationalization of health care, it seems to follow that patients deliberately and increasingly go abroad to obtain treatment outside the Member State of residence. Patients can be

---

[61] H. Legido-Quigley *et al.*, 'Patient mobility in the European Union', *British Medical Journal* 334 (2007), 188–90. See also M. Rosenmöller *et al.*, 'Patient mobility: the context and issues', in Rosenmöller, McKee and Baeten (eds.),

motivated to do so for various reasons: because they are confronted with waiting times at home; because the specific treatment is not available or is forbidden in their country; because of the reputation of a specific provider or treatment centre in another Member State; or because care is cheaper abroad.[62] Patients compare what is available at home and abroad, and depending on their preferences, needs and abilities, might choose to travel to obtain care.

Patients can either be sent abroad by their health system or go on their own initiative, although the two situations may be interlinked and a clear distinction would be difficult to make: patients wanting to be treated abroad might first try to obtain authorization for reimbursement reasons or patients being denied authorization might ultimately choose to go anyway and possibly legally challenge the refusal afterwards before a court. In addition, treatment providers at home often play a key role in referring patients to treatment in another Member State, as reliable information on treatment options to the general public is still scarce and scattered.[63]

Hereunder we will address the situation of patients using either the Treaty-based or the coordination route to obtain cover for treatment in another Member State. Also, special attention will be given to people living in border regions, as well as to patients getting treatment abroad in the context of pre-arranged – mostly bilateral – schemes. Finally, we will also mention purely private patients.

The remaining scope of prior authorization

As set out above, citizens in the EU fall under the principle of free movement of goods and services and are free to take up medical treatment or buy medical goods throughout the European Union.[64] Any measure that would hinder the free delivery of services and supply of goods – and its corollary of free reception of services and goods – needs to be justified on grounds of public policy, public security or public health or by overriding reasons of general interest. This also applies to the field of statutory health cover.[65] As already outlined, the

---

Patient mobility, above n.59, pp. 6–7; and Glinos and Baeten, 'A literature review', above n.2, pp. 18–21.

[62] Glinos and Baeten, 'A literature review', above n.2, pp. 18–21.

[63] Palm, Wismar and Ernst, 'Assessing possible directions', above n.51, p. 19.

[64] Joined Cases 286/82 and 26/83, *Luisi and Carbone* [1984] ECR 00377; and Case C-159/90, *SPUC* v. *Grogan* [1991] ECR I-04685.

[65] See above.

ECJ has defined the ambit of access to statutorily covered treatment not requiring prior authorization outside the state of affiliation.

Patients are free to take up non-hospital care in any Member State and claim for reimbursement with their social security system according to the tariffs and modalities applied there. In other words, treatment is covered as though it were provided in the Member State of affiliation – which also means that the treatment must be covered by the statutory system of the patient's home state. Member States have only gradually modified their administrative practices accordingly. Luxembourg and Belgium were among the first to apply 'open borders' for outpatient care.[66] Austria already applied a system of partial reimbursement of non-pre-authorized care abroad before the first rulings of the Court.[67] Germany introduced reforms in 2004 stipulating that non-hospital care is exempt from the prior authorization requirement,[68] while France and the Netherlands changed their respective legislation along similar lines in 2005.[69] With the new cross-border health care patients' rights proposal, it is expected that non-hospital care received in another Member State will be reimbursed without any additional condition up to the level of costs that would have been assumed had the same or similar health care been provided in the Member State of affiliation, without exceeding the actual costs of health care received (Articles 6(2) and 7). In cases where Member States do not have an existing set of defined reimbursement levels, they are required to put in place a mechanism for calculation based on objective, non-discriminatory criteria known in advance (Article 6(4)).

For hospital services – or, more precisely, services requiring planning in order *to guarantee a rationalized, stable, balanced and accessible*

---

[66] Initially, Belgium limited reimbursement for non-hospital care provided in another Member State without prior authorization to a ceiling of coverage up to €500 (later extended to €1000). This limitation was abolished in 2005. Also, the arrangement was, subject to certain conditions, further extended to day hospitalization, clinical laboratory analyses and pharmaceuticals purchased abroad.

[67] Palm *et al.*, 'Implications of recent jurisprudence', above n.36, p. 47.

[68] D. S. Martinsen, *EU for the patients: developments, impacts, challenges*, Report 6 (Stockholm: Swedish Institute for European Policy Studies, 2007), p. 37.

[69] M. Coucheir and Y. Jorens, 'Patient mobility in the European Union – the European framework in relation to patient mobility', Report written for the European 6th Framework Project 'Europe for Patients', European Commission, DG Research (2007).

supply of hospital services[70] – the ECJ accepted that reimbursement could be made subject to prior authorization for as long as it could be considered to be necessary, proportionate and based on objective, non-discriminatory criteria that are knowable in advance.[71] The ECJ argued that a large outflow of patients to be treated in other Member States would be liable to put at risk the very principle of having contractual arrangements with hospitals and, consequently, undermine all the planning and rationalization carried out in this vital sector to avoid the phenomena of hospital overcapacity, imbalance in the supply of hospital medical care and logistical and financial wastage.[72] In the *Stamatelaki* case, the absolute exclusion of any treatment in private hospitals abroad from statutory cover under the Greek legislation was considered by the ECJ to be a disproportionate measure, especially since restrictions on access to care in private Greek institutions were less severe.[73] As mentioned earlier, the European Commission in its new proposal for a directive has limited the use of prior authorization systems for statutory reimbursement along the same lines (Article 8(3–4)). It also obliges Member States to specify in advance and in a transparent way the criteria for refusal of prior authorization (Article 9(3)).

Although it is up to Member States to further define the scope of their authorization policies within these limits,[74] the ECJ has made clear that authorization cannot be refused for health care that is part of the statutory benefit package in the state of affiliation and that cannot be obtained there within medically justifiable time limits.[75] To properly assess the latter concept of 'undue delay' – the lack of timely access to the treatment at home – the competent institution is required to take account of all the circumstances of each individual case, including the patient's medical condition. In the cases of Mrs Van Riet and Mrs Watts, the ECJ made clear that, although Member States are entitled to institute a system of waiting lists to manage the supply

---

[70] Case C-157/99, *Geraets-Smits and Peerbooms*, above n.22, para. 81.
[71] See above.
[72] Case C-157/99, *Geraets-Smits and Peerbooms*, above n.22, para. 106.
[73] Case C-444/05, *Stamatelaki*, above n.22, paras. 27, 38.
[74] On the national practices in terms of prior authorization, see Y. Jorens, 'Cross-border health care: the use of E112 form', Training and Reporting on European Social Security (2007), p. 14; Coucheir and Jorens, 'Patient mobility', above n.69.
[75] Case C-157/99, *Geraets-Smits and Peerbooms*, above n.22, para. 103.

of treatments and to set priorities on the basis of available resources and capacities, the existence of waiting lists in itself could not justify a refusal to authorize hospital treatment in another Member State.[76] Only if the waiting time does not exceed the period that is acceptable in light of an objective medical assessment of the clinical needs of the person concerned, taking into consideration the medical condition, the history and probable course of the illness, the degree of pain and/ or the nature of the disability at the time when the authorization is sought, can authorization for treatment in another Member State be refused.[77] This reasoning has effectively opened up new opportunities for patients in the EU – rights that they might not have in their home system. When Mrs Watts brought her case in front of the High Court, the English judge in charge examined domestic legislation and human rights law to conclude that they did not constitute a basis for providing National Health Service (NHS) patients with a right to treatment. Yet, turning to EU law, the judge conceded that the freedom to seek and provide services in the EU entitles English patients to look for treatment abroad. As the Department of Health appealed against this decision, the *Watts* case reached the ECJ in early 2004.[78]

In order to establish more certainty around the concept of undue delay, some countries have started to introduce so-called 'time-dependent' guarantees, giving patients the right to be treated outside the national system and to go abroad for care if treatment is not available in the home system within specified time periods. Such treatment guarantees were introduced in 2002 in Denmark[79] and in 2004 in Norway.[80] The Irish National Treatment Purchase Fund (NTPF) has a similar effect of guaranteeing NHS patients timely access by commissioning services from the private sector, and there appears to be a shift in the approach among the English judiciary too (see above). Denmark has

---

[76] Case C-385/99, *Müller-Fauré*, above n.22, para. 92; Case C-372/04, *Watts*, above n.22, para. 75.

[77] Case C-157/99, *Geraets-Smits and Peerbooms*, above n.22, para. 104; Case C-372/04, *Watts*, above n.22, paras. 67–70, 119.

[78] J. Montgomery, 'Impact of EU law on English healthcare law', in E. Spaventa and M. Dougan (eds.), *Social welfare and EU law* (Oxford: Hart, 2003), pp. 145–56.

[79] Indenrigs- og Sundhedsministeriet, *Resultater paa sundhedsomraadet* (Copenhagen: Ministry of the Interior and Health, 2004).

[80] Trygdeetaten, *Bidrag til behandling i utlandet etter paragraf 5–22* (Oslo: Trygdeetaten/National Insurance Administration, 2004).

been one of the few Member States to adapt a revised national health policy following the *Kohll* and *Decker* rulings and later to implement a health reform to address waiting lists.[81] The 2002 reform guaranteeing Danish patients the right to be treated by a non-contracted (foreign) hospital if treatment is not available from a contracted provider within two months can be seen as a reaction to the *Geraets-Smits and Peerbooms* ruling.[82] Indeed, the preparatory documents on the reform make an explicit link between the ruling and the opening up of the Danish public system to allow access to publicly paid treatments outside the statutory system independently of whether care is provided in Denmark or another Member State. Since 1 October 2007, the waiting time criterion has been further reduced to one month.[83]

Other countries have also softened their policies by incorporating new rights into national law. In France, reforms in 2004–5 on the reimbursement of costs replaced the term 'abroad' with 'outside a Member State of the European Union or party to the agreement on the European Economic Area', thus signalling that restitution of health care consumed in EU/EEA Member States is not considered to be an exemption to the territoriality principle but rather to be a *right* of insured persons (subject to certain conditions allowed by the ECJ).[84] In Sweden, a series of cases brought before the Supreme Administrative Court regarding reimbursement by the national health insurance system for non-emergency care provided in Germany and France[85] also led to the Swedish authorities revising their policy towards treatment abroad after the national court recognized the right to compensation for care – even hospital care – that would have been reimbursed by the Swedish health care system if the care had been delivered in Sweden.[86]

---

[81] D. S. Martinsen, 'Towards an internal health markets with the European court', *West European Politics* 28 (2005), 1035–56.

[82] D. S. Martinsen, 'The Europeanization of welfare – the domestic impact of intra-European social security', *Journal of Common Market Studies* 43 (2005), 1027–54.

[83] Martinsen, *EU for the patients*, above n.68.

[84] Coucheir and Jorens, 'Patient mobility', above n.69.

[85] Case No. 6790–01, *Stigell* v. *The National Social Insurance Board*, Swedish Supreme Administrative Court; Case No. 6396–01, *Wistrand* v. *National Social Insurance Board*, Swedish Supreme Administrative Court; Case No. 5595–99, *Jelinek* v. *National Social Insurance Board*, Swedish Supreme Administrative Court.

[86] T. Palmqvist, 'Answers to questionnaire on the impact of EU law on national health care systems', Swedish Ministry of Health and Social

The increased choice options for patient via the access routes to care abroad sometimes also has implications for the way access to care is regulated nationally. Following the *Müller-Fauré* ruling of the ECJ, the Netherlands reviewed the principle that patients seeking care with non-contracted providers would not be covered at all. Recent French legislation is also illustrative in this respect. In mid-2004, a system of mild gatekeeping was adopted in France as part of the reorganization of the sickness insurance scheme. The new system foresees that people can register with an attending doctor of their choice (GP or specialist) who will be responsible for coordinating the patient's treatment pathway. If a patient chooses not to register or to see another doctor without prior referral, the amount of restitution from the sickness fund will be reduced. Yet a circular from May 2005 exempts insured French people from following the treatment pathway when in another Member State, and recognizes the right to choose an attending doctor in another Member State on the condition that the foreign health professional exercises the profession lawfully in the country of establishment and accepts the responsibility of being attending doctor according to French practices.[87]

Adjustments to the coordination route

Even if, in light of Articles 49 and 50 EC, the scope for denying cover of deliberate treatment in another Member State was seriously reduced, the general requirement of a prior authorization, which traditionally had also been provided for under Article 22(1)(c) of Regulation 1408/71/EEC and which is formalized through the granting of an E112 form, was upheld by the ECJ.

Given that insured persons under the coordination route are granted rights that they would not otherwise have, as they may claim reimbursement in accordance with the legislation of the place of stay, the ECJ in its *Inizan* judgement explicitly confirmed the consistency of the coordination route with Articles 49 and 50 EC on the freedom to provide services. Indeed, the Community legislator is free to accord

Affairs, 1 December 2006; questionnaire organized and sent to Member States by Observatoire social européen; U. Bernitz, 'Everyone's right to health care in Europe: the way forward', Paper prepared for the European Parliament Committee Meeting on Cross-Border Aspects of Health Services, 24 January 2007, pp. 3–4.
[87] Coucheir and Jorens, 'Patient mobility', above n.69.

rights and advantages in order to ensure freedom of movement for workers and also to attach conditions to or determine the limits thereof.[88] Nevertheless, the ECJ reinterpreted the provision of Article 22 in light of Articles 49 and 50 on two points.

First, the scope for denying prior authorization was aligned to the conditions set out above. From the *Inizan* ruling, it became clear that Member States could not take into account normal waiting times in order to assess whether they should authorize treatment abroad under the Social Security Regulation.[89] Whereas Article 22(2) initially stated that prior authorization may not be refused if the treatment in question is covered by the home state but cannot be given within the time normally necessary, the ECJ clarified that this should be understood in such a way that the request for authorization could not be turned down whenever treatment that is the same or equally effective for the patient – and that is part of the statutory benefit package – cannot be obtained without undue delay in the Member State of residence.[90] Since then, this change has been incorporated into Article 20(2) of the new Regulation 883/04/EC. It should be noted in this respect that Member States may grant authorizations for treatment in another Member State on a much wider basis even when the treatment is available without undue delay. Article 22(2) of the Regulation merely indicates when such authorizations may not be refused, but it does not set any limits as to when they may be granted.[91]

Since the conditions according to which prior authorization cannot be refused under Article 22(2) of Regulation 1408/71/EEC were completely aligned with the terms defined by the ECJ in the *Geraets-Smits and Peerbooms* ruling (see above), the 'coordination route' would be given priority in cases of undue delay. In its proposal on cross-border patient rights, the Commission stipulated that, whenever the conditions of Articles 22(1)(c) and 22(2) of Regulation 1408/71/EEC are met, the insured person shall always be granted an authorization pursuant to the Social Security Regulation (Article 9(2) *in fine*). The alternative mechanism put in place by the Directive is more specifically designed to provide a solution for citizens who may have

---

[88] Case C-56/01, *Inizan*, above n.15, paras. 22–3.
[89] Jorens, 'Cross-border health care', above n.74, p. 4.
[90] Case C-56/01, *Inizan*, above n.15, para. 45.
[91] Case C-368/98, *Vanbraekel*, above n.15, para. 31.

other reasons to travel to another country to receive treatment.[92] The Commission acknowledges that there are downsides to this procedure, as people would 'bear the financial risk of any additional costs arising'.[93] For that reason, the social security coordination procedure is given priority over the Directive, since '[t]he patient should not be deprived of the more beneficial rights guaranteed by Regulation 1408/71/EEC and 883/04/EC when the conditions are met'.[94]

If the level of payment in accordance with Article 22(1)(c) of Regulation 1408/71/EEC turns out to be lower than that to which the person would have been entitled if he/she had received (hospital) treatment in the competent Member State, an additional reimbursement covering the difference must be granted to the insured person by the competent institution.[95] This is the second improvement the ECJ has introduced on the basis of Articles 49 and 50 EC. This additional financial guarantee applies to the socially insured who were – or should have been – authorized to seek treatment in another Member State under the Social Security Regulation. Otherwise, this lower level of cover may deter or even prevent persons from accessing providers of medical services established in other Member States and therefore constitute an unjustified restriction of the freedom to provide services within the meaning of Article 49 EC.[96]

In addition, where hospital treatment is provided free of charge by a national health service and no tariff for reimbursement therefore exists in the legislation of the competent Member State, the ECJ specified that any possible user charge the patient would be required to bear in accordance with the legislation of the Member State of treatment should be additionally covered by the competent state up to the difference between the cost, objectively quantified, of the equivalent treatment in the home state and the amount reimbursed pursuant to the legislation of the treatment state, if the latter would be lower – with the total amount invoiced for the treatment received in the host

[92] European Commission, 'Proposal', above n.54, Consideration No. 21. See, further, European Commission, 'Patients' rights in cross-border care', Citizen's Summary, 2 July 2008, http://ec.europa.eu/health/ph_overview/co_operation/healthcare/docs/citizens_summary_En.pdf.

[93] European Commission, 'Proposal', above n.54, Explanatory Memorandum, p. 5.

[94] *Ibid.*, Consideration No. 22.

[95] Case C-368/98, *Vanbraekel*, above n.15, para. 53.

[96] *Ibid.*, paras. 43–52.

Member State as a maximum.[97] In this context, it should also be noted that Article 22 only grants a right to reclaim the costs of medical services received by the insured person in the host Member State. There is no right to reimbursement by the competent institution for the costs of travel, accommodation and subsistence that the insured person and any accompanying person incurred in the territory of the latter Member State, with the exception of the costs of accommodation and meals in hospital for the insured person him/herself.[98]

Whereas these additional financial guarantees were established in cases where prior authorization under Article 22(1)(c) of Regulation 1408/71/EEC are wrongly denied, this principle could also be extended to the more frequent case of occasional care delivered to a tourist, student or any other person requiring treatment while temporarily residing in the territory of another Member State (see below). Recently, the Commission has referred Spain to the ECJ over the refusal to grant additional reimbursement of the costs incurred for hospital care required during a temporary stay in another Member State.[99] Such an extension would not be without financial consequences for national security institutions, and, more significantly, would impose on them a heavy administrative burden.[100]

Improving access to care for people living in border regions

While at the periphery of Member States, border regions deserve particular attention as poles of often intense mobility. Due to short distances, the relative scarcity of facilities in peripheral areas and strong bonds among the populations (common languages, shared culture and a certain natural propensity to move across borders), border regions have more potential for patient mobility, which can reach relatively significant levels in concentrated areas. From a patient perspective, it is mainly proximity and familiarity that make people seek health care across the border. There appears to be a link between motivations and distance: the stronger the linguistic and cultural affinity and the shorter the distance to the border, the more likely it is that incentives

---

[97] Case C-372/04, *Watts*, above n.22, para. 131.
[98] Case C-466/04, *Acereda-Herrera* [2006] ECR I-05341.
[99] European Commission, 'Spain: reimbursement of the cost of hospital care required during a temporary stay in another Member State', Press Release No. IP/08/328, 28 February 2008.
[100] Coucheir and Jorens, 'Patient mobility', above n.69.

such as reputation of providers, ease of travel and familiarity with going abroad will encourage people to travel. Vice versa, longer distances to the foreign provider require stronger push factors to make patients travel for treatment (e.g., long waiting times, dissatisfaction or lack of specific services in the home system).[101]

As European integration has traditionally focused on the movement of workers, the particular situation of border region populations was translated into specific health care rights for frontier workers.[102] This category of workers, living and working on either side of the border, benefited from an unconditional double access to the health systems in both the working and residence state. Some Member States decided to extend these entitlements to the family members of frontier workers. In the context of the modernization of the social security coordination instrument, this extension has now been integrated into the new Regulation 883/04/EC.[103] Furthermore, the benefit of double access is also extended to retired frontier workers. After retirement, a frontier worker can continue a treatment that was already started in the Member State where he/she last pursued his/her activity as an employed or self-employed person.[104] Beyond the case of continuation of treatment, Member States can also decide to maintain retired frontier workers' unconditional right to treatment in their former working state. This would only apply to persons who have worked for at least two years as frontier workers in the five years preceding the effective date of old age or invalidity pension. Furthermore, both the former working state as well as the competent Member State that is to cover the medical expenses of the retired frontier worker in his/her state of residence have to have opted for this possibility and have to be listed

---

[101] R. G. Frost, 'Follow-up treatment of breast cancer patients in Flensburg of citizens from Southern Jutland County', Southern Jutland County (2000), p. 13; N. Boffin and R. Baeten, 'Dutch patients evaluate contracted care in Belgian hospitals: results of a mail survey', Observatoire social européen (2005); Glinos and Baeten, 'A literature review', above n.2, pp. 59–75.

[102] 'Frontier worker' is defined as any person pursuing an activity as an employed or self-employed person in a Member State and who resides in another Member State to which he/she returns as a rule daily or at least once a week. Article 1(f), Regulation 883/04/EC, above n.18.

[103] Article 18(2), Regulation 883/04/EC, above n.18. It should be noted that Member States have been given the possibility of opting out of this extension to family members, through their inclusion in Annex III.

[104] Article 28(1), Regulation 883/04/EC, above n.18. 'Continuation of treatment' means the continued investigation, diagnosis and treatment of an illness.

in Annex V. This will also apply to family members of retired frontier workers for as long as they already benefit from the extension under Article 18(2) in the period prior to retirement of the frontier worker or his/her death.[105]

Despite these extensions, which still mainly depend on Member States' discretion, the notion of 'frontier worker' was not replaced by 'frontier resident' in the new Social Security Regulation. To respond to local needs, specific arrangements have therefore been set up to allow patient mobility in border regions.[106] Local stakeholders have long been active in setting up these kinds of arrangements, with the aim of achieving cross-border complementarity between facilities and improving services available to the local populations. The function of these arrangements is generally to simplify access procedures for cross-border care, mainly through developing a relaxed version of the E112 procedure, which automatically grants prior authorization for cross-border care for people living in a border region. A series of regional projects involving local hospitals, statutory health insurers and health authorities along the borders between France and Belgium and between the Netherlands, Germany and Belgium have taken this approach to facilitating patient flows. Another approach is that of cross-border contracting between a funding body (statutory health insurer or health authority) and a hospital, between two statutory health insurers or between two hospitals. There is a concentration of contractual agreements on the borders between the Netherlands and its two neighbours, Germany and Belgium, but contracts also exist on the border between Denmark and Germany, and between Scandinavian regions. It should be noted that border region arrangements of either type can cover selected treatments, such as elective care, and can cover the entire border region population or just segments of it.

Contractual arrangements for planned care

In recent years, a growing number of health care funding bodies have started to explore the third patient mobility route by contracting with

---

[105] Article 28(3), Regulation 883/04/EC, above n.18.

[106] Besides the extension of the double access to family members of frontier workers, Belgium also abolished the requirement of prior authorization for any hospital care and renal dialysis performed in an institution situated less than 25 km from the Belgian border for any Belgian insured person residing less than 15 km from the border.

foreign providers. This has partly been a result of Member States adapting to the ECJ rulings by changing national legislation.

As a structural arrangement that controls patient flows while allowing mobility, contracting offers a way for purchasers to combine the concerns of sustainability and cost controls with those of satisfying a population's needs and expectations.[107] Cross-border contracts can either follow the rules of the social security coordination instrument or apply their own rules and tariffs established through negotiation between the contracting partners. These new practices and mechanisms, establishing parallel sub-systems of tariffs, quality standards and legal conditions can lead to new pressures. As public authorities are not necessarily aware of or involved in contractual processes, it may challenge the functioning of national health systems and change relations between stakeholders and actors.[108]

Patients who are given the opportunity to go abroad by their home funding body may do so in a pre-arranged setting. In several countries, long waiting lists have prompted public authorities to offer patients faster access abroad, or authorities have chosen not to deliver specific services within the country, for example, when population numbers do not justify it. In both cases, patients are 'sent abroad' to receive care that is part of the domestic benefit package. This implies that the practical aspects of the cross-border route, including medical appointments and travelling, are organized by the purchasing body, and that expenses are covered by the competent body.

Examples of countries that have set up structures for sending patients abroad include England, Ireland, Norway and the Netherlands. In December 2004, a paragraph was inserted into the Dutch law on contractual agreements between insurers and hospitals in order to provide a legal basis for Dutch insurers to contract with foreign hospitals that are part of the social security system of the state of establishment.[109] Yet, as early as 2002, at a time when the Netherlands was referred to the ECJ, the Dutch authorities had advised health insurers to conclude contracts with foreign providers if they planned to systematically offer their affiliated members access to cross-border care. The English NHS

---

[107] Glinos, Baeten and Boffin, 'Cross-border contracted care', above n.59, pp. 97–118.
[108] *Ibid.*
[109] Coucheir and Jorens, 'Patient mobility', above n.69.

set up two short-lived schemes in 2001–3 to send waiting list patients
to Germany, France and Belgium; in the same period, the Norwegian
health service created a 'patient bridge', which, for three years, channelled patients to Scandinavian and other countries; in Ireland, the
National Treatment Purchase Fund, in place since 2002, allows waiting list patients access to private hospitals in Ireland and the United
Kingdom. All these initiatives have emerged after the early landmark
ECJ rulings, and it could be suggested that the (pending) court cases,
together with domestic factors, such as highly unpopular waiting lists
and mounting political pressure from public dissatisfaction, might have
led Member States to look abroad to tackle shortages.[110] It is probably
no coincidence that all the countries that have made overseas arrangements are based on benefit-in-kind and, with the notable exception of
the Netherlands, are NHS-based systems, considered to be more prone
to capacity problems. Another characteristic is that arrangements are
based on cross-border contracting between the NHS (health insurers
in the Dutch case) and foreign providers.

The contracts make it possible for the sending country to define all
aspects of the cross-border care route, including medical and quality standards, procedures used, services given, prices, length of stays,
numbers of patients going abroad, etc., and thereby control patient
movements and costs while ensuring that patients receive care that
fulfils national criteria and expectations.[111] On the other hand, however, contracting can present challenges to the receiving country,
depending on the approach taken by the contracting parties.

A different approach is to embed contracts in bilateral framework
agreements signed between the competent authorities of the states
involved. In early 2003, such an agreement was signed between
Belgium and England.[112] Belgian health authorities were concerned

---

[110] College voor zorgverzekeringen, 'Grensoverschrijdende zorg', Circulaire
02/021, 2 May 2002; K. Lowson, P. West, S. Chaplin and J. O'Reilly,
'Evaluation of treating patients overseas', York Health Economics
Consortium, Department of Health (England), July 2002, www.dh.gov.uk/
en/Publicationsandstatistics/Publications/PublicationsPolicyAndGuidance/
DH_4005742.

[111] For an inventory of the elements that cross-border contracts might include,
see High Level Group on Health Services and Medical Care, 'Guidelines on
purchase of treatment abroad', 9 November 2005, http://ec.europa.eu/health/
ph_overview/co_operation/mobility/docs/highlevel_2005_017_en.pdf.

[112] UK Department of Health and Belgium, 'A framework for cross-border
patient mobility and exchange of experience in the field of health care

that cross-border contracts would put the integrity of the national system at risk and therefore sought an accord that clearly stated that foreign patients could not be given priority over Belgian patients and that official Belgian tariffs would be adhered to in the contracts.[113] Yet, in most cases, such bilateral agreements do not exist and stakeholders are not bound to follow national requirements regarding tariffs, medical procedures, quality standards, etc. Instead, contracting parties negotiate on these aspects, which generally results in the purchasers imposing the requirements in force in their system on the foreign providers receiving the patients. New elements might thus be introduced into the receiving system that can have adverse effects if parallel circuits are created in which it becomes lucrative to treat foreign (commercial) patients compared to domestic patients.[114] This is potentially a problem when contracts are made with hospitals that serve patients from the publicly financed system in their country. In this respect, the issue of applying different pricing for foreign patients was also mentioned as a concern in the public consultation undertaken by the Commission.[115]

It should be mentioned that Member States can take a different approach to sending patients abroad for care that is not available at home. Since the 1970s, Malta has had a bilateral agreement with the United Kingdom for sending Maltese patients requiring highly specialized treatments to United Kingdom hospitals (mainly in London). The scheme is rooted in a waiver agreement that assumes that the cost of treating large numbers of United Kingdom tourists in Malta is equivalent to the cost of treating far smaller numbers of Maltese patients with diseases requiring highly specialized equipment and facilities in the United Kingdom.[116] Luxembourg, being a small country surrounded by larger neighbours, has taken the approach of granting prior authorizations for planned care (based on Regulation 1408/71/EEC) more liberally than most other Member States.

between Belgium and England', Common Framework between the UK Department of Health and Belgium, 3 February 2003.

[113] I.A. Glinos, N. Boffin and R. Baeten, 'Contracting Cross-border Care in Belgian Hospitals: An Analysis of Belgian, Dutch and English Stakeholder Perspectives', Observatoire social européen, August 2005, pp. 29–30.

[114] Glinos, Baeten and Boffin, 'Cross-border contracted care', above n.59.

[115] European Commission, 'Consultation', above n.7.

[116] N. A. Muscat *et al.*, 'Sharing capacities – Malta and the United Kingdom', in Rosenmöller, McKee and Baeten (eds.), *Patient mobility in the EU*, above

Private patients

As noted above, citizens in the EU are, in principle, free to seek any health care, where they want and from whatever provider available – the only limitation being their ability to pay for it or the conditions set out by public and private funding systems for health care. When patient mobility occurs because the desired care is not part of the national benefit package and patients have to pay out-of-pocket or through private insurance cover, a series of particular issues may arise as patients seek treatment on their own initiative. Although the data are far from complete, there are clear indications of 'private' patients travelling within the EU for cheaper treatments[117] (dental care, aesthetic surgery, etc.) or for care that is outlawed or non-existent at home (e.g., abortion and late term abortion, fertility treatments, genetic screening, as well as (unapproved) alternative treatment methods for various serious diseases). As these mobile patients go abroad on their own initiative, often based on information found through Internet sources, they are not necessarily supported in their selection of foreign providers and may face issues related to quality and safety of care, as well as obtaining appropriate after-care when returning home. This patient group might be in an altogether more delicate situation due to the ethical controversies surrounding the care they seek abroad.

B. People in need of care while temporarily abroad

Apart from patients moving across borders, Europeans in general increasingly travel across the European Union for work, study or leisure. Consequently, situations where people need to receive medical attention while temporarily staying in another Member State have become ever more frequent. As their length of stay and their familiarity with the country of stay vary, the needs of these groups in terms of access to and

---

n.59, pp. 119–36; J. M. Cachia, 'Cross-border care: provision of highly specialized hospital services to island populations – a case study of the Maltese Islands', Ministry of Health (2004).

[117] T. Albreht, R. P. Brinovec and J. Stalc, 'Cross-border care in the south: Slovenia, Austria and Italy', in Rosenmöller, McKee and Baeten (eds.), *Patient mobility in the EU*, above n.59, pp. 9–21; J. Cienski, 'Polish health services quick to cash in on eager EU patients', *Financial Times*, 20 June 2005, p. 4; A. Cojean, 'Tourisme dentaire en Hongrie: beaux sourires de ... Budapest!', *Le Monde*, 20 August 2005, pp. 18–21; Glinos and Baeten, 'A literature review', above n.2.

use of health care facilities will differ considerably. While tourists will mainly need emergency care, people staying longer in another Member State might need access to the full range of health care services.

Extending the right to occasional care abroad

To accommodate this situation, the scope of the coordination route has been progressively extended. Where, initially, Article 22(1)(a) of Regulation 1408/71/EEC only granted access to treatment during a temporary stay[118] in another Member State for 'immediately necessary care', this was widened towards 'benefits in kind which become necessary on medical grounds during a stay in the territory of another Member State, taking into account the nature of the benefits and the expected length of the stay'.[119] This change was also motivated by the introduction of the European Health Insurance Card (EHIC) as of 1 May 2004, to replace the E111 form,[120] which was part of the EU Action Plan on Skills and Mobility,[121] aimed at promoting the mobility of citizens and particularly that of workers in the context of the Lisbon strategy. To enable a more easy and uniform access to health care for EU citizens while temporarily staying outside their state of affiliation, an alignment of rights was required with the categories of pensioners and their family members, who on the basis of Article 31 of the Regulation were exempted from the condition of urgency. The ECJ had already indicated that the right of a (Greek) pensioner to benefits in kind during a temporary stay in another Member State could not be made subject to the condition that the illness he suffered from had manifested itself suddenly and was not linked to a

---

[118] In the context of this Regulation, the difference between temporary stay and (more) permanent stay (residence) is important for the definition of entitlements.

[119] European Parliament and Council Regulation 631/2004/EC amending Council Regulation 1408/71/EEC on the application of social security schemes to employed persons, to self-employed persons and to members of their families moving within the Community, and Council Regulation 574/72/EEC laying down the procedure for implementing Regulation 1408/71/EEC, in respect of the alignment of rights and the simplification of procedures, OJ 2004 No. L100/1.

[120] European Commission, 'Communication concerning the introduction of the European health insurance card', COM (2003) 73 final, 17 February 2003.

[121] European Commission, 'Action plan of the Commission on skills and mobility', COM (2002) 72 final, 13 February 2002.

pre-existent pathology of which he was aware.[122] Clearly, the ECJ wanted to prevent the situation that citizens suffering from a chronic condition would be excluded from their right to mobility.

Although the EHIC was promoted as a sort of European passport for citizens, it was not intended to create any new entitlements or to establish an unconditional right to medical care across the EU. Since, by the abolition of the emergency requirement, it became difficult to distinguish occasional (E111 form) from planned cross-border care (E112 form), two additional criteria were introduced to assess the medical need for care while abroad: the nature of the benefits and the expected length of stay. As a method to implement these elements in practice, the Administrative Commission on Social Security for Migrant Workers suggested that it should be determined whether the medical treatment was aimed at enabling the insured person to continue his/her stay under medically safe conditions pending treatment by his/her usual doctor so as to prevent him/her from being obliged to return home for treatment.[123] To clarify certain aspects, the Administrative Commission recognized the applicability of Article 22(1)(a) for benefits in kind provided in conjunction with pregnancy and childbirth.[124] Furthermore, in line with Article 22(1)(a), it included kidney dialysis and oxygen therapy in a non-exhaustive list of benefits in kind that, in order to be provided during a stay in another Member State, require, for practical reasons, a prior agreement between the person concerned and the institution providing the care.[125]

Although the Administrative Commission clearly mentions that the European Health Insurance Card is not meant to cover situations

[122] Case C-326/00, *IKA* v. *Ioannidis* [2003] ECR I-01703.
[123] Administrative Commission on Social Security for Migrant Workers, 'Guidelines for uniform application of Article 22(1)(a)(i) by the social security institutions of the Member States', CASSTM Note 376/03, Annexe 1a; Decision No. 194 of the Administrative Commission on Social Security for Migrant Workers concerning the uniform application of Article 22(1)(a)(i) of Council Regulation 1408/71/EEC in the Member State of stay, OJ 2004 No. L104/127.
[124] Decision No. 195 of the Administrative Commission on Social Security for Migrant Workers on the uniform application of Article 22(1)(a)(i) of Regulation 1408/71/EEC as regards health care in conjunction with pregnancy and childbirth, OJ 2004 No. L160/133.
[125] Decision No. 196 of the Administrative Commission on Social Security for Migrant Workers of 23 March 2004 pursuant to Article 22(1a), OJ 2004 No. L160/135.

where the aim of the temporary stay is to receive medical treatment, it cannot be excluded that it would be used to bypass prior authorization for planned care, especially since under the coordination route the benefit basket of the host country applies, and patients could be motivated to seek care that would not be reimbursed – or reimbursed to a lesser extent – in the state of affiliation. The assessment of whether the conditions are met lies in the hands of the treating care provider. To prevent any abuse, it is recommended that social security institutions should instruct these providers[126] and cooperate with each other. The fear of abuse should not lead to the duplication of medical examinations by the competent institution in the home state[127] nor to any penalization of the insured persons. In the context of urgent vitally necessary treatment, the Court considered that a person covered by an E111 or E112 form cannot be required to return to the competent Member State to undergo a medical examination there. It highlights that the competent institution, once it has consented, by issuing the E111 or E112 form, to one of its insured persons receiving medical treatment in a Member State other than the competent Member State, is bound by the findings of the doctors authorized by the institution of the Member State of stay, acting within the scope of their office, during the period of validity of the form. They are clearly best placed to assess the state of health of the person concerned and the immediate treatment required by that state. This would even extend to the decision of transferring the patient to a hospital establishment in another state, even if that state is not a Member State.[128]

---

[126] Administrative Commission on Social Security for Migrant Workers, 'Practical information for health care providers receiving European health insurance card holders', CASSTM Note 376/03, Annexe 1b.

[127] Reference is made to Case C-344/89, *Martinez Vidal* [1991] ECR I-3245, in which the ECJ ruled that, in the case of recognition of invalidity, the competent institution is required to take into account any documents and reports drawn up by institutions of any other Member State in order to avoid repetition of examinations.

[128] Case C-145/03, *Keller* [2005] ECR I-2529, paras. 50–63. The reasoning of the Court is based on a sharing of responsibilities between the competent institution and the institution of the Member State of stay, in correlation with the Community framework on the mutual recognition of professional qualifications. However, some have pointed to some inconsistencies in the ruling as regards respecting the logic of Article 22 and the division of responsibilities upon which it relies. Coucheir and Jorens, 'Patient mobility', above n.69.

Whereas the main reason for introducing the European Health Insurance Card was to modernize and simplify the administrative practice for receiving occasional care across the European Union,[129] practical problems still may handicap the coordination route. Firstly, since Article 22 obliges holders of European Health Insurance Cards to comply with local rules in regard to accessing care, reimbursement might be refused if they seek care with providers who are working outside the statutory health care system in the host state. The situation may be exacerbated given that patients often do not know the foreign health care system or the language of the country. Furthermore, it is reported that, in certain Member States, some providers would not accept the card, with patients ending up having to pay for the care themselves and then to claim reimbursement back home.[130] In principle, the coordination route provides for the possibility of reimbursement by the competent institution back home according to the applicable tariffs in the state of treatment in the case that formalities could not be completed during the stay.[131] However, given all these practical stumbling blocks and the

[129] The different paper forms used (E110, E111, E119, E128) were replaced by one card, which, at a later stage, should also allow for electronic communication between competent institutions in different Member States. Also, citizens can no longer be required to first contact the social security institution before seeing a health care provider.

[130] M. Rosenmöller and M. Lluch, 'Meeting the needs of long-term residents in Spain', in Rosenmöller, McKee and Baeten (eds.), *Patient mobility in the EU*, above n.59, pp. 59–78.

[131] Article 34(1), Regulation 574/72/EC, above n.13, provides for the possibility to reimburse costs at the request of the person involved on his return home. In principle, reimbursement is adjudged according to the applicable tariffs in the state of stay. When necessary, this state will be called on to provide the relevant information on these tariffs. On the other hand, the institution of the place of residence may reimburse at its own tariffs, with the consent of the person involved, if these tariffs allow for reimbursement and if the total costs do not exceed the amount set by the Administrative Commission (see Decision No. 176 concerning reimbursement by the competent institution in a Member State of the costs incurred during a stay in another Member State by means of the procedure referred to in Article 34(4) of Regulation 574/72/EEC, OJ 2000 No. L243/42) and without the consent of the person involved, if the state of stay does not dispose of any reimbursement rates (Article 34(5)). Also, the proposal for the Regulation laying down the procedure for implementing Regulation 883/2004/EC, which is supposed to replace Regulation 574, provides for similar provisions under Article 25(6–7). See European Commission, 'Proposal for a Regulation of the

complexity of the coordination route, patients in some cases could use the Treaty-based route to directly claim reimbursement according to home state tariffs. This would be clearly the case for outpatient care services purchased in another Member State that are part of the home state benefit package. Member States remain in charge of fixing the reimbursement levels to which patients are entitled, although these have to be based on objective, non-discriminatory and transparent criteria. Also, the systematic refusal of the EHIC by providers in some countries and the need to respond to certain demands for better and more adapted treatment (in the individual's own language) has pushed some national health insurers to directly contract foreign providers in certain foreign regions popular with holidaymakers. This has become possible as Member States have adapted national legislation to the ECJ rulings. In 2004, German health care reforms were implemented to allow cross-border contracts provided that the services covered are included in the German benefit basket; that the foreign providers are part of the statutory system of the country of establishment; and that the requirements of German law are incorporated into the contracts.[132] Indeed, several German sickness funds have opened up contractual routes for affiliated members travelling in the EU.[133]

European Parliament and of the Council laying down the procedure for implementing Regulation 883/2004/EC on the coordination of social security systems', COM (2006) 16 final, 31 January 2006.

[132] A. Schneider, 'Grenzüberschreitende Inanspruchnahme von Krankenhausleistungen aus der Sicht des BMGS', *Zeitschrift fur europaishes Sozial- und Arbeitsrecht* 10 (2004), 413–5.

[133] The German sickness funds AOK Rheinland and Techniker Krankenkasse (TK) have had contracts with Dutch and Belgian hospitals on the Northern Sea coast line since 2003 as a result of German tourists having difficulties in getting their E111 forms accepted or even recognized by providers. Due to the same problems with accessing Austrian emergency facilities following ski injuries, TK has been in contract negotiations with University Hospital of Innsbruck. Nebling and Schemken, 'Cross-border contracting', above n.59. Some German insurers (such as Taunus BKK) have started making direct contracts with individual German doctors who have settled down on the Spanish coast where there is an important concentration of German tourists (for example, in Majorca). Rosenmöller and Lluch, 'Meeting the needs', above n.130. This not only creates an entire German health care network in another country, but also breaks with German practices, as direct contracts between purchasers and individual providers are not allowed on German territory but have to be concluded with the *Krankenversicherung*, the doctors association. Glinos, 'Cross-border collaboration', above n.58.

Taking into account the changing health care needs of people retiring to other countries

Pensioners retiring to a different Member State than their home country justify special attention because of their particular features. This 'high risk' population group presents specific age-related health care needs and raises related financial questions about who is to cover their health care costs.[134]

According to official figures, in July 2006 more than 300 000 United Kingdom citizens were receiving their pension in another Member State, with top destination countries being Ireland (103 667), followed by Spain (76 357) and France, Italy and Germany (with more than 30 000 United Kingdom pensioners each).[135] In December 2004, more than 50 000 German citizens were receiving their pension from the German statutory pension insurance in another Member State: 16 375 in Austria, followed by some 12 000 both in France and in Spain.[136] These data should be treated with caution due to likely underreporting, as not all residents actually submit an E121 form[137] or register with authorities in the new Member State, even though they reside there for more than three months per year. These so-called 'false tourists' are likely to regularly travel between their country of origin and the new country where they use the European Health Insurance Card or private insurance to access health services.

The 'false tourism' phenomenon could even be stimulated by the fact that pensioners, when registering in the new Member State, lose their right to directly access care in their former home country. The ECJ confirmed that Article 22(1)(c) and (i) of Regulation 1408/71/EEC also applies to a pensioner and members of his/her family who officially reside in a Member State other than the one that is liable for

---

[134] Rosenmöller and Lluch, 'Meeting the needs', above n.130.

[135] H. Legido-Quigley and D. La Parra, 'The health care needs of UK pensioners living in Spain: an agenda for research', *Eurohealth* 13 (2007), 14–8.

[136] Verband Deutscher Rentenversicherungsträger, *VDR Statistik*, Vol. 152 – Rentenbestand (Frankfurt am Main: VDR, 2004), Table 18, p. 23.

[137] Under the Social Security Regulation, form E121 constitutes the certified statement required for the purposes of registering a pensioner and members of his/her family with the institution of their place of residence in accordance with Article 28 of Regulation No. 1408/71, above n.13, and Article 29 of Regulation 574/72/EC, above n.13. This form is provided by the competent institution in the Member State granting the pension and in charge of covering the health care costs, following the rules established in Articles 27–8, Regulation 1408/71/EC, above n.13.

payment of that pension, and who wishes to get medical treatment in another Member State, even if that would be the state paying for his/her pension, as laid down by Article 28 of that same Regulation.[138] Furthermore, the prior authorization and the related E112 form need to be issued by the institution of the place of residence.[139] This also follows from the fact that all health care costs for this particular group are systematically covered on the basis of a yearly lump sum to be paid by the competent institution in the Member State liable for paying the pension to the new Member State of residence.[140] As a compensation for this lump sum payment, the financial liability for this group is integrally transferred to the institution in the state of residence, which has to be considered as competent to grant authorization for care abroad. As explained, in so far as treatment can be provided within medically acceptable time-limits, the residence state can refuse to cover for the pensioner wishing to return for medical reasons to his/her country of origin. To ease this situation, it is explicitly provided for under the new Social Security Regulation that, similar to the double access right for frontier workers, Member States can opt for the possibility of granting their pensioners residing in another Member State a permanent right to return for care in their territory at the expense of the competent institution.[141] Furthermore, in an attempt to rebalance the financial costs for pensioners between Member States, the rule of lump sum coverage between states for the category of pensioners has been abolished,[142] thus shifting responsibility for granting prior authorization back to the competent Member State – i.e., the state paying for the pension. This not only disrupts the logic behind the entire lump sum system but also increases administrative complexity.

4. Towards a community framework for safe, high-quality and efficient care?

Although consecutive rulings of the ECJ, as well as legislative proposals and decisions of the Administrative Commission on Social Security

---

[138] Case C-156/01, *van der Duin* v. *Wegberg/ANOZ* [2003] ECR I-7045, para. 51.
[139] *Ibid.*, para. 56.
[140] Article 36, Regulation 1408/71/EC, above n.13; Article 95, Regulation 574/72/EC, above n.13.
[141] Articles 2, 27, Regulation 883/04/EC, above n.18, which requires these Member States to be listed in its Annexe IV.
[142] Articles 4, 5, 27, Regulation 883/04/EC, above n.18.

for Migrant Workers, have further clarified different issues regarding the rules applicable to treatment received outside the state of affiliation, still more clarity is called for.[143] However, as was expressed throughout the public consultation that the European Commission's Directorate-General for Health and Consumer Protection organized between September 2006 and January 2007, this demand for clarity is not limited to the sole question of entitlements to reimbursement, nor is it limited to legal clarity. Indeed, it was increasingly understood that, if medical treatment throughout the European Union was to become a more common option for patients, it did not suffice to remove obstacles to the reimbursement of that care, but the establishment of a clear and transparent framework for ensuring the safety, quality and efficiency of those health services was also required. This acknowledgment of the need for so-called 'flanking measures',[144] next to clarification on the entitlement to statutory coverage for cross-border care, basically constitute the more adaptive approach announced by the European Commission after the exclusion of health care from the Services Directive.

In general, the observed diversity of quality and safety policies throughout the EU[145] were considered by many respondents to the consultation to be a major stumbling block to promoting the increased use of cross-border care. Given the lack of commonly agreed standards and of data to assess quality, the need to guarantee safe, high-quality and efficient cross-border care is, in the first place, addressed by clarifying what Member States need to do to ensure the clinical oversight of medical treatment. In its proposal, the Commission confirmed that the Member State of treatment should be entrusted with the task of ensuring that the common principles for health care – as set out in the Council Conclusions on 'common values and principles in the EU

---

[143] European Commission, 'Summary report of responses to the consultation regarding "Community action on health services"', Health and Consumer Protection Directorate-General, http://ec.europa.eu/health/ph_overview/co_operation/mobility/docs/health_services_rep_En.pdf.

[144] See Y. Jorens, 'General regulatory framework: competition and regulation in the internal market – what mixture is best for Europe?', in Federal Ministry of Health, *The social dimension in the internal market, perspectives of health care in Europe, conference documentation* (Berlin: Federal Ministry of Health, 2007), p. 19.

[145] H. Legido-Quigley *et al.*, 'Quality and safety', in Wismar *et al.* (eds.), *Cross-border healthcare*, above n.4.

health systems'[146] – are also met in the case of cross-border treatment. In particular, this implies that every Member State must ensure that treatment given to patients from other Member States is provided according to clear quality and safety standards of health care defined by that Member State, taking into account international medical science and generally recognized good medical practice, and that mechanisms are in place to both ensure that providers are able to meet these standards and that they are monitored and, where necessary, sanctioned (Article 5(a-b)). This minimum core set of obligations is meant to establish confidence in the quality and safety of health care provision throughout the EU. It is commonly agreed that, given the diversity of strategies and of levels of development in this field, only a non-regulatory and process-oriented approach would be feasible from an EU perspective.[147] While Member States remain responsible for setting the standards in their country, the Commission is allowed to develop guidelines or standards in order to facilitate the implementation of the above-mentioned provisions (Article 5(3)).[148]

Linked to this, the fear of harm arising from treatment in other countries is another aspect that calls for additional guarantees. While research indicates that in 10% of cases harm arises directly from medical intervention, the risk could be even greater for cross-border treatment due to insufficient information, inadequate assessment prior to surgery or lack of follow-up afterwards.[149] In this respect, lack of clarity and distrust centres on patient rights and liability issues. Although the Commission's proposal was renamed 'Directive on the application of patients' rights in cross-border health care', it only addresses individual patient rights to a limited extent. The Member State of treatment is also held responsible for ensuring that

---

[146] Council Conclusions on common values and principles in EU Health Systems, 2733rd Employment, Social Policy, Health and Consumer Affairs Council Meeting, Luxembourg, 1–2 June 2006, www.eu2006.at/en/News/Council_Conclusions/0106HealthSystems.pdf.

[147] Palm, Wismar and Ernst, 'Assessing possible directions', above n.51.

[148] In December 2008, the Commission adopted a Communication and a Proposal for a Council Recommendation on patient safety, including the prevention and control of health care associated infections: http://ec.europa.eu/health/ph_systems/patient_eu_en.htm.

[149] A survey conducted in the UK suggested that 18% of respondents reported complications following treatment abroad, including infections. BBC, 'Overseas ops "harm one in five" ', *BBC News*, 20 March 2008.

appropriate remedies and compensation mechanisms are in place when patients suffer harm from health care and that they can make complaints (Article 5(d)). Member States are also required to impose professional liability insurance or similar arrangements upon health care professionals (Article 5(e)). However, this does not rule out the possibility of Member States extending domestic liability coverage to patients seeking health care abroad, especially when this is deemed necessary (Recital 15).[150] Moreover, the fundamental right to privacy in the context of data processing is also mentioned as a responsibility of Member States (Article 5(f)). In this context, the consultation has drawn attention to the importance of ensuring continuity of care between different treating professionals and institutions when addressing cross-border care and the need to ensure timely exchange of personal patient data. Although the proposal also lists continuity of care as one of the areas of uncertainty to be addressed, it only reaffirms that this data transfer needs to take place in respect of the relevant provisions of the Data Protection Directive and, more specifically, in respect of patients' rights to have access to personal data concerning their health. The proposal explicitly reaffirms this right in the context of patients receiving care outside their home state (Article 6(5)). Experts have supported the idea of improving legal guarantees with respect to the use of and access to medical files.[151]

Another important component of a framework for ensuring optimal care throughout the EU is informed choice. In the first place, patients should know what the applicable rules are. This is why the new proposals reaffirm that, in cases where a patient or a provider temporarily move, the actual provision of health care is governed by the rules of the Member State of treatment (Article 11). Entitlements to statutory reimbursement are governed by the Member State of affiliation (Article 6(2–3)). Apart from the applicable legislation, there is a clear consensus that insufficient information is available on cross-border treatment. This not only refers to the availability of understandable information

---

[150] As a way of ensuring fair treatment, some countries, such as Denmark and Sweden, extend liability coverage provided by their national public no-fault insurance – which normally only applies to medical errors occurring on the national territory – when referring patients to providers abroad.

[151] Palm, Wismar and Ernst, 'Assessing possible directions', above n.51, p. 53. See Chapter 13 in this volume on the protection provided by Article 8 of the Data Protection Directive in the context of electronic health records.

regarding entitlements to statutory coverage or to the legal position with respect to liability and patient rights, but also links to the availability of treatment options throughout the Union and related information on quality and clinical outcomes. Obscurity surrounding the medical, financial and practical implications of seeking health care abroad is considered an obstacle to free movement and another source of distrust for patients. However, as experts also have pointed out, there is an opportunity and equity cost related to increasing the level of information on cross-border options, while, at the same time, information on domestic options also is not optimal.[152] While the European Commission proposes to entrust the Member State of treatment with the basic and general responsibility of providing all relevant information to enable patients to make informed choices, including information on availability, prices, cover, outcomes and professional liability (Article 5(c)), the Member State of affiliation is obliged to inform its citizens on entitlements and related administrative procedures, including mechanisms for appeal and redress, as well as terms and conditions that would apply whenever harm is caused following treatment abroad (Article 10(1–2)). In addition, patients should be informed about prior authorization systems (Article 8(5)).[153] The proposal also seeks to ensure that decisions about reimbursement of health care incurred in another Member State are taken in a timely manner. Where a period of fifteen calendar days is considered normal, this should be shorter if urgency requires.[154] The elements that were listed by the ECJ to define 'undue delay' in an individual case are here used to assess the time limits within which Member States should deal with individual requests (Article 9(4)). To combine all efforts in terms of improving information, the Commission proposes to establish national contact points for cross-border care in all Member States, which should provide and disseminate available information, as well as assist patients in protecting their rights, seeking appropriate redress and facilitating the out-of-court settlement of disputes arising from cross-border health care (Article 12).

[152] Palm, Wismar and Ernst, 'Assessing possible directions', above n.51, p. 17.
[153] Minimal requirements for these information obligations, especially when Member States need to address citizens coming from abroad, are not specified in the proposal. Only the case of information about entitlements is left to the Commission, which is assisted by a special Committee of Member States representatives, under Article 19, in developing a standard Community format, Article 10(3).
[154] European Commission, 'Proposal', above n.54, Consideration No. 33.

Finally, it is also increasingly understood that patient mobility is not just a matter of enabling patients to seek treatment elsewhere but also requires cooperation and mutual assistance among Member States, ranging from specific collaboration in border regions to overall coordination and monitoring. European cooperation is considered to add value to the individual actions of Member States because of the scale or nature of the health care concerned.[155] The Commission's proposal establishes a general duty of cooperation (Article 13) necessary for the implementation of all provisions contained in the Directive. More specific areas of cooperation are defined in recognizing medicines prescriptions throughout the Union (Article 14), developing European reference networks (Article 15), achieving interoperability for e-health applications (Article 16), collecting statistical and other complementary data for monitoring cross-border care (Article 17), and in assessing new health technologies (Article 18). The actual implementation of cooperation in these fields, however, depends greatly on the willingness of Member States to invest in it.

5. Conclusions

After more than ten years of public attention to the relatively modest phenomenon of patient mobility in the European Union, the much advocated need for legal clarity and certainty has still not been achieved. With the jurisprudence of the ECJ, an alternative, less restrictive and less cumbersome procedure was created on the basis of the principle of free movement of services and goods for the statutory cover of health care delivered outside the state of affiliation. The new procedure not only has a different legal base than the traditional social security coordination mechanism, but also applies a different concept of equal treatment: whereas under the latter cross-border patients are treated as though they were insured in the country of treatment, under the Treaty-based route they are treated as though the treatment were provided in the country of affiliation. As a consequence, different legislation applies in terms of benefit packages, applicable tariffs and conditions, as well as formalities that need to be observed. Despite consecutive rulings of the ECJ and attempts to align and codify procedures, the situation is still confused. Member

---

[155] European Commission, 'A Community framework', above n.14, p. 6.

States have only reluctantly started to review their administrative practices in terms of relaxing conditions for treatment outside their territory. Moreover, the review and modernization of the social security coordination framework could not integrate both routes, nor has it led to the simplification of administrative procedures and the resolution of practical problems, such as the acceptance of the European Health Insurance Card. Despite all this, the coordination route still applies and was not ruled out by the ECJ; in many respects, it remains preferable to the free choice route established through case-law, as it provides better social protection and certainty for patients.

Through the ECJ's rulings, and also through developments in the field enacted by health care actors (sickness funds, providers, local and regional authorities, etc.), options for patients to obtain cover for treatment outside their home state have increased, thereby challenging the territoriality foundations of health care systems.[156] Even where prior authorization is upheld, the discretionary power of Member States to apply it has been restricted. In fact, authorization can only be refused if the same treatment or a treatment that is equally effective for the patient can be obtained without undue delay in the Member State of residence. Prior authorization is only one of the instruments policy-makers use to control costs and ensure safe, high quality and efficient health services within their statutory health system. Its curtailment by the ECJ, therefore, had a significant symbolic meaning, announcing potentially even more far-reaching clashes between the objectives pursued within national health policy and obligations under EU law.[157] Some argue that the freedom of services approach puts too great an emphasis on patient choice at the expense of the fundamental values of European health care systems, particularly efficiency, solidarity and equality of access.[158] This is probably also why Member States initially reacted so vigorously to the ECJ jurisprudence and became more willing afterwards to engage in a political debate on the issue. The exclusion of health care from the Services Directive in 2006 was perhaps less related to the inclusion of Article 23 codifying ECJ case-law on patient mobility than to other provisions and obligations extending the internal market approach to new regulatory

---

[156] Martinsen, *EU for the patients*, above n.68.
[157] See Chapters 7, 8 and 9 in this volume on health services and competition.
[158] Hervey and Trubek, 'Freedom to provide health care', above n.37.

instruments or areas that were not even directly linked with the issue of mobility or that did not contain any cross-border elements. This is probably why, despite its limited scope and impact, patient mobility has attracted so much political attention over the years. It has opened the door towards aligning health systems overall with market logic and entrepreneurialism, which had become apparent in the systems or were introduced by reforms in the late 1980s and early 1990s.[159]

The need for more governance on patient mobility is not only motivated by the need for more legal certainty as to the application of internal market rules on health care. The uncertainties go beyond legal questions. As patient mobility types and patterns have diversified and motivations for patients to seek treatment outside their home state have changed, so too has the debate on patient mobility moved from being merely a matter of entitlements towards other issues, including quality of care, liability, responsibility, safety of care received abroad, etc. As indicated by the process enacted by the 2003 High Level Process of Reflection on Patient Mobility and Health Care Developments in the EU, there is an increasingly felt need to directly coordinate health care systems through closer cooperation between actors across borders and the creation of a common framework for ensuring safe, high-quality and efficient health care provision throughout the Union. However, some kind of legal framework is needed to embed these 'flanking measures' and steer the processes. This is what the European Commission has been aiming to do by developing a 'more adapted' legislative proposal after health services were excluded from the Services Directive.

The proposal for a new framework will still need to make it through the legislative process. In addition, it remains to be seen whether it will be able to effectively change the context for organizing and regulating health care provision throughout the EU. Considering the wide diversity in how health systems are structured, financed and regulated, the proposal developed by the Commission remains relatively vague and minimal. Since no minimal standards are provided for many of the obligations to be taken on by Member States and no concrete measures are being proposed

[159] R. B. Saltman, R. Busse and E. Mossialos, *Regulating entrepreneurial behaviour in European health care systems* (Buckingham: Open University Press, 2002).

for cross-border cooperation, much will depend on the willingness of Member States. As to the question of entitlements to cover for health care provided in another Member State, the new proposal by the Commission seems to go even further than the previous Article 23 in the Services Directive. It sheds more doubts in terms of the applicable benefit package, the use of prior authorization for hospital treatment in another Member State, as well as the conformity of conditions and formalities to which statutory reimbursement can be made subject. In this way, the proposal may not sufficiently reassure Member States as to their control over patient flows and its financial implications. On the other hand, the final proposal, to some extent, reinstates the traditional social security coordination mechanism as the preferred route, whenever the conditions for its application apply. It recognizes that this procedure provides more financial certainty for patients.

Meanwhile, developments of a different nature are taking place that are likely to change the outlook and patterns of patient mobility and cross-border care, creating new challenges for health systems. Besides a growing commercial drive in health care combined with increased access to information about treatment options, developments in e-health are likely to raise new legal questions as to what legislation applies in a specific case.[160] Furthermore, other legal and ethical problems could arise from more controversial interventions that may be entirely or partially outlawed at home due to bioethical concerns.[161] Although no systematic research has been carried out yet on these patient flows, anecdotal evidence from across Europe provides examples of couples travelling to other countries for fertility treatments and pre-implantation genetic diagnosis, women seeking to have an abortion or to give birth under anonymity when giving up the child for adoption, cases of people going abroad for euthanasia, stem cell therapy, gene treatments against cancer or to carry out genital mutilation. Considering these developments, any legal framework to be developed for cross-border care should be sufficiently flexible to progressively incorporate novel aspects.

For all these reasons, the question of who is actually steering the policy of increased mobility in health care has become more pressing than ever. While national governments initiated the discussion

[160] See Chapter 13 in this volume.   [161] See Chapter 6 in this volume.

on patient mobility, the Commission has gradually put itself in the driving seat of the political process. But, here also, we can observe divergent actions from different Directorates-General, with different approaches and objectives. Stakeholders and the European Parliament have played a significant role in taking health services and the reimbursement of cross-border care out of the 'horizontal' Services Directive. High level processes and groups have, until now, been unable to reach a consensus over this issue, or to design a desirable framework. With the proposed new Community framework on the application of patients' rights in cross-border health care, we are entering a new phase, which, it is hoped, will lead to clearer guidance for patients, administrations and actors in the field as to what the future might bring. If not, the European Court of Justice cannot but continue its work of interpreting primary and secondary Community legislation and playing the role of policy-maker.

13 | The EU legal framework on e-health

STEFAAN CALLENS

1. Introduction

The European single market in health care is developing despite the existence of many different health care systems. With cross-border activities in health care increasing, patients tend to be treated in other Member States more often than in the past, especially since there are waiting lists in some countries. Moreover, doctors ask for more and varied telematic information from their colleagues than previously, and health care professionals, hospitals and laboratories use more and more information and communication technology (ICT) applications to communicate health data for treatment and other purposes. Many health care players (like sickness funds, hospitals, laboratories, etc.) are European health care actors and feel the need to communicate health data between Member States for treatment and other purposes. Consumers, on the other hand, use the Internet to search for medical information or to order medicinal products from pharmacies that are located in other countries. Many of these developments are related to e-health.[1] E-health describes the application of information and communication technologies across the whole range of functions that affect the health care sector. According to the European Commission, e-health comprises the following four interrelated categories of applications: (a) clinical information systems; (b) telemedicine and home care, personalized health systems and services for remote patient monitoring, teleconsultation, telecare, telemedicine and teleradiology; (c) integrated regional/ national health information networks, distributed electronic health record systems and associated services such as e-prescriptions or e-referrals; and (d) secondary usage of non-clinical systems (such

---

[1] See S. Boillat and S. Callens, 'The sale of medicinal products by mail-order in Europe', *Yearbook of European Medical Law* (2005), 57–62.

561

as specialized systems for researchers, or support systems such as billing systems).[2]

Despite the fact that health services are excluded from the application of the Directive on Services in the Internal Market (Directive 2006/123/EC of 12 December 2006),[3] it is obvious that the Commission has enacted many rules related to health care and that these rules have an important impact on health care systems, including the creation of an EU legal framework for e-health. This chapter aims to describe this legal framework and some European policy initiatives on e-health. It will not analyse whether or not e-health is having an important effect on health care systems,[4] but rather how European rules have been created that are important for the functioning of e-health, and therefore also for health care players and health care systems.[5] It is clear that e-health in itself has an impact on health care. Health care systems are part of wider systems, such as social welfare systems and society. Therefore, evolutions in society, such as developments regarding information and telecommunication technology, as well as rules related to ICT, will influence health care systems. Section two describes some important European rules that may apply to e-health but which often are not known by actors in the health care system. These relate to the processing of personal data, the delivery of information society services, the use of medical devices, the conclusion of contracts at a distance and agreements that may have an influence on the competition between undertakings. Section three deals with European Union policy related to e-health. Despite the fact that many existing rules can be applied to e-health and despite the attention given to it by the Commission, there are still important issues that have to be clarified at the EU level in order to ensure that e-health

[2] eHealth Taskforce, 'Accelerating the Development of the eHealth Market in Europe', eHealth Taskforce Report (2007), p. 10.

[3] European Parliament and Council Directive 2006/123/EC on services in the internal market, OJ 2006 No. L376/36.

[4] For the impact of some e-health developments, see www.ehealth-impact. org. See also E. Mossialos, S. Thomson and A. Ter Linden, 'Information technology law and health systems in the European Union', *International Journal of Technology Assessment in Health Care* 20 (2004), 498.

[5] It is clear that other legal rules may be important for e-health, such as the rules on intellectual property rights or the Notification Directive 98/34/EC. Since these rules do not pose specific issues related to e-health, they are not described in this chapter.

will play an even more important role in health care systems than is the case today. Therefore, section four lists some key issues and provides suggestions for legal initiatives at the EU level.

2. European legal instruments related to e-health

A. *The Data Protection Directive*

On 24 October 1995, the Council adopted Directive 95/46/EC on the protection of individuals with regard to the processing of personal data and on the free movement of such data (the Data Protection Directive).[6] The Directive contains several important principles that require compliance from e-health actors that process personal data concerning health. If national health care systems or other e-health actors create health grids, electronic national records or information systems that may be used for treatment, quality review or research purposes, they have to comply with the principles of the Data Protection Directive.

The Data Protection Directive aims to protect individuals with regard to the processing of personal data, and at the same time allows the free movement of such data. The Directive applies to the processing of personal data wholly or partly by automatic means, and to the processing of personal data by other means, which form part of a filing system or are intended to form part of a filing system. Article 8 of the Directive prohibits the processing of personal data concerning health. However, this prohibition does not apply where the processing of health data[7] is required, for example, for the purposes of preventive medicine, medical diagnosis, the provision of care or treatment

---

[6] The 'Data Protection' Directive, Council Directive 95/46/EC on the protection of individuals with regard to the processing of personal data and on the free movement of such data, OJ 1995 No. L281/31.

[7] Case C-101/01, *Lindqvist* [2003] ECR I-12971. The ECJ stated in *Lindqvist* that the act of referring, on an Internet page, to various persons and identifying them by name or by other means constitutes 'the processing of personal data wholly or partly by automatic means' within the meaning of Article 3(1) of the Data Protection Directive (above n.6). Such processing of personal data in the exercise of charitable or religious activity is not covered by any of the exceptions in Article 6(2). In this case, the fact that it was mentioned on the Internet that an individual had injured her foot and was on half-time leave on medical grounds constitutes personal data concerning health within the meaning of Article 8(1) of the Data Protection Directive.

or the management of health care services, and where such data are processed by a health professional subject under national law or rules established by national competent bodies to the obligation of professional confidentiality or by another person also subject to an equivalent obligation of confidentiality.

According to the Data Protection Directive, personal data used in e-health projects must be processed fairly and lawfully. Furthermore, data must be collected for specified, explicit and legitimate purposes and not further processed in a way that is incompatible with those purposes. The data must be adequate, relevant and not excessive in relation to the purposes for which they are collected and must be kept in a form that permits identification of data subjects for no longer than is necessary and only for the purposes for which the data was collected or is required for further processing. Data subjects also have to be informed about the processing of their personal data.

Regarding the transfer of data between Member States, for example, for treatment purposes, in the case of e-health projects a data controller established in the territory of one Member State can be sure that in transferring data to another controller established in another Member State this data will be correctly protected, since the second Member State will provide for a similar level of protection of personal data.[8] With regard to the transfer of data to third countries, the Directive stipulates that the Member States shall provide that the transfer of personal data that are undergoing processing, or are intended for processing after transfer, may take place only if, without prejudice to compliance with national provisions adopted pursuant to the other provisions of the Directive, the third country in question ensures an adequate level of protection.[9] The adequacy of the level of protection afforded by the third country will be assessed in light of all the circumstances surrounding a data transfer operation or set of data transfer operations. Particular consideration is given to the nature of the data, the purpose and duration of the proposed processing operation or operations, the country of origin and country of final destination, the rules of law, both general and sectoral, in force in the third

[8] Article 25, 'Data Protection' Directive, above n.6.
[9] See also H. Rowe, 'Data transfer to third countries: the role of binding corporate rules', *Computer Law & Security Report* 19 (2003), 490–496.

country in question, and the professional rules and security measures that are complied with in that country.[10]

Since personal data (including personal data concerning health) is often transferred between the EU and the United States, and since there was uncertainty about the impact of the 'adequacy' standard on personal data transfers from the European Community to the United States, the United States Department of Commerce issued the 'Safe Harbor Principles' under its statutory authority to foster, promote and develop international commerce. The European Commission has recognized these Safe Harbor Principles in Decision 2000/520/EC of 26 July 2000.[11] These principles were developed in consultation with industry and the general public to facilitate trade and commerce between the United States and the European Union. They are intended for use solely by United States organizations receiving personal data from the European Union for the purpose of qualifying for the 'Safe Harbor' and the presumption of 'adequacy' it creates. The Safe Harbor Principles consist of seven principles and a few frequently asked questions (FAQs). FAQ 14 deals with the relationship between the Safe Harbor Principles and pharmaceutical and medical products. If personal data is collected in the EU and transferred to the United States for pharmaceutical research or other purposes, Member State law applies to the collection of the personal data and to any processing that takes place prior to the transfer to the United States. However, the Safe Harbor Principles apply to the data once they have been transferred to the United States. It should be noted that research

---

[10] For exceptions to Article 25 of the 'Data Protection' Directive, see Article 26(1) and Article 26(2) of the Directive; see also I. Andoulsi *et al.*, 'Bottlenecks and challenges and RTD responses for legal, ethical, social and economic aspects of healthgrids', Roadmap I 2008, p. 21, http://eu-share. org/deliverables.html. The Data Protection Directive also states that Member States may authorize a transfer or a set of transfers of personal data to a third country that does not ensure an adequate level of protection of personal data, where the controller adduces adequate safeguards through appropriate contractual clauses between the sender and the recipient of the personal data. In this context, the European Commission has proposed standard contractual clauses that ensure an adequate level of protection of transferred personal data.

[11] Commission Decision 2000/520/EC pursuant to European Parliament and Council Directive 95/46/EC on the adequacy of the protection provided by the safe harbour privacy principles and related frequently asked questions issued by the US Department of Commerce, OJ 2000 No. L215/7.

data are often uniquely key-coded at their origin by the principal investigator so as not to reveal the identity of individual data subjects, and pharmaceutical companies sponsoring such research do not receive the key. The unique key code is held only by the researcher, so that he/she can identify the research subject under special circumstances. Therefore, the transfer of data coded in this way from the European Union to the United States does not constitute a transfer of personal data that is subject to the Safe Harbor Principles.[12]

B. *The E-commerce Directive*

Directive 2006/123/EC on services in the internal market does not apply to non-economic services of general interest and to health care services. Nevertheless, health care actors that utilize e-health may be considered to be providing information society services and may have to comply with another important directive related to services, the Directive 2000/31/EC on certain legal aspects of information society services in the internal market (the so-called 'E-commerce Directive').[13]

The E-commerce Directive applies to information society services that are defined as any service normally provided for remuneration, at a distance, by electronic means,[14] for the processing (including digital compression) and storage of data, and at the individual request of a recipient of a service.[15] 'At a distance' means that the service is provided without the parties simultaneously being present.[16] Since the economic activities of an information society service can consist of

[12] Commission Decision 2000/520/EC, above n.11, Annexe II – frequently asked questions 14, 1 and 7. The issue of data transfer is a delicate issue as the SWIFT has shown; see Article 29, Data Protection Working Party, 'Opinion 10/2006 on the processing of personal data by the Society for Worldwide Interbank Financial Telecommunication (SWIFT)', WP 128, 22 November 2006.

[13] The Directive on Electronic Commerce, European Parliament and Council Directive 2000/31/EC on certain legal aspects of information society services, in particular electronic commerce, in the internal market, OJ 2000 No. L178/1. For more guidance on the Directive, see S. Callens, 'Telemedicine and the E-Commerce Directive', *European Journal of Health Law* 9 (2002), 93–109.

[14] Communication by phone, fax or mobile phone does not fall under the Directive.

[15] The recipient can be a patient or a physician asking for an opinion.

[16] P. Van Eecke, 'Electronic Health Care Services and the E-Commerce Directive', in J. Dumortier, F. Robben and M. Taeymans (eds.), *A decade of research@the crossroads of law and ICT* (Ghent: Larcier, 2001), p. 369.

services giving rise to online contracting, several e-health applications can be the subject of an information society service. The E-commerce Directive may apply to online medicine purchases, as well as to services consisting of the transmission of information via a communication network, or that provide access to a communication network. The E-commerce Directive may also be applicable to the use of electronic research registers by physicians who pay a fee to access a file, to physicians who use a web site to promote their activities, or for the sending of medical information among physicians against remuneration.[17]

The Directive obliges e-health actors who act as an information society service to provide the recipients of the service and competent authorities with easily, directly and permanently accessible information on the service providers and, where their activity is subject to an authorization scheme, the particulars of the relevant supervisory authority, any professional body or similar institution with which they are registered, as well as which professional titles they have obtained, which Member State has granted these titles, which applicable professional rules in the Member State of establishment are applicable and what means exist to access them. According to the Directive, Member States must ensure that e-health actors who act as information society services indicate any relevant codes of conduct to which they subscribe and information on how those codes can be consulted electronically.[18]

Member States have to ensure that the take-up and pursuit of the activity of an information society service provider (including an e-health actor) may not be made subject to prior authorization or any other requirement having equivalent effect (Article 4(1)). Article 4(1) shall be without prejudice to authorization schemes that are not specifically and exclusively targeted at information society services, or that are covered by Directive 97/13/EC on a common framework for general authorizations and individual licences in the field of

---

[17] See also *ibid.*, p. 375.
[18] In order to facilitate the free provision of services in general, there are specific rules aimed at the abolition of obstacles to the free movement of persons and services, which extend the possibility of pursuing professional activities under the original professional title. European Parliament and Council Directive 2005/36/EC on the recognition of professional qualifications, OJ 2005 No. L255/22, can also be applicable. Yet the Directive does not cover the situation where the health professional and the patient are not simultaneously present. (European Commission, 'Telemedicine for the benefit of patients, healthcare systems and society', Commission Staff Working Paper, SEC (2009) 943, June 2009); see Chapter 14 in this volume.

telecommunications services. This very important principle, as laid down in Article 4 of the E-commerce Directive, is a major challenge for national e-health networks or telemedicine projects for which the competent public authorities want to provide reimbursement under certain conditions.

C. *Medical Device Directives*

The Medical Device Directives[19] harmonize the rules pertaining to the free circulation of medical devices in the EU. Products that fall within their scope must meet all applicable essential safety and administrative requirements and must bear an EC-conformity mark to show that they comply with the Directive. Such products may then be sold throughout the European Economic Area without, in principle, being the subject of additional national legislation. These Medical Device Directives are of importance for the e-health sector, especially with regard to medical software that is used in many e-health applications. The Medical Device Directives define a medical device as any instrument, apparatus, appliance, software, material or other article, whether used alone or in combination, together with any accessories, including the software intended by its manufacturer to be used specially for diagnostic and/or therapeutic purposes and necessary for its proper application, intended by the manufacturer to be used for human beings for, among other things, the purpose of diagnosis, prevention, monitoring, treatment or alleviation of disease, injury or handicap and the control of conception. Software for general purposes, when used in an e-health project, is not a medical device. However, software in its own right, when specifically intended by the manufacturer to be used for one or more of the medical purposes set out in the definition of a medical device, is a medical device.

In the context of the Directive, manufacturers are obliged to place on the market or to put into service only medical devices that do not compromise the safety and health of patients, users and other persons, when properly installed, maintained and used in accordance

---

[19] European Parliament and Council Directive 2007/47/EC amending Council Directive 90/385/EEC on the approximation of the laws of the Member States relating to active implantable medical devices, Council Directive 93/42/EEC concerning medical devices and Directive 98/8/EEC concerning the placing of biocidal products on the market, OJ 2007 No. L247/21.

with their intended purpose. The manufacturer must design and manufacture medical devices in such a way that some essential requirements are met, such as taking into account the generally acknowledged state-of-the-art and to eliminate or reduce risks as much as possible. Devices that are in accordance with national provisions that have transposed the existing European harmonized standards will be presumed by EU Member States to be compliant with the essential requirements laid down by the Directive.[20] Devices other than those that are custom-made or intended for clinical investigation must bear an EC-conformity mark when placed on the market.[21] Clinical evaluation is also required and it will remain to be seen how this obligation will be fulfilled by medical software vendors. Directive 2007/47/EC of 5 September 2007, amending Directive 90/385/EEC on the approximation of the laws of the Member States relating to active implantable medical devices,[22] Council Directive 93/42/EC concerning medical devices[23] and Directive 98/8/EC concerning the placing of biocidal products on the market[24] clarify that clinical evaluation is needed for every medical device.[25] This clinical evaluation can be done in different ways – for instance, by means of a critical evaluation based on the scientific literature in that area or by means of results from a clinical investigation, or by combining both methods.[26] For active implantable devices and Class III devices, there must always be a clinical investigation.[27] Therefore, clinical investigation will be necessary for medical implantable software or software listed under Class III.[28]

D. Directive on Distance Contracting

E-health business may involve the conclusion of contracts. These contracts contain the description of the various parties' obligations and,

---

[20] Article 5, Directive 93/42/EC concerning medical devices, OJ 1993 No. L169/1.
[21] Article 4, *ibid.*   [22] Directive 2007/47/EC, above n.19.
[23] Directive 93/42/EC, above n.20.
[24] Directive 98/8/EC concerning the placing of biocidal products on the market, OJ 1998 No. L123/1.
[25] Directive 2007/47/EC, above n.19, Recital 8.   [26] *Ibid.*, Annexe 10, 1.1.
[27] *Ibid.*
[28] Medical devices are divided into classes. For the classification rules, see Directive 93/42/EC, above n.20, Annexe IX.

often, special clauses. A contract related to e-health concluded between a professional and a consumer (for example, a contract between a patient and a tele-expert or a contract between a patient and a pharmacist regarding the delivery of medicinal products) may be the subject of a contract at a distance. The Directive on Distance Contracting[29] will apply to any contract concerning goods or services concluded between a supplier and a consumer under an organized distance sales or service-provision scheme run by the supplier, who, for the purpose of the contract, makes exclusive use of one or more means of distance communication up to and including the moment at which the contract is concluded. In good time prior to the conclusion of any distance contract, the consumer shall be provided with sufficient information on the identity of the supplier, the main characteristics of the services, the price of the services, the arrangements for payment, delivery or performance, and the existence of a right of withdrawal. Consumers must receive written confirmation or confirmation in another durable medium available and accessible to them of the information mentioned above, in good time, during the performance of the contract, unless the information already has been given, with the same provisos, prior to conclusion of the contract. For any distance contract, consumers will have a period of at least seven working days in which to withdraw from the contract without penalty and without giving any reason.

E. Directive on Electronic Signatures

E-health projects often require the use of electronic signatures. Essential in an information society, the European Union has promoted the use of electronic signatures, which are to be treated as equal to hand-written signatures. An electronic signature is a generic technology-neutral term covering the methods by which electronic records can be signed and can be created by different technologies. The electronic signature is a key tool to ensure confidentiality, integrity and authenticity in the transfer of health data between electronic sources. Article 3(7) of the Directive on Electronic Signatures[30] states

---

[29] European Parliament and Council Directive 97/7/EC on the protection of consumers in respect of distance contracts, OJ 1997 No. L144/19.

[30] European Parliament and Council Directive 1999/93 on a Community framework for electronic signatures, OJ 2000 No. L13/12.

that Member States may make use of electronic signatures in the public sector subject to possible additional requirements. However, such requirements shall be objective, transparent, proportionate and non-discriminatory, and shall relate only to the specific characteristics of the application concerned. Such requirements may not constitute an obstacle to cross-border services for citizens.

F. Competition law

The European Union seeks to create a single internal market characterized by open competition. Therefore, a system of competition law has been developed whose central aim is to prevent the disruption of free competition or to neutralize any such disruption.[31]

Community competition rules prohibit undertakings from participating in anti-competitive activities, such as agreements to set prices or abuse of dominant position.[32] Article 81 of the EC Treaty prohibits all agreements between undertakings, decisions by associations of undertakings and concerted practices that may affect trade between Member States and that have as their object or effect the prevention, restriction or distortion of competition within the common market. Article 82 prohibits abuse of a dominant position by one or more undertakings. Article 86 of the EC Treaty is also important in the area of health care, permitting as it does partial exemption from the competition rules for some undertakings. This article states that undertakings entrusted with the operation of services of general economic interest shall be subject to the rules contained in this Treaty, in particular the rules on competition, in so far as the application of such rules does not obstruct the performance, in law or in fact, of the particular tasks assigned to them. The development of trade must not be affected to such an extent as would be contrary to the interests of the Community.

The rules of European competition law, for example, can apply to electronic networks. Independent health care practitioners may have a common computer server to exchange patient information. Such collaboration does not come under the prohibition of cartels, if some

---

[31] For a detailed description of the competition rules, see Chapters 7 and 8 in this volume.
[32] Articles 81 and 82 EC.

conditions are fulfilled. Firstly, the electronic system in principle may not be used for the exchange of competitively sensitive information about prices, turnover,[33] etc., as the exchange of such information can lead undertakings to no longer compete with one another. Secondly, an information network, in principle, has to be open. If the participants of a network benefit from this network and these economic benefits cannot be achieved by others who do not participate, a situation will be created where it will be very hard for health care practitioners to establish themselves in the market.[34]

3. EU policy related to e-health and its impact on health care systems

The Commission was and still is aware that e-health and/or telemedicine may contribute to delivering better quality of care and to a better involvement of patients in the management and follow-up of their health condition.[35]

In December 1999, the Commission launched the so-called 'e-Europe initiative' ('e-Europe – an information society for all'). The initiative was a political enterprise to ensure that the European Union would fully benefit from the changes brought about by the burgeoning information society. The e-Europe Action Plan initially identified ten areas where action at a European level would add value. These actions were revised in view of the Lisbon European Council in 2000,[36] and the actions were clustered around three main objectives: first, a cheaper, faster and secure Internet; second, investing in people and skills; and, third, stimulating the use of the Internet. This initiative saw the start

---

[33] See also A. Beurden, 'The European perspective on e-health', in S. Callens (ed.), *E-health and the law* (Den Haag: Kluwer, 2003), pp. 106–8.

[34] Dutch National Competition Authority, 'Richtsnoeren voor de Zorgsector', Report of the Dutch National Competition Authority (2001), www. zemagazine.nl/dsc?c=getobject&s=obj&objectid=11882&!sessionid=11zy SrobBaqys7l54qVBDU@t5G78Ld!zmQ!2Az1JIodvhoUhCp3M4aGxJh@ OuGEX&!dsname=bsl.

[35] European Commission, 'Questionnaire, tele-medicine', I2010 eHealth sub group Members (2007), p. 2; European Commission, 'A lead market initiative for Europe', COM (2007) 860 final, 21 December 2007, p. 5.

[36] The e-Europe Action Plan 2002 was adopted by the Commission on 14 June 2000 and endorsed by the European Council in Feira, Portugal on 19–20 June 2000, http://ec.europa.eu/information_society/eeurope/2002/ action_plan/pdf/actionplan_En.pdf.

of the Health Online Action, underlining that the European Union recognizes the strategic importance of fully exploiting new technologies in health care.[37] Policy actions detailed under the Health Online Action were as follows: to ensure that primary and secondary health care providers have a health telematics infrastructure in place, including regional networks; to identify and disseminate best practice in electronic health services in Europe, and to set benchmarking criteria; to establish a set of quality criteria for health-related web sites; to establish health technology and data assessment networks; and to publish a Communication on the 'legal aspects of e-health'.[38]

The High Level Committee on Health has established a Working Group on Health Telematics. This Working Group was asked to review the introduction of information and communication technology (ICT) in the health sector, the factors promoting or inhibiting its development, and areas where Community legislation could be beneficial. The Group considered particular applications of ICT in health; namely, health cards, virtual hospitals and provision of health-related information to health professionals and patients. Their report was accepted by the High Level Committee on Health in April 2003.[39]

E-health still receives a great deal of attention at the EU level, and the Commission has invested in several research programmes related to this area.[40] Moreover, in 2004, it established an Action Plan for a European E-health Area,[41] in which health and health care formed a key part of the Commission's vision for an information society where a new generation of computerized clinical systems, advanced telemedicine services and health network applications improve health, continuity of care and allow citizens to be more involved in, and assume greater responsibility for, their own health. The Commission believed that e-health would be an instrument for restructured, citizen-centred health care systems, which, at the same time, respects the diversity of Europe's multicultural,

---

[37] Beurden, 'The European perspective', above n.33, pp. 99–103. See also http://ec.europa.eu/information_society/eeurope/ehealth/index_en.htm.

[38] See the e-Europe Action Plan 2002, above n.36.

[39] http://ec.europa.eu/health/ph_overview/Documents/ hlch_health_telematics_final_report_en.pdf.

[40] European Commission, 'eHealth portfolio of projects', European Commission Information Society and Media (2007), http://ec.europa.eu/information_ society/activities/health/docs/publications/fp6upd2007/fp6intro1.pdf.

[41] European Commission, 'e-Health – making healthcare better for European citizens: an action plan for a European e-Health Area', COM (2004) 356 final, 30 April 2004.

multilingual health care traditions.[42] The Commission was and still is of the opinion that e-health can be an important tool for creating a citizen-centred health system,[43] and that it can facilitate cooperation between health actors[44] in Europe. According to the Commission, e-health will enable higher-quality, effective health care that is safe, empowering and accessible for patients and cost-effective for governments.[45] It is of no surprise that, in its report of 21 December 2007, the Commission considered e-health to be one of the six leading markets in Europe.[46]

Nevertheless, the Commission has observed a low take-up of telemedicine applications in real-life medicine. It is now identifying the barriers and triggering factors for greater use of e-health applications, and has issued, on 4 November 2008, a Communication on telemedicine for the benefit of patients, healthcare systems and society.[47] According to the Commission, Member States should have assessed and adapted by the end of 2011 their national regulations enabling wider access to telemedicine services. Issues such as accreditation, liability, reimbursement, privacy and data protection should be addressed.[48] The Commission has also drawn up a report on accelerating the development of the European e-health market, stating that the prospective return on e-health investment is relatively high when compared to the costs inherent in the health sector.[49] In its recent proposal for a directive on the application of patients' rights in cross-border health care,[50] the

[42] *Ibid.* [43] *Ibid.*

[44] See also the recent European Commission, 'Commission Recommendation of 2 July 2008 on cross-border interoperability of electronic health records', C (2008) 3282 final, 2 July 2008.

[45] European Commission and Member States, 'eHealth Conference 2007 Final Declaration', 17 April 2007. See also European Commission, 'A lead market initiative', above n.35.

[46] European Commission, 'A lead market initiative', above n.35.

[47] European Commission, 'Communication from the Commission to the European Parliament, the Council, the European Economic and Social Committee and the Committee of the Regions on telemedicine for the benefit of patients, healthcare systems and society', COM (2008) 689 final, 4 November 2008.

[48] The Working Paper of the Commission, European Commission, 'Telemedicine for the benefit of patients, healthcare systems and society', above n. 18, aims to provide additional information supporting the communication of 4 November 2008.

[49] eHealth Taskforce, 'Accelerating the Development', above n.2, p. 5.

[50] European Commission, 'Proposal for a European Parliament and Council Directive on the application of patients' rights in cross-border healthcare', COM (2008) 414 final, 2 July 2008.

Commission referred also (albeit rather briefly) to e-health. Article 16 of this proposal states that the Commission shall:

[A]dopt specific measures necessary for achieving the interoperability of information and communication technology systems in the health care field, applicable whenever Member States decide to introduce them. Those measures ... shall specify in particular the necessary standards and terminologies for inter-operability of relevant information and communication technology systems to ensure safe, high-quality and efficient provision of cross-border health services.

Despite the attention given to several legal issues related to e-health at the EU level, it is our opinion that a more detailed legal framework is needed to allow the use of this activity in health care systems, and one that takes into account all the interests at stake, such as data protection, public health, quality of care, cost–effectiveness, etc. The issues that need more European involvement are related to legal provisions (for example, rules are needed on liability and reimbursement matters; see section four, subsections B and C below) and to new technical developments (for example, the existence of health grids, electronic health records, e-health platforms, and further use of genetic data and tissue; see section four, subsection A).

4. Legal challenges to promote e-health

A. *New challenges due to new e-health applications*

Electronic health records and e-health platforms

Several Member States are shifting from using electronic health insurance cards to electronic health records or e-health platforms[51] in order to

---

[51] In Belgium, a new law establishing an 'e-health platform' was passed on July 2008 and published in the Official Journal on 13 October 2008. The e-health platform will be a protected electronic exchange platform where all healthcare practitioners can exchange information with due regard for privacy rules. The e-health platform aims to optimize the quality and continuity of health care, optimize the safety of patients, promote administrative simplification, and support health policy-making. The aim is to exchange information among all actors in the health care sector, with guarantees for information safety and privacy protection. In contrast to an electronic health record, the e-health platform will be a decentralized way of storing and exchanging medical data. The e-health platform itself does not contain much data but indicates nevertheless the places where relevant data can be found.

make available health data for medical treatment and allied purposes. It is argued by public authorities that electronic health records may improve quality of care[52] and patient safety and they also can be used as an instrument to control the rising demand for (and cost of) health services.[53] Electronic health records should facilitate the appropriate treatment of patients by providing health professionals with a better knowledge of a patient's history and previous interventions by other medical practitioners.[54] According to the Commission, improvements in patient safety can be achieved if information concerning patients is managed in a more systematic manner by everyone involved in health care provision or standards.[55] However, the use of electronic health records that contain data supplied by several health actors poses new risks, with some legal consequences (see below).

The Data Protection Commission at the European level, the so-called Article 29 Data Protection Working Party,[56] has adopted an interesting document on the processing of personal data relating to health in electronic health records (EHR).[57] This document aims to provide guidance on the way to apply the data protection legal framework to electronic health record systems. The analysis of the Working Party is certainly necessary, since many health care players do not always seem to know how to comply with the Data Protection Directive. The Working Party also has made an important recommendation for politicians, in that it recommends the laying down of special safeguards for the electronic health record system within a special

[52] However, secure and fast access to patient information will require the interoperability of health records.

[53] European Commission, 'e-Health', above n.41, p. 5. The lack of standards has pushed up the cost of development and customization, which has held back the e-health industry from more substantial investment in e-health solutions. See European Commission, 'e-Health', above n.41, p. 13.

[54] *Ibid.*, p. 8.

[55] European Commission and Member States, 'eHealth Conference 2007 Declaration', above n.45.

[56] See Articles 29 and 30, 'Data Protection' Directive, above n.6. Article 29 sets up a Working Party on the protection of individuals with regard to the processing of personal data, hereinafter referred to as 'the Working Party'. The Working Party advises and makes recommendations on all matters relating to the protection of persons with regard to the processing of personal data in the Community.

[57] Article 29 Data Protection Working Party, 'Working document on the processing of personal data relating to health in electronic records', WP 131, 15 February 2007.

comprehensive legal framework. This framework has to provide for, among other things, the following safeguards: it should be possible for patients, at any time, to prevent the disclosure of, and access to, their personal data; only relevant information should be entered into an EHR and it might be useful to create different data modules within an EHR system with different access requirements; a special arbitration procedure should be set up for disputes over the correct use of data in EHR systems; and a single special institution must be given responsibility for the proper handling of access requests.[58]

Together with the Working Party, we believe that new European general principles and data protection preconditions for establishing a nationwide EHR system or an e-health platform, as well as their applicable safeguards, are welcome, since this area poses potential new risks. The data contained in electronic health records or e-health platforms are used increasingly for purposes other than treatment, and health care actors are becoming more global (for instance, they are becoming part of European groups). Therefore, there are more opportunities to process health data among several Member States and/or third parties. There is also the risk that data may be more readily available to a wider circle of recipients.[59] In compiling existing medical information about an individual from different sources, with the result of allowing easier and more wide-spread access to this sensitive information, EHR systems introduce a new risk scenario. More categories of people may gain access to data if hospitals, pharmacies, laboratories, sickness funds, etc., that process health data become members of (international) groups. The Article 29 Working Party has stated that explicit consent must be given in order to process health data in an EHR.

It is true that the Data Protection Directive does allow for the processing of health data without explicit consent. Article 8(3) of the Data Protection Directive, for example, allows for processing by a health professional subject to confidentiality rules for the purposes of preventive medicine, medical diagnosis, the provision of care or treatment or the management of health care services. However, the Working Party is of the opinion that Article 8(3) cannot serve as the sole legal basis

---

[58] *Ibid.*, p. 13.
[59] *Ibid.*, p. 5. See also European Commission, 'Commission Recommendation', above n.44, p. 18.

for the processing of personal data in an EHR system. EHR systems provide direct access to a compilation of existing documentation about a person's medical treatment from different sources (hospitals, health care professionals, etc.) and throughout their lifetime. These systems transgress the traditional boundaries of the individual patient's direct relationship with a health care professional or institution. Therefore, it is not certain whether the processing of health data in an EHR system can be allowed without the explicit consent of the patient. The Article 29 Working Party is not convinced that relying only on the obligation to practise professional confidentiality provides sufficient protection.[60] If more people are allowed access to records because such records are kept by European actors, more specific safety measures must be taken and patients must be asked for consent as to which categories of people may have access to their records.

We not only need to reflect on the impact of Article 8(3) of the Directive[61] in light of patient rights related to EHR systems, we also need to reflect on the legal rules regarding the processing of personal health data for purposes other than treatment purposes, such as research and quality review. Better and more specific provisions in the Directive for the further use of health data are needed, as the use of such data takes place increasingly within a globalized context of health care actors, and in several Member States where national rules regarding certain types of processing differ. Indeed, globalization in health care has become a reality, since not only pharmaceutical companies but also sickness funds, patients groups, research institutes, hospitals and laboratories are becoming part of an increasing number of European-wide organizations or groups.

This globalization of health care actors requires more harmonized rules for health data processing, particularly as the exchange of data between European e-health actors will not be limited to the treatment

---

[60] Article 29 Data Protection Working Party, 'Working document', above n.57, p. 12.

[61] Article 8(1), 'Data Protection' Directive, above n.6, prohibits the processing of personal data. Article 8(1) 'shall not apply where processing of the data is required for the purposes of preventive medicine, medical diagnosis, the provision of care or treatment or the management of health care services, and where those data are processed by a health professional subject under national law or rules established by national competent bodies to the obligation of professional secrecy or by another person also subject to an equivalent obligation of secrecy'. Article 8(3), 'Data Protection' Directive.

of patients – the data also can be processed for evaluation, research or statistical purposes. Currently, harmonized rules in this area are lacking. Several Member States have formulated strict rules for the processing of medical data for research purposes, while other Member States have more flexible rules. Article 8 of the Directive leaves too much room for different legislation in the Member States, which is not good for the establishment of an internal market in which international quality review projects, epidemiological studies, clinical trials and post-marketing surveillance projects are emerging. It is regretful that Article 8 does not contain more specific rules for the processing of medical data for research purposes, as more specific rules at the European level are needed.[62]

Health grids

Initiatives to analyse the impact of health grids in health care systems have existed for several years. A grid is a new technology that aims to enhance the services already offered by the Internet. It offers rapid computation, large scale data storage and flexible collaboration by harnessing the power of a large number of commodity computers or clusters of other basic machines. The grid was devised for use in scientific fields, such as particle physics and bioinformatics, in which large volumes of data, or very rapid processing, or both, are necessary.[63] A grid has also been used in some ambitious medical and health care applications.[64] However, there is a tension between the spirit of the grid paradigm and the requirements of medical or health care applications. On the one hand, the grid stores data in the most convenient way according to performance criteria. On the other hand, a hospital or other health care institution is required to maintain control of the

---

[62] Since EHR systems may contain a large amount of data over a long period of time, the new European legal framework should also foresee, among other things, the need for a comprehensive logging and documentation of all processing steps that have taken place within the system, combined with regular internal checks and follow-up on correct authorization, and regular internal and external data protection auditing. See also European Commission, 'Commission Recommendation', above n.44, Point 14(k). It will also be an important challenge for legislators to guarantee that all groups in society (including single parents, homeless persons, the elderly and disabled, isolated communities, etc.) have equal access to electronic health records. See also European Commission, 'e-Health – making healthcare better', above n. 41, p. 15.

[63] See www.initiative.healthgrid.org.   [64] *Ibid.*

confidential patient data and to remain accountable for its use at all times.[65] Health grids provide doctors, researchers and health system planners with the opportunity to support areas of health care such as medical imaging and image processing, modelling the human body for therapy planning, pharmaceutical research and development, epidemiological studies and genomic research, and treatment development. However, in order to be truly effective, such grid applications must draw together huge amounts of data from disparately located computers – which implies data sharing across jurisdictions and the sharing of responsibilities by a range of different data controllers.[66] The Supporting and Structuring HealthGrid Activities and Research in Europe (SHARE) Report[67] illustrates the applicability of the European Data Protection Directive to grids. Since not all Member States have transposed the Directive in the same way, and since the Directive itself allows Member States to adopt legislative measures to restrict the scope of some obligations and rights, there are differences in the level of protection granted to personal data between EU Member States, which might be a problem for the implementation of the health grid technology throughout the whole territory of the European Union.[68] According to the SHARE project, if health grids are really to grow to their full potential and deliver their promises, adjustments must be made to national and supranational legislation. This implies the development and adoption of robust guidelines developed specifically for the health grid context, which address the balancing of interests between an individual's privacy and medical advancement.[69]

Further use of genetic data and tissue

E-health will create the situation where the difference between human tissue and computer data that refer to human tissue becomes very small. Since DNA sequences of samples can be analysed via and stored

---

[65] *Ibid.*

[66] SHARE, 'Bottlenecks and challenges and RTD responses for legal, ethical, social and economic aspects of healthgrids', Roadmap I (2008), p. 19. SHARE is a European initiative supporting the grid concept and the introduction of new technologies in the medical sector that involve e-health or e-infrastructures in medical research. Its main goal is to ensure the successful take-up of health grids by creating a roadmap for essential technology development in the future. See www.healthgrid.org.

[67] *Ibid.*   [68] *Ibid.*, p. 19.   [69] *Ibid.*, p. 25.

on computers, the distinction between the processing of human tissue and the processing of health data diminishes. E-health will enhance this further use of human tissue and genetic data as human tissue and blood, and the (genetic) data derived from tissue, is increasingly being used and stored for treatment and other purposes, such as research. The pharmaceutical industry, for example, collects human tissue when carrying out clinical trials on certain medicinal products. This is the issue of storing pharmacogenetic samples. Pharmacogenetics is the study and understanding of the genetic variation between individuals underlying differential responses to drug treatment.[70] University centres also often store blood and human tissue samples that can be used for research purposes, and countries collect biological samples on a very large scale and create population banks.[71] Several European documents already refer to the use of human tissue, such as Directive 2004/23/EC on setting quality and safety standards for the donation, procurement, testing, processing, preservation, storage and distribution of human tissues and cells[72] and Regulation 1394/2007/EC on advanced therapy medicinal products.[73] However, these documents remain too vague to provide health care systems with clear and detailed rules on the further use of genetic data and tissue. It will be a challenge for Europe to provide a more detailed legal framework with rules governing the (further) processing of tissue and data, an issue

---

[70] European Commission Group of Experts, 'Ethical, legal and social aspects of genetic testing: research, development and clinical applications', Report of the Independent Expert Group (2004), http://ec.europa.eu/research/conferences/2004/genetic/pdf/report_En.pdf.

[71] J. A. Bovenberg, *Property rights in blood, genes and data. Naturally yours?* (Leiden: Martinus Nijhoff Publishers, 2006), p. 23.

[72] Directive 2004/23/EC on setting quality and safety standards for the donation, procurement, testing, processing, preservation, storage and distribution of human tissues and cells, OJ 2004 No. L102/48.

[73] Regulation 1394/2007/EC of the European Parliament and of the Council on advanced therapy medicinal products and amending Directive 2001/83/EC and Regulation 726/2004/EC, OJ 2007 No. L324/12. At the level of the Council of Europe, we can refer to the Council of Europe Additional Protocol to the Convention on Human Rights and Biomedicine concerning Transplantation of Organs and Tissues of Human Origin, Strasbourg, 24 January 2002, in force 1 May 2006, ETS No. 186, http://conventions.coe.int/treaty/en/treaties/html/186.htm; as well as to Recommendation Rec(2006)4 on research on biological materials of human origin, Strasbourg, 15 March 2006, https://wcd.coe.int/ViewDoc.jsp?id=977859. Rules regarding the use of human tissue and blood often differ between the Member States.

that goes beyond national boundaries and is becoming a European, and also an international, concern.

B. *Towards more guidelines on the reimbursement criteria for telemedicine*

The E-commerce Directive does not regulate the reimbursement of telemedicine services, which falls under the competence of the Member States.[74] European and international telemedicine projects have often failed because they are too expensive for patients, and reimbursement by their health insurance funds[75] is not possible.[76] The recent Commission Communication on telemedicine for the benefit of patients, health care systems and society of 4 November 2008 states clearly that the lack of legal clarity with regard to, for example, reimbursement is a major challenge for telemedicine and that, in some Member States, for a medical act to be legally recognized as such, the presence of the patient and the health professional in the same place is required.[77]

An essential condition for reimbursement is indeed never fulfilled in the domain of telemedicine since reimbursement requires the physical presence of the (tele) physician with the patient at the moment of performing the medical action. This refusal to reimburse medical costs if there is no physical presence might have been reasonable in a period without ICT. It could be argued that a physician who only listens to a patient on the telephone cannot indeed make a good diagnosis, and therefore reimbursement by public authorities for this kind of service could be refused. However, the revolution in the ICT sector today makes it sometimes possible to collect the required medical information for a diagnosis at a distance without being physically

---

[74] If there is a cross-border element, the European rules on free movement will be engaged.

[75] S. Callens, 'Tele-medicine and European law', *Telehealth Law* 2 (2002), 34–40.

[76] The Standing Committee of European Doctors has recommended a reimbursement of telemedical services by national social security systems in the same way as any other form of medical service. Standing Committee of European Doctors, 'The practice of tele-medicine in Europe: analysis, problems and CPME recommendations', 2002M/027 (2002), p. 18.

[77] European Commission, 'Communication from the Commission', above n.47, p. 8.

present. The question is then whether, under those circumstances, it is still reasonable to refuse reimbursement just because a physician does not see a patient physically.

The question arises as to whether or not the criterion of physical presence for the reimbursement of treatment forms an obstacle to the free movement of services – that is, whether there is a barrier to the free movement of services if the telemedicine treatment or diagnostic services carried out by a physician in country X on a patient situated in country Y is not reimbursed due to the physical presence requirement. The counter-argument may be that it is an issue of objective public interest and that the Member States should decide themselves whether or not the criterion of physical presence is needed for the reimbursement of medical interventions. The Member States can, indeed, owing to a lack of harmonization at Community level, determine for themselves the conditions under which a person can or must subscribe to a social security regime and under which the right to benefits exists.[78]

However, the Court of Justice has regularly stressed that Member States also have to comply with Community law in the implementation of social security systems.[79] Simple mention of a rule of social security law does not exclude the application of Articles 49 and 50 of the EC Treaty.[80] In the *Kohll* case, the Court of Justice stressed that the requirement of prior consent by the insured person's health insurance fund, before the patient can claim (ambulatory) medical costs in another Member State, is a barrier to the free delivery of services.[81] In the case of telemedicine, Member State legislation that requires a physical presence for reimbursement purposes does not forbid a patient from having recourse to a telephysician established in another Member State. It only makes the reimbursement thereof impossible. In a certain sense, the physical presence condition may impede medicine at a distance by a physician established abroad, as

---

[78] H. D. C. Roscam Abbing, 'Public health insurance and freedom of movement within the European Union', *European Journal of Health Law* (1999), 1–6.

[79] See, for example, Case C-120/95, *Decker* v. *Caisse de Maladie des Employés Privés* [1998] ECR I-1831, para. 23; Case C-158/96, *Kohll* v. *Union des Caisses de Maladie* [1998] ECR I-1931, para. 19; Case C-157/99, *Geraets-Smits and Peerbooms* [2001] ECR I-5473.

[80] See also Chapter 11 in this volume.

[81] Case C-158/96, *Kohll*, above n.79, para. 35.

well as the possibility, for example, of a Belgian patient consulting a telephysician in another European country. However, the condition of physical presence applies both to telemedicine treatment carried out by Belgian or foreign physicians, as well as to traditional medical treatments applied in situ. Thus, the measure is applicable without exception and is therefore not a formally discriminatory measure. However, it may still fall within Articles 49 and 50 EC, as it constitutes a deterrent to the cross-border provision of services.[82] Alongside the justifications mentioned in Article 46 of the EC Treaty (in particular, public health reasons), Member States may view the physical presence condition as an imperative reason in the common interest that justifies an obstacle to the trade in services.[83]

However, whether or not the reimbursement of medicine at a distance does in fact have an important effect on the financial balance of social security systems still needs to be examined. It seems to us that the reimbursement of certain types of telemedical interventions will have to be accepted. If the safety of patients is guaranteed and if the telemedical treatment is cost neutral, it is to be expected that exceptions to the physical presence requirement will have to be allowed under Community law.[84] It is obvious that guidance (at the European level) can be given as to the criteria that (tele) health sessions will have to comply with for reimbursement purposes.[85] However, these criteria must always comply with the principle of Article 4 of the E-commerce Directive (see above).

---

[82] See Case C-55/94, *Gebhard* [1995] ECR I-4165; Case C-384/93, *Alpine Investments* [1995] ECR I-1141.

[83] Case C-158/96, *Kohll*, above n.79, para. 41; S. Callens, 'International tele-medicine and the law', in *Proceedings of the 13th World Congress on Medical Law*, Vol. 1 (Helsinki: World Congress on Medical Law, 2000).

[84] Concerning the reimbursement of medical treatment received abroad, see Chapter 12 in this volume.

[85] The recent proposal for a directive on the application of patients' rights in cross-border health care, European Commission, 'Proposal', above n.50, refers in its Article 16 to e-health, but this article remains quite vague. It states that the Commission 'shall adopt specific measures necessary for achieving the interoperability of information and communication technology systems in the healthcare field, applicable whenever Member States decide to introduce them. Those measures … shall specify in particular the necessary standards and terminologies for inter-operability of relevant information and communication technology systems to ensure safe, high-quality and efficient provision of cross-border health services.'

C. Towards a European legal framework on liability and telemedicine

One of the important questions in cases of liability and telemedicine will be whether or not the telemedical transaction is the most suitable approach for the treatment of patients. Physicians must always consider whether or not telemedicine poses an increased risk for a patient – for instance, in an emergency situation where a delay in providing the necessary medical intervention would pose a greater risk to the patient than a prompt intervention with telehealth. On other occasions, however, telehealth might not offer the best method,[86] since telemedicine might not allow the physician to effectively resolve problems during the transaction. Furthermore, telemedicine makes it difficult to alter the course of a procedure in order to address complications that may surface during surgery.[87] One has to take into account that an online session can be disrupted or fail during the procedure without any direct access by the tele-expert to the patient. It can well be expected that, compared to traditional medical treatments, a greater variety of people undoubtedly will be held liable if something goes wrong during the telemedical session. The technical failure of some devices used during a telemedical session can lead to liability claims against software producers or Internet providers. In the case of a defective medical device, the Product Liability Directive[88] has to be considered. This Directive establishes the general principle that a producer is liable for damages caused by a defect in its product. A product is defective when it does not provide the safety that a person is entitled to expect, taking all circumstances into account, including the presentation of the product, the use to which it reasonably could be expected to be put and the time at which the product was put into circulation.[89]

---

[86] D. A. Crolla, 'Health care without walls: responding to telehealth's emerging legal issues', *Health Law in Canada* 19 (1998), 6.

[87] *Ibid.*

[88] Council Directive 85/374/EEC on the approximation of the laws, regulations and administrative provisions of the Member States concerning liability for defective products, OJ 1985 No. L210/29.

[89] Telemedicine might sometimes, however, make it easier to know who made a mistake, since tele-operations may be taped and be kept together with the file. This could facilitate answering the question of what went wrong during the session. B. Sluyters, 'Telegeneeskunde', *Tijdschrift voor Gezondheidsrecht* (1999), 273.

The issue of liability becomes very important in the case of 'telemonitoring', whereby medical devices are implanted to monitor and follow the patient. We might think, for example, of patients suffering from cardiac conditions.[90] These devices send electronic messages about the patient's health situation to the doctor in charge at specific regular intervals. However, the device may not always contain an alarm system for emergency situations and does not always include twenty-four-hour assistance. The question then is whether physicians should hesitate to use these new medical methods, despite their technological efficiency, for fear of the burden of unclear liability. Would the doctor be held liable for not responding immediately to a message received during his absence? Written and oral information about the patient using the device and how information received by the doctor will be handled is important. Patients will have to be informed accurately – and in such a way that they can understand – of the doctor's limited availability and, for example, that the medical device has no alarm. Doctors are obliged to ensure the continuity of health care for any treatment under-taken, including postoperative care and follow-up. Doctors must take all the necessary measures during their absences to guarantee the quality of their health care services to their patients. Therefore, it is pref-erable for doctors to organize their practices so that they inform their patients of absences, permit a suitably competent colleague to access their professional mailbox during any absence – albeit with due respect for professional confidentiality and privacy – and inform patients of the possibility of contacting this substitute.

We believe that the EU should play an important role even with regard to the liability issue if e-health actors are submitted to different liability schemes.[91] Some countries, like France and Belgium, recently enacted so-called 'no-fault' legislation related to health care.

The no-fault issue is already contained in the Product Liability Directive[92] but is increasingly being expanded to other domains,

---

[90] For the importance of teleradiology in Europe, see European Commission, 'Communication from the Commission', above n.47, p. 4.

[91] It is a good thing that the Commission has stated in European Commission, 'Communication from the Commission', above n.47, p. 9, that, by the end of 2011, Member States should have assessed and adapted their national regulations enabling wider access to telemedicine services and that issues such as liability and reimbursement should be addressed.

[92] For the relationship between e-health and product liability and medical devices see C. Van Doosselaere *et al.*, 'eHealth … But is it legal?', *Eurohealth* 13 (2007), 2.

such as the delivery of health care. However, many countries do not use the no-fault standard with regard to the treatment of patients by health care professionals. No-fault liability rules state that if a patient is harmed, he/she is compensated regardless of the intent or negligence of the health care practitioner. If something goes wrong during a medical intervention, adequate compensation for patients might indeed be considered to be an important right. It is not good for patients or health care professionals if this right is regulated differently across the European Union, as this will not promote the use of telemedicine and the access to health care it allows. Therefore, EU legislation should require Member States to provide similar rules for compensation, which would enhance the free movement of patients and of health care services, and, in the final analysis, also access to health care and e-health. The no-fault rules should also cover damage caused in country X by a tele-expert located in country Y. Currently, some no-fault laws, such as the Belgian law, only apply to damage caused in Belgium. However, it is questionable whether this rule conforms to the EU Treaty, since it will not regulate damage caused in Belgium by a tele-expert working from abroad in the same way as the damage caused in Belgium by a tele-expert working in Belgium.

5. Conclusion

Many health care players (such as sickness funds, hospitals, laboratories, etc.) are now European health care actors and may feel the need to communicate health data between Member States for treatment and other purposes. Through the enactment of European rules that can be applied to e-health, the Commission has created quite an important legal framework for e-health, and therefore also for health care systems. Moreover, the Commission has given specific attention to e-health through the launch, in 1999, of its e-Europe initiative – 'e-Europe – an information society for all' – which included the Health Online Action. The Commission has also invested in several research programmes and, in 2004, established an Action Plan for a European E-health Area. The Commission continues to refer to the importance of e-health,[93] as well as the legal barriers to effective

---

[93] See Article 16 of European Commission, 'Proposal for a European Parliament and Council Directive', above n.50. See also European Commission, 'Commission Recommendation', above n.44.

e-health.[94] Some European instruments – such as the Data Protection
Directive, the E-commerce Directive, the Medical Devices Directives
and the Distance Contracting and Competition Rules Directive – play
an important role for health care systems, through the use of e-health
applications.

However, despite these rules and policy attention, the existing legal
framework is not yet complete. The current European rules often
remain too vague. The issues confronting health care players have to
be addressed at the European level, as some important legal issues,
as well as technological developments, need a clear legal answer.
Regarding the legal issue, specific attention should be given to the
need to enact European criteria on the reimbursement of e-health
activities and on the (no-fault) liability issue. Before e-health can play
an important role for health care players and health care systems,
while respecting the interests of patients, health care providers and
public authorities, the European Union will also have to provide a
clear answer to the challenges caused by new technical developments,
such as e-health platforms, electronic health records, health grids and
the further use of genetic data and tissue.

[94] See European Commission, 'Communication from the Commission',
above n.47.

14 | *EU law and health professionals*

MIEK PEETERS, MARTIN MCKEE AND
SHERRY MERKUR

1. Introduction

In November 2005, a young French woman received the world's first ever face transplant. The operation was carried out in Amiens, France, by a team that was mainly French but contained one Belgian. This case exemplified very visibly the benefits that free movement of health professionals can bring to the delivery of the increasingly complex health care being provided in Europe. The benefits of professional mobility extend far beyond the very specialized care involved in that exceptional case. Within Europe, there are both surpluses and shortages of health professionals. The opening of borders offers a means to ensure that appropriate health professionals and potential patients are brought together, whether through movement of patients or, as is discussed in this chapter, movement of professionals. In addition, there are particular issues that arise in border areas, where patients may live closer to a hospital across the border than to one in their home state.[1] Especially where these areas are sparsely populated, it is simply good management of resources to ensure that health professionals can also move across borders, working in the most appropriate facilities, wherever they are situated.

Yet there are also dangers. The large economic differences between Member States, which have grown substantially with the two most recent enlargements to the European Union, pose a challenge for the poorer countries. A plentiful supply of health professionals, coupled with formidable physical barriers to migration, meant that, during the communist era, wages were very low in comparison with other occupations. The facilities in which health care was delivered reflected this situation. Cheap labour reduced the incentive to invest in labour-saving technology, which, in any case, was expensive and,

---

[1] H. Legido-Quigley *et al.*, 'Patient mobility in the European Union', *British Medical Journal* 334 (2007), 188–90.

in some cases, unobtainable because of western restrictions on the export of technology with potential security implications, such as computers. As a result, the inherited infrastructure was often highly dependent on large numbers of staff.[2] The removal of borders within Europe has allowed many of the next generation of health professionals needed to staff these facilities to move west, in some cases beyond the EU to the United States, thereby threatening the viability of many traditional facilities.[3] Although a study conducted in 2005–6 in six Member States by the High Level Group on Health Services and Medical Care suggested that health professional mobility was then still limited, they noted the potential for it to increase.[4] The challenges are not confined to those countries losing health professionals. Western European countries face problems too, sometimes of their own making.[5] The chaos associated with the implementation of a new postgraduate medical training system in the United Kingdom in 2007 was in part due to the expectations raised across Europe and beyond among doctors considering movement to the United Kingdom.[6]

A particular concern relates to the situation where health professionals cross borders intermittently (to provide a service rather than to become established). This could compromise continuity of care, especially where complex after-care is needed or where a patient with a chronic disorder subsequently develops complications.[7]

---

[2] M. McKee, 'Cochrane on Communism: the influence of ideology on the search for evidence', *International Journal of Epidemiology* 36 (2007), 269–73.

[3] M. M. Bala, and W. M. Lesniak, 'Poland is losing its doctors', *British Medical Journal* 331 (2005), 235; L. Starkiene *et al.*, 'The future prospects of Lithuanian family physicians: a 10-year forecasting study', *BioMed Central: Family Practice* 6 (2005), 41.

[4] European Commission, 'Work of the High Level Group in 2006', HLG/2006/8, 10 October 2006.

[5] M. A. Garcia-Perez, C. Amaya and A. Otero, 'Physicians' migration in Europe: an overview of the current situation', *BioMed Central Health Services Research* 7 (2007), p. 201.

[6] C. Black *et al.*, 'MTAS (UK Medical Training Application Service): which way now? Interview by Rebecca Coombes', *British Medical Journal* 334 (2007), 1300.

[7] K. Hendrickx, 'Buitenlandse 'eendagschirurgen' aan de slag in Belgische klinieken', *De Morgen*, 15 March 2008. As highlighted in this journal article, the Belgian association of esthetical surgeons denounced the 'blitz surgery' of French and Italian aesthetic surgeons, who just come to perform specific operations and then disappear.

This chapter examines the European legal framework within which health professionals operate. It concentrates mainly on the arrangements by which health professionals move between Member States. However, the reach of European law extends far beyond their professional mobility. Like other workers, they are subject to the panoply of legislation on issues as diverse as pension provision, discrimination, and health and safety. Clearly, it is neither possible nor especially useful to review all of these areas. There is, however, one area that will be considered in more detail. This is the Working Time Directive, which, as will be discussed, is having profound and largely unintended consequences for health professionals and the configuration of health care delivery in Europe.

2. Mobility of health professionals

A. Introduction

The legal framework for patients seeking medical treatment in an EU Member State other than the one in which they are insured has been the subject of intense discussion for over a decade.[8] For many years, governments and others were in a state of denial, taking the view that the Treaty provisions provided adequate safeguards to prevent patients moving across borders at the expense of funders, save in very limited circumstances. This view was maintained even though academic commentators had long advised otherwise.[9] The *Kohll*[10] and *Decker*[11] cases shattered this complacency and, although the immediate implications of those cases applied to only a very narrow set of circumstances, unleashed a series of legal challenges that progressively expanded the circumstances in which patients could obtain treatment abroad without prior authorization. Although this issue is addressed elsewhere in this book, it illustrates several important

---

[8] M. McKee, E. Mossialos and P. Belcher, 'The influence of European Union law on national health policy', *Journal of European Social Policy* 6 (1996), 263–86.

[9] P. G. Svensson and P. Stephenson, 'Health care consequences of the European economic community in 1993 and beyond', *Social Science and Medicine* 35 (1992), 525–9.

[10] Case C-158/96, *Kohll* v. *Union des Caisses de Maladie* [1998] ECR I-1931.

[11] Case C-120/95, *Decker* v. *Caisse de Maladie des Employés Privés* [1998] ECR I-1831.

points that must be borne in mind when reading this chapter. First, the failure by European governments to provide a sound legislative basis for health care in Europe has created a vacuum that the Court has been forced to fill.[12] As it can only decide on those cases brought before it, some of which have been highly atypical, it has often left as many questions unresolved as it has answered. Second, this is an area that has been afflicted with numerous unintended consequences. Here, however, the subject under consideration is the movement of health professionals.

Professionals working in the health sector were the first professional group to be the subject of secondary European legislation facilitating free movement. This follows directly from the EC Treaty, which explicitly mentions the need for coordination of health professions (Article 47(3)). The first group to receive attention was doctors. The so-called 'Doctors' Directives', Directives 75/362/EEC and 75/363/EEC (later codified in the Doctors' Directive, Directive 93/16/EEC),[13] have become the model for sectoral directives for other health professions: nurses responsible for general care, dentists, veterinary surgeons, midwives and pharmacists. The remaining categories of health professionals fell under the scope of the general directives.

These Directives – subsequently consolidated into the single Directive 2005/36/EC (see below) – on the recognition of professional qualifications, contrary to what might be expected from their title, not only regulate the 'take up' and 'access' to the profession, but also coordinate professional rules concerning the 'pursuit' of the profession, such as the requirements related to presentation of documents and the applicability of national (disciplinary) measures. Thus, the Directive(s) on the recognition of professional qualifications provide the legal basis for all forms of mobility for health professionals, whether they are establishing themselves in another Member State or simply providing services on an occasional or temporary basis.

This section examines the European regulatory framework for the recognition of health professional qualifications, taking the old

---

[12] P. Kanavos and M. McKee, 'Cross-border issues in the provision of health services: are we moving towards a European health care policy?', *Journal of Health Services Research Policy* 5 (2000), 231–6.
[13] Council Directive 93/16/EEC to facilitate the free movement of doctors and the mutual recognition of their diplomas, certificates and other evidence of formal qualifications, OJ 1993 No. L165/1.

Directives as a starting point, before moving on to the consolidating Directive 2005/36/EC.[14] It asks to what extent the old and new legislation succeeds in ensuring the benefits of free movement while avoiding the pitfalls, in particular in relation to patient safety. Finally, it will highlight the issue of free movement of (para)medical students.

B. *Before Directive 2005/36/EC: sectoral and general directives*

Sectoral and general directives

The rights enshrined in the Treaties establishing free movement of workers and services and freedom of establishment for regulated professions formed the basis of secondary legislation that sought to coordinate the rules of Member States concerning access and the pursuit of a profession. The general principle underpinning this body of legislation has been that of mutual recognition. Thus, Member States were required to accept that a qualification obtained elsewhere met a minimum level, measured almost exclusively in terms of the length of study. This approach was driven by the philosophy of the internal market, wherein mobility took priority over other considerations.

Directive 2005/36/EC on the recognition of professional qualifications, which was to be implemented by Member States by the end of October 2007, consolidated two earlier types of directives: sectoral and general ones.

Sectoral directives related to a named profession and provided for automatic recognition of diplomas where the training required for the award of the diploma met the minimum requirements. Many health professions were the subject of a sectoral directive (doctors, nurses, dentists, midwives, pharmacists and veterinary surgeons). The procedure of automatic recognition of basic professional qualifications obliged every Member State to act positively in response to every request for recognition. They could not decline someone with one of the diplomas listed in the relevant directive (for example, by requiring that the applicant undertake further examination). The fact

---

[14] European Parliament and Council Directive 2005/36/EC on the recognition of professional qualifications, OJ 2005 No. L255/22–142; M. Peeters, 'Free movement of medical doctors: the new Directive 2005/36/EC on recognition of professional qualifications', *European Journal of Health Law* 12 (2005), 373–96.

that a qualification is on that list implies that the training entailed in obtaining it meets the minimum requirements.

The recent enlargements of the EU into central and eastern Europe gave rise to a specific issue concerning qualifications. Prior to 1991, physicians in the three Baltic states trained under the Soviet medical system, with narrow specialization at undergraduate level. This also applied to some physicians from the central European countries who had trained in the USSR, especially those working in the public health, or sanitary-epidemiological service. This was not comparable with medical training acquired in the rest of Europe. In addition, some other qualifications obtained in countries before they acceded to the EU did not meet the criteria for mutual recognition. In response, the system of 'acquired rights' was created. This served as a mechanism that permitted the recognition of diplomas for which training was commenced before a certain date (the reference date) and therefore did not meet (all) the minimum requirements. This reference date was usually either the initial date of the entry into force of the Directive or the date of accession of the Member State, where it only became a member after the entry into force of the Directive. However, other reference dates were possible where a Member State sought a specific derogation, including those that arose following German unification. If the minimum requirements were not met, then they could have been compensated for by proof of having obtained appropriate professional experience. A so-called 'certificate of acquired rights' issued by the home state was required to accompany the diploma, and to state that the person had been engaged effectively and lawfully in the relevant activities for at least three of the five years prior to the date of issue of the certificate.

In addition to these 'general' acquired rights, there were 'specific' rights created on the occasion of the 2004 enlargement in relation to the Soviet Union, Czechoslovakia and Yugoslavia. These applied to diplomas for which training began in one of these states before they broke into independent successor states, with the date of break-up acting as the reference date. In these cases, a certificate of acquired rights issued by authorities in the successor states must also confirm that the professional qualifications in question have the same legal effect as ones issued currently in that Member State.

Finally, there were 'special' acquired rights, where particular professions in individual countries had been subject to specific requirements, such as Polish nurses and midwives. If the training begun before the 'reference date' was in full conformity with the minimum training requirements of the Directive in question, then the home Member State could have issued a so-called 'certificate of conformity', stating that the relevant diploma was covered by the Directive and that it complied with the minimum training requirements.[15]

At each enlargement of the European Union, therefore, the sectoral directives have been modified so as to remove any barriers to the adoption of the *acquis communautaire*. The official titles of the relevant diplomas from new Member States were listed in the 'recognition lists' of the relevant sectoral directives.

As far as coordination of the *pursuit* of a profession is concerned, measures within the sectoral directives generally differed depending on whether they applied to the right of free establishment or to the free movement of services, although a few applied to *both*. The latter obliged host Member States to inform the incoming professionals about health and social security legislation, provide information on ethical issues and to guarantee that they have acquired the necessary language skills. They also allowed the host Member State to ask, in case of legitimate doubt, to confirm that the diploma, certificate or title was compliant with the minimum requirements listed in the relevant directive.

Measures to facilitate the pursuit of a profession by a migrant doctor wishing to *establish* him/herself in another Member State involved rules about documents and oaths. When a host Member State required that its citizens produce a certificate of good standing, of physical or mental health, and/or an oath or solemn declaration before practising the profession, it could ask the same from another EU citizen. However, it had to accept equivalent documents if the home Member State did not require such certificates, and had to permit an appropriate form of oath or declaration for foreign doctors.

Other measures related to cases where there was evidence that a migrant doctor may have been guilty of professional misconduct or was unfit to practice. If the host Member State obtained knowledge of a serious matter involving the migrant doctor that occurred outside its territory before the individual moved, it could – but did not have to – inform the Member State of origin. If disciplinary, legal or administrative measures were initiated in the host Member State, the Member State of origin had an obligation to forward all necessary information regarding disciplinary action or criminal penalties previously imposed.

There were circumstances in which a health professional could seek to provide *services* on a temporary or occasional basis in one Member State without becoming established there. Examples included short-term visits to undertake a particular procedure, as might be the case where a world-renowned specialist joined a surgical team conducting an unusually complex operation, or where the health professional remained in his or her Member State of establishment but examined images from a patient in another Member State.

The decision to grant permission to a foreign health professional to provide 'services' involved legislation that was, overall, rather more flexible than that dealing with establishment. Here, registration bodies faced certain constraints. Host Member States were explicitly obliged to exempt doctors providing services, on this basis, from any requirement to obtain authorization from or to join or register with a professional body. They could – but did not have to – take measures to implement procedures on professional conduct in their territory, by requiring either automatic temporary registration, pro forma membership of a professional organization or registration in a central register, provided that this did not delay or in any way complicate the provision of services or impose additional costs on the person providing the services. The sectoral directives also forbade any measure that compelled registration with a public social security body involved in settlement of accounts for services rendered, such as a sickness fund. The doctor only had to inform this body in advance or, in urgent cases, subsequently about the services provided.

Furthermore, the host Member State could request certain documents from the service provider: a prior declaration that informed the host Member State that he/she had provided services previously, a certificate of legal establishment and a certificate that the person held the necessary diploma, certificate or title. Telemedicine provides an interesting case, as the health professional does not physically move to the territory of another Member State so only the 'service' itself moves. This seemed to be excluded from the scope of the directives, which applied only when the service involved a 'temporary stay' in its territory. Telemedicine includes a wide range of cross-border services whereby the health professional remains in his or her Member State of establishment but, for example, examines images from a patient in another Member State, or even operates on this patient by means of telesurgery. This is clearly an area where case-law is likely to fill the gap.

General directives arose when it became clear that, beyond those professions that were common to all Member States and where there was some very general consensus about what the terms meant (however, see below), there was a myriad of others where there was much less agreement. Often, a particular set of tasks was the responsibility of professionals with different titles in different Member States, or a package of care was the responsibility of a single profession in one Member State but divided among several elsewhere. As a consequence, a more general provision was needed that allowed for mutual – but not automatic – recognition of diplomas and other qualifications, without prior harmonization or coordination of the training requirements. The basic assumption was that every person who had obtained a professional qualification in a Member State possessed the necessary skills to practise that profession in another Member State, even if the duration and nature of training were different. Nevertheless, the host Member State was not *ipso iure* obliged to recognize their diplomas. The Member State where the individual sought employment could decide each case separately and could impose, as appropriate, compensating measures such as an aptitude test or an adaptation period. The general system included three directives: Directive 89/48/EEC concerned diplomas awarded by higher education establishments on completion of professional education of at least three years; Directive 92/51/EEC concerned programmes at a level corresponding to secondary education, possibly complemented by professional training or experience; and Directive 99/42/EC concerned qualifications in respect of professional activities not covered by the first two Directives.

For the *pursuit* of a profession, the general directives, unlike the sectoral ones, did not distinguish between establishment and provision of services. They simply coordinated the rules on required documents and oaths, as in the sectoral directives (see above). The relationship between the sectoral and general systems could be qualified as *lex specialis derogat legi generali*. Hence, the general system did not apply to general practitioners and most specialist doctors, general nurses, dentists, veterinary surgeons, midwives and pharmacists. It applied to all the other regulated health professions that had not been dealt with in the sectoral directives. Examples included specialist nurses, specialist pharmacists, specialist dentists, psychologists, physicians, chiropractors, osteopaths and opticians. The range of possible professions created certain problems. For example, Portugal and Spain, when implementing the Directive, included in their domestic legislation an exhaustive list of professions included within its scope. They excluded those of pharmacist-biologist and hospital pharmacist, respectively, however, thus creating a barrier to the free movement of these individuals. As a consequence, the Commission referred both countries to the European Court of Justice.[16]

Shortcomings

The minimum training requirements of the sectoral directives were established to guarantee the *quality* of training. In the famous cases *Kohll* and *Decker*, the Court concluded for the first time that, since the conditions of taking up and practising the medical profession were regulated by the Doctors' Directive, the quality of doctors within the EU was sufficiently guaranteed. Therefore, arguments based on public health concerns could not be used to justify limiting the free movement of patients. Theoretically, the Court simply applied the logic of the sectoral approach. The Directive was designed to facilitate free movement by precluding questions about the equivalence of the diplomas once minimum training standards were met. In the more recent case of *Stamatelaki*,[17] the Court followed the same reasoning. The argument that cross-border care could be restricted because the Greek social security institutions could not check the quality of treatment provided in private hospitals abroad was rejected because the Doctors' Directive rendered this unnecessary.

Actual practice was, however, slightly different. In many countries, there was evidence of distrust of foreign health professionals. The official minimum standards were seen as inadequate, as they ignored the content of training and the level of competence reached.

---

[16] See European Commission, 'Professional qualifications: infringement proceedings against Portugal and Spain', Press Release No. IP/06/1789, 13 December 2006.

[17] Case C-444/05, *Stamatelaki* [2007] ECR I-1385.

Furthermore, the acquired rights' system meant that even these minimum requirements did not always have to be met. While the general directives were based on the concept of mutual trust, even a brief review of the reality reveals that this had often been absent, with compensating measures often leading to cumbersome administrative processes that impeded free movement. The general system, however, offered more possibilities for quality assurance, as it permitted the host Member State to require these measures. It also overcame a problem with the sectoral system,[18] which was seen as slow to respond to changes in clinical practice – in particular, the emergence of new specialities – as it involved the co-decision procedure where the European Parliament and Council decided together, advised by advisory committees and groups of national officials.

One obvious issue to be considered in relation to mobility within Europe was the ability to communicate. According to the sectoral directives, host Member States had to ensure that professionals acquired the language skills necessary to communicate with their patients. The rule allowed – although not explicitly – host Member States to require that candidates have certain language skills in order to be allowed to practise. This was confirmed in the *Haim II* case,[19] which considered the situation of a dentist. The Court concluded that the reliability of the communication between the dentist and his patient; the administrative authorities; and the professional organizations was an imperative reason of general interest justifying that the admission as dentist is subject to linguistic requirements. How these were assessed was left to the discretion of the Member State, although the linguistic standard required could not be more than was required to do the job, establishing the principle of proportionality, whereby Member States could not demand systematic language exams. However, for medical doctors, this could be challenging, as the duty of the doctor to inform the patient in clear and comprehensible language and the reciprocal right of the patient to give informed consent demanded a high level of linguistic ability. However, the necessary language skills would differ among specialities and it seemed reasonable to require less profound knowledge from a pathologist than from a psychiatrist. On the other hand, the general

---

[18] F. Van Overmeiren, '*Kohll* en *Decker* anders bekeken: de mobiliteit van gezondheidsmedewerkers in de Europese Unie', *Tijdschrift voor Sociaal Recht* 2 (2004), 354.

[19] Case C-424/97, *Haim II* [2000] ECR I-5123.

directives – unlike the sectoral ones – contained no stipulations about linguistic knowledge. A strict interpretation of the directives therefore created a paradox. The host Member State must ensure that a nurse providing general care had sufficient linguistic knowledge but needs not to do so for a specialist practitioner covered by the general system.

There were also some problems with the provisions on the pursuit of the profession. The exchange of information between Member States was far from optimal. Since the exchange of information was largely voluntary, doctors who were temporarily unable to practise their profession in one Member State may have been able to operate freely in a different one.[20] It was also necessary to consider sanctions against doctors whose standards were found to be inadequate. What should the host[21] Member State decide on the basis of information received? Could it simply forbid the doctor to practise on the basis of a decision made elsewhere? Should the Member State look at the underlying facts and then decide using its own legal instruments? In the absence of any explicit rules, the only guidelines seemed to be the non-discrimination rule and the principle of prohibition of obstacles to free movement, both based on Articles 39, 43 and 49 of the EC Treaty.

According to the non-discrimination[22] rule, Member States could not refuse a foreign doctor for reasons other than those they could invoke to stop their own nationals from pursuing the profession. The non-discrimination rule was, however, extremely difficult to apply in practice. Standards of practise differed enormously among the Member States. There were also certain activities that were forbidden in some states but not in others, such as performing an abortion. The situation was complicated further as Member States use different legal instruments, procedures and norms underlying disciplinary proceedings.[23] This raised the question of whether an individual

[20] H. Nys, *Medisch recht* (Leuven: Acco, 2001), p. 73.
[21] Or the home Member State when confronted with a sanction taken by the host country.
[22] It forbids also indirect discrimination. This is the case when a different treatment, not on the basis of nationality, but on the basis of another, legal criterion has the same disadvantageous effect.
[23] H. D. C. Roscam Abbing, 'Medical practice and disciplinary measures in the European Union', in P. Lens and G. Van der Wal (eds.), *Problem doctors, a conspiracy of silence* (Amsterdam: IOS Press, 1997), pp. 247–61; and H. D. C. Roscam Abbing, 'The right of the patient to quality of medical practice and the position of migrant doctors within the EU', *European Journal of Health Law* 4 (1997), 347–60.

banned from practising in his/her home country because of actions such as abortion or euthanasia could be penalized in another where they are legal. Other questions related to how to deal with cases that were not yet resolved. The general principle of innocence until proven guilty was enshrined in the European Convention for the Protection of Human Rights and Fundamental Freedoms. Yet some Member States also had mechanisms whereby someone accused of misconduct was suspended without loss of pay pending resolution of the facts. This was clearly not possible where the health professional sought to move to another Member State. Another issue related to events that took place long ago, especially where the length of disqualification imposed varied between the Member States.

In addition to the requirement that it should be non-discriminatory, the decision could not, according to the settled case-law of the Court,[24] hamper or otherwise make freedom of establishment, services and workers less attractive. Nevertheless, there were two ways that a national measure that was discriminatory and/or hampered movement may be justified. First, there was a limited list of grounds (among others, public health) set out in Articles 39, 46 and 55 of the Treaty. However, the Court ruled that such measures must be proportionate to the goal being pursued.[25] Second, there was the Court's so-called 'rule of reason'.[26] Measures that indirectly discriminated or hampered free movement could be justified if they fulfilled four conditions: they must be applied in a non-discriminatory manner; they must be justified by imperative requirements in the general interest; they must be able to achieve the objective being pursued; and they must not go beyond what is necessary in order to achieve the objective being pursued (the proportionality requirement). It could be argued that the Doctors' Directive, by offering no guidelines in this matter whatsoever, hampered true free movement. This could only be achieved by legal certainty, in the form of rules for coordination.

---

[24] See, for example, Case C-19/92, *Kraus* [1993] ECR I-1663; Case C-113/89, *Rush Portuguesa* [1990] ECR I-01417; P. Schoukens, *De sociale zekerheid van de zelfstandige en het Europees gemeenschapsrecht: de impact van het vrije verkeer van zelfstandigen* (Leuven: Acco, 2000), p. 313.

[25] Case C-101/94, *Commission v. Italy* [1996] ECR I-02691. See also Schoukens, *De sociele zekerheid*, above n.24, p. 326.

[26] Case C-55/94, *Gebhard* [1995] ECR I- 4165. See also K. Lenaerts and P. Vanuffel, *Europees recht in hoofdlijnen* (Antwerp, Apeldoorn: Maklu, 2008), p. 219.

The lack of any concrete criterion to distinguish between the provision of a 'service' and an 'establishment' also caused much legal uncertainty. This difference was important because more flexible rules applied to the provision of services. Often, it was a factual matter to distinguish between a service and an establishment. The key issue was how long an economic activity should continue before it changed from a 'service' to 'establishment'. European case-law did not provide any concrete guidelines. In the _Gebhard_ case, the Court ruled that the temporary nature of the activities in question had to be determined in light of their duration, regularity, periodicity and continuity.[27] This did not preclude the provider of services, within the meaning of the Treaty, from creating some infrastructure in the host Member State (including an office, chambers or consulting rooms) in so far as this was necessary for performing the services in question.

Another problematic issue was the lack of clarity about payment or reimbursement of the costs incurred by the patient. As described above, it was forbidden for the host Member States to oblige foreign doctors who provided services on a temporary basis in their territory to register with a social security body. However, in some countries, such as Belgium, the patient could only be reimbursed if his or her doctor was registered with the social security body. Service providers had, however, a duty to 'inform' these bodies. The purpose of doing so was far from clear. Was it to register the professional with the social security body to ensure that the care provided was covered by insurance? The Court confirmed that this provision did not seek to remove all remaining obstacles to the refund of medical services by an insurance institution with whom the health care professional was not registered.[28] According to the Directive, Member States seemed free to decide whether or not to refund payment for such services. Yet, according to the rulings in the cases of _Kohll_ and _Decker_, they were not at all free to decline to do so. Refusing reimbursement to an insured patient treated by a doctor established in another country could be seen as an infringement of the principle of free movement. This was clearly an area that required resolution.

[27] Case C-55/94, _Gebhard_, above n.26.
[28] Case C-232/99, _Commission v. Spain_ [2002] ECR I-4235.

Telemedicine, where providers do not move, also raises many as yet unresolved issues. At present, the only provisions that exist are vague, deriving from Treaty provisions on free movement of services and some Court cases[29] stating that any restriction on the free provision of services is unlawful, unless justified by objective public interests, such as public health.

C. *Directive 2005/36/EC*

Background

The proposal for a new Directive on the recognition of professional qualifications, which was launched in 2002, had the broad objective of creating a more uniform, transparent and flexible regime. The European Parliament, the Council and the Commission agreed that it was important to prepare an accessible, consolidated version of the legal provisions on mutual recognition of professional qualifications. The underlying philosophy of the new Directive is explicitly deregulatory, reflecting a view that professional regulation, rather than being seen as a protection for the public, is instead an obstacle to the operation of the market. Thus, the Commission's proposal[30] was based on the continuing liberalization of services, a reduction in barriers to recognition of qualifications, and more flexibility to update the provisions of the Directive in the light of changing circumstances. All of these goals need to be viewed in light of the Lisbon Agenda, which seeks to transform Europe into the world's most dynamic and competitive economy by 2010.

The new Directive,[31] which covers all professional qualifications in any sector (not just health), combines the two systems (sectoral and general), allowing the same mechanisms to apply: the '[g]eneral system (for the recognition of evidence of training)' (Chapter I) and the sectoral system (renamed as '[r]ecognition on the basis of the coordination of minimum training conditions' (Chapter III)). There is, however, a third, completely new system. This is '[r]ecognition

---

[29] See for example Joined Cases C-34/95 to C-36/95, *De Agostini* [1997] ECR I-03843.

[30] European Commission, 'Amended proposal for a European Parliament and Council Directive on the recognition of professional qualifications', COM (2004) 317 final, 20 April 2004.

[31] Directive 2005/36/EC, above n.14

on the basis of professional experience' (Chapter II). This applies primarily to areas such as industrial production, craftsmanship and trade, where individuals who are clearly qualified to undertake a role may not possess any official qualifications.

Automatic recognition on the basis of the coordination of minimum training conditions

For all health professions falling under the scope of the former sectoral system – i.e., doctors, general practitioners and specialist doctors, nurses responsible for general care, dentists, dental practitioner and specialist dentists, veterinary surgeons, midwives and pharmacists – exactly the same mechanism continues to apply: automatic recognition on the basis of a completion of minimum training requirements (Article 21). However, the system now is called simply '[r]ecognition on the basis of the coordination of minimum training conditions'. As explained above, the procedure of automatic recognition of basic professional qualifications obliges every Member State to respond positively to every request for recognition. They cannot challenge the registration of someone with one of the diplomas listed in Annex V of the Directive by, for example, requiring that the applicant take another examination.

The situation with specialist qualifications in medicine and dentistry is more complicated. Again, there is a system based on mutual recognition, also involving specification of the duration of study. However, although some specialities, such as general surgery or neurosurgery are essentially the same in all Member States, others are not. Thus, in many Member States, dermatovenerology exists as a distinct speciality, whereas in others dermatology and specialization in sexually transmitted diseases are distinct categories. Moreover, the activities undertaken by doctors working in public health, and the corresponding skills required, vary greatly, so that this is only recognized as a speciality in a few Member States. There is also the difficulty of overlapping terminology, which is seen in the case of family medicine and general practice.[32]

Automatic mutual recognition only applies when the speciality exists in either all or in at least two Member States. In the latter case,

---

[32] I. Caixeiro, 'UEMO: lobbying letter from the Working Group on Specialist Training', *PrimaryCare* 8 (2008), 15–6.

the recognition is limited to the Member States where the speciality exists. A problem arising from the diversity of specializations is the potential to create an almost endless list of those recognized in only a few Member States. To overcome this problem, while retaining those already recognized, new applications will be permitted only if the specialities exist in two fifths of Member States (Article 26).[33] However, future medical specialties that do not meet this criterion will fall under the scope of the general system. This implies that host Member States can take compensatory measures in such cases. It is important to stress that individual Member States nevertheless remain free to agree among themselves the automatic recognition of medical and dental specialities common to them but not falling within the terms of this Directive.[34]

The minimum requirements for the training of doctors, general practitioners and specialist doctors, nurses responsible for general care, dentists, dental practitioners and specialist dentists, veterinary surgeons, midwives and pharmacists are listed in Articles 24–5, 31, 34–6, 44 and 46 of the Directive.[35] By creating a single committee to monitor and propose periodic revisions to the Directive, the Commission seeks to ensure easier updating of the criteria being used. This is designed to address criticisms that those criteria have, in the past, failed to adapt to the rapidly changing health system context. A comitology committee (Article 58) replaces the various advisory committees existing in the former system, which some in the Commission viewed as cumbersome, although others saw them as providing necessary safeguards, based on their detailed knowledge of the professions concerned. This quest for simplicity also reflected the challenges posed by the many more languages in use following recent enlargements. Another change

---

[33] 'The new provision ensures that Community procedures (notification, comitology) are required only if a certain "critical mass" of Member States are actually involved. This is justified in relation to the existing rules on the grounds of reducing the procedural burden. Otherwise, all 27 Member States would be called upon to vote by qualified majority, using the comitology procedure, on requests from (in some cases) only two Member States, who would anyway remain completely free to achieve mutual recognition on a bilateral basis'. European Parliament, 'Draft recommendation for second reading. Common position adopted by the Council with a view to the adoption of a Directive of the European Parliament and of the Council on the recognition of professional qualifications. Council common position', 13781/2/2004 – C6–0008/2005 – 2002/0061(COD).

[34] Directive 2005/36/EC, above n.14.   [35] *Ibid.*

brought in by the new Directive is the incorporation of professional organizations in the comitology committee. The system of acquired rights (see above) has been maintained (Article 23).

There are some specific provisions for specialized doctors (Article 27), general practitioners (Article 30), general nurses (Article 33), dental practitioners (Article 37), veterinary surgeons (Article 39) and midwives (Article 43). Third country diplomas fall outside the scope of automatic recognition enshrined in the Directive and national authorities must make other provisions for deciding on the registration of health professionals holding them. However, the provisions adopted are subject to European law, in that Directive 2001/19/EC[36] requires Member States to examine not only the qualification held by the migrant but also whether he or she has acquired experience and/or training in another Member State. This followed the Court's decision in the *Vlassopoulou* case.[37] The Court ruled that a Member State, when deciding whether to permit an individual to practise a profession that is, according to national law, only open on the basis of a diploma or professional qualification, must take into consideration any diplomas, certificates and other evidence of formal qualification that the person concerned has obtained in another Member State in order to practise that same profession. In doing so, it must compare the knowledge and abilities certified by those diplomas with the knowledge and qualifications required in its national rules. This view was reinforced in the *Haim I* case,[38] where it was ruled that when competent national authorities have to check whether the nationally-prescribed practical training has been met, they must take into consideration the professional experience of the person concerned, including any professional experience obtained in

---

[36] This Directive modified both the former sectoral directives and the general ones and is also called the SLIM-Directive. Directive 2001/19/EC of the European Parliament and of the Council of 14 May 2001 amending Council Directives 89/48/EEC and 92/51/EEC on the general system for the recognition of professional qualifications and Council Directives 77/452/EEC, 77/453/EEC, 78/686/EEC, 78/687/EEC, 78/1026/EEC, 78/1027/EEC, 80/154/EEC, 80/155/EEC, 85/384/EEC, 85/432/EEC, 85/433/EEC and 93/16/EEC concerning the professions of nurse responsible for general care, dental practitioner, veterinary surgeon, midwife, architect, pharmacist and doctor, OJ 2001 No. L206/1.

[37] Case C-340/89, *Vlassopoulou* [1991] ECR I-2357.

[38] Case C-319/92, *Haim* [1994] ECR I-425.

another Member State. In the *Hocsman* case,[39] the Court extended this approach to include diplomas and experience obtained in third countries. Dr Hocsman obtained his basic medical training as doctor in Argentina. In Spain, where this training was recognized, he obtained a specialist diploma as a urologist, going on to practise as such for some time. He then became an EU citizen. In France, he was denied the right of establishment because his basic diploma was not recognized. The Court ruled that:

[W]here, in a situation not regulated by a directive on mutual recognition of diplomas, a Community national applies for authorisation to practise a profession access to which depends, under national law, on the possession of a diploma or professional qualification, or on periods of practical experience, the competent authorities of the Member State concerned must take into consideration all the diplomas, certificates and other evidence of formal qualifications of the person concerned and his relevant experience, by comparing the specialised knowledge and abilities certified by those diplomas and that experience with the knowledge and qualifications required by the national rules.

In this way, established jurisprudence goes beyond the Directive, which only mentions the obligation to consider diplomas and experience obtained in another Member State. Thus, it is not possible simply to refuse to recognize a third country diploma without giving it due consideration. There are a few other issues that arise in relation to diplomas obtained outside the EU. One is the question of what happens when someone who obtained such a qualification and has it recognized in one Member State seeks to work in another one. In such cases, the Member State that the individual wishes to move to is not obliged to accept the decision of the first state.

Another issue relates to training obtained partly outside the EU. This was addressed in the *Tennah-Durez* case.[40] The Court interpreted 'third country diploma' narrowly as only those diplomas that are actually awarded by a third country. In order to qualify as an EU diploma, it is not necessary that the training is undertaken entirely in a Member State. An Algerian woman, who had obtained Belgian nationality, had undertaken most of her undergraduate medical

[39] Case C-238/98, *Hocsman* [2000] ECR I-066231-6623.
[40] Case C-110/01, *Tennah-Durez* [2003] ECR I-6239.

education in Algeria but then completed the last year of her course in Belgium. Having obtained her medical diploma, she moved to France, where she was denied the right of establishment. The Court ruled that it is not relevant where the training was undertaken; at stake was whether the training meets the minimum requirements of the Doctors' Directive. The competent authority to make that judgement is the Belgian state. The Member State that awards the diploma approves the training undertaken in order to obtain it. In this way, a diploma awarded by a Member State provides a 'doctor's passport', enabling the holder to move within the EU without having his/her professional qualification opened to challenge, except in some very special circumstances, discussed below, which apply equally to nationals of the host country.

The general system

As explained earlier, under the general system the host Member State can decide each case on its own merits and can, as appropriate, impose compensating measures such as an aptitude test or an adaptation period. Compensation measures are allowed when the training undertaken by the applicant is up to one year less than that required by the host Member State, when the professional role includes professional activities that do not exist in the home Member State, or where there are differences in specific aspects of the training (Article 14). Following the *Vlassopoulou*[41] and *Haim I*[42] cases, host Member States must always take into consideration the diplomas, certificates and other evidence of formal qualification, as well as the experience that the applicant has obtained in another Member State in order to practise that profession, by comparing the knowledge and abilities certified by those diplomas with the knowledge and qualifications required by national rules (Article 14(5)). Although the new Directive addresses all professional qualifications, there is one important way in which health professions are treated differently. Reflecting one of the underlying goals of the new approach, which is to facilitate greater cross-border provision of services, the new Directive bans compensation measures

---

[41] Case C-340/89, *Vlassopoulou*, above n.37.
[42] Case C-319/92, *Haim*, above n.38.

when they concern services. In this case, compensating measures are seen as a potential infringement of the free movement of services. Specifically, host Member States can no longer restrict the free provision of services for any reason relating to professional qualifications as long as the service provider is legally established in another Member State (Article 5(1)). However, quite explicitly, this does not apply to health professions (and public safety professions) (Article 7(4)). For them, the old rules remain applicable, thus permitting compensation measures.

Directive 2005/36/EC introduced so-called 'common platforms' (Article 15). Common platforms are sets of criteria for professional qualifications that can compensate for the considerable differences that have been identified between the training requirements for certain professions in different Member States. These differences are identified by comparing the duration and content of the training in at least two thirds of the Member States, but including all the Member States where the profession has been regulated. The criteria adopted are agreed as attesting to a sufficient level of competence. Common platforms may be notified to the Commission by the Member States or by professional organizations. When an applicant has a qualification that satisfies the criteria set out in the common platform, as adopted through a comitology procedure, the host Member State will have to waive the compensating measures. The system recalls the scheme of automatic recognition on the basis of minimum training requirements contained in the sectoral system. Article 15(4) does, however, stress that Member States remain competent to determine the professional qualifications required for the pursuit of professions in their territory and for the organization of education and professional training. Moreover, if a Member State considers that a common platform no longer offers adequate guarantees of professional qualifications, it shall inform the Commission accordingly (Article 15(5)).

Concerning third country diplomas, where a profession does not fall under the scope of the automatic recognition system, each Member State is free to recognize it or not. Such diplomas fall within the scope of the general scheme, on condition that the holder has three years' professional experience in the Member State that recognized that diploma (Article 3(3)).

Pursuit of the profession

Establishment versus provision of services

The new Directive merges all coordinating rules concerning the pursuit of the profession (automatic recognition, general system and recognition on the basis of professional experience).

a. Establishment The provisions of Directive 2005/36/EC facilitating the pursuit of a profession by a migrant health professional primarily involve the coordination of rules concerning documents and oaths (Articles 50–1), as in the old directives. When deciding whether to grant permission for *establishment* by a foreign health professional, host Member States can apply their national rules fully, as long as these do not infringe the right of establishment. An example of a national rule doing this was the requirement for the applicant to cancel his or her registration in their home Member State. The Court found that this was too absolute and general in nature to be justified.[43] In a recent case,[44] the European Court had to rule on a German regional quota for psychotherapists joining the social security system. At stake was not the existence of the quota as such, but rather the acquired rights of psychotherapists already recognized as 'German sickness fund physiotherapists'. The Court stated that by failing to grant the same acquired right to psychotherapists working in the health insurance system of another Member State, Germany breached the right of free establishment. In a case concerning the advertisement of services and the right to establishment the Court[45] has stated that an Italian provision forbidding the advertisement of aesthetic medical and surgical treatments on national television is an infringement of the right of establishment, given that such advertisements are allowed under certain circumstances on local television.

---

[43] Case 96/85, *Commission* v. *France* [1986] ECR 1475.
[44] Case C-456/05, *Commission* v. *Germany* [2007] ECR I-10517.
[45] Case C-500/06, *Corporacion Dermoestetica SA* [2008] ECR I-5758. It is interesting to note that the issue of advertising by health professionals also has been brought before the Court in relation to competition law, arguing that liberal professions must be seen as 'undertakings' and that advertising is indispensable for free competition. However, the Court found that the Belgian law prohibiting dental care providers from engaging in advertising did not infringe Articles 81 and 10 of the EC Treaty, nor could it be seen as a (forbidden) agreement between undertakings. See the recent Case C-446/05, *Doulamis* [2008] ECR I-1377.

There are also cases pending on the establishment of pharmacists. These two joined cases[46] concern a decree by the Spanish region of Asturias regulating pharmacies. The Commission initiated infringement proceedings against Italy, Austria, Spain[47] and, later, Germany concerning national legislation restricting the right to operate chains of pharmacies.

b. Provision of services As was already the case with the old sectoral directives, the decision on whether to grant permission to a foreign health professional to provide 'services' on an occasional or temporary basis involves legislation that is, overall, rather more flexible than with establishment. As already noted, a key objective of Directive 2005/36/EC was to facilitate greater freedom in providing services. Previously, only the sectoral directives took a more flexible approach to services compared with establishment. The new Directive includes a separate Title (II) covering the provision of services that are common to all systems of recognition.

It is recognized that there is potential to use the procedures related to provision of services to circumvent the more stringent requirements of establishment. Thus, to avoid such 'masked establishment',[48] Article 5(2) clarifies that Title II (dedicated to the provision of services) shall 'only' apply where the service provider moves to the territory of the host Member State to pursue, on a temporary and occasional basis, his/her profession. In defining a 'service' in this way, the Directive implements the case-law from the *Gebhard* case,[49] which implies that the temporary character of the service should be assessed on a case-by-case basis, taking into account the duration, frequency and continuity of

---

[46] Joined Cases C-570/07 and C-571/07, *Pérez and Gómez* (judgment pending).
[47] European Commission, 'Internal market: infringement proceedings concerning Italy, Austria and Spain with regard to pharmacies', Press Release No. IP/06/858, 28 June 2006. See also Chapter 11.
[48] A European provision cannot in any way benefit some citizens to the detriment of others. It is therefore necessary to avoid 'masked establishment' – that is to say, where provisions relating to the free provision of services allow a migrant to avoid the provisions relating to the right of establishment in the country where he/she pursues his/her activities, in fact by enabling him/her to benefit, without any reason, from more advantageous regulations than those laid down for national citizens. See European Parliament, 'Draft recommendation', above n.33.
[49] Case C-55/94, *Gebhard*, above n.26.

the activity. This does not prevent the provider of services from equipping him/herself with infrastructure in the host Member State, in so far as such infrastructure is necessary for the purpose of performing the services in question. As a consequence, EU citizens may find it almost impossible, in practice, to differentiate 'services' and 'establishment'. Unfortunately, the Directive missed the opportunity to set a concrete time limit (sixteen weeks per year was initially suggested) to distinguish between these concepts. It is, however, crucial to differentiate them because of the different legal bases under which they operate.

The provision of services across borders where the health professional does not physically move, as with telemedicine, remains excluded from the scope of this application under Articles 1 and 2. This is another area where legal clarification is needed. Despite some explicit exceptions (see below), the Directive establishes the principle that host Member States can fully apply their own professional rules to the incoming service provider (Article 1(3)). Rules of this kind relate, for example, to the organization of the profession and professional standards, including those concerning ethics, supervision and liability. The case-law of the Court of Justice, such as the *Van Binsbergen* case,[50] however, shows that the application of professional rules is not unconditional. Although the Court in general agrees upon the principle that rules governing the activities of professionals in host Member States apply to service providers, the application of these requirements does not seem to be unconditional. They must be justified objectively by the need to ensure that professional rules of conduct are observed. The rules are thus to be judged on a case-by-case basis. If called upon to do so in litigation, Member States will have to justify their actions when applying their national rules and it is up to the Court to judge them, balancing free movement – and, more generally, the internal market – and public health.

The host Member State can ask for a prior declaration the first time a service provider moves into its territory (Article 7(1–2)). The declaration should be written and the service provider may supply it by any appropriate means. Such a declaration must be renewed once for each year that the professional intends to provide services. In a currently pending procedure,[51] France has to justify its requirement that

[50] Case 33–74, *Van Binsbergen* [1974] ECR 1299.
[51] European Commission, 'Professional qualifications: infringement procedures against France, Greece and Spain', Press Release No. IP/06/888, 29 June 2006.

incoming services employing doctors, dentists and midwives produce such a declaration for each service and for each patient seen. As well as declarations, host Member States may require proof of nationality, evidence of professional qualifications and an attestation of legal establishment. The latter must certify that the person is 'not prohibited from practising even temporarily'. Explicit exceptions in the Directive relating to the applicability of host Member State rules to service providers include two important exemptions (Article 6), as was the case with the old sectoral directives. Host Member States cannot require that incoming service providers register with a professional organization or with a social security body. However, a temporary registration or membership pro forma with the host professional organization is possible. To lighten the administrative burden for the incoming service provider, this occurs automatically. The competent authority will therefore send the written declaration and required documents to the professional organization. The second prohibition, involving registration with a social security body, implies that the unclear situation regarding the payment or reimbursement of the costs for the patient (see above) remains.

At the time of writing, Estonia[52] has been confronted with a reasoned opinion from the Commission in view of its rules prohibiting the recognition of medical prescriptions made out by medical practitioners who are qualified to act in their Member State of establishment but not registered in Estonia. The Commission takes the view that these provisions restrict both the freedom of health professionals to provide services as well as patients' rights, and that they are contrary to Article 40 of the EC Treaty.

Quality: continuing to practise

As noted above, professional mobility is based on the mutual recognition of professional qualifications, which assumes that someone registered to practise in one Member State is competent to do so in all others. As noted above, however, the actual practice is slightly different. There seems to be distrust towards foreign health professionals in some countries. Yet existing systems of regulation are seen by many as failing in

---

[52] European Commission, 'Free movement of services: infringement proceedings against Estonia and Portugal', Press Release No. IP/08/1033, 26 June 2008.

their pursuit of their primary goals: provision of a system of professional accountability; ensuring that basic standards of care do not fall below those that are acceptable; and promoting continuing improvements in quality of care.[53] Specifically, the acquisition of a qualification, perhaps many years previously, is no longer seen as sufficient evidence of fitness to practise. There is also increasing recognition that some skills decline over time, an effect found to be present in a number of aspects of care in a recent systematic review of sixty-two studies.[54] In a number of countries, one response has been the introduction of periodic revalidation and requirements to undertake lifelong learning. These developments are not, however, recognized by the existing European legal framework. Progress has been limited. At a 2006 meeting of the High Level Group on Health Services and Medical Care, the group concluded that 'there is no clear consensus reached on which concrete actions to develop in order to take forward issues such as CPD [continuing professional development]'.[55] The introduction of revalidation mechanisms, which aim to 'demonstrate that the competence of doctors is acceptable', draws on the experiences of the United States, Canada, Australia and New Zealand.[56] In Europe, practice varies.[57] In its most basic form, it involves participation in continuing medical education (CME), which is designed to keep physicians up to date on clinical developments and medical knowledge. The broader concept of continuing professional development (CPD) includes CME, along with the development of personal, social and managerial skills. More demanding methods incorporate peer review, external evaluation and practice inspection.

[53] T. A. Brennan *et al.*, 'The role of physician specialty board certification status in the quality movement', *Journal of the American Medical Association* 292 (2004), 1038–43; K. Sutherland and S. Leatherman, 'Does certification improve medical standards?', *British Medical Journal* 333 (2006), 439–41.

[54] N. K. Choudhry, R. H. Fletcher and S. B. Soumerai, 'Systematic review: the relationship between clinical experience and quality of health care', *Annals of Internal Medicine* 142 (2005), 260–73.

[55] European Commission, 'Report on the work of the High Level Group', above n.4.

[56] L. Southgate and M. Pringle, 'Revalidation in the United Kingdom: general principles based on experience in general practice', *British Medical Journal* 319 (1999), 1180–3; D. H. Irvine, 'Everyone is entitled to a good doctor', *The Medical Journal of Australia* 186 (2007), 256–61.

[57] S. Merkur *et al.*, 'Physician Revalidation in Europe', *Clinical Medicine* 8 (2008), 371–6.

However, it is important to recognize that, within Europe, there are very differing traditions of how the professions and the state should interact, which will shape the nature of systems in assessing continuing fitness to practise. Even within countries, there are differences in the approaches advocated, a situation that is not helped by the very weak evidence base that such systems are effective. Thus, in the United Kingdom, the majority of public as well as family doctors believe that physicians should be assessed regularly to ensure their knowledge and skills are up to date.[58] Yet some commentators – most notably, Onora O'Neill in her 2002 Reith Lectures – have argued cogently that overzealous regulation could be harmful.[59]

Currently, the Netherlands and Germany have explicit revalidation systems in place. Since 2005, Dutch physicians have had to undertake CME and undergo a visit by peers every five years. Revalidation is a requirement to remain on the medical register. The visits (*visitatie*), by a team of three other doctors, including one recently visited and one about to be, involve a comprehensive assessment of practice, with ongoing discussions on monitoring adherence to clinical guidelines and patient input. While physicians in Germany receive their licence to practise from regional ministries and are regulated through their regional chambers (professional associations), the 2004 Social Health Insurance (SHI) Modernization Act introduced revalidation requirements for physicians at the federal level. Germany's revalidation scheme requires physicians to fulfil CME requirements every five years (250 credit points of approximately 45 minutes each). Physicians contracted with the SHI funds and working in ambulatory care are not subject to detailed regulations on the topics that must be covered by CME. In contrast, specialists working in hospitals have to show that 70% of their vocational training has been on topics concerning their speciality. Radiologists are subject to an additional recertification procedure if they read mammograms. These programmes are voluntary for purely private physicians. In the event of non-compliance, the Regional Associations of SHI Physicians can reduce reimbursement rates after one year by 10% and after two years

[58] Ipsos MORI, 'Attitudes to medical regulation and revalidation of doctors' research among doctors and the general public', Research Study Conducted for Department of Health, MORI (2005).

[59] O. O'Neill, *A question of trust* (Cambridge: Cambridge University Press, 2002).

by 25%. If the CME certificate is not achieved within two years after the due date, accreditation may be withdrawn. All regions, except for one (Baden Wurttemberg), have implemented a computer-based registration system for CME. At the end of June 2009, the CME system will be reviewed for the first time. It is expected that participation in CME should be combined with quality assurance systems, thus promoting a broader system of CPD.

In the United Kingdom, the General Medical Council has proposed that physicians would have to prove their fitness to practise. Current proposals are that revalidation should include two requirements: relicensure to permit practise as a medical practitioner, and additional recertification to practise as a general practitioner or specialist.[60] Relicensure, every five years, would be based on a revised model of appraisal used in the National Health Service, but applied to all doctors wherever they work. Recertification procedures would be speciality specific, led by the Royal Colleges. Physicians who failed in either process would spend a period of time in supervised practise. In some other countries, including Austria, Belgium, France and Spain, programmes are heavily dependent upon participation in CME as the mechanism to maintain physician competence.

Austria, Belgium and France also take their systems a step further by including peer review. There is a mandatory CME programme for licensed medical doctors in Austria, the *Diplom-Fortbildungs-Programm*. Although legal responsibility resides with the Austrian Medical Chamber, the actual implementation of the programme rests with the Academy of Physicians. Physicians must acquire CME credits, 80% of which have to be acquired through speciality-related certified CME programmes, with 27% of the total within the physician's particular speciality. Undergoing peer review is another means of accumulating such credits, and certificates are awarded over a three-year cycle.

Also, in Belgium there is a legal obligation for general practitioners and specialists to comply with set standards and the pursuit of accreditation is supported by financial incentives. Accreditation is granted by the Institut national d'assurance maladie-invalidité/Rijksinstituut

---

[60] L. Donaldson, 'Good doctors, safer patients: proposals to strengthen the system to assure and improve the performance of doctors and to protect the safety of patients', Report for the UK Department of Health, 14 July 2006.

voor ziekte- en invaliditeitsverzekering (INAMI/RIZIV) for a period of three years if the physician meets additional requirements, including participation in CME and peer review. While accreditation is not required, it enables physicians to charge higher reimbursable fees to patients, boosting a physician's annual salary by about 4%.[61] In order to keep their professional title, general practitioners are required to regularly maintain and develop their knowledge, skills and medical performance by undertaking at least twenty hours (200 credits) of continuing professional development annually, including four hours in group peer review.[62] Hospital physicians are required to participate in the peer review process, regardless of whether they seek accreditation.

In France, CME and medical audit (known as the Evaluation of Professional Practices (EPP)) have been introduced. Both are intended to be compulsory, with participation assessed every five years. However, they have come under criticism by the Inspector General of Social Affairs as neither system is monitored. Furthermore, because the legal status of the institutions responsible for the regulation of CME and EPP requirements are not the same, EPP has been difficult to implement and enforcement has been delayed.

In Spain, CME is reported as fragmented, but there is growing interest in developing certification and recertification schemes in the regions, which are responsible for the provision of health care. National legislation has identified the need for these programmes and the medical colleges have established voluntary CME systems. In 1998, the Spanish Commission of Continuing Education of Health Professionals initiated a nationwide CME system based on Catalonia's experience, but by 2005 it had been implemented by only nine regional commissions (out of seventeen).

In a Europe where the right to professional mobility is enshrined in law, on the basis that all Member States have in place effective systems to ensure quality of care, diversity on this scale in the absence of any European legal framework creates obvious problems, and the reasoning that a sufficient level of quality is assured through formal

---

[61] C. Peck *et al.*, 'Continuing medical education and continuing professional development: international comparisons', *British Medical Journal* 320 (2000), 432–5.

[62] Arrêté ministerial du 21 Février 2006 fixant les critères d'agrément des médecins generalists, *Moniteur Belge* 1 (2006), 10277.

qualifications, as enshrined in European secondary law and followed by the Court of Justice, therefore seems unrealistic.

The European Accreditation Council for CME (EACCME) was established in January 2000 by the European Union of Medical Specialists to provide a practical instrument to improve the quality of CME in Europe. By recognizing high quality specialist education, it connects the existing and emerging accreditation systems in Europe and act as a clearing house for accreditation of CME and credits.[63]

Practices allowed

Within Europe, there is considerable diversity in the roles undertaken by different professionals. For example, nurses prescribe drugs and manage clinics treating chronic diseases in some countries but have much more limited roles in others.[64] Directive 2005/36/EC does not envisage any coordination of these roles, despite the obvious implications for someone trained in a system where, for example, the nursing role is extremely restrictive and then moves to one where it is more expansive. In the *Bouchoucha* case,[65] the Court judged that, given the lack of a Community definition of 'medical activities', Member States are free to regulate these activities as they see fit. At stake was a complaint by a holder of a British diploma in osteopathy. According to the Court, the French rule requiring that a qualified medical doctor provide osteopathic treatments does not breach the right of free establishment.

The same reasoning was followed in the *Gräbner* case.[66] The Court ruled that the German requirement of being a qualified medical doctor in order to practise the profession of *'Heilpraktiker'* (lay health practitioner) did not obstruct the free movement of services or the right to free establishment. So far, the Court seems to respect the Member State's choice to reserve certain activities for persons with a specific qualification, such as medical doctors.[67]

---

[63] See also the EACCME web site, www.uems.net/main.php?category=6.
[64] M. McKee, C.-A. Dubois and B. Sibbald, 'Changing professional boundaries', in C.-A. Dubois, M. McKee and E. Nolte (eds.), *Human resources for health in Europe* (Maidenhead: Open University Press, 2006), pp. 63–78.
[65] Case C-61/89, *Bouchoucha* [1990] ECR I-3551.
[66] Case C-294/00, *Gräbner* [2002] ECR I-6515.   [67] *Ibid.*, para. 48.

Disciplinary matters

Member States are required to exchange information regarding 'disciplinary action or criminal sanctions taken or any other serious, specific circumstances' that are likely to be relevant for the pursuit of the profession, while respecting the EU's privacy legislation. The effective and timely exchange of information about health professionals between Member States is important to protect patient safety. The 'Health Care Professionals Crossing Borders Project' is relevant here. This project seeks to facilitate an efficient proactive method of information exchange. This informal initiative, which originated under a Dutch EU Presidency, is led by the Alliance of United Kingdom Health Regulators on Europe (AURE), a consortium of bodies regulating the various health professions in the United Kingdom, and brings together all health care regulators across the European Economic Area. In October 2005, it developed a model of information exchange known as the 'Edinburgh Agreement'. Among its other activities, it has developed a 'European Certificate of Current Professional Status'. Member States were expected to implement this certificate scheme by the time that Directive 2005/36/EC came into force in October 2007. Nevertheless, some problems remain. As was the case with the old directives, the new Directive does not stipulate anything about the possible extraterritorial effect of those measures. So, it is still not clear what the host Member State is supposed to decide on the basis of information received, or what the home Member State should do when confronted with a sanction taken by the host country. As noted above, the only guidelines seem to be the principles of non-discrimination and the prohibition on hampering free movement, both based on Articles 39, 43 and 49 of the Treaty, which can be extremely difficult to apply in practice. However, as was discussed in relation to revalidation, the extent to which medical practice is regulated by the state varies enormously among Member States, as do the legal instruments and procedures employed, and the norms underlying disciplinary proceedings.[68] To complicate matters further, the situation is changing. An example is the intention in the United Kingdom to apply the civil standard of proof in cases of alleged professional misconduct, where guilt will be assessed on the balance of probabilities, instead of the

---

[68] Roscam Abbing, 'Medical practice', above n.23, pp. 247–61; Roscam Abbing, 'The right of the patient', above n.23.

previous criminal standard, where it was judged on the basis of being beyond reasonable doubt. The principle of non-discrimination would suggest that the standards of the Member State to which the professional was seeking to move should be applied. However, this clearly raises issues concerning the ability to take evidence and reach conclusions about events in another legal jurisdiction.

The situation is complicated further by the way in which national data protection legislation is interpreted, which is sometimes used as a reason not to allow Member States to exchange information, a rationale that is entirely contrary to the European legislation, which was intended to facilitate its transfer where necessary. There does seem to be a need to establish a European legal duty[69] to exchange such data. Finally, it should be noted that, although not yet in use, the new Directive does offer the possibility to introduce professional cards that would summarize a person's training, experience and any penalties incurred (Preamble, Point 32).

As this brief review shows, there is clearly much legal uncertainty that, unless resolved, will continue to hamper true freedom of movement.

D. Access to training: free movement of students

Some Member States restrict access to (para)medical training by applying a system of so-called *numerus clausus*. Controls on the number of health professionals are used by these Member States as a tool for planning, seeking to avoid overproduction in the health sector. A 1986 European Court of Justice case[70] is relevant in this regard. The Court confirmed that no rule of the European Communities *obliges* Member States to restrict the access of medical students. The Italian Court had consulted the Court to clarify this issue, as Italy had imposed no restrictions but was concerned that it might have to, an issue that was controversial given the high number of medical graduates seeking jobs in Italy at that time. Differing policies among Member States have led to problems. Students in Member States that

[69] As proposed by the Alliance of UK Health Regulators on Europe in its 'Response to the EC Consultation regarding Community action on health services', January 2007.

[70] Joined Cases 98/85, 162/85 and 258/85, *Bertini and Bisignani and Others* [1986] ECR 1885.

apply the *numerus clausus* system can obtain training in a neigh-bouring Member State, by using their right of free movement, which precludes them being discriminated against on the basis of nation-ality. Austria and Belgium face a special situation in this regard. Between 30% and 50% of medical students in Austria are German. Germany and Austria both apply strict *numerus clausus* systems. Belgium (Wallonia) also has a high proportion of medical students from France.[71] The European Court of Justice[72] stated clearly that Austria's requirements for holders of a secondary education diploma from other Member States to prove that they have met conditions governing access to higher education in their home Member State (e.g., having passed an entrance exam or obtained a grade to qualify for the *numerus clausus* system in the home Member State) was in breach of the European principle of non-discrimination. This judg-ment was heavily criticized. As a reaction to this judgment, Austria amended its Universities Act, imposing a quota by which 75% of the places for medical and dental studies could be reserved for holders of an Austrian secondary education diploma (with 20% for other EU diplomas and 5% for third country diplomas). Having received a let-ter of formal notice from the Commission, Austria argued the quota was necessary because of potential shortages of health care profes-sionals practising in Austria. The Commission, confronted by prima facie evidence, therefore decided to suspend the infringement case (1998/2308) for five years in order to give the Austrian authorities the opportunity to provide supplementary data supporting the argument that the measure is necessary and proportionate.[73]

A similar situation arose with a decree from the French commu-nity in Belgium (*Communauté française*) in June 2006, which sought to limit the number of non-Belgian students in certain (para)medical studies by imposing a quota of 70% reserved places for students who are resident in Belgium. The quota covers nine separate subject areas in total, including medical and veterinary studies. The French

---

[71] K. Groenendijk, 'Free movement of workers in Europe 2005', European Report, European Commission Employment, Social Affairs, and Equal Opportunities (2006).

[72] Case C-147/03, *Commission v. Austria* [2005] ECR I-07963.

[73] European Commission, 'Access to higher education: the Commission suspends its infringement cases against Austria and Belgium', Press Release No. IP/07/1788, 28 November 2007.

community provided evidence that this was necessary to maintain sufficient territorial coverage and quality in its public health system. The Commission also decided to suspend this infringement case (2006/4760) for five years in order to give the authorities the opportunity to provide supplementary data.[74] It is apparent that applying the *numerus clausus* system to control access to training does not seem to be an effective planning tool when only some Member States do so. Students will simply go to another Member State for training and return to their home Member States with their diplomas, where they will be recognized on the basis of Directive 2005/36/EC. Restricting the pursuit of the profession within the framework of social security is another planning tool. Instead of restricting the number of students – or access to training – it restricts the number of health professionals that can participate in the social security system (see the above discussion on the German regional restriction imposed on psychotherapists) – or access to the pursuit of the profession within the framework of the social security system. The situation continues to evolve. Belgium recently adopted a similar measure in relation to physiotherapists. As it applied to students already in training, it led to a major debate on acquired rights. Given the findings of the recent German case, any measure that only protected the acquired rights of Belgian students may be in breach of European law.

E. *Ethical recruitment guidelines*

As already noted, free movement of health professionals poses a potential threat of 'brain drain'. Recruitment of health professionals from other Member States and from outside the European Union (a situation that, in some cases, is facilitated by European law on third country diplomas), may exacerbate existing shortages of health personnel in the countries of origin. This has risen rapidly up the international agenda, as increasing numbers of western European countries have engaged in active recruitment of foreign health personnel, especially nurses.[75] This issue was addressed by the High Level Group on Health

---

[74] *Ibid.*
[75] See, for example, www.nurses.be; a recruitment firm established in Belgium, specialized in recruiting nurses in Romania and Bulgaria.

Services and Medical Care in 2006[76] and, on 7 April 2008, a Code of Conduct on Ethical Cross-border Recruitment and Retention in the Hospital Sector was signed by the European Federation of Public Service Unions (EPSU) and the European Hospital and Healthcare Employers Association (HOSPEEM), representing, respectively, health care unions and employers.[77] It is, however, purely a voluntary agreement. The opposite situation has occurred in the United Kingdom, where there is a tradition of foreign doctors working as junior doctors, with some progressing to substantive senior posts in the United Kingdom, while others return to their countries of origin, in many cases having gained valuable experience. A new computerized system for the recruitment of medical training posts was introduced in 2007. The system was a spectacular failure but, during the course of its prolonged collapse, it became clear that it was attracting over 10 000 applicants from outside the European Union and it was likely that, even if only a fraction of them were successful, many British graduates would be unemployed. In February 2008, the Secretary of State for Health announced a ban on such applicants. This ban was challenged in the British courts by the British Association of Physicians of Indian Origin on the grounds that health ministers did not have the authority to change immigration law.[78] In May 2008, the United Kingdom Law Lords supported them, but on the specific grounds that the Secretary of State had acted unlawfully by simply announcing the change of policy on a web site managed by a nongovernmental organization, rather than bringing it before parliament where she would have had to defend her position publicly.

3. The Working Time Directive

As can be seen in several places in this book, European legislation not specifically directed at the health sector can have a profound and even unintended impact on it. One of the clearest examples is the

---

[76] European Commission, 'Report on the work of the High Level Group', above n.4.
[77] European Federation of Public Service Unions, 'EPSU-HOSPEEM code of conduct and follow up on ethical cross-border recruitment and retention in the hospital sector', European Federation of Public Service Unions (2007).
[78] J. Carvel, 'Doctors from outside EU barred from consultant training', *The Guardian*, 7 February 2008.

Working Time Directive. With its legal basis in Article 137 of the EC Treaty, it pursues a social objective – the protection of the health and safety of workers and the improvement of their working conditions – as fundamental goals and without reference to the internal market.

The initial Working Time Directive 93/104/EC[79] was amended by Directive 2000/34/EC[80] and later consolidated in Directive 2003/88/EC,[81] which function as *lex specialis* in relation to Directive 89/391/EEC.[82] The latter contains general principles concerning the safety and health of workers at work and remains fully applicable to the areas covered by the Working Time Directive, without prejudice to more stringent and/or specific provisions in the later Directive. The Working Time Directive lays down minimum periods of daily and weekly rest, annual leave, and maximum weekly working time, as well as regulating certain aspects of night work, shift work and working patterns. The Directive applies to most workers and to all in the health sector. Yet, for many years there was a collective denial among many governments that the Working Time Directive would ever be applied to hospital staffing, perhaps because the consequences were so great. Only a very few countries, such as the Netherlands and the United Kingdom, made any substantive provision for its effects. The *SIMAP*[83] ruling shattered this complacency (see below). Only in 2000 were doctors in training explicitly included in its scope of application, when it was decided to implement it over five years from 1 August 2004. Requirements on rest periods came into force at once, but the length of the working week is being reduced progressively until it reaches forty-eight hours in August 2009. A generation ago, doctors worked extremely long hours, posing a threat to their own health and the health of their patients.[84] For example, surgeons who missed a

---

[79] Council Directive 93/104/EC concerning certain aspects of the organization of working time, OJ 1993 No. L307/18.

[80] European Parliament and Council Directive 2000/34/EC amending Directive 93/104/EC concerning certain aspects of the organisation of working time to cover sectors and activities excluded from that Directive, OJ 2000 No. L195/41.

[81] European Parliament and Council Directive 2003/88/EC concerning certain aspects of the organisation of working time, OJ 2003 No. L299/9.

[82] Council Directive 89/391/EEC on the introduction of measures to encourage improvements in the safety and health of workers at work, OJ 1989 No. L183/1.

[83] Case C-303/98, *SIMAP* [2000] ECR I-07963.

[84] M. McKee and N. Black, 'Does the current use of junior doctors in the United Kingdom affect the quality of medical care?', *Social Science and Medicine* 34 (1992), 549–58.

night's sleep made 20% more errors and took 14% longer to perform a simulated operation than those at the start of a shift. For many, therefore, the Working Time Directive was a welcome initiative.[85]

An immediate problem was how to deal with on-call responsibilities, with many differing views.[86] This has since been clarified in case-law by the European Court of Justice, which defined 'working time' and 'on-call service'. However, this was only the beginning of a lengthy discussion on how to implement the rulings, given the many practical difficulties involved (see Box 14.1).

It is now apparent that implementation of the Directive, as interpreted by the Court, will pose a threat to the survival of small hospitals serving dispersed populations.[87] To ensure twenty-four-hour, year-round coverage in a speciality, the rota must include up to ten doctors. This is far in excess of the number actually employed in some specialities, even in quite large hospitals. Furthermore, although the overall hours worked are less, the resulting shift patterns can be very disruptive of family life. Finally, reduced hours, coupled with a transfer of much care out of hospitals, greatly reduce opportunities for training.

A. The contents of the Directive

It is important to stress that Member States are free at any time to apply laws that go further than the Directive (Article 15) to protect the health and safety of workers. The minimum requirements include: a forty-eight-hour maximum working week, including overtime (Article 6); a minimum of eleven hours of continuous rest in every twenty-four-hour period (Article 3), a rest break after every six hours worked (Article 4); a minimum period of twenty four hours of continuous rest in each seven-day period (Article 5); and a minimum of four weeks' paid annual leave (Article 7). Night workers should not work longer than eight hours in any twenty-four-hour period where their work involves special hazards

---

[85] N. J. Douglas, 'Sleep, performance and the European Working Time Directive', *Clinical Medicine* 5 (2005), 95–6.

[86] R. Baeten and Y. Jorens, 'The impact of EU law and policy', in Dubois, McKee and Nolte (eds.), *Human resources*, above n.64, pp. 214–34.

[87] B. Rechel, C.-A. Dubois and M. McKee, *The health care workforce in Europe: learning from experience* (Copenhagen: WHO Regional Office for Europe on behalf of the European Observatory on Health Systems and Policies, 2006).

Box 14.1 Experience in implementing the European Working Time Directive in the United Kingdom

The implications of the Directive have been reported on most extensively from the United Kingdom. One study was undertaken in a stroke unit that had a senior doctor in training based on the ward each weekday to provide regular input at times when other members of the rehabilitation team were working. During weekdays in the three months following the implementation of the Directive, none of the most junior doctors in the training grades were present on 52% of the days, while on 42% of the days none of the more senior doctors in training were present. On 28% of days, no doctor in training attended the ward. Although it is especially important to ensure medical involvement in the assessment of such patients during normal working hours, the implementation of the Directive substantially reduced the opportunities to do so.[88]

Another study examined the provision of neonatal care in three hospitals providing obstetric services.[89] It concluded that, although some rationalization was possible by having only one hospital providing the most complex care, by requiring senior staff to work night shifts (although they questioned how sustainable this was in the long term), and by enhancing the roles of nonmedical staff, implementation of the Working Time Directive would ultimately require a major reconfiguration of services. However, this would require careful planning and coordination of hospital services at the regional level at a time when the English Department of Health was seeking to increase competition between facilities.[90]

---

or heavy physical or mental strain (Article 8). Night workers are entitled to a free health assessment, and should be transferred to day work, whenever possible, if they develop health problems related to night

---

[88] M. O. McCarron, M. Armstrong and P. McCarron, 'Effect of the European Working Time Directive on a stroke unit', *Quality and Safety in Health Care* 15 (2006), 445–6.

[89] C. Campbell and S. A. Spencer, 'The implications of the Working Time Directive: how can paediatrics survive?', *Archives of Disease in Child* 92 (2007), 573–5.

[90] C. Ham, *When politics and markets collide: reforming the English National Health Service* (Birmingham: Health Services Management Centre, 2007).

work (Article 9). More generally, night and shift workers should have dedicated health and safety protection, including access to protection and prevention services or facilities appropriate to the nature of their work (Article 12). Article 16 lays down reference periods during which these requirements should be fulfilled. For example, for the forty-eight-hour week, this is averaged over four months.

It was not until the *SIMAP*[91] and *Jaeger*[92] judgments in the European Court of Justice that 'working time', in relation to on-call duties, was defined in the health sector. The Directive defines 'working time' as the period a worker is working, at his/her employer's disposal and carrying out his/her activity or duties (Article 2(1)). Many employers had assumed that time spent awaiting emergency calls but not actually working was excluded from working time.

In the *SIMAP* case, the Court ruled that on-call duty by doctors counts as working time when they are present at the facility but when they are on call from home, it only counts when they are actually working. The *Jaeger* case between the German municipal authorities and Dr Jaeger was brought before the Court to clarify whether on-call duty hours in the emergency department were to be considered working time. The authorities argued that German law distinguishes between 'readiness for work', 'on-call service' and 'stand-by', stating that only 'readiness for work' constitutes actual work that is eligible for payment, while the others are considered resting time, as no professional tasks are performed. However, the Court ruled in favour of Dr Jaeger, stating that his on-call hours at Kiel municipal hospital were to be considered to be working time, regardless of whether he actually treated patients or rested. Thus, this ruling further clarified that being present in the hospital but not carrying out activities must be seen as 'working time', even when the doctor is resting. An example of how on-call work in Hungary relates to payment within the framework of the Working Time Directive is presented in Box 14.2.

B. Derogations and opt-outs

Derogations from the minimum requirements do, however, remain possible under the conditions of Article 17. They should be set out in

---

[91] *Ibid.*
[92] Case C-151/02, *Jaeger* [2003] ECR I-8389.

Box 14.2 Experience in implementing the European Working Time Directive in Hungary

Doctors in Hungary can undertake on-call work for eighteen consecutive hours or twenty-four hours in emergencies; however, differentiation is made between on-call work (e.g., surgeons), qualified on-call work (e.g., doctors working in drug clinics, anaesthesiology or neurotraumatics) and 'silent' on-call work, as stated in the Labour Code and Government Decree 233/2000 on the Application of the Public Employees Act to Health Care. Wages are calculated according to the amount of actual work involved, but, when this was not recorded, or there is no collective agreement, then only four to six hours of on-call duty is regarded as actual work. Therefore, it is quite common for doctors to begin their regular eight-hour shift after spending twenty-four hours on-call, and only receive payment for six hours of work during the on-call period.[93]

In April 2005, a Hungarian doctor decided to challenge these regulations though the Hungarian labour courts on the basis that they conflicted with the Working Time Directive. He argued that, according to the ECJ, if a doctor has to remain at his/her workplace when on call, then the total time has to be considered to be working time, regardless of whether he/she had undertaken any actual work. If the higher courts share the same opinion, then the health care system of Hungary will face a significant crisis. The Hungarian Chamber of Doctors estimated that around 25000 Hungarian doctors were in a similar situation, and may be able to recover the wages they have lost.[94] The state has tried to resolve the dispute without setting a legal precedent.

---

laws, regulations, administrative provisions or (collective) agreements and should provide compensatory rest ensuring at least the same degree of protection. Derogations from the rest requirements (in Articles 3, 4 and 5), the eight-hour night work schedule (Article 8), and the reference periods (Article 16) are explicitly allowed where (health) services must

---

[93] É. Magyar, 'Jogharmonizáció immáron, bentro'l'' szemlélve: a munkaidő szabályozásának lehetséges irányai I', *Munkaügyi Szemle* 5 (2004), 19–23.
[94] L. Dux, 'Working time of Hungarian doctors one year after 2004', *Transition Studies Review* 13 (2006), 23–5.

ensure continuity of care (Article 17(3)(c)(i)). As mentioned previously, for doctors in training there is a specific transitional period before full implementation of the 'forty-eight-hour week' requirement (Article 17(5)) in Directive 2000/34/EC, which takes 'the specific nature of activities of doctors in training into account' (Preamble, Point 7). Although intended to be implemented by 2009, a Member State can request the Commission to grant a further delay of three years, but must justify its case. In no case has a doctor in training been allowed to work more than fity-eight hours per week since August 2007, fifty-six hours since September 2007, and will be prevented from working more than fifty-two hours from September 2009.

There is, however, a potential escape clause for governments, as Member States can decide to allow individual workers to opt out of the forty-eight-hour limit (Article 22). However, as confirmed in the case of *Pfeiffer*,[95] consent should be given expressly and freely by the individual and referral to a collective agreement is not sufficient. Some have done so, specifically to alleviate some of the problems created by the *SIMAP* case. Cyprus, France, Germany, Malta, the Netherlands, Slovenia and Spain have done so, but only for health workers, while the United Kingdom has enabled all workers to do so.

C. Moving forward

There are some measures that can ameliorate the problems outlined above. There is substantial scope to transfer responsibility for many conventionally medical roles to other health care professionals. Of course, this must be accompanied by corresponding improvements in the status and pay of those taking on these extended roles.[96] There is also much scope for cross-cover of activites, for example, by different sub-specialties within surgery. However, in many cases, the only feasible solution is the merger of small hospitals, potentially creating problems with access to services.[97] There is also considerable scope

---

[95] *Ibid.*
[96] McKee, Dubois and Sibbald, 'Changing professional boundaries', above n.64, pp. 63–78.
[97] M. McKee, *Reducing hospital beds. What are the lessons to be learned?* (Copenhagen: WHO Regional Office for Europe on behalf of the European Observatory on Health Systems and Policies, 2004).

for greater efficiency in training, in particular making much greater use of actors performing the roles of patients and using simulators, but this has enormous financial consequences for medical schools.

Notwithstanding the scope for such changes, there remains a broad consensus that the existing legislation poses serious problems, largely because the Court has interpreted 'working time' in a way that is different to that envisaged by some of those who enacted the original Directive. Consequently, the European Commission launched a public consultation on the Directive in early 2004. In September 2004, it proposed updating key aspects of the Directive, suggesting that the inactive time spent on call would not be considered to be working time, while compensatory rest should be provided after seventy-two hours. An individual opt-out would remain possible but subject to stricter conditions. However, the European Parliament fundamentally amended this Commission proposal in May 2005 on its first reading, stating that waiting time should be considered entirely as working time.[98] The European Commission then presented a new proposal in an attempt to reach a compromise.[99] It has, however, proven extremely difficult to achieve an agreement within the Council, with a meeting of employment ministers during the 2006 Finnish Presidency concluding that, at that time, there was no prospect of reaching a consensus.[100] A sticking point has been the insistence, by Cyprus, France, Greece, Italy and Spain, that the opt-out should be phased out over time, while others, such as the United Kingdom, want it to remain indefinitely. It is also clear that there is no enthusiasm for treating health care as a special case.

In the second half of 2007, the Portuguese Presidency proposed that: (a) the opt-out would be seen as an *exception to the general rule* of a forty-eight-hour working week in the EU; (b) implementation of the opt-out must be laid down by collective agreement, agreement between the social partners or by national law; and (c) a

---

[98] European Parliament Legislative Resolution on the proposal for a Directive of the European Parliament and Council amending Directive 2003/88/ EC concerning certain aspects of working time (COM (2004) 0607 – C6–0122/2004 – 2004/0209 (COD)), P6_TA-PROV(2005)0175, 11 May 2005.

[99] European Commission, 'Amended proposal for a European Parliament and Council Directive amending Directive 2003/88/EC concerning certain aspects of the organisation of working time', COM (2005) 246 final, 31 May 2005.

[100] R. Watson, 'European Working Time Directive: battles in time', *British Medical Journal* 334 (2007), 770–1.

weekly limit of working hours would be set for workers who agree to the opt-out, among other stipulations.[101] Agreement on the Working Time Directive and similar measures applying to temporary agency work[102] was postponed in December 2007, after the British prime minister threatened to boycott the Treaty signing ceremony in Lisbon. He argued that giving enhanced rights to temporary workers would damage the flexible employment market in the United Kingdom[103] and linked the issue to the EU Treaty. Nevertheless, a majority of Member States are in favour of action to help agency workers.[104] In the meantime, there have been complaints, upheld by the European Ombudsman, that the Commission is not dealing with infringement complaints on the Working Time Directive in a timely manner.[105] In June 2008, the Council finally reached a political agreement on the Commission proposal. This agreement considered active on-call time at the workplace to be working time, in contrast with inactive on-call time, which does not have to be regarded as working time unless national law so provides.[106] This position was endorsed by the European Commission[107] but rejected again by the European

[101] 2837th Council Meeting on Employment, Social Policy, Health and Consumer Affairs, Doc. No. 16139/07 (Press 284), Luxembourg, 5–6 December 2007.

[102] The Council sought to reach political agreement on two draft directives: amending Directive 2003/88/EC and establishing working conditions for temporary agency workers. Due to difficulties in finding separate solutions for these drafts, the Portuguese Presidency decided that there would be added value in working on a simultaneous and integrated solution.

[103] The United Kingdom Government was concerned that if agency workers were treated equally to permanent workers, flexible employment would become less useful.

[104] European Citizen Action Service, 'EU ministers bow to Brown over working time, temp work', *EurActiv*, 7 December 2007, www.euractiv.com.

[105] European Citizen Action Service, 'Ombudsman urges Commission: "get going on working time"', *EurActiv*, 19 September 2007, www.euractiv.com.

[106] Common Position (EC) No. 23/2008 of 15 September 2008 adopted by the Council, acting in accordance with the procedure referred to in Article 251 of the Treaty establishing the European Community, with a view to the adoption of a Directive of the European Parliament and of the Council amending Directive 2003/88/EC concerning certain aspects of the organisation of working time, OJ 2008 No. C254/26.

[107] Communication from the Commission to the European Parliament pursuant to the second subparagraph of Article 251(2) of the EC Treaty concerning

Parliament at its second reading.[108] The Parliament reconfirmed its view that non-active on-call time should also be considered as waiting time. By April 2009, the Parliament and Council had failed to find a compromise during the conciliation process, including the issue of on-call time, concluding a five-year effort to agree a revision of the Directive. This is the first time that no agreement could be found through the conciliation process since the Amsterdam Treaty, which significantly extended the scope of the co-decision procedure. The Commission is left with three options: do nothing; start infringement procedures against the Member States that are facing problems complying with the European Court of Justice judgements on on-call time calculations; or come up with a new proposal to revise the Directive.

4. Conclusion

Mutual recognition of diplomas and the coordination of rules regarding the pursuit of a profession enabled the large-scale cross-border movement of health professionals within the European Union. Yet, as was realized as long ago as the fourteenth century when the Venetian Republic introduced quarantine to counteract the hazards of free trade, free movement can conflict with public health. Here, the concern relates to patient safety. Once again, the search for a coherent legal framework involves the quest for balance between the internal market and public health.

The legal framework provided by Directive 2005/36/EC contains shortcomings and fails to resolve legal uncertainty. Examples reviewed in this chapter include the lack of coordination of disciplinary measures, of continuing professional development systems and of potential problems concerning cross-border payment or reimbursement of costs

the Common Position of the Council on the adoption of a proposed Directive of the European Parliament and of the Council amending Directive 2003/88/EC concerning certain aspects of the organisation of working time, COM/2008/0568 final – COD 2004/0209.

[108] European Parliament Legislative Resolution of 17 December 2008 on the Council Common Position for adopting a Directive of the European Parliament and of the Council amending Directive 2003/88/ EC concerning certain aspects of the organisation of working time (10597/2/2008 – C6–0324/2008 – 2004/0209(COD)).

by social security bodies. The lack of a clear definition of 'services' in relation to 'establishment', the exclusion of telemedicine from its scope of application, and the system of acquired rights exemplify the missed opportunities. A more active harmonization of training requirements and the conditions under which individuals pursue health professions seems to be needed. The principle of free movement will only be accepted by European citizens when they can overcome mistrust of the quality of training provided in some other Member States and when the remaining legal issues discussed above are resolved. Yet the challenges involved are profound. Within the EU, there are very different views about the acceptable relationship between the state and the health professional. Those countries with strong traditions of liberal professions would find it quite unacceptable to have the very high level of state control seen in, for example, the United Kingdom, where the activities undertaken by family doctors are set out in an extremely detailed payment schedule. Similarly, there are great differences in how countries view misdemeanours by health professionals that are unrelated to their professional work. Thus, a British doctor recently appeared before the General Medical Council (the professional regulator) accused (but subsequently acquitted) of disorderly behaviour at a football match when off duty. In particular, an especially intrusive role for the state may raise concerns in those new Member States where, within living memory, there were many examples of victimization of health professionals on political grounds. It seems especially unlikely that Member States with such diverse cultures would be able to achieve any meaningful agreement at a European level, much less give the European institutions the power to enforce some pan-European model.

Turning to the Working Time Directive, this is clearly a law that was enacted for the best possible reasons, seeking to abolish into history the horrendous working schedules that existed a generation ago. However, the specific characteristics of the health care sector have made it extremely difficult, in practice, to create provisions that would be appropriate in that sector. The health care sector stands out as being extremely labour intensive, yet demands continuity of care. To achieve this, it traditionally made maximum use of its personnel – especially doctors in training – who were, albeit often reluctantly, willing to work such long hours to optimize exposure to experience and in the knowledge that it would only last a few years. The challenges faced by governments, professionals and other health care providers are formidable. The process of adaptation will be long and difficult but, in the long run, these changes are needed. The Working Time Directive provides a much needed incentive to make the best possible use of scarce human resources.

As is apparent from many chapters in this book, European Community law does not always take account of the specific characteristics of health care. Health systems in Europe differ greatly and are continually changing. This makes it difficult to ensure that relevant EU legislation takes account of the implications for health care. The challenge is to find compromises between the need to promote effective, equitable and efficient health care, while adhering to the underlying principles of EU law.

15 | The EU pharmaceuticals market: parameters and pathways

LEIGH HANCHER

1. Introduction

The European Union pursues two major objectives in its policy on pharmaceutical products: its policies strive to secure a high level of public health and innovation and, at the same time, provide support for a competitive industry that ensures that Europe continues to benefit from new medicines.

The first objective requires that access to medicines and treatments is affordable and that medicines are safe and effective, but also, increasingly, that patients should receive the information necessary to make informed choices about their own treatment. The second objective requires enhancing the competitiveness of Europe's pharmaceutical sector. The competence to intervene in the market, and the related tools with which the EU institutions pursue – or, rather, attempt to reconcile – these two objectives are by no means similar in legal scope or nature. Although the European Union has now created a centralized licensing agency, the European Medicines Agency (EMEA), and also enjoys extensive legislative powers to determine what might be termed the 'regulatory pathway' for authorizing the marketing of new products in accordance with strict criteria on safety, quality and efficacy, it has less direct influence on what can be termed the commercial or 'market pathway' – the prices and conditions under which products are purchased by national heath care providers and insurance companies, and, indeed, patients. The role of the Member States in defining the ways they provide access to medicines, the price of those medicines and how patients and consumers gain access to information on pharmaceutical products is still crucial in determining overall policy, even though a certain amount of secondary legislation adopted at the European level is of increasing importance in shaping the market pathway.

With respect to the second objective – ensuring the broader competitiveness of the industry – the picture has always been complex, given the very processes of competition in the pharmaceutical market and the Union's overriding goal – and, indeed, constitutional duty – to create an integrated European market. On the one hand, the extensive level of harmonization and, indeed, centralization of the rules governing product licensing or marketing authorization allows the European-based industry to register and market their products across all twenty-seven Member States of the European Union. On the other hand, national rules and regulations on price and profit controls and marketing more generally can have a major impact on the competitiveness of the industry.

The persistence of national regulation that hold down prices and profits, and results in market fragmentation, is often claimed to be a major factor in explaining the alleged difference in the strengths of the European-based research industry as compared to its American counterparts. The European Federation of the Pharmaceutical Industries and Associations (EFPIA) claims that, between 1990 and 2005, research and development (R&D) investment in the United States grew 4.6 times, while in Europe it grew by only 2.8 times, and that the United States still dominates the biopharmaceutical field, accounting for three quarters of the world's biotechnology revenues and R&D spending.[1] According to Intercontinental Marketing Services (IMS) data, 66% of sales of new medicines marketed since 2001 are generated from the United States market, compared with 24% from the European market.[2] And according to the European Commission, if Europe was once known as the 'world's pharmacy' (where, until 1998, seven out of ten new medicines originated in Europe), today this has fallen to about three out of ten.[3] Europe's industry, rightly or wrongly, is hence perceived by the sector, as well as policy-makers at the European level, to be facing serious challenges, matched only by those facing public health, challenges driven by demographic change

[1] See EFPIA, 'The Pharmaceutical Industry in Figures 2007', www.efpia. org. See also G. Verheugen, Commissioner for Enterprise and Industry, 'Delivering better information, better access and better prices', Speech to the Pharmaceutical Forum, SPEECH/06/547, Brussels, 29 September 2006, www. europa.eu.

[2] IMS Health data is available on www.imshealth.com.

[3] See the European Commission, 'Public-Private Research Initiative to boost the competitiveness of Europe's pharmaceutical industry', Press Release No. IP/08/662, 30 April 2008.

and the high cost of innovative treatments. Europe, it is alleged, is losing competitive ground not only to the United States, but also to China, India and Singapore.

Yet the most persistent issue in European policy towards the sector is how to deal with market fragmentation.[4] Traditionally, the Commission, parallel traders and generic competitors have relied upon the twin principles of free movement and undistorted competition to 'correct' obstacles to trade and competition that result from divergent national price and profit control legislation. This type of intervention is largely ad hoc and ex post, however, and has not succeeded in addressing the research-based industry's concerns that the returns it needs to generate new products can be guaranteed. On the contrary, the continued presence of parallel imports and the Commission's continued, if passive, support of it, is a persistent thorn in the industry's flesh. At the same time, national governments are reluctant to surrender sovereignty on pricing and profit controls and, by implication, an important part of their national health budgets to the European institutions. Hence, further attempts to harmonize price control legislation at the European level have been more or less abandoned following the adoption of the framework Price Transparency Directive in 1989.[5] Instead, coordination and consensus-building has taken place through various stakeholders' forums, commencing with the so-called 'Bangemann' rounds in the 1990s,[6] and the G10 Medicines Group in 2002. The latter reached agreement on fourteen recommendations, and expressed its wish to continue its work further. In response, in 2005, the Commission set up the High Level Pharmaceutical Forum, which is discussed below. This type of informal consensus-building

---

[4] See also A. Gambardella, L. Orsenigo and F. Pammolli, 'Global competitiveness in pharmaceuticals – a European perspective', Report prepared for DG Industry, November 2000, http://ec.europa.eu/enterprise/library/enterprise-papers/pdf/enterprise_paper_01_2001.pdf.

[5] Council Directive 89/105/EEC of 21 December 1988 relating to the transparency of measures regulating the prices of medicinal products for human use and their inclusion in the scope of national health insurance systems, OJ 1989 No. L40/8.

[6] For an appraisal of the Bangemann rounds and the G10 process, see L. Hancher, 'The pharmaceuticals market: competition and free movement actively seeking compromises', in M. McKee, E. Mossialos and R. Baeten (eds.), *The impact of EU law on health care systems* (Brussels: PIE-Peter Lang, 2002), pp. 235–75.

has become the preferred policy approach in an attempt to find a politically acceptable balance between the competing interests of the Member States and those of the European Union's institutions, as well as the competing objectives of public health demands and those of the research-based industry.

The simultaneous pursuit of these various objectives at the EU level has always called for a delicate balancing exercise between competing interests. If anything, this balancing exercise has become more complex in the enlarged EU of twenty-seven Member States, given the considerable differences in health care budgets across the EU, as well as the increased mobility of the sector itself, which can source not only production but also research in more conducive climates, such as China, India and Singapore. But there are other factors that complicate the picture further, and not least the changing impact of European and national competition law and policy on the sector, and the resulting possibilities and constraints that this implies for the Commission, the Member States, payers and industry alike. Important developments in the case-law of the European courts and the national competition authorities and courts may indicate that many of the traditional assumptions about the role and impact of competition policy towards the pharmaceutical sector may need to be re-assessed. But the tools to ensure affordable access to safe and effective medicines by increasingly proactive patients who are better informed on medicines and health treatment choices must also evolve to meet new demands, especially as national budget constraints dictate the need for effective pricing and reimbursement policies – policies that increasingly require a demonstration of the relative effectiveness and efficacy of new products before they can be eligible for reimbursement. The dynamics of these processes may thrust the European institutions (and, in particular, the Commission) into new roles – roles that go beyond merely creating an internal market in which products can move freely from one market to another and patients can access products from different sources, but that leave the Member States' responsibility for managing health care budgets broadly intact. As a result, the extent to which individual Member States traditionally have also been able to strike a balance between the two objectives of promoting innovation while securing affordability through price and profit regulation may have to be re-assessed.

This chapter examines these dynamics, in light of the changes to the competition policy 'tool kit', which has been an important feature of the European pharmaceutical market for several decades, and draws some tentative conclusions on the potentially changing role of the European Union in the pharmaceutical sector. In particular, it will highlight a shift in preferences for certain of the traditional tools at the disposal of the European institutions to promote the creation of a single pharmaceuticals market. Whereas, in the past, the Commission, supported by the jurisprudence of the European courts, relied primarily on the rules on free movement of goods to condone if not actively stimulate parallel importation of pharmaceutical products into higher priced markets, recent policy and legal developments suggest that the EC competition rules may also function as effective 'tools' to pursue this goal. Against this background, this chapter will argue that the 'regulatory' and 'market' pathways are intersecting in new and challenging ways for the major stakeholders in the European Union – that is, the Member States, the different parts of the pharmaceutical industry, including the research-based industry, the generic manufacturers as well as parallel importers, wholesalers and, last but not least, health care providers and health insurance bodies, and patients. The intersection of these regulatory and market pathways may have important consequences for the way in which major policy issues confronting these various stakeholders could develop. These include the role of generics versus research-based products, pricing issues, including the emergence of value-based pricing, as well as other areas of pharmaceutical regulation, including its extension to cover clinical trials, orphan and paediatric medicines, and, further, direct marketing of prescription-based products to patients, all of which will determine the continued attractiveness of the European market for innovative medicines, as well as access and affordability for patients. As this chapter will seek to explain and illustrate, both regulation and European competition law can shape how these two pathways intersect; as such, they can impose both constraints on and, at the same time, offer opportunities for the different stakeholders involved.

The second section of this chapter will briefly outline the parameters of competition in the industry and explain the three types of competition that typify it. It will then go on to examine recent regulatory developments and their impact on these processes of competition, as well as new developments in the application of ex post competition controls in the regulatory pathway to promote generic competition.

The next sections examine potential challenges to the Commission's traditional policy on parallel imports and how this may affect the market pathway in the future. The final section reviews the current endeavours of the recently created Pharmaceutical Forum to deliver new methods to reconcile the objectives of securing affordable access to pharmaceutical products while promoting competitiveness, and considers the scope for soft-law solutions at the intersection of the regulatory and market pathways. The chapter ends with some tentative conclusions.

2. The parameters for competition in the European pharmaceutical market

The European pharmaceutical market is characterized by three types of competition.

A. *Therapeutic competition*

Competition between new, patented, innovative products is often referred to as therapeutic competition: research-based pharmaceutical companies compete to develop therapies that are superior to existing or future drugs developed by their competitors and then try to persuade the relevant national 'payers' to pay for or reimburse a significant part of the price for these products. Market exclusivity may be protected not only by patents and other generally applicable intellectual property rights, but also by specific regulation pertaining to marketing authorization procedures. Regulatory data protection provisions in Community legislation ensure that regulatory authorities cannot use clinical and other data submitted by the original developer of a product to subsequently assess applications from competitors for marketing authorizations for generic versions of the product for a certain period of time.

This type of competition also enjoys a relatively benign environment in the sense that European competition law generally encourages joint research and development, licensing, co-marketing and co-distribution arrangements as long as the advantages of cooperation outweigh any negative impact on competition. The fact that many government payers hold significant (or even monopsonistic) purchasing power may also shield dominant companies from allegations of abusive conduct.

B. Generic competition

The second type of competition comes from generic products. As will be discussed below, this type of competition is increasingly encouraged at the European and national levels, although the research-based industry is also protected from generic competition by a number of legal and regulatory instruments that aim to encourage R&D by granting innovative products a de facto market exclusivity in the 'regulatory pathway', at least for a specified period of time.

The advent of a generic (or non-patented) version of a leading product on the market once both patent and regulatory data protection periods have expired can have a substantial impact on prices – leading to price falls of up to 80%. A report from the British Office of Fair Trading (OFT) on the United Kingdom's price and profit regulation scheme (PPRS) published in mid-2007 found that almost 83% of prescription items in the United Kingdom are now written generically compared to just 51% in 1994.[7] The European Generics Medicines Association (EGA) claims that demand for generic medicines has grown in the last two decades to account for nearly 50% of medicines consumed in the twenty-seven EU Member States today.[8] As such, the research-based industry has made repeated attempts to prevent or delay registration and marketing of generic copies of their leading products. As a result of recent amendments to the European product licensing regime, however, this strategy is increasingly unattractive and companies are resorting to other tactics. As we will discuss in greater detail below, the application of Article 82 EC (which prohibits the abuse of a dominant position) is now becoming of greater importance in determining the legality of certain industry tactics to delay or deter generic competition.

Generic competition is also referred to as inter-brand competition, and this term covers competition from generic and, increasingly, so-called 'bio-similar' products. The High Level Group on Innovation and the Provision of Medicines (also referred to as the G10 Medicines Group), established by the European Commission in 2001 in order to provide a consultative forum on moving European pharmaceutical policy forward,[9] had called upon EU Member States to secure the development of a competitive generic market in the European Union

[7] www.oft.gov.uk/shared_oft/reports/comp_policy/oft885.pdf.
[8] See www.egagenerics.com/doc/ega_factsheet-01.pdf.
[9] See also Chapter 4 in this volume.

(Recommendation 4).[10] In its Communication of 1 July 2003, the Commission had stated that 'generic medicines can provide signifi- cant savings to health care providers, however, their use must be bal- anced with sufficient incentives to develop innovative products'.[11] The successor to the G10 Medicines Group, the Pharmaceutical Forum (discussed below), endorsed the importance of this Recommendation in its Progress Report on 29 September 2006.

C. *Intra-brand competition*

The final type of competition takes the form of intra-brand competi- tion – usually, in the form of parallel imports of cheaper products from low-priced Member States into higher-priced markets. As a result of enlargement in 2004 and again in 2007, the extent of price differentials across the European Union has widened substantially. The European Commission, relying on the past jurisprudence of the European courts on the application of the EC Treaty rules on free movement and compe- tition, has generally taken a positive standpoint on parallel imports as a way of cementing the internal market in pharmaceuticals. Certain of the recommendations adopted by the G10 Group in May 2002 hinted that this generally benign approach might have to be reconsidered, at least in so far as there was legal scope to do so. Nevertheless, in its sub- sequent Communication on parallel imports in 2003,[12] the Commission seemed to maintain its traditional pro-parallel trade line.[13]

D. *Consequences*

The impact of these different processes of competition on the two objectives of European Union policy on the pharmaceutical sector is complex and controversial. The gradual creation of a centralized

[10] For an examination of the processes leading to the work of the G10 and a discussion of these recommendations, see Hancher, 'The pharmaceuticals market', above n.6.
[11] European Commission, 'A stronger European-based pharmaceutical industry for the benefit of the patient – a call for action', COM (2003) 383 final, 1 July 2003, p. 16.
[12] European Commission, 'Communication on parallel import of proprietary medicinal products for which marketing authorisations have already been granted', COM (2003) 839 final, 30 December 2003.
[13] *Ibid.*, p. 6.

regime for granting marketing authorizations, culminating in the establishment of the EMEA in 1993, has been primarily fashioned with a view to facilitating simultaneous market access across the entire European union for new, innovative products – and, as such, to stimulate therapeutic competition. At the same time, however, this process of centralization also offers generic products the promise of wider market access, and can stimulate inter-brand competition once patents and other intellectual property rights expire. Generics can stimulate innovation through competition and also by creating significant 'financial headroom' for innovation, in the sense that national health care budgets can direct the savings from the use of competitive generic equivalents to finance reimbursement of new, truly innovative products. In addition, a number of generic companies have produced their own new chemical entities (NCEs) (for example, Aztromycin, Glatiramer Acetate, Deferiprone and Vinpocetine).

At the same time, it must be stressed that national marketing authorization procedures have not been entirely displaced by the ongoing process of centralization and harmonization: national regulations still play an important role in the European pharmaceutical market. Hence, a product originally licensed in Greece, for example, cannot be automatically exported to a higher-priced market such as the Netherlands and marketed there; national authorization is still required, albeit subject to the requirement that the Dutch authorities recognize the procedures followed by their Greek counterparts. In other words, significant regulatory barriers to free movement and competition across the entire European Union still remain. Regulation marks the boundary lines between the three processes of competition identified above. It follows that any attempts to modify regulation and to harmonize national rules will have a profound impact on these very processes of competition and the interests of the different stakeholders who benefit in very different ways from them. Constructing and refining the European 'regulatory' pathway therefore always involves a delicate balancing of competing interests. This process can be characterized as an ongoing but complex and controversial attempt at the European level to strike a balance between the competing objectives of maintaining a favourable economic environment for innovative products while securing affordable access for patients to medicines in general.

Recent developments in European and national competition law (which are now largely based on the same principles as a result of the adoption of the so-called 'Modernization' Regulation 1/2003/EC)[14] have only contributed to that complexity and controversy. We will consider these developments in further detail below, but the evolution of the European regulatory framework for product licensing or marketing authorization will be examined in greater detail in the next section, with a view to examining the way in which it has sought to strike a balance between competing interests and provide counter-balancing mechanisms in what may be termed the 'regulatory pathways'.

3. Recent developments in the 'regulatory' pathway

It is not the intention here to examine the complex and detailed body of secondary legislation – that is, the various European directives and regulations for the approval of new products or for their generic equivalents. This body of legislation has evolved piecemeal since the adoption of the first Directive 65/65/EEC into what are known as the centralized and decentralized licensing regimes.[15] It covers not only the process of product approval, but also many aspects of the subsequent marketing of pharmaceutical products, including labelling, packaging and distribution. Policy in the regulatory pathway falls primarily within the remit of the European Commission's Directorate-General for Enterprise and Industry (DG Industry), and its central task has been to further the realization of the single market for pharmaceutical products, with the Directorate-General for Competition (DG Competition) playing an increasingly proactive role in this respect, as is discussed below. The following subsections will examine certain topical issues in the regulatory pathway with a view to highlighting their impact on the potential for stimulating therapeutic, inter-brand and intra-brand competition.

A. *The centralized and decentralized licensing regime*

In order to market a pharmaceutical product within the EU, a brand name drug manufacturer must obtain a marketing authorization covering the Member States in which the drug will be marketed. This body of law has primarily evolved with the aim of creating, through

---

[14] Council Regulation 1/2003/EC on the implementation of the rules on competition laid down in Articles 81 and 82 of the Treaty, OJ 2003 No. L1/1.

[15] For an analysis of the evolution of the European licensing regime from 1965 through to 1988, see L. Hancher, *Regulating for competition: government, law and the pharmaceutical industry in the United Kingdom and France* (Oxford: Clarendon Press, 1990).

harmonization, a single European market for newly patented and innovative products, which must be subjected to extensive testing and screening before they can be put on the market. Since the adoption of the first EEC Directive in 1965, in the wake of the thalidomide crisis, a Community-wide system of market authorization based on common principles for prior testing and screening of new medicinal products and a complex technical body of regulation has evolved, culminating in 1995 in the creation of the European Medicines Agency – the centralized European agency responsible for licensing new products, as well as issuing guidelines on various stages in the development and eventual administration of medicinal products. As this subsection will briefly explain, national governments have not been prepared to allow full centralization or total harmonization of each and every aspect of pre- and post-marketing regulation at the Community level, and have retained important powers both in the regulatory and, most particularly, in the market pathways.

Following an extensive review of the operation of the EMEA in 2000, the existing body of regulations was further streamlined. The EMEA remains primarily linked to the Commission through the Directorate-General for Enterprise and Industry (DG Industry) (responsible for the internal pharmaceutical market) and not the Directorate-General for Health and Consumer Protection (DG SANCO) (responsible for health and consumer protection policy). There are currently two methods for obtaining a marketing authorization: (a) either through a centralized application to the EMEA for a marketing authorization covering the entire territory of the EU; or (b) through a decentralized application for an authorization covering only an individual Member State, which can be recognized by other Member States under the mutual recognition procedure (MRP). This general scheme is governed now by Regulation 726/2004/EC[16] (replacing Regulation 2309/93/EC, which laid down the centralized procedure and established the EMEA) and Directive 2001/83/EC on the community code relating to medicinal products for human use (as amended by, *inter alia*, Directive 27/2004/EC),[17] which

---

[16] European Parliament and Council Regulation 726/2004/EC laying down Community procedures for the authorisation and supervision of medicinal products for human and veterinary use and establishing a European Medicines Agency, OJ 2004 No. L136/1.

[17] European Parliament and Council Directive 2004/27/EC amending Directive 2001/83/EC on the Community code relating to medicinal products for human use, OJ 2004 No. L136/34.

sets out the general rules applicable to medicinal products, including
the procedures for marketing authorization and mutual recognition.
Regulation 726/2004/EC has again been recently amended in January
2007 to extend the centralized procedure to paediatric medicines.[18]

Under the centralized procedure, a drug manufacturer must submit
to the EMEA for consideration a detailed dossier containing quality,
safety and efficacy information about the drug.[19] This application is
considered by the Committee for Medicinal Products for Human Use,
and, if granted by a Commission Decision, the marketing authorization will be valid in all Member States. Use of the centralized procedure is mandatory for biotechnology medicines, products containing
NCEs, for the treatment of certain disorders and diseases, and is
optional for other NCEs and sufficiently innovative products. Under
the MRP, the application for a national marketing authorization is
made to a single Member State (known as the reference Member State
(RMS)) and, if granted by this RMS, then the MRP, which is codified
in EU legislation, provides that other Member States must approve
the marketing authorization. In practice, the RMS coordinates the
MRP and prepares an assessment report on the medicinal product,
which is sent (along with the approved information leaflets and packaging) to the other Member States selected by the applicant. Unless a
Member State raises an objection on the grounds of potential serious
risk to public health, the drug is given marketing approval in all the
EU Member States selected by the applicant.

B. *Patent protection and the supplementary patent certificate regime*

In the EU, patents generally last for a maximum of twenty years starting from the date the patent application was filed. During that time,
the patent holder has an exclusive right to prevent third parties from
making, using, selling, importing or stocking the patented product (or
method of production) that falls within the claims of the patent. Once
a patent for a drug has been filed, preclinical and clinical testing will

---

[18] European Parliament and Council Regulation 1901/2006/EC on medicinal
products for paediatric use and amending Regulation 1768/92/EEC,
Directive 2001/20/EC, Directive 2001/83/EC and Regulation 726/2004/EC,
OJ 2006 No. L378/1.
[19] See also Chapter 3 in this volume.

commence with a view to marketing authorization. However, given that, as a result of the adoption of increasingly stricter premarketing regulation, obtaining the necessary authorization is a lengthy process that can last between six to twelve years, and so the product is patent-protected for considerably less than twenty years after first marketing. In other words, 'effective patent protection' is much shorter than twenty years.

To meet the concerns of the research-based industry, which argued that, due to the adoption of stricter premarketing regulation, it was not being given sufficient opportunity to reap the benefits of its R&D and investment, the EU introduced the Supplementary Patent Certificate (SPaC) regime in 1992.[20] An SPaC is granted if, at the date of application, the innovative drug is protected by a basic patent in force, a valid marketing authorization is in place and the product has not already been subject to such a certificate. The application must be filed in each country where protection is sought, within six months of the grant of the first marketing authorization. An SPaC extends the period of the patent protection for up to five years, or fifteen years from the first marketing authorization in the EU, whichever is less. It extends the protection conferred by the patent and, hence, it covers the same rights (and limitations) as the patent itself. The issue of whether the SPaC only protects the product in question in the specific form stated in the marketing authorization or whether it protects the active substance in the specific, authorized form and all other forms protected by the basic patent arose in the case of *Farmitalia Carlo Erba*. The Court affirmed that protection extends to the active ingredients, so that a third party cannot obtain market authorization for the same active substance merely by using a different form of it.[21]

Clinical trials and pharmacovigilance – limited harmonization so far

Not all the stages of the development and subsequent testing of a new therapy are subject to centralization, however. Certain crucial stages of the process are only subject to partial harmonization. The regulation of clinical trials remains primarily a national matter, albeit

---

[20] Council Regulation 1768/92/EEC concerning the creation of a supplementary protection certificate for medicinal products, OJ 1992 No. L182/1.
[21] Case C-392/97, *Farmitalia Carlo Erba* [1999] ECR I-5553.

that the procedures for conducting trials are harmonized on the basis
of Council Directive 2001/20/EC, the terms of which are currently
under review. This Directive has been the subject of heated debate and
criticism and is generally considered to have failed to achieve its stated
goals. Monitoring the potential adverse effects of products already on
the market – pharmacovigilance – is also primarily a national activity and relies on spontaneous reports from patients and doctors. On
the one hand, the current regulations are considered by the industry
to be fragmented, contradictory and unclear and are thus in urgent
need of consolidation and rationalization. On the other hand, patient
organizations and some national regulators claim that the current
system is not sufficiently transparent or sufficiently independent from
the interests of the industry.[22] The Commission launched a consultation process in April 2006 in order to obtain a variety of views on
the current functioning of the EU pharmacovigilance system, followed by a consultation based on draft proposals for changes to the
current legislation. The results of this second consultation exercise
have been analysed in a document published on DG Industry's web
site in April 2008, and are expected to lead to the adoption of more
detailed proposals for further amendments to Directive 2001/83/EC,
including a strengthened role for the EMEA and a better institutionalized embedding of the advisory Pharmacovigilance Committee into
the current European and national systems. In particular, the EMEA
could be given explicit tasks to strengthen transparency and communication and make public more information on the benefits and risks
of medicines.[23]

Remaining gaps

At the same time, there are still crucial issues that are not subject to
harmonization at all. Although, since 1992, the relevant European
legislation has banned advertisement to the public of medicines subject to prescription and has only allowed advertising for other medicines under certain conditions, information provided to patients is not
harmonized at all. Although the Commission has launched various
initiatives on this ongoing public debate, and it has now focused on the

[22] See also G. Permanand, E. Mossialos and M. McKee, 'Regulating medicines
in Europe: the EMEA, marketing authorisations, transparency and
pharmcovigilance', *Clinical Medicine* 6 (2006), 87–90.
[23] Available at http://ec.europa.eu/enterprise/phabiocom/comp_new.htm.

need to address the lack of a Community framework on information to patients, the legal situation has not changed. As we will explain below, however, the attempts now being made to address this lacuna provide a poignant illustration of the policy pitfalls that can arise when the 'regulatory' pathway threatens to extends into highly sensitive – and primarily national – areas.

4. Generic competition in the regulatory pathway

This section will first focus on a number of recent developments that are illustrative of the European Union's (and particularly the Commission's) ongoing attempts to strike a balance between the competing objectives of maintaining a favourable economic environment for innovative products while securing affordable access for patients to medicines in general. Recent changes at the European level have facilitated the licensing of generic products and, to a certain extent, 'bio-similar' medicines.

At first sight, the amended EU legislation (that is, Directive 2004/27/EC[24] and Regulation 726/2004/EC,[25] which entered into force in late 2005) has exerted a major impact on the regulatory pathway for generic medicines, since it:

- permits generic R&D before patent expiry (the so-called 'Bolar' scheme);
- allows marketing of generics even where the original product has been withdrawn from the market for commercial reasons;
- provides a more efficient system for the registration of generic medicines (through the decentralized or mutual recognition procedures);
- ensures greater harmony between newly-approved generic medicines and older-approved originator products; and
- provides clear scientific and legal definitions of generic and bio-similar medicines – definitions that were not contained in earlier EU legislation.

The amended regime is again a useful illustration of the EU's continuing attempt to strike a balance between the competing interests

---

[24] Directive 2004/27/EC, above n.17.
[25] Regulation 726/2004/EC, above n.16.

of the R&D-based sector and those of the public and private health care institutions that benefit from greater generic competition. Nevertheless, it is claimed that, despite these improvements, there is much to be done, as the EU generic industry operates in a highly complex regulatory environment in Europe – an environment that creates barriers to market entry that do not exist in other parts of the world, such as the United States. In particular, the new legislation has increased the overall period of time that generic manufacturers must wait before registering their products. Certain Member States do not allow generic licensing applications until the original patent expires, while others create limitations on receiving applications for market authorization or for pricing status while the original patent remains in place.

A. Data exclusivity

Directive 2004/27/EC, which had to be implemented at the national level by 30 October 2005, introduced a number of important amendments to the provisions governing data exclusivity in Directive 2001/83/EC.[26] As this 2004 Directive did not replace the earlier 2001 Directive, the latter measure remains in force, as amended.

Data exclusivity has proved complex in the context of the so-called 'abridged application' procedure for marketing a generic drug. In principle, the regulatory authorities can only process a generic application after a certain number of years following the granting of the first marketing authorization of the originator or innovative medicine. The principle of data exclusivity hence precludes authorities for a reasonable period of time from using or relying on the original registration or the data submitted by the innovator for the benefit of third parties seeking to market a copy of the product without producing their own data. After the period of data exclusivity ends, the originator's data can be relied upon by the authorities to approve the marketing of copy products, thereby obviating the need for the second applicant to repeat trials already conducted by the originator. Article 8(3) of the amended 2001 Directive states that the results of preclinical tests and clinical trials must be submitted with the application for a marketing

---

[26] Directive 2001/83/EC on the Community code relating to medicinal products for human use, OJ 2001 No. L311/67.

authorization of a particular drug. Article 10(1) allows a generic producer, once data exclusivity has expired (as well as the patent protection and, where relevant, supplementary patent protection (see above)), to submit an application for authorization without submitting the data referred to in Article 8(3)(i) – the so-called 'abridged' procedure. Hence, the authorities can use the original application as a reference, but this provision does not give the generic manufacturer access to the original research data.

B. From data exclusivity to marketing exclusivity

Originally, a Member State had to grant data exclusivity for either six or ten years from initial authorization. While a number of countries granted a ten-year protection period, a number opted for the shorter period. Under the 2001 Directive, generic manufacturers could only apply for an authorization once the patent, the SPaC and data exclusivity had expired. This meant that the total protection period was effectively extended for about another twelve months in practice, while the application for the authorization for the generic drug was being processed. The 2004 Directive introduces a number of changes.

8+2+1 Year data and marketing exclusivity

Generic manufacturers will be barred from referring to the results of preclinical and clinical tests of the original, innovative drug until eight years have elapsed from the date of authorization of the latter. Hence, in some Member States, the data exclusivity period has been extended by two years, but in others reduced by two. However, a new term – 'marketing exclusivity' – has been introduced to prevent the marketing of a generic drug during the two years following the data exclusivity period.

The period of marketing exclusivity runs in parallel with the data exclusivity but lasts for ten years. And so, at the end of the first period (data exclusivity), there is an additional two years market exclusivity, which runs from the end of the data exclusivity period. The two year additional market exclusivity period can be extended by one year if, during the eight year data exclusivity period, the innovative company obtains an authorization for one or more new therapeutic indications, which, during the scientific evaluation prior to their authorization, are held to bring a significant clinical benefit in comparison with existing therapies. Together these amendments form the so-called '8+2+1' rule. In practice, this means that a generic company must wait for eight years before submitting its marketing application and must wait a further two (or three) years, during which time that application can be processed. The 2004 Directive (Article 10(6)), however, serves to protect the interests of generic competition by allowing generic producers to commence research and development work on a product before patent (or SPaC) expiry – this is the so-called 'Bolar' scheme, which takes its name from the United States equivalent. Consequently, carrying out the necessary studies and trials will no longer constitute patent infringement.

A generic medicinal product is now defined in the 2004 Directive and this has put an end to much of the controversy – and litigation – generated by the 'essential similarity' test, which had not been defined in earlier directives. Both the European Court of Justice (ECJ) and the English High Court had been prepared to interpret this concept in favour of the generic manufacturer.[27] Article 10(2)(b) of the 2004 Directive defines a generic medicinal product as meaning:

[A] medicinal product which has the same qualitative and quantitative composition in active substances and the same pharmaceutical form as the reference medicinal product and whose bioequivalence with the reference product has been demonstrated by appropriate bioavailability studies. The different salts, esters, ethers, shall be considered to be the same active substance, unless they differ significantly in properties with regard to safety and/or efficacy. In such cases, additional information providing proof of the safety and/or efficacy of the various salts, esters and so on of an authorised active substance must be supplied by the applicant.

This new definition provides clarity as to when the abridged procedure (or hybrid abridged procedure) should be applied. Nevertheless, it contains vague concepts, such as when two drugs differ significantly regarding safety or efficacy, and it is likely that the different components of the definition – which has to be implemented into national

---

[27] Case C-106/01, *Novartis* [2004] ECR 1–4403; Case C-36/03, *Approved Prescription Services* [2004] ECR I-11583; Case C-74/03, *SmithKline Beecham* [2005] ECR I-595; *The Case of R (on the Application of Merck Sharp and Dohme Ltd)* v. *The Licensing Authority* [2005] EWHC 710 (Admin).

law – will require further clarification from the courts. In particular, the registration and use of generic medicines is allegedly hampered due to a lack of EU-wide harmonization of indications of reference products (also known as 'originators') on which the generic applicant must base its common European-wide approval. This, in part, is attributed to patents being granted on particular uses of products and to allowing data exclusivity for 'new' indications, which in fact do not represent any real innovatory value,[28] as well as the extension of the types of properties eligible for intellectual property rights (IPR) protection in general, through the combination of patent, trade-mark and patent. The scope of IPR includes not only methods of treatment but also methods of treatment and action mechanisms, while IPR may also be invoked for packaging, delivery profiles and dosing, screening methods, etc.[29] Further delays in bringing generics to the market are attributed to market approval/authorization or licensing processes, as well as the granting of substitution/reimbursement status (see below).

C. Bio-similar medicines or products

The concept of a bio-similar product was introduced into EU legislation in 2003 and further defined in Directive 2004/27/EC. In essence, the registration process for this type of product allows a manufacturer to submit an application for an authorization for a product claimed to be similar to another biological medicine. The rationale for creating this new licensing route is that biological medicines or biologics do not usually meet all the conditions to be considered as a generic (see Recital 15 of the Directive). Given the complexity of biological molecules, and the fact that they are produced in living organisms, it is virtually impossible for applicants to produce an identical copy of a reference biological product. Hence, the licensing route is based on the principle that biologics are not chemical drugs and that the generic approach is very unlikely to be applicable to biologics: dissimilar

---

[28] See, in particular, M. N. Graham Dukes, 'Priority medicines and the world', *Bulletin of the WHO* 83 (2005), 321–400.

[29] See the presentation of E. Larson, 'Evolution of IPR and pharmaceutical discovery and development', Paper presented at the Conference on 'Intellectual Property Rights: How Far Should They Be Extended?', Washington, DC, 22 October 2001.

products are not biogenerics. The three main eligibility criteria are, first, that the product must be a biological medicine. In legal terms, this means any type of biologic, including not only blood-derived products but all vaccines or products derived from gene/cell therapy, etc. Secondly, the reference product must have been authorized within the European Community, although it is not required that the reference product still be authorized at the time that the bio-similar application is filed. Thirdly, the application has to be submitted after the expiry of the data exclusivity period (the 8+2+1 rule discussed above).

Commission officials have acknowledged this to be one of the most complex issues that the European Community has faced in the area of pharmaceuticals in the last five years. In particular, as regards the kind of data required to file a bio-similar application, the EU legislation is based on the principle that a uniform approach is unworkable in this area. The type and amount of preclinical and clinical data are not predefined in legislation but are determined on a case-by-case basis. Thus, the requirements to demonstrate safety, efficacy and quality of a bio-similar product are class-specific and the amount of information required can range from that required for an 'abridged' generic application to being nearly as complete as a full, stand-alone application. The legislation makes specific reference to the obligation of compliance with detailed scientific guidelines to be produced by the EMEA, and the first of these guidelines was released in November 2004. These guidelines make it clear that the quality attributes in the bio-similar and reference products should not be identical, as minor molecular structural differences are inherent to biologics. However, these differences must be justified on scientific grounds and must be considered on a case-by-case basis in relation to their potential impact on safety and efficacy.

The EMEA approved the first two bio-similar products in the EU in 2006. By mid-2008, five authorizations had been granted, and two more were expected to be granted by the end of 2008. One application for an interferon was given a negative scientific opinion in June 2006 because of major concerns regarding comparability with the originator product, including impurities. A debate has also arisen as to whether the European regulatory framework can also be used to evaluate interchangeability – i.e., is a bio-similar product actually interchangeable in medical practice with the reference product? The EMEA does not consider that it has the legal competence – either through the legislation provisions or on the basis of its guidelines – to conduct this type of assessment.[30]

The generic manufacturers' association, the EGA, predicts that by 2010 highly expensive biopharmaceutical products will make up 25% of pharmaceutical sales in the EU and 50% of new applications. As a result, bio-similar medicinal products will become, in its view, a necessary component of future health care management policies. It claims that even a 20% price reduction on six off-patent biopharmaceutical products would save the EU Member States some €1.6 billion per year. The Association claims that, while the regulatory pathway for bio-similars has now been established, much remains to be done to establish a market pathway at the national levels.[31]

D. *Competition law and the regulatory pathway: the AstraZeneca Case*

As discussed above, the European institutions have sought to strike a balance between the objectives of stimulating innovation while securing affordable access through regulation ex ante – regulation securing rights to data exclusivity and, more recently, marketing exclusivity in the interests of the research based industry – while at the same time harmonizing the marketing authorization procedures for generic products. The Commission has, however, considered it necessary to expand this 'tool kit' in the form of stricter ex post control on certain practices on the part of the research based industry – practices that have consisted in using the regulatory pathway to frustrate the market pathway for generic competitors.

In June 2005, the Commission imposed a fine of €60 million on AstraZeneca (AZ) for abusing its dominant position in the market for proton pump inhibitors by delaying generic market entry of generic copies of its best-selling product, Losec, through its use of procedures before national patent offices and regulatory authorities.[32] This

---

[30] See testimony of N. Rossignol, Administrator, Pharmaceuticals Unit, European Commission Directorate-General for Enterprise & Industry, before the HELP Committee on 8 March 2007, http://help.senate.gov/ Hearings/2007_03_08/Rossignol.pdf.

[31] See EGA, 'Building a 'market pathway' for bio-similar medicines', Press Release, 3 May 2007, www.bogin.nl/ega-press.

[32] Commission Decision 2006/857/EC of 15 June 2005 relating to a proceeding under Article 82 of the EC Treaty and Article 54 of the EEA Agreement (Case COMP/A.37.507/F3, *AstraZeneca*), OJ 2006 No. L332/24.

case is particularly significant because it confirms that the behaviour of pharmaceutical companies before regulatory and other authorities can be considered abusive, whereas it was previously considered that this was unlikely, if only because these procedures were open to all competitors regardless of the market share of the leading manufacturer. AZ developed a central strategy to protect Losec's market position in Europe after expiry of the basic patent on the active ingredient – omeprazole. AZ sought to obtain additional patent protection through the SPaC regime of up to five years in a number of countries by providing national patent offices not with the required date of the first marketing authorization of Losec in the EU but with the date the product was first reimbursed (a later date).

The Commission found that AZ's 'misleading representations' to the patent authorities were abusive, since they were part of a centralized strategy to prevent generic market entry. The Commission was not persuaded by the argument that the terms of the EC Regulation relevant to the information to be submitted to the patent offices (Regulation 1768/92/EEC) was not clear, nor was its view changed by the fact that questions on the interpretation of the Regulation had been referred to the ECJ, which had only clarified the scope of Articles 3, 13 and 19 of the Regulation in a ruling in 2003.[33] According to the evidence in the Commission's possession, AstraZeneca concealed from the national patent offices the date upon which it had received its first marking authorization for Losec as the marketing authorization was given prior to the cut-off dates provided for in the Regulation.

The Commission also found a second type of abuse in AZ's strategy of selectively withdrawing the market authorization of Losec in favour of an improved version – Losec MUPS – in the four countries where, due to the specific market situation, generic competitors, as well as parallel importers, would have been able to launch generic copies unless the 'reference product' was made unavailable. AZ attempted to ensure this by withdrawing its own market authorizations for Lozec in capsule form (the original formulation) and applying for a new authorization based on a tablet formulation. At the time these practices were implemented, they could (and did) give rise to foreclosure effects on the market, since generic producers could only obtain a marketing authorization and parallel importers could

---

[33] Case C-127/00, *Hässle AB* v. *Ratiopharm* [2003] ECR I-14781.

only obtain import licences if there was an existing reference market authorization for the original corresponding medicinal product.

Subsequent changes to Directive 2001/83/EC as introduced by Directive 2004/27/EC, as discussed above, should make it impossible to repeat this specific conduct. The amended legislation provides that: (a) all marketing authorizations granted for the same medicinal product (including not only the initial marking authorization but also subsequent marketing authorizations relating to change in strength, pharmaceutical form, administration route or presentation of the product) shall be considered to belong to the same 'global' marketing authorization (Article 6(1)); and (b) a generic marketing authorization shall be granted even if the reference product is not authorized in the Member State in which the application is submitted, as long as it is authorized in any other EU or EEA Member State (Article 10(1)).

The *AstraZeneca* decision represents an important plank in the Commission's strategy of dealing strictly with any restrictions on parallel imports and on market access for generic products. Indeed, it is the first time that the Commission has relied on Article 82 to penalize conduct before national patent offices and regulatory authorities responsible for marketing authorizations. In particular, it marks an interesting extension of the case-law on Article 82 with regard to the exercise of intellectual property rights by dominant companies, and the decision has raised question marks as to how this fits in with the Commission's wider review of Article 82, in which it has considered the need to adopt a more economics-based approach (as opposed to a form-based approach) to allegedly abusive practices.[34]

The recent case-law on the application of the competition rules to intellectual property rights has focused on the question of whether the grant of compulsory licences for intellectual property rights could be imposed on dominant companies by competition authorities. The ECJ has ruled in a series of cases that the exercise of an exclusive right and, more specifically, the refusal of only a company holding a dominant position to grant a licence for an intellectual property right may, in

---

[34] European Commission, 'Discussion Paper on Article 82', DG Competition Discussion Paper (2006), p. 7, http://ec.europa.eu/comm/competition/antitrust/art82/discpaper2005.pdf.

certain exceptional circumstances, constitute an abuse of a dominant position.[35] In the *IMS* case, the Court held that in order for such a refusal to be regarded as abusive it must prevent the emergence of a new product for which there is potential demand, be without objective justification and capable of eliminating all competition on the relevant market.[36] In the *AstraZeneca* case, the Commission not only examined the exercise of intellectual property rights but also possible abuses in obtaining, protecting and extending these very rights. The Commission has essentially argued that the dichotomy between the existence of an IPR and its exercise has gradually been abandoned in the case-law and has been replaced by the concept of the subject matter of the right in question.[37] Furthermore, the Commission held that the use of public procedures and regulations may, in specific circumstances, constitute abuse, as this concept is not limited to behaviour in the market only.

As regards the second issue, the economics-based approach to Article 82, a report published in July 2005 pointed out that, with regard to a 'refusal to deal' case, the competition authorities should be particularly reluctant to intervene when the source of the bottleneck is an intellectual property right, since any intervention may reduce the incentive to innovate.[38] In other words, the Commission should conduct a full balancing exercise and take into account not only the exclusionary effects of the conduct vis-à-vis generic drug companies, but also the potential pro-competitive effects and efficiencies of the conduct, as well as the effects that its own enforcement actions might have on the innovative sector. In the *AstraZeneca* case, the Commission distinguished marketing authorizations, which, unlike patents, SPaC and data exclusivity, are not intended to reward innovation but instead merely bestow the right to sell products on the market.[39]

[35] Joined Cases C-241/91 P and C-242/91 P, *Magill* [1995] ECR I-743.
[36] Case C-418/01, *IMS* [2004] ECR I-5039.
[37] Commission Decision 2006/857/EC, above n.32, para. 741; Case C-223/01, *AstraZeneca* [2003] ECR I-11809; Case C-238/87, *Volvo Veng* [1988] ECR 6211.
[38] J. Gual *et al.*, 'An economic approach to Article 82', Report by the EAGCP, July 2005, http://ec.europa.eu/comm/competition/publications/studies/eagcp_july_21_05.pdf.
[39] See also N. De Souza, 'Competition in pharmaceuticals: the challenges ahead post AstraZeneca', European Commission, Competition Policy Newslettter No. 1 (2007), pp. 39–43.

The Commission's decision has now been appealed to the Court of Justice[40] but, in the meantime, the Commission has launched similar investigations into alleged abusive conduct by Boehringer – which is believed to have been involved in similar practices[41] – and, in January 2008, the Commission launched a sector-wide inquiry – the most wide-ranging and flexible tool in its competition tool-kit, allowing it to consider the industry as a whole, rather than focusing on specific companies or practices.[42]

E. The Commission Inquiry

The Commissioner for Competition has now publicly acknowledged that 'generic competition is an area which has suffered from under-enforcement in the past', and has taken action accordingly. The launch of the Commission's anti-trust, sector-wide inquiry on 16 January 2008, unusually, was heralded by dawn raids at the offices of at least eight major pharmaceutical companies. In May 2008, the inquiry was extended to a further eighty companies. The Commission's major concerns are its perception that fewer new pharmaceuticals are being brought to market and that the entry of generic pharmaceuticals may be being 'delayed'. The objective of the inquiry is to obtain a better understanding of competition in the sector and to determine whether these two concerns result from anti-competitive practices. The inquiry will focus on two particular issues: agreements between pharmaceutical companies, such as settlements in patent disputes, and establishing whether companies have created artificial barriers to product entry, through misuse of patent rights, vexatious litigation or other means. This latter concern obviously arises from the Commission's investigation into AstraZeneca, and it is clear that the Commission will review registration and litigation

---

[40] Case T-321/05, *AstraZeneca* v. *Commission* (judgment pending); registered in OJ 2005 No. C271/24.
[41] Case COMP/39.246, *Boehringer* (judgement pending), details of initiation available at http://ec.europa.eu/comm/competition/antitrust/cases/decisions/39246/initiations.pdf.
[42] Case COM/D2/39.514 initiating an inquiry into the pharmaceutical sector pursuant to Article 17 of Council Regulation 1/2003/EC, above n.14. See also European Commission, 'Antitrust: Commission launches sector inquiry into pharmaceuticals with unannounced inspections', Press Release No. IP/08/49, 16 January 2008.

strategies that are designed to extend the effective patent life of a 'blockbuster' product.

Anti-competitive agreements

The Commission has not previously considered patent settlement agreements in any detail, nor has there been any finding of infringement in relation to such agreements in the past. In contrast, this area has been a hot topic in United States anti-trust practice for some time. The latter is heavily influenced by the relevant legislation, including the Drug Price Competition and Patent Term Restoration Act of 1984 (commonly known as the Hatch-Waxman Act amendments), which does not have a direct European equivalent. These arrangements typically arise in the context of settlement of patent infringement claims between a manufacturer of branded pharmaceuticals and a manufacturer of a new generic product. Settlements of such claims have raised complex anti-trust concerns, particularly where the settlements provide for delayed entry of the generic into the market, with a 'reverse' payment from the patent holder to the alleged infringer. The United States courts of appeals have taken different approaches to these arrangements, with some holding that such settlements are per se an illegal allocation of markets. In addition, the principal United States anti-trust regulators appear to hold different views on the issue. The Federal Trade Commission views reverse settlements as anti-competitive while the Department of Justice appears to take a less formalistic standpoint.[43]

The Commission has stated that its inquiry will not challenge intellectual property law protection, but the launching of the inquiry seems to indicate the Commission's willingness to get to grips with the impact of competition on the patent strategies of manufacturers, particularly towards the end of a product's patent life. The launching of the inquiry raises complex legal and policy questions as to where the boundary lies between legitimate protection of patent rights and anti-competitive conduct. Much will depend on the follow-up steps taken on completion of the Commission's final report, scheduled for spring 2009. Enforcement action against particular firms is not necessarily

---

[43] G. Robert and F. Falconi, 'Patent litigation settlement agreements in the pharmaceutical industry: marrying the innovation bride and competition groom product', *European Competition Law Review* 27 (2006), 524–33.

an inevitable outcome of a sector-wide inquiry. Indeed, previous Commission inquiries have resulted in a wide range of outcomes. The adoption of legislation dealing with particular areas of concern is one possibility (for example, measures in relation to payment systems and consumer credit as a result of the retail banking sector inquiry), but there are also examples of the Commission encouraging industry participants to address issues themselves (as, for example, in the business insurance inquiry).

5. Developments in the marketing pathway

In this section, we will focus on issues relating to the post-authorization of prescription-only products and, in particular, examine the issue of the provision of information to patients on medicines and direct-to-consumer advertising of these products, the present regulation of which is currently under review.

A. *Pricing and marketing*

Although the introduction of new medicinal products into European and national markets is subject to extensive, but closely harmonized, regulatory procedures, two key features of the marketing pathway – pricing and the provision of information to patients – remain primarily the preserve of Member States.

Indeed, only a minimal level of harmonization has been achieved with respect to pricing and profit controls, whereas the increasingly sensitive issue of access to information for patients is entirely a matter for the Member States, subject only to the common basic principle, as enshrined in Directive 2001/83/EC, that advertising of prescription products to the public is prohibited.[44] Attempts to reform the essentially procedural requirements introduced by the Price Transparency Directive of 1989 have met strong resistance and, instead, the European Union has sought to evolve a wider policy consensus on the substance of national price and profit control through a series of political initiatives based on consultation and coordination and the development of general guiding principles. In the meantime, however, the Commission has continued to support intra-brand competition

---

[44] Directive 2001/83/EC, above n.26.

by relying on the fundamental principles of free movement and competition. Recent case-law at both the European and national levels suggests that the scope for the application of competition-based principles, as a result of the introduction of a more economics-based approach, may be more restricted in the future. These developments are examined in the next subsection below.

B. Intra-brand competition: the setting sun?

Parallel trade in the pharmaceutical sector has been the subject of decades of heated dispute and litigation between industry players and wholesalers, as well as the European Commission and Member States. Economic studies are advanced on both sides of the debate. There are studies to support the contention that parallel trade is a key factor undermining European pharmaceutical competitiveness by diminishing revenue flows and reducing innovation potential, and yet it brings no clear benefit to consumers, since gains accrue mainly to the traders rather than the health care buyers (or payers) or patients.[45] But, equally, there are studies that identify a positive impact for this latter group as the research-based industry attempts to keep market share by lowering prices.[46]

Nevertheless, the Commission's prevailing view, as last expressed in its Communication of 2003,[47] is that parallel trade should be supported as a lawful form of trade within the European Union. In addition, parallel trade affects market practices. Pharmaceutical companies claim that the often volatile activities of wholesalers result in an unpredictability of demand and intricate supply chain problems. This complicates the allocation of resources for these companies and may have a detrimental effect on their ability to ensure the appropriate level of stock to meet patient needs in each EU Member State. In response, the research-based companies have resorted to dual-pricing strategies

---

[45] P. Kanavos *et al.*, 'The economic impact of pharmaceutical parallel trade in European Union Member States: a stakeholder analysis', London School of Economics and Political Science (2004), http://mednet3.who.int/prioritymeds/report/append/829Paper.pdf.
[46] M. Ganslandt and K. E. Maskus, 'Parallel imports and the pricing of pharmaceutical products: evidence from the European Union', Swedish Research Institute of Industrial Economics Working Paper No. 622 (2004).
[47] European Commission, 'Communication on parallel import', above n.12.

and supply quota systems. Supply quota systems come in a variety of forms, but usually they involve a restriction of supplies to wholesalers commensurate with the latter's requirements in the domestic market, plus a limited margin. Dual pricing strategies seek to reduce the price differential between geographical markets and, as a result, the incentive for arbitrage in the form of parallel trade. Manufacturers set a standard price for unregulated markets as well as export products, but may agree a discounted price in regulated markets.

From an EU competition law perspective, the first strategy may give rise to a breach of Article 81(1) EC if the supply quotas result from an agreement with the wholesalers concerned; if there is no consensus – that is, if the wholesalers oppose the quota – then the quota system can only be caught if the company imposing it unilaterally is dominant in the relevant product and geographical markets.[48] Dual pricing strategies, however, may be subject to Articles 81 and 82 EC if there is agreement between the supplier and the wholesaler and, in the case of Article 82, the supplier is dominant. Recent case-law at the European and national levels indicates, albeit cautiously, that both strategies may be pursued under certain conditions. In a number of respects, the Commission's standpoint in its 2003 Communication on parallel imports now appears to be undermined.

C. *The GlaxoSmithKline Case: dual pricing upheld*

On 27 September 2006, the Court of First Instance (CFI) handed down its long-awaited judgment on the Commission's decision to refuse to grant an exemption under Article 81(3) of the EC Treaty to a dual pricing system operated by GlaxoSmithKline (GSK) in Spain.[49] GSK was compelled under Spanish law to charge reduced wholesale prices for sales on the Spanish domestic market, but imposed higher prices for parallel export by its wholesale customers, prices that were equivalent to the prices it originally applied to register in Spain. The Commission, taking its traditional formal approach to clauses in agreements leading to export bans as a 'per se' restriction of competition, had concluded that any attempt to limit parallel exports was

---

[48] Case T-41/96, *Bayer AG v. Commission* [2000] ECR II-3383; Joined Cases C-2/01 P and C-3/01 P, *BAI and Commission v. Bayer* [2004] ECR I-23.
[49] Case T-168/01, *GlaxoSmithKline Services v. Commission* [2006] ECR II-2969.

contrary to Article 81(1) and as a so-called 'hard-core' restriction, was not eligible for exemption. The CFI rejected the Commission's approach that GSK's policy had the object of restricting competition but upheld the Commission's reasoning as regards to the effects of the arrangements on competition. Nevertheless, it concluded that the Commission should have fully examined the legal and economic context of the pharmaceuticals sector, and should have carried out a full balancing exercise of all the relevant evidence before reaching a conclusion on Article 81(3). Hence, the CFI referred the decision back to the Commission. In the meantime, appeals to the ECJ were lodged by the Commission and by GSK, as well as by two European wholesalers' associations (the European Association of Euro-Pharmaceutical Companies (EAEPC) and Aseprofar) against the CFI ruling.[50]

This judgment will have significant repercussions for future Commission policy. In the past, the Commission has always contended that, while it was broadly sympathetic to the claims of the research-based industry that divergent national price and profit regulations that give rise to parallel trade could threaten their capacity for innovation and their global competitiveness, its hands were tied by the jurisprudence of the Courts, which supported parallel trade as an important stimulus to completing the internal pharmaceuticals market. That the Commission had already entertained doubts as to the wisdom of this approach was evident in its 1998 Communication on the single market in pharmaceuticals, where it recognized that unless parallel trade could operate dynamically on prices, it creates inefficiencies because the financial benefit accrues to the parallel trader and not to the national health care system or to patients.[51]

Although it is not possible to examine the judgment in full detail here, it may be noted that the CFI rejected the Commission's main argument that the arrangements must be considered to be per se contrary to Article 81(1) because they have the object of restricting parallel trade.

---

[50] See Case C-501/06, *GlaxoSmithKline Services Unlimited* v. *Commission* (not yet reported); Case C-513/06, *Commission* v. *GlaxoSmithKline Services Unlimited* (not yet reported); Case C-515/06, *European Association of Euro-Pharmaceutical Companies* v. *GlaxoSmithKline Services Unlimited* (not yet reported); and Case C-519/06, *Asociación de exportadores españoles de productos farmacéuticos* v. *GlaxoSmithKline Services Unlimited* (not yet reported).

[51] European Commission, 'Communication on the single market in pharmaceuticals', COM (98) 588 final, 25 November 1998.

The CFI concluded that, as the prices of the relevant medicine were to a large extent shielded from the free play of supply and demand due to national regulatory controls, it cannot be taken for granted that parallel trade tends to produce prices that increase the welfare of final consumers. In other words, there is no automatic protection for parallel trade under Article 81, but rather this activity must be shown to have given final consumers the advantage of effective competition in terms of supply or in respect of price, rather than simply benefiting the parallel traders as such. Therefore, GSK was correct to maintain that, in the specific legal and economic context, the Commission could not merely presume, in the absence of a more detailed examination of the essential characteristics of the sector, that the parallel trade restricted by GSK's sales conditions would have a beneficial impact on the prices charged to final consumers and, as a result, that this policy would have the object of restricting competition. Importantly, however, the CFI stated that, even though the clause was attributable to, and allowed by, the regulatory context, this did not mean that it could not be said to infringe competition rules.

Therefore, the CFI concluded that, even if GSK's pricing was merely consistent with the regulatory context, this did not justify the pricing policy as such for the purposes of Article 81. It then went on to consider the application of the exemption criteria as provided for in Article 81(3). GSK had argued that the higher revenues resulting from the dual pricing scheme contributed to efficiency by means of increased capacity for R&D expenditure. This, in turn, facilitated innovation, which, it argued, is the determining parameter on inter-brand competition. As GSK financed its investment in R&D from its own funds, and not from borrowing, any reduction in its returns undermined its capacity to innovate. At the same time, the parallel exports did not compete on price and therefore had no pro-competitive effect on the market.

GSK also argued that these issues had to be assessed in the context of the Commission's Communication of 1998,[52] where precisely these characteristics of the pharmaceutical market were acknowledged. The CFI concluded that the Commission had failed to undertake a rigorous examination of these arguments and, in particular, that it should have examined whether a parallel trade led to a loss

[52] *Ibid.*

of efficiency for the industry in general and for GSK in particular. The evidence on which the Commission had relied was ambiguous, as it had failed to compare the gain in efficiency for intra-brand competition with a loss of efficiency in inter-brand competition. The CFI set the required standard of proof that it expected in such a case at a high level: the Commission was not entitled to reject GSK's efficiency and innovation arguments on the grounds that the advantages claimed by GSK would not necessarily be achieved. The Commission was required to consider whether it was more likely than not that the claimed advantages would be achieved. Therefore, the Commission had not properly substantiated its conclusions on the ineligibility of the arrangements for exemption under Article 81(3) nor had it properly balanced the available evidence in reaching its final conclusion.[53]

D. *Abuse of a dominant position*

A related question dealt with by the Court was whether or not it was abusive conduct, contrary to Article 82(c), for a dominant company to refuse to supply to a parallel exporter. It reasoned that GSK was responding to, rather than creating, different pricing areas and Article 82 only prohibits a dominant company from applying artificial price differences between Member States. As each Member State constituted a distinct national market due to different national pricing and profit controls, it was possible for GSK to apply different prices because different markets exist. This line of reasoning reflects case-law at the national levels, in particular in the lower-price Member States, including France, Greece and Spain, to the effect that a refusal by a dominant company to supply an exporter so as to prevent the exploitation of price differences in the destination market will not constitute abuse of a dominant position.

E. *Supply quotas and refusals to supply*

The Greek Syfait Case
The Greek Competition Commission (HCC) issued a decision on 5 September 2006, shortly before the CFI ruling in the *GlaxoSmithKline*

---

[53] The EAEPC lodged a complaint against Pfizer for the introduction of a similar system on 17 October 2005, but at the time of writing no formal action had been taken on this.

v. *Commission* case discussed above, also concerning a complaint against GSK for its refusal to supply certain quantities of three products – Imigran, Lamctal and Serevent – to Greek wholesalers trading outside Greece. GSK initially discontinued supplies in 2000, but subsequently resumed supplies in 2001 on the basis of restrictive quotas. On reference to the ECJ, the Advocate General concluded that, in the circumstances of the case, it was not abusive for GSK to refuse to supply the orders, taking into account the pervasive regulation of price and distribution in the Member States that were imposed upon rather than made or chosen by the pharmaceutical companies. The ECJ declined to rule on the reference, finding that the Greek Competition Commission was not a court that was entitled to make such a reference, but the Greek Commission went on to rule that GSK did not abuse its dominant position when it applied the quota system, although cutting off supplies for the initial period did amount to an abuse. It may be noted that the HCC did not assess GSK's supply quota system on the grounds that this was under review by the Commission.

Nevertheless, the ECJ is now confronted with several references from the Greek courts to which the ruling of the Competition Commission has now been appealed. In particular, the Greek Appeal Court asked the Court for further guidance on the nature and scope of the duties of the national competition authority to apply Community competition rules in the same way to markets that function competitively as to those in which competition is distorted by state intervention. The Court was asked to give further guidance on the criteria for establishing abuse in the event that the 'standard' approach does not apply and to consider whether an approach entailing the balancing of interests is appropriate. If this indeed is correct, what interests are to be compared? Is the answer affected by the fact that the ultimate consumer/patient derives limited financial advantage from the parallel trade, and should account be taken of the interests of social insurance bodies in cheaper medicinal products? The Court took a rather traditional, formal approach, however, and held that any refusal by a pharmaceuticals company in a dominant position to meet orders sent to it by wholesalers involved in parallel exports constitutes an abuse, although such a company must "be in a position to take steps that are reasonable and in proportion to the need to protect its own commercial interests".[54]

[54] Joined Cases C-468/06 to C-478/06, *Sot. Lélos Kai Sia EE (and Others)* v. *GlaxoSmithKline AEVE* [2008] ECR I-7139, paras. 69–70.

In the meantime, EAEPC has sought the annulment of a Commission decision rejecting three complaints against GSK. The Commission, in fact, rejected the complaint on the basis that the Greek authorities were dealing with the case and EAEPC, in turn, appealed this decision to the CFI.[55]

The French Competition Council and the Paris Court of Appeal

The previous year (20 December 2005), the French Competition Council (FCC) held that GSK, Pfizer, Merck Sharp & Dohme (MSD), Lily, Sanofi and others had not abused any dominant position in refusing to supply certain exporters. When the price of a product is regulated, it should not be regarded as abusive to refuse to supply such products to another operator that is not itself active on the market affected by the price regulation and that only seeks to purchase the products in order to export at a profit. Furthermore, the competition tribunal dismissed allegations of discrimination in favour of wholesalers with mixed operations involving domestic and exporting activities and to the detriment of purely exporting wholesalers. It also concluded that a difference in treatment could be justified in light of the public service obligations resting on the wholesalers with domestic activities.[56] However, the FCC appears to have concluded that a quota system for pure exporters would not be justified and would be anti-competitive, and that it would keep this subject under review. Furthermore, the French tribunal rejected the argument that Article 81 should be applied even if there was no evidence of an agreement between the companies to target wholesalers who exported.

In a separate ruling, the Paris Court of Appeal, again relying on the Commission's 1998 Communication, doubted that, even assuming that the suppliers in question were in a dominant position, their

---

[55] Case T-153/06, *European Association of Euro-Pharmaceutical Companies v. Commission*. The Commission relied on Article 13 of Regulation 1/2003/ EC, above n.14. Removed from register on 28 February 2008.

[56] Article 81(2) of Directive 2001/83 provides that the holder of a marketing authorization for a medicinal product and the distributors of that product must ensure appropriate and continued supplies of the product to pharmacies and persons authorized to supply medicinal products so that the needs of patients in the member state in question are covered.

decision to limit the supplies of certain products to wholesalers on the basis of allocations of a quantity of products by reference to the market shares that they had in the French market would, in itself, constitute abuse.

The Spanish Tribunal for Fair Trading

In dealing with the same question, the Spanish Tribunal for Fair Trading doubted if the companies involved could be held to be dominant, given the degree of market regulation and the purchasing power of the national health system, so that suppliers did not have the independence of action normally associated with a dominant position. Furthermore, it stated that there could be no abuse of any dominant position, as a company in such a position could not be required to initiate commercial relations with all customers or potential customers who request it. The complainant, who had never had regular, stable or continuous dealings with the manufacturer, GSK, had access to alternative sources of supply, such as other distributors.

F. *Implications*

This recent spate of cases at the European and national levels indicates that conventional competition law methodology is not always being adhered to and that courts and competition authorities at both levels are willing to recognize the specific characteristics of parallel trade and arbitrage between high and low-priced markets. The different national regulatory conditions must be taken into account, not only to assess the agreements at issue but also to understand the position of the different parties in the relevant market. Competition analysis depends on the delimitation of a relevant product[57] and a relevant geographic market. In these recent cases, there is a discernable trend, culminating in the recent case of *GlaxoSmithKline* v. *Commission*, towards

---

[57] In most cases, a preliminary idea of the appropriate market definition is obtained by looking at the products grouped together in Level 3 of WHO's Anatomical Therapeutic Classification (ATC) scheme. The Commission generally uses these ATC Level 3 categories as the starting point of its analysis of the relevant market. In many cases, this category will be the relevant product market, although the Commission (and national authorities) may conclude that the market should be narrower. IMS sales data is also grouped according to the ATC categories so market share data is relatively easy to obtain.

recognition of the fact that wholesalers who purchase products for the purposes of parallel export are operating in a different geographical market that is outside the market of the Member State of export, and as suppliers into the higher-priced Member States of import. This is of importance because it makes it harder to sustain the argument that companies who are at first sight dominant because they have high market shares cannot necessarily restrict competition in the sense that their action would eliminate competition in a substantial part of the relevant market. Furthermore, and as indicated above, the CFI also suggested that it was necessary to assess what form of competition should be given priority with a view to ensuring the maintenance of effective competition, inter-brand or intra-brand? This prioritization would have to be based on careful economic analysis. As many commentators have observed, the burden on the Commission and also, of course, on national courts and authorities, is daunting. Full assessment of the efficiency argument involves addressing in detail whether a company such as GSK, as a rational operator facing competitive pressures at the innovation level, would invest a significant part of the increased funding that would result from dual pricing in R&D. The economics of innovation is a global matter that must be weighed in a balancing exercise against the restrictive effects of parallel trade between individual EC Member States. And this assessment must be prospective.[58] This is a long way from the simple 'per se' approach that had formed the cornerstone of Commission practice (and rhetoric) until now.

Decentralization of competition law enforcement

A further trend that is already evident from the number of cases on the application of Articles 81 and 82 now being decided by the national competition authorities and courts, discussed above, is the impact of the so-called 'modernization' of European competition law on the Community tool kit. Regulation 1/2003/EC, which came into force on 1 May 2004, removed the Commission's exclusive right to apply Article 81(3) to exempt anti-competitive agreements, as well as the

---

[58] See, for an outline of the economic approach to assessing the impact of parallel trade on competition, CRA International, European Competition Practice, 'Parallel trade in pharmaceuticals: more harm than good?', Competition Memo, March 2008, www.crai.com/ecp/assets/Parallel_Trade_in_Pharmaceuticals.pdf.

prior notification procedure. The Regulation also provides for various mechanisms to coordinate the application of Article 81 EC by the national competition authorities, including a network, the European Competition Network (ECN), to provide a framework for applying and developing the EC competition rules at the national level. To enhance the effectiveness of the ECN, a number of subgroups have been established, some with a sectoral focus. In 2005, the ECN Pharmaceuticals subgroup was established. It is intended that this group will function as a valuable vehicle to support its members' enforcement and advocacy efforts in the pharmaceutical sector, as well as a better and more consistent approach to the application of the European competition rules.

As part of the modernization strategy, the Commission is also promoting private damages actions for infringements of competition law. It is acknowledged that private enforcement of European competition law before national courts is widely underdeveloped. Since the case of *Courage v. Crehan*,[59] it has become apparent that some form of remedy should be available to those who have suffered financial harm as a result of infringements of Article 81 and 82 EC. Damages actions must be brought at the national level and must comply with the relevant legal and procedural requirements of the relevant Member State. As was recently noted in a report on private enforcement produced for the Commission, an 'astonishing level of diversity' characterizes national rules and procedures.[60] Efforts by the Commission aimed at dealing with the various barriers to action faced by private plaintiffs, albeit cautious in nature, are likely to mean that private enforcement could become an important complement to public enforcement in the future.[61] The spectre of United States experience looms large, including massive settlement agreements on brand name manufacturers

---

[59] Case C-453/99, *Courage and Crehan* [2001] ECR I-6297.
[60] E. Clark, M. Hughes and D. Wirth, 'Study on the conditions of claims for damages in case of infringement of EC competition rules – analysis of economic models for the calculation of damages', Ashurst Report for the European Commission (2004), http://ec.europa.eu/comm/competition/ antitrust/actionsdamages/study.html; D. Waelbroeck, D. Slater and G. Even-Shosan, 'Study on the conditions of claims for damages in case of infringement of EC competition rules – comparative report', Ashurst Report for the European Commission (2004), http://ec.europa.eu/comm/ competition/antitrust/actionsdamages/study.html.
[61] European Commission, 'Damages actions for breach of the EC antitrust rules', Green Paper, SEC (2005) 1732, 19 December 2005. The follow-up White

for engaging in the types of practices that the Commission recently condemned in the *AstraZeneca* case. The Commission imposed a fine of €60 million in that case. On the other side of the Atlantic, the manufacturers of BuSpar, Taxol and Platinol agreed to damages award settlements amounting to US$535 million, US$135 million and US$50 million, respectively. But public enforcement, too, is taking on a new dimension in Europe, as some Member States have opted to criminalize certain anti-trust offences. The industry remains a major target for investigation and litigation, but the potential penalties are becoming more severe and far-reaching. Against this background, the industry may welcome rather than resist legislative reforms that bring greater clarity with respect to their rights and, as such, may be more favourably disposed to centralized, legislative solutions.

6. Further efforts at policy compromise: the role of the pharmaceutical forum

Set up to track the further implementation of the non-binding G10 recommendations, published in 2002, this high level political platform for discussion[62] – which was chaired by the Commissioners of Health and of Enterprise, and in which the major stakeholders[63] at the EU and national levels took part – set up three expert working groups to come up with guidelines for further action on a number of key issues, which are discussed below. The Pharmaceutical Forum, which met annually between 2005 and 2008, concluded its work with a final report in October 2008. It sought to provide the political mandate for further reform, as well as a broader platform for discussion on competitiveness and public health issues. It was supported by a Steering Committee, chaired by DG

Paper on private enforcement is European Commission, 'Damages actions for breach of the EC antitrust rules', White Paper, COM (2008) 165 final, 2 April 2008.

[62] See G. Verheugen, 'Future post-G10 pharmaceutical strategy', Speech to the EFPIA, SPEECH/05/311, Brussels, June 2005.

[63] These include the EFPIA, the EGA, the European Self-Medication Industry, EuropaBio, the European Association of Full-Line Wholesalers, the European Patients Forum, the Standing Committee of European Doctors, the Pharmaceutical Group of the European Union, Association Internationale de la Mutualité and the European Social Insurance Platform. In addition, ministries from each Member State are invited and three representatives from the European Parliament are members.

SANCO and DG Industry.[64] The constitution of the Forum marked a continuation of the policy of the open method of coordination as the better way to proceed towards balancing the interests of the industry and those of national health care systems in the 'market pathway'. As the Commissioner for Enterprise stressed in his speech to the first Forum meeting, it is not the intention to produce new European legislation but to find better ways of learning from each other.

Even if it was not the mandate of these working groups (WGs) to draft new legislation, their final recommendations could well form the basis for a further restructuring of the regulatory framework or pathway. Their reports may also result in additional functions being transferred from the national to the European level, or even the creation of new functions. A Second Progress Report was published by the Forum in July 2007, outlining concrete results and implementation proposals, albeit that further implementation, as such, will be developed through concrete work packages following the political direction given by the Forum in the course of 2008.[65] The Commission adopted a new Communication with three legislative tools on the future of the single market in pharmaceuticals in December 2008, drawing on the work of the Forum.[66] The EFPIA has called upon the Commission to use this as an opportunity to

---

[64] Membership of this Committee was restricted to seven Member States and representatives of the European Parliament and the ten stakeholders mentioned above.

[65] The First and Second Progress Reports are available via the Commission's web site, http://ec.europa.eu/enterprise/phabiocom/comp_pf_en.htm. The Final Report of the Forum was published in October 2008 and is available at http://ec.europa.eu/pharmaforum/docs/final_conclusions_en.pdf.

[66] Whilst finalizing this book, the European Commission launched the so-called 'pharmaceutical package', which includes a communication to launch reflections on ways to improve market access and the price-setting mechanism and a proposal to enable citizens to have access to information on prescription-only medicines. European Commission, 'Communication on safe, innovative and accessible medicines: a renewed vision for the pharmaceutical sector', COM (2008) 666 final, 10 December 2008; European Commission, 'Proposal for a directive amending, as regards information to the general public on medicinal products subject to medical prescription, Directive 2001/83/EC on the Community Code relating to medicinal products for human use', COM (2008) 663 final, 10 December 2008; and European Commission, 'Proposal for a regulation amending, as regards information to the general public on medicinal products for human use subject to medical prescription, Regulation (EC) No. 726/2004 laying down Community procedures for the authorisation and supervision

develop a strategic vision for the sector, which should recognize the need for the future EU regulatory framework to deliver high quality, science and risk-based decision-making that will accommodate the global nature of drug development and retain the confidence of all stakeholders through excellence in execution of its responsibilities. It remains to be seen if the two Commissioners responsible, as well as the other stakeholders represented at the Forum, will subscribe to this approach. Again, a careful balancing of competing interests through a difficult consensus-building process is the order of the day.

The most sensitive topic, following established tradition, was undoubtedly pricing policy, but the WG on relative effectiveness and the WG on information to patients also faced their own challenges.

A. *Pricing*

The key task of the WG on pricing was to examine alternative pricing and reimbursement mechanisms to support Member States in fulfilling their commitment to the G10 recommendations, as well as towards the public health objectives of offering equal access to medicines at affordable overall cost. Although the WG aimed to help Member States meet the rising challenges of high expenditure, inequality of access and calls for earlier access to innovative products by exchanging information on different pricing mechanisms, it is for Member States themselves to decide how to implement the mechanism that suits them best.

Yet the future direction of pricing and profit regulation can also have an impact on the interaction between the processes of therapeutic and generic competition. Generic manufacturers now also claim that it is important to ensure that national pricing and profit control systems can ensure that the long-term sustainability of the EU-based generic medicines industry is maintained so that it can compete effectively on EU and global markets. This means not only that pricing and reimbursement approvals and substitution status should be automatic once they have obtained a market authorization or licence, but also that the pricing of generic medicines should not be linked to a constant,

of medicinal products for human and veterinary use and establishing a European Medicines Agency', COM (2008) 662 final, 10 December 2008. See http://ec.europa.eu/enterprise/pharmaceuticals/pharmacos/pharmpack_en.htm.

set percentage of the originator product (for example, always 25% to 50% lower than the originator).[67] This form of linkage allegedly enables originators to force generic competitors out of the market by constantly lowering prices to the point where generic manufacturers cannot remain on the market or afford to enter a market. Hence, calls from this quarter are now heard for further amendments to the Price Transparency Directive (Directive 89/105/EEC)[68] in order to ensure automatic pricing and reimbursement approvals in cases where the price request is lower than the comparable originator product.[69]

External expert reports commissioned by the WG on pricing have developed a detailed overview of the application of different pricing and reimbursement practices in the Member States and have compared six specific techniques in greater detail. The WG was also asked to examine ways to increase transparency, consistency and interchangeability of information regarding prices, price components and related issues – including through collaboration with the Transparency Directive Committee (made up of Member States only). In this respect, the work of this WG, which draws upon the input of a much wider range of stakeholders, could increase pressure for reform of this measure, which has been criticized for being too narrow in scope (see below in relation to the discussion on relative effectiveness assessments) and inadequately enforced at the national level.

The aim is to improve consensus at the national level on general principles and good practices when performing relevant assessments and to encourage national authorities to set up a data sharing network both prior to and after a market authorization has been awarded. The requisite 'tool box' to encourage effective data sharing was developed over the course of 2007–8, but Annex A to the report recommends the promotion of generic products through demand-side as well as supply mechanisms. The reports from this WG also stress that affordability has a European dimension. A similar price level leads to a different level of affordability depending on the economic situation of

---

[67] See EGA, 'EGA urges price de-linkage for off-patent medicines at EU High Level Forum on Pharmaceuticals', Press Release, 26 June 2007, www.bogin. nl./ega-press.

[68] Council Directive 89/105/EEC, above n.5.

[69] See Contribution by the EGA to the Pharmaceutical Forum Pricing Working Group, 7 November 2006, www.egagenerics.com/doc/ega_pwgcontributionIIAT_2006–11–06.pdf.

each Member State, as the WG states. The WG goes on to suggest that attention should be given to measures that allow companies to offer medicines at affordable prices in each European market. Limiting price control only to nationally-used volumes would allow differential prices. Furthermore, the WG recommends that manufacturers should commit to register and supply all EU markets at reasonable prices. These types of recommendations may also support manufacturer policies on dual pricing, or non-extraterritoriality as it is also known, as discussed above. The EFPIA has called for clear guidelines in this area, as opposed to harmonizing legislation, and has condemned the 'commoditization of clinically-different medicines in reference price systems' as rewarding imitation (i.e., generic competition) and stifling incremental innovation.[70] As we noted in section two above, the EGA (the generic association) has also called for guidelines to reward generic products and stimulate their uptake in health budgets.

Regarding the WG's overall recommendations, as presented in the Forum's final report,[71] therefore, these relate to three main issues: (i) increasing access to medicines with a specific focus on access issues around orphan products and smaller markets; (ii) better incentivising and rewarding innovation which serves public health needs; and (iii) optimal use of resources via the 'toolbox' approach and use of so-called 'guiding principles' for policy-makers and national authorities.

B. Relative effectiveness

The WG on relative effectiveness assessments (REAs)[72] aimed to support Member States in applying relative effectiveness assessment

---

[70] EFPIA, 'Response to the Commission's Consultation on the future of the single market in pharmaceuticals for human use in Europe, the future of pharmaceuticals for human use in Europe – making Europe a hub for safe and innovative medicines', EFPIA Views (2007), www.efpia.org.

[71] The Final Report of the Forum was published in October 2008 and is available at http://ec.europa.eu/pharmaforum/docs/final_conclusions_en.pdf.

[72] 'Relative effectiveness' is defined as the extent to which an intervention does more good than harm compared to one or more intervention alternatives for achieving the desired results when provided under the usual circumstances of practice. Relative effectiveness assessments (REAs) are carried out to investigate to what extent a medicinal product does more good than harm compared to one or more other medicinal products or alternative health interventions for achieving the desired result when provided under the usual circumstances of practice. The working group has agreed that the quality of life dimension should be part of the assessment of relative effectiveness.

systems in order to allow containment of pharmaceutical costs, as well as a fair reward for innovation. The REAs should help identify the most valuable medicines, both in terms of clinical efficiency and cost–effectiveness, and thus help governments set a fair price for these medicines. So far, the draft proposals stress the potential for improving both the principles and practicality of sharing and using data for relative effectiveness assessments. Issues related to cost–effectiveness have not been discussed at this stage, however. In some quarters, there was some optimism that the Forum would recommend extending the procedural requirements of the Transparency Directive of 1989 to REA procedures as a means of speeding up the time taken for new products to go through each and every regulatory hoop. Although the case-law of the ECJ has required strict application of the Directive to all measures affecting price and reimbursement, including insurance coverage, REA procedures are not (yet) covered by the various timetables imposed under the Directive.[73] The research industry and a number of Member States remain resolutely opposed to a pan-European assessment of relative effectiveness.

Amongst the WG's final recommendations, therefore, were that: (i) there was a need for working definitions and good practice guidelines and principles for relative effectiveness assessment - this with a view to ensuring a balance between growing medicine costs (and those of healthcare more generally) and measures to promote innovation, towards ensuring the most effective medicines make it to market; and (ii) there was need for a clear understanding of the current state-of-play regarding national approaches and barriers/challenges to overcome.

C. Patient information

Finally, the WG on information to patients advised the Forum on ways to improve the quality of, and access to, information on authorized medicines and related health areas. So far, this is the only WG in which certain stakeholders have distanced themselves from the results.[74] A key aim for the research-based industry is to reform the

---

[73] Case C-229/00, *Commission* v. *Finland* [2003] ECR 1–5727.

[74] See the Joint ESIP and AIM Position Statement on Information to Patients on Diseases and Treatment Options, attached to Annex B of the Second Progress

existing legal framework, which is claimed to be anachronistic and no longer a reflection of the demands of the 'empowered patient'. Again, self-regulation is the preferred way forward.

The majority of the members of the WG, however, agreed upon core quality principles, as well as a toolbox of good practice to help patients evaluate information. Data sharing and a European database for patient information is also under discussion, as is a form of model information package produced by a 'public–private partnership' – that is, industry, patients, carers, health professionals and the relevant national authorities. Different regulation techniques to validate, ex ante, an agreed common core set of information are also being explored, including an ex ante validation system, which could provide a system for national authorities to assess and validate information provided to patients on diseases and treatment options prior to its provision to the general public, and co-regulation mechanisms, which would include a review process that would be built on ex post controls, including sanctions and self-regulation, according to agreed codes of practice.

The WG's final recommendations thus focused on: (i) ensuring better availability of and access to information for patients and citizens more generally; (ii) better quality of information including that all stakeholders achieve consensus over core principles of good information (it also recommended that the ban on the direct to consumer advertising of medicines remain in place); and (iii) participation and involvement of all relevant stakeholders towards generating the best and most up-to-date information possible.

***

Much of the work streams of the working groups seems to point in the direction of the promotion of shared general or core principles and shared information, but there is also more than a hint of a suggestion that the Commission itself could play a key role in building up and managing European-wide databases[75] on pricing, relative effectiveness

---

Report of 26 June 2007, http://ec.europa.eu/enterprise/phabiocom/docs/pf_20070626_esip_aim_joint_statement.pdf.

[75] A first step in this direction was in fact made in late 2006 with the launch of the European database – www.eudrapharm.eu – which currently contains information, in English, on centrally authorized medicines. Later phases will add the information in all the other official languages, together with improved search functions. The aim is to include information on all authorized medicines in the EU.

and perhaps on patient information, eventually taking on a policing role to ensure the quality and reliability of the data it will be called on to acquire and manage. This last topic has also resurfaced in the context of the report on current practice with regard to provision of information to patients on medicinal products, which the Commission is required to produce on the basis of Article 88(a) of Directive 2001/83/EC.[76] On the basis of its recent consultation exercise, the Commission has announced that it intends to propose to the European Parliament and the Council a series of amendments to Directive 2001/83/EC. The Commission indicated the policy objectives that will be pursued by its intended proposals – namely, that, while the ban on direct-to-consumer advertising of prescription products will be maintained, a framework will be introduced to ensure access by patients to objective non-promotional information about the benefits and risks of medicines. This, in turn, requires the introduction of measures to ensure a clear distinction between promotional and non-promotional information and on the roles of different players in providing that information.[77] In a follow-up public consultation document on its legal proposal on information to patients, the Commission proposes to place continued emphasis on co-regulation – that is, the involvement of public authorities and a mix of stakeholders including health care professionals, patient organizations and the pharmaceutical industry. These co-regulatory bodies would be responsible for adopting a code of conduct on information to patients and monitoring and following up all information activities by the industry.[78]

Irrespective of the eventual legal form that these and the other measures discussed here are likely to take, it may be observed that progress on building up the requisite 'toolbox' for assessing relative effectiveness, and informing patients on this type of issue, will surely take European policy (and perhaps regulation) in the direction of encouraging (or compelling) national authorities to examine and compare therapeutic effectiveness, at least in the context of their pricing and

---

[76] Directive 2001/83/EC, above n.26.
[77] See, further, European Commission, 'Report on current practice with regard to provision of information to patients on medicinal products', COM (2007) 862 final, 20 December 2007.
[78] The consultation document is available at http://ec.europa.eu/enterprise/pharmaceuticals/pharmacos/docs/doc2008/2008_02/info_to_patients_consult_200802.pdf.

reimbursement management schemes.[79] Attempts to include a 'needs' criterion or a comparative efficacy criterion for marketing authorization in the early days of European harmonization met with considerable resistance, not least from the industry, and were abandoned.[80]

7. Conclusion

The organization of the demand side of the market for medicinal products – the 'market pathway' – has always been the preserve of Member States. Subject to the very limited procedural constraints imposed by the Price Transparency Directive of 1989, they may opt for the system of price or profit control that suits their own policy needs best. Diversity of approach is a fact of life in the twenty-seven EU Member States, and it is unlikely that we will see any attempts to introduce Union-wide harmonizing legislation on price control in the near future. However, increasingly, national price and profit control regimes aim not only to deliver lower prices for patients, but also value for money. Value-based pricing, as the recent Office of Fair Trading report in the United Kingdom has stressed, could lead to a more effective use of health budgets, not only keeping prices down but also releasing funds that could be used to give patients better access to medicines and other treatment, which they may currently be denied. Over time, value-based pricing would also give companies stronger incentives to invest in drugs for those medicinal conditions where there is greatest patient need. Options to introduce ex post value-based pricing or ex ante value-based pricing (probably in addition to ex post controls) are under consideration in the United Kingdom and are being debated at the EU Pharmaceutical Forum.

It is unlikely that these types of principles will be incorporated in binding legislation: guidelines and self-regulatory instruments offer more scope for flexibility and for balancing European and national interests. A pan-European approach to relative effectiveness is likely to be resisted on the grounds that any assessment remains intrinsically linked to national specificities and priorities. Inevitably, however, the options considered within the Forum and its WGs will put greater

[79] See n. 66.
[80] See Hancher, *Regulating for competition*, above n.15, Chapter 4.

emphasis not just on comparing therapeutic efficacy and value of different types of products, but on setting up new pathways, mechanisms and even institutions for coordinating and comparing experiences between, and facilitating inter-exchangeability across, the national levels.

Such developments could result in a new role for the European institutions – and, in particular, the Commission – which may not only be facilitative, in the sense of providing the necessary data to enable such comparisons, but also even prescriptive if it becomes involved in policing the accuracy and reliability of this type of data. Follow up pressure from various stakeholders in the Pharmaceutical Forum's WGs could also lead to extension of the procedural requirements of the Price Transparency Directive – the only legal regulatory instrument that regulates the market pathway – to new areas such as REAs. The scope of the Directive could be extended to impose more exacting standards on the compilation of value assessments, as well as for the regulatory timetables involved.

More importantly, spillover effects into the supply side, the regulatory pathway and into the myriad of regulations that govern marketing authorizations, data exclusivity and SPaCs cannot be ruled out if comparative therapeutic data also could be used in decisions by European as well as national authorities in making these regulatory decisions. As we have seen, data generated in this 'regulatory pathway' are subject to a considerable amount of protection, and to the benefit of the research-based industry. This chapter has also indicated that, here too, balances have been struck between the competing objectives of rewarding innovation and promoting generic competition and parallel trade. In the future, new balances may have to be struck – for example, patent and other IPR protection could be prolonged in exchange for better, safer and more affordable innovation.[81]

However, the further streamlining of legislation governing the regulatory pathway no longer appears to be the main method of balancing the competing interests and objectives that have traditionally characterized policy in the sector. The *AstraZeneca* case, and the launching of the sector-wide inquiry, which was discussed in detail in this chapter, makes it clear that not only legislation but also the application of

---

[81] See S. Garattini and V. Bertele, 'How can we regulate medicines better?', *British Medical Journal* 335 (2007), 803–5.

competition law can be used to strike a balance between competing interests in the regulatory pathway. It will be interesting to see if, and to what extent, similar demands for European-wide protection will be called for by the innovative industry if it is under pressure to produce comparative efficacy data for national price control and reimbursement agencies. The pressure is surely likely to rise as coordination of data sharing and evaluation techniques across the Member States becomes more streamlined. Here, again, the regulatory and market pathways may well begin to intersect, offering, perhaps indirectly, greater potential, after all, for a European-wide, substantive approach to price and profit control.

As has also been argued in this chapter, decentralization of competition law enforcement is also an important new development affecting the industry, but decentralization does not necessarily imply isolated national action: on the contrary, here, too, the Commission – and Commission policy – is very much a driving factor. Nevertheless, as national courts and authorities are required to engage in complex economic and market analysis when applying competition law principles in this market, the Commission's preferred formalistic approach to protecting parallel imports and intra-brand competition is certainly under challenge at the national as well as European levels. The recent application of competition law principles to prevent abuse of regulatory practices may prove to be an interesting ex post complement to ex ante balancing exercises in the regulatory pathway. Irrespective of which pathway will prove the most effective route to dealing with market fragmentation, it is unlikely that the delicate balancing act that lies at the basis of European pharmaceutical policy and all of its legal manifestations is likely to become more complex.

Bibliography

1. Literature

Abraham, J. and Lewis, G., *Regulating medicines in Europe: competition, expertise, and public health* (London: Routledge, 2000).

Adams, H. and Nys, H., 'Comparative Reflections on the Belgian Euthanasia Act 2002', *Medical Law Review* 11 (2003), 353–76.

Alber J., 'The European Social Model and the United States', *European Union Politics* 7 (2006), 393–419.

Albreht T., Brinovec, R.P. and Štalc, J., 'Cross-border care in the south: Slovenia, Austria and Italy', in Rosenmöller, M., McKee, M. and Baeten, R. (eds.), *Patient mobility in the European Union: learning from experience* (Copenhagen: WHO Regional Office for Europe on behalf of the European Observatory on Health Systems and Policies, 2006).

Albreht, T., Cesen, M., Hindle, D., Jakubowski, E., Kramberger, B., Petric, V.K., Premik, M. and Toth, M., *Health care systems in transition: Slovenia* (Copenhagen: WHO Regional Office for Europe on behalf of the European Observatory on Health Systems and Policies, 2002).

Aleksandrova, S., 'The Bulgarian health care reform and Health Care Act 2004', *Medicine and Law* 26 (2007), 1–14.

Alston, P., 'Assessing the strengths and weaknesses of the European Social Charter's advisory system', in de Búrca, G. and de Witte, B. (eds.), *Social rights in Europe* (Oxford: Oxford University Press, 2005).

Altenstetter, C., 'Health care in the European Community', in Hermans, G., Casparie, A.F. and Paelinck, J.H., (eds.), *Health care in Europe after 1992* (Leiden: Dartmouth, 1992).

Alter, K.J., *Establishing the supremacy of European law: the making of an international rule of law in Europe* (Oxford: Oxford University Press, 2001).

Amato-Gauci, A. and Ammon, A., 'Annual epidemiological report on communicable diseases in Europe', Report on the status of communicable diseases in the EU and EEA/EFTA countries, ECDC (2007).

Andoulsi, I., Herveg, J., Stroetmann, V., Stroetmann, K., Dobrev, A., Van Doosselaere, C. and Wilson, P., 'Bottlenecks and challenges and RTD responses for legal, ethical, social and economic aspects of health-grids', Roadmap I (2008).

Arai-Takahashi, Y., *The margin of appreciation doctrine and the principle of proportionality* (New York: Intersentia, 2002).

Armstrong, K.A., 'Mutual recognition', in Barnard, C. and Scott, J. (eds.), *The legal foundations of the single European market* (Oxford: Hart, 2002).

Arrowsmith, S., *The law of public and utilities procurement* (London: Sweet and Maxwell, 2005).

ASPECT Consortium, 'Tobacco or health in the European Union: past, present and future', The ASPECT Report (2004).

Bach, S., 'International Mobility of Health Professionals: Brain Drain or Brain Exchange?', WIDER Research Paper No 2006/82 (2006), UNU-World Institute for Development Economics Research.

Bache, I. and George, S., *Politics in the European Union* (Oxford: Oxford University Press, 2006).

Bache, I. and Jordan, A., 'Britain in Europe and Europe in Britain', in Bache, I. and Jordan, A. (eds.), *The Europeanization of British politics* (Basingstoke: Palgrave Macmillan, 2008).

Bachinger, E. and McKee, M., 'Tobacco policies in Austria during the Third Reich', *International Journal of Tuberculosis and Lung Disease* **11** (2007), 1033–7.

Baeten, R., 'Health care on the European political agenda', in Degryse, C. and Pochet, P., (eds.), *Social developments in the European Union 2002* (Brussels: ETUI, Observatoire social européen, Saltsa, 2003).

'Health care: after the court, the policy-makers get down to work', in Degryse, C. and Pochet, P. (eds.), *Social developments in the European Union 2004* (Brussels: ETUI-REHS, Observatoire social européen, Saltsa, 2005).

Baeten R., 'The potential impact of the services directive on healthcare services', in Nihoul, P. and Simon, A.-C. (eds.), *L'Europe et les soins de santé* (Brussels: De Boeck/Larcier, 2005).

Baeten, R., 'Health and social services in the internal market', in Degryse, C. and Pochet, P. (eds.), *Social developments in the European Union 2006* (Brussels: ETUI-REHS, Observatoire social européen, Saltsa, 2007).

Baeten, R. and Jorens, Y., 'The impact of EU law and policy', in Dubois, C-A., McKee, M. and Nolte, E. (eds.), *Human resources for health in Europe* (Maidenhead: Open University Press, 2006).

Baeyens, A., 'Implementation of the Clinical Trials Directive: Pitfalls and Benefits', *European Journal of Health Law* **8** (2001), 293.

Baker, S. and Wu, L., 'Applying the market definition guidelines of the EC Commission', *European Competition Law Review* **19** (1998), 273–81.

Bala, M. M. and Lesniak, W. M., 'Poland is losing its doctors', *British Medical Journal* **331** (2005), 235.

Ballet, J., 'The Belgian Supreme Court held that obligatory opening and closing hours for pharmacists violate the Competition Act', *Concurrences*, January 2008, www.concurrences.com/abstract_bulletin_web.php3?id_article=15370.

Barani, L., 'Hard and soft law in the European Union: the case of social policy and the open method of coordination', *The Constitutionalism Web-Papers* (2006).

Barnard, C., 'EU citizenship and the principle of solidarity', in Spavanta, E. and Dougan, M., (eds.), *Social welfare and EU law* (Oxford: Hart, 2005).

EC employment law (Oxford: Oxford University Press, 2006).

Barnard, C., 'Solidarity and new governance in social policy', in de Búrca, G. and Scott, J. (eds.), *New governance and constitutionalism in Europe and the US* (Portland: Hart, 2006).

Barnard, C. and Deakin, S., 'Market access and regulatory competition', in Barnard, C. and Scott, J. (eds.), *The legal foundations of the single European market: unpacking the premises* (Oxford: Hart, 2002).

Barnes, D. E. and Bero, L. A., 'Industry-funded research and conflict of interest: an analysis of research sponsored by the tobacco industry through the Center for Indoor Air Research', *Journal of Health Politics, Policy and Law* **21** (1996), 515–42.

Barr, N., *The economics of the welfare state*, 3rd ed. (Oxford: Oxford University Press, 1998).

Bartosch, A., 'The relationship of public procurement and state aid surveillance – the toughest standard applies?', *Common Market Law Review* **35** (2002), 551–76.

Bates, C., Connolly, G. and Jarvis, M., *Tobacco additives: cigarette engineering and nicotine addiction* (London: Action on Smoking and Health, 1999).

Bergmann, H. and Röhling, F., 'The German Federal Cartel Office vetoes a merger of two public hospitals *(Greifswald University Hospital/Wolgast Hospital)*', *e-Competitions Law Bulletin* No. 12733 (2006).

Bernitz, U., 'Everyone's right to health care in Europe: the way forward', Paper prepared for the European Parliament Committee Meeting on Cross-Border Aspects of Health Services, 24 January 2007.

Beurden, A., 'The European perspective on e-health', in Callens, S. (ed.), *E-health and the law* (Den Haag: Kluwer, 2003).

Bevers, M., 'Rationale behind new strategy', British American Tobacco, Bates No. 325123195–325123196 (2000).

Beyleveld, D. and Brownsword, R., *Human dignity in bioethics and biolaw* (Oxford: Oxford University Press, 2001).

Biggs, H., *Euthanasia, death with dignity and the law* (Oxford: Hart, 2001).

Black, C., Maxwell, P., Marshall, M., Rees, M. and Dolphin, T., 'MTAS (UK Medical Training Application Service): which way now?' Interview by Rebecca Coombes', *British Medical Journal* 334 (2007), 1300.

Blanpain, N. and Pan Ké Shon, J.-L., 'L'assurance complémentaire maladie: une diffusion encore inégale', *INSEE Première* 523 (1997).

Bocognano, A., Couffinhal, A., Dumesnil, S. and Grignon, M., *Which coverage for whom? Equity of access to health insurance in France* (Paris: CREDES, 2000).

Boffetta, P., Agudo, A., Ahrens, W., Benhamou, E., Benhamou, S., Darby, S. C., Ferro, G., Fortes, C., Gonzalez, C. A., Jockel, K. H., Krauss, M., Kreienbrock, L., Kreuzer, M., Mendes, A., Merletti, F., Nyberg, F., Pershagen, G., Pohlabeln, H., Riboli, E., Schmid, G., Simonato, L., Tredaniel, J., Whitley, E., Wichmann, H. E., Winck, C., Zambon, P. and Saracci, R., 'Multicenter case-control study of exposure to environmental tobacco smoke and lung cancer in Europe', *Journal of National Cancer Institute* 90 (1998), 1440–50.

Boffin N. and Baeten, R., *Dutch patients evaluate contracted care in Belgian hospitals: results of a mail survey* (Brussels: Observatoire social européen, 2005).

Boillat, S. and Callens, S., 'The sale of medicinal products by mail-order in Europe', *Yearbook of European Medical Law* (2005), 57–62.

Bolkestein, F., 'Letter from the European Commission to the Dutch Minister of Health, Welfare and Sport', Ministry of Health, Welfare and Sport, 25 November 2003.

Borrás, S. and Greve, B., 'Concluding remarks: new method or just cheap talk?', *Journal of European Public Policy* 11 (2004), 329–36.

Börzel, T. and Risse, T., 'When Europe hits home. Europeanization and domestic change', *European Integration Online Papers* 4 (2000), http://eiop.or.at/eiop/texte/2000–015a.htm.

Bovenberg, J. A., *Property rights in blood, genes and data. Naturally yours?* (Leiden: Martinus Nijhoff, 2006).

Bovens, M., 'New forms of accountability and EU governance', *Comparative European Politics* 5 (2007), 104–20.

Bovis, C., 'The regulation of public procurement as a key element of European economic law', *European Law Journal* 4 (1998), 220–42.

'Recent case law relating to public procurement: a beacon for the integration of public markets', *Common Market Law Review* 39 (2002), 1025–56.

'Financing services of general interest in the EU: how do public procurement and state aids interact to demarcate between market forces and protection?', *European Law Journal* 11 (2005), 79–109.

EC *public procurement: case law and regulation* (Oxford: Oxford University Press, 2006).

'Developing public procurement regulation: jurisprudence and its influence on law making', *Common Market Law Review* 43 (2006), 461–495.

Bowis, J., 'European Parliament report on patient mobility and health-care developments in the European Union', A6–0129/2005, 29 April 2005.

Boyle, P., d'Onofrio, A., Maisonneuve, P., Severi, G., Robertson, C., Tubiana, M. and Veronesi, U., 'Measuring progress against cancer in Europe: has the 15% decline targeted for 2000 come about?', *Annals of Oncology* 14 (2003), 1312–25.

Boyle, S., 'What foundation trusts mean for the NHS', A report for the Overview and Scrutiny Committee of the Royal Borough of Kensington and Chelsea, January 2004, www.rbkc.gov.uk/howwegovern/your-council/oscreport_foundationtrusts.pdf.

Brennan, T.A., Horwitz, R.I., Duffy, F.D., Cassel, C.K., Goode, L.D. and Lipner R.S., 'The role of physician specialty board certification status in the quality movement', *Journal of the American Medical Association* 292 (2004), 1038–43.

Breuil-Genier, P., 'Généraliste puis spécialiste: un parcours peu fréquent', *INSEE Première* 709 (2000).

Brillat, R., 'The supervisory machinery of the ESC: recent developments and their impact', in de Búrca, G. and de Witte, B. (eds.), *Social rights in Europe* (Oxford: Oxford University Press, 2005).

Buonanno, L., Zablotney, S. and Keefer, R., 'Politics versus science in the making of a new regulatory regime for food in Europe', *European Integration Online Papers* 5 (2001).

BUPA Ireland, *Risk equalisation* (Dublin: BUPA Ireland, 2003).

Busse, R. and van Ginneken, E., 'Access to healthcare services within and between countries of the European Union', in Wismar, M., Palm, W., Figueras, J., Ernst, K. and van Ginneken, E. (eds.), *Cross-border healthcare: mapping and analysing health systems diversity* (Copenhagen: WHO Regional Office for Europe on behalf of the European Observatory on Health Systems and Policies, forthcoming 2009).

'Cross-border healthcare data', in Wismar, M., Palm, W., Figueras, J., Ernst, K. and van Ginneken, E. (eds.), *Cross-border healthcare: mapping and analysing health systems diversity* (Copenhagen: WHO

Regional Office for Europe on behalf of the European Observatory on Health Systems and Policies, 2009).

Cabral, P., 'The internal market and the right to cross-border medical care', *European Law Review* (2004), 673–85.

Cachia, J. M., 'Cross-border care: provision of highly specialized hospital services to island populations – a case study of the Maltese Islands', Ministry of Health (2004).

Cadreau, M., 'An economic analysis of the impacts of the health systems of the European single market', in Kyriopoulos, J., Sissouras, A. and Philalithes, J. (eds.), *Health systems and the challenge of Europe after 1992* (Athens: Lambrakis Press, 1991).

Caduff, L. and Bernauer, T., 'Managing risk and regulation in European food safety governance', *Review of Policy Research* **23** (2006), 153–67.

Caixeiro, I., 'UEMO: lobbying letter from the Working Group on Specialist Training', *PrimaryCare* **8** (2008), 15–6.

Callens, S., 'International tele-medicine and the law', *Proceedings of the 13th World Congress on Medical Law*, Vol. 1 (Helsinki: World Congress on Medical Law, 2000).

'Tele-medicine and E-Commerce Directive', *European Journal of Health Law* **9** (2002), 93–109.

'Tele-medicine and European law', *Telehealth Law* **2** (2002), 34–40.

Campbell, C. and Spencer, S. A., 'The implications of the Working Time Directive: how can paediatrics survive?', *Archives of Disease in Child* **92** (2007), 573–5.

Carlson, S., 'World Congress of Smokers Rights Groups (SRGs)', Philip Morris, Bates No. 2500041706–9 (1982).

Carvel, J., 'Doctors from outside EU barred from consultant training', *The Guardian*, 7 February 2008.

Centre for European Policy Studies, 'Making antitrust damages actions more effective in the EU: welfare impact and potential scenarios', Report for the European Commission (2008), http://ec.europa.eu/comm/competition/antitrust/actionsdamages/files_white_paper/impact_study.pdf.

Chalmers, D., Hadjiemmanuil, C., Monti G. and Tomkins, A., *European Union law* (Cambridge: Cambridge University Press, 2006).

Chapman, S., 'The future of smoke-free legislation', *British Medical Journal* **335** (2007), 521–2.

Chavrier, G., 'Etablissement public de santé, logique économique et droit de la concurrence', *Revue de Droit Sanitaire et Social* **2** (2006), 274–87.

Chérot, J. Y., 'Financement des obligations de service public et aides d'état', Revue Europe (2005), 5.

Chiti, E., 'The emergence of a Community administration: the case of European agencies', *Common Market Law Review* 37 (2000), 309–43.

Choudhry, N. K., Fletcher, R. H. and Soumerai, S. B., 'Systematic review: the relationship between clinical experience and quality of health care', *Annals of Internal Medicine* 142 (2005), 260–73.

Christensen, T. and Lægreid, P., 'Regulatory agencies – the challenge of balancing agency autonomy and political control', *Governance: An International Journal of Policy, Administration and Institutions* 20 (2007), 499–520.

Cienski, J., 'Polish health services quick to cash in on eager EU patients', *Financial Times*, 20 June 2005.

Clark, E., Hughes, M. and Wirth, D., 'Study on the conditions of claims for damages in case of infringement of EC competition rules – analysis of economic models for the calculation of damages', Ashurst Report for the European Commission (2004), http://ec.europa.eu/competition/antitrust/actionsdamages/economic_clean_en.pdf.

Clergeau, C., 'European food safety policies: between a single market and a political crisis', in Steffen, M. (ed.), *Health governance in Europe: issues, challenges and theories* (London: Routledge, 2005).

Cohen, D., 'EU residents may be able to travel to any member state for care from 2010', *British Medical Journal* 355 (2007).

Cohen, J. E., Milio, N., Rozier, R. G., Ferrence, R., Ashley, M. J. and Goldstein, A. O., 'Political ideology and tobacco control', *Tobacco Control* 9 (2000), 263–7.

Cohen, P., 'The separation of purchaser from provider in health care systems and European Community law: the case of the British National Health Service', LSE Discussion Paper No.1 (1994).

Cojean, A., 'Tourisme dentaire en Hongrie: beaux sourires de ... Budapest!', *Le Monde*, 20 August 2005.

Colin, C. and Maisonneuve, H., 'Misleading information on environmental tobacco smoke in the French lay press', *International Journal of Epidemiology* 26 (1997), 240–1.

Collignon, S., Dehousse, R., Gabolde, J., Jouen, M., Pochet, P., Salais, R., Sprenger, R. and Zsolt de Sousa, H., 'The Lisbon strategy and the open method of co-ordination. 12 Recommendations for an effective multi-level strategy', Notre Europe Policy Paper No. 12 (2005).

Conant, L., 'Individuals, courts, and the development of European social rights', *Comparative Political Studies* 39 (2006), 76–100.

Cooper, Z. and Le Grand, J., 'Choice, competition and the political left', *Eurohealth* 13 (2008), 18–20.

Cornelissen, R., 'The principle of territoriality and the Community regulations on social security', *Common Market Law Review* 3 (1996), 439–471.

Coucheir, M. and Jorens, Y., 'Patient mobility in the European Union – the European Framework in relation to patient mobility', Report written for the European 6th Framework project 'Europe for Patients'', European Commission, DG Research (2007).

Craig, P., 'The nature of the Community: integration, democracy and legitimacy', in Craig, P. and de Búrca, G. (eds.), *The evolution of EU law* (Oxford: Oxford University Press, 1999).

Craig, P. and de Búrca, G., *EU law* (Oxford: Oxford University Press, 2007).

Craig, P. and Harlow, C. (eds.), *Lawmaking in the European Union* (Deventer: Kluwer, 1998).

Crolla, D. A., 'Health care without walls: responding to telehealth's emerging legal issues', *Health Law in Canada* 19 (1998), 1–19.

Crombez, C., 'The democratic deficit in the European Union: much ado about nothing?', *European Union Politics* 4 (2003), 101–20.

Curwen, P., 'Social policy in the European Community in light of the Maastricht Treaty', *European Business Journal* 4 (1992), 17–26.

Daintith, T., 'The techniques of government', in Oliver, D. and Jowell, J. L. (eds.), *The changing constitution* (Oxford: Clarendon Press, 1994).

Davey Smith, G. and Phillips, A. N., 'Passive smoking and health: should we believe Philip Morris's "experts"?', *British Medical Journal* 313 (1996), 929–33.

Davies, A. C. L., *Accountability: a public law analysis of government by contract* (Oxford: Oxford University Press, 2001).

Davies, G., 'Welfare as a service', *Legal Issues of European Integration* (2002), 27–40.

'The process and side-effects of harmonisation of European welfare states', Jean Monnet Working Paper No. 02/06 (2006), 1–64.

Dawes, A., 'Bonjour Herr Doctor: national healthcare systems, the internal market and cross-border medical care within the EU', *Legal Issues of European Integration* (2006), 167–82.

de Búrca, G., 'Towards European welfare?', in de Búrca, G., (ed.), *EU law and the welfare state: in search of solidarity* (Oxford: Oxford University Press, 2005).

de Búrca, G. and Scott, J., 'Introduction: new governance, law and constitutionalism', in de Búrca, G. and Scott, J., (eds.), *Law and new governance in the EU and US* (Oxford: Hart, 2006).

De Haan, J., 'The new Dutch law on euthanasia', *Medical Law Review* 10 (2002), 57.

de la Porte, C. and Pochet, P., 'Supple co-ordination at EU level and key actor's involvement', in de la Porte, C. and Pochet, P. (eds.), *Building social Europe through the open method of co-ordination* (Brussels: PIE-Peter Lang, 2002).

De Ruiter, R., 'To prevent a shift of competences? Developing the open method of coordination: education, research and development, social inclusion and e-Europe', PhD Thesis, European University Institute (2007).

De Schutter, O., 'Fundamental rights and the transformation of governance in the European Union', Reflexive Governance in the Public Interest, Working Paper REFGOV-FR-13 (2007).

De Souza, N., 'Competition in pharmaceuticals: the challenges ahead post AstraZeneca', European Commission, *Competition Policy Newsletter* No. 1 (2007), 39–43.

de Vries, S.A., 'Patiëntenzorg in Europa na Watts: Wiens zorg?', *SEW – Tijdschrift voor Europees en Economisch Recht* 55 (2007), 132–40.

Dearlove, J.V., Bialous, S.A. and Glantz, S.A., 'Tobacco industry manipulation of the hospitality industry to maintain smoking in public places', *Tobacco Control* 11 (2002), 94–104.

Dehousse, R., 'Integration v regulation? On the dynamics of regulation in the European Community', *Journal of Common Market Studies* 30 (1992), 383–402.

'Constitutional reform in the European Community: are there alternatives to the majoritarian avenue?', *West European Politics* 18 (1995), 118–36.

'Regulation by networks in the European Community: the role of European agencies', *Journal of European Public Policy* 4 (1997), 246–61.

'Integration through law revisited: some thoughts on the juridification of the European political process', in Snyder, F. (ed.), *The Europeanisation of law; the legal effects of European integration* (Oxford: Hart, 2000).

Dehousse, R. (ed.), *L'Europe sans Bruxelles? Une analyse de la méthode ouverte de coordination* (Paris: L'Harmattan, 2004).

Dehousse, R., 'Delegation of powers in the European Union: the need for a multi-principals model', Draft Discussion Paper Connex 2–3, Centre d'études européennes de Sciences Po, 12 November 2006.

den Exter, A., 'Blending private and social health insurance in the Netherlands: challenges posed by the EU', in Flood, C.M., Roach, K. and Sossin, L. (eds.), *Access to care, access to justice: the legal debate over private health insurance in Canada* (Toronto: University of Toronto Press, 2005).

Department of Health, and Children, 'Private health insurance', White Paper, Department of Health and Children (1999).

'Submission to the European Commission's study on voluntary health insurance in the European Union', Department of Health and Children (2001).

'Tánaiste announces increase in means test for GP Visit Card', Department of Health and Children, 26 June 2006.

Department of Health, and Children, 'Government approves reform measures for Private Health Insurance market', Department of Health and Children, 25 April 2007.

Dethier, J.-J. and Shapiro, T., 'Constitutional rights and the reform of social entitlements', in Bokros, L. and Dethier, J.-J. (eds.), *Public finance reform during the transition. The experience of Hungary* (Washington, DC: World Bank, 1988).

DG SANCO, 'Summary of the comments received on the consultation paper on the advisability and feasibility of establishing fees for EFSA', August 2007, http://ec.europa.eu/food/consultations/sum_cons_Efsa_fees_En.pdf.

Diethelm, P. A., Rielle, J. C. and McKee, M., 'The whole truth and nothing but the truth? The research that Philip Morris did not want you to see', *Lancet* 366 (2005), 86–92.

Dineson, T. V., 'Interim report on the Hen-Ry promotion campaign', Philip Morris, Bates No. 2023270359–60 (1989).

Donaldson, C., Gerard, K. and Jan, S. (eds.), *Economics of health care financing: the visible hand* (London: Macmillan Press, 2003).

Donaldson, L., *Good doctors, safer patients: proposals to strengthen the system to assure and improve the performance of doctors and to protect the safety of patients* (London: Department of Health, 2006).

Donovan, K. O., 'Taking a neutral stance on the legal protection of the fetus', *Medical Law Review* 14 (2006), 115–23.

Douglas, N. J., 'Sleep, performance and the European Working Time Directive', *Clinical Medicine* 5 (2005), 95–6.

Doyle, L., 'Brussels stubs out cash for anti-smoking group', *The Guardian*, 10 October 1996.

Dubois, C.-A., McKee, M. and Nolte, E., *Human resources for health in Europe* (Maidenhead: Open University Press, 2006).

du Marais, B. and Sakon, A., 'According to the French State Council, the tariff that public hospitals levy on private activities of medical doctors employed as civil servants can partly be related to a market price', *Concurrences* (2007), 148–50.

Duncan, B., 'Health policy in the European Union: how it's made and how to influence it', *British Medical Journal* 324 (2002), 1027–30.

Durand-Zaleski, I., *The health system in France* (New York: The Commonwealth Fund, 2008).

Dux, L., 'Working time of Hungarian doctors one year after 2004', *Transition Studies Review* 13 (2006), 23–5.

Eberlein, B., 'Formal and informal governance in single market regulation', in Christiansen, T. and Piattoni, S. (eds.), *Informal governance in the European Union* (Cheltenham: Edward Elgar, 2004).

Eberlein, B. and Grande, E., 'Beyond delegation: trans-national regulatory regimes and the EU regulatory state', *Journal of European Public Policy* 12 (2005), 89–112.

Eberlein, B. and Kerwer, D., 'Theorising the new modes of European Union governance', *European Integration Online Papers* 6 (2003), http://eiop.or.at/eiop/texte/2002–005a.htm.

'New governance in the European Union: a theoretical perspective', *Journal of Common Market Studies* 42 (2004), 121–42.

Ecorys Nederland BV, 'Study of regulatory restrictions in the field of pharmacies', Report commissioned by the European Commission, DG Internal Market and Services, 22 June 2007, http://ec.europa.eu/internal_market/services/docs/pharmacy/report_En.pdf.

El Amin, A., 'EU's food agency battles attempts to hijack science', *Food Quality News*, 21 September 2006, www.foodqualitynews.com/Legislation/EU-s-food-agency-battles-attempts-to-hijack-science.

Erhel, C., Mandin, L. and Palier, B., 'The leverage effect. The open method of co-ordination in France', in Zeitlin, J. and Pochet, P. (eds.) (with Magnusson, L.), *The open method of co-ordination in action: the European employment and social inclusion strategies* (Brussels: PIE-Peter Lang, 2005).

Esping-Anderson, G., *The three worlds of welfare capitalism* (London: Polity Press, 1989).

European Commission, 'Liberalisation of insurance in the single market: update and questions', *Single Market News* 11 (1998), 1–8.

'Commission scrutinises Belgian law on supplementary health insurance provided by private sickness funds', Press Release No. IP/06/1781, 13 December 2006.

European Commission, 'Insurance: Commission scrutinises exemption of Irish Voluntary Health Insurance Board from EU rules', Press Release No. IP/07/87, 24 January 2007.

Everson, M., Majone, G., Metcalfe, L. and Schout, A., 'The role of specialised agencies in decentralising EU governance', Report presented to the Commission (2000), http://ec.europa.eu/governance/areas/group6/contribution_en.pdf.

Faber, J.-C., 'The European Blood Directive: a new era of blood regulation has begun', *Transfusion Medicine* **14** (2004), 257–73.

Faculty of Public Health, *A CAP on health: the impact of the EU Common Agricultural Policy on public health* (London: Faculty of Public Health, 2007).

Fallsberg, L., 'Patients' rights in Europe', *European Journal of Health Law* **10** (2003), 5.

Farrell, A.-M., 'The emergence of EU governance in public health: the case of blood policy and regulation', in Steffen, M. (ed.), *Health governance in Europe* (London: Routledge, 2005).

Fenton, R. A., 'Catholic doctrine versus women's rights: the new Italian law on assisted reproduction', *Medical Law Review* **14** (2006), 73–107.

Ferrera, M., 'European integration and national social citizenship: changing boundaries, new structuring?', *Comparative Political Studies* **33** (2003), 611–52.

'Towards an 'open' social citizenship?' The new boundaries of welfare in the European Union', in de Búrca, G., (ed.), *EU law and the welfare state: in search of solidarity* (Oxford: Oxford University Press, 2005).

The boundaries of welfare: European integration and the new spatial politics of social protection (Oxford: Oxford University Press, 2005).

Ferrera, M. and Gualmini, E., *Rescued by Europe? Social and labour market reforms in Italy from Maastricht to Berlusconi* (Amsterdam: Amsterdam University Press, 2004).

Ferriman, A., 'Vilified for attacking tobacco', *British Medical Journal* **320** (2000), 1482.

Fessenko, D., 'The Bulgarian NCA clears state aid in the form of compensation for public transportation services under national state aid rules *(Elena Avtotransport)*', *e-Competitions Law Bulletin* No. 13146 (2007).

Fidler, A. H., Haslinger, R. R., Hofmarcher, M. M., Jesse, M. and Palu, T., 'Incorporation of public hospitals: a "silver bullet" against overcapacity, managerial bottlenecks and resource constraints? Case studies from Austria and Estonia', *Health Policy* **81** (2007), 328–38.

Figueras, J., Saltman, R. and Sakellarides, C. (eds.), *Critical challenges for health care reform* (Buckingham: Open University Press, 1998).

Follesdahl, A. and Hix, S., 'Why there is a democratic deficit in the EU: a response to Majone and Moravcsik', European Governance Papers (EUROGOV) No. C-05–02 (2005), https://www.connex-network. org/eurogov/pdf/egp-connex-C-05–02.pdf.

France, G., 'Cross-border flows of Italian patients within the European Union', *European Journal of Public Health* **7** (1997), Supp: 18–25.

Frank, S., *A new model for European medical device regulation – a comparative legal analysis in the EU and the USA* (Groningen: Europa Law, 2003).

Fredman, S., 'Transformation or dilution: fundamental rights in the EU social space', *European Law Journal* 12 (2006), 41–60.

Friends of the Earth Europe, 'Throwing caution to the wind – a review of the European Food Safety Authority and its work on genetically modified foods and crops', November 2007.

Frost, R. G., 'Efterbehandling af brystkraeftpatienter i Flensborg af borgere fra Soenderjyllands Amt', Soenderjyllands Amt (2000).

Gabara, I. I., 'Why the EU's tobacco policy is up in smoke', *Wall Street Journal Europe*, 10 October 1996.

Gambardella, A., Orsenigo, L. and Pammolli, F., 'Global competitiveness in pharmaceuticals – a European perspective', Report prepared for DG Industry, November 2000, http:///ec.europa.eu/enterprise/library/enterprise-papers/pdf/enterprise_paper_01_2001.pdf.

Ganslandt, M. and Maskus, K. E., 'Parallel imports and the pricing of pharmaceutical products: evidence from the European Union', Working Paper No.622, Swedish Research Institute of Industrial Economics (2004).

Garattini, S. and Bertele, V., 'Adjusting Europe's drug regulation to public health needs', *Lancet* 358 (2001), 64–7.
'How can we regulate medicines better?', *British Medical Journal* 335 (2007), 803–5.

Garcia-Perez, M. A., Amaya, C. and Otero, A., 'Physicians' migration in Europe: an overview of the current situation', *BioMed Central Health Services Research* 7 (2007), 201.

Garran, R., 'Setback for RYO: EU tobacco tax harmonisation', *Tobacco International* (1995), 43–5.

Geradin, D. and Petit, N., 'The development of agencies at EU and national levels: conceptual analysis and proposals for reform', Jean Monnet Working Paper No. 01/04 (2004).

Geyer, R., *Exploring European social policy* (Cambridge: Polity Press, 2000).

Gibis, B., Koch, P. and Bultman, J., 'Shifting criteria for benefit decisions', in Saltman, R., Busse, R. and Figueras, J. (eds.), *Social health insurance systems in western Europe* (Maidenhead: Open University Press, 2004).

Giddens, A., Diamond, P. and Liddle, R. (eds.), *Global Europe, social Europe* (Cambridge: Polity, 2006).

Gilmore, A. and McKee, M., 'Tobacco policy in the European Union', in Feldman, E. A. and Bayer, R. (eds.), *Unfiltered: conflicts over tobacco policy and public health* (Cambridge, MA: Harvard University Press, 2004).

Gilmore, A., Österberg, E., Heloma, A., Zatonski, W., Delcheva, E. and McKee, M., 'Free trade versus the protection of health: the examples of alcohol and tobacco', in McKee, M., MacLehose, L. and Nolte, E. (eds.), *Health policy and European Union enlargement* (Maidenhead: Open University Press, 2004).

Giorello, M., 'Gestions in house, entreprises publiques et marchés publics: la CJCE au croisement des chemins du marché intérieur et des services d'intérêt économique général', *Revue du Droit de l'Union européenne* (2006), 23–50.

Glinos, I., 'Cross-border collaboration', in Wismar, R., Palm, W., Figueras, J., Ernst, K. and van Ginneken, E. (eds.), *Cross-border healthcare: mapping and analysing health systems diversity* (Copenhagen: WHO Regional Office for Europe on behalf of the European Observatory on Health Systems and Policies, 2009).

Glinos I. and Baeten, R., 'A literature review of cross-border patient mobility in the European Union', Brussels: Observatoire social européen, 2006.

Glinos, I., Baeten, R. and Boffin, N., 'Cross-border contracted care in Belgian hospitals', in Rosenmöller, M., McKee, M. and Baeten, R. (eds.), *Patient mobility in the European Union: learning from experience* (Copenhagen: WHO Regional Office for Europe on behalf of the European Observatory on Health Systems and Policies, 2006).

Glinos, I., Boffin, N. and Baeten, R., Cross-border care in Belgian Hospitals: an analysis of Belgian, Dutch and English stakeholder perspectives, Brussels: Observatoire social européen, 2005.

Goldsmith, Lord, 'A charter of rights, freedoms and principles', *Common Market Law Review* 38 (2001), 1201–16.

Gostin, L. O., *Public health law: power, duty, restraint* (Berkeley: University of California Press, 2000).

Graham Dukes, M. N., 'Priority medicines and the world', *Bulletin of the WHO* 83 (2005), 321–400.

Greer, S. L., 'Uninvited Europeanization: neofunctionalism and the EU in health policy', *Journal of European Public Policy* 13 (2006), 134–52.

'Choosing paths in European Union health policy: a political analysis of a critical juncture', *Journal of European Social Policy* 18 (2008), 219–31.

'Ever closer union: devolution, the European Union, and social citizenship rights', in Greer, S. L. (ed.), *Devolution and social citizenship rights in the United Kingdom* (Bristol: Policy Press, 2008).

'Power struggle: the politics and policy consequences of patient mobility in Europe', OSE Policy Paper No. 2 (2008).

The politics of European Union health policies (Buckingham, Open University Press, 2009).

Greer, S. L., da Fonseca, E. M. and Adolph, C., 'Mobilizing bias in Europe: lobbies, democracy, and EU health policymaking', *European Union Politics* 9 (2008), 403–33.

Gribnau, H., 'Soft law and taxation: the case of the Netherlands', *Legisprudence* 1 (2008), 291–326.

Groenendijk, K., 'Free movement of workers in Europe 2005', European Report, European Commission Employment, Social Affairs, and Equal Opportunities (2006).

Gruning, T. and Gilmore, A., 'Germany: tobacco industry still dictates policy', *Tobacco Control* 16 (2007), 2.

Gruning, T., Gilmore, A. B. and McKee, M., 'Tobacco industry influence on science and scientists in Germany', *American Journal of Public Health* 96 (2006), 20–32.

Gual, J., Hellwig, M., Perrot, A., Polo, M., Rey, P., Schmidt, K. and Stenbacka, R., 'An economic approach to Article 82', Report by the EAGCP, July 2005, http://ec.europa.eu/comm/competition/publications/studies/eagcp_july_21_05.pdf.

Gyselen, L. and Kyriazis, N., 'Article 86: the monopoly power measurement issue revisited', *European Law Review* 11 (1986), 134–48.

Haas, P. M., 'Introduction: epistemic communities and international policy coordination', *International Organization* 46 (1992), 1–35.

Hackshaw, K., Law, M. R. and Wald, N. J., 'The accumulated evidence on lung cancer and environmental tobacco smoke', *British Medical Journal* 315 (1997), 980–8.

Ham, C., *When politics and markets collide: reforming the English national health service* (Birmingham: Health Services Management Centre, 2007).

Ham, C. and Robert, G. (eds.), *Reasonable rationing: international experience of priority setting in health care* (Buckingham: Open University Press, 2003).

Hamel, M.-P. and Vanhercke, B., 'The OMC and domestic social policymaking in Belgium and France: window dressing, one-way impact, or reciprocal influence?', in Heidenreich, M. and Zeitlin, J. (eds.), *Changing European employment and welfare regimes: the influence of the open method of coordination on national labour market and social welfare reforms* (London: Routledge, 2009).

Hamilton, G. J., 'Private insurance for all in the Dutch health care system?', *European Journal of Health Law* 10 (2003), 53–61.

'A new private universal Dutch health insurance in the Netherlands', in den Exter, A. (ed.), *Competitive social health insurance yearbook 2004* (Rotterdam: Erasmus University Press, 2005).

Hancher, L., *Regulating for competition. Government, law, and the pharmaceutical industry in the United Kingdom and France* (Oxford: Clarendon Press, 1990).

'The European pharmaceutical market: problems of partial harmonisation', *European Law Review* 15 (1990), 9–33.

'Creating the internal market for pharmaceutical medicines – an Echternach jumping procession?', *Common Market Law Review* 28 (1991), 821–53.

'The pharmaceuticals market: competition and free movement actively seeking compromises', in McKee, M., Mossialos, E. and Baeten, R. (eds.), *The impact of EU law on health care systems* (Brussels: PIE-Peter Lang, 2002).

Hantrais, L., *Social policy in the European Union* (Basingstoke: Palgrave Macmillan, 2007).

Harris, D. S., 'Memo on public relations effort being conducted by Hen-Ry', Philip Morris, Bates No. 2023270361–2 (1989).

Hatton, C. and Kauranen, S. A., 'The Irish Competition Authority settles an alleged price-fixing dispute in the health sector relating to medical examination reports to life insurance companies', *e-Competitions Law Bulletin* No. 13967 (2007).

Hatzopoulos, V. G., *Le principe communautaire d'équivalence et de reconnaissance mutuelle dans la libre prestation de services* (Brussels: Bruylant, 1999).

Hatzopoulos, V. G., 'Do the rules on internal market affect national health care systems?', in McKee, M., Mossialos, E. and Baeten, R. (eds.), *The impact of EU law on health care systems* (Brussels: PIE-Peter Lang, 2002).

Hatzopoulos, V. G., 'Killing national health and insurance systems but healing patients? The European market for health care services after the judgments of the ECJ in *Vanbraekel* and *Peerbooms*', *Common Market Law Review* 39 (2002), 683–729.

'Health law and policy, the impact of the EU', in de Búrca, G., (ed.), *EU law and the welfare state: in search of solidarity* (Oxford: Oxford University Press, 2005).

'The ECJ case law on cross-border aspects of the health services', DG Internal Policies of the Union Briefing Note, IP/A/IMCO/FWC/2006–167/C3/SC1, January 2007, www.europarl.europa.eu/comparl/imco/studies/0701_healthserv_ecj_en.pdf.

'Why the open method of coordination is bad for you: a letter to the EU', *European Law Journal* 13 (2007), 309–42.

Hatzopoulos, V. G. and Do, T. U., 'The case law of the ECJ concerning the free provision of services: 2000–2005', *Common Market Law Review* 43 (2006), 923–91.

Hatzopoulos, V. and Stergiou, H., 'Public procurement law and health care: From theory to practice', in Van de Gronden, J., Krajewski, M., Neergaard, U. and Szyszczak, E. (eds.), *Health Care and EU Law* (The Hague: Asser Press, forthcoming).

Hauray, B., *L'Europe du médicament: politique- expertise- intérêts privés* (Paris: Presses de Sciences Po, 2006).

Heidenreich, M. and Zeitlin, J. (eds.), *Changing European employment and welfare regimes: the influence of the open method of coordination on national labour market and social welfare reforms* (London: Routledge, 2009).

Hemerijck, A., *Revisiting productive welfare for continental Europe* (The Hague: Netherlands Scientific Council for Government Policy, 2007).

Hendrickx, K., 'Buitenlandse 'eendagschirurgen' aan de slag in Belgische klinieken', *De Morgen*, 15 March 2008.

Hendriks, A., 'The right to health', *European Journal of Health Law* 5 (1998), 89–116.

Hervey, T. K., 'Legal issues concerning the Barber Protocol', in O'Keeffe, D. and Twomey, P. (eds.), *Legal issues of the Maastricht Treaty* (London: Wiley-Chancery, 1994).

'Buy baby: the European Union and regulation of human reproduction', *Oxford Journal of Legal Studies* 18 (1998), 207–33.

European social law and policy (London: Longman, 1998).

'Social solidarity: a buttress against internal market law?', in Shaw, J. (ed.), *Social law and policy in an evolving European Union* (Oxford: Hart, 2000).

'The legal basis of European Community public health policy', in McKee, M., Mossialos, M. and Baeten, R. (eds.), *The impact of EU law on health care systems* (Brussels: PIE-Peter Lang, 2002).

'The right to health in European Union law', in Hervey, T. K. and Kenner, J. (eds.), *Economic and social rights under the EU Charter of Fundamental Rights: a legal perspective* (Oxford: Hart, 2003).

'We don't see a connection: "the right to health" in the EU Charter and European Social Charter', in de Búrca, G. and de Witte, B. (eds.), *Social rights in Europe* (Oxford: Oxford University Press, 2005).

'The European Union and the governance of health care', in de Búrca, G. and Scott, J. (eds.), *New governance and constitutionalism in Europe and the US* (Portland: Hart, 2006).

'EU law and national health policies: problem or opportunity?', *Health Economics, Policy and Law* 2 (2007), 1–6.

'New governance responses to healthcare migration in the EU: the EU guidelines on block purchasing', *Maastricht Journal of European and Comparative Law* **14** (2007), 303–33.

Hervey, T. K. and Kenner, J. (eds.), *Economic and social rights under the EU Charter of Fundamental Rights: a legal perspective* (Oxford: Hart, 2003).

Hervey, T. K. and McHale, J., *Health law and the European Union* (Cambridge: Cambridge University Press, 2004).

Hervey, T. and Trubek, L., 'Freedom to provide health care services within the EU: an opportunity for hybrid governance', *Columbia Journal of European Law* **13** (2007), 623–49.

Holland, W. W., Mossialos, E. and Permanand, G., 'Public health priorities in Europe', in Holland, W. W. and Mossialos, E. (eds.), *Public health policies in the European Union* (Aldershot: Ashgate, 1999).

Hoogervorst, H., 'Letter from the Dutch Minister of Health, Welfare and Sport to the European Commissioner for the Internal Market', Ministry of Health, Welfare and Sport, 8 October 2003.

Hooghe, L. and Marks, G., *Multi-level governance and European integration* (Lanham: Rowman and Littlefield, 2001).

Houtepen, R. and ter Meulen, R., 'New types of solidarity in the European welfare state', *Health Care Analysis* **8** (2000), 329–340.

Idot, L., 'Droit social et droit de la concurrence: confrontation ou cohabitation (à propos de quelques développements récents)', *Europe* **9** (1999), 4–8.

'Les services d'intérêt général économique et les règles de concurrence', in Louis, J. V. and Rodriguez, S. (eds.), *Les services d'intérêt économique général et l'UE* (Belgium: Bruylant, 2006).

Indenrigs-og Sundhedsministeriet, *Resultater paa sundhedsomraadet* (Copenhagen: Ministry of the Interior and Health, 2004).

Irvine, D. H., 'Everyone is entitled to a good doctor', *The Medical Journal of Australia* **186** (2007), 256–61.

Jacobson, K. and Vifell, A., 'Integration by deliberation? On the role of committees in the OMC', Paper prepared for the Workshop on 'Forging Deliberative Supranationalism in the EU', Florence, 7–8 February 2003.

Jenkins-Smith, H. C. and Sabatier, P., 'Evaluating the advocacy coalition framework', *Journal of Public Policy* **14** (1994), 175–203.

Jepsen, M. and Serrano Pascual, A., 'The concept of ESM and supra-national legitimacy-building', in Jepsen, M. and Serrano Pascual, A. (eds.), *Unwrapping the European social model* (Bristol: Policy Press, 2006).

Jones, A. and Sufrin, B., *EC competition law*, 2nd ed. (Oxford: Oxford University Press, 2004).

Joossens, L., 'Comments on Commission report COM (95) 285 final on the approximation of taxes on cigarettes', International Union Against Cancer, September 1996.

Joossens, L. and Raw, M., 'Are tobacco subsidies a misuse of public funds?', *British Medical Journal* 30 (1996), 832–5.

Jordan, A. and Schout, A., *The coordination of the European Union: exploring the capacities of networked governance* (Oxford: Oxford University Press, 2006).

Jorens, Y., 'The evolution of social policy in the European Union', Polityka Spoleczna (2005), 26–9.

'Cross-border health care: the use of the E112 form', Training and Reporting on European Social Security (2007).

'General regulatory framework: competition and regulation in the internal market – what mixture is best for Europe?', Federal Ministry of Health, *The social dimension in the internal market, perspectives of health care in Europe, conference documentation* (Berlin: Federal Ministry of Health, 2007).

Jorens, Y. and Coucheir, M., 'The European legal framework in relation to provider mobility', Europe for Patients Project, Deliverable to the European Commission, WP 2, unpublished (2005).

Jorens, Y., Coucheir, M. and Van Overmeiren, F., 'Access to health care in an internal market: impact for statutory and complementary systems', *Bulletin Luxembourgeois des questions sociales* 18 (2005), 1–136.

Joseph, C., Morgan, D., Birtles, R., Pelaz, C., Martin-Bourgon, C., Black, M., Garcia-Sanchez, I., Griffin, M., Bornstein, N. and Bartlett, C., 'An international investigation of an outbreak of Legionnaires disease among UK and French tourists', *European Journal of Epidemiology* 12 (1996), 215–9.

Jupille, J., *Procedural politics: issues, influence and institutional choice in the European Union* (Cambridge: Cambridge University Press, 2004).

Kaczorowska, A., 'A review of the creation by the ECJ of the right to effective and speedy medical treatment and its outcomes', *European Law Journal* (2006), 345–70.

Kanavos, P., Costa-I-Font, J., Merkur, S. and Gemmill, M., 'The economic impact of pharmaceutical parallel trade in European Union Member States: a stakeholder analysis', London School of Economics and Political Science (2004), http://mednet3.who.int/prioritymeds/report/append/829Paper.pdf.

Kanavos, P. and McKee, M., 'Cross-border issues in the provision of health services: are we moving towards a European health care policy?', *Journal of Health Services Research Policy* 5 (2000), 231–6.

Kassim, H., Menon, A., Peters, B. G. and Wright, V. (eds.), *The national co-ordination of EU policy: the European level* (Oxford: Oxford University Press, 2001).

Kassim, H., Peters, B. G. and Wright, V. (eds.), *The national co-ordination of EU policy: the domestic level* (Oxford: Oxford University Press, 2000).

Kelly, B., 'An emerging mental health strategy of the European Union. A multi-level work in progress', *Health Policy* (forthcoming 2009).

Kenner, J., 'Economic and social rights in the EU legal order: the mirage of indivisibility', in Hervey, T. K. and Kenner, J. (eds.), *Economic and social rights under the EU Charter of Fundamental Rights: a legal perspective* (Oxford: Hart, 2003).

EU employment law: from Rome to Amsterdam and beyond (Oxford: Hart, 2003).

Kerschbaumer, K., 'Public-private partnerships in Eastern Europe', *Eurohealth* 13 (2007), 7–9.

Kessler, F., 'Droit de la concurrence et régimes de protection sociale: un bilan provisoire', in Kovar, R. and Simon, D. (eds.), *Service public et Communauté européenne: entre l'intérêt général et le marché*, Vol. I (Paris: La Documentation française, 1998).

Kling, F., 'Ban on tobacco advertising not legal', *Tobacco Journal International* 4 (2000), 58.

Koski, A., Sirén, R., Vuori, E. and Poikolainen, K., 'Alcohol tax cuts and increase in alcohol-positive sudden deaths: a time-series intervention analysis', *Addiction* 102 (2007), 362–8.

Krajewski, M., 'Providing legal clarity and securing policy space for public services through a legal framework for services of general economic interest: squaring the circle?', *European Public Law* 14 (2008), 377–98.

Krajewski, M. and Farley, M., 'Non-economic activities in upstream markets and the scope of competition law after *FENIN*', *European Law Review* 32 (2007), 111–24.

Krapohl, S., 'Credible commitment in non-independent regulatory agencies: a comparative analysis of the European agencies for pharmaceuticals and foodstuffs', *European Law Journal* 10 (2004), 518–38.

'Thalidomide, BSE and the single market: an historical-institutionalist approach to regulatory regimes in the European Union', *European Journal of Political Research* 46 (2007), 25–46.

Kvist, J. and Saari, J. (eds.), *The Europeanisation of social protection* (Bristol: Policy Press, 2007).

Kyprianou, M., 'The new European healthcare agenda', Speech at the European Voice Conference on 'Healthcare: Is Europe Getting Better?', Brussels, 20 January 2005.

Laffan, B. and Lindner, J., 'The budget', in Wallace, H., Wallace, W. and Pollack, M. (eds.), *Policy-making in the European Union* (Oxford: Oxford University Press, 2005).

Lafontaine, C., 'National law on pharmacies and its non-application by a Member State's public authorities – *DocMorris* again leading the way to accomplish freedom of establishment', *Zeitschrift für Europarechtliche Studien* 9 (2006), 301–40.

Law, M.R., Morris, J.K. and Wald N.J., 'Environmental tobacco smoke exposure and ischaemic heart disease: an evaluation of the evidence', *British Medical Journal* 315 (1997), 973–80.

Lee, K., Buse, K. and Fustukian, S., *Health policy in a globalising world* (Cambridge: Cambridge University Press, 2002).

Lee, R. and Morgan, D., 'In the name of the father? Ex parte *Blood*: dealing with novelty and anomaly', *Modern Law Review* 60 (1997), 840–56.

Legido-Quigley, H. and La Parra, D., 'The health care needs of UK pensioners living in Spain: an agenda for research', *Eurohealth* 13 (2007), 14–8.

Legido-Quigley, H., Glinos, I., Baeten, R. and McKee, M., 'Patient mobility in the European Union', *British Medical Journal* 334 (2007), 188–90.

Legido-Quigley, H., Glinos, I.A., Washe, K., van Beek, B., Cule Cucic, C. and McKee, M., 'Quality and safety', in Wismar, M., Palm, W., Figueras, J., Ernst, K. and van Ginneken, E. (eds.), *Crossborder healthcare: mapping and analysing health systems diversity* (Copenhagen: WHO Regional Office for Europe on behalf of the European Observatory on Health Systems and Policies, 2009).

Legido-Quigley, H., McKee, M., Nolte, E. and Glinos, I., *Assuring the quality of health care in the European Union* (Copenhagen: WHO Regional Office for Europe on behalf of the European Observatory on Health Systems and Policies, 2008).

Leibfried, S., 'Social policy. Left to judges and the markets?', in Wallace, H., Wallace, W. and Pollack, M. (eds.), *Policy-making in the European Union* (Oxford: Oxford University Press, 2005).

Leibfried, S. and Pierson, P., *European social policy: between fragmentation and integration* (Washington, DC: Brookings, 1995).

Lenaerts, K. and Heremans, T., 'Contours of a European social union in the case-law of the European Court of Justice', *European Constitutional Law Review* 2 (2006), 101–15.

Lenaerts, K. and Vanuffel, P., *Europees recht in hoofdlijnen* (Antwerp, Apeldoorn: Maklu, 2008).

Levidow, L. and Carr, S., 'Europeanising advisory expertise: the role of "independent, objective and transparent" scientific advice in agri-biotech regulation', *Environment and Planning C: Government and Politics* 25 (2007), 880–95.

Liddle, R. and Lerais, R., 'Europe's social reality', Consultation Paper, Bureau of European Policy Advisors (2007).

Logminiene, Z., 'Hospital sector reform in Lithuania', *Eurohealth* 7 (2001), 70–3.

Lopez-Santana, M., 'Soft Europeanization? The differential influences of European soft law on employment policies, processes and institutional configurations in EU Member States', PhD thesis, University of Michigan (2006).

Lowson, K., West, P., Chaplin, S. and O'Reilly, J., 'Evaluation of treating patients overseas', York Health Economics Consortium, Department of Health (England), July 2002, www.dh.gov.uk/en/Publicationsandstatistics/Publications/PublicationsPolicyAndGuidance/DH_4005742

Lynskey, O., 'The Irish Competition Authority settles price-fixing proceedings in the health insurance sector', *e-Competitions Law Bulletin* No. 14004 (2007).

Maarse, H., 'Health insurance reform (again) in the Netherlands: will it succeed?', *Euro Observer* 4 (2002), 1–3.

Mabbett, D., 'Social regulation and the social dimension in Europe: the example of insurance', *European Journal of Social Security* 2 (1997), 241–57.

MacLehose, L., Brand, H., Camaroni, I., Fulop, N., Gill, O. N., Reintjes, R., Schaefer, O., McKee, M. and Weinberg, J., 'Communicable disease outbreaks involving more than one country: systems approach to evaluating the response', *British Medical Journal* 323 (2001), 861–3.

Magnette, P., 'The politics of regulation in the European Union', in Geradin, D., Muñoz, R. and Petit, N. (eds.), *Regulation through agencies in the EU: a new paradigm of European governance* (Cheltenham: Edward Elgar, 2005).

Magyar, E., 'Jogharmonizáció immáron "bentro'l" szemlélve: a munkaido´ szabályozásának lehetséges irányai I', *Munkaügyi Szemle* 5 (2004), 19–23.

Majone, G., 'The European Community between social policy and social regulation', *Journal of Common Market Studies* 31 (1993), 153–70.

'The rise of the regulatory state in Europe', *West European Politics* 17 (1994), 77–101.

'A European regulatory state', in Richardson, J. (ed.), *European Union: power and policy-making* (London: Routledge, 1996).

Regulating Europe (London: Routledge, 1996).

'The agency model: the growth of regulation and regulatory institutions in the European Union', *European Institute of Public Administration (EIPAScope)* **3** (1997), 1–6.

'The credibility crisis of Community regulation', *Journal of Common Market Studies* **38** (2000), 273–302.

'Delegation of regulatory powers in a mixed polity', *European Law Journal* **8** (2002), 319–39.

'The politics of regulation and European regulatory institutions', in Hayward, J. and Menon, A. (eds.), *Governing Europe* (Oxford: Oxford University Press, 2003).

Dilemmas of European integration: the ambiguities and pitfalls of integration by stealth (Oxford: Oxford University Press, 2005).

Mann, J., Gruskin, S., Grodin, M. A., Annas, G. A. (eds.), *Health and Human Rights: A Reader* (London: Routledge, 1999).

Martin, C. J., 'Nature or nurture? Sources of firm preference for national health reform', *American Political Science Review* **89** (1995), 898–913.

Martin, D. and Martin, D. B., 'Why Philip Morris needs the United Kingdom', Memorandum to Gerard Wirz, Philip Morris, Bates No. 2501207805–09 (1992).

Martinsen, D. S., 'The Europeanization of welfare – the domestic impact of intra-European social security', *Journal of Common Market Studies* **43** (2005), 1027–54.

'Towards an internal health market with the European court', *West European Politics* **28** (2005), 1035–56.

'EU for the patients: developments, impacts, challenges', Report 6, Swedish Institute for European Policy Studies (2007).

Martinsen, D. S. and Vrangbaek, K., 'The Europeanization of health care governance: implementing the market imperatives of Europe', *Public Administration* **86** (2007), 169–84.

Masseria, C., 'Access to care and health status inequalities in a context of healthcare reform', Synthesis Report, Peer Review and Assessment in Social Inclusion, Hungary, 17–18 January 2007.

Maucher, M., 'Analysis of the replies of all European Union Member States' governments to the questionnaire of the Social Protection Committee preparing the Communication on social and health services of general interest', Observatory for the Development of Social Services in Europe, 16 September 2005, www.soziale-dienste-in-europa.de/Anlage25573/auswertung-antworten-ms-mitteilung-sgdai-ed.pdf.

Maynard, A., 'European health policy challenges', *Health Economics* **14** (2005), Supp 1: 255–63.

McCarron, M.O., Armstrong, M. and McCarron, P., 'Effect of European working time directive on a stroke unit', *Quality and Safety in Health Care* **15** (2006), 445–6.

McDaid, D. and Wiley, M.M., *Ireland: health system review* (Copenhagen: WHO Regional Office for Europe on behalf of the European Observatory on Health Systems and Policies, 2009).

McGowan, F. and Wallace, H., 'Towards a European regulatory state', *Journal of European Policy* **3** (1996), 560–76.

McHale, J., 'Enforcing health care rights in the English Courts', in Burchill, R., Harris, D. and Owers A. (eds.), *Economic, social and cultural rights: their implementation in UK law* (Nottingham: University of Nottingham Human Rights Centre, 1999).

McKee, M., *Reducing hospital beds. What are the lessons to be learned?* (Copenhagen: WHO Regional Office for Europe on behalf of the European Observatory on Health Systems and Policies, 2004).

'A European alcohol strategy: will the opportunity be missed?', *British Medical Journal* **333** (2006), 871–2.

'Cochrane on Communism: the influence of ideology on the search for evidence', *International Journal of Epidemiology* **36** (2007), 269–73.

McKee, M. and Black, N., 'Does the current use of junior doctors in the United Kingdom affect the quality of medical care?', *Social Science and Medicine* **34** (1992), 549–58.

McKee, M., Dubois, C.-A. and Sibbald, B., 'Changing professional boundaries', in Dubois, C.-A., McKee, M. and Nolte, E. (eds.), *Human resources for health in Europe* (Maidenhead: Open University Press, 2006).

McKee, M. and Gilmore, A., 'Smokeless tobacco: seeing the whole picture', *International Journal of Epidemiology* **36** (2007), 805–8.

McKee, M. and Mossialos, E., 'Health policy and European law: Closing the gaps', *Public Health* **120** (2006), Supp: 16–20.

McKee, M., Mossialos, E. and Baeten, R. (eds.), *The impact of EU law on health care systems* (Brussels: PIE-Peter Lang, 2002).

McKee, M., Mossialos, E. and Belcher, P., 'The influence of European Union law on national health policy', *Journal of European Social Policy* **6** (1996), 263–86.

McKee, M. and Ryan, J., 'Monitoring health in Europe: opportunities, challenges and progress', *European Journal of Public Health* **13** (2003), Supp: 1–4.

McKee, M. and Steyger, E., 'When can the European Union restrict trade on grounds of public health?', *Journal of Public Health Medicine* **19** (1997), 85–6.

Merkin, R. and Rodger, A., *EC insurance law* (London: Longman, 1997).

Merkur, S., Mossialos, E., Long, M. and McKee, M., 'Physician revalidation in Europe', *Clinical Medicine* 8 (2008), 371–6.

Merola, M. and Medina, C., 'De l'arrêt Ferring à l'arrêt Altmark: continuité
ou revirement dans l'approche du financement des services publics',
Cahiers de Droit Européen 5–6 (2003), 639–94.

Metz, A., 'Innovation in governance? Six proposals for taming open
co-ordination', Center for Applied Policy Research (C.A.P.) Working
Papers Policy Analysis 1 (2005).

Milenkovic Kramer, A., 'Health insurance in Slovenia', unpublished report
(2006).

Ministry of Health Welfare, and Sport, 'Do you have compulsory or private
health insurance? A single new-style health insurance for everybody as
of 1 January 2006', Brochure of the Ministry of Health, Welfare and
Sport (2005).

Mladovsky, P., 'To what extent are Roma disadvantaged in terms of health
and access to health care? What policies have been introduced to foster health and social inclusion?', Research Note for the European
Commission, DG Employment and Social Affairs (2007).

Montgomery, J., 'Impact of EU law on English healthcare law', in
Spaventa, E. and Dougan, M. (eds.), *Social welfare and EU law*
(Oxford: Hart, 2003).

Monti, G., *EC competition law* (Cambridge: Cambridge University Press,
2007).

Moravcsik, A., 'In defense of the "democratic deficit": reassessing the legitimacy of the European Union', *Journal of Common Market Studies*
40 (2002), 603–34.

Moreno, L. and Palier, B., 'The Europeanisation of welfare: paradigm
shifts and social policy reforms', in Taylor-Gooby, P. (ed.), *Ideas
and welfare state reform in western Europe* (Basingstoke: Palgrave
Macmillan, 2005).

MORI, 'Attitudes to medical regulation and revalidation of doctors'
research among doctors and the general public', Research Study
Conducted for Department of Health, MORI (2005).

Morris, P., 'Communication – smokers' organizations', *Infotopics:
Summaries of Public Information* 6 (1987), 39.

'Smoking restrictions 3-year plan', Phillip Morris Corporate Affairs
Europe (undated).

Mossialos, E., Dixon, A., Figueras, J. and Kutzin, J. (eds.), *Funding
health care: options for Europe* (Buckingham: Open University Press,
2002).

Mossialos, E. and Le Grand, J. (eds.), *Health care and cost containment in
the European Union* (Aldershot: Ashgate, 1999).

Mossialos, E. and McKee, M., 'Is a European health care policy emerging?', *British Medical Journal* 323 (2001), 248.

Mossialos, E. and McKee, M. (with Palm, W., Karl, B. and Marhold, F.), *The influence of EU law on the social character of health care systems* (Brussels: PIE-Peter Lang, 2002).

Mossialos, E. and Permanand, G., 'Public health in the European Union: making it relevant', LSE Health Discussion Paper No. 17 (2000).

Mossialos, E. and Palm, W., 'The European Court of Justice and the free movement of persons in the European Union', *International Social Security Review* 56 (2003), 3–29.

Mossialos, E. and Thomson, S., 'Voluntary health insurance in the European Union: a critical assessment', *International Journal of Health Services* 32 (2002), 19–88.

Voluntary health insurance in the European Union (Copenhagen: World Health Organization, 2004).

Mossialos, E., Thomson, S. and Ter-Linden, A., 'Information technology law and health systems in the European Union', *International Journal of Technology Assessment in Health Care* 20 (2004), 498–508.

Muscat, N. A., Grech, K., Cachia, J. M. and Xuereb, D., 'Sharing capacities – Malta and the United Kingdom', in Rosenmöller, M., McKee, M. and Baeten, R. (eds.), *Patient mobility in the European Union – learning from experience* (Copenhagen: WHO Regional Office for Europe on behalf of the European Observatory on Health Systems and Policies, 2006).

Mutualité Chrétienne, 'L'Hospi Solidaire, parce que l'hospitalisation ne doit pas être un luxe', www.mc.be/fr/100/campagne_hospi/index.jsp.

Nebling, T. and Schemken, H.-W., 'Cross-border contracting: the German experience', in Rosenmöller, M., McKee, M. and Baeten, R. (eds.), *Patient mobility in the European Union: learning from experience* (Copenhagen: WHO Regional Office for Europe on behalf of the European Observatory on Health Systems and Policies, 2006).

Nemeth, K., 'European insurance law: a single insurance market?', EUI Working Paper LAW No 2001/4 (2001).

Neuman, M., Bitton, A. and Glantz, S., 'Tobacco industry strategies for influencing European Community tobacco advertising legislation', *Lancet* 359 (2002), 1323–30.

Newdick, C., 'Citizenship, free movement and health care: cementing individual rights by corroding social solidarity', *Common Market Law Review* 43 (2006), 1645–68.

Nickless, J., 'The internal market and the social nature of health care', in McKee, M., Mossialos, E. and Baeten, R. (eds.), *The impact of EU law on health care systems* (Brussels: PIE-Peter Lang, 2002).

Nolte, E. and McKee, M., *Does health care save lives? Avoidable mortality revisited* (London: Nuffield Trust, 2004).

Nys, H., 'Physician involvement in a patient's death: a continental European perspective', *Medical Law Review* 7 (1999), 208–46.

'Comparative health law and the harmonization of patients' rights in Europe', *European Journal of Health Law* 8 (2001), 317–31.

Medisch recht (Leuven: Acco, 2001).

Odudu, O., *The boundaries of EC competition law* (Oxford: Oxford University Press, 2006).

Offe, C., 'The European model of "social" capitalism: can it survive European integration?', *Journal of Political Philosophy* 11 (2003), 437–69.

Office of Fair Trading, 'Health insurance: a second report by the Office of Fair Trading', Office of Fair Trading (1998).

'The Competition Act 1998 and public bodies', Policy Note No. 1/2004, OFT 443, August 2004.

O'Leary, S., 'Solidarity and citizenship rights in the Charter of Fundamental Rights of the European Union', in de Búrca, G., (ed.), *EU law and the welfare state: in search of solidarity* (Oxford: Oxford University Press, 2005).

Oliver, A. and Mossialos, E., 'Health system reform in Europe: looking back to see forward?', *Journal of Health Policy Politics and Law* 30 (2005), 7–28.

O'Neill, O., *A question of trust* (Cambridge: Cambridge University Press, 2002).

Ong, E.K. and Glantz, S.A., 'Tobacco industry efforts subverting International Agency for Research on Cancer's second-hand smoke study', *Lancet* 355 (2000), 1253–9.

Oortwijn, W.J., Ling, T., Mathijssen, J., Lankhuizen, M., Scoggins, A., van Stolk, C. and Cave, J., *Interim Evaluation of the Public Health Programme 2003–2008* (Santa Monica: RAND Corporation, 2007).

Organisation for Economic Co-operation, and Development, *Private health insurance in OECD countries: compilation of national reports* (Paris: OECD, 2001).

O'Rourke, R., *European food law* (London: Sweet & Maxwell, 2005).

Palm, W., 'Voluntary health insurance and EU insurance directives: between solidarity and the market', in McKee, M., Mossialos, E. and Baeten, R. (eds.), *The impact of EU law on health care systems* (Brussels: PIE-Peter Lang, 2002).

Palm, W., Nickless, J., Lewalle, H. and Coheur, A., 'Implications of recent jurisprudence on the coordination of healthcare protection systems', General report produced for the Directorate-General for Employment, Social Affairs and Equal Opportunities of the European Commission (2000).

Palm, W., Wismar, M. and Ernst, K., 'Assessing possible directions for the Community action on healthcare services: summary of the expert panels', in Wismar, M., Palm, W., Figueras, J., Ernst, K. and van Ginneken, E. (eds.), *Cross-border healthcare: mapping and analysing health systems diversity* (Copenhagen: WHO Regional Office for Europe on behalf of the European Observatory on Health Systems and Policies, 2009).

Palmqvist, T., 'Answers to questionnaire on the impact of EU law on national health care systems', Swedish Ministry of Health and Social Affairs, 1 December 2006, Questionnaire organized and sent to Member States by Observatoire social européen.

Palu, T. and Kadakmaa, R., 'Estonian hospital sector in transition', *Eurohealth* 7 (2001), 61–4.

Paolucci, F., Schut, E., Beck, K., Greb, S., Van de Voorde, C. and Zmora, I., 'Supplementary health insurance as a tool for risk selection in mandatory basic health insurance markets: a five country comparison', *Health Economics, Policy and Law* 2 (2007), 173–92.

Peck, C., McCall, M., McLaren, B. and Rotem, T., 'Continuing medical education and continuing professional development: international comparisons', *British Medical Journal* 320 (2000), 432–35.

Peers, S., 'Can the Treaty of Lisbon be ratified or implemented? A legal analysis', *Statewatch Paper*, 19 June 2008.

Peers, S. and Ward, A., *The EU Charter of Fundamental Rights: politics, law and policy* (Oxford: Hart, 2004).

Peeters, M., 'Free movement of medical doctors: the new Directive 2005/36/EC on recognition of professional qualifications', *European Journal of Health Law* 12 (2005), 373–96.

'Free movement of medical doctors in the EU', *Medicine and Law* 26 (2007), 231–44.

Peeters, M. and Schoukens, P., 'Vrij verkeer van zorgverstrekkers in de Europese Unie', *Acta Hospitalia* 4 (2004), 15–71.

Pennings, G., 'Belgian Law on medically assisted reproduction and the disposition of supernumerary embryos and gametes', *European Journal of Health Law* 14 (2007), 251.

Permanand, G., *EU pharmaceutical regulation: the politics of policymaking* (Manchester: Manchester University Press, 2006).

'Commentary on "health policy and European law": closing the gaps', *Public Health* 120 (2006), Supp: 21–2.

Permanand, G. and Mossialos, E., 'Constitutional asymmetry and pharmaceutical policy-making in the European Union', *Journal of European Public Policy* 12 (2005), 687–709.

Permanand, G., Mossialos, E. and McKee, M., 'Regulating medicines in Europe: the European Medicines Agency, marketing authorisation, transparency and pharmacovigilance', *Clinical Medicine* 6 (2006), 87–90.

Perry, N., Broeders, M., de Wolf, C., Törnberg, S., Holland, R., von Karsa, L., *European guidelines for quality assurance in breast cancer screening and diagnosis* (Brussels: European Commission, 2006).

Pestieau, P., *The welfare state in the European Union: economic and social perspectives* (Oxford: Oxford University Press, 2006).

Pieters, D. and van den Bogaert, S., *The consequences of European competition law for national health policies* (Antwerp: Maklu Uitgevers, 1997).

Pilkington, P. and Gilmore, A.B., 'The Living Tomorrow Project: how Philip Morris has used a Belgian tourist attraction to promote ventilation approaches to the control of second hand smoke', *Tobacco Control* 13 (2004), 375–8.

Pochmarski, R., 'Working in Europe without frontiers, mutual recognition of diplomas in the enlarged EU', Report of the International Seminar, 'From Mutual Recognition to Mutual Communication', Warsaw, September 2004.

Poiares Maduro, M., *We the Court: the European Court of Justice and the European economic constitution* (Oxford: Hart, 1998).

Prosser, T., *The limits of competition law: markets and public services* (Oxford: Oxford University Press, 2005).

Puig-Junoy, J., 'Managing risk selection incentives in health sector reforms', *International Journal of Health Planning and Management* 14 (1999), 287–311.

Quero, A., 'Report by the working group 3a. Establishing a framework for decisionmaking regulatory agencies', SG/8597/01EN, Preparation of the White Paper on Governance Work – Improving the Exercise of Executive Responsibilities, June 2001.

Radaelli, C., 'Europeanization: solution or problem', in Cini, M. and Bourne, A. (eds.), *European Union studies* (Basingstoke: Palgrave Macmillan, 2006).

Rajmil, L., Borrell, C., Starfield, B., Fernandez, E., Serra, V., Schiaffino, A. and Segura, A., 'The quality of care and influence of double health care coverage in Catalonia (Spain)', *Archives of Disease in Childhood* 83 (2000), 211–4.

Randall, E., 'Not that soft or informal: a response to Eberlein and Grande's account of regulatory governance in the EU with special reference to the European Food Safety Authority (EFSA)', *Journal of European Public Policy* 13 (2006), 402–19.

Rechel, B., Dubois, C.-A. and McKee, M., *The health care workforce in Europe: learning from experience* (Copenhagen: WHO Regional Office for Europe on behalf of the European Observatory on Health Systems and Policies, 2006).

Rednak, A. and Smrekar, T., 'Evropa žuga Sloveniji zaradi zdravstvenih zavarovanja', *Finance*, 4 May 2007.

Reerink, A. and Rosenberg, E., 'Neelie Kroes over staatssteun aan nieuwe zorgstelsel', NRC Handelsblad, 5 October 2005.

Reintjes, R., 'International and European responses to the threat of communicable disease', in Coker, R., Atun, R. and McKee, M. (eds.), *Health systems and the challenge of communicable disease: experiences from Europe and Latin America* (Buckingham: McGraw Hill, 2008).

Reintjes, R., Thelen, M., Reiche, R. and Csohan, A., 'Benchmarking national surveillance systems: a new tool for the comparison of communicable disease surveillance and control in Europe', *The European Journal of Public Health* 17 (2007), 375–80.

Rice, N. and Smith, P., 'Strategic resource allocation and funding decisions', in Mossialos, E., Dixon, A., Figueras, J. and Kutzin, J. (eds.), *Funding healthcare: options for Europe* (Maidenhead: Open University, 2002).

Robert, G. and Falconi, F., 'Patent litigation settlement agreements in the pharmaceutical industry: marrying the innovation bride and competition groom product', *European Competition Law Review* 27 (2006), 524–33.

Robertson, G., 'A social Europe: progress through partnership', *European Business Journal* 4 (1992), 10–6.

Robertson, J., 'Protecting embryos and burdening women: assisted reproduction in Italy', *Human Reproduction* 19 (2004), 1693–6.

Rocard, M., 'Mission mutualité et droit communautaire: rapport de fin de mission', Government of France (1999).

Roscam Abbing, H. D. C., 'Human tissue and consumer protection from a European perspective', *European Journal of Health Law* 2 (1995), 298–304.

'Medical practice and disciplinary measures in the European Union', in Lens, P. and Van Der Wal, G. (eds.), *Problem doctors, a conspiracy of silence* (Amsterdam: IOS Press, 1997).

'The right of the patient to quality of medical practice and the position of migrant doctors within the EU', *European Journal of Health Law* 4 (1997), 347–60.

'Public health insurance and freedom of movement within the European Union', *European Journal of Health Law* (1999), 1.

Rosenmöller, M. and Lluch, M., 'Meeting the needs of long-term residents in Spain', in Rosenmöller, M., McKee, M. and Baeten, R. (eds.), *Patient mobility in the European Union: learning from experience* (Copenhagen: WHO Regional Office for Europe on behalf of the European Observatory on Health Systems and Policies, 2006).

Rosenmöller, M., McKee, M., Baeten, R. and Glinos, I. A., 'Patient mobility: the context and issues', in Rosenmöller, M., McKee, M. and Baeten, R. (eds.), *Patient mobility in the European Union: learning from experience* (Copenhagen: WHO Regional Office for Europe on behalf of the European Observatory on Health Systems and Policies, 2006).

Ross, M., 'Article 16 EC and services of general interest: from derogation to obligation?', *European Law Review* 25 (2000), 22–38.

'Promoting solidarity: from public services to a European model of competition', *Common Market Law Review* 44 (2007), 1057–80.

Rossi, J., 'Competition law enforcement mechanisms', *Law in Transition* (2004), 78–84, www.ebrd.com/pubs/legal/lit041m.pdf.

Rowe, H., 'Data transfer to third countries: the role of binding corporate rules', *Computer Law and Security Report* 19 (2003), 490.

Rowland, D., *Mapping communicable disease control administration in the UK* (London: Nuffield Trust, 2006).

Rubene, A., 'The Latvian Competition Council fines the medical gas monopolist for the application of an unfair and discriminating price', *e-Competitions Law Bulletin* No. 16460 (2006).

Rupprecht, F., Tissot, B. and Chatel, F., 'German health care system: promoting greater responsibility among all system players', INSEE Studies No. 42 (2000).

Sabel, C. and Zeitlin, J., 'Learning from difference: the new architecture of experimentalist governance in the EU', *European Law Journal* 14 (2008), 271–327.

Saltman, R. B., Busse, R. and Mossialos, E., *Regulating entrepreneurial behaviour in European health care systems* (Buckingham: Open University Press, 2002).

Sandier, S., Paris, V. and Polton, D., *Health care systems in transition: France* (Copenhagen: WHO Regional Office for Europe on behalf of the European Observatory on Health Systems and Policies, 2004).

Sauter, W., 'Services of general economic interest (SGEI) and universal service obligations (USO) as an EU law framework for curative health care', TILEC Discussion Paper, DP 2007–029, Tilburg University, September 2007.

Schäfer, A., 'Beyond the Community method: why the open method of coordination was introduced to EU policy-making', *European Integration Online Papers* **8** (2004), 10.

Scharpf, F., 'A new social contract? Negative and positive integration in the political economy of European welfare states', EUI Working Paper RSC 96/44 (1996).

Governing in Europe: effective and democratic? (Oxford: Oxford University Press, 1999).

'The European social model: coping with the challenges of diversity', *Journal of Common Market Studies* **40** (2002), 645–70.

'Problem-solving effectiveness and democratic accountability in the EU', Max Planck Institute for the Study of Societies MPIfG Working Paper 03/1 (2003).

Schneider, A., 'Grenzüberschreitende Inanspruchnahme von Krankenhausleistungen aus der Sicht des BMGS', *Zeitschrift fur europaishes Sozialund Arbeitsrecht* **10** (2004), 413–5.

Schoukens, P., *De sociale zekerheid van de zelfstandige en het Europees gemeenschapsrecht: de impact van het vrije verkeer van zelfstandigen* (Leuven: Acco, 2000).

Schreyögg, J., Stargardt, T., Velasco-Garrido, M. and Busse, R., 'Defining the "health benefit basket" in nine European countries: evidence from the European Union Health BASKET Project', *European Journal of Health Economics* **6** (2005), Supp: 2–10.

Schröter, H., 'Kommentierung der Artikel 81–83 EGV', in H. von der Groeben and J. Schwarze (eds.), *Kommentar zum Vertrag über die Europäische Union und zur Gründung der europäischen Gemeinschaft*, Vol. 2, 6th ed. (Baden Baden: Nomos Verlag, 2003).

Schulz, A. and de Douhet, J., 'French Competition Council vs. GSK France: who is the predator?' esapience Centre for Competition Policy, June 2007.

Schweitzer, H., 'Competition law and public policy: reconsidering an uneasy relationship. The example of Art. 81', EUI Working Papers 2007/30 (2007).

Scientific Committee on Emerging, and Newly Identified Health Risks (SCENIHR), 'Health Effects of Smokeless Tobacco Products', Health and Consumer Protection Directorate General, February 2008, http://ec.europa.eu/health/ph_risk/committees/04_scenihr/docs/scenihr_o_013.pdf.

Scott, C., 'Agencies for European regulatory governance: a regimes approach', in Geradin, D., Muñoz, R. and Petit, N. (eds.), *Regulation through agencies in the EU: a new paradigm of European governance* (Cheltenham: Edward Elgar, 2005).

Sécurité Sociale, 'Contrat responsable', Sécurité Sociale (2008), www.securite-sociale.fr/comprendre/reformes/reformeassmal/decrets/maitrise/20050930.htm.

Senden, L., *Soft law in European Community law* (Oxford: Hart, 2004).

'Soft law, self-regulation and co-regulation in European law: where do they meet?', *Electronic Journal of Comparative Law* 9 (2005), 18–9.

Skjærseth, J. B., Stokke, O. S. and Wettestad, J., 'Soft law, hard law, and effective implementation of international environmental norms', *Global Environmental Politics* 6 (2006), 104–20.

Slaughter, A.-M., *A new world order* (Princeton: Princeton University Press, 2004).

Slob, A. and Smakman, F., *Evaluation of the civil society dialogue at DG Trade: assessment of relevance, effectiveness and efficiency of CSD policy and procedures* (Rotterdam: ECORYS for DG Trade, 2006).

Slovenia Business Week, 'Government responds to EU's warning over health insurance', *Slovenia Business Week* 18 (2007).

Slot, P. J., 'Applying the competition rules in the healthcare sector', *European Competition Law Review* 24 (2003), 580–93.

Slot, P. J. and Johnston, A., *An introduction to competition law* (Oxford, Portland: Hart, 2006).

Sluyters, B., 'Telegeneeskunde', *Tijdschrift voor Gezondheidsrecht* (1999), 273.

Smismans, S., 'EU employment policy: decentralisation or centralisation through the open method of coordination?', European University Institute Working Paper LAW No. 2004/1 (2004).

Southgate, L. and Pringle, M., 'Revalidation in the United Kingdom: general principles based on experience in general practice', *British Medical Journal* 319 (1999), 1180–3.

Spanish Presidency, 'The Europe of Health', Unpublished paper from the Spanish Presidency of the EU in preparation of the informal Ministerial Debate in Malaga, Madrid, 24 January 2002.

Spaventa, E., 'From Gebhard to Carpenter: towards a (non-)economic European Constitution', *Common Market Law Review* 41 (2004), 743–73.

Standing Committee of European Doctors, 'The practice of tele-medicine in Europe: analysis, problems and CPME recommendations', 2002M/027 (2002).

Starkiene, L., Smigelskas, K., Padaiga, Z. and Reamy, J., 'The future prospects of Lithuanian family physicians: a 10-year forecasting study', *BioMed Central: Family Practice* 6 (2005), 41.

Stein, H., 'The Treaty of Amsterdam and Article 129: a second chance for public health in Europe?', *Eurohealth* **3** (1997), 4–8.

Steyger, E., 'The proposed Dutch health insurance system in the light of European Law', in den Exter, A. (ed.), *Competitive social health insurance yearbook 2004* (Rotterdam: Erasmus University Press, 2005).

Stjernø, S., *Solidarity in Europe: the history of an idea* (Cambridge: Cambridge University Press, 2005).

Stone Sweet, A., 'Judicial authority and market integration in Europe', in Ginsburg, T. and Kagan, R. A. (eds.), *Institutions and public law: comparative approaches* (Frankfurt: PIE-Peter Lang, 2005).

Sutherland, K. and Leatherman, S., 'Does certification improve medical standards?', *British Medical Journal* **333** (2006), 439–41.

Swedish Competition Authority (SCA), 'Assessment for improving consumer welfare in health and elderly care', English Summary (2007), www.kkv.se/upload/Filer/ENG/Publications/rap_2007–3_summary. pdf.

Svensson, P. G. and Stephenson, P., 'Health care consequences of the European economic community in 1993 and beyond', *Social Science and Medicine* **35** (1992), 525–9.

Sylvest, J. and Adamsen, C., 'The impact of the European Court of Justice case law on national systems for cross-border health services provision', Briefing Note, DG Internal Policies of the Union, IP/A/ALL/ FWC/2006–105/LOT 3/C1/SC1 (2007).

Szyszczak, E., 'Competition law and services of general economic interest', Paper presented at the ERA Conference on 'European Economic Integration and National Social Protection Systems: Towards a New Form of Internal Market', Brussels, 31 May-1 June 2007.

Talbot-Smith, A. and Pollock, A., *The new NHS, a guide* (New York: Routledge, 2006).

Taylor, G. and Millar, M., ' "The appliance of science': the politics of European food regulation and reform', *Public Policy and Administration* **17** (2002), 125–46.

Taylor-Gooby, P., 'Introduction: open markets versus welfare citizenship: conflicting approaches to policy convergence in Europe', *Social Policy and Administration* **37** (2003), 539–54.

   'Open markets and welfare values', *European Societies* **6** (2004), 29–48.

Thatcher, M., 'Delegation to independent regulatory agencies: pressures, functions and contextual mediation', *West European Politics* **25** (2002), 125–47.

Thatcher, M. and Stone Sweet, A., 'Theory and practice of delegation to non-majoritarian institutions', *West European Politics* **25** (2002), 1–22.

The Competition Authority, *Competition in the private health insurance market* (Dublin: The Competition Authority, 2007).

Thomson, S., 'What role for voluntary health insurance?', in Kutzin, J., Cashin, C. and Jakab, M. (eds.), *Implementing health financing reform: lessons from countries in transition* (Copenhagen: WHO Regional Office for Europe on behalf of the European Observatory on Health Systems and Policies, 2009).

Thomson, S., Foubister, T. and Mossialos, E., *Financing health care in the European Union: Challenges and policy responses* (Copenhagen: WHO on behalf of the European Observatory on Health Systems and Policies, 2009).

Thomson, S. and Mossialos, E., 'Choice of public or private health insurance: learning from the experience of Germany and the Netherlands', *Journal of European Social Policy* 16 (2006), 315–27.

'Editorial: EU law and regulation of private health insurance', *Health Economics Policy and Law* 2 (2007), 117–24.

'Regulating private health insurance in the European Union: the implications of single market legislation and competition policy', *Journal of European Integration* 29 (2007), 89–107.

Timmins, N., 'European law looms over NHS contracts', *Financial Times*, 15 January 2007.

Tobacco Advisory Group of the Royal College of Physicians, *Harm reduction in nicotine addiction: helping people who can't quit* (London: Royal College of Physicians, 2007).

Tobes, B., *The right to health as a human right in international law* (Antwerp: Intersentia, Hart, 1999).

Tomaszefska, M., 'The Polish Office for Competition and Consumer Protection holds that the National Health Fund has imposed its dominant position by imposing low purchase prices of health services (Narodowy Fundusz Zdrowia)', *e-Competitions Law Bulletin* No. 13674 (2007).

Toplak, S., 'Constitutional Court failed to please Vzajemna and Adriatic', *The Finance Business Daily Newspaper*, 17 September 2005, www.finance-on.net/show.php?id=137526.

Treib, O., Bähr, H. and Falkner, G., 'Modes of governance: towards conceptual clarification', *Journal of European Public Policy* 14 (2007), 1–20.

Trubek, L., 'New governance practices in US healthcare', in de Búrca, G. and Scott, J. (eds.), *New governance and constitutionalism in Europe and the US* (Portland: Hart, 2006).

Trubek, L., Nance, M. and Hervey T. K., 'The construction of a healthier Europe: lessons from the fight against cancer', *Wisconsin International Law Journal* 26 (2008), 804–44.

Trubek, D. and Trubek, L., 'Hard and soft law in the construction of social Europe: the role of the open method of co-ordination', *European Law Journal* 11 (2005), 343–64.

'New governance and legal regulation: complementarity, rivalry or transformation', *Columbia Journal of European Law* 13 (2007), 539–64.

Trygdeetaten, *Bidrag til behandling i utlandet etter paragraf 5–22* (Oslo: Trygdeetaten, National Insurance Administration, 2004).

Tsebelis, G. and Geoffrey, G., 'The institutional foundations of intergovernmentalism and supranationalism in the European Union', *International Organization* 55 (2001), 357–90.

Ugland, T. and Veggeland, F., 'Experiments in food safety policy integration in the European Union', *Journal of Common Market Studies* 44 (2006), 607–24.

Vagliasindi, M. and Campbell, L., 'The EBRD: promoting transition through competition', *Law in Transition* (2004), 35–45, www.ebrd. com/pubs/legal/lit041g.pdf.

Van Asselt, M., Vos, E. and Rooijackers, B., 'Science, knowledge and uncertainty in EU risk regulation', in Everson, M. and Vos, E. (eds.), *Uncertain risks regulated* (London: Routledge-Cavendish, 2009).

van de Ven, W.P., Beck, K., van de Voorde, C., Wasem, J. and Zmora, I., 'Risk adjustment and risk selection in Europe: six years later', *Health Policy* 83 (2007), 162–79.

van de Ven W. P and van Vliet, R.C., 'How can we prevent cream skimming in a competitive health insurance market? The great challenge for the 90s', in Zweifel, P. and Frech III, H. (eds.), *Health economics worldwide (developments in health economics and public policy)* (Amsterdam: Kluwer, 1992).

Van den Abeele, E., 'Adoption of the Services Directive: a Community big bang or a velvet revolution?', in Degryse, C. and Pochet, P. (eds.), *Social developments in the European Union 2006* (Brussels: ETUI-REHS, Observatoire social européen, Saltsa, 2007).

van der Gronden, J., 'Is a Member State entitled to introduce regulated competition into the health care sector under EC law? Reaction to the contribution of E. Steyger', in den Exter, A. (ed.), *Competitive social health insurance yearbook 2004* (Rotterdam: Erasmus University Press, 2005).

van der Mei, A.P., 'Cross-border access to health care within the EU: some reflections on *Geraets-Smits and Peerbooms* and *Vanbraekel*', *Medical Law* (2002), 289–315.

Free movement of persons within the European Community, cross-border access to public benefits (Oxford: Hart, 2001).

'Cross-border access to medical care: non-hospital care and waiting lists', *Legal Issues of European Integration* 31 (2004), 57–67.

van der Mei, A.P. and Waddington, L., 'Public health and the Treaty of Amsterdam', *European Journal of Health Law* 5 (1998), 129–54.

van Doorslaer, E., Masseria, C. and Koolman, X., 'Inequalities in access to medical care by income in developed countries', *Canadian Medical Association Journal* 174 (2006), 177–83.

Van Dosselaere, C., Wilson, P., Herveg, J. and Silber, D., 'eHealth ... But is it legal?', *Eurohealth* 13 (2007), 2.

Van Eecke, P., 'Electronic health care services and the e-Commerce Directive', in Dumortier, J., Robben, F. and Taeymans, M. (eds.), *A decade of research @ the crossroads of law and ICT* (Ghent: Larcier, 2001).

van Gerven, M. and Beckers, M., 'Unemployment protection reform in Belgium, Finland, the Netherlands and the UK. Policy learning through OMC?', in Heidenreich, M. and Zeitlin, J. (eds.), *Changing European employment and welfare regimes: the influence of the open method of coordination on national labour market and social welfare reforms* (London: Routledge, 2009).

Van Overmeiren, F., '*Kohll* en *Decker* anders bekeken: de mobiliteit van gezondheidsmedewerkers in de Europese Unie', *Tijdschrift voor Sociaal Recht* 2 (2004), 331–83.

Vanhercke, B., 'The social stakes of economic and monetary union: an overview', in Pochet, P. and Vanhercke, B. (eds.), *Social challenges of economic and monetary union*, Work and Society Series No. 18 (Brussels: European Interuniversity Press, 1998).

'Political spill-over, changing advocacy coalition, path dependency or domestic politics? Theorizing the emergence of the social protection OMC's', Paper presented at the Conference on 'Governing Work and Welfare in an Enlarged Europe', Madison, University of Wisconsin, 19–20 May 2006.

'Is the OMC growing teeth? The governance turn in EU social policy co-ordination', Second Year Paper, University of Amsterdam (2007).

Varkevisser, M., Capps, C. and Schut, F., 'Defining hospital markets for antitrust enforcement: new approaches and their applicability to the Netherlands', *Health Economics Policy and Law* 3 (2008), 7–29.

Visser, J., 'The OMC as selective amplifier for national strategies of reform. What the Netherlands want to learn from Europe', in Zeitlin, J. and Pochet, P. (eds.), *The open method of co-ordination in action: the European employment and social inclusion strategies* (Brussels: PIE-Peter Lang, 2005).

Vos, E., 'European administrative reform and agencies', European University Institute Working Papers No. RSC 2000/31 (2000).

'Reforming the European Commission: what role to play for EU agencies?', *Common Market Law Review* 37 (2000), 1113–34.

'Independence, accountability and transparency', in Geradin, D., Muñoz, R. and Petit, N. (eds.), *Regulation through agencies in the EU: a new paradigm of European governance* (Cheltenham: Edward Elgar, 2005).

Vos, E. and Wendler, F., 'Food safety regulation at the EU level', in Vos, E. and Wendler, F. (eds.), *Food safety regulation in Europe* (Antwerp: Intersentia, 2006).

Vujicic, M. and Zurn, P., 'The dynamics of the health labour market', *International Journal of Health Planning and Management* 21 (2006), 101–15.

Vzajemna, 'Dispute put forward to High Court regarding the new Health Care and Health Insurance Act No. U-I-277/05', Vzajemna, 22 December 2005.

Waelbroeck, D., Slater, D. and Even-Shosan, G., 'Study on the conditions of claims for damages in case of infringement of EC competition rules – comparative report', Ashurst Report for the European Commission (2004), http://ec.europa.eu/competition/antitrust/actionsdamages/comparative_report_clean_En.pdf.

Wagstaff, A., van Doorslaer, E., van der Burg, H., Calonge, S., Christiansen, T., Citoni, G., Gerdtham, U.G., Gerfin, M., Gross, L., Hakinnen, U., Johnson, P., John, J., Klavus, J., Lachaud, C., Lauritsen, J., Leu, R., Nolan, B., Peran, E., Pereira, J., Propper, C., Puffer, F., Rochaix, L., Rodriguez, M., Schellhorn, M. and Winkelhake, O., 'Equity in the finance of health care: some further international comparisons', *Journal of Health Economics* 18 (1999), 263–90.

Warden, J., 'UK adheres to Formula One exemption', *British Medical Journal* 315 (1997), 1397–402.

Wasem, J., 'Regulating private health insurance markets', Paper prepared for the Four Country Conference on 'Health Care Reforms and Health Care Policies in the United States, Canada, Germany and the Netherlands', Ministry of Health, Welfare and Sport, Amsterdam, 23–25 February 1995.

Watson, R., 'European antismoking group loses grant', *British Medical Journal* 311 (1995), 10.

'MEPS back tougher health warnings on cigarette packets', *British Medical Journal* 322 (2001), 7.

'European Working Time Directive: battles in time', *British Medical Journal* 334 (2007), 770–1.

Weatherill, S., *Law and integration in the European Union* (Oxford: Clarendon, 1995).

'Competence creep and competence control', *Yearbook of European Law* 23 (2004), 1–55.

Weiler, J.H.H., 'The Community system: the dual character of supra-nationalism', *Yearbook of European Law* 1 (1982), 267–306.

The constitution of Europe (Cambridge: Cambridge University Press, 1999).

'A constitution for Europe? Some hard choices', *Journal of Common Market Studies* 40 (2002), 563–80.

White, R., *EC social security law* (Harlow: Longman, 1999).

Wicks, E., *Human rights and health care* (Oxford: Hart, 2006).

Wilks, S., 'Agency escape: decentralization or dominance of the European Commission in the modernization of competition policy?', *Governance: An International Journal of Policy, Administration, and Institutions* 18 (2005), 431–52.

Winterstein, A., 'Nailing the jellyfish: social security and competition law', *European Competition Law Review* 6 (1999), 324–33.

Wirtschafts- und Sozialwissenschaftliches Institut (WSI), 'Liberalization, privatization and regulation in the German Healthcare Sector/ Hospitals', November 2006.

Wismar, M., Palm, W., Figueras, J., Ernst, K., van Ginneken, E. (eds.), *Cross-border healthcare: mapping and analysing health systems diversity. Assessing possible directions for the Community action on healthcare services* (Copenhagen: WHO Regional Office for Europe on behalf of the European Observatory on Health Systems and Policies, 2009).

Wismar, M., Busse, R. and Berman, P., 'The European Union and health services – the context', in Busse, R., Wismar, M. and Berman, P. (eds.), *The European Union and health services: the impact of the single European market on Member States* (Amsterdam: IOS Press, 2002).

World Health Organization, *International health regulations* (Geneva: WHO, 2005).

Yates, J., *Private eye, heart and hip* (Edinburgh: Churchill Livingstone, 1995).

Zeitlin, J., 'Social Europe and experimentalist governance: towards a new constitutional compromise?', in de Búrca, G., (ed.), *EU law and the welfare state: in search of solidarity* (Oxford: Oxford University Press, 2005).

'Introduction: the open method of co-ordination in question', in Zeitlin, J. and Pochet, P. (eds.) (with Magnusson, L.), *The open method of co-ordination in action: the European employment and social inclusion strategies* (Brussels: PIE-Peter Lang, 2005).

Zeitlin, J. and Pochet, P. (eds.) (with Magnusson, L.), *The open method of co-ordination in action: the European employment and social inclusion strategies* (Brussels: PIE-Peter Lang, 2005).

Zeitlin, J. and Trubek, D. (eds.), *Governing work and welfare in a new economy* (Oxford: Oxford University Press, 2003).

Zilgavis, P., 'The European Convention on Biomedicine: its past, present and future', in Garwood-Gowers, A., Tingle, J. and Lewis, T. (eds.), *Healthcare law: the impact of the Human Rights Act 1998* (London: Cavendish, 2001).

2. Cases (Numerical Order)

A. *Decisions of the European Court of Justice*

Case 9/56, *Meroni v. High Authority* [1958] ECR 133.

Case 26/62, *Van Gend en Loos* [1963] ECR 1.

Case 6/64, *Costa v. ENEL* [1964] ECR 585.

Case 9/70, *Grad v. Finanzamt Traunstein* [1970] ECR 825.

Case 11/70, *International Handelsgesellschaft mbH v. Einfuhr* [1970] ECR 1125.

Case 39/72, *Commission v. Italy* [1973] ECR 101.

Case 127/73, *Belgishe Radio en Televisie et Société Belge des Auteurs, Compositeurs et Editeurs v. SV SABAM et NV Fonior* [1974] ECR 313.

Case 8/74, *Procureur du Roi v. Dassonville* [1974] ECR 837.

Case 15/74, *Centrafarm v. Sterling Drug* [1974] ECR 1147.

Case 33/74, *Van Binsbergen* [1974] ECR 1299.

Case 41/74, *Van Duyn v. Home Office* [1974] ECR 1337.

Case 36/75, *Rutili* [1975] ECR 1219.

Case 43/75, *Defrenne v. SABENA (No. 2)* [1976] ECR 455.

Case 71/76, *Thieffry* [1977] ECR 765.

Case 117/77, *Bestuur van het Algemeen Ziekenfonds Drenth-Platteland v. G. Pierik* [1978] ECR 825.

Case 120/78, *Cassis de Dijon* [1979] ECR 649.

Case 148/78, *Ratti* [1979] ECR 1629.

Case 182/78, *Pierik* [1979] ECR 1977.

Case 44/79, *Hauer v. Land-Rheinland-Pfalz* [1979] ECR 321.

Case 53/80, *Koninklijke Kaasfabriek Eyssen BV* [1981] ECR 409.

Case 104/81, *Kupferberg* [1982] ECR 3641.

Case 40/82, *Commission v. United Kingdom (Turkeys)* [1982] ECR 2793.

Case 238/82, *Duphar* [1984] ECR 523.
Joined Cases 286/82, and 26/83, *Luisi and Carbone* [1984] ECR 377.
Case 107/83, *Klopp* [1984] ECR 2971.
Case 152/84, *Marshall* [1986] ECR 723.
Case 205/84, *Commission* v. *Germany* [1986] ECR 3755.
Case 96/85, *Commission* v. *France* [1986] ECR 1475.
Joined Cases 98/85, 162/85,and 258/85, *Michele Bertini and Giuseppe Bisignani and others* v. *Regione Lazio and Unità sanitarie locali* [1986] ECR 1885.
Case 118/85, *Commission* v. *Italy* [1987] ECR 2599.
Case 221/85, *Commission* v. *Belgium* [1987] ECR 719.
Case 66/86, *Ahmed Saeed Flugreisen and Silver Line Reiseburo BmbJ* v. *Zentrale sur Bekampfung unlaurteren Wettbewerbs e V* [1989] ECR 803.
Case 263/86, *Belgium* v. *Humbel* [1988] ECR 5365.
Case 292/86, *Gulling* [1988] ECR 11.
Case 143/87, *Stanton* [1988] ECR 3877.
Joined Cases 154/87, and 155/87, *Wolf* [1988] ECR 3897.
Case 238/87, *Volvo Veng* [1988] ECR 6211.
Case 5/88, *Wachauf* [1989] ECR 2609.
Case C-18/88, *Régie des télégraphes et des téléphones (RTT)* v. *GB-Inno-BM SA* [1991] ECR-5941.
Joined Cases C-54/88, C-91/88,and C-14/89, *Criminal proceedings against Eleonora Nino and others* [1990] ECR I-3537.
Case C-61/89, *Bouchoucha* [1990] ECR I-3551.
Case C-113/89, *Rush Portuguesa Ltd* v. *Office national d'immigration* [1990] ECR I-1417.
Case C-213/89, *Factortame* [1990] ECR I-2433.
Case C-260/89, *ERT* [1991] ECR-I-2925.
Case C-288/89, *Gouda* [1991] ECR I-4007.
Case C-340/89, *Vlassopoulou* [1991] ECR I-2357.
Case C-344/89, *Martinez Vidal* [1991] ECR I-3245.
Case C-41/90, *Höfner and Elser* v. *Macrotron* [1991] ECR I-1979.
Case C-76/90, *Säger* v. *Dennemeyer* [1991] ECR I-4221.
Case C-159/90, *SPUC* v. *Grogan* [1991] ECR I-04685.
Case C-179/90, *Merci Convencionali Porto di Genova* v. *Siderugica Gabrielli* [1991] ECR I-5889.
Case C-204/90, *Bachmann* [1992] ECR I-249.
Case C-300/90, *Commission* v. *Belgium* [1992] ECR I-305.
Case C-351/90, *Commission* v. *Luxembourg* [1992] ECR I-3945.
Case C-106/91, *Ramrath* [1992] ECR I-3351.
Joined Cases C-159/91, and 160/91, *Poucet and Pistre* [1993] ECR I-637.

Case C-185/91, *Reiff* [1993] ECR I-5801.

Joined Cases C-241/91 P, and 242/91 P, *Magill* [1995] ECR I-743.

Case C-320/91, *Procureur du Roi* v. *Paul Corbeau* [1993] ECR I-2533.

Case C-19/92, *Kraus* [1993] ECR I-1663.

Case C-37/92, *Vanacker and Lesage* [1993] ECR I-4947.

Case C-109/92, *Wirth* [1993] ECR I-6447.

Case C-275/92, *Customs and Excise Commissioners* v. *Schindler and Schindler* [1994] ECR I-1039.

Case C-319/92, *Haim II* [1994] ECR I-425.

Case C-364/92, *SAT Fluggesellschaft* v. *Eurocontrol* [1994] ECR I-43.

Case C-387/92, *Banco Exterior de España* [1994] ECR I-877.

Case C-393/92, *Municipality of Almelo and Others* v. *NV Energiebedrift Ijsselmij* [1994] ECR I-1477.

Case C-153/93, *Delta* [1994] ECR I-2517.

Case C-384/93, *Alpine Investments* [1995] ECR I-1141.

Case C-387/93, *Banchero* [1995] ECR I-4663.

Case C-392/93, *R* v. *HM Treasury ex parte British Telecommunications PLC* [1996] ECR I-1631.

Case C-55/94, *Gebhard* [1995] ECR I-4165.

Case C-96/94, *Centro Servizi Spediporto* [1995] ECR I-2883.

Case C-101/94, *Commission* v. *Italy* [1996] ECR I-2691.

Case C-157/94, *Commission* v. *Netherlands* [1997] ECR I-5699.

Case C-238/94, *José García* [1996] ECR I-1673.

Case C-272/94, *Guiot and Climatec* [1996] ECR I-1905.

Joined Cases C-34/95 to C-36/95, *De Agostini* [1997] ECR I-3843.

Case C-70/95, *Sodemare* [1997] ECR I-3395.

Case C-120/95, *Decker* v. *Caisse de Maladie des Employés Privés* [1998] ECR I-1831.

Case C-343/95, *Cali and Figli* v. *Servizi Ecologici Porto di Genova* [1997] ECR I-1580.

Joined Cases C-359/95 P, and 379/95 P, *Ladbroke Racing* [1997] ECR I-6265.

Case C-398/95, *SETTG* [1997] ECR I-3091.

Case C-8/96, *Mac Quen* [2001] ECR I-837.

Case C-44/96, *Mannesmann Anlangebau Austria* [1998] ECR I-73.

Case C-67/96, *Albany International* v. *Stichting Bedrijfspensioenfonds Textielindustrie* [1999] ECR I-5751.

Case C-158/96, *Kohll* v. *Union des Caisses de Maladie* [1998] ECR I-1931.

Case C-360/96, *Gemeente Arnhem* v. *BFI Holding* [1998] ECR I-6821.

Case C-38/97, *Librandi* [1998] ECR I-5955.

Case C-75/97, *Maribel* [1999] ECR I-3671.

Case C-76/97, *Tögel* [1998] ECR-5357.

Joined Cases C-115/97 to C-117/97, *Brentjens* v. *Stichting Bedrijfspensioenfonds* [1999] ECR I-6025.

Case C-174/97, *P* [1998] ECR I-1303.

Case C-200/97, *Ecotrade* [1998] ECR I-7907.

Case C-219/97, *Drijvende Bokken* [1999] ECR I-6121.

Case C-256/97, *Déménagements-Manutention Transport SA (DMT)* [1999] ECR I-3913.

Case C-392/97, *Farmitalia Carlo Erba* [1999] ECR I-5553.

Case C-424/97, *Haim* [2000] ECR I-5123.

Case C-107/98, *Teckal* [1999] ECR I-8121.

Joined Cases C-180/98 to C-184/98, *Pavlov a.o.* [2000] ECR I-6451.

Case C-225/98, *Commission* v. *France* [2000] ECR I-7445.

Case C-238/98, *Hocsman* [2000] ECR I-6623.

Case C-239/98, *Commission* v. *France* [1999] ECR I-8935.

Case C-296/98, *Commission* v. *France* [2000] ECR I-3025.

Case C-303/98, *SIMAP* v. *Conselleria de Sanidad* [2000] ECR I-7963.

Case C-324/98, *Telaustria* [2000] ECR I-745.

Case C-367/98, *Commission* v. *Portugal* [2002] ECR I-4731.

Case C-368/98, *Vanbraekel* [2001] ECR I-5363.

Case C-376/98, *Germany* v. *EP and Council (Tobacco Advertising)* [2000] ECR I-8419.

Case C-405/98, *Gourmet International* [2001] ECR I-1795.

Case C-157/99, *Geraets-Smits and Peerbooms* [2001] ECR 5473.

Joined Cases C-223/99, and C-260/99, *Agora and Excelsior* [2001] ECR I-3605.

Case C-232/99, *Commission of the European Communities* v. *Kingdom of Spain* [2002] ECR I-4235.

Case C-274/99 P, *Connolly* v. *Commission* [2001] ECR I-1611.

Case C-309/99, *J. C. J. Wouters et al.* v. *Algemene Raad van de Nederlandse Orde van Advocaten* [2002] ECR I-1577.

Case C-324/99, *DaimlerChrysler,* [2001] ECR I-9897.

Case C-385/99, *Müller-Fauré* [2003] ECR I-4509.

Case C-453/99, *Courage and Crehan* [2001] ECR I-6297.

Case C-475/99, *Ambulanz Glöckner* v. *Landkreis Südwestpfalz* [2001] ECR I-8089.

Case C-483/99, *Commission* v. *France* [2002] ECR I-4781.

Case C-503/99, *Commission* v. *Belgium* [2002] ECR I-4809.

Case C-127/00, *Hässle AB* v. *Ratiopharm* [2003] ECR I-14781.

Case C-218/00, *Cisal di Battistello Venanzio* v. *INAIL* [2002] ECR I-691.

Case C-229/00, *Commission* v. *Finland* [2003] ECR I-5727.

Case C-280/00, *Altmark Trans GmbH* [2003] ECR I-7747.
Case C-294/00, *Deutsche Paracelsus Schulen* v. *Gräbner* [2002] ECR I-6515.
Case C-326/00, *IKA* v. *Ioannidis* [2003] ECR I-01703.
Case C-355/00, *Freskot* v. *Elliniko Dimosio* [2003] ECR I-5263.
Case C-463/00, *Commission* v. *Spain* [2003] ECR I-4581.
Joined Cases C-2/01 P, and C-3/01 P, *BAI and Commission* v. *Bayer* [2004] ECR I-23.
Case C-56/01, *Inizan* v. *Caisse primarie d'assurance maladie des Hauts de Seine* [2003] ECR I-2403.
Case C-101/01, *Lindqvist* [2003] ECR I-12971.
Case C-106/01, *Novartis* [2004] ECR I-4403.
Case C-110/01, *Tennah-Durez* [2003] ECR I-6239.
Case C-156/01, *van der Duin* v. *Wegberg/ANOZ* [2003] ECR I-07045.
Case C-198/01, *Consorzio Industrie Fiammiferi (CIF) Autorita Garante della Concorrenza e del Mercato* [2003] ECR I-8055.
Joined Cases C-264/01, C-301/01, C-354/01, and C-355/01, *AOK Bundesverband* [2004] ECR I-2493.
Case C-223/01, *AstraZeneca* [2003] ECR I-11809.
Case C-322/01, *DocMorris* [2003] ECR I-14887.
Joined Cases C-397/01, and C-403/01, *Pfeiffer* [2004] ECR I-8835.
Case C-418/01, *IMS* [2004] ECR I-5039.
Case C-491/01, *R* v. *Secretary of State for Health, ex parte British American Tobacco and Imperial Tobacco* [2002] ECR I-11453.
Case C-496/01, *Commission* v. *France*, [2004] ECR I-2351.
Case C-8/02, *Leichtle* [2004] ECR I-2641.
Case C-151/02, *Jaeger* [2003] ECR I-8389.
Case C-434/02, *André* v. *Landrat des Kreises Herford* [2004] ECR I-11825.
Case C-36/03, *Approved Prescription Services* [2004] ECR I-11583.
Case C-74/03, *SmithKline Beecham* [2005] ECR I-595.
Case C-140/03, *Commission* v. *Greece*, [2005] ECR I-3177.
Case C-145/03, *Keller* [2005] ECR I-2529.
Case C-147/03, *Commission of the European Communities* v. *Republic of Austria* [2005] ECR I-7963.
Case C-205/03 P, *Federacion National de Empresas de Instrumentacion Cientifica Medica Tecnica y Dental (FENIN)* v. *Commission of the European Communities* [2006] ECR I-6295
Case C-210/03, *Swedish Match AB* [2004] ECR I-11893.
Case C-231/03, *Coname* [2005] ECR I-7287.
Case C-234/03, *Contse* [2005] ECR I-9315.
Case C-380/03, *Germany* v. *EP and Council (Tobacco Advertising No. 2)* [2006] ECR I-11573.

Case C-458/03, *Parking Brixen* [2005] ECR I-8612.

Case C-532/03, *Commission* v. *Ireland (Ambulance Services)* [2007] ECR I-11353.

Joined Cases C-94/04, and C-202/04, *Cipolla e.a.* [2006] ECR I-11421.

Joined Cases C-295/04 to C-298/04, *Manfredi* [2006] ECR I-6619.

Joined Cases C-338/04, C-359/04,and C-360/04, *Placanica* [2007] ECR I-1891.

Case C-372/04, *Yvonne Watts* v. *Bedford Primary Care Trust, Secretary of State for Health* [2006] ECR I-4325.

Case C-466/04, *Acereda-Herrera* [2006] ECR I-5341.

Case C-444/05, *Aikaterini Stamatelaki* v. *NPDD Organismos Asfeliseos Eleftheron Epangelmation (OAEE)* [2007] ECR I-1385.

Case C-507/03 *Commission* v *Ireland, An Post* [2007] ECR I-168.

Case C-446/05, *Doulamis* [2008] ECR I-1377.

Case C-456/05, *Commission* v. *Germany* [2007] ECR I-10517.

Case C-119/06, *Commission* v. *Italy, Ambulance Services* [2007] ECR I-168.

Joined Cases C-468/06 to C-478/06, *Sot. Lelos kai Sia EE* [2008] ECR I-7139.

Case C-489/06, *Commission* v. *Hellenic Republic* (not yet reported).

Case C-500/06, *Corporacion Dermoestetica SA* v. *To Me Group Advertising* [2008] ECR I-5785.

Case C-501/06-P, *GlaxoSmithKline Services Unlimited* v. *Commission* (not yet reported).

Case C-513/06-P, *Commission* v. *GlaxoSmithKline Services Unlimited* (not yet reported).

Case C-515/06-P, *European Association of Euro-Pharmaceutical Companies* v. *GlaxoSmithKline Services Unlimited* (not yet reported).

Case C-519/06-P, *Asociación de exportadores españoles de productos farmacéuticos* v. *GlaxoSmithKline Services Unlimited* (not yet reported).

Case C-531/06, *Commission* v. *Italy* (judgment pending).

Case C-169/07, *Hartlauer Handelsgesellschaft mbH* v. *Wiener Landesregierung and Oberösterreichische Landsergierung* (not yet reported).

Joined Cases C-171/07, and C-172/07, *Apothekerkammer des Saarlandes and others* and *Neumann-Seiwert* (not yet reported).

Joined Cases C-570/07, and C-571/07, *Pérez and Gómez* (judgment pending).

B. Decisions of the Court of First Instance

Case T-106/95, *FFSA* v. *Commission* [1997] ECR II-229.

Case T-41/96, *Bayer AG* v. *Commission* [2000] ECR II-3383.

Joined Cases T-172/98, and T-175/98 to T-177/98, *Salamander* [2000] ECR II-2487.

Case T-319/99, *FENIN* v. *Commission* [2003] ECR II-357.

Case T-326/99, *Olivieri* v. *Commission and European Agency for the Evaluation of Medicinal Products* [2003] ECR II-06053.

Case T-123/00, *Thomae* v. *Commission* [2002] ECR II-5193.

Case T-311/00, *British American Tobacco (Investments) Ltd* v. *Commission* [2002] ECR II-2781.

Case T-168/01, *GlaxoSmithKline Services* v. *Commission* [2006] ECR II-2969.

Case T-133/03, *Schering-Plough Ltd* v. *Commission and EMEA*. Order of the CFI, OJ 2008 C.37/22.

Case T-289/03, *British United Provident Association Ltd (BUPA) and Others* v. *Commission* [2008] ECR II-81.

Case T-321/05, *AstraZeneca* v. *Commission* (judgment pending).

3. Directives (Numerical Order)

Council Directive 64/221/EEC on the co-ordination of special measures concerning the movement and residence of foreign nationals which are justified on grounds of public policy, public security or public health, OJ 1964 No. L56/850.

Council Directive 65/65/EEC on the approximation of provisions laid down by law, regulation or administrative action relating to proprietary medicinal products, OJ 1965 No. L22/369.

Council Directive 73/239/EEC on the coordination of laws, regulations and administrative provisions relating to the taking-up and pursuit of the business of direct insurance other than life assurance, OJ 1973 No. L 228/3.

Council Directive 75/318/EEC on the approximation of the laws of Member States relating to analytical, pharmacotoxicological and clinical standards and protocols in respect of the testing of medicinal products, OJ 1975 No. L147/1.

Council Directive 75/319/EEC on the approximation of provisions laid down by law, regulation or administrative action relating to medicinal products, OJ 1975 No. L147/13.

Council Directive 76/207/EEC, on the implementation of the principle of equal treatment for men and women as regards access to employment, vocational training and promotion, and working conditions, OJ 1976 No. L39/40.

Council Directive 77/187/EEC on the approximation of the laws of the Member States relating to the safeguarding of employees' rights in the event of transfers of undertakings, businesses or parts of businesses, OJ 1977 No. L61/26.

Commission Directive 80/723/EEC on the transparency of financial relations between Member States and public undertakings, OJ 1980 No. L195/35.

Council Directive 83/477/EEC on the protection of workers from the risks related to exposure to asbestos at work (second individual Directive within the meaning of Article 8 of Directive 80/1107/EEC), OJ 1983 No. L263/25.

Council Directive 83/570/EEC amending Directives 65/65/EEC, 75/318/EEC and 75/319/EEC on the approximation of provisions laid down by law, regulation or administrative action relating to proprietary medicinal products, OJ 1983 No. L332/1.

Council Directive 85/374 on the approximation of the laws, regulations and administrative provisions of the Member States concerning liability for defective products, OJ 1985 No. L210/29.

Council Directive 87/22/EEC on the approximation of national measures relating to the placing on the market of high-technology medicinal products, particularly those derived from biotechnology, OJ 1987 No. L15/38.

Council Directive 88/357/EEC on the coordination of laws, regulations and administrative provisions relating to direct insurance other than life assurance and laying down provisions to facilitate the effective exercise of freedom to provide services and amending Directive 73/239/EEC, OJ 1988 No. L172/1.

Council Directive 88/378/EEC on the approximation of the laws of the Member States concerning the safety of toys, OJ 1988 No. L187/1.

Council Directive 89/105/EEC relating to the transparency of measures regulating the prices of medicinal products for human use and their inclusion in the scope of national health insurance systems, OJ 1989 No. L40/8.

Council Directive 89/391/EEC on the introduction of measures to encourage improvements in the safety and health of workers at work, OJ 1989 No. L183/1.

Council Directive 89/552/EEC on the coordination of certain provisions laid down by law, regulation or administrative action in Member States concerning the pursuit of television broadcasting activities, OJ 1989 No. L298/23.

Council Directive 89/622/EEC on the approximation of the laws, regulations and administrative provisions of the Member States concerning the labelling of tobacco products, OJ 1989 No. L359/1.

Council Directive 89/654/EEC concerning the minimum safety and health requirements for the workplace (first individual Directive within the meaning of Article 16(1) of Directive 89/391/EEC), OJ 1989 No. L393/1.

Council Directive 89/665/EEC on the coordination of the laws, regulations and administrative provisions relating to the application of review procedures to the award of public supply and public works contracts, OJ 1989 No. L395/33.

Council Directive 90/425/EEC concerning veterinary and zootechnical checks applicable in intra-Community trade in certain live animals and products with a view to the completion of the internal market, OJ 1990 No. L224/29.

Council Directive 91/440/EEC for the development of community rail, OJ 1991 No. L237/25.

Commission Directive 91/356/EEC laying down the principles and guidelines of good manufacturing practice for medicinal products for human use, OJ 1991 No. L193/30.

Council Directive 92/25/EEC on the wholesale distribution of medicinal products for human use, OJ 1992 No. L113/1.

Council Directive 92/26/EEC concerning the classification for the supply of medicinal products for human use, OJ 1992 No. L113/5.

Council Directive 92/27/EEC on the labelling of medicinal products for human use and on package leaflets, OJ 1992 No. L113/8.

Council Directive 92/41/EEC amending Directive 89/622/EEC on the approximation of the laws, regulations and administrative provisions of the Member States concerning the labelling of tobacco products, OJ 1992 No. L158/30.

Council Directive 92/49/EEC on the coordination of laws, regulations and administrative provisions relating to direct insurance other than life assurance, (third 'non-life insurance' Directive), OJ 1992 No. L228/23.

Council Directive 92/50/EEC relating to the coordination of procedures for the award of public service contracts, OJ 1992 No. L209/1.

Council Directive 92/78/EEC amending Directives 72/464/EEC and 79/32/EEC on taxes other than turnover taxes which are levied on the consumption of manufactured tobacco, OJ 1992 No. L316/1.

Council Directive 92/80/EEC on the approximation of taxes on manufactured tobacco other than cigarettes, OJ 1992 No. L316/10.

Council Directive 93/42/EEC concerning medical devices, OJ 1993 No. L169/1.

Council Directive 93/16/EEC to facilitate the free movement of doctors and the mutual recognition of their diplomas, certificates and other evidence of formal qualifications, OJ 1993 No. L165/1.

Council Directive 93/37/EEC concerning the coordination of procedures for the award of public works contracts, OJ 1993 No. L199/54.

Council Directive 93/38/EC coordinating the procurement procedures of entities operating in the water, energy, transport and telecommunications sectors, OJ 1993 No. L82/39.

Council Directive 93/39/EEC amending Directives 65/65/EEC, 75/318/EEC and 75/319/EEC in respect of medicinal products, OJ 1993 No. L214/22.

Council Directive 93/104/EC concerning certain aspects of the organization of working time, OJ 1993 No. L307/18.

Council Directive 95/46/EC on the protection of individuals with regard to the processing of personal data and on the free movement of such data, OJ 1995 No. L281/31.

Council Directive 96/62/EC on ambient air quality assessment and management, OJ 1996 No. L296/1.

European Parliament, and Council Directive 97/7/EC on the protection of consumers in respect of distance contracts, OJ 1997 No. L144/19.

European Parliament, and Council Directive 98/43/EC on the approximation of the laws, regulations and administrative provisions of the Member States relating to the advertising and sponsorship of tobacco products, OJ 1998 No. L213/9.

Council Directive 1999/81/EC amending Directive 92/79/EEC on the approximation of taxes on cigarettes, Directive 92/80/EEC on the approximation of taxes on manufactured tobacco other than cigarettes and Directive 95/59/EC on taxes other than turnover taxes which affect the consumption of manufactured tobacco, OJ 1999 No. L211/47.

European Parliament, and Council Directive 1999/93 on a Community framework for electronic signatures, OJ 2000 No. L13/12.

European Parliament, and Council Directive 2000/31 on certain legal aspects of information society services, in particular electronic commerce, in the internal market (Directive on electronic commerce), OJ 2000 No. L178/1.

European Parliament, and Council Directive 2000/34/EC amending Directive 93/104/EC concerning certain aspects of the organisation of working time to cover sectors and activities excluded from that Directive, OJ 2000 No. L195/41.

Council Directive 2000/43/EC implementing the principle of equal treatment between persons irrespective of racial or ethnic origin, OJ 2000 No. L180/22.

European Parliament, and Council Directive 2000/60/EC establishing a framework for Community action in the field of water policy, OJ 2000 No. L327/1.

Council Directive 2000/78/EC establishing a general framework for equal treatment in employment and occupation, OJ 2000 No. L303/16.

European Parliament, and Council Directive 2001/12/EC modifying Directive 91/440/EEC, OJ 2001 No. L75/1.

European Parliament, and Council Directive 2001/20/EC on the approximation of the laws, regulations and administrative provisions of the Member States relating to the implementation of good clinical practice in the conduct of clinical trials on medicinal products for human use, OJ 2001 No. L121/34.

European Parliament, and Council Directive 2001/37/EC on the approximation of the laws, regulations and administrative provisions of the Member States concerning the manufacture, presentation and sale of tobacco products, OJ 2001 No. L194/26.

European Parliament, and Council Directive 2001/83/EC on the Community code relating to medicinal products for human use, OJ 2001 No. L311/67.

Council Directive 2002/10/EC of 12 February 2002 amending Directives 92/79/EEC, 92/80/EEC and 95/59/EC as regards the structure and rates of excise duty applied on manufactured tobacco, OJ 1992 No. L46/26.

European Parliament, and Council Directive 2002/49/EC relating to the assessment and management of environmental noise, OJ 2002 No. L189/1.

European Parliament, and Council Directive 2002/98/EC setting standards of quality and safety for the collection, testing, processing, storage and distribution of human blood and blood components and amending Directive 2001/83/EC, OJ 2003 No. L33/30.

European Parliament, and Council Directive 2003/33/EC on the approximation of the laws, regulations and administrative provisions of the Member States relating to the advertising and sponsorship of tobacco products, OJ 2003 No. L152/16.

European Parliament, and Council Directive 2003/88/EC concerning certain aspects of the organisation of working time, OJ 2003 No. L299/9.

European Parliament, and Council Directive 2004/17/EC coordinating the procurement procedures of entities operating in the water, energy, transport and postal service sectors, OJ 2004 No. L134/1.

European Parliament, and Council Directive 2004/18/EC on the coordination of procedures for the award of public works contracts, public supply contracts and public service contracts, OJ 2004 No. L134/114.

European Parliament, and Council Directive 2004/23/EC on setting standards of quality and safety for the donation, procurement, testing, processing, preservation, storage and distribution of human tissues and cells, OJ 2004 No. L102/48.

European Parliament, and Council Directive 2004/27/EC amending Directive 2001/83/EC on the Community code relating to medicinal products for human use, OJ 2004 No. L136/34.

European Parliament, and Council Directive 2004/38/EC on the right of citizens of the Union and their family members to move and reside freely within the territory of the Member States amending Regulation 1612/68/EEC and repealing Directives 64/221/EEC, 68/360/EEC, 72/194/EEC, 73/148/EEC, 75/34/EEC, 75/35/EEC, 90/364/EEC, 90/365/EEC and 93/96/EEC, OJ 2004 No. L158/77.

European Parliament, and Council Directive 2005/36/EC on the recognition of professional qualifications, OJ 2005 No. L255/22.

Directive 2005/81/EC, amending Directive 80/723/EEC on the transparency of financial relations between Member States and public undertakings as well as on financial transparency within certain undertakings, OJ 2005 No. L312/47.

European Parliament, and Council Directive 2006/12/EC on waste, OJ 2006 No. L114/1.

Council Directive 2006/97/EC adapting certain Directives in the field of free movement of goods, by reason of the accession of Bulgaria and Romania, OJ 2006 No. L363/107.

European Parliament, and Council Directive 2006/123/EC on services in the internal market, OJ 2006 No. L376/36.

European Parliament, and Council Directive 2007/44/EC of 5 September 2007 amending Council Directive 92/49/EEC and Directives 2002/83/EC, 2004/39/EC, 2005/68/EC and 2006/48/EC as regards procedural rules and evaluation criteria for the prudential assessment of acquisitions and increase of holdings in the financial sector, OJ 2007 No. L247/1.

European Parliament, and Council Directive 2007/47/EC amending Council Directive 90/385/EEC on the approximation of the laws of the Member States relating to active implantable medical devices, Council Directive 93/42/EEC, concerning medical devices and Directive 98/8/EEC concerning the placing of biocidal products on the market, OJ 2007 No. L247/21.

European Parliament, and Council Directive 2007/66/EC amending Council Directives 89/665/EEC and 92/13/EEC with regard to improving the effectiveness of review procedures concerning the award of public contracts, OJ 2007 No. L335/31.

European Parliament, and Council Directive 2008/27/EC amending Directive 2001/18/EC on the deliberate release into the environment of genetically modified organisms, as regards the implementing powers conferred on the Commission, OJ 2008 No. L81/45.

European Parliament, and Council Directive 2009/81/EC on the coordination of procedures for the award of certain works, contracts, supply contracts and service contracts, OJ 2009 K216/71.

4. Decisions (Numerical Order)

Council, and Representatives of the Governments of the Member States Decision 88/351/EC adopting a 1988 to 1989 plan of action for an information and public awareness campaign in the context of the 'Europe against cancer' programme, OJ 1988 No. L160/52.

Council, and Ministers for Health of the Member States Decision 91/317/EEC adopting a plan of action in the framework of the 1991 to 1993 'Europe against AIDS' programme, OJ 1991 No. L175/26.

Commission Decision 2000/520 pursuant to European Parliament, and Council Directive 95/46/EC on the adequacy of the protection provided by the safe harbour privacy principles and related frequently asked questions issued by the US Department of Commerce, OJ 2000 No. L215/7.

Council Decision 2002/187/JHA setting up Eurojust with a view to reinforcing the fight against serious crime, OJ 2002 No. L63/1.

European Parliament, and Council Decision 2002/1786/EC adopting a programme of Community action in the field of public health (2003–2008), OJ 2002 No. L271/1.

Commission Decision 2004/858/EC setting up an executive agency, the 'Executive Agency for the Public Health Programme', for the management of Community action in the field of public health, pursuant to Council Regulation 58/2003/EC, OJ 2004 No. L369/73.

Commission Decision 2005/842/EC on the application of Article 86(2) of the EC Treaty to state aid in the form of public service compensation granted to certain undertakings entrusted with the operation of services of general economic interest, OJ 2005 No. L312/67.

Council Decision 2006/702/EC on Community strategic guidelines on cohesion, OJ 2006 No. L291/11.

European Parliament, and Council Decision 2006/1982/EC concerning the Seventh Framework Programme of the European Community for research, technological development and demonstration activities (2007–2013), OJ 2006 No. L412/1.

European Parliament, and Council Decision 2007/1350/EC establishing a second programme of Community action in the field of health (2008–13), OJ 2007 No. L301/3.

Council Decision 2007/198/Euratom establishing the European Joint Undertaking for ITER and the Development of Fusion Energy and conferring advantages upon it, OJ 2007 No. L90/58.

Council Decision 2008/203/EC implementing Regulation 168/2007/EC as regards the adoption of a Multi-annual Framework for the European Union Agency for Fundamental Rights for 2007–2012, OJ 2008 No. L63/14.

Commission Decision 2008/351/EC amending Decision 2000/57/EC as regards events to be reported within the early warning and response system for the prevention and control of communicable diseases, OJ 2008 No. L117/40.

Commission Decision 2008/544/EC amending Decision 2004/858/EC in order to transform the Executive Agency for the Public Health Programme into the Executive Agency for Health and Consumers, OJ 2008 No. L173/27.

5. Regulations (Numerical Order)

Council Regulation 1408/71/EEC on the application of social security schemes to employed persons and their families moving within the Community, OJ 1971 Sp.Ed. Series I, p. 416.

Council Regulation 574/72/EEC fixing the procedure for implementing Regulation 1408/71/EEC on the coordination of social security schemes for persons moving within the Community, OJ 1971 Sp.Ed. Series I, p. 159.

Council Regulation 337/75/EEC establishing a European Centre for the Development of Vocational Training, OJ 1975 No. L39/1.

Council Regulation 1365/75/EEC on the creation of a European Foundation for the improvement of living and working conditions, OJ 1975 No. L139/1.

Council Regulation 1210/90/EEC on the establishment of the European Environment Agency and the European Environment Information and Observation Network, OJ 1990 No. L120/1.

Council Regulation 1360/90/EEC establishing a European Training Foundation, OJ 1990 No. L131/1.

Council Regulation 1768/92/EEC concerning the creation of a supplementary protection certificate for medicinal products, OJ 1992 No. L182/1.

Council Regulation 302/93/EEC on the establishment of a European Monitoring Centre for Drugs and Drug Addiction, OJ 1993 No. L36/1.

Council Regulation 2309/93/EEC laying down Community procedures for the authorization and supervision of medicinal products for human and veterinary use and establishing a European Agency for the Evaluation of Medicinal Products, OJ 1993 No. L214/1.

Council Regulation 40/94/EC on the Community trade mark, OJ 1994 No. L11/1.

Council Regulation 2062/94/EC establishing a European Agency for Safety and Health at Work, OJ 1994 No. L216/1.

Council Regulation 2063/94/EC amending Regulation 1360/90/EEC establishing a European Training Foundation, OJ 1994 No. L216/9.

Council Regulation 2100/94/EC on Community plant variety rights, OJ 1994 No. L227/1.

Council Regulation 2965/94/EC setting up a Translation Centre for bodies of the European Union, OJ 1994 No. L314/1.

Council Regulation 3294/94/EC amending Regulation 302/93/EEC on the establishment of the European Monitoring Centre for Drugs and Drug Addiction, OJ 1994 No. L341/7.

Commission Regulation 542/95/EC concerning the examination of variations to the terms of a marketing authorization falling within the scope of Council Regulation 2309/93/EEC, OJ 1995 No. L55/15.

Council Regulation 1643/95/EC amending Regulation 2062/94/EC establishing a European Agency for Safety and Health at Work, OJ 1995 No. L156/1.

Council Regulation 2506/95/EC amending Regulation 2100/94/EC on Community plant variety rights, OJ 1995 No. L258/3.

Council Regulation 2610/95/EC amending Regulation 2965/94/EC setting up a Translation Centre for bodies of the European Union, OJ 1995 No. L268/1.

Council Regulation 1572/98/EC amending Regulation 1360/90/EEC establishing a European Training Foundation, OJ 1998 No. L206/1.

Council Regulation 933/1999/EC amending Regulation 1210/90/EEC on the establishment of the European Environment Agency and the European Environment Information and Observation Network, OJ 1999 No. L117/1.

European Parliament, and Council Regulation 1784/1999/EC on the European Social Fund, OJ 1999 No. L213/5.

Council Regulation 2454/1999/EC amending Regulation 1628/96/EC relating to aid for Bosnia and Herzegovina, Croatia, the Federal Republic of Yugoslavia and the former Yugoslav Republic of Macedonia, in particular by the setting up of a European Agency for Reconstruction, OJ 1999 No. L299/1.

Council Regulation 2666/2000/EC on assistance for Albania, Bosnia and Herzegovina, Croatia, the Federal Republic of Yugoslavia and the Former Yugoslav Republic of Macedonia, repealing Regulation 1628/96/

EC and amending Regulations 3906/89/EEC and 1360/90/EEC and Decisions 97/256/EC and 1999/311/EC, OJ 2000 No. L306/1.

Council Regulation 2667/2000/EC on the European Agency for Reconstruction, OJ 2000 No. L306/7.

European Parliament, and Council Regulation 1049/2001/EC regarding public access to European Parliament, Council and Commission documents, OJ 2001 No. L145/43.

Council Regulation 2415/2001/EC amending Regulation 2666/2000/EC on assistance for Albania, Bosnia and Herzegovina, Croatia, the Federal Republic of Yugoslavia and the Former Yugoslav Republic of Macedonia and Regulation 2667/2000/EC on the European Agency for Reconstruction, OJ 2001 No. L327/3.

European Parliament, and Council Regulation 178/2002/EC laying down the principles and requirements of food law, establishing the European Food Safety Authority and laying down procedures in matters of food safety, OJ 2002 No. L31/1.

European Parliament, and Council Regulation 1406/2002/EC establishing a European Maritime Safety Agency, OJ 2002 No. L208/1.

European Parliament, and Council Regulation 1592/2002/EC on common rules in the field of civil aviation and establishing a European Aviation Safety Agency, OJ 2002 No. L240/1.

Council Regulation 1/2003/EC on the implementation of the rules on competition laid down in Articles 81 and 82 of the EC Treaty, OJ 2003 No. L1/1.

Council Regulation 58/2003/EC laying down the statute for executive agencies to be entrusted with certain tasks in the management of Community programmes, OJ 2003 No. L11/1.

Council Regulation 859/2003/EC extending the provisions of Regulation 1408/71/EEC and Regulation 574/72/EEC to nationals of third countries who are not already covered by those provisions solely on the ground of their nationality, OJ 2003 No. L124/1.

European Parliament, and Council Regulation 460/2004/EC establishing the European Network and Information Security Agency, OJ 2004 No. L77/1.

European Parliament, and Council Regulation 631/2004/EC amending Council Regulation 1408/71/EEC on the application of social security schemes to employed persons, to self-employed persons and to members of their families moving within the Community, and Council Regulation 574/72/EEC laying down the procedure for implementing Regulation 1408/71/EEC, in respect of the alignment of rights and the simplification of procedures, OJ 2004 No. L100/1.

European Parliament, and Council Regulation 851/2004/EC establishing a European Centre for disease prevention and control, OJ 2004 No. L142/1.

European Parliament, and Council Regulation 726/2004/EC laying down Community procedures for the authorization and supervision of medicinal products for human and veterinary use and establishing a European Medicines Agency, OJ 2004 No. L136/1.

European Parliament, and Council Regulation 851/2004/EC establishing a European Centre for disease prevention and control, OJ 2004 No. L142/1.

European Parliament, and Council Regulation 881/2004/EC establishing a European railway agency (Agency Regulation), OJ 2004 No. L220/3.

European Parliament, and Council Regulation 883/2004/EC on the coordination of social security systems, OJ 2004 No. L166/1.

Council Regulation 1321/2004/EC on the establishment of structures for the management of the European satellite radio-navigation programmes, OJ 2004 No. L246/1.

Council Regulation 2007/2004/EC establishing a European Agency for the Management of Operational Cooperation at the External Borders of the Member States of the European Union, OJ 2004 No. L349/1.

Council Regulation 768/2005/EC establishing a Community Fisheries Control Agency and amending Regulation 2847/93/EEC establishing a control system applicable to the common fisheries policy, OJ 2005 No. L128/1.

European Parliament, and Council Regulation 1080/2006/EC on the European Regional Development Fund and repealing Regulation 1783/1999/EC, OJ 2006 No. L210/1.

European Parliament, and Council Regulation 1081/2006/EC on the European Social Fund and repealing Regulation 1784/1999/EC, OJ 2006 No. L210/12.

Council Regulation 1083/2006/EC laying down general provisions on the European Regional Development Fund, the European Social Fund and the Cohesion Fund and repealing Regulation 1260/1999/EC, OJ 2006 No. L210/25.

European Parliament, and Council Regulation 1901/2006/EC on medicinal products for paediatric use and amending Regulation 1768/92/EEC, Directive 2001/20/EC, Directive 2001/83/EC and Regulation 726/2004/EC, OJ 2006 No. L378/1.

European Parliament, and Council Regulation 1907/2006/EC concerning the Registration, Evaluation, Authorisation and Restriction of Chemicals (REACH), establishing a European Chemicals Agency, amending Directive 1999/45/EC and repealing Council Regulation 793/93/EEC and Commission Regulation 1488/94/EC as well as Council Directive 76/769/EEC and Commission Directives 91/155/ EEC, 93/67/EEC, 93/105/EC and 2000/21/EC, OJ 2006 No. L396/1.

European Parliament, and Council Regulation 1922/2006/EC on establishing a European Institute for Gender Equality, OJ 2006 No. L403/9.

European Parliament, and Council Regulation 1924/2006/EC on nutrition and health claims made on foods, corrected version at OJ 2006 No. L44/1.

Council Regulation 168/2007/EC establishing a European Union Agency for Fundamental Rights, OJ 2007 No. L53/1.

European Parliament, and Council Regulation 863/2007/EC establishing a mechanism for the creation of Rapid Border Intervention Teams and amending Council Regulation 2007/2004/EC as regards that mechanism and regulating the tasks and powers of guest officers, OJ 2007 No. L199/30.

Commission Regulation 1422/2007/EC amending Directives 2004/17/EC and 2004/18/EC of the European Parliament and of the Council in respect of their application thresholds for the procedures for the award of contracts, OJ 2007 No. L317/34.

European Parliament, and Council Regulation 1137/2008 EC adapting a number of instruments subject to the procedure laid down in Article 251 of the Treaty to Council Decision 1999/468/EC, with regard to the regulatory procedure with scrutiny – Adaptation to the regulatory procedure with scrutiny OJ 2008 No. L311/1.

6. Commission Documents (Chronological Order)

European Commission, 'Communication concerning the consequences of the judgment given by the Court of Justice on 20 February 1979 in Case 120/78 *Cassis de Dijon*', OJ 1980 No. C256/2.

'Technical harmonisation and standards, a new approach', COM (85) 19 final, 31 January 1985.

'Completion of the internal market', White Paper, COM (85) 310 final, 14 June 1986.

'Social protection in Europe', COM (93) 531 final, 26 April 1994.

'European social policy, options for the Union', Green Paper, COM (93) 551 final, 17 November 1993.

'European social policy. A way forward for the Union', White Paper, COM (94) 333 final, 27 July 1994.

'The future of social protection, framework for a European debate', COM (95) 466 final, 31 October 1995.

'Communication on services of general interest in Europe', COM (96) 443 final, 11 September 1996.

'Report from the Commission to the Council, the European Parliament, the Economic and Social Committee and the Committee on the Response to the Resolution of the Council and the Ministers for Health and the Member States Meeting on banning smoking in places open to the public', COM (96) 573 final, 14 November 1996.

'General principles of food law in the European Union', Green Paper, COM (97) 176 final, 30 April 1997.

'Communication on the development of public health policy in the European Community', COM (98) 230 final, 15 April 1998.

'Communication on the single market in pharmaceuticals', COM (98) 588 final, 25 November 1998.

'A concerted strategy for modernising social protection', COM (99) 347 final, 14 July 1999.

'Progress achieved in relation to public health protection from the harmful effects of tobacco consumption', COM (99) 407 final, 8 September 1999.

'Food safety', White Paper, COM (99) 719 final, 12 January 2000.

'Services of general interest in Europe', COM (2000) 580 final, 20 September 2000.

'Proposal for a European Parliament and Council Directive amending Directive 2001/83/EC on the Community code relating to medicinal products for human use', COM (2001) 404 final, 26 November 2001.

'European governance', White Paper, COM (2001) 428 final, 25 July 2001.

'The future of health care and care for the elderly: guaranteeing accessibility, quality and financial viability', COM (2001) 723 final, 5 December 2001.

'Action plan of the Commission on skills and mobility', COM (2002) 72 final, 13 February 2002.

'Draft proposal for a European Parliament and Council Regulation on action by Member States concerning public service requirements and the award of public service contracts in passenger transport by rail, road and inland waterway', COM (2002) 107 final, 21 February 2002.

'Operating framework for the European agencies', COM (2002) 718 final, 11 December 2002.

'Proposal for a Joint Report. Health care and care for the elderly: supporting national strategies for ensuring a high level of social protection', COM (2002) 774 final, 3 January 2003.

'Communication concerning the introduction of the European health insurance card', COM (2003) 73 final, 17 February 2003.

'Amended proposal for a European Parliament and Council Directive amending Directive 2001/83/EC on the Community code relating to medicinal products for human use', COM (2003) 163 final, 3 April 2003.

'Services of general interest', Green Paper, COM (2003) 270 final, 21 May 2003.

'A stronger European-based pharmaceutical industry for the benefit of the patient – a call for action', COM (2003) 383 final, 1 July 2003.

'Communication on parallel import of proprietary medicinal products for which marketing authorisations have already been granted', COM (2003) 839 final, 30 December 2003.

'Proposal for a European Parliament and Council Directive on services in the internal market', COM (2004) 2 final, 5 March 2004.

'Communication from the Commission – report on competition in professional services', COM (2004) 83 final, 9 February 2004.

'Follow-up to the high level reflection process on patient mobility and healthcare developments in the European Union', COM (2004) 301 final, 20 April 2004.

'Amended proposal for an European Parliament and Council Directive on the recognition of professional qualifications', COM (2004) 317 final, 20 April 2004.

'e-Health – making healthcare better for European citizens: An action plan for a European e-Health Area', COM (2004) 356 final, 30 April 2004.

'Proposal for a European Parliament and Council Decision establishing a Programme of Community action in the field of Health and Consumer Protection 2007–13', COM (2005) 115 final, 6 April 2005.

'Amended proposal for a Directive of the European Parliament and of the Council amending Directive 2003/88/EC concerning certain aspects of the organisation of working time', COM (2005) 246 final, 31 May 2005.

'Promoting the mental health of the population: towards a strategy on mental health for the European Union', Green Paper, COM (2005) 484 final, 14 October 2005.

'Communication on public-private partnerships and community law on public procurement and concessions', COM (2005) 569 final, 15 November 2005.

'Community Framework for state aid in the form of public service compensation', OJ 2005 No. C297/4.

'Annual policy strategy for 2007, boosting trust through action', COM (2006) 122 final, 14 March 2006.

'Communication on the International Health Regulations', COM (2006) 552 final, 26 September 2006.

'Interpretative Communication on the Community law applicable to contract awards not or not fully subject to the provisions of the public procurement directives', OJ 2006 No. C179/2.

'Towards a Europe free from tobacco smoke: policy options at EU level', Green Paper, COM (2007) 27 final, 30 January 2007.

'Communication pursuant to the second subparagraph of Article 251(2) of the EC Treaty concerning the common position of the Council on the adoption of a European Parliament and Council Decision establishing a second Programme of Community action in the field of Health (2007–2013)', COM (2007) 150 final, 23 March 2007.

'Organ donation and transplantation: policy actions at EU level', COM (2007) 275 final, 30 May 2007.

'Together for health: a strategic approach for the EU 2008–2013', White Paper, COM (2007) 630 final, 23 October 2007.

'Communication from the Commission – a single market for 21st century Europe', COM (2007) 724 final, 20 November 2007.

'Communication on "a single market for 21st century Europe" – services of general interest, including social services of general interest: a new European commitment', COM (2007) 725 final, 20 November 2007.

'A lead market initiative for Europe', COM (2007) 860 final, 21 December 2007.

'Report on current practice with regard to provision of information to patients on medicinal products', COM (2007) 862 final, 20 December 2007.

'Amended Proposal for a Directive of the European Parliament and of the Council on the taking-up and pursuit of the business of insurance and reinsurance (SOLVENCY II)', COM (2008) 119 final, 21 April 2008.

'The way forward', COM (2008) 135 final; and SEC (2008) 323, 11 March 2008.

'Proposal for a European Parliament and Council Directive on the application of patients' rights in cross-border healthcare', COM (2008) 414 final, 2 July 2008.

'A Community framework on the application of patients' rights in cross-border healthcare', COM (2008) 415 final, 2 July 2008.

'Communication on telemedicine for the benefit of patients, healthcare systems and society', COM (2008) 689 final, 4 November 2008.

'Communication on safe, innovative and accessible medicines: a renewed vision for the pharmaceutical sector', COM (2008) 666 final, 10 December 2008.

'Interpretive Communication on the application of Community law on public procurement and concessions to institutionalised public-private partnerships (IPPV)', OJ 2008 No. C 91/02.

'Proposal for a directive of the European Parliament and of the Council amending, as regards information to the general public on medicinal products subject to medical prescription, Directive 2001/83/EC on the Community Code relating to medicinal products for human use', COM (2008) 663 final, 10 December 2008.

'Proposal for a regulation of the European Parliament and of the Council amending, as regards information to the general public on medicinal products for human use subject to medical prescription, Regulation (EC) No. 726/2004 laying down Community procedures for the authorisation and supervision of medicinal products for human and veterinary use and establishing a European Medicines Agency', COM (2008) 662 final, 10 December 2008.

7. Secretary-General of the Commission Documents

European Commission 'Report on the application of internal market rules to health services – implementation by the Member States of the Court's Jurisprudence', Commission Staff Working Paper, SEC (2003) 900, 28 July 2003.

'Damages actions for breach of the EC antitrust rules', Green Paper, SEC (2005) 1732, 19 December 2005.

'Consultation regarding Community action on health services', SEC (2006) 1195/4, 26 September 2006.

'Frequently asked questions concerning the application of public procurement rules to social services of general interest', Commission Staff Working Document, SEC (2007) 1514, 20 November 2007.

'Frequently asked questions in relation with Commission Decision of 28 November 2005 on the application of Article 86(2) of the EC Treaty to state aid in the form of public service compensation granted to certain undertakings entrusted with the operation of services of general economic interest, and of the Community framework for state aid in the form of public service compensation', Commission Staff Working Document, SEC (2007) 1516, 20 November 2007.

'Recommendation on cross-border interoperability of electronic health records', C (2008) 3282 final, 2 July 2008.

'Telemedicine for the benefit of patients, healthcare systems and society', Commission Staff Working Document, SEC(2009)943 final, June 2009.

8. Treaty provisions

A. EC Treaty

Article 3(g) EC.
Article 5(1) EC.
Article 18 EC.
Article 28 EC.
Article 37 EC.
Article 39 EC.
Article 43 EC.
Article 46(1) EC.
Article 49 EC.
Article 81 EC.
Article 82 EC.
Articles 83–85 EC.
Article 87 EC.
Article 95 EC.
Article 152 EC.
Article 152(1) EC.
Article 152(4) EC.
Article 152(5) EC.
Article 230 EC.
Article 232 EC.
Article 234 EC.
Article 249 EC.

B. Treaty on European Union

Article 6(1) TEU.
Article 7 TEU.
Article 46 TEU.

Index